THE OXFORD HANDBOOK OF

MANAGEMENT CONSULTING

THE OXFORD HANDBOOK OF

MANAGEMENT CONSULTING

Edited by

MATTHIAS KIPPING

and

TIMOTHY CLARK

OXFORD

UNIVERSITY PRESS

OXFORD
UNIVERSITY PRESS

Great Clarendon Street, Oxford OX2 6DP

Oxford University Press is a department of the University of Oxford.
It furthers the University's objective of excellence in research, scholarship,
and education by publishing worldwide in

Oxford New York

Auckland Cape Town Dar es Salaam Hong Kong Karachi
Kuala Lumpur Madrid Melbourne Mexico City Nairobi
New Delhi Shanghai Taipei Toronto

With offices in

Argentina Austria Brazil Chile Czech Republic France Greece
Guatemala Hungary Italy Japan Poland Portugal Singapore
South Korea Switzerland Thailand Turkey Ukraine Vietnam

Oxford is a registered trade mark of Oxford University Press
in the UK and in certain other countries

Published in the United States
by Oxford University Press Inc., New York

© Oxford University Press 2012

British Library Cataloguing in Publication Data
Data available

Library of Congress Cataloging in Publication Data
Data available

Typeset by SPI Publisher Services, Pondicherry, India
Printed in Great Britain
on acid-free paper by
MPG Books Group, Bodmin and King's Lynn

ISBN 978-0-19-923504-9

1 3 5 7 9 10 8 6 4 2

CONTENTS

PART 1 HISTORICAL DEVELOPMENT OF MANAGEMENT CONSULTING

PART 2 DISCIPLINARY AND THEORETICAL PERSPECTIVES

PART 3 CONSULTING AS A KNOWLEDGE BUSINESS

PART 4 CONSULTANTS AND MANAGEMENT FASHION

PART 5 CONSULTANTS AND THEIR CLIENTS

PART 6 NEW AVENUES FOR RESEARCH

Acknowledgements

Editing a book such as this is an intensely collaborative process. We are enormously grateful to all the contributors for their support and for responding so conscientiously and considerately to our comments on the various drafts of their chapters. David Musson at Oxford University Press was a constant support, responding to our queries and offering advice at key points. Emma Lambert, also at Oxford University Press, was especially helpful in assisting us to prepare the manuscript for submission. And Elizabeth Stone did an excellent job at diligently copy editing the completed manuscript. We are also appreciative of the help of Lourdes Watts, Fiona Bell, and Kath Pickford who, at various times, have assisted with the preparation of different aspects of the manuscript. Tim Clark would like to acknowledge the financial assistance of the Leverhulme Trust for their funding of the project entitled 'Tipping Points: Mathematics, Metaphors and Meanings'. Finally, we would both like to acknowledge all our colleagues at the Durham Business School and the Schulich School of Business for their support and encouragement and, last not least, our families for being so patient during this long-lasting project.

LIST OF FIGURES

List of Tables

Notes on the Contributors

Stephen Ackroyd is Emeritus Professor of Organizational Analysis at Lancaster University Management School. His early research was into organizational misbehaviour and was completed whilst working as a consultant. In the course of his career, Stephen has researched public sector organizations and the professions (especially medicine, law, and business consultants), as well as conducting a longitudinal study of the organizational forms and strategies of the largest British companies. His recent books include: *Realist Perspectives on Management and Organisation* (with S. Fleetwood, Routledge 2000), *The Organization of Business* (Oxford University Press 2002), *The New Managerialism and the Public Service Professions* (with I. Kirkpatrick and R. Walker, Palgrave Macmillan 2005), *The Oxford Handbook of Work and Organization* (with R. Batt and others, Oxford University Press 2006), and *Redirections in the Study of Expert Labour* (with D. Muzio and J-F. Chanlat, Palgrave Macmillan 2006). Stephen is currently working on updating his books *Organizational Misbehaviour* and *The Organization of Business*.

Mats Alvesson is Professor of Business Administration at the University of Lund, Sweden, and at University of Queensland Business School, Australia. He is Honorary Professor at University of St Andrews and Visiting Professor at Exeter University. Research interests include critical theory, gender, power, management of professional service (knowledge-intensive) organizations, leadership, identity, organizational image, organizational culture and symbolism, qualitative methods, and philosophy of science. Recent books include *Interpreting Interviews* (Sage 2011), *Metaphors We Lead By: Understanding Leadership in the Real World* (with Andre Spicer (eds), Routledge 2011), *Oxford Handbook of Critical Management Studies* (with Todd Bridgman and Hugh Willmott (eds), Oxford University Press 2009), *Understanding Gender and Organizations* (Sage 2009, 2nd ed., with Yvonne Billing), *Reflexive Methodology* (Sage 2009, 2nd ed., with Kaj Skoldberg), *Changing Organizational Culture* (with Stefan Sveningsson, Routledge 2008), *Knowledge Work and Knowledge-Intensive Firms* (Oxford University Press 2004).

N. Anand is Professor of Organizational Behaviour at IMD, Lausanne. His research interests include professional service firms, organizational design, institutional change, and the regulation of emotion in social networks.

Jos Benders holds the Chair of Organization Concepts at Tilburg University and is a Guest Professor at the Centre for Sociological Research of the Katholieke Universiteit

Leuven. His research interests include (fashionable) organization concepts, new technology in organizations, 'lean' management in health care, self-directed work teams, and late medieval coinage in the Low Countries. He is co-author and author of a wide range of publications, and has published in such journals as *Human Relations*, *Information and Management*, *Journal of Management Studies*, *Numismatic Chronicle*, and *Organization*.

Pojanath Bhatanacharoen is a postdoctoral researcher at Durham University. She splits her time between Durham Business School and the Institute of Hazard, Risk and Resilience, working on multidisciplinary project 'Tipping Points', with particular focus on the diffusion of popular ideas and management fashion. Pojanath's background is in political science. Her thesis, completed at Newcastle University, explored the relationships and dynamics between the influence, power, decision-making, negotiation strategies, and institutional designs of the European Union and World Trade Organization.

Kyle Bruce is a senior lecturer at the Graduate School of Management, Macquarie University, Australia. He has published papers on the historiography of scientific management and human relations, institutional theory in economics, organization studies and international business, US inter-war business history, the history of US economic and management thought, and evolutionary economics, strategy, and the theory of the firm.

Timothy Clark is Professor of Organizational Behaviour at Durham Business School, Durham University. In the last decade he has conducted a series of research projects into consultancy work and speaker–audience interaction during management guru lectures. The publications emanating from these projects include *Management Speak* (with David Greatbatch, Routledge 2005), and, most recently, *Management Consultancy: Knowledge and Boundaries in Action* (with Andrew Sturdy, Robin Fincham, and Karen Handley, Oxford University Press 2008). He is currently working on a multidisciplinary project examining the emergence and nature of 'Tipping Points'.

Barbara Czarniawska is Professor of Management Studies at Gothenberg Research Institute, School of Business, Economics and Law at the University of Gothenburg, Sweden. She takes a feminist and constructionist perspective on organizing, recently exploring connections between popular culture and the practice of management, and the organization of news production. As methodologist, she explores techniques of fieldwork and the applications of narratology in social sciences. Recent books in English include: *A Theory of Organizing* (Edward Elgar 2008) and *Organizing in the Face of Risk and Threat* ((ed.), Edward Elgar 2009).

Robert J. David is Associate Professor of Strategy and Organization and Cleghorn Faculty Scholar at the Desautels Faculty of Management, McGill University. He is also Director of the Centre for Strategy Studies in Organization at McGill. Dr. David studies the evolution of management practices, organizational forms, and industries from an institutional perspective. He serves on the editorial board of *Organization Science* and as an associate editor at *Journal of Management Inquiry*, and recently co-edited volume 21 of *Research in the Sociology of Work*, entitled *Institutions and Entrepreneurship*. Dr. David holds a Ph.D. in Organization Theory from Cornell University.

Timothy Devinney (B.Sc. CMU; M.A., M.B.A., Ph.D. Chicago) is Professor of Strategy at the University of Technology, Sydney. He has held positions at the University of Chicago, Vanderbilt, UCLA, and Australian Graduate School of Management, and has been a visitor at many other universities. He has published six books and more than eighty articles in leading journals including *Management Science*, *The Academy of Management Review*, *Journal of International Business Studies*, *Organization Science*, and the *Strategic Management Journal*. He is a fellow of the Academy of International Business, a recipient of an Alexander von Humboldt Research Award, and a Rockefeller Foundation Bellagio fellow. He is Past-Chair of the International Management Division of the AOM and Co-editor of *AOM Perspectives*. He is currently on the editorial board of over ten of the leading journals, Director of the SSRN International Management Network, and co-editor of the Advances in International Management series.

Lars Engwall is Professor of Business Studies at Uppsala University, Sweden, and has held visiting positions in European and US institutions. He has published widely in the management area, particularly on organizations such as newspapers, banks, and universities as well as on the creation and diffusion of management knowledge. Among his publications are *Mercury Meets Minerva* (Pergamon Press 2009 [1992]), *Management Consulting* (with Matthias Kipping (eds), Oxford University Press 2002), *The Expansion of Management Knowledge* (with Kerstin Sahlin-Andersson (eds), Stanford University Press 2002), and *Reconfiguring Knowledge Production* (with Richard Whitley and Jochen Gläser (eds), Oxford University Press 2010). He is a member of a number of learned societies.

James Faulconbridge is a senior lecturer in Economic Geography at Lancaster University, UK. His work examines the globalization of professional/business services including advertising, executive search, law and management consultancy, and the spaces of learning and knowledge within firms. He has published extensively in journals including *Economic Geography*, *Environment and Planning A*, *The Journal of Economic Geography*, and *Work, Employment and Society*. He has also co-written the book, *The Globalization of Advertising: Agencies, Cities and Spaces of Creativity*, published in 2010 by Routledge.

Michael Faust is a senior researcher at the Sociological Research Institute (SOFI) at Göttingen University, Germany. He obtained a Diploma in Economics, a doctoral degree, and his Habilitation in Sociology from Tübingen University. His research covers the sociology of work and industry and organization studies. He has published on the decentralization of the firm, changing roles of middle managers, international production networks, the rise of Shareholder Value, and the development of management consulting in Germany, often in a comparative perspective.

Robin Fincham is Emeritus Professor of Organizational Behaviour at Stirling Management School, Stirling University, UK. His work has focused on topics of information technology and the computing occupations; also management knowledge and processes of knowledge sharing, and, recently, issues of expert labour and the corporate professions. The role of management consultants as change agents has been a continuing topic across a number of these areas. His published work includes *Management Consultancy: Knowledge and Boundaries in Action* (Oxford University Press 2008) with Andrew Sturdy, Timothy Clark, and Karen Handley.

R. Edward Freeman is University Professor at the University of Virginia, Elis and Signe Olsson Professor of Business Administration at the Darden School, and Academic Director of the Business Roundtable Institute for Corporate Ethics. From 1987 to 2009 he was Director of Darden's Olsson Center for Applied Ethics, one of the world's leading academic centres for the study of ethics. He is the author or editor of over 20 volumes in the areas of stakeholder management, business strategy, and business ethics as well as more than 100 articles in a wide variety of publications. Freeman has a Ph.D. in Philosophy from Washington University and a B.A. in Mathematics and Philosophy from Duke University.

Michal Frenkel is a senior lecturer of Sociology and Organization Studies at the Hebrew University of Jerusalem. Her research looks at the transformation of ethnic, racial, and gendered social orders, in the context of the cross-national transfer of management knowledge and practices. Her articles on the role of geopolitical and centre-periphery power relations in shaping organizational practices, and on the global transformation of work–family organizational policies, have appeared in top international journals such as the *Academy Management Review, Organization Science, Organization Studies, Organization*, and others.

Kerim Galal studied Information Systems at the University of Münster and the School of Economics and Management in Lund, Sweden. He spent three years as a research assistant at the Chair of Strategy and Organization at the European Business School in Oestrich-Winkel. In his research he has focused on the consulting business. Today, he works as the executive assistant to the CEO of DEKRA SE.

Heidi Gardner is Assistant Professor of Organizational Behavior at Harvard Business School. Her research examines the design of knowledge-intensive work. She has published articles in the *Academy of Management Journal* and *Journal of Organizational Behavior*, and several chapters in edited volumes. Before academia, Gardner worked as a strategy consultant for McKinsey & Co. in London, Johannesburg, and New York. She earned a Master's degree from the London School of Economics and a Ph.D. from London Business School.

David Greatbatch is Visiting Professor at Durham Business School, Durham University. His research focuses on public speaking and interpersonal communication in organizational settings, drawing on ethnomethodology and conversation analysis. He is currently undertaking projects on organizational storytelling and the use of oratory by organizational leaders. He has published widely in journals such as *American Journal of Sociology*, *American Sociological Review*, *Human Relations*, *Language in Society*, *Law and Society Review*, *Sociology of Health and Illness*, and *The Leadership Quarterly*. He co-authored *Management Speak* (Routledge 2005) with Timothy Clark.

Royston Greenwood is the TELUS Professor of Strategic Management at the University of Alberta, and Visiting Professor at the Saïd Business School, University of Oxford. He received his Ph.D. from the University of Birmingham in the UK. His research interests include the management of organizational design and change, usually from the perspective of institutional theory, and his favoured empirical settings involve professional service firms. In 2009 he was elected a fellow of the Academy of Management.

Stefan Heusinkveld is Associate Professor at VU University Amsterdam, the Netherlands. His research concentrates on the production and consumption of management ideas and, in particular, the role of management consultants and management gurus. Stefan's work has appeared in various journals such as *Organization Studies*, *Human Relations*, *Management Learning*, *Information and Management*, *Technovation*, *Quality and Quantity*, and *Journal of Organizational Change Management*. His book on knowledge-based innovation in consultancies will be published by Routledge in 2012.

Andrew Jones is Professor of Economic Geography, Department of Geography, Environment and Development Studies, Birkbeck College, University of London. His research has focused on the transnationalization of firms in financial and business services, as well as a wider interest in the global knowledge economy. He has published over 35 journal articles and book chapters, as well as the book *Management Consultancy and Banking in an Era of Globalization* (Palgrave Macmillan). He is currently the Chair of the RGS–IBG Economic Geography Research Group and the book review editor of *The Journal of Economic Geography*.

Nicole Jung is Professor of Business Administration at Deutsche Bundesbank University of Applied Sciences, Germany. Her most recent work focuses on client–consultant relationships. Further research interests include organizational behaviour, management fashions, human resource management, and power and control. Nicole graduated in Business Administration and British and American Studies. She received her doctoral degree from Mannheim University in 2010 and was Visiting Scholar at Stanford University.

Elisabeth Kelan is a senior lecturer in Work and Organisations in the Department of Management at King's College London. Prior to this appointment she was a senior research fellow at London Business School. She received her Ph.D. from the London School of Economics and Political Science. She has published one monograph and various articles in journals like *Human Relations*, *Journal of Business Ethics*, and *Gender,*

Work and Organization. Her research interests lie in the area of gender in organizations, diversity, identities, and organizational cultures.

Alfred Kieser is Professor Emeritus of Organizational Behaviour at Mannheim University. His research interests include the history of organization, management fashions, consulting, and organizational learning. He has published in, among other journals, *Administration Science Quarterly*, *Journal of Management Inquiry*, *Journal of Management Studies*, *Organization Science*, *Organization Studies*, and *Organization*. He has published two textbooks on organization theory (in German). He received an honorary doctoral degree from the University of Munich and is a member of the Heidelberg Academy of Sciences.

Matthias Kipping is Professor of Strategic Management and Chair in Business History at the Schulich School of Business, York University, Toronto, Canada. He obtained his doctorate from the University of Munich and additional degrees in France and the United States and held previous appointments in the United Kingdom and Spain. He has published widely on management consultancy and its evolution, co-edited, with Lars Engwall, a volume on *Management Consulting: Emergence and Dynamics of a Knowledge Industry* (Oxford University Press 2002), and is currently finalizing a manuscript tentatively entitled *From Racket to Riches: The Management Consultancy Business in Historical and Comparative Perspectives*, also to be published by Oxford University Press.

Ian Kirkpatrick is Professor in Work and Organization at Leeds University Business School and Director of the Leeds Social Science Institute. His research interests are in the effects of new management and employment practices on the role of professionals in public and private services. Ian has published widely in leading journals including, most recently, *Public Administration*, *Work, Employment and Society*, and the *British Journal of Industrial Relations*. He is currently Chair of a Framework 7 European COST Action, focusing on the relationship between medicine and management, and also subeditor of the British Sociological Association journal, *Work, Employment and Society*.

Dean Krehmeyer is the Executive Director of the Business Roundtable Institute for Corporate Ethics and co-author of the report, *Breaking the Short-Term Cycle: Discussion and Recommendations on How Corporate Leaders, Asset Managers, Investors, and Analysts Can Refocus on Long-Term Value*. He facilitates seminars for boards of directors and senior corporate executives. Mr Krehmeyer, previously with A. T. Kearney and Deloitte & Touche LLP, has an MBA from the Darden School and an M.S. in Accounting and a B.S. in Commerce from the University of Virginia.

Megan S. McDougald received her Ph.D. in Organizational Analysis from the University of Alberta. She has worked extensively as a management consultant in the areas of change management, strategic planning and balanced scorecard for clients in North America, Australia, and the United Kingdom. Her areas of research interest include:

social capital, professional service firms, and mergers and acquisitions. She is particularly interested in how professional service firms transfer their social capital (or their clients and staff) when they undergo a merger or acquisition. She currently works in the Research Services Office at the University of Alberta.

Carmelo Mazza holds a Ph.D. in Organization Theory from IESE Business School, Barcelona, Spain. He has taught in several business schools throughout Europe and is currently Affiliate Professor at IE Business School in Madrid. His research interests range from the institutionalization of practices in media/cultural industries to the study of the consulting profession. His recent studies on the university reforms in Europe have led to several publications and conferences. Carmelo Mazza has published articles in several high-rated journals including *Organization Studies*, *Journal of Organizational Behavior*, *Organization, and Human Relations*, in which he is also active as a reviewer.

Timothy Morris is Professor of Management Studies at the Saïd Business School, University of Oxford. He has a Master's degree and doctorate from the London School of Economics. His research interests are concerned with the nature and patterns of change and processes of innovation in professional organizations. He has studied firms in a range of sectors including law, architecture, executive search, accounting, and management consulting. His publications include several books, contributions to numerous edited collections, and papers in leading American and European management journals.

Daniel Muzio is Professor of Leadership and Organization at the University of Manchester as well as a visiting professor at Luiss University, in Rome. His research interests include the sociology of the professions, organizational theory, and the management of professional services firms. He has published in several leading management, sociology, and law journals, and co-edited a book *Redirections in the Study of Expert Labour: Established Professions and New Expert Occupations* for Palgrave Macmillan (2008).

Natalia Nikolova (Ph.D. University of Cologne) is a senior lecturer of Management at the University of Technology, Sydney, specializing in the areas of management consulting, professional business services, and the creative industries. Natalia has published in academic journals and books and her work has been presented and recognized at a number of international conferences. In 2008, she received the Best Paper Award of the Management Consulting Division at the Academy of Management. In 2007, Natalia published a book entitled *The Client–Consultant Relationship in Professional Business Service Firms*.

Ansgar Richter is Professor of Strategy and Organization at EBS Business School in Wiesbaden, Germany. He studied philosophy and economics in Germany and at the London School of Economics, and has been a visiting scholar at the University of California at Berkeley, Stanford University, and INSEAD. He also has several years of experience as a management consultant with a leading strategy consulting company. In his research he investigates the organization and strategy of professional service firms.

Nicole J. Saam is Professor of Methods of Empirical Social Research at Friedrich-Alexander University Erlangen-Nürnberg, Germany. She studied political science, economics, and sociology, and has worked at the institutes of sociology of the universities of Munich, Mannheim, Leipzig, Marburg, Erfurt, and Augsburg. Her research fields include social theory, social science methodology, sociology of organizations, and political sociology.

Denis Saint-Martin is Professor in the Département de science politique, Université de Montréal, Canada, where he teaches public administration and policy. He is also the Director of the European Union Center of Excellence. He has published widely in the field of public management and comparative politics. One of his books, *Building the New Managerialist State: Consultants and the Politics of Public Sector Reform in Comparative Perspective* (Oxford University Press 2000, re-edited in 2004) won the US Academy of Management Best Book Award for 2001–2. He is currently working in the area of welfare state redesign and on the Watergate Effect, a comparative research project that looks at the regulation of ethics in politics from an historical-institutionalist perspective.

Yehouda Shenhav (Ph.D. Stanford University 1985) is Professor of Sociology at Tel-Aviv University and a senior editor for *Organization Studies*. Until recently he was Head of Advanced Studies at the Jerusalem Vanleer Institute and Editor of *Theory and Criticism* (1999–2009). Among his recent books are: *Manufacturing Rationality: The Foundations of the Managerial Revolution* (Oxford University Press 2003), *The Arab Jews* (Stanford University Press 2006), and *Beyond the Green Line* (Polity Press, forthcoming).

Andrew Sturdy is Professor of Organizational Behaviour and Head of the Department of Management at the University of Bristol, UK. His research and policy interests are mainly around issues of power and identity in the production and use of management ideas, especially in relation to management consultancy and organizational change. His most recent book is *Management Consultancy*, (Oxford University Press 2009, with Karen Handley, Tim Clark, and Robin Fincham). He is currently researching the organization and dynamics of internal consultancy.

Richard C. S. Trahair completed a Ph.D. in the Psychology Department, University of Melbourne, taught Social Psychology, researched industrial relations at Broken Hill (1958–67), and published in *Human Relations*. At La Trobe University (1968–2001), he taught industrial sociology and political psychology, published the biography of Elton Mayo (Transaction 1984), medical works for Oxford University Press, and on eponyms in the social sciences, *Utopias and Utopians*, and Cold War espionage (1994–2004) for Greenwood Press. He is currently writing a biography of Eric Trist.

Vera Wendlandt (M.Sc.Ec.) studied Economics at Münster University, Germany, where she focused on the economics of hybrid organizations and the traffic and energy sectors. After finishing her studies in 2007, she started working as a management consultant for logistics service providers near Frankfurt, which is also her current position. In 2008 she began her doctoral studies on organizational phenomena in the traffic sector at Münster University, which will be completed in 2012. During her doctoral studies Vera Wendlandt worked for one year, from 2009 to 2010, as a research assistant under the direction of Ansgar Richter, Ph.D.

Andreas Werr is Professor at the Stockholm School of Economics and Head of the Center for People and Organization. His research interests focus on the acquisition, application, and development of knowledge and expert e-work. Andreas has carried out extensive research on the use of management consultants and the management of professional service firms. His work has been published in journals such as *Organization Studies*, *Organizational Change Management*, and *The MIT Sloan Management Review*.

Christopher Wright is Professor of Organizational Studies at the University of Sydney. He has published extensively on the diffusion of management knowledge, organizational and workplace change, and is the author of several monographs including *The Management of Labour: A History of Australian Employers* (Oxford University Press 1995). His current research focuses on the role and impact of internal consultancy on organizational change and innovation, and business responses to climate change.

....

CHAPTER 1

RESEARCHING MANAGEMENT CONSULTING: AN INTRODUCTION TO THE HANDBOOK

....

MATTHIAS KIPPING
TIMOTHY CLARK[*]

In a relatively short period of time management consultants and management consultancy have come to occupy a significant role in modern organizations. Many major decisions in a wide range of organizations and sectors are made with the assistance of management consultants. The impact of their advice is hard to avoid. Indeed, whether we are aware of it or not, many of us will have experienced the outcome of some kind of consultancy-led initiative or programme. It is, we will argue later, this sense of influence and power, combined with concerns in relation to their accountability, that has heightened the profile of management consulting in the academic literature and made it a thriving area of research.

This volume brings together contributions from leading scholars to provide a comprehensive and authoritative overview of the extant literature on management consulting. This Handbook is therefore designed to present the full range of research and thinking on management consulting, dispersed amongst different disciplines, subdisciplines, and conceptual approaches. Each chapter reviews and critically reflects upon the existing research on a specific topic or theme before identifying potentially productive avenues for future research. Individually, they demonstrate the diversity of conceptual and empirical approaches and relate these to one another so that overlaps, parallel concerns, and areas of synergy are identified. Collectively, the range of topics covered demonstrates that although there is a fast expanding and rich body of research on management consulting itself, it has also been used as an illustration by scholars working in a number of disciplines to provide an example to broader questions. Research into management consulting is therefore an interdisciplinary endeavour and as such provides a route into a number of critical issues that have occupied social science over the last fifty years or so. These issues include the shifting nature of organizations, the rise of management, the nature of knowledge, professions, fashion, and the post-industrial economy. These chapters not only provide an unrivaled insight into management consulting as an activity but also enable readers to develop their broader knowledge and become better informed and more rounded social scientists.

As will be discussed at various points in this volume, definitions of management consultancy are problematic because the permeable boundaries of the industry have resulted in significant shifts over time in the composition of the industry. This means that what comprises consulting work is dynamic, ever shifting, and contested as new firms enter the industry and techniques deemed formerly appropriate, change. Although the industry is characterized by periodic structural shifts, at its heart it is an advisory activity built on the client–consultant relationship. However, many definitions of management consulting derive from industry bodies that have an interest in presenting the activity in a very positive light. The following is an example of an early definition of management consulting from the Association of Consulting Management Engineers (ACME) (quoted by Higdon 1969: 306):

> Management consulting is the professional service performed by specially trained and experienced persons in helping managers identify and solve managerial and operating problems of the various institutions of our society...This professional service focuses on improving the managerial, operating, and economic performance of these institutions.

This definition has been echoed in many subsequent definitions (such as Kubr 2002: 3–4), where consultants are frequently portrayed, and indeed like to be portrayed, as experts who draw on a professional knowledge-base to help solve client problems of various kinds. They are often 'seen as synonymous with the role of professional helpers remedying illness in client organizations' (Fincham and Clark 2002: 7). As a number of the chapters in this volume demonstrate, the nature of consulting knowledge and the degree to which it has been able to professionalize are vigorously debated issues in the literature (Kipping and Wright, Chapter 8; Kirkpatrick, Muzio, and Ackroyd, Chapter 9; Werr, Chapter 12; Morris, Gardner, and Anand, Chapter 14; Jung and Kieser, Chapter 16; Nikolova and Devinney, Chapter 19). In a later section this Introduction will discuss the rise of consulting, but it is important to note here that it is perhaps this chimeral ability to avoid precise definition and to be able to constantly reinvent its core services to meet ever changing understandings of the problems that beset contemporary organizations, which partly underpins its growing economic importance. As an industry, management consulting has proved very adaptable, as it has sought to sustain demand for its services in a context that, occasionally, radically alters.

In terms of structure, the first section of this introductory chapter details the merits of management consulting as a research topic, highlighting three reasons why it has attracted the attention of researchers: (i) While not necessarily big in overall revenue terms, it grew quickly, faster than the economy as a whole in many Western nations, especially since the 1980s; (ii) it employed many smart, or at least well-educated people, becoming an example of the kind of knowledge work many saw as the future of economic and business activity; and (iii), probably most importantly, its activities impacted an ever wider number of organizations and even society as a whole. The subsequent section will provide a chronological overview of the evolution of research on management consulting (for earlier reviews, see Armenakis and Burdg 1988; Mohe and Seidl 2009). It will show that interest in the industry was originally limited, mainly confined to the business and even general press as well as a few investigative journalists, but that this interest accelerated in the 1950s and reached a first high point in the late 1960s with the publication of a small number of influential books. From the mid-1970s attention grew and diversified, with research involving, in addition to journalists, consultants themselves and academics from a variety of backgrounds. Academic research in particular, but also more popular accounts of management consulting, have exploded since the 1990s, following on from the unprecedented growth and visibility of the industry. The final section of this Introduction will briefly explain how this Handbook has chosen to present the current state-of-the-art thinking in academic research as well as promising avenues for its future development.

1.1 ASSESSING THE IMPORTANCE OF MANAGEMENT CONSULTANTS

Today, consultants are ubiquitous in the business world even beyond their advisory role. They frequently pop up when one leafs through business magazines, attends business events, or checks the shelves of bookstores or billboards at airports. There is hardly an issue of any leading business magazine that does not have an article referring to management consulting firms or individual celebrity consultants and management gurus. According to some accounts (e.g. Faust 2002), consultants have actually replaced academics, and even managers, as the leading 'experts' on business matters, and as such are influential in determining our understanding of contemporary organizational issues. They have not only become a pre-eminent 'reference source' but also (co-)author articles in popular academic journals, have written many bestselling management books, and even, in some cases, publish their own periodicals (Clark, Bhatanacharoen, and Greatbatch, Chapter 17; Engwall, Chapter 18; both this volume). Consequently, there seems little doubt that consultants are highly visible. However, what are the reasons for their importance and do they merit being the focus of sustained research? In the following three sections we explore different potential answers to these questions.

1.1.1 Consulting as an Economic Activity

There is little doubt that management consulting is a business, even if most consultants try to think of themselves—and portray themselves—as 'trusted professional advisors'. Management consulting has indeed become an important economic activity. Since its boundaries are not well delineated and shift over time, it is notoriously difficult to obtain any accurate statistics on the size of the management consulting market, globally or for different countries, regions, and sectors. Estimates tend to be provided by industry groups, such as the European Federation of Management Consultancies Associations (FEACO—Fédération Européenne des Associations de Conseils en Organisation), or industry experts, such as Kennedy Consulting Research. Kubr (2002), who has written a widely used *Guide to the Profession*, estimated the global market to be worth US$102 billion in 1999, with Europe accounting for $33 billion, as compared to a total of $28.3 billion in 1992 (with these totals equivalent to, respectively, $133.5 and $44 billion in 2010). According to FEACO, in 2010, the European consulting market had an estimated value of €85 billion, with 'business consulting' (rather than IT consulting, outsourcing, and a few other activities) accounting for 43 per cent of this total. Taking business consulting only, and applying the same proportion as that of ten years earlier, suggests that the global market in 2010 had a value of around $150 billion. If one takes all consulting revenues into account the resulting market size would be closer to $350 billion.

One should take all of these data as, at best, providing an order of magnitude, which will vary widely depending on what is included, given the vague boundaries between business and IT consulting (and even outsourcing) and with much of the market dominated by individual practitioners and small firms (see Faulconbridge and Jones, Chapter 11, this volume; Keeble and Schwalbach 1995). Nor do these estimates take into account the size of internal consultancy activities, which have attracted attention only very recently (see, e.g., Wright 2009; Sturdy and Wright 2011). Given the above, plus the growth of markets other than those of North America and Europe, the above estimate of $150 billion is probably on the low side. The largest consulting firm is (by most measures) IBM Global Business Services, which alone had revenues of $18.2 billion in 2010, which would translate into a 12 per cent market share—highly unlikely in what continues to be a very fragmented market. Nevertheless, not all of its activities can probably be counted as management consulting. Against this backdrop, $350 billion seems a somewhat more realistic estimate of market size, since this would give IBM an approximate share of 5 per cent.

Whatever their reliability in detail, these figures do show that the market has grown significantly relative to the early 1990s (despite some setbacks following the bursting of the Internet bubble in the early 2000s, lack of confidence after the Enron collapse in 2001, and the 2008 economic/financial crisis). This growth has at least partially contributed to a surge in academic interest from the 1990s onwards (see below). The recent rise of management consulting as an economic activity becomes even more pronounced when comparing the current industry size to the late 1950s, when the first more comprehensive market and firm data were available (Higdon 1969: 21). At the time, the US was by far the largest market with estimated revenues for close to 2,000 consulting firms reaching $426 million (equivalent to $3.45 billion in 2010) in 1954 and $850 million with 2,700 consultancies in 1968 (a 2010 equivalent of $5.33 billion). These numbers once again do not include the tens of thousands of individual consultants acting as sole-traders. In comparison, the UK—even if also a relatively developed market—was only estimated to generate total revenue of £4 million in 1956 (corresponding to just under £80 million or $123 million in 2010), with the big four firms accounting for about three quarters of this amount (Tisdall 1982: 9). In 2010 it had grown 100-fold, generating fee income of just under £8 billion or $23.5 billion. The UK market seems to have remained fairly concentrated with the Management Consulting Association's (MCA's) now fifty-five member firms accounting for an estimated 70 per cent of total turnover (http://www.mca.org.uk/about-us accessed 14 June 2011), even if the late 1980s and early 1990s also saw a significant growth of individual and small and medium-sized consultancies (Keeble and Schwalbach 1995).

Throughout most of this period, therefore, consulting has grown faster than the economies of many Western nations, partially by expanding globally (Kipping 1999). The leading firms in terms of revenue also grew much bigger. In 1968, the largest firm in the US was the Stanford Research Institute with $60 million in revenues ($376 million in 2010 dollars), which corresponded to a market share of about 7 per cent. Among those firms that are still significant today, the biggest then were Booz Allen with $50 million ($313 million in 2010) and McKinsey estimated between $22–5 million (with $24 million equivalent to $150 million in 2010), corresponding to market shares of 5.9 and 2.8 per cent respectively. Today's firms are significantly bigger in absolute terms but do not seem to have increased their market share. Some of the market leaders in the 1960s actually have a lower share today. For example, with respective revenues of $5 and $6.6 billion in 2009 Booz Allen and McKinsey only accounted for approximately 1.4 and 1.9 per cent of a market estimated at $350 billion (see, respectively, Booz Allen Hamilton 2009 and Forbes 2010). This suggests that the market might have undergone some structural change since the 1950s as consulting has been both absorbed and appropriated by other occupational groups (for more details, see Kipping 2002; McDougald and Greenwood, Chapter 5; Galal, Richter, and Wendlandt, Chapter 6; both this volume).

However, while the overall size in terms of markets and firm revenues is important, it is still small when compared to many other industries. This might explain why little of the extant research examines the industry structure or competition among the incumbent firms, or changes among those firms (e.g. through exit and entry). Thus, there are few if any studies that use approaches from economics, including 'old' or 'new' industrial organization or population ecology (see for details Saam, Chapter 10, this volume; Clark 1995). Neither have there been traditional strategy studies, based, for example, on Porter's (1980) Five Forces framework. Much of this has to do with the lack of statistical data on the industry and their lack of reliability, arising from the already mentioned blurred and fluid boundaries. The industry has a very fragmented nature, with highly visible and increasingly large professional service providers operating alongside a myriad of smaller niche firms and a plethora of individual consultants. But it also shows that, as a business, management consulting does not seem to be of major importance. According to FEACO (2010: 9), for instance, management consulting accounted for an estimated 0.7 per cent of European GDP in 2010 (up from 0.24 per cent in 1998 and 0.53 per cent in 2000). Other reasons, therefore, seem to better account for the broad interest it has received over recent decades.

1.1.2 The Human Element in Consulting

One of the reasons for the attention paid to management consulting can be found in the human resources it employs. As the above mentioned Forbes (2010) entry on McKinsey notes, somewhat casually, '[t]he firm is among the largest hirers of newly minted MBAs in the United States'. Ruef (2002) has traced the rise of management consulting as an employer for a large business school in the western US between 1933 and 1997, showing that their share increased from a meagre 2 per cent in the mid-1940s to just under one quarter of all graduates by the 1990s. In general, management consultancies developed a complex—often complementary, sometimes competitive—relationship with business schools (for details see David, Chapter 4; Engwall, Chapter 18; both this volume). Consulting firms have actually become so important for business school graduates that there are specialized websites tracking their reputation and/or offering resources to help potential hires land a job with a consultancy (e.g., vault.com and wetfeet.com).

But management consultancies do not only target postgraduate MBAs. Indeed, the major source of new talent in the largest consulting firms consists of recruits fresh out of undergraduate programmes. For example, in the late 1990s, according to the managing director of Andersen Consulting, now Accenture, the company received 3 million applications per year worldwide (Films of Record 1999). While an astonishing number at first sight, it is less surprising when considering both the attraction of (under)graduates to the industry and the size of Andersen Consulting, which had grown to over 70,000 employees by 2000 (http://www.accenture.com/us-en/company/overview/history/Pages/growth-global-leader.aspx accessed 7 June 2011). In addition, there is significant turnover among consulting staff due, on the one hand, to the consultancy's up-or-out policies and, on the other, the possible recognition among employees that the job is not so glamorous after all, given, among other issues, the long hours, extensive travel, and, for junior consultants, limited client exposure (Alvesson, Chapter 15, this volume; Armbrüster 2006).

Yet, it is not the sheer numbers of consultants that have attracted most of the attention (after all, employment in the sector in absolute terms is not that high), but their 'quality'. Consultants have become, for many, synonymous with a new type of employee, the 'knowledge worker', a type that has attracted significant attention in the popular and in the more academic management literature. The term was apparently first coined by Peter Drucker in his 1959 book *The Landmarks of Tomorrow*. A number of futurologists such as Alvin Toffler (1971) and Daniel Bell (1973) noted the macroeconomic shift from manufacturing to services in many advanced Western economics from the 1960s (Stehr 1994). Critical to these economic and social changes was the emerging prominence of a host of knowledge occupations such as accounting, law, IT services, employment agencies, and management consulting. Their rise has been seen as synonymous with the development of a new economy in which knowledge and intellectual abilities have become the key source of competitive advantage for companies (e.g., Lloyd and Sveiby 1987; Eisenhardt and Santos 2001; Newell et al. 2002). At the same time, because their key assets are in their heads, knowledge workers are seen as highly mobile, which creates numerous problems in terms of hiring and retaining talent (e.g. Drucker 2002). Management consultancies themselves have made a contribution to further exacerbating this issue, by encouraging their client firms to be very active in 'the war for talent'—the title of a book by three McKinsey consultants (Michaels, Handfield-Jones, and Axelrod 2001).

While there has been some research about what it actually means for consultants to be defined as 'knowledge workers' (see Alvesson, Chapter 15, this volume, and 2004), studies looking at how consulting firms manage their knowledge have been more numerous (Werr, Chapter 12; Heusinkveld and Benders, Chapter 13; both this volume) and are part of a much larger literature on knowledge management in which consultancies have been, once again, seen as providing an example for other companies, given the (supposed) knowledge-intensive nature of their business (e.g. Hansen, Nohria, and Tierney 1999; Alvesson 2004). But knowledge was not the only area where consultants were considered to be exemplary, even trendsetting. There was another area related to the idea that consultants are 'professionals'—a term they or the firms they work for often use to describe themselves.

Consultants were not included in the original academic research and debates on professionalism and professional occupations (e.g. Larson 1977; Abbott 1988), in part because of the lack of awareness of their activities but also because they had not reached formal professional status (McKenna 2006). However, they became more interesting as a result of changes observed in traditional professions, such as accounting and law, which gradually loosened their previous professional obligations and drifted towards a new type of organization, the professional service firm (PSF). PSFs became a focus of attention in organization and management theory and were used as examples for a process, which saw traditional professional partnerships adopt more features of 'normal' organizations, evolving towards what are widely called 'managed professional businesses' (MPB) (Hinings 2005; Von Nordenflycht 2010). Much of this research ultimately focused on the traditional professions, namely accounting and law, but some researchers began to examine the case of consulting, where PSFs had predated external professions, and therefore never let the latter develop fully, while looser associations between consulting and professionalism—often in purely discursive form—continued to persist (Gross and Kieser 2006; Leicht and Lyman 2006; Kipping 2011; Muzio, Kirkpatrick, and Kipping 2011). Nevertheless, for consulting, much of the discussion centred around the reasons why consultants had failed to develop a professional status in the first place (Kirkpatrick, Muzio, and Ackroyd, Chapter 9, this volume). This was another issue in which consultants were somewhat more central in the research interest.

1.1.3 Consultants as Promoters of Organizational (and Societal) Change

A third reason for the attention paid to management consultants does not concern the liveliness of their own business or the human resources behind it, but rather the considerable impact it is believed they have on other organizations (for a critical review, see Sturdy 2011). Indeed, they are frequently portrayed as shadowy figures operating in the background but exercising considerable influence. This has clearly been the most important reason for the interest shown towards them both in the business press and academic research, since their influence by far exceeds their importance both in terms of size of economic activity and employment. As research has shown, their influence has been widespread. They have not only influenced commercial/business organizations, but also governments (Saint-Martin, Chapter 22, this volume) and a variety of other organizations, including non-governmental organizations (NGOs), trade unions, and the church (Macdonald 2006; also Capron 2000). Their impact has not only been exerted through the advice they have sold, but also, if not more importantly, through their more general pronouncements on major issues such as regulation or health care (Kipping and Wright, Chapter 8, this volume), and even the future of capitalism (Barton 2011), and, last but not least, through former consultants occupying leading positions in business, politics, and society (Kipping 2012).

Their influence is not only recent. Some, like Marsh (2008: 35–40) go back as far as antiquity, highlighting how Plato and others as outsiders shaped Greek society and polity. Possibly even more famous is Machiavelli and his advice given to the prince (2003) in *The Prince* (pp. 43–6). However, most would argue that management consulting only emerged with the 'visible hand' (Chandler 1977) of management since the second industrial revolution in the second half of the nineteenth century (Wright and Kipping, Chapter 2, this volume; for a divergent opinion McKenna 2006). Some of the earliest and most detailed studies of how consultants tried to change organizations—and frequently encountered resistance in doing so—cover this period. There is, in particular, the book by Aitken (1960), examining the failed introduction of scientific management methods at the US government arsenal in Watertown in the early twentieth century, which even led to a congressional investigation (providing, in turn, much of the material for the study). At that time, the US Congress also invited well-known consultants to give their opinion on important economic issues, for example, the regulation of rates for railway companies (Quigel 1992). Some of them, most prominently Frederick Taylor, also gave occasional lectures at the newly founded business schools, in his case, Harvard (Engwall, Chapter 18, this volume).

In terms of the actual impact of consultants, the literature is—probably not surprisingly—divided. The extent and effect of this impact has been one of the major issues debated vigorously in both the popular and academic literature. Many of the studies mentioned above have highlighted the resistance of those concerned, in these cases the workers, against the organizational changes introduced, mostly concerning the introduction of scientific management methods (for example, Littler 1982, Downs 1990; for studies highlighting the resistance or at least reluctance of middle managers, see Cailluet 2000; Kipping 2000; Kipping and Armbrüster 2002). There are very few studies that actually claim, based on empirical evidence, that consultants have done harm to the organizations they advise. There are, however, a number of cases discussed by journalists and based on court documents, where clients have alleged that the consultants did not deliver the results they promised and, in one case, were even accused of having caused the company's bankruptcy (see O'Shea and Madigan 1997). It should be noted that all of these cases were eventually settled out of court and that O'Shea and Madigan (1997) also discuss cases where the consultants, supposedly, had a positive influence. On the other hand, there are a number of authors, many of them action researchers, who highlight the positive effect of their own work and the work of other organizational development consultants (see below; also Trahair and Bruce, Chapter 3, this volume). Indeed, as Fincham and Clark (2002) point out, many of the key authors in organizational development were reflecting on and describing their own practice. It is unsurprising that they present such a positive picture of the consulting process and its potential benefits to clients.

The majority of the literature, however, remains rather neutral or uncertain when it comes to the evaluation of the effect that consultants have. A sizeable number of commentators agree that consulting interventions lead to organizational change, but they differ in terms of its depth and directionality (see Faust, Chapter 7, this volume). There are those who believe that consultants disseminate very similar organizational templates to their client organizations, leading them ultimately to convergence in organizational form or to display 'isomorphism' (e.g. Hagedorn 1955; Chandler 1962; DiMaggio and Powell 1983). Others argue that most organizations will not blindly copy these templates, but adapt, hybridize, or, more generally, 'translate' them (see also Nikolova and Devinney, Chapter 19, this volume). Another view, and currently possibly the dominant one among researchers, sees the changes, if they take place at all, as mainly superficial. Following in the footsteps of Abrahamson (1991, 1996), they argue that consultants—and other actors in what they term the management fashion arena—induce managers to adopt new ideas, but, just like fashionable clothes, shed them as quickly and replace them with new fashions launched by those same actors (see below; also Jung and Kieser, Chapter 16; Clark, Bhatanacharoen, and Greatbatch, Chapter 17; both this volume). This, some suggest, might not necessarily cause immediate harm, but the ever changing nature of consultancy-led techniques at the least leads to cynicism among those affected inside an organization.

Whatever the differences in opinion, and there continue to be many, it is clear that the main reason that management consulting has attracted such a broad interest can be found in the (at least supposed) impact they have had on a broad range of organizations and even on society at large. This interest seems to have been particularly strong after the industry 'exploded' in the 1990s and early twenty-first century—making consultants much more visible actors in the economy. But, as the following section will show, there has been even earlier research covering a number of different issues (some of them already addressed above). This section will provide both an overview of the evolution of this research and a snapshot of the current situation.

1.2 Extant Research: Evolution and Current State

The following discussion will provide a chronological overview of research publications addressing the management consulting industry—research being broadly defined as encompassing investigative work emanating from scholars, journalists, and self-reflecting practitioners. As has been widely noted elsewhere, and as this section will confirm, more narrowly defined academic research on management consulting took off primarily in the 1990s. Nevertheless, there were studies examining the industry and its actors before then, usually written by journalists, sometimes commissioned by the consultancies themselves or their associations. Occasionally, and more by accident rather than design, consultants also appeared on the radar of scholars working on a number of different issues. Moreover, despite the surge in interest directed at management consultancy, even today the research output has remained on the margins of the mainstream (defined as the top-ranked, US-based management journals), with much of it being published in the form of monographs, edited volumes, and articles in European-based journals. Many of the scholars, journalists, and (former) practitioners publishing during the recent research boom from the 1990s have taken a broadly critical stance towards the industry and its activities, whereas most of the earlier publications had adopted a more neutral or even a positive tone.

1.2.1 Early Research on Consulting

The early investigative work on management consultancy came from three rather different sources: the (business) press, which has probably shown both the earliest and the most consistent interest almost since the inception of management consulting; the consultancies themselves as well as their associations; and scholars, with most of them 'stumbling across' the industry while researching other issues (e.g. Jackall 1988).

Journalistic accounts of consulting firms and, in particular, of their eponymous founders go back to the beginning of the twentieth century (if not further). Thus, the already mentioned resistance of workers to the introduction of scientific management at the Watertown arsenal prompted not only the intervention of the US Congress but also a reaction in the press, with an editorial in the *New York Evening Post* in 1914, for example, supporting Frederick W. Taylor and his system (Aitken 1960: 231). In addition to Taylor, who is widely seen as the 'father' of scientific management and the 'grandfather' of management consulting (Tisdall 1982; Wright and Kipping, Chapter 2, this volume), other leading industrial engineers (and by extension the consulting firms they founded) also received their fair share of attention.

However, at least in the first half of the twentieth century, much of the public interest was not due to their consulting, but their social activities. For example, Charles Bedaux, whose firm was the most important consultancy during the first half of the twentieth century, attracted most of the attention for the adventurous expeditions he organized though the Rocky Mountains and the Sahara. And he received even more publicity by hosting the wedding between Wallis Simpson and the Duke of Windsor, the former King Edward VIII, at his château in the Loire Valley as well as organizing the Duke's subsequent trips to Nazi Germany and to the United States—the latter was eventually abandoned in the face of significant opposition from organized labour (for details on all of these see, in particular, Christy 1984; for his consulting activities, see Wright and Kipping, Chapter 2, this volume). Thus, of the 20 articles published about Bedaux in the *New York Times* between 1930 and 1944 (when he committed suicide), only two dealt specifically with his consulting activities—one of them, incidentally, with his mission 'to Reorganize Economy of Greece' (published on the first page of the newspaper on 2 August 1938). Since the 1950s, press articles dealt more frequently with a new breed of consultancies and, in particular, with their more prominent representatives, including Booz Allen Hamilton and McKinsey (McKenna 2006; Kipping 2012; about their rise, see also David, Chapter 4, this volume).

Journalists and freelance authors are also behind some of the first broad overviews of the industry. An exemplar is Higdon's (1969) book entitled *The Business Healers*, which draws on data from the US-based Association of Management Consulting Engineers (ACME), earlier press articles, interviews with consultants and their clients, as well as personal observations. Like many of his later emulators Higdon provides an overview of the industry and its activities, but focuses on the most visible firms at the time, dedicating entire chapters to Booz Allen Hamilton, '[t]he mammoth among management consulting firms' (p. 112); McKinsey, the firm with the 'self admitted reputation for working with the uppermost of those on *Fortune's* 500 list' (p. 148); and George S. May, 'The Most Brazenly Resourceful Self-Publicist of Our Time' and, in the eyes of most industry insiders 'the black sheep of management consulting' (p. 149). Jean-Jacques Servan-Schreiber's (1968) book on *The American Challenge*, published as the French original *Le défi américain* in 1967, should also be mentioned. While examining the threat to European companies posed by US multinationals, he, in passing, highlighted the role of Booz Allen Hamilton, Arthur D. Little, and McKinsey in disseminating an 'American-style management that is, in its own special way, unifying Europe' (pp. 38–9)—an observation much quoted and investigated in the later literature (see, for example, Kipping 1999: 209; McKenna 2006: 165).

The consultants themselves wrote books long before the publication of *In Search of Excellence* (Peters and Waterman 1982), which is often regarded as the starting point for management bestsellers authored by celebrity consultants (Jung and Kieser, Chapter 16; Clark, Bhatanacharoen, and Greatbatch, Chapter 17; both this volume). To mention but a few, in addition to Taylor's works there are, for instance, Harrington Emerson's books:

Efficiency as a Basis for Operations and Wages (1909) and *The Twelve Principles of Efficiency* (1912); James O. McKinsey's *Budgetary Control* published in 1922 (Wolf 1978); and Maynard, Stegemerten, and Schwab's (1948) *Methods Time Measurement*. However, like today, these books usually tried to summarize and publicize the consultants' ideas rather than reflecting on their and the industry's activities.

There are exceptions, like C. B. Thompson's (1917) *The Theory and Practice of Scientific Management*, which examines the implementation and effects of the diverse systems as well as the reactions of those concerned. He relies on 'consulting engineers' for part of his information (p. 36) and also includes some reflections upon the role of consultants in this process. However, it was not until the 1970s or even the 1980s, that consultants themselves showed more interest in their own activities and, in particular, the evolution of their own firms and the industry as a whole. There are surprisingly few memoirs of consultants, probably due to the secrecy with which the industry has surrounded itself in order to protect client confidentiality. And the few that exist were usually limited to internal use (e.g. Neukom 1975 for McKinsey). This has changed only recently, when a series of former consultants wrote sensationalist and—usually—damning accounts based on their own experiences (e.g. Ashford 1998; Pinault 2000; Craig 2005).

In terms of academic research, there were numerous, usually comparative, studies of the different systems of scientific management that were disseminated by individual consultants or a few larger consulting firms (for an overview, see Wright and Kipping, Chapter 2, this volume), but they paid little attention to these consulting activities per se. The same is true for the books written about the inventors and early proponents of these different systems, and, in particular, Taylor. Thus, in their overview of the 13 'pioneers' of scientific management, Urwick and Brech (1945) did not include either Harrington Emerson or Charles Bedaux, who through their commercial consulting activities had made a major contribution to disseminating these ideas (Wright and Kipping, Chapter 2, this volume). But, for that same reason, they were looked down upon, even ostracized by the 'purists' within the movement. This lack of recognition within the academic literature lasted until the 1980s (e.g. Merkle 1980; Nelson 1980). It was only then that another school of thought, that is, labour process theory, recognized the roles consultants had in imposing scientific management onto workers (see below for more details). This 'discovery' seems to have prompted other researchers to pay closer attention to consulting in their own work (e.g. Nelson 1992, 1995).

Another stream of academic research concerned with consulting comes from the literature on organizational development (OD). This is related to what today is called 'action research', when academics were deeply involved with the subjects they were researching and, as a result, often also gave advice (for two early examples, see Trahair and Bruce, Chapter 3, this volume). Much of this literature was written by individuals actively engaged in consulting and focused on using behavioural science methods to build and sustain an organization's problem-solving capability (Beckhard 1969; Bennis 1969; French and Bell 1995). Perhaps Schein (1969) provided the definitive statement on this approach to consulting when he identified the distinctiveness of the OD practitioner as a process consultant, whose role he defined as 'a set of activities on the part of the con-sultant which helps the client to perceive, understand, and act upon process events which occur in the client's environment' (p. 9). From this perspective consulting is a joint endeavour in which the consultant uses their expertise in 'processes at the individual, interpersonal, and intergroup levels' (ibid.) to build capacity in the client to diagnose and resolve the problem should it occur again.

Finally, there was a concluding remark in Chandler's (1962) *Strategy and Structure* on the spread of the multidivisional form of organization, where he noted 'the very signifi-cant role that management consultants [...] have had in bringing about the adoption of the new structure as well as introducing many other administrative innovations and practices' (pp. 381–2)—though without providing any additional details. While made somewhat in passing at the time, it would eventually lead to his own quip that 'a man-ager once advised a colleague that he could save the $100,000 fee that McKinsey & Company was charging corporations to oversee their reorganization by reading a copy of Chandler's *Strategy and Structure*, which could be purchased for $2.95' (John 1997: 152, n. 2, which refers to a 1984 chapter by Chandler). The original observation would also be echoed more than 20 years later by DiMaggio and Powell (1983) in an article, which established the foundation for research on the role of management consultants in the diffusion of management ideas/fashions (see below).

Overall therefore, prior to World War II interest in consulting was almost exclusively limited to a few articles in the business and general press, and many of these dealt with the more 'newsworthy' private lives and adventures of the most visible consultants. In this respect they were celebrities of their time who happened to be consultants. Interest grew from the 1950s and increasingly involved, in addition to journalists, the consultants themselves and academics who, in the case of OD, were often personally involved in consulting activities. A first high point was reached in 1969 with the publication of the books by Higdon and Schein. What unites all of these authors is their generally positive attitude towards management consultancy and their belief that it could make a positive difference if correctly applied and used. This was to change from the mid-1970s onwards, which also saw a broadening of the approaches towards the industry.

1.2.2 Growing Interest and Divergence

While research activity occurred from the 1990s onwards, slightly lagging with the growth of the industry itself, there were a number of significant publications during the mid-1970s, which in many ways shaped the directions of the studies to come. Much of the new dynamic no longer came from the business press and journalists, but from the consultants themselves and from academia, where opinions became increasingly divided between those seeing management consulting as positive (and even providing normative advice on how to become a good consultant) and others who started to exam-ine the impact that consultants had on client organizations, but diverged in terms of evaluating it—positively or negatively (see also Section 1.1.3 above).

The business press continued to write about the industry at an accelerating pace (see Kipping (2012) for an overview of articles in *Business Week*). But there was some change in tone with not all reporting being positive. For instance, two lawyers wrote a popular book that was highly critical of the US government's use of outside advisors (Guttman and Willner 1976; see also Saint-Martin, Chapter 22, this volume). The press in general seemed to pay more attention to the growing influence of consultants and became more alert towards possible downsides. Thus, it appears that the sales methods used by George S. May, which had already been criticized by Higdon (see above), also prompted some negative reaction in the European press, not only for his firm, but for consulting in general (Wright and Kipping, Chapter 2, this volume).

Possibly prompted by these criticisms, in order to ascertain their own position in the emerging 'management fashion arena' (Faust 2002; Jung and Kieser, Chapter 16, this volume), consultancies began to become more active in publishing. This not only concerned books intended for managers, like the already mentioned bestseller *In Search of Excellence* by McKinsey consultants Peters and Waterman (1982), but others that examined their own industry or firm. Thus, Tisdall (1982) wrote a book about management consulting in the UK, commissioned by the Institute of Management Consultants (IMC). Her book also seems to have been motivated by the growing success of US consultancies in the UK (see Ferguson 2001; McKenna 2006), since it focuses mainly on the home-grown firms and their associations, the MCA, and the IMC. The accounting firms, which had also started to develop consulting activities after World War II (see McDougald and Greenwood, Chapter 5, this volume) were among the most active in publishing their histories, probably because many of them originated in the nineteenth century and at the time reached milestones in their development (e.g. Coopers & Lybrand 1984; Spacek's 1989 oral history of Arthur Andersen). Among the consulting firms, Arthur D. Little had its centenary history written by a journalist from the *New Yorker* (Kahn 1986). This was aimed at claiming its position among the leading management consultancies, which it only entered after World War II through operations research, having previously provided contract research for the chemical and natural resources industries. Additional firms, once again mainly accounting-based ones, followed, with similar commissioned histories in the subsequent decade (e.g. Allen and McDermott 1993; Jones 1995).

Most importantly, the 1980s also saw an increase in academic attention towards management consultancy. Thus, the work on OD consulting continued with some of the most influential publications being published as updated editions (e.g., French and Bell 1995). Furthermore, this work branched out into a much more normative literature, which tried to provide guidelines and advice for those wanting to offer consultancy services; a section whose numbers were swelling as the industry overall grew and as many of the middle managers who had been made redundant as a result of de-layering joined their ranks. Similarly, a growing series of publications sought to make the insights from the work of the consultants available to others, in particular managers and management students (e.g. Biech 1999; Rasiel 2001). Others, recognizing the rise of knowledge-intensive firms, developed titles specifically focusing on how to manage these firms (e.g. Maister 1993). Since the 1990s, dedicated textbooks have been published for the growing number of consulting courses (e.g. Wickham 1999; Biswas and Twitchell 2001).

Taken together, all of these books might subsequently have become the most successful parts of consulting-related publications in terms of sales. But with very few exceptions—namely O'Mahoney's (2010) recent textbook—they contain little if any research, and will therefore not be discussed further. Another important exception was first published by the International Labour Office in 1976 under the title *Management Consulting: A Guide to the Profession*. While in part aimed at offering advice to consulting practitioners, it also provides an in-depth overview and analysis of the industry and its various facets. This is probably still the single most comprehensive contribution to the literature from a practical perspective and is currently in its fourth edition (Kubr 2002).

At the same time, other academics became interested in consulting, albeit usually tangentially. Their work, however, foreshadowed some of the subsequent developments during the 1990s, when scholarly interest in the industry accelerated, as some might say, 'exploded' (Ernst and Kieser 2002). First of all, there were some studies that looked at consulting from a labour perspective. These studies examined cases where consultants had contributed to the degradation of work and the deskilling of workers posited by Braverman (1974). The most comprehensive work of this kind was conducted by Littler (1982) based on several case studies of UK firms, whose consultant was Bedaux. Subsequently, there were a growing number of studies, also by labour historians, examining the reaction and resistance of workers to this process (e.g. Downs 1990). Bedaux, in particular, received increasing attention in terms of his personal life (Christy 1984) and his consulting activities (Kreis 1990). Consulting received even greater academic attention as labour process theory morphed into critical management studies, where the focus extended beyond the politics of work organization and capitalism into a more general critique of managerialism, hegemony, and power (see below; also Nikolova and Devinney, Chapter 19; Czarniawska and Mazza, Chapter 21; both this volume).

Second, mirroring the remarks by Chandler (1962) and Servan-Schreiber (1968), DiMaggio and Powell (1983: 152) highlighted that '[l]arge organizations choose from a relatively small set of major consulting firms, which, like Johnny Appleseeds, spread a few organizational models throughout the land'. Their widely cited article became a kind of manifesto for what has since been called 'neo-institutionalism' in management and organization theory. And their example of consultancies as a force for mimetic isomorphism has significantly influenced subsequent studies of consultants as transmitters of organizational templates (even if that idea was first voiced by Hagedorn 1955), leading to many studies of diffusion. Unlike labour process theory, this was a more neutral view, which is why it was eventually questioned by more critical scholars and those seeing a translation rather than transmission process at work (for details, see Faust, Chapter 7, this volume).

1.2.3 Current State of the Art: Some Light, Many Dark Spots

The past two decades saw a general increase in publications on consulting from all the sources mentioned above, including, in particular, from former consultants, some of whom wrote some very harsh criticisms of the industry based on their own experiences (see above). Journalists also showed an increased interest in the industry, both using them as 'experts' on management matters and examining the consulting firms and their role in more depth. While some of their accounts were almost 'hagiographic', such as Edersheim (2004) on McKinsey's Marvin Bower, many others took a more critical stance, for example O'Shea and Madigan (1997), who used court filings to identify some of their (alleged) failures, or Byrne (2002), who, following the Enron collapse, highlighted that many other firms advised by McKinsey had gone bankrupt.

More importantly, from the point of view of this Handbook, is the fact that this period also saw academic research on management consulting come into its own, that is, it treated the industry and its rapid growth as a phenomenon worthy of examination per se. Many researchers adopted a 'critical approach' (Clark and Fincham 2002). Much of this work is summarized in the chapters of this Handbook. This section, therefore, only provides some more general remarks about the features of this research, as it has evolved over the last two decades and presents itself at the time of writing (in mid-2011).

First of all, it is necessary to stress the importance of the work by Abrahamson (esp. 1991, 1996, 2011), who has drawn the attention of researchers towards the notion of 'management fashions' and of 'fashion-setting communities', and how the latter, which include management consultancies, produce ideas to be consumed by managers. This sparked research on the different waves of management fashions, usually based on a bibliometric approach which, although criticized for its somewhat simplistic assumptions and methodological shortcomings (e.g. Clark 2004), nevertheless highlighted the tremendous impact and influence of fashionable ideas. More importantly, this research also drew attention to the different actors within the fashion-setting communities, not least the management consultants (e.g. David and Strang 2006), who had so far remained fairly marginal, or rather, tangential in the interests of scholars. However, much of the research and the subsequent publications on the topic emanated from Europe and were published in European-based journals or, even more frequently, in the form of monographs or contributions to edited volumes. This is all the more surprising as the industry itself originated in the United States, where it continues to have its largest market today (Wright and Kipping, Chapter 2, David, Chapter 4, both this volume; McKenna 2006; Kipping 2012).

The explanation for this can be found in the fact—and this is the second important observation about the extant academic literature—that research on management consultants has found it difficult to meet the two most important conditions for publication in the top-rated management journals in North America: the need to contribute to a major theoretical concern and to collect systematic, ideally quantitative data as the basis for statistical analysis and hypothesis testing. Consulting has yet to find its 'grand' theory (see Salaman 2002) and, from what has already been noted above, is an industry difficult to put into databases—partially due its unclear and fluid boundaries, and partially due to the reluctance of the main actors to share information for fear of breaching client confidentiality. Sturdy and colleagues (2009) note the lack of research based on observations of the detailed mechanics of the client–consultant relationship in situ. Much of the empirical research on consulting has therefore been conducted in the form of semi-structured interviews or observational studies—which only rarely find their way into these top-rated journals—or by historians, who are more used to incomplete data and more amenable to either filling gaps through triangulation or living with the idea that certain facts are 'possible' or 'likely' (rather than certain within a particular confidence interval).

Some consulting research has been able to attach itself to bigger questions and therefore find its way into those journals—but this has been and continues to be an exception. This concerns research that has dealt with the issue of knowledge management, which was quite fashionable in the 1990s, where some empirical studies led to publications in leading US journals such as *Academy of Management Journal, Administrative Science Quarterly*, and *Strategic Management Journal* (e.g. Hansen and Haas 2001). But even with respect to the knowledge-management strategies being pursued in consultancies, the vast majority of the research was published either in practitioner-oriented journals (less interested in formal rigour) or European outlets, which have tended to value the interest in the phenomenon per se—something that is now also changing. Slightly more successful were studies of management consulting that addressed the widely debated issues around PSFs and their evolution (see above; also Kirkpatrick, Muzio, and Ackroyd, Chapter 9; Morris, Gardner, and Anand, Chapter 14; this volume), but even here most of the cases came from the more central, 'traditional' professions such as accounting and law, since they offered, by definition, more comprehensive and complete data (for overviews, see Hinings 2005; Von Nordenflycht 2010).

What should also be noted here is that the lack of publications in top-rated US journals is by no means a reflection of the 'quality' of the extant literature. Rather, although the topic has attracted few scholars from the United States (something that is apparent by looking at the contributors to this Handbook), the literature is more varied in its underlying theoretical frameworks and, possibly, somewhat more critical than it might have been otherwise—and this is, we believe, ultimately a good thing.

Third, it needs to be highlighted that different academic disciplines have contributed to a very different degree to consulting research. In this respect, sociology—as well as management and organization studies based on sociological approaches—and economics present the opposite ends of the spectrum (see, respectively, Faust, Chapter 7, Saam, Chapter 10, both this volume; also Armbrüster 2006). While research based on the former abounds, at least in relative terms, economists have produced little to elucidate the management consulting industry, with almost all studies coming from heterodox, in particular neo-institutional rather than orthodox, neo-classical economics. This is not surprising given the lack of data for econometric analysis and the complexity of the phenomenon, which make formalization, for example through game theoretical modelling, close to impossible. A similar dichotomy can be found between history and geography.

The former has produced a large body of—usually atheoretical—research, not only in English but also in many other languages, tracing the industry's development either in particular countries or focusing on particular types of service, such as strategy or scientific management (see Part I in this volume for the latter and also above). A geographic perspective, by contrast, has only informed a handful of major studies despite significant potential, which could have linked the consulting phenomenon to important issues such as globalization (and spatial dislocation) or the rise and role of cities (see, for details, Faulconbridge and Jones, Chapter 11, this volume).

The chapters in this volume attempt to reflect the diverse, albeit skewed, nature of the extant academic literature. They also attempt to highlight possible avenues for future research within existing approaches. Thus, the final chapters in this Handbook point to important issues, where management consulting has yet to become the object of serious study, including, in no particular order, ethics, postcolonialism, and gender. The next subsection gives an overview of the Handbook's structure and briefly summarizes the main contribution of each of the chapters.

1.3 STRUCTURE AND CONTRIBUTION OF THE HANDBOOK

This book is not the first attempt at summarizing the extant academic literature and offering a kind of stepping stone for future research. While geared more towards practitioners, Kubr (2002) also provides an overview of some of that literature. Two edited volumes were published in 2002 with more of an academic focus. Clark and Fincham (2002) brought together some of the leading critical researchers on management consultancy. Although not intended to imply that these commentators and researchers shared identical views about consulting as an activity, the label 'critical' was used to highlight the fact that client demand for consulting cannot be assumed. Building on Alvesson's (1993) observation that consulting is beset by ambiguities in relation to the nature of its knowledge (i.e., its constant churn), its perceived value (i.e., is it superior to other forms of knowledge on organizations?), and its relation to the outcomes of a project (i.e., did consultants make the difference?), it is argued that consultants have to actively convince clients of their value and worth. The critical approach therefore emphasizes the inherent vulnerability of consulting to shifting perceptions of its legitimacy and value and the need to constantly establish its credibility via a range of strategies. By contrast, the contributions in Kipping and Engwall (2002) took a more comparative and historical perspective, examining the development of the industry in a wide range of countries, focusing in particular on how consultants gained legitimacy, how they managed their knowledge, and how they interacted with their clients. Finally, concurrently with this Handbook, Avakian and Clark (2012) are publishing a double volume collection of many of the key publications on management consulting. These two volumes complement this Handbook in that they provide ready access to many of the works that have most influenced thinking about management consulting and are frequently referenced in the subsequent chapters.

In terms of its structure, this Handbook is organized around some of the dominant themes in the literature. Thus, the first part focuses on the history of the industry, which not only reflects the fact that management consultants have influenced organizations for over a century, but also the strength of historical research on the industry. The chapters are organized chronologically, with Wright and Kipping examining the important origins of consulting in engineering and scientific management (see also above). Breaking with some perceived wisdom they show how consultants contributed significantly to the spread of these approaches, some of which continue to be applied today. The next chapter by Trahair and Bruce traces the trajectories of two of the pioneers of the human relations school, Elton Mayo and Eric Trist, whose ideas influenced many human resources (HR) consultancies and whose action research also prefigured some of the later OD consulting. David, in the following chapter, focuses on the institutional context, in which strategy consulting emerged and expanded in the United States, suggesting that changes in this context created opportunities subsequently exploited by a number of still well-known consultancies. The next two chapters (by, respectively, McDougald and Greenwood, and Galal, Richter, and Wendlandt) focus on firms that entered management consulting later from different origins—respectively, accounting and information technology. In both cases, they not only show how these firms eventually or became pre-eminent players in the industry, but also explain the consequences of this evolution for the organization, management and continuing resilience of these firms.

The second part of this Handbook provides extensive overviews of the various disciplinary approaches in the research on consulting, highlighting the significant differences in their respective contributions. Sociological perspectives, as shown in the chapter by Faust, have so far dominated much of the extant research. He subdivides the rich literature into two major perspectives, institutional and cognitive–cultural on the one hand, relational and structural on the other, and argues for an increased dialogue, if not integration, between the two. In another broad-based overview, Kipping and Wright examine management consulting from one of the key debates in the social sciences—the extent to which national business systems are converging. While the relevant literature seems to point towards convergence, there are also counter indications depending, to a large extent, on the level of analysis. As mentioned by Faust and discussed above, one of the major sociological questions concerns the nature and role of professionalism and professionalization in management consulting. The quite extensive extant research is examined in depth by Kirkpatrick, Muzio, and Ackroyd, who focus on the reasons why professionalism has remained rather weak and what consequences this has had for the industry. The final two chapters in this part of the Handbook discuss two academic disciplines, which so far have contributed relatively little to our understanding of the management consulting phenomenon: economics (discussed by Saam) and geography (summarized by Faulconbridge and Jones). In both cases, management consulting has only received marginal attention. This is unsurprising for economics, where mainstream approaches either lack the data or the tools to deal with its complexity. It is more surprising for geography, where issues of proximity and distance play an important role for consulting success with clients, and where consultants have played an important part in the decisions about the (re)location of economic activities.

The next three parts develop in greater depth three of the issues that have found most attention in the previous literature: knowledge management, relationship with manage-ment fashion, and consultant–client interaction. The chapters in the part on knowledge management address the notion that, at their core, management consultants are creators and disseminators of management knowledge and have therefore been viewed as exem-plars of knowledge-management processes. Werr begins with a broad overview examin-ing the nature of consulting knowledge, how it is shared within the firm, whether these processes impact on performance, and how consultancies create new knowledge. Heusinkveld and Benders pick up on the last theme and explore how consultancies engage in 'new concept development' and then apply this knowledge in different client contexts. Morris, Gardner, and Anand draw on the literature on professional service firms to initially examine the different macrostructural arrangements adopted by con-sulting firms and how these have changed over time. Following this they discuss the microstructural arrangements, which underpin how work is organized in these firms. Alvesson's chapter completes this part by identifying the special features of knowledge work and what these imply for the management of knowledge workers, their retention, and identities. This chapter stresses the importance of normative control within consult-ing firms.

The chapters in the fourth part of this Handbook focus on the relationship between management consulting and fashion. Jung and Kieser examine the nature of manage-ment fashions, their importance in generating client demand, and the role that consult-ants play as members of a 'management fashion arena'. Clark, Bhatanacharoen, and Greatbatch look at a group of celebrity consultants known as management gurus. They stress how their celebrity status is founded on their ability to create and disseminate fashionable management ideas through bestselling management books and lectures. Engwall's chapter turns to examining the relationship between business schools and strategy consulting in terms of the former's supply of graduates, their role in fostering 'celebrity consultants', and the way in which these consultancies have emulated various features of business schools.

The fifth part of this Handbook focuses on a core and much researched aspect of consulting—the client–consultant relationship. Nikolova and Devinney provide a detailed overview of the literature on this relationship by identifying three broad and contrasting models: the expert/functionalist, the social learning perspective, and the critical approach. The features of each model are explored in relation to a common set of factors (nature of consulting, nature of client–consultant interaction, power relations). Fincham seeks to rebalance the current focus on the consultant side of the relationship by stressing the role of clients. His chapter demonstrates how such an approach can generate new understanding in relation to the knowledge creation, power, and dependency in the client–consultant relationship, and the notion of the client itself. Czarniawska and Mazza adopt a social constructivist perspective to examine the client–consultant relationship; drawing on Luhmann, the role of consultants as merchants of meaning; and, drawing on ideas from anthropology, consulting as a 'liminal condition'. Saint-Martin looks at the role of consultants in central government, why their use has expanded and the possible consequences of the growing influence of consultants for the operation of government (both positive and negative).

The final section of this Handbook is intended to be exploratory by considering how to develop existing areas of focus in terms of potential gaps but also identifying new approaches that are currently absent from the literature but have strong potential to contribute to broadening our understanding consulting work. In this respect Sturdy draws together a number of the themes of earlier chapters and introduces others to identify productive areas for future research in terms of empirical, theoretical, and methodological focus, as well as addressing the absence of importance groups such as employees, unions, and citizens. Krehmeyer and Freeman discuss how different approaches from the literature on ethics could expand our understanding of consulting work, help focus on the codes of ethics that operate within the consulting industry, as well as assist in addressing debates around the ethics of consulting (i.e., confidentiality, client's interest, conflicts of interest). Kelan reviews the literature on gender in consulting to illustrate that many of the broader endemic organizational gender issues are present within consulting. This chapter emphasizes the fact that future work would benefit from examining the gendered nature of the career model, consulting skills, and the notion of the ideal consultant. The final chapter of this Handbook by Frenkel and Shenhav considers the implications of a post-colonial perspective for future thinking and research on consulting work. Their main point is that studies examining consulting work at a global level, and in emerging markets in particular, need to move away from such stereotypes as 'Western-advanced' and 'Third World-developing' since these perpetuate historical power relations and a 'sense of supremacy', with the former shaping the latter in their own image. To overcome this imbalance and to ensure appropriate prominence for and sensitivity to non-Western interests they propose a 'hybrid space', which actively recognizes the immediate market conditions of the relationship as well as the 'historically situated geopolitical context'.

Individually, the chapters offer authoritative overviews of the key themes in the extant and emergent literature on management consulting. Collectively, they demonstrate the breadth of empirical and theoretical approaches adopted, the opportunities to extend these, and the degree to which work in this area is highly interdisciplinary. As we stated at the outset of this chapter, research on management consulting is a vibrant area of study which generates important insights that contribute to broader debates in business and management and the social sciences. We very much hope that the contributions in this Handbook will galvanize readers into conducting research that further expands our understanding of management consulting.

NOTE

* We are grateful to Pojanath Bhatanacharoen, Robin Fincham, Andrew Sturdy, and Chris Wright for their helpful comments on an earlier version of this chapter.

REFERENCES

Abbott, A. (1988). *The System of Professions: An Essay on the Division of Expert Labor*. Chicago: University of Chicago Press.

Abrahamson, E. (1991). 'Managerial Fads and Fashions: The Diffusion and Rejection of Innovations'. *Academy of Management Review*, 16/3, 586–612.

Abrahamson, E. (1996). 'Management Fashion'. *Academy of Management Review*, 21/1, 254–285.

Abrahamson, E. (2011). 'The Iron Cage: Ugly, Uncool, and Unfashionable', *Organization Studies*, 32/5, 615–629.

Aitken, H. (1960). *Taylorism at Watertown Arsenal: Scientific Management in Action, 1908–1915*. Cambridge, MA: Harvard University Press.

Allen, D. G. and McDermott, K. (1993). *Accounting for Success: A History of Price Waterhouse in America 1890–1990*. Boston: Harvard Business School Press.

Alvesson, M. (1993). 'Organizations as Rhetoric: Knowledge Intensive Firms and the Struggle with Ambiguity', *Journal of Management Studies*, 30/6, 997–1019.

Alvesson, M. (2004). *Knowledge Work and Knowledge-Intensive Firms*. Oxford: Oxford University Press.

Armenakis, A.A. and Burdg, H.B. (1988). 'Consultation Research: Contributions to Practice and Directions for Improvement'. *Journal of Management*, 14/2, 339–365.

Ashford, M. (1998). *Con Tricks: The Shadowy World of Management Consultancy and How to Make it Work for You*. London: Simon & Schuster.

Avakian, S. and Clark, T. (2012). *Management Consultants—Volumes 1 and 2 (Part of the International Library of Critical Writings on Business and Management Series)*. Cheltenham: Edward Elgar.

Barton, D. (2011). 'Capitalism for the Long Term'. *Harvard Business Review*, 89/3 (March), 84–91.

Beckhard, R. (1969). *Organizational Development*. Reading, MA: Addison-Wesley.

Bell, D. (1973). *The Coming of Post-Industrial Society: A Venture in Social Forecasting*. New York: Basic Books.

Bennis, W.G. (1969). *The Nature of Organization Development*. Reading, MA: Addison-Wesley.

Biech, E. (1999). *The Business of Consulting: The Basics and Beyond*. San Francisco, CA: Jossey-Bass Pfeiffer.

Biswas, S. and Twitchell, D. (2001). *Management Consulting: A Complete Guide to the Industry*. 2nd edn. New York: John Wiley & Sons.

Booz Allen Hamilton (2009). *Annual Report for 2009*. http://www.boozallen.com/about/annual-report accessed 14 June 2010.

Braverman, H. (1974). *Labor and Monopoly Capital: The Degradation of Work in the Twentieth Century*. New York: Monthly Review Press.

Byrne, J. A. (2002). 'Inside McKinsey'. *Business Week*, 8 (July), 54–62.

Cailluet, L. (2000). 'McKinsey, Total-CFP et la *M-Form*: Un exemple français d'adaptation d'un modèle d'organisation importé'. *Entreprises et Histoire*, 25 (October), 26–45.

Capron, M. (2000). 'Les experts des comités d'entreprise en France: une coopération originale avec les représentants des salariés'. *Entreprises et Histoire*, 25 (October), 93–103.

Chandler Jr, A. D. (1962). *Strategy and Structure: Chapters in the History of the Industrial Enterprise*. Cambridge, MA: MIT Press.

Chandler Jr, A. D. (1977). *The Visible Hand: The Managerial Revolution in American Business*. Cambridge, MA: Belknap Press.

Christy, J. (1984). *The Price of Power: A Biography of Charles Eugène Bedaux*. Toronto: Doubleday.

Clark, T. (1995). *Managing Consultants: Consultancy as the Management of Impressions*. Buckingham: Open University Press.

Clark, T. (2004). 'The Fashion of Management Fashion: A Surge Too Far?' *Organization*, 11/2, 297–306.

Clark, T. and Fincham, R. (2002). *Critical Consulting: New Perspectives on the Management Advice Industry*. Oxford: Blackwell.

Coopers & Lybrand (1984). *The Early History of Coopers & Lybrand. Fiftieth anniversary, 1898–1948*. Reprint. New York: Garland.

Craig, D. (2005). *Rip Off! The Scandalous Inside Story of the Management Consulting Money Machine*. London: The Original Book Company.

David, R. J. and Strang, D. (2006). 'When Fashion is Fleeting: Transitory Collective Beliefs and the Dynamics of TQM Consulting'. *Academy of Management Journal*, 49/2, 215–233.

DiMaggio, P. and Powell, W. (1983). 'The Iron Cage Revisited: Institutional Isomorphism and Collective Rationality in Organizational Fields'. *American Sociological Review*, 48 (April), 147–160.

Downs, L. L. (1990). 'Industrial Decline, Rationalization and Equal Pay: The Bedaux Strike at Rover Automobile Company'. *Social History*, 15/1: 45–73.

Drucker, P. F. (1959). *The Landmarks of Tomorrow: A Report on the New 'Post-Modern' World*. London: Heinemann.

Drucker, P. F. (2002). 'They're Not Employees, They're People'. *Harvard Business Review*, 80/2 (February), 70–77.

Edersheim, E. H. (2004). *McKinsey's Marvin Bower: Vision, Leadership, and the Creation of Management Consulting*. Hoboken, NJ: John Wiley & Sons.

Eisenhardt, K. M. and Santos, F. M. (2001). 'Knowledge-Based View: A New Theory of Strategy?' In A. Pettigrew, H. Thomas, and R. Whittington (eds), *Handbook of Strategy and Management*. London: Sage, 139–164.

Emerson, H. (1909). *Efficiency as a Basis for Operations and Wages*. New York: The Engineering Magazine.

Emerson, H. (1912). *The Twelve Principles of Efficiency*. New York: The Engineering Magazine Company.

Ernst, B. and Kieser, A. (2002). 'In Search of Explanations for the Consulting Explosion'. In K. Sahlin-Andersson and L. Engwall (eds), *The Expansion of Management Knowledge: Carriers, Flows, and Sources*. Stanford, CA: Stanford University Press, 47–73.

Faust, M. (2002). 'Consultancies as Actors in Knowledge Arenas: Evidence from Germany'. In M. Kipping and L. Engwall (eds), *Management Consulting: Emergence and Dynamics of a Knowledge Industry*. Oxford: Oxford University Press, 146–163.

FEACO (2010). *Survey of the European Management Consultancy 2009/2010*. Brussels: Fédération Européenne des Associations de Conseils en Organisation (FEACO).

Ferguson, M. (2001). *The Rise of Management Consulting in Britain*. Aldershot: Ashgate.

Films of Record (1999). *Masters of the Universe*, Channel 4 (UK), London.

Fincham, R. and Clark, T. (2002). 'Introduction: The Emergence of Critical Perspectives on Consulting'. In T. Clark and R. Fincham (eds), *Critical Consulting: New Perspectives on the Management Advice Industry*. Oxford: Blackwell, 1–18.

Forbes (2010). 'McKinsey'. In 'America's Largest Private Companies'. Available at http://www. forbes.com/lists/2010/21/private-companies-10_McKinsey-Co_IPPW.html accessed 30 September 2011.

French, W. L. and Bell, C. H. (1995). *Organization Development: Behavioural Science Interventions for Organization Improvement*. Englewood Cliffs, NJ: Prentice-Hall.

Gross, C. and Kieser, A. (2006). 'Are Consultants Moving Towards Professionalization?' In R. Greenwood, R. Suddaby, and M. McDougald (eds), *Professional Service Firms* (*Research in the Sociology of Organizations*, vol. 24). Oxford: JAI Press, 69–100.

Guttman, D. and Willner, B. (1976). *The Shadow Government: The Government's Multi-Dollar Give-Away of its Decision-Making Powers to Private Management Consultants, Experts and Think Tanks*. New York: Pantheon.

Hagedorn, H. (1955). 'The Management Consultant as Transmitter of Business Techniques'. *Explorations in Entrepreneurial History*, 7, 164–173.

Hansen, M. T. and Haas, M. R. (2001). 'Competing for attention in knowledge markets: Electronic document circulation in a management consulting company'. *Administrative Science Quarterly*, 46/1, 1–28.

Hansen, M. T., Nohria, N. and Tierney, T. (1999). 'What is your strategy for managing knowledge ?', *Harvard Business Review*, 77/2, 106–16.

Higdon, H. (1969). *The Business Healers*. New York: Random House.

Hinings, C. R. (2005). 'The Professions'. In S. Ackroyd, R. Batt, P. Thompson, and P. S. Tolbert (eds), *The Oxford Handbook of Work and Organization*. Oxford: Oxford University Press, 485–507.

Jackall, R. (1988). *Moral Mazes: The World of Corporate Managers*. Oxford: Oxford University Press.

John, R. R. (1997). 'Elaborations, Revisions, Dissents: Alfred D. Chandler Jr's, "The Visible Hand" after Twenty Years'. *Business History Review*, 71/2, 151–200.

Jones, E. (1995). *True and Fair: The History of Price Waterhouse*. London: Hamish Hamilton.

Kahn, E. J. (1986). *The Problem Solvers: A History of Arthur D. Little, Inc.* Boston: Little Brown.

Keeble, D. and Schwalbach, J. (1995). 'Management Consultancy in Europe'. ESRC Centre for Business Research, University of Cambridge, Working paper no. 1.

Kipping, M. (1999). 'American Management Consulting Companies in Western Europe, 1910s to 1990s: Products, Reputation, and Relationships'. *Business History Review*, 73/2, 190–220.

Kipping, M. (2000). 'Consultancy and Conflicts: Bedaux at Lukens Steel and the Anglo-Iranian Oil Company'. *Entreprises et Histoire*, 25, 9–25.

Kipping, M. (2002). 'Trapped in Their Wave: The Evolution of Management Consultancies'. In T. Clark and R. Fincham (eds), *Critical Consulting: New Perspectives on the Management Advice Industry*. Oxford: Blackwell, 28–49.

Kipping, M. (2011). 'Hollow from the Start? Image Professionalism in Management Consulting'. *Current Sociology*, 59/4 (July), 530–550.

Kipping, M. (2012). *From Racket to Riches: The Management Consultancy Business in Historical and Comparative Perspective*. Oxford: Oxford University Press.

Kipping, M. and Armbrüster, T. (2002). 'The Burden of Otherness: Limits of Consultancy Interventions in Historical Case Studies'. In M. Kipping and L. Engwall (eds), *Management Consulting: Emergence and Dynamics of a Knowledge Industry*. Oxford: Oxford University Press, 203–221.

Kipping, M. and Engwall, L. (eds) (2002). *Management Consulting: Emergence and Dynamics of a Knowledge Industry*. Oxford: Oxford University Press.

Kreis, S. (1990). 'The Diffusion of an Idea: A History of Scientific Management in Britain, 1890–1945'. Unpublished PhD dissertation, University of Missouri-Columbia.

Kubr, M. (2002 [1976]). *Management Consulting: A Guide to the Profession*. Geneva: International Labour Office.

Larson, M. S. (1977). *The Rise of Professionalism: A Sociological Analysis*. Berkeley, CA: University of California Press.

Leicht, K. T. and Lyman, E. C. M. (2006). 'Markets, Institutions and the Crisis of Professional Practice'. *Research in the Sociology of Organizations*, 24, 17–44.

Littler, C. (1982). *The Development of the Labour Process in Capitalist Societies: A Comparative Analysis of Work Organisation in Britain, the USA, and Japan*. London: Heinemann.

Lloyd, T. and Sveiby, K-E. (1987). *Managing Know How: Add Value by Valuing Creativity*. London: Bloomsbury.

Macdonald, S. (2006). 'Babes and Sucklings: Management Consultants and Novice Clients'. *European Management Journal*, 24/6, 411–421.

Machiavelli, N. (2003). *The Prince*. London: Longman.

Maister, D. (1993). *Managing the Professional Service Firm*. New York: Free Press.

Maynard, H. B., Stegemerten, G. J., and Schwab, J. L. (1948). *Methods Time Measurement*. New York: McGraw-Hill.

McKenna, C. (2006). *The World's Newest Profession: Management Consulting in the Twentieth Century*. New York: Cambridge University Press.

McKinsey, J. O. (1922). *Budgetary Control*. New York: Ronald Press.

Merkle, J. E. (1980). *Management and Ideology: The Legacy of the International Scientific Management Movement*. Berkeley, CA: University of California Press.

Michaels, E., Handfield-Jones, H., and Axelrod, B. (2001). *The War for Talent*. Boston: Harvard Business School Press.

Mohe, M. and Seidl, D. (2011). 'Theorizing the Client–Consultant Relationship from the Perspective of Social-Systems Theory', *Organization*, 18: 3–22.

Muzio, D., Kirkpatrick, I., and Kipping, M. (2011). 'Professions, Organizations and the State: Applying the Sociology of the Professions to the Case of Management Consultancy', *Current Sociology*, 59/6: 805–24.

Nelson, D. (1980). *Frederick W. Taylor and the Rise of Scientific Management*. Madison: University of Wisconsin Press.

Nelson, D. (ed.) (1992). *A Mental Revolution: Scientific Management since Taylor*. Columbus: Ohio State University Press.

Nelson, D. (1995). 'Industrial Engineering and the Industrial Enterprise'. In N. R. Lamoreaux and D. M. G. Raff (eds), *Coordination and Information: Historical Perspectives on the Organization of Enterprise*. Chicago: University of Chicago Press, 35–50.

Neukom, J. G. (1975). *McKinsey Memoirs: A Personal Perspective*. New York: Privately Printed.

Newell, S., Scarbrough, H., Swan, J., and Robertson, M. (2002). *Knowledge Work and Knowledge Workers*. London: Palgrave.

O'Mahoney, J. (2010). *Management Consultancy*. Oxford: Oxford University Press.

O'Shea, J. and Madigan, C. (1997). *Dangerous Company: The Consulting Powerhouses and the Businesses They Save and Ruin*. London: Nicholas Brealey.

Peters, T. J. and Waterman Jr, R. H. (1982). *In Search of Excellence: Lessons from American Best-Run Companies*. New York: Harper & Row.

Pinault, L. (2000). *Consulting Demons: Inside the Unscrupulous World of Global Corporate Consulting*. Chichester: John Wiley & Sons.

Porter, M. E. (1980). *Competitive Strategy*. New York: Free Press.

Quigel Jr, J. P. (1992). 'The Business of Selling Efficiency: Harrington Emerson and the Emerson Efficiency Engineers, 1900–1930'. Unpublished PhD dissertation, Pennsylvania State University.

Rasiel, E. M. (2001). *The McKinsey Way: Using the Techniques of the World's Top Strategy Consultants to Help You and Your Business*. New York: McGraw Hill Professional.

Ruef, M. (2002). 'At the Interstices of Organizations: The Expansion of the Management Consulting Profession, 1933–1997'. In K. Sahlin-Andersson and L. Engwall (eds), *The Expansion of Management Knowledge: Carriers, Flows, and Sources*. Stanford, CA: Stanford University Press, 74–95.

Schein, E.H. (1969). *Process Consultation: Its Role in Organization Development*. Reading, MA: Addison-Wesley.

Servan-Schreiber, J. J. (1968). *The American Challenge*. New York: Atheneum.

Spacek, L. (1989). *The Growth of Arthur Andersen & Co., 1928–1973: An Oral History*. New York: Garland.

Stehr, N. (1994). *Knowledge Societies*. London: Sage.

Sturdy, A. (2011). 'Consultancy's Consequences? A Critical Assessment of Management Consultancy's Impact on Management', *British Journal of Management*, 22, 517–530.

Sturdy, A. and Wright, C. (2011). 'The Active Client: The Boundary-Spanning Roles of Internal Consultants as Gatekeepers, Brokers and Partners of their External Counterparts'. *Management Learning*, 42/5, 485–505.

Sturdy, A., Clark, T., Fincham, R., and Handley, K. (2009). *Management Consultancy in Action: Relationships, Knowledge and Power*. Oxford: Oxford University Press.

Thompson, C. B. (1917). *The Theory and Practice of Scientific Management*. Boston: Houghton Mifflin.

Tisdall, P. (1982). *Agents of Change: The Development and Practice of Management Consultancy*. London: Heinemann.

Toffler, A. (1971). *Future Shock*. London: Pan Books.

Urwick, L. and Brech, E. (1945). *The Making of Scientific Management*. Vol. I: *Thirteen Pioneers*. London: Pitman.

Von Nordenflycht, A. (2010). 'What is a Professional Service Firm? Towards a Theory and Taxonomy of Knowledge Intensive Firms'. *Academy of Management Review*, 35/1, 155–174.

Wickham, P. A. (1999). *Management Consulting*. London: FT Prentice Hall.

Wolf, W. B. (1978). *Management and Consulting: An Introduction to James O. McKinsey*. Ithaca: Cornell University Press.

Wright, C. (2009). 'Inside Out? Organizational Membership, Ambiguity and the Ambivalent Identity of the Internal Consultant'. *British Journal of Management*, 20/3, 309–322.

PART 1

....

HISTORICAL DEVELOPMENT OF MANAGEMENT CONSULTING

....

....

CHAPTER 2

THE ENGINEERING ORIGINS OF THE CONSULTING INDUSTRY AND ITS LONG SHADOW

....

CHRISTOPHER WRIGHT
MATTHIAS KIPPING

2.1 INTRODUCTION

....

WHILE the engineering origins of management have been extensively analysed (Chandler 1965; Shenhav 1999), a coherent analysis of the engineering origins of management consulting has yet to be provided. These origins have largely fallen into the cracks of history, because of two 'myths' perpetuated by much of the extant literature. The first of these concerns the almost mythical role attributed to the towering figure of Frederick W. Taylor as the 'father' of scientific management (Copley 1923; Nelson 1980), and, according to some, the 'grandfather' of management consulting (Tisdall 1982; Kanigel 1997;). He and his ideas have obsessed generations of scholars—an obsession that has obscured the contributions of other actors, who, at least from the perspective of the nascent consulting industry, were equally, if not more, important. More generally, the focus on the 'pioneers of scientific management' (Urwick and Brech 1945) has obscured the role of myriads of less well-known individuals (Nelson 1992, 1995) and, even more importantly, the role of several consulting firms that implemented these ideas in a large number of organizations around the world.

The second myth concerns the suggestion that these individuals and organizations, known at the time as 'efficiency experts' or industrial engineers, were not 'real' consultants. The origins of 'true' or 'modern' consulting, so that story goes, lie with those advising top managers on strategy and organization, not those who used stop-watches to speed up employees' work on the shop floor. Invented to a certain extent by James O. McKinsey and, more importantly, Marvin Bower, to distinguish their firm, McKinsey & Co., as the pre-eminent brand of 'corporate advisers', this view has been perpetuated in recent accounts of the industry's history (McKenna 2006). This view, nevertheless, remains a historical construction. For instance, rather than eschewing operational efficiency, McKinsey's own promotional brochure from 1957 lists the following three among its seven 'fields of specialization': 'Manufacturing and Operations' (which included 'Wage incentive and supervisory incentive plans'), 'Office, Plant, and Warehouse Operating Methods and Procedures', as well as 'Personnel Management and Labor Relations' (McKinsey & Co. 1957).

Similarly, in terms of raw numbers, engineering-based firms remained dominant for a long time. In the mid-1930s, efficiency consultants such as Bedaux and Emerson already employed several hundred consultants in many offices around the world (see below), while the firm founded by James O. McKinsey in 1926 had less than thirty people in their Chicago and New York offices and Booz Allen & Hamilton, another of the 'modern' management consultancies founded in 1914, only eleven (McKenna 1995: 54). And even around 1960, the 'gilded age' of the strategy consultants according to McKenna (2006: ch. 6), the largest and internationally most active US consultancies were actually George S. May and H. B. Maynard, both of which focused on operational improvement. Thus, based on its highly successful Methods-Time-Measurement (MTM) system, the latter employed about 330 consultants in eight European offices at the end of the 1960s, while McKinsey employed less than half that number in six offices (Kipping 1999: 205, 210). However, the purpose of this chapter is not to diminish the importance of the corporate strategy consultants, whose growth and institutionalization is examined in detail by David (Chapter 4, this volume), but to re-emphasize the significance of the industrial engineering origins of consultancy, and correct the historical record regarding the myth of management consulting as solely the province of boardroom advisers. For our account, we draw on the limited and rather dispersed literature that exists on this topic and, where necessary, complement it with our own research.

The chapter is subdivided in four main sections, organized chronologically. The first of these revisits the origins of scientific management and the role of Taylor and his allies in seeking to diffuse this distinctive model of management to a broader business audience. Despite the emphasis accorded to Taylor and the early 'gurus' of scientific management in many management histories (e.g. Wren 2005), the contribution of consultants to the way in which this system was diffused, adapted, and translated across companies, industries, and nations has yet to receive significant attention from researchers. In the second part of the chapter, we emphasize the pivotal role played by the early efficiency consultants, focusing in particular on the firms established by Harrington Emerson and Charles E. Bedaux. These consultants proved adept at spreading the techniques of scientific management as a codified consulting methodology, and we examine their origin, their (internal) organization, their international expansion, and their influence. The third section of the chapter outlines the post-World War II growth of efficiency consulting and the role of firms such as H. B. Maynard and George S. May, which, although less well known today than Booz Allen & Hamilton and McKinsey & Co., were amongst the largest and most pervasive of the global consultancies during the 1950s and 1960s. In the fourth section, we chronicle the demise of these consultancies as (independent) organizations, which started, slowly yet steadily, in the early 1970s and reached something of an end point in 2008, when Accenture acquired what little was left of Maynard & Co. (O'Connell 2008). In addition, and perhaps more importantly, we look at the lasting influence of industrial engineering, which has shaped contemporary management practices such as quality management, lean production, and business process re-engineering (BPR). The chapter concludes by outlining areas where further research is needed on the history and continued role of efficiency consulting and its impact on management practice.

2.2 TAYLOR, SCIENTIFIC MANAGEMENT, AND THE LIMITS OF DIFFUSION

Extant research on the development of scientific management has focused predominantly on the founding role of Frederick W. Taylor, his creation of the principles of scientific management, and the small and close-knit group of 'disciples' (such as Sanford Thompson, Carl Barth, Henry Gantt, and Frank and Lillian Gilbreth) that followed Taylor and fought for what they viewed as a radical reconceptualization of industrial management: the so-called 'mental revolution' (Nelson 1992). The initial spread of Taylor's technique and ideas was largely based on the publications of his method (Taylor 1903, 1911), his role as a consulting engineer to a number of industrial companies (including Bethlehem Steel—the site of the famous pig-iron experiment), his lectures at Harvard University, the publicity generated first by the so-called Eastern Rate Case of 1910, when the reformist lawyer and later Supreme Court justice Louis Brandeis argued that the application of 'scientific management' would enable the railway companies to increase wages without raising their rates, and then by the controversy that followed the strike against the 'Taylor System' at the government's Watertown Arsenal, which led to a Congressional investigation (Aitken 1960; Wren 2005).

For both management researchers and critics, Taylor's system of scientific management is seen as having a profound impact on the nature of industrial work and even our broader society (e.g. Braverman 1974; Merkle 1980; Locke 1982; Wren 2005). However, while the origins of scientific management and the life of Frederick Taylor have been extensively documented, how these practices and ideas became diffused more broadly throughout industry, societies, and globally is less well articulated. As studies both at the time and more recently have shown, the immediate impact of Taylor and his disciples in diffusing scientific management to American industry during the early 1900s was limited. For example, following Taylor's death in 1915, C. Bertrand Thompson's 1917 survey of scientific management practice found only 113 industrial plants applying the full Taylor system (Thompson 1917). Similarly, Nelson's (1991) analysis for the 1920s, found only a sparse use of the full scientific management system in US factories, with the use of these methods most pronounced in labour-intensive and batch assembly settings, rather than the larger modern and capital-intensive industries such as automobiles and steel. While Taylor and his disciples worked hard to promote the benefits of scientific management through extensive lectures, publications, tours, and through consulting to selected companies—in a way not dissimilar to current 'gurus' (see Clark, Bhatanacharoen, and Greatbatch, Chapter 17, this volume)—existing histories have tended to neglect the diffusion process beyond these initial 'pioneers'.

What seems clear is that the actual process of the diffusion of scientific management by Taylor and his disciples was always constrained whilst it was limited to ad hoc inter-personal exchanges and small, individual consulting applications. Taylor's efforts in proselytizing his method were not motivated by a desire to make money, but rather to gain professional recognition and, more broadly, to improve management–labour relations (Nelson 1980). However, beyond the publication of the theory and practice of scientific management, and the later formation of associations and organizations such as the Taylor Society and the International Committee of Scientific Management (Comité International de l'Organisation Scientifique (CIOS)), which served to institutionalize scientific management thinking and practice (Merkle 1980; Cayet 2005), more extensive diffusion required the commercialization of the scientific management technique as a consulting service. This point has been highlighted by Littler (1978: 187), who notes how the application of new management models often involves 'an historical lag between the ideas of intellectuals and those of active practitioners. Priests and warriors never think alike.' It was the formation of dedicated management consultancies in the early decades of the twentieth century that acted as 'carrying organizations' (Sahlin-Andersson and Engwall 2002) for the diffusion of these practices on a far broader scale than was possible by the originators of the system (Littler 1982; Guillén 1994). Moreover, as the embryonic research on these early consulting firms suggests, they not only played a major role in the diffusion of scientific management, but also formed the basis for the growth of management consulting as the defined business activity we recognize today.

2.3 THE EARLY EFFICIENCY CONSULTANTS

Very few of the pioneering scientific management engineers set up lasting consulting organizations. They usually offered advice on an ad hoc basis individually or in small groups, and so did a large number of less well-known individual consulting engineers (Nelson 1992). Frank Gilbreth and his wife Lillian established a consultancy called Gilbreth Inc., but they apparently did not employ anybody else. In any case, the Gilbreths focused more on developing and defending their own ideas about micromotion and fatigue against criticism from Taylor and his disciples rather than advising companies (Price 1992). After Frank Gilbreth's early death in 1924, Lillian continued to proselytize their ideas for another five decades (Lancaster 2004). C. Bertrand Thompson, mentioned above, opened an office in Paris in 1918 and so did Wallace Clark, a disciple of Henry Gantt, who apparently also had offices in London, Berlin, Prague, Warsaw, Geneva, and Athens. However, all of these offices were closed at the outset of World War II if not before (Moutet 1975: 32–34). The two firms that had a lasting impact on the international diffusion of scientific management and the emergence of consulting as a business activity were those founded by Harrington Emerson and Charles E. Bedaux in 1907 and 1916 respectively.

2.3.1 The Emerson Engineers

Probably the first to establish a proper consulting organization with employees and several offices was one of Taylor's competitors: Harrington Emerson (1853–1931). So far, his consulting activities have received little attention in the literature. The most comprehensive account can be found in an unpublished Ph.D. dissertation by Quigel (1992), who focuses on his life, the system he devised as well as its application, and also provides some details on the consulting organization that Emerson created in 1907. After a six-year tenure as professor of modern languages at the State University of Nebraska, followed by mixed success as a venture capitalist and entrepreneur, Harrington Emerson decided in the early 1900s to become an efficiency engineer. He had become acquainted with Taylor's and others' work at the meetings of the American Society of Mechanical Engineers, and with scientific management in general through several of the ventures he had been involved in (Quigel 1992: ch. 2). On this basis, he developed a somewhat different, proprietary system to optimize work practices and introduce payment-by-results (Sanders 1926; Balderston 1930). Emerson published his ideas in several books, including *Efficiency as a Basis for Operation and Wages* (1919).

But more important from our point of view were his activities as a consultant. Among his most notable and widely publicized early assignments was the reorganization of the machine and locomotive repair shops of the Santa Fe Railroad, which he conducted between 1904 and 1907, assisted by a few time study engineers, including his brother Samuel (Quigel 1992: ch. 3). Taylor looked down upon Emerson's work, suggesting that his efforts there 'were perhaps one quarter of the way towards scientific management' (quoted by Quigel 1992: 146), an opinion shared by many other 'purists' (ibid.: 146–149). Nevertheless, in terms of the actual diffusion of scientific management *and* the origins of consulting as a business activity, this project carries a double significance. First, according to Chandler (1965) railways had been the birthplace of managerial enterprise and this was the first time a large railway had actually introduced scientific management methods. Second, the publicity generated by this project helped Emerson attract new clients to such an extent that he hired additional consulting engineers and established his own consulting organization in 1907, originally called the Emerson Company Engineers and renamed the Emerson Efficiency Engineers in 1913 (Quigel 1992: ch. 5).

The Emerson Efficiency Engineers was arguably the first management consulting firm and it was quite successful. It employed its own efficiency engineers, thirty of them between

1913 and 1918, subdivided into five 'grades': apprentice, assistant, sub-associate, associate, directing officer. In addition to its 'regular' employees, it also drew on a broad range of 'affiliated specialists' (Quigel 1992: 289–294). In terms of geographic scope, by 1917, according to its own brochure, the consultancy had offices, called 'agencies', in New York, Pittsburgh, Chicago, Philadelphia, and Tacoma. It also had a short-lived presence outside the United States just before World War I. An Italian engineer named A. M. Morrini had studied the Emerson system in a number of US companies (Christy 1984: 27–35). In 1914, he returned to Europe and established a small office in Paris, where he and a few consulting engineers applied the Emerson system to metalworking and automobile firms. However, after the outbreak of World War I, Morrini closed the office and went back to the United States (Moutet 1975: 31–33).

In 1919 under pressure from his own brother Samuel and younger associates, Emerson reorganized the consultancy—giving the former more power over decision-making—and renamed it the Emerson Engineers. This was the prelude to a more profound shake-up in 1925, when Emerson himself was removed from the firm by 'the younger men over whom', according to his own recollection, he 'had ruled somewhat despotically over the last fifteen years' and who wanted 'to run things to suit themselves' (quoted by Quigel 1992: 288). Emerson subsequently continued to promote the cause of scientific management and advised several foreign governments on transportation policy. The Emerson Engineers thrived at least until the 1950s (unfortunately, after 1925 Quigel's study follows the trail of the man rather than the firm).

Emerson was of crucial importance for the nascent consulting industry. During his tenure, the consultancy advised nearly 200 companies in improving their operational efficiency; these included well-known firms such as Bethlehem Steel, Alcoa, and General Motors. According to Quigel (1992: 279) it was, in particular, the consultancy's 'orientation towards achieving immediate gains and meeting the specific needs of clients [that] not only facilitated management's acceptance of efficiency engineering but also expanded the role of the consulting engineer'. Another measure of Emerson's impact during the inter-war period can be found in a survey of different wage payment systems, conducted by the National Industrial Conference Board (NICB 1930). While not statistically representative, the survey covered 1,214 plants, employing a total of almost 800,000 workers. The first important finding was that only a minority were operating under sophisticated payment-by-results systems. Most workers were either paid piece rates or time wages. Among the competing systems, Emerson's came in third with a total of 9,252 workers being paid according to his system, very close to the Halsey system (9,953 workers), which came second. Both were vastly outnumbered by the 33,177 workers operating under another consultancy-driven efficiency programme: the Bedaux system.

2.3.2 Bedaux and the Global Expansion of Consulting

The firm established by Charles Eugène Bedaux (1886–1944) in 1916 marked the true beginnings of consulting as a business activity. Unlike Taylor or even Emerson, Bedaux had no interest in promoting scientific management as a way of industrial (and human) betterment, but saw it largely as a money-making exercise—which is probably the main reason why Urwick and Brech (1945) did not include him in their book on the *Pioneers of Scientific Management*. His is a typical fairy-tale story of the poor immigrant becoming not only rich but also famous—albeit with an unhappy ending. His life has been chronicled by a number of authors (Flanner 1945; Bedaux 1979; Christy 1984). However, most of his biographers did not focus on his consulting activities but rather on his very active social life, his highly publicized expeditions through the Sahara and the Rocky Mountains (the latter also the subject of a documentary called 'Champagne Safari'), and, most importantly, his alleged, hotly debated but yet to be proven, collaboration with the Nazis during World War II (see also Linne 1996). The important role of the Bedaux efficiency system has been highlighted by a number of authors examining the implementation and consequences of scientific management (Littler 1982; Downs 1990). But the development and role of his consultancy only became a central topic of research more recently, notably with the work of Kreis (1992) and Kipping (1997, 1999; see also Tisdall 1982; and Ferguson 2002, who ignores much of the earlier literature).

Born in a Paris suburb in 1886 as the son of a railway engineer, Bedaux never completed his secondary school education. After a colourful youth, in 1906 he left hurriedly for the United States, where he initially worked as a manual labourer. While Bedaux might have become acquainted with scientific management then, he probably started seeing it as a money-making opportunity when acting as a translator for the above mentioned Italian engineer Morrini, who had come to the United States to study the Emerson system. In 1914, he followed Morrini first to France and then, after the outbreak of World War I, back to the United States. Here, he developed his own system of work measurement and payment-by-results, the Bedaux system. It standardized all human efforts according to a single unit of measurement, the so-called 'B', defined as a fraction of a minute of activity plus a fraction of a minute of rest. Workers were expected to achieve a minimum of 60 B per hour and received bonuses for higher B values (Laloux 1950).

Compared to its competitors, the Bedaux system was not necessarily more efficient but—at least according to Harvard Business School professor, T. H. Sanders (1926: 19)—more flexible and broad-based in its applications and able to be used for 'general management purposes, as well as for technical cost-accounting purposes' (see also Balderston 1930). This, together with Bedaux's widely acknowledged talent as a salesman, contributed to the rapid expansion of the consulting firm, which he first established in Grand Rapids, Michigan, in 1916, but quickly moved to Cleveland, Ohio, in 1918. Bedaux and his growing number of collaborators, whom he drew from some of the most prestigious engineering schools, including MIT, soon started to expand their activities from the Midwest to the rest of the United States. Among his American clients were a large number of well-known firms, including the Chicago meat packer Swift, American Rolling Mill, Eastman Kodak, B. F. Goodrich, Du Pont, and General Electric. As Table 2.1 shows, his activities and his organization saw a considerable expansion from the mid-1920s onwards.

Table 2.1 Growth of the Bedaux consultancy, 1918–1931

Year	Number of Offices	Consulting Engineers	Plants Using Bedaux	Plants with Work in Progress
1918	1	2	1	2
1925	2	19	70	15
1928	7	94	161	72
1930	9	176	399	81
1931	10	205	509	123

Source: Kreis 1992: 157, based on Bedaux 1932: 9.

Within the United States, Bedaux moved the main office to New York and opened additional offices in Boston, Chicago, and Portland. Outside the United States, Bedaux established his first foreign office in London in the United Kingdom in 1926, quickly followed by offices in Germany, Italy, and France. By the end of the 1930s his firm had become truly global, not only covering the United States and Western Europe, but also Scandinavia, Eastern Europe, Africa, and Australia (Kipping 1999; Wright 2000). Despite significant labour hostility towards the Bedaux system in many countries (Littler 1982; Kreis 1992; Wright 1995), the firm's international growth was significant, with more than 1,000 plants utilizing the system and the consultancy counting many of the world's leading companies among its clients. Bedaux not only provided consultancy services to companies, he also advised governments (Greece) and even travelled to the Soviet Union to compare his own system with practices there, namely Stakhanovism (Christy 1984: 130–135, 192).

To reflect the growth and geographic extension of his firm, Bedaux created a decentralized organization structure with an international holding, first located in New York, then transferred to Amsterdam. He maintained the links between the different country-based operating companies through interlocking board memberships and regular meetings of his major staff (Kipping 1999: 200). In addition to his own international expansion, Bedaux became the progenitor of the consulting industry in several countries, most notably the United Kingdom. Here, his success led to a number of spin-off consultancies, namely Production Engineering (PE), Urwick, Orr and Partners (UOP), and Personnel Administration (PA). Together with his own subsidiary, these went on to form the basis of management consulting in the UK and dominated the industry there at least until the 1970s (Tisdall 1982; Ferguson 2002). Bedaux's consultancy played a similar, albeit somewhat less significant, role in France, where his office employed about eighty consulting engineers and had advised 350 companies before World War II (Moutet 1997: 211–216), and in Italy, where he first worked with Giovanni Agnelli's Fiat (Faliva and Pennarola 1992: 9–15, 186).

By the end of the 1920s, Bedaux himself had become rich and an international socialite. He bought a château in the Loire Valley where he hosted reunions of company employees as well as lavish parties. It was here that the former King Edward VIII, then the Duke of Windsor after his abdication, wed the American divorcée Wallis Simpson, a friend of Bedaux's wife Fern. Subsequently, Bedaux organized the highly controversial trip of the Duke to Nazi Germany, which caused significant negative publicity for the consultancy in Britain and the United States. His damaged reputation, as well as the outbreak of World War II, had serious consequences for his consulting firm. Already, in 1938, the British subsidiary had forced him to relinquish majority ownership in exchange for a one-off license payment, and had renamed itself Associated Industrial Consultants (AIC). During the war, Bedaux remained in France, even after German occupation. To avoid confiscation of his consultancy due to his US nationality, Bedaux transferred ownership of the international holding in Amsterdam and of the French subsidiary to his brother Gaston (Christy 1984: 205).

In November 1942, while in North Africa on behalf of the French Vichy regime to explore possibilities for the construction of a pipeline and railway across the Sahara, Bedaux was captured by the US army. He was transferred to Miami, questioned, and finally charged with trading with the enemy. But before facing trial, he committed suicide on 14 February 1944 (Flanner 1945: II, 44–45, and III; Christy 1984: chs 19 and 20; see also the *New York Times*, 20 February 1944). During World War II, the head of his US consultancy, Albert Ramond, had already tried to repair Bedaux's damaged reputation by speaking and publishing widely on how to promote the war effort through better co-operation between management and the unions, and the use of the Bedaux incentive system (for example, 'Bedaux Reformed', *Time*, 19 January 1942). After the suicide, Ramond followed the earlier example of the British subsidiary and renamed the consultancy Albert Ramond and Associates to avoid any further association with Bedaux's name and negative reputation.

Thus, while Bedaux's once globally dominant consultancy firm had largely disintegrated by 1945, many of its constituent parts and spin-offs continued to thrive, notably in the United Kingdom. Moreover, the post-World War II period also saw the surge of a new set of efficiency-oriented consulting firms.

2.4 THE EXPANSION OF EFFICIENCY CONSULTING AFTER WORLD WAR II

The efficiency engineers thrived during World War II because of the need to rapidly increase output and integrate a large number of unskilled, mainly female, employees into the workforce. This trend was reinforced in the post-war period as companies (often prompted by government) sought to increase productivity and reduce labour costs. This benefited the existing efficiency consultancies, which now also integrated ideas from the emerging human and industrial relations schools (see Trahair and Bruce, Chapter 3, this volume). Thus, in the late 1950s, the Emerson Engineers conducted a landmark study at ESSO's Fawley refinery near Southampton in the United Kingdom, which led to a pioneering and widely publicized agreement about the sharing of productivity gains between management and trade unions (Tisdall 1982: 65–71).

However, in the United Kingdom, the main beneficiaries from the productivity drive were Bedaux's former subsidiary AIC, and its spin-offs PE, UOP, and PA (see above). Much of their consulting work continued the legacy of Bedaux, focusing on the use of time study and related wage incentive schemes to establish new effort norms in manufacturing settings. By the mid-1950s these so-called 'Big Four' consultancies were thought to account for three quarters of a total UK market estimated at £4 million (Tisdall 1982: 9). They reached their apex in 1970, when they employed a total of 2,400 consultants, according to the statistics of the British Management Consultancies Association, compared to less than 400 for the four leading US strategy firms in the whole of Europe in 1969 (Kipping 1999: 210). Bedaux's widow Fern tried to rebuild the consulting firm in Continental Europe after the war and, by the end of the 1960s, the 'Bedaux Group' claimed to have offices in Paris, Milan, Amsterdam, Madrid, Barcelona, and Frankfurt (advertisement in 'Les sociétés de service', *Les dossiers de l'entreprise*, 10 March 1969, p. 36). Its activities appeared most important in Spain, where the Bedaux consultancy had opened its first office in 1953 and already employed almost 100 consultants in 1960 (Kipping 2009).

Moreover, during this period a number of new efficiency consultancies came to the fore, based either on a further development of the existing work study and payment-by-results systems or on a more active, often rather controversial, approach when selling their services. Among the former, Harold B. Maynard and his Methods Engineering Council (MEC) was the most prominent, whereas George S. May was without any doubt the most (in)famous of the latter.

2.4.1 Maynard and Methods-Time-Measurement (MTM)

One of the most successful and influential consultancies during the immediate post-war decades was the MEC established in Pittsburgh in 1934 by the American industrial engineer Harold B. Maynard. A key innovation that led to the success of this firm was the development of a new technique of work study known as Methods-Time-Measurement (MTM). Working on a productivity project at the large American manufacturer Westinghouse Corporation, Maynard and his colleagues Gus Stegemerten and Jack Schwab, became convinced that greater efficiencies could be achieved if work methods were designed scientifically prior to the establishment of time standards. Maynard and his team had already developed a system for rating work effort (Maynard, Stegemerten, and Lowry 1927) and, by using micromotion film techniques, they established a vast collection of time standards for elementary human motions in industrial work. Unlike traditional time study, the industrial engineer using this 'predetermined' library could calculate standard times for job tasks based upon the basic motion elements involved. This gave standards an apparent rigour and also reduced the potential for worker resistance that often accompanied direct stop-watch observation (Maynard, Stegemerten, and Schwab 1948).

The MTM technique proved a major success for Maynard's MEC consultancy, which became the most prominent of the post-war breed of 'efficiency engineers', installing the system in a broad range of North American manufacturers, as well as retail and insurance companies. Like Bedaux, Maynard's technique and his consultancy also spread internationally, with the global diffusion of MTM first occurring in countries on opposite sides of the world: Australia and Sweden. In the case of Australia, MTM was first applied in 1950 at refrigeration manufacturers Kelvinator, following a six-week visit by Maynard, sponsored by local management consultancy W. D. Scott & Co. Scott had met Maynard at the 1947 CIOS conference in Stockholm and subsequently negotiated an agreement with MEC to assist in the application of the MTM system among Australian clients, and later in the UK, Asia, and Africa (Wright 2000, 2002).

In Sweden, the managing director of the Volvo car company is credited with the introduction of MTM to local industry, with the first application occurring at the company's engine factory in Skövde in 1950 (Glimstedt 1998; Laring et al. 2002). The rapid adoption of MTM and its public availability led to the establishment of MTM associations and societies, and broader moves to professionalize the fledgling occupation of industrial engineers. By contrast, in the UK, the earlier influence of the Bedaux system and traditional time study appear to have stymied attempts to introduce MTM amongst British companies. Indeed, it was not until Australian consultants W. D. Scott carried out an MTM study for the British parent of biscuit manufacturer Peak Freens in 1957 that MTM began to be used in the UK, with prominent clients including the London Transport Board as well as leading banks and insurance companies (Wright 2000).

Post-war manufacturing growth resulted in increasing business interest in industrial engineering or 'work study' as it was labelled in the UK, which became an increasingly fashionable management specialism in post-World War II industrial companies (ILO 1957). Other predetermined work measurement systems were developed by consultants and enjoyed varying levels of application. Notable amongst these was the Work Factor system developed by American industrial engineers in the 1940s (Quick, Duncan, and Malcolm 1962). Limitations in the applicability of MTM to a broader range of work settings such as low volume production, maintenance, clerical, and office work also led to new consultancy products including the Master Standard Data (MSD) system (Crossan and Nance 1962), and the Clerical Work Measurement system of Paul B. Mulligan and Associates. Maynard's consultancy responded to these developments with new and adapted methodologies including MTM General Purpose Data and Universal Maintenance Standards (UMS) in the early 1960s (Porter 1964). By the late 1960s, Maynard had become the largest American consultancy in Europe with about 330 consultants and offices in eight countries (Kipping 1999: 205).

2.4.2 George S. May: Giving Consulting a Bad Name

Other US productivity consultancies also thrived in the post-war decades of economic growth and manufacturing expansion. For example, the consultancy established by

George S. May in Chicago in 1925 equally focused on efficiency improvement and cost reduction. It utilized a forceful sales technique that May had learnt early in life selling bibles. A flamboyant character, May dressed in bright shirts and ties, ran a country club, and staged the 'World's Championship of Golf'. In marketing his firm's services he aggressively sought out clients through mass mail-outs of letters and promotional pamphlets, and 'cold-calling' company executives (Stryker 1954; Higdon 1969). Indeed, in contrast to other consulting firms, which shunned advertising, May's direct-mail division, operating on an annual budget of $1 million, 'deposits from 8,500 to 20,000 pieces of sales matter in the Chicago post office every day' (Stryker 1954: 140). May's aggressive selling techniques and advertising prevented his firm gaining membership of the Association of Consulting Management Engineers (ACME), which had been established in 1933 by Harold B. Maynard, Edwin Booz, James O. McKinsey, and others to improve professional standards in the emerging consulting industry and shunned consultants advertising their services (Higdon 1969).

Despite such industry rejection, the George S. May Company proved extraordinarily successful, with a promotional brochure from the late 1960s estimating the firm had surveyed 150,000 businesses and earned $200 million in fees since its inception (ibid.: 151). It was also one of the first American consultancies to establish a permanent presence in Western Europe after World War II, with May opening an office in Dusseldorf in 1955, following his participation at a golf tournament there (Higdon 1969; Kipping 1999: 205–206). Ten years later, the consultancy listed offices in nine European countries and by the mid-1960s it employed about 1,000 consultants worldwide and ranked in the top ten of global management consultancies. But May's sales methods, controversial in the United States, proved inappropriate in Europe. In the 1960s, German newspapers reported that clients were complaining that the promises of his salesmen, both in terms of cost reductions and revenue improvements, were seldom fulfilled (Ricke 1989: 32). The literature has reported similar complaints and even law suits from Italy and the UK (Tisdall 1982: 64–65; Faliva and Pennarola 1992: 75–77).

While these troubles signaled the end of its oversees activities, the consultancy continued to thrive in the United States, despite the death of its founder, aged 71, in 1962. George S. May International remained in the ownership of the family and focused increasingly on small and medium-sized businesses, providing a range of consulting and training services, centred on sales and operations. At the onset of the twenty-first century the consultancy had annual revenues of $100 million and, in February 2011, named Kerry Sam Jacobs, the founder's granddaughter as its new president (http://www.georgesmay.com/ accessed 10 December 2011). Incidentally, May was not the only consultancy to use such aggressive sales techniques. Another efficiency consultant who followed a similar path was Alexander Proudfoot, who had worked for May, and who established a consultancy in Chicago in 1946 based around a codified proprietary model of cost reduction and efficiency improvement (Higdon 1969: 229–248). Like May, Proudfoot employed an aggressive marketing approach, which stressed tangible improvements as a result of the company's technique, and enjoyed significant success, expanding to Europe and being ranked the fourth largest consulting firm in terms of revenues in the early 1970s, before further global expansion to Africa and Australia in the 1980s (Kennedy Research Group 1996). It still exists today as part of the UK-based and publicly quoted Management Consulting Group (http://www.mcgplc.com/ accessed 10 December 2011).

Thus, engineering-based consultancies continued to play an important role in the industry after World War II, even dominating it in many countries throughout the 1960s, the supposed 'gilded age' of the strategy consultants (McKenna 2006). After 1945, the internationally successful efficiency consultants that derived from the original pioneers, in particular Bedaux, were joined by a new breed of service providers, who made their mark either based on improved, and less controversial, measurement techniques, in particular Maynard's MTM system, or on aggressive sales methods, for which George S. May was the most (in)famous example. But from the late 1960s onwards, these firms declined in relative importance and visibility. While many of them have disappeared today, either being absorbed or vanishing completely, many of their ideas have lived on and some even saw a revival in more recent periods.

2.5 THE LASTING INFLUENCE OF THE EFFICIENCY CONSULTANTS

2.5.1 Decline and Reinvention

After reaching new heights during the 1960s, the consultants focusing on operational efficiency on the shop floor and in offices gradually saw their numerical importance and public visibility erode. There is some speculation in the extant literature about the reasons for these developments—and the parallel rise of McKinsey & Co. and others. It might have been related to the change in production methods, with machines replacing human labour, or the more general decline in manufacturing activities in the industrialized countries (Wright 2000). It is also possible that the worldwide expansion of the diversified and decentralized multidivisional form of organization provided managers with new types of challenges that the efficiency consultants could not address (Kipping 2002). During the post-World War II period there was also the—related—rise of executives with, first, a sales and marketing, and then a finance, background, who had little interest in manufacturing and operational efficiency (Fligstein 1990: 280–287).

Whatever the reasons, as the existing research shows, it was in the United States that the decline of the efficiency consultancies was more pronounced and started earlier. Thus, while still active in the 1950s (see above), the Emerson Engineers did not appear on the first ever list of the fifty largest US consultancies by 1968 revenue, compiled by Higdon (1969), although they supposedly survived until the 1980s (McKenna 2006: 38). Bedaux's former US subsidiary, operating under the name Albert Ramond and Associates since 1945, did appear on Higdon's list ranked forty-fourth and with eighty consultants employed. And, in a 1982 consulting directory, it was listed with headquarters in Chicago, offices in New York and Toronto, and twelve named principals, offering 'a complete range of services in the field of management and industrial consulting' (Wasserman and McLean 1982: 212). Maynard was still tenth on the 1968 list with 450 consultants, but it also declined and in 2008 Accenture acquired what was left of it (O'Connell 2008). George S. May was also a significant presence in the late 1960s with 400 consultants, and Alexander Proudfoot ranked eighth largest with 300 consultants. Despite a troubled reputation, both May and Proudfoot still exist today as mid-tier consultancies (see above).

In Europe and Australia, the efficiency consultancies retained their importance somewhat longer because they managed to expand the range of their services (Tisdall 1982; Wright 2000). This was, for example, the case with Urwick, Orr and Partners, which also offered management by objectives and corporate reorganization (Channon 1973). Maybe for that particular reason, that is, to expand into those services, it was acquired by Price Waterhouse in 1985 and was the first of the Big Four to disappear (Jones 1995). Mere shadows of their former selves, AIC, renamed Inbucon, and PE, merged in 1987 and were first acquired by Cray Group in 1993 and then by the UK-based IT and HR consultancy Lorien in 1996 ('Lorien buy takes P-E out of Cray', *Management Consultancy*, 8 October 1996). Their trading names have now disappeared. PA, which had been the most international of the Big Four and also managed to diversify into IT services, not only survived, but is still among the top twenty consultancies in Britain and the top fifty worldwide (Kennedy Information 2004). The Bedaux name itself vanished in 1985, when the Spanish consultancy, which had been declining already, was acquired by the German strategy and organization firm Roland Berger (Kipping 2009: 72).

While most of the original efficiency consultancies disappeared, operations and efficiency-based consultancy services did not. Indeed, some of the most famous management consultancies that are usually viewed as strategic advisers have, for much of their history, also provided operational efficiency services. This is particularly the case for A. T. Kearney, a spin-off from the firm founded in 1926 by James O. McKinsey (Higdon 1969; McKenna 2006). Other international consultancies also diversified into selling operational efficiency methodologies. Indeed, as demonstrated in Table 2.2, despite their association as 'strategy houses', consultancies like McKinsey & Co. and Booz Allen & Hamilton continued to generate a significant proportion of their revenues from operational efficiency work, and the latest generation of IT-based consultancies such as PricewaterhouseCoopers (now part of IBM Consulting) and Accenture also have large and significant operational efficiency practices. During the 1990s, the fashion for re-engineering created significant demand for consulting services, as banks and other large service companies sought to improve efficiencies and reduce costs through the downsizing and 'delayering' of their organizations (Fincham and Evans 1999). These developments suggest that beyond the existence of specific efficiency consultancies, the broader influence and impact of efficiency techniques is still significant although it has yet to be examined systematically by the relevant literature.

Table 2.2 Largest consulting practices in operations management, 2003

Rank	Firm Name	2003 Ops Mgmt Consulting Revenue ($ mil.)	Share of Firm's Global Consulting Revenue	2003 Global Consulting Revenue ($ mil.)
1	IBM	$1,959.0	15%	$12,955.0
2	McKinsey & Co.	$839.7	28%	$3,000.0
3	Deloitte	$769.6	13%	$5920.0
4	Booz Allen & Hamilton	$605.1	30%	$2,017.0
5	CSC	$583.3	17%	$3,350.0
6	A. T. Kearney	$567.0	67%	$846.0
7	Accenture	$453.4	5%	$8,272.0
8	PA Consulting	$241.1	44%	$548.0
9	Gedas	$205.7	29%	$705.7
10	Roland Berger	$156.0	25%	$625.0

Source: Based on Kennedy Information (2004), Consultants News, October, p. 4.

2.5.2 Impact and Survival of Efficiency Ideas

It is clear from the extant research that Taylorism and scientific management have significantly shaped workplace practices around the globe, even if detailed studies of different countries such as France (Humphreys 1986), Britain (Littler 1982; Whitston 1996), Japan (Tsutsui 1998), the Soviet Union (Wren 1980), and Australia (Wright 1993) found marked variations in the extent of application. While researchers vary widely in terms of how they define scientific management from specific workplace practices—for example, time and motion study and related wage incentive schemes (Littler 1982; Wright 1993), through to a far more amorphous management 'philosophy' or ideology (Merkle 1980)—they have tended to focus on the early application of scientific management, only rarely extending this analysis beyond World War II. This is partly a function of the widespread obsession with Taylor, which, as we have shown, has obscured the role of individual industrial engineers and consulting firms that were central to the diffusion of the new methods. The lack of interest in, and knowledge of, the lasting influence of industrial engineering and the related consulting firms is also due to a—partially understandable—focus on new rather than established ideas and their proponents. From such a perspective, McKinsey and other similar firms appear more 'modern' (McKenna 1995, 2006), and thus more worthy of attention, even if at a global level they were dwarfed by the efficiency-based consultancies during the inter-war period and only started to gain the upper hand during the mid- to late 1960s.

In terms of the actual ideas, some authors have stressed the lasting influence of Taylorism in the broader sense, showing how its fundamental principles have influenced subsequent management ideas/fashions such as operations research/linear programming (Waring 1991), Japanese quality management, and 'lean production' (Tsutsui 1998), or, more recently, BPR (Conti and Warner 1994; Pruijt 1998), an area of significant consulting activity during the 1990s (Fincham and Evans 1999). Others see it as the first example of a 'rational' as opposed to a 'normative' kind of management (Barley and Kunda 1992) or as one of two fundamental schools of thought about modern management—the other emanating from Henri Fayol (Hatchuel and Glise 2004). However, little research has sought to examine the influence of industrial engineering after World War II, when it reached is zenith. For example, the research that does exist suggests post-war consultancies were important in the establishment of internal industrial engineering capabilities within manufacturing firms, and that 'work study' and 'methods engineers' represented something of an elite within leading post-war companies, such as the UK chemical giant ICI (Reader 1975; Wright 1995). With few exceptions (Glimstedt 1998; Wright 2000), there has been no research on the MTM system, its implementation, and consequences, despite its widespread use in factories around the world. More generally, the formation of professional associations of industrial engineers (in which consultants often played a key role) highlights another avenue through which the ideas of efficiency engineering may have achieved further influence and application, and about which little is known.

In terms of contemporary application, broader industrial engineering techniques of quality management and process redesign continue to be central to the management of a wide range of manufacturing and service settings, and examples can still be found of time study-based work measurement in sectors such as retail, where specialist efficiency consultancies diffuse computer-based systems of work standards for measuring the productivity of supply chain operations (Wright and Lund 1998). More generally, the global relocation of labour-intensive manufacturing to China and other Asian countries (Gamble, Morris, and Wilkinson 2004), suggests there is a continued, and possibly significant, role for industrial engineers and efficiency consultants in these newly industrialized regions. To date, however, a comprehensive analysis of the extent and forms of industrial engineering practice and the role consultancies play in spreading such ideas in different country settings is lacking.

2.6 CONCLUSIONS

Discussions of the origins of management consulting as an occupation and industry have tended to downplay efficiency engineering as a founding influence. 'Modern' management consulting has often been defined as advising senior managers about issues of organizational structure and strategy, rather than the more micro concerns of efficiency on the shop floor or in the office (e.g. McKenna 2006). However, as our chapter shows, such a view glosses over a significant body of historical research, which suggests the first management consultants were indeed 'efficiency engineers' and that much of the growth of the global consulting industry up until the 1960s was based on such work.

Indeed, according to the extant, even if limited, literature, these early management consultants were central to the broader dissemination and application of the ideas and practices of industrial engineering. Despite the academic focus on Frederick Taylor and his model of 'scientific management' as one of the most influential ideas of the twentieth century, as well as the hostility of Taylor and his disciples towards what they considered aberrations from their own 'pure' system, it was the early management consultants such as Bedaux and later on Maynard that acted as the conduits for the broader spread and application of these ideas in industry and around the world. The literature surveyed in this chapter not only demonstrates the significance of the industrial engineering origins of management consulting, it begins the process of drawing the historical links to contemporary consulting practice. Despite the different content of what was being disseminated, these consulting organizations were remarkably similar to the supposedly 'modern' consultancies and in many ways more advanced—most certainly in terms of their global scope.

While there is a growing body of historical research regarding the early engineering origins of consulting, significant gaps remain in our understanding of the impact and influence of these ideas both on the broader consulting industry and upon management more generally. For example, as we have noted, despite the widespread application of consulting methodologies such as MTM, detailed research into the global spread of this technique and its influence has yet to be undertaken. Similarly, the role of efficiency consultants in the promotion of an industrial engineering profession both globally, and in different country settings, would fill significant gaps in our knowledge regarding the history of management more generally. We also need to understand better why these consultancies declined, at least in relative terms, from the late 1960s.

Of more contemporary interest, we still know surprisingly little about the activities of the remaining operational efficiency consultants, despite the fact that industry observers estimate this segment contributes as much as 25 per cent of global industry revenues (Kennedy Information 2004). While contemporary management fashions such as BPR, quality management, and Six Sigma have been a focus of critical academic research, the role of consultancies in promoting, and more importantly, implementing these techniques has received far less attention (for exceptions see Werr, Stjernberg, and Docherty 1997; Fincham and Evans 1999). Finally, as is the case for research on management consulting more generally, we know very little about how consulting is developing in emerging economies (see also Frenkel and Shenhav, Chapter 26, this volume). Given the global relocation of labour-intensive manufacturing to these economies, it seems likely that in these locations the older style shop floor engineering will continue as a central form of organizational life. The role of consultancies in these settings represents a further important area for future research.

References

Aitken, H. (1960). *Taylorism at Watertown Arsenal: Scientific Management in Action, 1908–1915.* Cambridge, MA: Harvard University Press.

Balderston, C. C. (1930). *Group Incentives: Some Variations in the Use of Group Bonus and Gang Piece Work.* Philadelphia: University of Pennsylvania Press.

Barley, S. R. and Kunda, G. (1992). 'Design and Devotion: Surges of Rational and Normative Ideologies of Control in Managerial Discourse'. *Administrative Science Quarterly*, 37/3, 363–399.

Bedaux, C. E. (1928). *Bedaux Measures Labour*. New York: International Bedaux Institute.

Bedaux, G. (1979). *La vie ardente de Charles E. Bedaux*. Paris: Privately published.

Braverman, H. (1974). *Labor and Monopoly Capital: The Degradation of Work in the Twentieth Century*. New York: Monthly Review Press.

Cayet, T. (2005). 'Organiser le travail, organiser le monde: étude d'un milieu international d'organisateurs-rationalisateurs durant l'entre-deux-guerres'. Unpublished Ph.D. dissertation, European University Institute, Florence.

Chandler Jr, A. D. (1965). 'The Railroads: Pioneers in Modern Corporate Management'. *Business History Review*, 39/1, 16–40.

Channon, D. F. (1973). *The Strategy and Structure of British Enterprise*. London: Macmillan.

Christy, J. (1984). *The Price of Power: A Biography of Charles Eugène Bedaux*. Toronto: Doubleday.

Conti, R. and Warner, M. (1994). 'Taylorism, Teams and Technology in "Reengineering" Work Organization'. *New Technology, Work and Employment*, 9/2, 93–102.

Copley, F. B. (1923). *Frederick W. Taylor: Father of Scientific Management*. New York: Harper & Row.

Crossan, R. M. and Nance, H. W. (1962). *Master Standard Data: The Economic Approach to Work Measurement*. New York: McGraw-Hill.

Downs, L. L. (1990). 'Industrial Decline, Rationalization and Equal Pay: The Bedaux Strike at Rover Automobile Company'. *Social History*, 15/1, 45–73.

Emerson, H. (1919). *Efficiency as a Basis for Operation and Wages*. New York: Engineering Magazine Co.

Faliva, G. and Pennarola, F. (1992). *Storia della consulenza di direzione in Italia: protagonisti, idee, tendenze evolutive*. Milan: Edizioni Olivares.

Ferguson, M. (2002). *The Rise of Management Consulting in Britain*. Aldershot: Ashgate.

Fincham, R. and Evans, M. (1999). 'The Consultants' Offensive: Reengineering: From Fad to Technique'. *New Technology, Work and Employment*, 14/1, 32–44.

Flanner, J. (1945). 'Annals of Collaboration: Equivalism I–III'. *New Yorker*, 21 (22 September), 28–47; (6 October), 32–45; (13 October), 32–48.

Fligstein, N. (1990). *The Transformation of Corporate Control*. Cambridge, MA: Harvard University Press.

Gamble, J., Morris, J., and Wilkinson, B. (2004). 'Mass Production is Alive and Well: The Future of Work and Organization in East Asia'. *International Journal of Human Resource Management*, 15/2, 397–409.

Glimstedt, H. (1998). 'Americanization and the "Swedish Model" of Industrial Relations: The Introduction of the MTM System at Volvo in the Postwar Period'. In M. Kipping and O. Bjarnar (eds), *The Americanization of European Business: The Marshall Plan and the Transfer of US Management Models*. London: Routledge, 133–148.

Guillén, M. (1994). *Models of Management: Work, Authority, and Organization in a Comparative Perspective*. Chicago: University of Chicago Press.

Hatchuel, A. and Glise, H. (2004). 'Rebuilding Management: A Historical Perspective'. In N. Adler, A. Shani, and A. Styhre (eds), *Collaborative Research in Organizations: Foundations for Learning, Change, and Theoretical Development*. Thousand Oaks, CA: Sage, 5–22.

Higdon, H. (1969). *The Business Healers*. New York: Random House.

Humphreys, G. G. (1986). *Taylorism in France, 1904–1920: The Impact of Scientific Management on Factory Relations and Society*. New York: Garland.

ILO (International Labour Organization) (1957). *Introduction to Work Study*. Geneva: International Labour Office.

Jones, E. (1995). *True and Fair: A History of Price Waterhouse*. London: Hamish Hamilton.

Kanigel, R. (1997). *The One Best Way: Frederick Winslow Taylor and the Enigma of Efficiency*. New York: Viking.

Kennedy Information (2004). *The Global Consulting Marketplace 2004–2006: Key Data, Trends and Forecasts*. Peterborough, NH: Kennedy Information Inc.

Kennedy Research Group (1996). 'Proudfoot Looks to Rebound'. *Consultants News*, September, 8.

Kipping, M. (1997). 'Consultancies, Institutions and the Diffusion of Taylorism in Britain, Germany and France, 1920s to 1950s'. *Business History*, 39/4, 67–83.

Kipping, M. (1999). 'American Management Consulting Companies in Western Europe, 1910s to 1990s: Products, Reputation, and Relationships'. *Business History Review*, 73/2, 190–220.

Kipping, M. (2002). 'Trapped in Their Wave: The Evolution of Management Consultancies'. In T. Clark and R. Fincham (eds), *Critical Consulting: New Perspectives on the Management Advice Industry*. Oxford: Blackwell, 28–49.

Kipping, M. (2009). 'Management Consultancies and Organizational Innovation in Europe'. In P. Fernández Pérez and M. B. Rose (eds), *Innovation and Entrepreneurial Networks in Europe*. London: Routledge, 61–80.

Kreis, S. (1992). 'The Diffusion of Scientific Management: The Bedaux Company in America and Britain, 1926–1945'. In D. Nelson (ed.), *A Mental Revolution: Scientific Management Since Taylor*. Columbus: Ohio State University Press, 156–174.

Laloux, P. (1950). *Le système Bedaux de calcul des salaires*. Paris: Editions Hommes et Techniques.

Lancaster, J. (2004). *Making Time: Lillian Moller Gilbreth; A Life Beyond 'Cheaper by the Dozen'*. Boston: Northeastern University Press.

Laring, J. Forsman, M., Kadefors, R., and Örtengren, R. (2002). 'MTM-based Ergonomic Workload Analysis'. *International Journal of Industrial Ergonomics*, 30/3, 135–148.

Linne, K. (1996). 'Ein Amerikanischer geschäftsmann und die Nationalsozialisten: Charles Bedaux'. *Zeitschrift für Geschichtswissenschaft*, 44, 809–826.

Littler, C. (1978). 'Understanding Taylorism'. *British Journal of Sociology*, 29/2, 185–202.

Littler, C. (1982). *The Development of the Labour Process in Capitalist Societies: A Comparative Analysis of Work Organization in Britain, the USA, and Japan*. London: Heinemann.

Locke, E. A. (1982). 'The Ideas of Frederick W. Taylor: An Evaluation'. *Academy of Management Review*, 7/1, 14–24.

Maynard, H. B., Stegemerten, G. J., and Lowry, S. M. (1927). *Time and Motion Study and Formulas for Wage Incentives*. New York: McGraw-Hill.

Maynard, H. B., Stegemerten, G. J., and Schwab, J. L. (1948). *Methods Time Measurement*. New York: McGraw-Hill.

McKenna, C. (1995). 'The Origins of Modern Management Consulting'. *Business and Economic History*, 24/1, 51–58.

McKenna, C. D. (2006). *The World's Newest Profession: Management Consulting in the Twentieth Century*. New York: Cambridge University Press.

McKinsey & Co. (1957). *Supplementing Successful Management*. New York: McKinsey & Co. (promotional brochure).

Merkle, J. (1980). *Management and Ideology: The Legacy of the International Scientific Management Movement*. Berkeley: University of California Press.

Moutet, A. (1975). 'Les origines du système de Taylor en France. Le point de vue patronal (1907–1914)'. *Le mouvement social*, 93, 15–49.

Moutet, A. (1997). *Les logiques de l'entreprise: l'effort de rationalization dans l'industrie française de 1919 à 1939*. Paris: Edition de l'EHESS.

NICB (National Industrial Conference Board) (1930). *Systems of Wage Payment*. New York: National Industrial Conference Board.

Nelson, D. (1980). *Frederick W. Taylor and the Rise of Scientific Management*. Madison: University of Wisconsin Press.

Nelson, D. (1991). 'Scientific Management and the Workplace, 1920–1935'. In S. Jacoby (ed.), *Masters to Managers: Historical and Comparative Perspectives on American Employers*. New York: Columbia University Press, 74–89.

Nelson, D. (ed.) (1992). *A Mental Revolution: Scientific Management Since Taylor*. Columbus: Ohio State University Press.

Nelson, D. (1995). 'Industrial Engineering and the Industrial Enterprise'. In N. R. Lamoreaux and D. M. G. Raff (eds), *Coordination and Information: Historical Perspectives on the Organization of Enterprise*. Chicago: University of Chicago Press, 35–50.

O'Connell, V. (2008). 'Stores Count Seconds to Trim Labor Costs'. *Wall Street Journal*, 17 November, A.1.

Porter, F. (1964). 'Predetermined Time Systems'. *Industrial Engineer* (September/October), 6–8.

Price, B. (1992). 'Frank and Lillian Gilbreth and the Motion Study Controversy, 1907–1930'. In D. Nelson (ed.), *A Mental Revolution: Scientific Management Since Taylor*. Columbus: Ohio State University Press, 58–76.

Pruijt, H. (1998). 'Multiple Personalities: The Case of Business Process Reengineering'. *Journal of Organizational Change Management*, 11/3, 260–268.

Quick, J. H., Duncan, J. H., and Malcolm, J. A. (1962). *Work-Factor Time Standards: Measurement of Manual and Mental Work*. New York: McGraw-Hill.

Quigel Jr, J. P. (1992). 'The Business of Selling Efficiency: Harrington Emerson and the Emerson Efficiency Engineers, 1900–1930'. Unpublished PhD dissertation, Pennsylvania State University.

Reader, W. J. (1975). *Imperial Chemical Industries: A History*. Oxford: Oxford University Press.

Ricke, M. (1989). 'Die Freiberufliche Unternehmensberatung 1900 bis 1960: Entstehung und entwicklung eines berufs im Deutschen Sprachgebiet'. Unpublished M. A. thesis, Institut für Sozial- und Wirtschaftsgeschichte, Ludwig-Maximilians-Universität Munich.

Sahlin-Andersson, K. and Engwall, L. (2002). 'Carriers, Flows, and Sources of Management Knowledge'. In K. Sahlin-Andersson and L. Engwall (eds), *The Expansion of Management Knowledge*. Stanford, CA: Stanford University Press, 3–32.

Sanders, T. H. (1926). 'Wage Systems: An Appraisal'. *Harvard Business Review*, 5/1, 11–20.

Shenhav, Y. A. (1999). *Manufacturing Rationality: The Engineering Foundations of the Managerial Revolution*. Oxford: Oxford University Press.

Stryker, P. S. (1954). 'The Relentless George S. May'. *Fortune*, 49 (June), 140–141 and 196–208.

Taylor, F. W. (1903). *Shop Management*. New York: Harper & Row.

Taylor, F. W. (1911). *The Principles of Scientific Management*. New York: Harper.

Thompson, C. B. (1917). *The Theory and Practice of Scientific Management*. Boston: Houghton Mifflin.

Tisdall, P. (1982). *Agents of Change: The Development and Practice of Management Consultancy*. London: Heinemann.

Tsutsui, W. (1998). *Manufacturing Ideology: Scientific Management in Twentieth Century Japan*. Princeton, NJ: Princeton University Press.

Urwick, L. and Brech, E. (1945). *The Making of Scientific Management*. London: Pitman.

Waring, S. P. (1991). *Taylorism Transformed: Scientific Management Theory Since 1945*. Chapel Hill: University of North Carolina Press.

Wasserman, P. and McLean, J. (eds) (1982). *Consultants and Consulting Organizations Directory*, 5th ed. Detroit: Gale Research Company.

Werr, A., Stjernberg, T., and Docherty, P. (1997). 'The Functions of Methods of Change in Management Consulting'. *Journal of Organizational Change Management*, 10/4, 288–307.

Whitston, K. (1996). 'Scientific Management and Production Management Practice in Britain Between the Wars'. *Historical Studies in Industrial Relations*, 1, 47–75.

Wren, D. (1980). 'Scientific Management in the U.S.S.R. with Particular Reference to the Contribution of Walter N. Polakov'. *Academy of Management Review*, 5/1, 1–11.

Wren, D. (2005). *The History of Management Thought*. 5th edn New York: John Wiley & Sons.

Wright, C. (1993). 'Taylorism Reconsidered: The Impact of Scientific Management Within the Australian Workplace'. *Labour History*, 64, 34–53.

Wright, C. (1995). *The Management of Labour: A History of Australian Employers*. Melbourne: Oxford University Press.

Wright, C. (2000). 'From Shopfloor to Boardroom: The Historical Evolution of Australian Management Consulting, 1940s to 1980s'. *Business History*, 42/1, 86–106.

Wright, C. (2002). 'Promoting Demand, Gaining Legitimacy and Broadening Expertise: The Evolution of Consultancy-Client Relationships in Australia'. In M. Kipping and L. Engwall (eds), *Management Consulting: Emergence and Dynamics of a Knowledge Industry*. Oxford: Oxford University Press, 184–202.

Wright, C. and Lund, J. (1998). '"Under the Clock": Trade Union Responses to Computerised Control in US and Australian Grocery Warehousing'. *New Technology, Work and Employment*, 13/1, 3–15.

CHAPTER 3

HUMAN RELATIONS AND MANAGEMENT CONSULTING: ELTON MAYO AND ERIC TRIST

RICHARD C. S. TRAHAIR
KYLE BRUCE

3.1 INTRODUCTION

THE acceptance of management ideas by the business community does not necessarily follow from their scientific credibility or from purely socio-economic and technological factors. For ideas to be taken up by practitioners, institutional circumstances have to be conducive, particularly those related to the activities of professional groups such as management consultants. Similarly, management ideas are not merely a set of techniques, but also an ideology that appeals to managers vis-à-vis providing a rationale for their 'right to manage'. Accordingly, the success or otherwise of management ideas has much to do with their rhetorical efficacy in legitimizing managerial authority, a process undoubtedly assisted by the (co)creation, reception, interpretation, and diffusion of such ideas by 'management intellectuals' such as consultants (Guillén 1994).

While much attention has been paid to the international diffusion of scientific management (Merkle 1980; Guillén 1994; Bloemen 1996; Cayet 2007; Nyland and Bruce 2011) and, partially, to the important role of management consulting within this (Kipping 1997; Wright and Kipping, Chapter 2, this volume), the international expansion of human relations and the concomitant role of consulting in the global spread of such ideas has received scant attention, with the possible exception of Guillén (1994). This is a serious omission. Following Alvarez (1998), Sahlin-Andersson and Engwall (2002), Engwall and

Kipping (2004), and Kipping, Engwall, and Üsdiken (2009) regarding the expansion of management knowledge generally, and Kipping (1997), and Wright and Kipping (Chapter 2, this volume) on the role of consulting in particular, the present chapter (a) examines the manner in which the human relations approach to management was 'packaged' and 'sold' to the business community and (b) critically assesses the role of management consulting in this process, focusing for both issues on the role of two of its main proponents: Elton Mayo and Eric Trist.

Mayo is widely considered the 'father' of the human relations 'school' of management due to his pivotal public relations role in interpreting and explicating the fabled Hawthorne studies as well as his dissemination of human relations ideas in the MBA and executive education curriculum at the Harvard Business School (Trahair 1984; Gillespie 1991; Bruce 2006; Bruce and Nyland 2011). Trist made seminal contributions to the field of organizational development, was a founding member of the Tavistock Institute of Human Relations, and played a key role in the establishment of the journal, *Human Relations* (Trist 1993; Trahair 2011). And while neither men were much interested in, or sympathetic towards, management consulting, many of their ideas as well as their technical procedures have found their way into consulting praxis; Mayo is best known for his employee interviewing and counselling techniques (Smith 1998), Trist for pioneering action research (Trist and Murray 1990). The chapter is organized as follows. First, a brief biographical sketch of the lives of these two men is provided. Second, it outlines their roles as consultants and also their impact on management practitioners. The chapter concludes with some comments on their respective contribution to the professionalization of management and management consulting.

3.2 GEORGE ELTON MAYO

3.2.1 His Life and Work

George Elton Mayo was born in Adelaide, a free settlement and the capital of South Australia, on 26 December 1880, into one of the city's most prominent families. Despite his siblings' academic and professional achievements in medicine and in law, the pale, anomic Elton failed to complete medical school three times and only found his niche as a mature-age student studying philosophy at the University of Adelaide, graduating with a bachelor's degree in 1911. Thereafter and until his arrival in the US in 1922 he lectured in philosophy (broadly conceived, and thus including economics, ethics, psychology, and politics) at the fledgling University of Queensland in Brisbane. During that time he also married Dorothea McConnel, who had been educated in Europe and emanated from one of Queensland's most respected and prominent families (for more details on his biography, see Trahair 1984, Bruce 2012).

While at the University of Queensland, Mayo became interested in medical psychopathology, primarily the new psychology of Sigmund Freud, Pierre Janet, and

Carl Gustav Jung, and was promoted to a professorship in 1919. Yet chafing under what he perceived as the working-class provincialism of Brisbane, Mayo sought an academic career in England and set sail in July 1922 via the west coast of the USA, wherein he had hoped to earn the remainder of his fare to the UK. This was not to be and following some rather desperate networking with grant and philanthropy officials, Mayo landed himself a research fellowship at the Wharton School in Philadelphia in 1923 where he remained until his Harvard appointment in 1926 (Trahair 1984; Hoopes 2003). As we will demonstrate below, these formative years were propitious inasmuch as they connected Mayo and John D. Rockefeller Jr (JDR Jr, hereafter) and thereby laid the path for Mayo's involvement in the ongoing Hawthorne studies, securing his reputation as a 'founding father' of the human relations 'school' (HRS, hereafter) of management.

Mayo's position at Wharton was financed by JDR Jr from his own personal funds following difficulties convincing the trustees of the foundation established in his mother's memory of the importance of Mayo's work. He became Mayo's financial and professional benefactor: either through his family's various philanthropic foundations or through his own personal wealth, JDR Jr and his philanthropic network funded Mayo's salary initially at Wharton and then again at Harvard; he either personally or via corporate contacts arranged access to firms for Mayo's industrial research (including Hawthorne); and, again, either personally or through contacts, JDR Jr continually assured Mayo a receptive business audience for his evolving human relations ideas (Bulmer and Bulmer 1981; Harvey 1982; Fisher 1983; Trahair 1984; Gillespie 1991; Magat 1999; O'Connor 1999a). Indeed, Mayo's ability to engage in his first serious applied work in industrial psychology in Philadelphia factories in no small measure owed much to Rockefeller connections (Bulmer and Bulmer 1981).

His consulting work whilst at Wharton, particularly that at Continental Mills, laid the foundations for his approach to interpreting the Hawthorne results in his 1933 *Human Problems*. Believing that the scientific study of individuals and human relationships at work must precede scientific management (SM, hereafter), he wanted to study workers and gauge how their past experiences, domestic life, and work conditions might precipitate pessimistic or 'obsessional reveries' or daydreams at work. In this respect, he applied the new medical psychoanalysis to factory problems and, after extensive interviews concerning unproductive fatigue and reveries, he likened factory workers to shell-shocked soldiers in need of serious psychological/psychiatric attention (Bruce 2012). He postulated that poor conditions and long hours resulted in fatigue and mild psychiatric disturbances which, he believed, might result in high labour turnover, low productivity, and industrial unrest. He dismissed workers' calls for a 'voice' over, and improvements to, wages and conditions as 'socialistic radicalism' and as symptomatic of some deeper psychosocial maladjustment. His major recommendation was for increased rest pauses or breaks and, as a consequence, labour turnover dropped and output rose (Trahair 1984). The way forward, he concluded, was *not* improved wages and conditions and industrial democracy, but, instead, the type of industrial psychological research he was presently engaged in.

'Discovering' a correlation between workers' productivity and their mental health won Mayo the enthusiasm of key Rockefeller foundation heads, particularly psychologist Beardsley Ruml, and it coalesced with JDR Jr's concern with improving industrial relations. JDR Jr's willingness to support social and industrial research evolved from the infamy that befell his family's name as a consequence of the 1914 Ludlow massacre in which six striking miners, two women, and eleven children were killed at the Rockefeller-owned Colorado Fuel and Iron (hereafter, CFI) company (Gitelman 1988; Rees 2010). In the aftermath of this tragedy JDR Jr engaged the public relations services of Clarence Hicks, a former YMCA official concerned with workers' welfare, and the industrial relations expertise of W. L. Mackenzie King, a future prime minister of Canada. Both urged JDR Jr to fund social science researchers whose work would help resolve 'the labor question' in a fashion amenable to Rockefeller interests and helped him establish the CFI Employee Representation (or Rockefeller) Plan that would both provide a venue in which management and employees could discuss issues of common concern, and would present the Rockefellers in a positive light (Fisher 1993). Although more progressive than those similarly established at other companies, the Plan nevertheless was designed to exclude independent unionism by improving communication and co-ordination within the firm and by developing what today would be called a 'high-involvement' or 'high-performance' human resource management regime (Kaufman and Taras 2000; Rees 2010).

Armed with Rockefeller funding and the support of Harvard Business School dean, Wallace Donham, Mayo arrived at Harvard in 1926 and remained there until his retirement in 1947. Mayo used Rockefeller lucre to hire gifted young acolytes who became collectively famous as the 'Harvard Human Relations Group' and raised the reputation of the Business School from its initial 'low status as a trainer of money grabbers into a high-prestige educator of socially conscientious administrators' (O'Connor 1999a; Hoopes 2003: 141). Donham, who would become a close friend to Mayo, planned to overcome the lack of national leadership among America's corporation executives by changing US management from a specialist occupation to a profession (Khurana 2007). This meant that Mayo's industrial research, and the teaching based upon it, needed to focus on human aspects of work, and that business school education should no longer involve the unreliable application of business policy with an organization chart or concentrate on business success by way of applied economics.

The 1940s were not kind to Mayo and he became increasingly alienated from his Harvard colleagues, a situation no doubt exacerbated by the retirement in 1942 of his oldest ally, Donham. Even his principal and most loyal acolyte, Fritz Roethlisberger, increasingly sought to distance himself from Mayo. Other members of the 'Human Relations Group' had also left the fold: Philip Cabot died in December 1941, Lawrence Henderson who had led the 'Pareto Circle' died in February 1942, Lloyd Warner had left for the University of Chicago, and T. M. Whitehead had left to serve in the US Army during World War II. Mayo doggedly hung on at Harvard despite the wish of the new dean, Donald David, that he leave. Mayo continued until the summer of 1947 when he retired to England. He lectured on industrial conflict at the National Institute of Industrial

Psychology, recommending that managers must interact with workers on the factory floor before spontaneous co-operation would replace bitter conflict between the two at work. He insisted again that the next generation of managers be taught social skills in tandem with technical skills, and that scientific investigations into industrial relations were necessary as a foundation for the education of tomorrow's managers. He hoped to find a position with the British Institute of Management, where his daughter Patricia Mayo worked, and went to talk with colleagues at the Tavistock Institute of Human Relations (TIHR, hereafter). Mayo worked too strenuously. In December 1947 he had a stroke and never fully recovered, dying an isolated and frail man on 1 September 1949 (Trahair 1984; Hoopes 2003).

3.2.2 His Main 'Advice' to Management

Mayo believed that during the industrialization of work leaders of industry rapidly changed the technological means by which work was to be undertaken in an effort to get an edge on their competitors and control market fluctuations. That technological change was too rapid and unplanned, and, consequently, seriously affected the personal and social life of people at work. The result was alienation or *anomie* as workers lost their sense of community, purpose, and function. Individuals experienced what was then called 'fatigue': today we call it 'stress'. Employees made different attempts to reduce that fatigue, and to enhance their control of valued aspects of their work. Above all else, they fell victim to obsessive thoughts, or as Mayo called them, 'pessimistic reveries'; they used compulsive and elaborate rituals of fun-seeking and other strange, irrational pastimes. In short, accompanying the goods and services they were paid to produce, they also produced mental and physical ill health that was serious enough to warrant medical attention and sometimes hospitalization (Mayo 1933; Trahair 1984; Wren and Greenwood 1998; Wren 2005).

Furthermore, too rapid technological changes had an effect on social relationships. The most constructive and understandable action that would follow was the workers' formation of social organizations to protect their values, relieve their distress, and help reduce the merciless rate of industrialization in a society that seemed to be treating them so badly. Almost in self-defence, when work groups were broken up by the too rapid and thoughtless application of technical change to work, employees founded their own informal working groups. They sought to enjoy the benefits from their work that being with others brings; they established their own rules of work; they controlled the effort they could safely expend; and they controlled the communications they were prepared to make to people above. These informal rules and groupings sometimes conflicted with the formal expectations of those in charge. Both those in charge and their employees could see how futile these kinds of work organization were (Mayo 1933; Trahair 1984; Wren and Greenwood 1998; Wren 2005).

Mayo considered these human, social, and political problems in both general and specific terms. In general, he always sought solutions through extending two activities:

scientific research and education based on that research. When he was more specific, he spoke, for example, of fatigue or distress from dissatisfaction with work. He recommended proper relaxation and rest, according to the results of studies at work and in the laboratory. Also he recommended altering the conditions of work, and treating employees so that the effect of fatigue would diminish. And he recommended counselling for individuals with a purposeless life, lack of security, and the loss of social function. He further recommended that employees could be encouraged to participate in decisions that affected their chances and standing at work, and to collaborate in actions following those decisions (Trahair 1984).

As is well known, it was Mayo's closest disciple, Fritz Roethlisberger (with General Electric (GE)'s William Dickson) in the 1939 *Management and the Worker*, who provided a more accurate and encyclopaedic outline of the Hawthorne studies, particularly in relation to the later Bank Wiring Room studies that began in December 1931 (Bruce 2006). Between 1932 and 1935 Mayo had little to do with Hawthorne as his time was consumed with travel and popularizing the earlier experiments. Mayo used Rockefeller funding to get *Management and the Worker* published with Harvard University Press, and in it Roethlisberger and Dickson gave more formal expression to Mayo's insights concerning the individual–working group dynamic: they employed the terms *formal* and *informal organization* to capture this inter-human relations phenomenon (Bruce 2006; Bruce and Nyland 2011). For them, the Bank Wiring Room studies suggested that the group of workers studied 'possessed an intricate social organization in terms of which much of their conduct was determined'. It was this social code rather than individual malady that resulted in output restriction, as it served as a 'protective mechanism' insulating the group from outside changes in work conditions and personal relations (Roethlisberger and Dickson 1939: 525). In sum, in a much cited stanza,

> (t)he study of the bank wiremen showed that their behavior at work could not be understood without considering the *informal organization* of the group and the relation of this informal organization to the total social organization of the company. The work activities of this group, together with their satisfactions and dissatisfactions, had to be viewed as manifestations of a complex pattern of interrelations. In short, the work situation of the bank wiring group had to be treated as a *social system*; moreover, the industrial organization of which this group was a part also had to be treated as a social system. (Ibid.: 551; emphasis added)

So, therefore, organizations came to be viewed as social systems, wherein we find a number of individuals working towards common goals but each bringing to the work situation a number of different, personally and socially conditioned goals or aspirations (ibid.: 553–554). The aim of the organization, or more realistically its management, is to somehow temper these individual goals so they are congruent with those of the organization. These notions, along with an embryonic discussion of organizational or corporate culture, can be found in *Management and the Worker* and they infuse any meaningful contemporary discussion of organizational behaviour, motivation, and human resource management.

3.2.3 How Mayo 'Sold' Human Relations

3.2.3.1 *Early Contacts with Businesses*

It must be emphasized from the outset that Mayo abhorred mixing with businessmen, believing them to be uncouth and unsophisticated, and he especially despised visiting company plants and factories on consulting assignments. This said, following his field-work in Philadelphia and perhaps in a bid to gain recognition and further academic employment, Mayo began proselytizing on the benefits of industrial psychology. Critical for his latent human relations ideas to reach a receptive audience were, first, his roles with Rockefeller-owned big businesses as well as their professional think tanks, partic-ularly the clandestine Special Conference Committee and also Industrial Relations Counselors (IRC, hereafter), JDR Jr's industrial relations consulting company. Particularly important in the context of the latter was his friendship with IRC head, Arthur H. Young. In October 1927, Young arranged for Mayo to address a group of indus-trialists concerning what psychology could offer industry. Known as 'The Lunchers', who met at the Harvard Club in New York, many of the attendees were from leading American industrial organizations and met periodically to discuss and co-ordinate labour policies. Corporations represented included Standard Oil of New Jersey, General Electric, Bethlehem Steel, DuPont, General Motors, US Rubber, Goodyear, Westinghouse, International Harvester, and the Irving Trust. Key to the activities of the group was the need to legitimate management authority without limiting the prerogatives of owner-ship (Nyland and Bruce 2012).

Mayo's address had two critical consequences. First, the personnel director of Western Electric invited Mayo to consult in the ongoing Hawthorne studies, thus precipitating the most public and enduring aspect of the diffusion of his knowledge claims concern-ing human motivation, worker irrationality, and the need for a managerial elite. Less well known, but perhaps of equal consequence, Mayo was invited to a private meeting with JDR Jr, from which came a consulting assignment to research possible causes of improper functioning of the (CFI) Industrial Plan and the possible use of forces to bring about a more co-operative relationship between management and employees. Two months after Mayo's 'investigation' into the limited success of the Rockefeller Plan, he received a retainer from IRC and, as a something of a *quid pro quo*, Young was invited to lecture at the Harvard Business School. Thereafter, Mayo and Young became close friends and Mayo benefited greatly from the connections made through Young. Mayo accompanied Young to Geneva as an 'expert industrial relations advisor' when IRC established a branch at the International Labour Organization (ILO) in Geneva. Young, in fact, was a crucial bridge and broker between Mayo and JDR Jr in that he drew Mayo into the inner circle of industrial relations executives of major corporations, fostered his involvement in the Hawthorne studies, and ensured Western Electric and AT&T executives under-stood the importance of Mayo's research (Trahair 1984; Smith 1987). Mayo's consulting assignment at Hawthorne was attractive to JDR Jr and other philanthropy officers because this research promised 'a technology of social control that could confront problems of industrial unrest and individual maladjustments among workers' (Gillespie 1991: 112–113).

3.2.3.2 *Mayo and Hawthorne*

Mayo first visited the Hawthorne plant (one of Western Electric's largest manufacturing sites in Chicago) for two days in April 1928, then for four days in 1929, and then he began a deeper involvement in the ongoing experiments in 1930. The experiments had commenced in 1924 and the results were so inconclusive and confusing to management at Western Electric that it was crucial Mayo's interpretation of the data 'proved' his preconceived ideas and furnished a shared account of the investigations amongst different parties: namely, to managers at Hawthorne; to Harvard researchers; to top Harvard Business School administrators; to Rockefeller philanthropies underwriting Mayo's interpretations; and to conservative big business interested in control over their companies. The key findings were widely construed as demonstrating that once the irrationalities of workers are removed, or ameliorated, they will respond positively to non-economic incentives and be motivated to increase their productivity. Though there were five sets of independent experiments, the key findings were actually based on a study of only six women (two of whom were replaced) at a workbench—the Relay Assembly studies—over some five years! In November 1928 Mayo reported his interpretation of the findings of the relay assembly studies to members of the Special Conference Committee, a clandestine group of influential industrialists concerned with how to deal with worker unrest in their organizations. They were very impressed, particularly now that his latent theories were cloaked in facts and figures and emphasized that changes in supervision solved worker maladjustment and improved productivity (Trahair 1984; Gillespie 1991). The poorly designed study of six unrepresentative staff was sufficient for big business to accept Mayo's theory and be 'enrolled' in his research programme; such was the need for acceptance of Mayo's knowledge claims as an explanation of worker behaviour and as a way to control society (Bruce and Nyland 2011).

It is important to emphasize that, contrary to the textbook orthodoxy, Mayo did *not* direct, control, or initiate the research at Hawthorne; he was a consultant, publicist, and a therapist to those who *did* direct, control, and initiate the research. Many social scientists were invited by the management to give their views on the research being done in the personnel department; Mayo impressed the management more than did the others, so he was called upon more often to help personnel managers make sense of their research. Mayo's other major contribution was to help in reporting the extension of research into observations in the firm's Bank Wiring Room, which found that some people who are socially unskilled can actually be quite productive should their work surroundings be propitious, while others who are exceedingly capable may not be so in an inappropriate milieu. Results showed that abstract managerial principles, for example, efficiency campaigns to maximize shareholder interests, fail because relations between managers and work group members are unknown or not recognized, and consequently workers create their own work procedures. Working under abstract work policies regulations and following formalized practices led workers into conflict with management and prevented efficient collaboration. In the Hawthorne studies, without supervision employees overcame conflict between what they wanted and what was possible, and achieved a high degree of collaboration and productivity. It was this that led to the conclusion that the reorganization of modern industry should be based first on knowledge of how to achieve effective collaboration (Carey 1967; Trahair 1984; Gillespie 1991; Smith 1998; Wren and Greenwood 1998).

3.2.3.3 *Consulting Engagements Elsewhere*

Although Mayo's role at Hawthorne was mainly interpretive, he had attempted independent consulting projects elsewhere, with limited success. His Harvard colleagues thought the study of fatigue, monotony, and morale had no proper place in the training of men for business; also, it was thought that it would need close and time-consuming instruction for young men to understand the human problems at work. Such instruction was thought to be too costly, and the return on it was difficult to justify in business terms. Also students themselves resisted the study of human problems in industrial causation because it was a new, undeveloped field in business administration, and much higher salaries could be earned outside personnel (Trahair 1984).

Mayo's ideas were resisted outside Harvard Business School, not by business leaders so much as by those whose immediate influence at work would be most affected by the changes he advocated. This problem had arisen at the Continental Mills. Mayo's assistant, Emily Osborne, wrote that she and Mayo had gained the confidence and co-operation of departmental heads and leaders, that is, higher management and employees, but little or no support from middle management or foremen. They feared results from research would reflect upon them badly, so they impeded it. Usually Mayo aimed to study fatigue and its effects by first seeing employees who came to the firm's dispensary for medical attention from the industrial nurse. While she took the employees' blood pressure, they would talk about their preoccupations. This information revealed to Mayo the human problems at work, and the production, labour, and organizational difficulties at the plant. With this information he could identify those parts of the plant where his research could bring benefit. But middle management and foremen, fearing that organizational change arising from Mayo's research would undermine their control, saw no benefits for themselves in co-operating with the firm's dispensary, and kept the latter well away from their administrative activity. They would tolerate it only to satisfy the company's insurers (Trahair 1984).

In the American Rubber Company, Mayo and his assistant managed to collect data on workers and overcome some of the resistance of middle management. But suddenly demand fell for the company's product and the production manager had no time for the introduction of rest pauses or similar recommendations. As with Hawthorne in 1932, the Depression closed out Mayo. The Boston Manufacturing Co. wanted Mayo to follow techniques of F. W. Taylor's scientific management by centralizing control, raising morale, and cutting costs. He was there less than one month.

Although research at William Carter Knitwear had shown that rest pauses could help smooth production, Mayo never learned whether or not the firm heeded his advice (Trahair 1984).

3.2.3.4 *Executive Education*

The second means of securing a business audience for his knowledge claims was Mayo's pivotal role in the Harvard executive education programme, the so-called 'Cabot Weekends'. Regardless of Mayo's motives, 'what mattered was that were was an audience of social scientists, foundation officials, corporate executives, and managers ready to listen to and support Mayo's approach'. His mild criticism of them was 'the prelude to a program offering them more efficient techniques of control' (Gillespie 1991: 110). Held for one weekend a month, beginning in January 1935 and ending in December 1941, these workshops were composed of young executives—the future captains of industry and finance—from America's largest corporations, including Western Electric, AT&T, Standard Oil, Nabisco, J. P. Morgan, American Tobacco, Du Pont, IBM, and US Steel (Cruickshank 1987).

In practice, the Cabot Weekends were just one part of a particular model of leadership training emphasized by Harvard Business School dean, Donham, focusing on business managers as elites or statesmen presiding over a rapidly deteriorating society (Cruickshank 1987). This view received particular impetus from Donham's shared involvement with Mayo in the Harvard Pareto Circle who, as an epistemic community, felt the need to defend capitalism against socialistic threats and who invoked Pareto specifically to counter Marx (O'Connor 2008). Given the subject matter of the Cabot Weekends was about clarifying social and human problems in industry, Cabot shaped many of these meetings around talks by Mayo and Roethlisberger, and subsequently other HRS figures such as T. N. Whitehead and George Lombard, particularly as 'the enthusiastic response by businessmen toward the Hawthorne findings suggested that the School might pursue new directions in executive education' (Trahair 1984; Cruickshank 1987: 190). As Roethlisberger (1977: 86–87) notes, 'Cabot at this time must have felt that Mayo's diagnosis of the ills of modern industrial civilization wanted an audience of responsible businessmen. He bought together some the outstanding business leaders of the time and bought them Mayo in person.'

This is an important point because the Hawthorne researchers took for granted the necessity of complete managerial hegemony in the workplace. As Gillespie (1991: 268) notes, 'Human Relations became an attractive ideology for a technocratic and managerial class trying to reconcile its expanded power with the principles of liberal democracy.' In this way, Mayo made a strong case that his ideas and methods would develop the requisite managerial elite needed to save civilization by training these leaders at Harvard (O'Connor 1999b). As he himself asserted, 'Human Relations, in the form of skills taught to business leaders and administrators, could ensure social collaboration in the factory and in society at large and win the war against Communism' (1949, cited in Gillespie 1991: 246).

3.3 ERIC LANSDOWN TRIST

3.3.1 His Life and Work

Eric Trist, an only child, was born in 1909 in Dover, England. His father was a sea captain and his mother a governess in Scotland and both were inclined to education, his mother more so than his father. At the local secondary school Trist was an excellent student, and his teachers, recognizing his scholarly abilities, encouraged him to sit for a university scholarship. He went to Pembroke College, Cambridge, in October 1928. Much influenced by Ivor A. Richards and F. R. Leavis, Trist completed a first degree in English and then studied psychology under Frederic C. Bartlett. He became interested more in psychoanalysis—not popular at Cambridge—than experimental psychology, and was drawn to the social psychology of Kurt Lewin whom he would first meet briefly at one of Bartlett's tea parties. Excited by Lewin's article on Galilean and Aristotelian methods in psychology (Lewin 1931), Trist made a career mistake—so he would often tell—when he appeared uncritical of Lewin's work, not sufficiently detached, too involved, and over-impressed by it. His fellow scholars at Cambridge, and especially Bartlett—as Trist said years later—found him 'guilty of enthusiasm' (Trist 1993). Nevertheless, he graduated in May 1933 with not only first-class honours in psychology, but also a Distinction Star, an award not given since World War I. With support from senior academics and an outstanding degree, he was awarded a Commonwealth Fund Fellowship and went to Yale (1933–1935) where he studied postgraduate anthropology with Edward Sapir. Sapir's concept of culture interested Trist because it came from the internal world of a person, was shared with others, and was not a fixed force to which one responded passively (Trahair forthcoming).

He was greatly disappointed at not being accepted in the Psychology Laboratory at Cambridge and so, unable to find academic work, he decided to be a school-teacher. At the last minute he was offered a research position in a three-year Pilgrim Trust study of unemployment in Dundee under the direction of the former student of Bartlett, Oscar A. Oeser. The fieldwork was a 'baptism of fire' to Trist (Trist 1993). Dundee's economic depression distressed Trist and his wife, Virginia. He learned that long-term unemployment, especially in the jute industry, was a well-established element of Scotland's industrial culture. He and his wife worked to show men, women, and children in Dundee that through education they could ameliorate their economic distress. He spent one year as the acting head of Oeser's department at St Andrews University, and was unimpressed by the internal conflicts and irrationalities of university funding and administration. In May 1940 Trist began work at London's Maudsley Psychiatric Hospital as a clinical psychologist under Aubrey J. Lewis, and constructed tests for effects of brain damage and war neurosis (Trahair forthcoming).

While at the Maudsley, in late 1941 Trist became acquainted with social psychiatry, not much accepted at the Maudsley then, but more so among medical staff at the Tavistock

Clinic. Many of the staff from the Clinic within the Army Psychiatric Corps wanted Trist, as a psychologist, to join them and undertake applied research into new ways to select officers for the British Army. Prevented from quitting the Maudsley, Trist volunteered to join the army; with his wife and son he went to Edinburgh to work on the experimental stage of the War Office Selection Board (WOSB), on procedures for finding more effective officers for the army (Trist and Murray 1990). Psychological work on this problem occupied Trist until the middle of 1943 when Dr. A. T. Macbeth Wilson asked Trist to help plan and develop Civil Resettlement Units (CRU) for repatriated prisoners of war. This began Trist's active work in the therapeutic community (Wilson, Trist, and Curle 1990). He began to see that his work on officer selection and prisoner-of-war resettlement was not cognate with the tight bureaucratically based authority exercised in an army. Nevertheless, while both WOSB and CRU procedures were founded on social and psychoanalytic psychology and the professional use of democratic authority, they were remarkably successful organizations inside the military. At that time such thought and procedures were well outside mainstream psychology and psychiatry in Great Britain.

In February 1946, Trist, who had been co-opted into the 'Tavistock Group' late in 1945, was chosen, due to his creative and highly regarded organizational skills, to set out the way for a new organization. It would be associated with, but not part of, the post-war medical work of the Tavistock Clinic, and be known legally as the Tavistock Institute of Human Relations (TIHR). The TIHR became the centre of Trist's working life until 1966 when he accepted a chair of Organizational Behavior and Social Ecology in the management school at the University of California, Los Angeles. After three years he accepted a similar position at the Wharton School. He was made emeritus in 1978, and then accepted a similar professorship in the Faculty of Environmental Studies at York University, Toronto, where in 1983 he was made Doctor of Laws (Honoris). After retirement Trist suffered ill health during the 1980s—heart attacks, bypass surgery, diabetes, a hip fracture—but continued to work on several projects. In 1984, he left Philadelphia and retired in Gainesville, Florida. In retirement, Trist travelled to England often, also to India, to Scandinavian countries, and to Scotland where he consulted on the Craigmillar artistic project. His final important work centred on the publication of an anthology on the work of the Tavistock Institute (Trahair forthcoming).

3.3.2 His Aim: The Application of Science to Organizations

An important role in the development of Trist's early views on industrial society was played by his shock at the inhumane effect of the 1930s Depression, and although he was never a member of the Communist Party of Great Britain, he found sympathy for some of its humane goals until clear evidence of brutality in Soviet Russia could not be ignored. The alienation of workers from productive employment, the ideas and research of Kurt Lewin, and effective studies and research in the British Army, demonstrated to Trist the complexity of resolving human and social problems inside a well-established bureaucracy, the value of a clinician's patient, scientifically oriented observation, and the fact that carefully controlled changes in operating procedures could help integrate the gratification of individual needs with the aims of an organization.

In the establishment of the TIHR and its administration, and his research into coal production, Trist was able to establish what became known as the socio-technical system approach to the study of organizations. In this he was helped considerably by an Australian social scientist, Fred E. Emery, who provided Trist and his associates with the first coherent and thorough account of the characteristics of the technical system (Emery 1959). In England the connection between technology and work organization was made around this time by Woodward (1958), and Burns and Stalker (1961). In this theoretical contribution, the argument was that in humanizing industry it was necessary to look beyond the ideas attributed to Mayo that spontaneous co-operation comes from friendliness towards workers, which then leads to individual adjustment to a task, better co-operation and higher production, less absenteeism, less waste, and greater ease of supervision. Socio-technical theory and practice tended to explore the possibility of basic, limited, structural changes to industry in the hope that these would help reduce alienating people from productive activity.

Trist was invited to join the Tavistock Group towards the end of 1945 and he accepted the consulting assignment of drawing up the administrative and managerial structure of what would become the TIHR. He helped design the TIHR procedures for the selection of staff, training of social scientists in the field, pursuit of funding from the British government, industry, and abroad, and especially the founding and editing of the journal *Human Relations*. Also, he worked informally as a counsellor and psychological adviser until 1966 to colleagues who regularly brought him both personal and research problems that had arisen in their work (Trahair forthcoming).

Trist worked on the application of social science to work and industry and many of his publications appeared in the three-volume anthology of the Tavistock Institute, and were listed in his memoirs. One important aspect of this application concerned the bureaucratic control of work through the use of science in the management of work. In the 1960s and 1970s Trist and Emery set forth the view that public and private organizations were best understood as 'open systems', rather than 'logico-economic' arrangements. Also they advanced the view that, importantly, organizations existed in different types of environments, and, consequently, managed change in the organizations would only be successful to the extent that awareness of the environment was realistic rather than it being regarded merely as an economic marketplace. Finally, Trist held the view that industrial civilization would benefit most when the quasi-religious passion for bureaucracy as the preferred form of domination at work gave way to participative democracy, and when the tightly supervised competitive 'team' was induced to become an autonomous and self-regulating group, and that the goal of industrial organizations was best achieved with efficient, creative, and gratifying use of human effort (Trahair forthcoming).

Trist worked on many research projects and issues: leadership and the effect of its absence in educational groups, family networks, conflict in a coal mine, withdrawal from work, and the psychology of culture (Trist and Murray 1990). He studied coal mining groups and developed his socio-technical theory (Trist and Bamforth 1951; Trist et al. 1963). Trist's coal industry studies (Trist et al. 1963) centred on how a traditional work system functioned with a group of six, self-selected members, all 'mates', equally paid, enjoying considerable autonomy in their tasks, and requiring personal adaptability. Trist and his fellow researchers found that the work was psychologically gratifying, meaningful, and challenging. This traditional system was replaced quickly by the introduction of an economically compelling coal-face conveyor, different jobs, and new work relations.

Newly mechanized technology failed to provide a work system fitting to use the miners' shared experience, ability, and commitment; productive performance fell, spontaneous characteristics of work cycles faded, and superiors struggled to co-ordinate new tasks and to smooth production flow. Work groups competed for variable pay rates and status, blamed other groups for slow-downs, and devoted envy-driven energy to uncooperative work. Trist then found a mine where job specialization and mechanistic thinking were absent. Here the traditional single-place mining system was integrated with the new longwall technology. The integration was achieved by moving groups from task to task, maintaining some multi-skilling and specializing tasks of machine work, and ultimately restored the continuity between task performance from shift to shift. Consequently, outside supervision was rarely needed, composite workgroups became cohesive and responsible for the allocation of tasks and the assignment of men, interest in job rotation emerged, pay rates were governed by interdependence not competition, and absenteeism fell (Trahair forthcoming).

A comprehensive account of the socio-technical system appeared first by Trist's colleague Emery (1959), whose capacity to put social and psychological theories into practice would complement Trist's work (Trist, Emery, and Murray 1997a). Socio-technical theory looked beyond Mayo's idea that spontaneous co-operation comes from friendliness towards workers, leading to individual adjustment to a task, better co-operation, higher production, less absenteeism, less waste, better housekeeping, and greater ease of supervision. Although new social processes and technological advances were extraordinarily well integrated, organizational changes could not be introduced into UK coal industry. Industrial authorities had little interest in a study they had not controlled; the larger socio-political system was too threatened by economically effective changes. In response Trist and Emery devised a fresh perspective on organizational change with open systems theory and a new theory on organizational environments (Emery and Trist 1963).

Trist's next important contribution was the 'Search Conference' with Emery (Emery 1996; Emery and Purser 1996), a participative method for changing organizations to achieve desirable and possible futures. The method is an alternative to conventional planning and traditional organizations that use elite groups—often supported by expert staff and external consultants—as the locus of control in the chain of command. Instead the Search Conference draws together people who normally work at the lower levels to establish plans for their shared system. During the 1960s eleven Search Conferences were held in England, Southeast Asia, Australia, Holland, Norway, France, and Canada. By 1993 it was well established in North America (Weisbord et al. 1992).

3.3.3 Trist as an Action Researcher

Trist did not find that conventional management consulting suited organizational change (Trist 1976) and used action research based on joint consultation rather than expert-only consultation. This meant that two or more action researchers worked openly as consultants with *all* willing participants at *all* levels in a client organization, never covertly for merely its managers. They would study the organization closely with its members, search with them for a better way, and then, with the clients' help, introduce agreed upon changes, systematically assess their value, and continue to seek better ways followed by further assessments. To promote objectivity such consultants worked in pairs, and discussed work relations with outside colleagues and with members of the organization, and published their findings in professional journals (Trist, Emery, and Murray 1997b).

In America, Trist's action-research consultancy in the coal mining industry lay behind an agreement between union and management to institute autonomous and participant work systems in Rushton, Pennsylvania. Although productivity improved, the experiment did not survive and autonomous work groups did not spread throughout the mine. After twelve years it was found that the experiment's failure was due to mining industry changes in the 1970s, work group fears, anger, rivalry, and envy not well understood by the researchers, and their unwitting recommendations unexpectedly aggravated the tense working relations (Susman and Trist 1993).

Two more action-research consultancies for Trist were in organizational change at General Foods Corporation (Ketchum 1975), and another elsewhere with academic colleague, Louis E. Davis (Archer 1975). The first study centred on explaining the difference between traditional engineering design and socio-technical design. By the end of 1971, Ketcham had gathered data and impressions, much as an anthropologist would, on plant visits, and then with Trist and a Harvard Business School colleague as his guides defined the task, strategies, and the ranking of important values for group discussion with personnel and operation executives. The aim was to diffuse socio-technical ideas and practices into an organization and have it change from within. Ketcham gradually introduced to the management a new way of working for and with people, deciding how to change work, educating themselves as they introduced changes, and expanding future plans. It was a long job. Each meeting used an open system, and clarified reward schedules, and, in time, the action-research scheme was accepted. Ketcham describes the effect of changes on goal-setting, the role of higher management, the experiences of threats, rivalry among peers, casualties resulting from the complexity and value differences evident during changes, the vagaries of elitism, the acceptance of variable job evaluation criteria and procedures, career issues, union acceptance, and critical evaluation of progress and problems.

The second consultancy had employed a theoretical model, guided briefly by Trist and Davis, of Archer's analysis of a workplace as a socio-technical system and had also established an action-research committee of superintendents, a general foreman, and a personnel officer (Archer 1975). Later Trist went to Jamestown, a manufacturing town in western New York State; he took graduate students with him to undertake an anthropological study of the community (Trist 1976). The report made proposals for socio-technical action research to help stabilize organizations and communities undergoing change. The research produced a new concept, 'the function of the continuant', that is, points of stability for an organization that sought change within itself. Furthermore, the concept helped deal more broadly with relations between Jamestown's firms, labour–management relations, and tensions within the community and among the researchers themselves.

3.4 THE HUMAN RELATIONS LEGACY AND MANAGEMENT CONSULTING

For management consulting, Trist's and Mayo's research differed with respect to industrial problems, their origins, conceptual level, research, and expertise. For Mayo industrial problems were an illness, best managed through proper education. But Trist contrasted research approaches towards industry by universities, management consultancies, and the TIHR (Trist 1976; Trist and Murray 1990: 27–32). In universities, problems need a theory and a method, are tackled abstractly, involve research then teaching, and should be properly discipline-bound. In traditional management consulting the problem belongs to one client, is concrete, requires research for a service to the client, and is done in an administrative division. In Trist's world, the problem originates from a wide field: it has an important past, requires research followed by action, and employs integrated fields of expertise and experience.

For Mayo the university was his starting point. The problem came not from a client, but from his scholarly observations on the stress that potential clients or dissatisfied entrepreneurs had unwittingly aroused among employees. By using a listening-post approach, Mayo's nurse would identify unhealthy variations in blood pressure levels and wild reveries in employees where stress and fatigue arose; next Mayo would diagnose and proscribe the therapy he alone thought appropriate, for example, controlled rest pauses and counselling, followed by talks to managers at weekend conferences.

In place of traditional management consultation procedure, Trist had the following advice: first, secure an understanding of the problem from the highest level of authority in the client organizations and focus on the values they uphold; second, offsite, use the Search Conference with these authorities to review the total organization, especially the origins of problems and current images of itself, have members find their shared images of the future, and decide actions required to realize the future through new principles of work design, work analysis, and autonomous primary work systems; third, at this level of authority aim for organizational change only where it is accepted, and might be valued. Fourth, select existing sites where management, unions, and local authorities operate, and establish a group of workers, employees, and specialists to study the local issues, and recommend action. In joint worker–management–local authority committees decide on project sites, assess them, and evaluate proposed changes. If group members value the socio-technical changes, then encourage them to work through the stress that changes arouse.

Trist has yet to attract criticism like that given to Mayo, but Cooke (2006) demonstrated that action research, originating as a detached, expert, and evidence-based procedure for involving all levels of participation in organizational change, may in fact be co-opted to managerial interests alone. Mayo's theory of human relations was based almost entirely on his personal political interpretation of worker motivation; this shaped the results of the Hawthorne investigations, and his career can be seen as the rise of causal knowledge above statistical fact and the emergence of high theory masquerading as factual evidence (Gillespie 1991). Given his reliance on JDR Jr the real motivation behind Mayo's theory was, arguably, that of psychological control over workers. While F. W. Taylor was supportive of improvements in workers' pay and conditions, Mayo and the HRS promised to eliminate such calls entirely. Mayo's conceptualization of managers as a natural elite, possessing the ability and,therefore, the right to rule workplaces and the nation is especially problematic, an issue discussed in great detail elsewhere (Rose 1978, 1990, 1998; Townley 1993; Miller and Rose 1995; Deetz 2003; Costea, Crump, and Amiridis 2008).

REFERENCES

Alvarez, J. L. (ed.) (1998). *The Diffusion and Consumption of Business Knowledge*. New York: St Martin's Press.

Archer, J. T. (1975). 'Achieving Joint Organizational, Technical, and Personal Needs: The Case of the Sheltered Experiment of Aluminum Casting Team'. In L. E. Davis and A. B. Cherns (eds), *The Quality of Working Life: Cases and Commentary*. London: Collier Macmillan, 253–268.

Bloemen, E. (1996). 'The Movement for Scientific Management in Europe Between the Wars'. In J-C. Spender and H. Kijne (eds), *Scientific Management: Frederick Winslow Taylor's Gift to the World?* Boston: Kluwer, 111–131.

Bruce, K. (2006). 'Henry Dennison, Elton Mayo and Human Relations Historiography'. *Management and Organizational History*, 1/2, 177–199.

Bruce, K. (2012). 'G. Elton Mayo'. In M. Witzel and M. Warner (eds), *The Oxford Handbook of Management Theorists*. Oxford: Oxford University Press, forthcoming.

Bruce, K. and Nyland, C. (2011). 'Elton Mayo and the Deification of Human Relations'. *Organization Studies*, 32/3, 383–405.

Bulmer, M. and Bulmer, J. (1981). 'Philanthropy and Social Science in the 1920s: Beardsley Ruml and the Laura Spelman Rockefeller Memorial, 1922–1929'. *Minerva*, 19/3, 347–407.

Burns, T. and Stalker, G. M. (1961). *The Management of Innovation*. London: Tavistock.

Carey, A. (1967). 'The Hawthorne Studies: A Radical Criticism'. *American Sociological Review*, 32, 403–416.

Cayet, T. (2007). 'A Scientific Management of Work? A Micro-International Perspective on the Internationalization of Management Ideas'. Paper presented at the European Business History Association (EBHA) conference, Geneva, 13–15 September.

Cooke, B. (2006). 'The Cold War Origin of Action Research as Managerialist Cooptation'. *Human Relations*, 59/5, 665–693.

Costea, B., Crump, N., and Amiridis, K. (2008). 'Managerialism, the Therapeutic Habitus and the Self in Contemporary Organizing'. *Human Relations*, 61/5, 661–685.

Cruickshank, J. (1987). *A Delicate Experiment: The Harvard Business School, 1908–1945*. Boston: Harvard Business School Press.

Deetz, S. (2003). 'Disciplinary Power, Conflict Suppression and HRM'. In M. Alvesson and H. Willmott (eds), *Studying Management Critically*. London: Sage, 23–45.

Emery, F. E. (1959). *Characteristics of Socio-Technical Systems*. London: Tavistock Institute, Document 527.

Emery, F. E. (1996). 'History of the Search Conference'. In M. Emery and R. E. Purser, *The Search Conference: A Powerful Method for Planning Organizational Change and Community Action*. San Francisco: Jossey-Bass, 292–306.

Emery, F. E. and Trist, E. L. (1963). 'The Causal Texture of Organizational Environments'. Paper presented at the International Congress of Psychology, Washington, September. Reprinted in *Human Relations*, 18 (1965), 21–32.

Emery, M. and Purser, R. E. (1996). *The Search Conference: A Powerful Method for Planning Organizational Change and Community Action*. San Francisco: Jossey-Bass.

Engwall, L. and Kipping, M. (2004). 'Introduction: The Dissemination of Management Knowledge'. *Management Learning*, 35/3, 243–253.

Fisher, D. (1983). 'The Role of Philanthropic Foundations in the Reproduction of and Production of Hegemony: Rockefeller Foundations and the Social Sciences'. *Sociology*, 17/2, 206–233.

Fisher, D. (1993). *Fundamental Development of the Social Sciences: Rockefeller Philanthropy and the United States Social Science Research Council*. Ann Arbor, MI: University of Michigan Press.

Gillespie, R. (1991). *Manufacturing Knowledge: A History of the Hawthorne Experiments*. Cambridge: Cambridge University Press.

Gitelman, H. (1988). *Legacy of the Ludlow Massacre: A Chapter in American Industrial Relations*. Philadelphia: University of Pennsylvania Press.

Guillén, M. F. (1994). *Models of Management: Work, Authority, and Organization in a Comparative Perspective*. Chicago: University of Chicago Press.

Harvey, C. E. (1982). 'John D. Rockefeller, Jr, and the Social Sciences: An Introduction'. *Journal of the History of Sociology*, 4, 1–31.

Hoopes, J. (2003). *False Prophets: The Gurus Who Created Modern Management and Why Their Ideas are Bad for Business Today*. Cambridge, MA: Perseus.

Kaufman, B. and Taras, D. (2000). *Nonunion Employee Representation: History, Contemporary Practice, and Policy*. Armonk, NY: M. E. Sharpe.

Ketchum, L. D. (1975). 'A Case Study of Diffusion'. In L. E. Davis and A.B. Cherns (eds), *The Quality of Working Life: Cases and Commentary*. London: Collier Macmillan, 138–163.

Khurana, R. (2007). *From Higher Aims to Hired Hands: The Social Transformation of American Business Schools and the Unfulfilled Promise of Management as a Profession*. Princeton, NJ: Princeton University Press.

Kipping, M. (1997). 'Consultancies, Institutions and the Diffusion of Taylorism in Britain, Germany and France, 1920s to 1950s'. *Business History*, 39/4, 67–83.

Kipping, M., Engwall, L., and Üsdiken, B. (2009). 'Preface: The Transfer of Management Knowledge to Peripheral Countries'. *International Studies of Management and Organization*, 38/4, 3–16.

Lewin, K. (1931). 'The Conflict Between Aristotelian and Galilean Modes of Thought in Contemporary Psychology'. *Journal of General Psychology*, 5, 141–177.

O'Connor, E. S. (1999a). 'The Politics of Management Thought: A Case Study of the Harvard Business School and the Human Relations School'. *Academy of Management Review*, 24/1, 117–131.

O'Connor, E. S. (1999b). 'Minding the Workers: The Meaning of "Human" and "Human Relations" in Elton Mayo'. *Organization*, 6/2, 223–246.

O'Connor, E. S. (2008). Personal communication with authors, email dated 14 May.

Magat, R. (1999). *Unlikely Partners: Philanthropic Foundations and the Labor Movement*. Ithaca, NY: ILR Press.

Mayo, E. (1933). *The Human Problems of an Industrial Civilization*. New York: Macmillan.

Merkle, J. E. (1980). *Management and Ideology: The Legacy of the International Scientific Management Movement*. Berkeley: University of California Press.

Miller, P. and Rose, N. (1995). 'Production, Identity, and Democracy'. *Theory and Society*, 24/3, 427–467.

Nyland, C. and Bruce, K. (2011). 'The ILO, the Taylor Society, and Managerial Opportunism'. Unpublished paper.

Nyland, C. and Bruce, K. (2012). 'The Demonization of Scientific Management and the Deification of Human Relations'. In N. Lichtenstein and E. Shermer (eds), *The American Right and Labor: Politics, Ideology, and Imagination*. Philadelphia: University of Pennsylvania Press.

Rees, J. (2010). *Representation and Rebellion: Employee Representation at the Colorado Fuel and Iron Company 1914–1942*. Boulder: University of Colorado Press.

Roethlisberger, F. J. (1977). *The Elusive Phenomena*. Cambridge, MA: Harvard Business School Press.

Roethlisberger, F. J. and Dickson, W. J. (1939). *Management and the Worker*. Cambridge, MA: Harvard University Press.

Rose, M. (1978). *Industrial Behaviour: Theoretical Developments since Taylor*. London: Penguin.

Rose, N. (1990). *Governing the Soul: The Shaping of the Private Self*. London: Routledge.

Rose, N. (1998). *Inventing Ourselves: Psychology, Power, and Personhood*. Cambridge: Cambridge University Press.

Sahlin-Andersson, K. and Engwall L. (2002). *The Expansion of Management Knowledge: Carriers, Flows, and Sources*. Paolo Alto, CA: Stanford University Press.

Smith, J. H. (1987). 'Elton Mayo and the Hidden Hawthorne'. *Work, Employment, and Society*, 1/1, 107–120.

Smith, J. H. (1998). 'The Enduring Legacy of Elton Mayo'. *Human Relations*, 51/3, 221–249.

Susman, G. and Trist, E. L. (1993). 'Action Resource in an American Underground Coal Mine'. In E. L. Trist, F. E. Emery, and H. Murray (eds), *The Social Engagement of Social Science: A Tavistock Anthology*, vol. 3: *The Socio-ecological Perspective*. Philadelphia: University of Pennsylvania Press, 416–450.

Townley, B. (1993). 'Foucault, Power/Knowledge and its Relevance for Human Resource Management'. *Academy of Management Review*, 18/3, 518–545.

Trahair, R. (1984). *The Humanist Temper: The Life and Work of Elton Mayo*. New Brunswick, NJ: Transaction Publishers.

Trahair, R. (forthcoming). *Tavistock Man: The Life and Work of Eric Trist*.

Trist, E. L. (1976). 'Action Research and Adaptive Planning'. In A. W. Clark (ed.), *Experimenting with Organisational Life: The Action Research Approach*. London: Plenum Press, 223–236.

Trist, E. L. (1993). 'Guilty of Enthusiasm'. In A. G. Bedeian (ed.), *Management Laureates: A Collection of Autobiographical Essays*. Greenwich, CT: JAI Press, 191–221.

Trist, E. L. and Bamforth, K. W. (1951). 'Some Social and Psychological Consequences of the Longwall Method of Coal-Getting'. *Human Relations*, 4, 1–38.

Trist, E. L. and Murray, H. (eds) (1990). *The Social Engagement of Social Science: A Tavistock Anthology*, I: *The Social Psychological Perspective*. Philadelphia: University of Pennsylvania Press.

Trist, E. L., Emery, F. E., and Murray, H. (eds) (1997a). *The Social Engagement of Social Science: A Tavistock Anthology*, vol. 3: *The Socio-Ecological Perspective*. Philadelphia: University of Pennsylvania Press.

Trist, E. L., Emery, F. E., and Murray, H. (1997b). 'Historical Overview: Consultancy Developments'. In E. L. Trist, F. E. Emery, and H. Murray (eds), *The Social Engagement of Social Science: A Tavistock Anthology*, vol. 3: *The Socio-Ecological Perspective*. Philadelphia: University of Pennsylvania Press.

Trist, E. L., Higgin, G. W., Murray, H. A., and Pollock, A. B. (1963). *Organizational Choice: Capabilities of Groups at the Coal Face Under Changing Technologies. The Loss, Re-Discovery and Transformation of a Work Tradition*. London: Tavistock.

Weisbord, M. R. et al. (1992). *Discovering Common Ground: How Future Search Conferences Bring People Together to Achieve Breakthrough Innovation, Empowerment, Shared Vision and Collaborative Action*. San Francisco: Berrett-Koehler.

Wilson, A. T. M., Trist, E. L., and Curle, A. (1990). 'Transitional Communities and Social Reconnection: The Civil Resettlement of British Prisoners of War'. In E. L. Trist and H. Murray (eds), *The Social Engagement of Social Science: A Tavistock Anthology*, I: *The Socio-Psychological Perspective*. Philadelphia: University of Pennsylvania Press, 88–112.

Woodward, J. (1958). *Industrial Organisation: Theory and Practice*. London: Oxford University Press.

Wren, D. (2005). *The Evolution of Management Thought*. New York: John Wiley & Sons.

Wren, D. and Greenwood, R. G. (1998). *Management Innovators: The People Who Have Shaped Modern Business*. New York: Oxford University Press.

CHAPTER 4

INSTITUTIONAL CHANGE AND THE GROWTH OF STRATEGY CONSULTING IN THE UNITED STATES

ROBERT J. DAVID[*]

4.1 INTRODUCTION

THE remarkable growth of the management consulting industry has puzzled scholars and practitioners alike. Today, the industry is a socially and economically prominent sector of organization life, but prior to World War I the industry was fledgling at best (Higdon 1969; Kipping 2002; McKenna 2006). This transformation has garnered considerable academic attention. One line of argument for the industry's growth emphasizes management consulting's efficacy in addressing organizational problems. For example, in his two-part treatise, Canback (1998, 1999) invokes transaction-cost economics and argues that external contracting for management advice is, on the whole, more efficient than an internal solution (see also Washburn 1996). Using a similar argument, McKenna (2006) posits that management consulting offers 'knowledge economies' that outweigh the costs of using consultants. A second line of scholarly work takes a more critical stance and describes how management consultants perpetuate demand for their services through their interaction with clients. For example, Clark (1995; Clark and Salaman 1998) employs a dramaturgical metaphor to explain how consultants manage clients' impressions of the value of consulting. Similarly, Ernst and Kieser (2002) elaborate a model in which consulting projects initiated to give managers control over uncertainty actually exacerbate this need, thereby creating a cycle of self-perpetuating demand. A third, related line of work takes a political view and sees consultants as competing with and displacing other management groups, principally senior and middle managers inside organizations (Sturdy 1997).

What is generally under-explored in these approaches is how changes in the wider social context facilitated management consulting's growth (cf. Kipping and Wright, Chapter 8, this volume). While existing studies acknowledge the importance of such macroscopic changes, they generally do not elaborate on them: the economic, interactionist, and political approaches are endogenous in nature, with a focus on the consulting process itself. This chapter seeks to redress this gap with a historical–institutional perspective. Specifically, the chapter elaborates on how broad institutional changes created *opportunities* for early management consulting firms to gain resources and legitimacy for their activities. Five such changes are discussed: the increased number and complexity of corporate organizations, the establishment of a large and permanent military–industrial complex during and following World War II, the increased corporatization of non-corporate sectors, the spread of business education, and the expansion of the business press.

This analysis of these institutional changes extends the work of two notable studies of management consulting's growth. In his paper and book on the history of management consulting, McKenna (1995, 2006) locates the impetus of the industry's growth in the Glass–Steagall Act of 1933, which he argues 'opened up a vacuum into which firms of management consultants rushed'. More recently, Ruef (2002) examined a series of labour market shifts that increased the attractiveness of management consulting to business school graduates. The present chapter extends this prior work by considering a broader set of institutional changes—changes in the distribution of organizational forms in society, normative shifts within organizations, and the emergence of complementary sectors—and by making explicit the links between these institutional changes and the growth of the strategy consulting field.

The analysis in this chapter focuses specifically on the field of strategy consulting as a subset of the larger management consulting industry in the United States. A number of existing explanations for the growth of management consulting also focus on strategy consulting firms, implicitly if not explicitly (for example, Canback 1998; Ernst and Kieser 2002; McKenna 2006). Strategy consulting firms were the 'second wave' of management consultants, coming after the 'efficiency experts', who applied Taylorist principles to the shop floor (Kipping 2002; Wright and Kipping, Chapter 2, this volume). More than their engineering-based predecessors, strategy consulting firms struggled to explain their methods and potential benefits, and thus faced greater legitimacy hurdles (McKenna 1995). It was during the 1920–1980 period that strategy consulting emerged as a distinct field and grew to substantial prominence, eclipsing the first wave of shop-floor consultants; by 1960, strategy consulting was on the cusp of a golden age and would dominate the industry in the ensuing decades (Kipping 2002; McKenna 2006). Strategy consulting expanded most rapidly in the United States, and indeed the institutional changes described in this chapter generally occurred first in that country (Chandler 1990; Fligstein 1990: 304).

This account of the growth of strategy consulting employs a historiographical approach (Kieser 1994; Ventresca and Mohr 2002) and draws upon material from a variety of archival sources: organizational histories, the business press, publications from industry associations, and the work of business historians. Quantitative data on historical trends were also collected from sources such as *County Business Patterns*, *Statistical Abstract of the United States*, and *Digest of Educational Statistics*. Unfortunately, no systematic data exist on the size of the management consulting industry (or its subfields) prior to the publication of industry directories in the 1970s. In summary, the objectives of this chapter are to: 1) describe how macro-institutional change provided a fertile context for the remarkable growth of strategy consulting; 2) complement existing explanations of consulting's growth, particularly explanations drawing on economic or interactionist perspectives; and 3) inductively generate insights about how institutional change affects industry evolution more generally.

4.2 Institutional Change and Opportunity Creation

This section explores how broad institutional changes allowed the field of strategy consulting to expand from its nascent state. While 'institutional change' can refer to a great many different types of change (David and Bitektine 2009), even changes within individual organizations, here it refers to structural or normative changes in organizational *fields* and *forms* (Scott 2001). Specifically, the chapter examines the emergence of (or fundamental change in) the following *types* of organizations: large corporations, governments, the military and military-related organizations, not-for-profits, business schools, and the business press. Its central thesis is that the emergence of (or changes in) these organizational forms created opportunities for strategy consulting firms—opportunities that early strategy consulting firms exploited. Without the changes outlined below, it is unlikely that strategy consulting would have attained the level of social and economic prominence that it has.

4.2.1 The Corporate Form

Increases in both the *number* and the *complexity* of corporate organizations have presented a burgeoning opportunity for strategy consulting. As Chandler (1962, 1977, 1990) and others have documented, the first half of the twentieth century saw the structure of American industry change from one of small, single-product, owner-run enterprises to one dominated by large, complex corporations (see also Berle and Means 1932; Presthus 1962; Fligstein 1990). Merger waves following World War I and World War II accelerated these changes and resulted in great increases in the number and complexity of corporate organizations (Chandler 1977: 477). Most large corporations adopted a multidivisional structure (M-form), characterized by dispersed, decentralized units (Fligstein 1990; Kipping 2002). Figures 4.1 and 4.2 show the changing nature of the organizational landscape in the twentieth century. As Figure 4.2 shows, by 1979 almost 90 per cent of large organizations had adopted the M-form, requiring complex systems for co-ordination, control, and decision-making.

The post-World War II period also witnessed extensive corporate diversification. Inhibited from pursuing related mergers by the Cellar–Kefauver Act of 1950, corporations sought growth through *un*related expansion (Fligstein 1990). The result was diversified conglomerates of unrelated businesses. Organizations that before the war had ten to twenty-five divisions typically expanded to forty or more in the post-war years. An extreme example is that of General Electric, which by 1955 had over one hundred operating divisions (Fligstein 1990: 234). By the mid-1960s, mergers were topping 2,000 per year. These changes further increased organizational complexity, as managers were often faced with distant markets, new products and processes, far-flung supply chains, and diverse sets of competitors.

As a result of the decentralization and diversification of US corporations, new managerial positions not present in the previously dominant, owner-managed, single-product firms were created (Chandler 1977: 411). For the first time, owners no longer administrated their enterprises and full-time salaried executives came to dominate large corporations, resulting in the need for new managerial skills, justifications, and excuses. Meanwhile, managerial functions such as marketing, finance, and product development became increasingly specialized, making cross-functional communication more difficult (Vernon 1971: 127). Finally, as Fligstein (1990: 292) noted, diversification often did not lead to higher profits, a situation which prompted the search for solutions.

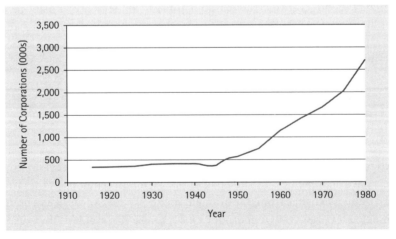

FIGURE 4.1 Number of corporations in the US

Source: Statistical Abstract of the United States.

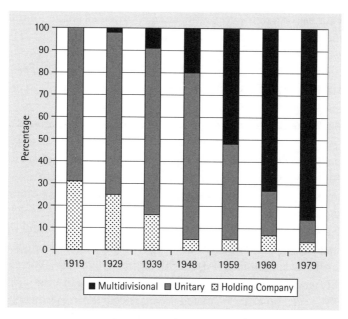

FIGURE 4.2 Structures of the 100 largest US firms
Source: Fligstein 1990: 336.

These changes in the organizational landscape created opportunities for early strategy consulting firms. For instance, in a landmark project begun in 1925, Edwin Booz (founder of Booz, Allen & Hamilton) was hired to reorganize US Gypsum in the wake of a multi-firm merger. Similarly, in 1935, US Steel—which had remained a federation of independent firms after it was formed through the merger of three large steel companies in 1901—commissioned a consortium of consulting firms that included McKinsey & Co. to help it integrate its activities. Retail firms, which were among the most diversified and ambitious firms of the pre-World War II period, were also frequent clients of early strategy consultants. For example, in the 1930s, Montgomery Ward enlisted the help of Edwin Booz as it opened a vast network of retail outlets and integrated backwards into manufacturing. During the same period, James O. McKinsey was hired to undertake a high-profile reorganization of Marshall Field, a large retailer that was feeling the ill effects of over-diversification.

The structural complexity, decentralized management, dispersed operations, and ambiguous authority structures of corporate organizations had essentially created the *opportunity* for strategy consulting firms to offer solutions to organizational problems and justifications for managerial actions. This does not imply, however, that consulting firms represented an optimal, or even effective, solution to organizational problems. Indeed, mimetic processes may have been at work: as large, prominent firms began to hire management consultants, smaller firms may have been prompted to 'follow the leaders' (DiMaggio and Powell 1983; Haveman 1993; Han 1994). The key analytic point here is that the evolution of the corporate sector provided a fertile context for strategy consulting, one which early firms capitalized upon.

4.2.2 Military–Industrial Complex

While increases in the number and complexity of corporate organizations occurred over an extended period, World War II provided an immediate (and lasting) stimulus to the strategy consulting field. As shown in Figure 4.3, the US military increased to over twenty-four times its pre-war size from 1939 to 1945; similarly, Figure 4.4 shows that US military spending also experienced a sharp increase, rising from $2.5 billion in 1939 to $162 billion in 1944 (1967 dollars).

This massive war effort created problems of co-ordination and control within the military, which management consultants could claim to address. Leading consulting firms, such as Booz, Allen & Hamilton and Arthur D. Little, were closely involved with the war effort, with partners and senior employees often occupying high-ranking military positions. A prominent example of war-related projects occurred in 1940, when Frank Knox, Secretary of the Navy, asked Edwin Booz to help him reorganize the entire US Naval organization (Bowman 1984). The navy was to double in size within two years, and Booz himself moved to Washington to manage the project. The firm also helped create the Army Services Forces, designed to help the army run more efficiently. In 1941, Richard Paget (then a Booz Allen partner) was named head of the navy's Office of the Management Engineer, and Mark Cresap (also a Booz Allen consultant) was appointed to a similar position in the army. Meanwhile, Arthur Tom Kearney, a senior partner at McKinsey & Co. (and later the founder of his own strategy consulting firm), was put in charge of reorganizing the War Production Board (McKenna 1996a: 103). This was the

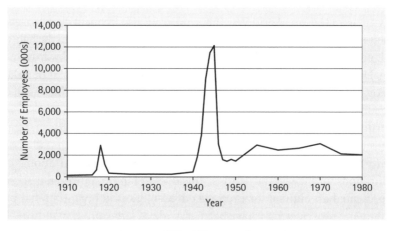

FIGURE 4.3 US military employment
Source: Statistical Abstract of the United States.

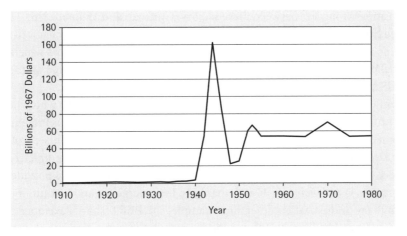

FIGURE 4.4 US military spending
Source: Statistical Abstract of the United States.

first time that personnel not trained in the military were given such key roles (Bowman 1984: 24).

Importantly, however, World War II was more than a one-time stimulus. Even though military employment and expenditures dropped markedly at the war's end, they remained well above pre-war levels (see Figures 4.3 and 4.4). Military-related demand for management consulting remained strong, as the military–industrial complex took on massive defence programmes (Hunt 1977: 16). In 1946, former Booz Allen partners Mark Cresap and Richard Paget, along with Paget's assistant in the navy, William McCormick, founded their own consulting firm (Cresap, McCormick & Paget) based primarily on military and related governmental assignments (Higdon 1969: 124). Booz, Allen & Hamilton itself also received a tremendous boost from the emerging military–industrial complex. For example, the firm undertook post-war projects for the Olin Corporation, makers of munitions, and for Sperry Gyroscope, makers of weapons systems. Between 1945 and 1948, Booz, Allen & Hamilton added eighteen partners to the ten that it had at the end of the war (Bowman 1984: 43). In 1958, as part of the landmark Polaris Missile project, Booz Allen developed a computer-based project management tool known as Program Evaluation and Review Technique, or PERT—a tool that soon gained wide prevalence in industry and gave the firm considerable visibility and recognition (Guttman and Willner 1976: 182). During the 1950s, Booz Allen added an additional forty-two partners, and by 1964 its military division alone had 275 clients and $6 million in annual revenue (Bowman 1984). The firm's work for the military continued through the 1960s and 1970s, with contracts related to the procurement of navy ships, the development of Trident submarines, and the management of NASA space missions.

The nature of the military–industrial complex also led to opportunities within government and industry: after the war had ended, high-ranking military personnel took positions with consulting firms, government departments, and in industrial organizations, creating strong ties between these sectors (Guttman and Willner 1976). Finally, as discussed below, the war precipitated an increase in the size of the federal government as well as the international expansion of American corporations, both of which created additional opportunities for management consultants (see Kipping 1999 on the expansion of US management consultants to Europe).

In sum, in the words of George Fry (a former Booz Allen partner who would later found a prominent firm of his own), 'the war proved to be a tremendous impetus for the management consulting business' (quoted in Higdon 1969: 123). This accords with Carroll, Delacroix, and Goodstein's (1988) argument that war can redirect resources among organizational forms (see also Stinchcombe 1965). The stimulus provided by the war, moreover, lasted well past its end, thanks to the emergence and institutionalization of the military–industrial complex; for example, the PERT chart developed by Booz Allen spread quickly from military to industrial application. The war thus not only served as an immediate stimulus for strategy consulting, but as an irreversible one.

4.2.3 The Corporatization of Non-Corporate Sectors

The post-war years also witnessed the increasing 'corporatization' of non-corporate sectors—that is, the spread of corporate beliefs, values, and practices to areas previously dominated by other institutional logics (e.g. professional, political) (Starr 1982; Alexander and D'Aunno 1990). Corporatization is similar to Weber's (1947: 186) *rationalization*, or an increase in the degree of cost-benefit calculation present in a sector of activity. As purveyors of rational management techniques from the corporate sector, strategy consultants benefited from this normative change. While corporatization also occurred in the educational and even religious fields (McKenna 1996b), the most important changes for the consulting industry were in government and health care.

4.2.3.1 *Federal, State, and Local Governments*

First, as the federal government in the United States increased in both size and complexity, it also became increasingly subject to corporate logic. As shown in Figure 4.5, federal civilian employment (i.e. excluding the military) rose from 800,000 or so in 1935 to almost 4 million in 1945, and stabilized at over 2 million in the post-war period. By 1947, the number of federal administrative units had increased to over 1,800 from less than 500 some twenty years earlier (Gervasi 1949; McKenna 1996a).

This growth, moreover, took place 'in a haphazard fashion' (Emmerich 1971: 47), as 'agency piled on agency and bureau on bureau' (Gervasi 1949: 4). As a result, the federal government faced severe problems of co-ordination and control, and came under increasing pressure for administrative reform. In a landmark reorganization effort, the Hoover Commission on Organization of the Executive Branch was established in 1947 'to bring into an integrated organization structure the numerous agencies left in the wake of war and demobilization' (Emmerich 1971: 82) and to 'achieve maximum economy and effectiveness of administration' (Gervasi 1949: 9). Hoover himself was an ardent

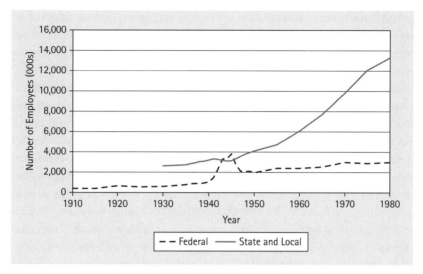

FIGURE 4.5 US government employment
Source: Statistical Abstract of the United States.

believer in 'orthodox administrative doctrine' and equated the presidential role with 'any other essentially *managerial* function' (Arnold 1976: 64; emphasis added). As such, Hoover applied a 'business' rather than 'political' logic to the reorganization, and, in a break with past federal task forces, recruited heavily from industry (Emmerich 1971; Arnold 1976). In fact, in the first high-profile use of management consultants by the federal government outside of the military, the commission hired management consulting firms to lead fifteen of its thirty-four policy studies, and thereby imparted 'the perspective of private business' and a 'general efficiency approach' to the federal government (Emmerich 1971: 85; McKenna 1996a: 102).

Consulting firms were given other higher-profile assignments within the federal government. In 1948, Robert Heller & Associates was hired to reorganize the US Post Office. In 1950, President Truman allocated $1 million for management consulting projects within the government, and in 1952 President Eisenhower hired McKinsey & Co. to provide advice on political appointments and to reorganize the White House (McKenna 1996a). Through the 1960s, the use of consultants continued to spread across federal agencies, as firms such as McKinsey & Co., Booz Allen, and Arthur D. Little took on projects for the Department of Transportation, the National Science Foundation (NSF), the Internal Revenue Service (IRS), and the US Olympic Committee (Guttman and Willner 1976).

As also shown in Figure 4.5, state and local governments grew at an even faster pace than the federal government. This growth was also accompanied by a shift towards corporate logic, often involving the creation of new organizational structures (e.g. lateral teams, chief executives) and the adoption of measurable performance criteria (Tolbert and Zucker 1983; Greenwood 1984; Hinings and Greenwood 1988). As with the federal government, this increase in size and change in logic created opportunities for management consultants. Moreover, federal grants to state and local governments were often administered by management consultants, encouraging the spread of consulting services down to the local level.

For example, strategy consulting firms were deeply involved in the 'Model Cities' programme of the 1960s, which was intended to address urban development problems. Firms such as McKinsey & Co., Booz Allen, and Fry Consultants helped install planning and evaluation systems in 144 cities as part of this programme; in fact, McKinsey & Co. was considered the *de facto* Model Cities administrator in New York City (Guttman and Willner 1976: 199). McKinsey's involvement in this and other New York City projects even led, in 1968, to the firm being given an official position within the city's government, as head of the Division of Program Budget Systems (Guttman and Willner 1976: 275). Strategy consulting firms also did considerable work on urban mass transit systems, such as Arthur D. Little's 1969 contract to manage the Center Cities Transportation Project for the Urban Mass Transit Authority (Guttman and Willner 1976: 257). Other examples of consulting work for state and local governments in the 1960s include Booz Allen projects to cut costs for the city of Seattle, reorganize Pasadena's school budget, and help the state of Connecticut study new ways of attracting industries (Higdon 1969: 13). In sum, in the years following World War II, increasing corporatization allowed strategy consulting firms to permeate various levels of public administration.

4.2.3.2 *Health care*

The corporatization of health care also created opportunities for management consultants. As Starr (1982) and Gray (1983, 1991) have described, health care in the United States has witnessed a shift away from the logics of community service and professional sovereignty towards those of commercialization, competition, and corporate control. This has led to practices in health care resembling those in the corporate sector, such as horizontal and vertical integration, diversification, and concentration of ownership (Starr 1982: 429). According to Alexander and D'Aunno (1990: 54), the result has been a 'decline in voluntarism and professional power in the health care sector; the introduction of new organizational forms (multihospital systems, specialized delivery organizations, corporate restructuring, and diversification); and the increased emphasis on running health care as a *business* rather than as a social service, including not only increases in business practices per se but also the adoption of symbols and language associated with business'. As these authors further noted, terms such as 'profit' and 'market', which were once considered taboo in the health care sector, have become widespread.

As with federal and local governments, the corporatization of health care was accompanied by increased use of strategy consultants. For example, in the 1960s, Cresap, McCormick & Paget undertook projects for Georgetown University Hospital in Washington, a children's hospital in Boston, and the Mount Sinai Hospital in New York City (McKenna 1996b). During the same period, Arthur D. Little consulted extensively for the National Cancer Institute (Kahn 1986). In 1970, when the New York City Health and Hospitals Corporation was formed to manage 18 New York City hospitals, it looked to consulting firms such as McKinsey & Co. to help implement reforms, including the drafting of legislation (Guttman and Willner 1976: 281).

In sum, as government and health care organizations became increasingly subject to corporate logic, they sought to adapt by adopting corporate practices. Because strategy consulting firms embody corporate logic, they represented readily available signals of conformity. In other words, what was important here was not the technical ability of strategy consultants to help clients become more 'efficient' or 'rational' but rather the *signals* that they provided of their clients' efforts to do so. By hiring strategy consultants, organizations in these sectors incorporated the 'rationalized myth' of corporate management in an effort to demonstrate consistency with their changed normative contexts (Meyer and Rowan 1977; Meyer 1986; Meyer, Boli, and Thomas 1994).

4.2.4 Business schools

The growth of management consulting owes much to the expansion of business education. The first school of business in the United States, the Wharton School, was founded at the University of Pennsylvania in 1881 by Joseph Wharton, a prominent industrialist (Sass 1982). By 1958, some 163 schools were granting over 55,000 degrees annually (Gordon and Howell 1959: 20–21). Overall, business degrees rose from 3 per cent of all degrees in 1919 to 13 per cent in 1958. By 1980, the number of business graduates in the United States had risen even more dramatically, to well over 200,000 per year. Figure 4.6 chronicles this growth, at both the bachelor and masters levels.

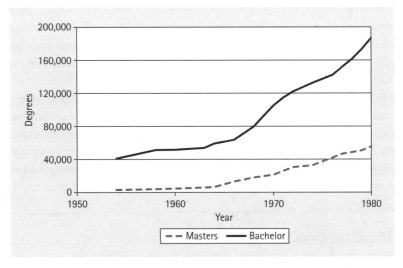

FIGURE 4.6 US business degrees conferred
Source: Digest of Educational Statistics.

Business schools have exerted symbiotic effects on the management consulting industry—and strategy consulting firms in particular—in three related ways. First, business schools produce graduates that can claim qualifications as management consultants. Like firms in established professions such as law and accounting, consulting firms could now send a strong signal of specialized human capital and expertise (Armbrüster 2004). This is a key element of professionalization, which leads to normative legitimacy (DiMaggio and Powell 1983; Abbott 1988). Again, what is important here is that the *claim* that business schools produce specialized human capital is widely accepted; the actual technical qualifications of business school graduates to practice management are largely unsubstantiated. Second, business schools facilitate the development, codification, and dissemination of managerial knowledge (Sahlin-Andersson and Engwall 2002). Business faculty members make their work visible at conferences, in business publications, and in the press, making both consulting firms and potential clients aware of new applications and ideas. In this way, business schools generate opportunities that can be appropriated by the consulting industry (see also Jung and Kieser, Chapter 16; Engwall, Chapter 18; both this volume).

Finally, because they are affiliated with universities (i.e. widely respected institutions), business schools impart legitimacy to the very notion of 'management knowledge' and 'management progress'. They give the field of management standing in the academic community, next to the sciences, medicine, and law (Khurana 2007; Engwall, Kipping, and Üsdiken 2010). Management consultants could thus claim to be purveyors of legitimated knowledge. In sum, business schools have allowed the management consulting industry to increase its legitimacy by both helping to define a jurisdiction for management and by producing 'experts' within this realm (Larson 1977; Abbott 1988; Kipping 2011). This is particularly important for strategy consulting firms, who base their expertise largely in the field of management itself rather than in engineering, accounting, and information technology as some other subgroups of management consultants do.

Early strategy consulting firms had strong ties to business schools. For example, James O. McKinsey was on the faculty at the University of Chicago, where he lectured in the morning and consulted in the afternoon (Wolf 1978). McKinsey & Co. would later hire extensively from business schools, particularly Harvard's (Higdon 1969). By the 1970s, consulting firms had become voracious consumers of MBA graduates (Ruef 2002). Meanwhile, consulting industry associations used the presence of business education to claim legitimacy for the industry. For example, in 1958, the Association of Consulting Management Engineers (the industry association that had come to represent elite strategy consulting firms) claimed that 'the immense growth in formal business training courses offered by universities and colleges' had produced many 'young specialists' who, even without prior business experience, had the requisite skills to become consultants (Amon et al. 1958: 21). Business schools had essentially allowed consulting firms—individually and collectively—to claim specialized expertise.

4.2.5 Business press

The expansion of the business press has also exerted symbiotic effects on the management consulting industry. Since the founding of the first specialized business publications in the late 1800s, the business press has grown phenomenally. For example, the *Wall Street Journal*, founded in 1889, went from 12,000 subscribers in 1910 to 1.8 million in 1980, while *Business Week* magazine went from 75,000 in 1930 to 800,000 in 1980. Figures 4.7 and 4.8 show the growth in circulation of the *Wall Street Journal* and three prominent business magazines, respectively.

This growth has benefited the management consulting industry in two main ways. First, the business press raised the awareness of the consulting industry itself through mostly laudatory coverage. Articles on consulting and consultants began to appear regularly in the post-war period, with titles such as 'Profit Engineers' (*Business Week* 1946) and 'Consultant Field Shows Big Growth' (Ryan 1953). Their tone was generally positive—articles outlined the nature of management consulting, extolled its benefits, and chronicled its recent growth. For example, Ryan (1953: 1) wrote: 'most of these firms stand ready to tackle almost any consulting problem or business survey assigned to them, and the variety of these problems has widened spectacularly in recent years'. Other articles profiled the large and successful firms—mostly strategy consulting firms—and trumpeted their successes. For example, in 'Slump or Boom, They Keep on Growing' (*Business Week* 1955: 142), McKinsey & Co. was profiled as a firm that can handle any kind of 'major, nonrecurring management problem', while in 'The Instant Executives' (*Forbes* 1967), the exploits of Booz, Allen & Hamilton at Hilton Hotels, the University of Alabama, and in the Chicago public school system were extolled. Of course, there was also some criticism of management consulting in the press. However, this was typically accompanied by advice on 'how to get the most' out of consulting engagements and avoid pitfalls.

Second, the business press has helped generate cycles of management fashion, which create demand for consulting services (David and Strang 2006; Jung and Kieser, Chapter 16, this volume). The press facilitates the process of *theorization*, or the propagation of public theories regarding the effectiveness of management techniques (Strang and

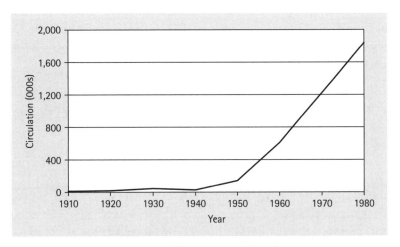

FIGURE 4.7 *Wall Street Journal* circulation

Source: Ayer Directory of Periodicals.

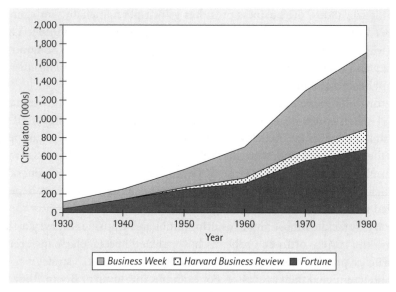

FIGURE 4.8 Leading business periodicals
Source: Ayer Directory of Periodicals.

Meyer 1993; Abrahamson 1996). Indeed, as Kieser (2002: 169) explained, public discourse surrounding a management concept gains momentum when 'widely read management magazines pick up the basic ideas' of the concept. With its bias towards the 'new' and 'successful' (Eccles and Nohria 1992), the business press allows management gurus, prominent CEOs, and consultants themselves to disseminate their prescriptions (Jackson 2001; Clark and Greatbatch 2002; Clark, Bhatanacharoen, and Greatbatch, Chapter 17, this volume). On the client side, moreover, the business press can generate anxiety among managers, as they read about success stories in other firms (Ernst and Kieser 2002). Waves of fashion can ensue, placing tremendous pressure on managers to act—a situation favourable to management consultants (David and Strang 2006). In sum, the business press contributes to the notion that the use of management consulting is both valuable and necessary.

4.3 IMPLICATIONS: INSTITUTIONAL CHANGE AND INDUSTRY EVOLUTION

As organizational theorists have long recognized, industry emergence and evolution is shaped by institutional forces (e.g. Stinchcombe 1965; Meyer 1986; Ruef 2000). In the institutional perspective, new organizational forms spread to the extent that they gain legitimacy, or become seen as the appropriate or natural way of effecting a particular action (DiMaggio 1991; Haveman and Rao 1997; Sine and David 2003; Sine, Haveman, and Tolbert 2005; Tolbert, David, and Sine 2011). Institutionalists recognize that industries can grow even in the absence of efficiency reasons (e.g. Granovetter and McGuire 1998; Sine, David, and Mitsuhashi 2007), in contrast to the economic perspective, which holds that only technically efficient or cost-effective organizations will proliferate (e.g. Chandler 1962; Williamson 1975). Consistent with the institutional perspective, the account of the expansion of strategy consulting offered in this chapter emphasizes legitimacy rather than efficiency: the institutional changes outlined here created opportunities for strategy consulting firms to gain pragmatic, normative, and cognitive legitimacy regardless of their technical benefits. In this way, the institutional environment facilitated rather than constrained innovation (Scott 2010). Specifically, the institutionalization of the decentralized, diversified corporate form and the military–industrial complex, the spread of corporate norms to non-corporate sectors, and the spread of business education and the business press all facilitated 'the generalized perception' (Suchman 1995: 574) that strategy consulting firms were desirable, proper, and appropriate. Without these institutional changes, strategy consulting would not have reached the social and economic prominence that it has.

The perspective in this chapter differs in important ways from prior analyses of management consulting's growth. McKenna (2006) argues that management consultants provide 'economies of knowledge' that outweigh their costs. His argument accords with those of practitioners, such as Canback (1998, 1999), who employ reasoning from transaction-cost economics to argue that management consultants provide a cost-effective solution to organizational problems. To date, there has been no systematic empirical analysis of these economic arguments for the growth of management consulting. There is, however, considerable anecdotal evidence to question the economic rationality of management consulting, and at best there is a paucity of evidence that consultants provide efficient outcomes (e.g. O'Shea and Madigan 1997; Pinault 2000; Clark and Fincham 2002; Kihn 2005). The institutional explanation advanced here avoids the functional assumption that strategy consulting grew because it is economically rational to hire consultants, and instead emphasizes the reasons that strategy consulting came to be seen as desirable, proper, and appropriate within its social setting. Importantly, an institutional perspective emphasizes context in a way that economic arguments do not (see Faust, Chapter 7, this volume). Indeed, the institutional changes described in this chapter were, on the whole, most pronounced in the United States during the period 1920–1980, and this is where strategy consulting experienced its most rapid growth (Chandler 1990; Fligstein 1990: 304).

The perspective advanced here also differs from prior work that emphasizes client–consultant interaction (e.g. Clark 1995; Ernst and Kieser 2002; Nikolova and Devinney, Chapter 19, this volume). Consistent with the institutional approach, work emphasizing client–consultant interaction tends to be sceptical of efficiency arguments for the growth of the consulting industry; these accounts, however, are inclined to locate the reasons for consulting's expansion in the psychological effects that consultants have on their clients. For example, Ernst and Kieser (2002) emphasize client insecurity and need for control as driving the growth of management consulting. The account presented here is at a different level of analysis, and does not speak directly to the nature of client–consultant interaction. Instead, it *embeds* this interaction within a changing institutional context. For example, the sense of insecurity that Ernst and Kieser (2002) discuss can result from (as these authors acknowledge) environmental complexity and media hype, the development of which are discussed here. Put another way, the dynamics of client–consultant interaction are institutionally situated, such that discussions of institutional change provide a necessary complement to interactionist explanations.

The analysis presented here has implications for theory and future research. Three such implications seem particularly noteworthy. First, this chapter directs attention to the role of the state as a legitimating force. Whereas past work has emphasized the state's power to *regulate* (and thus legitimate) new industries, it is suggested here that the state can legitimate through its ability to *consume* (see also Kipping and Saint-Martin 2005). As described above, governments at various levels have been voracious consumers of consulting services, providing resources and visibility. This was especially critical early in the industry's history, when its status was still in question. Even though the state did not confer professional status on consulting by regulating qualifications and mandating certification (Kirkpatrick, Muzio, and Ackroyd, Chapter 9, this volume; Kipping 2011), it nonetheless enhanced the industry's legitimacy by purchasing its services at the highest levels. In some cases, moreover, it put strategy consulting firms in positions of power, and required firms wishing to deal with the government to use these consultants. Future research on industry evolution should thus go beyond the state's regulative influence and include its ability to impart both tangible resources and legitimacy through its consumption patterns.

Second, this chapter suggests that the flow of institutional logics—sets of assumptions, values, and beliefs that define formal and informal rules of behaviour—across social sectors can result in the concomitant expansion of organizational forms. In previous work, institutional theorists have shown that changes in logics *within* sectors of activity can result in adaptive changes in organizational forms or the birth of new forms (Haveman and Rao 1997; Thornton and Ocasio 1999; Sine and David 2003). This chapter suggests that as the corporate logic spread outside of the corporate realm into new sectors, opportunities were created for strategy consultants as *carriers* of this logic. If organizational forms spread along with the logics they embody, future research on industry evolution should not only seek to understand changes in logics *within* focal sectors, but also track the spread of logics *across* sectors of activity.

Finally, this chapter suggests the importance of co-evolutionary dynamics as an interesting avenue for future research. While not emphasized here, reciprocal effects are clearly present between strategy consulting and the institutional environment. For example, just as the increasing complexity of large corporations created opportunities for management consulting firms, these firms have themselves contributed to the increasing complexity of corporate organizations; similarly, the management consulting industry has both benefited from and contributed to the corporatization of non-industrial sectors. And reciprocal effects exist between management consultants, business schools, and the business press (Engwall and Kipping 2002). These co-evolutionary relationships are likely to be non-linear and time-varying (Astley and Fombrun 1987; Baum and Singh 1994; Hunt and Aldrich 1998). Although our models for handling these complex systems of interaction are currently under-developed, reciprocal effects such as these present a promising area for future research. Computational models and simulations represent one avenue with which to explore such complex, reciprocal effects.

4.4 CONCLUSION

Consultants, managers, and many scholars typically assume that the growth of the management consulting industry reflects the benefits that it provides. Indeed, they 'take for granted that the industry should exist and function the way it does' (Canback 1998: 3). At least partially, this taken-for-grantedness stems from a general lack of understanding of the industry's history. When the origins and evolution of an industry are not recalled or well understood, it is easy to take the industry for granted (Berger and Luckmann 1967; Tolbert and Zucker 1996). This chapter directs attention to the broad institutional changes that facilitated the growth of strategy consulting. It intentionally avoids functional assumptions, and instead treats consulting's growth as a process to be explained rather than an ineluctable progression (Kieser 1994). The chapter elaborates on the opportunities that emerged over time, and illustrates how entrepreneurial actors seized these opportunities (Sine and David 2010; Tolbert, David, and Sine 2011). A fuller understanding of the field's evolution, combined with micro-level analysis of the consulting process itself, can overcome the taken-for-granted nature of management consulting and provide a richer understanding of its growth. This would be a welcome development, not only academically but especially for the many managers who hire consultants based on assumption or habit.

NOTE

* The helpful comments of the editors, Timothy Clark and Matthias Kipping, as well as those of Raghu Garud, Heather Haveman, Pamela Tolbert, and workshop participants at Cornell University, the Academy of Management meetings, and Durham University are gratefully acknowledged. The author also thanks the Social Sciences and Humanities Research Council of Canada and the Cleghorn Faculty Scholar Award (Desautels Faculty of Management, McGill University) for generous funding.

REFERENCES

Abbott, A. (1988). *The System of Professions: Essays in the Division of Expert Labor*. Chicago: University of Chicago Press.
Abrahamson, E. (1996). 'Management Fashion'. *Academy of Management Review*, 21, 254–285.
Alexander, J. A. and D'Aunno, T. A. (1990). 'Transformation of Institutional Environments: Perspectives on the Corporatization of U.S. Health Care'. In S. S. Mick and associates (eds),

Innovations in Health Care Delivery: Insights for Organization Theory. San Francisco: Jossey-Bass, 53–85.

Amon, R. F., Clifford, D. K., Dixon Jr, L. F., Grice, G. L., Jacobs Jr, C. E., Lee, D. C., Leiner Jr, F. C., and Shirley, R. W. (1958). *Management Consulting*. Technical report. Boston: Harvard University, Graduate School of Business Administration.

Armbrüster, T. (2004). 'Rationality and Its Symbols: Signalling Effects and Subjectification in Management Consulting'. *Journal of Management Studies*, 41, 1247–1269.

Arnold, P. E. (1976). 'The First Hoover Commission and the Managerial Presidency'. *Journal of Politics*, 38, 46–70.

Astley, G. and Fombrun, C. (1987). 'Organizational Communities: An Ecological Perspective'. In S. Bacharach and N. DiTommaso (eds), *Research in the Sociology of Organizations*. Greenwich, CT: JAI Press, 5, 163–185.

Baum, J. A. C. and Singh J. V. (1994). 'Organization-Environment Coevolution'. In J. Baum and J. Singh (eds), *The Evolutionary Dynamics of Organizations*. New York: Oxford University Press, 379–402.

Berger, P. L. and Luckmann, T. (1967). *The Social Construction of Reality: A Treatise in the Sociology of Knowledge*. Garden City, NJ: Doubleday.

Berle, A. A. and Means, G. C. (1932). *The Modern Corporation and Private Property*. New York: Macmillan.

Bowman, J. (1984). *Booz Allen & Hamilton: Seventy Years of Client Service, 1914–1984*. New York: Booz Allen & Hamilton.

Business Week (1946). 'Profit Engineers'. 16 February, 78–83.

Business Week (1955). 'Slump or Boom, They Keep on Growing'. 24 September, 136–145.

Canback, S. (1998). 'The Logic of Management Consulting (Part One)'. *Journal of Management Consulting*, 10/2, 3–11.

Canback, S. (1999). 'The Logic of Management Consulting (Part Two)'. *Journal of Management Consulting*, 10/3, 3–12.

Carroll, G. R., Delacroix, J., and Goodstein, J. (1988). 'The Political Environments of Organizations: An Ecological View'. In B. M. Staw and L. L. Cummings (eds), *Research in Organizational Behavior*, vol. 10. Greenwich, CT: JAI Press, 359–392.

Chandler Jr, A. D. (1962). *Strategy and Structure: Chapters in the History of the Industrial Enterprise*. Cambridge, MA: MIT Press.

Chandler Jr, A. D. (1977). *The Visible Hand: The Managerial Revolution in American Business*. Cambridge, MA: Belknap Press.

Chandler Jr, A. D. (1990). *Scale and Scope: The Dynamics of Industrial Capitalism*. Cambridge, MA: Belknap Press.

Clark, T. (1995). *Managing Consultants: Consultancy as the Management of Impressions*. Buckingham: Open University Press.

Clark, T. and Fincham R. (eds) (2002). *Critical Consulting: New Perspectives on the Management Advice Industry*. Oxford: Blackwell.

Clark, T. and Greatbatch, D. (2002). 'Collaborative Relationships in the Creation and Fashioning of Management Ideas: Gurus, Editors, and Managers'. In M. Kipping and L. Engwall (eds), *Management Consulting: Emergence and Dynamics of a Knowledge Industry*. New York: Oxford University Press, 129–145.

Clark, T. and Salaman, G. (1998). 'Telling Tales: Management Gurus' Narratives and the Construction of Managerial Identity'. *Journal of Management Studies*, 35, 137–161.

David, R. J. and Bitektine, A. B. (2009). 'The Deinstitutionalization of Institutional Theory? Exploring Divergent Agendas in Institutional Research'. In D. Buchanan and

A. Bryman (eds), *The Sage Handbook of Organizational Research Methods*. London: Sage, 160–175.

David, R. J. and Strang, D. (2006). 'When Fashion is Fleeting: Transitory Collective Beliefs and the Dynamics of TQM Consulting'. *Academy of Management Journal*, 49, 215–233.

DiMaggio, P. J. (1991). 'Constructing an Organizational Field as a Professional Project: U.S. Art Museums, 1920–1940'. In W. Powell and P. DiMaggio (eds), *The New Institutionalism in Organizational Theory*. Chicago: University of Chicago Press, 267–292.

DiMaggio, P. J. and Powell, W. W. (1983). 'The Iron Cage Revisited: Institutional Isomorphism and Collective Rationality in Organizational Fields'. *American Sociological Review*, 48, 147–160.

Eccles, R. G. and Nohria, N., with Berkley, J. D. (1992). *Beyond the Hype: Rediscovering the Essence of Management*. Cambridge, MA: Harvard University Press.

Emmerich, H. (1971). *Federal Organization and Administrative Management*. University, AL: University of Alabama Press.

Engwall, L. and Kipping, M. (2002). 'Introduction: Management Consulting as a Knowledge Industry'. In M. Kipping and L. Engwall (eds), *Management Consulting: Emergence and Dynamics of a Knowledge Industry*. Oxford: Oxford University Press, 1–16.

Engwall, L., Kipping, M., and Üsdiken, B. (2010). 'Public Science Systems, Higher Education and the Trajectory of Academic Disciplines: Business Studies in the United States and Europe'. In R. Whitley, J. Gläser, and L. Engwall (eds), *Reconfiguring Knowledge Production*. Oxford: Oxford University Press, 325–353.

Ernst, B. and Kieser, A. (2002). 'In Search of Explanations for the Consulting Explosion'. In K. Sahlin-Andersson and L. Engwall (eds), *The Expansion of Management Knowledge*. Stanford, CA: Stanford University Press, 47–73.

Fligstein, N. (1990). *The Transformation of Corporate Control*. Cambridge, MA: Harvard University Press.

Forbes (1967). 'The Instant Executives'. 15 November, 27–45.

Gervasi, F. (1949). *Big Government: The Meaning and Purpose of the Hoover Commission Report*. New York: McGraw-Hill.

Gordon, R. A. and Howell, J. E. (1959). *Higher Education for Business*. New York: Columbia University Press.

Granovetter, M. and McGuire, P. (1998). 'The Making of an Industry: Electricity in the United States'. In M. Callon (ed.), *The Law of Markets*. Oxford: Blackwell, 147–173.

Gray, B. H. (ed.) (1983). *The New Health Care for Profit*. Washington, DC: National Academy Press.

Gray, B. H. (1991). *The Profit Motive and Patient Care*. Cambridge, MA: Harvard University Press.

Greenwood, R. (1984). 'Incremental Budgeting: Antecedents of Change'. *Journal of Public Policy*, 4, 277–306.

Guttman, D. and Willner, B. (1976). *The Shadow Government*. New York: Pantheon.

Han, S. (1994). 'Mimetic Isomorphism and Its Effect on the Audit Services Market'. *Social Forces*, 73, 637–663.

Haveman, H. A. (1993). 'Follow the Leader: Mimetic Isomorphism and Entry into New Markets'. *Administrative Science Quarterly*, 38, 593–627.

Haveman, H. A. and Rao, H. (1997). 'Structuring a Theory of Moral Sentiments: Institutional and Organizational Coevolution in the Early Thrift Industry'. *American Journal of Sociology*, 102, 1606–1651.

Higdon, H. (1969). *The Business Healers*. New York: Random House.

Hinings, C. R. and Greenwood, R. (1988). 'The Normative Prescription of Organizations'. In L. G. Zucker (ed.), *Institutional Patterns and Organizations*. Cambridge, MA: Ballinger, 53–70.

Hunt, A. (1977). *The Management Consultant*. New York: John Wiley & Sons.

Hunt, C. S. and Aldrich, H. E. (1998). 'The Second Ecology: Creation and Evolution of Organizational Communities'. In B. M. Staw and L. L. Cummings (eds), *Research in Organizational Behavior*, vol. 20. Greenwich, CT: JAI Press, 267–301.

Jackson, B. (2001). *Management Gurus and Management Fashions*. London: Routledge.

Kahn Jr, E. J. (1986). *The Problem Solvers: A History of Arthur D. Little, Inc.* Boston: Little Brown.

Khurana, R. (2007). *From Higher Aims to Hired Hands: The Social Transformation of American Business Schools and the Unfulfilled Promise of Management as a Profession*. Princeton, NJ: Princeton University Press.

Kieser, A. (1994). 'Why Organizational Theory Needs Historical Analyses—and How This Should Be Performed'. *Organization Science*, 5, 608–623.

Kieser, A. (2002). 'Managers as Marionettes? Using Fashion Theories to Explain the Success of Consultancies'. In M. Kipping and L. Engwall (eds), *Management Consulting*. Oxford: Oxford University Press, 167–183.

Kihn, M. (2005). *House of Lies: How Management Consultants Steal your Watch and Then Tell You the Time*. New York: Warner Business Books.

Kipping, M. (1999). 'American Management Consulting Companies in Western Europe, 1920 to 1990: Products, Reputation, and Relationships'. *Business History Review*, 73, 190–220.

Kipping, M. (2002). 'Trapped in Their Wave: The Evolution of Management Consultancies'. In T. Clark and R. Fincham (eds), *Critical Consulting: New Perspectives on the Management Advice Business*. Oxford: Blackwell, 28–49.

Kipping, M. (2011). 'Hollow from the Start? Image Professionalism in Management Consulting'. *Current Sociology*, 59/4, 530–550.

Kipping, M. and Saint-Martin, D. (2005). 'Between Regulation, Promotion and Consumption: Government and Management Consultancy in Britain'. *Business History*, 47/3, 449–465.

Larson, M. S. (1977). *The Rise of Professionalism: A Sociological Analysis*. Berkeley: University of California Press.

McKenna, C. D. (1995). 'The Origins of Modern Management Consulting'. *Business and Economic History*, 24, 51–58.

McKenna, C. D. (1996a). 'Agents of Adhocracy: Management Consultants and the Reorganization of the Executive Branch, 1947–1949'. *Business and Economic History*, 25, 101–111.

McKenna, C. D. (1996b). 'Finding Profits in Non-Profits: The Influence of Management Consultants on the Third Sector'. Program on Non-Profit Organizations, Yale University, Working paper no. 235.

McKenna, C. D. (2006). *The World's Newest Profession: Management Consulting in the Twentieth Century*. New York: Cambridge University Press.

Meyer, J. W. (1986). 'Social Environments and Organizational Accounting'. *Accounting, Organizations, and Society*, 11, 345–356.

Meyer, J. W. and Rowan, B. (1977). 'Institutionalized Organizations: Formal Structure as Myth and Ceremony'. *American Journal of Sociology*, 83, 340–363.

Meyer, J. W., Boli, J., and Thomas, G. M. (1994). 'Ontology and Rationalization in the Western Cultural Account'. In W. R. Scott and J. W. Meyer (eds), *Institutional Environments and Organizations*. Thousand Oaks, CA: Sage, 9–27.

O'Shea, J. and Madigan, C. (1997). *Dangerous Company: The Consulting Powerhouses and the Businesses They Save and Ruin*. New York: Times Business.

Pinault, L. (2000). *Consulting Demons*. New York: Harper Business.

Presthus, R. (1962). *The Organizational Society*. New York: Alfred A. Knopf.

Ruef, M. (2000). 'The Emergence of Organizational Forms: A Community Ecology Approach'. *American Journal of Sociology*, 106, 658–714.

Ruef, M. (2002). 'At the Interstices of Organizations: The Expansion of the Management Consulting Profession, 1933–1997'. In K. Sahlin-Andersson and L. Engwall (eds), *The Expansion of Management Knowledge*. Stanford, CA: Stanford University Press, 74–95.

Ryan, J. R. (1953). 'Consultant Field Shows Big Growth'. *New York Times*, 3 December, section 3, 1.

Sahlin-Andersson, K. and Engwall, L. (2002). 'Carriers, Flows, and Sources of Management Knowledge'. In K. Sahlin-Andersson and L. Engwall (eds), *The Expansion of Management Knowledge*. Stanford, CA: Stanford University Press, 3–32.

Sass, S. A. (1982). *The Pragmatic Imagination*. Philadelphia: University of Pennsylvania Press.

Scott, W. R. (2001). *Institutions and Organizations*. 2nd edn. Thousand Oaks, CA: Sage.

Scott, W. R. (2010). 'Entrepreneurs and Professionals: The Mediating Role of Institutions'. In W. Sine and R. David (eds), *Institutions and Entrepreneurship (Research in the Sociology of Work)*, vol. 21. Bingley, UK: Emerald, 27–49.

Sine, W. D. and David, R. J. (2003). 'Environmental Jolts, Institutional Change, and the Creation of Entrepreneurial Opportunity in the U.S. Electric Power Industry'. *Research Policy*, 32, 185–207.

Sine, W. D. and David, R. J. (2010). 'Institutions and Entrepreneurship'. In W. Sine and R. David (eds), *Institutions and Entrepreneurship (Research in the Sociology of Work)*, vol. 21. Bingley, UK: Emerald, 1–26.

Sine, W. D., Haveman, H. A., and Tolbert, P. S. (2005). 'Risky Business? Entrepreneurship in the New Independent Power Sector'. *Administrative Science Quarterly*, 50, 200–232.

Sine, W. D., David, R. J., and Mitsuhashi, H. (2007). 'From Plan to Plant: Effects of Certification on Operational Start Up in the Emergent Independent Power Sector'. *Organization Science*, 18, 578–594.

Starr, P. (1982). *The Social Transformation of American Medicine*. New York: Basic Books.

Stinchcombe, A. L. (1965). 'Social Structure and Organizations'. In J. March (ed.), *Handbook of Organizations*. Chicago: Rand-McNally, 142–193.

Strang, D. and Meyer, J. W. (1993). 'Institutional Conditions for Diffusion'. *Theory and Society*, 22, 487–511.

Sturdy, A. (1997). 'The Dialectics of Consultancy'. *Critical Perspectives on Accounting*, 8, 511–535.

Suchman, M. C. (1995). 'Managing Legitimacy: Strategic and Institutional Approaches'. *Academy of Management Review*, 20, 571–610.

Thornton, P. H. and Ocasio, W. (1999). 'Institutional Logic and the Historical Contingency of Power in Organizations: Executive Succession in the Higher Education Publishing Industry, 1958–1990'. *American Journal of Sociology*, 105, 801–843.

Tolbert, P. S. and Zucker, L. G. (1983). 'Institutional Sources of Change in the Formal Structure of Organizations: The Diffusion of Civil Service Reform, 1880–1935'. *Administrative Science Quarterly*, 28, 22–39.

Tolbert, P. S. and Zucker, L. G. (1996). 'The Institutionalization of Institutional Theory'. In S. Clegg, C. Hardy, and W. Nord (eds), *Handbook of Organizational Theory*. London: Sage, 176–190.

Tolbert, P. S., David, R. J., and Sine, W. D. (2011). 'Studying Choice and Change: The Intersection of Institutional Theory and Entrepreneurship Research'. *Organization Science*, 22, 1332–1344.

Ventresca, M. J. and Mohr, J. W. (2002). 'Archival Research Methods'. In J. Baum (ed.), *The Blackwell Companion to Organizations*. Cambridge, MA: Blackwell, 805–828.

Vernon, R. (1971). *Sovereignty at Bay: The Multinational Spread of U.S. Enterprises*. New York: Basic Books.

Washburn, S. A. (1996). 'Challenge and Renewal: A Historical View of the Profession'. *Journal of Management Consulting*, 9, 47–53.

Weber, M. (1947 [1924]). *The Theory of Social and Economic Organization*. Trans. and ed. by A. M. Henderson and T. Parsons. New York: Oxford University Press.

Williamson, O. E. (1975). *Markets and Hierarchies: Analysis and Antitrust Implications*. New York: Free Press.

Wolf, W. B. (1978). *Management and Consulting: An Introduction to James O. McKinsey*. Ithaca, NY: New York State School of Industrial and Labor Relations.

CHAPTER 5

CUCKOO IN THE NEST? THE RISE OF MANAGEMENT CONSULTING IN LARGE ACCOUNTING FIRMS

MEGAN S. McDOUGALD
ROYSTON GREENWOOD

In 1966, Forbes concluded an article on whether accounting firms were taking over management consulting services with this observation, 'One thing is clear: the old image of the accountant as a silent, grim-faced man in a green eyeshade sitting apart from the mainstream of business is completely out of date. He's now a top management consultant and that role is going to grow.' (As quoted in Arthur Andersen & Co. 1988: 125)

5.1 INTRODUCTION

THIS chapter reviews the history of accounting, the rise of management consulting within large accounting firms, and the position of those firms within the consulting industry. We then outline two tensions that arose from the considerable growth in those services. Management consulting services, initially an add-on to supplement audit and assurance services, became the 'cuckoo in the nest'—threatening the status and position of accountants. The provision of consulting services also raised the potential conflict of interest that comes about when a firm provides both consulting and auditing services to the same client. This tension culminated in the Enron affair and resulted in the demise of Arthur Andersen, at the time a pre-eminent firm. Our theme is to raise and explore forces that push accounting firms into the consulting sector, and forces that pull them back. Resolution of these forces is an ongoing and unresolved challenge.

5.2 THE EVOLUTION OF ACCOUNTING AND THE RISE OF THE MULTI-DISCIPLINARY FIRM

5.2.1 Regulation of the Industry

In the UK, the Bankruptcy Act of 1831 was the first government recognition of accounting through its creation of the office of 'official assignee'—a court official, who could be an accountant or person of similar standing, charged with performing investigative work and preparing balance sheets for bankrupts (Jones 1995). The Act has been called the 'first official recognition of accountants by the State' (Woolf 1912). This recognition continued with the passage of the Joint Stock Companies Act 1844, and the Companies Clauses Consolidation Act 1845, which legislated that businesses must be formally incorporated and required the annual appointment of auditors to examine the accounts and balance sheets of all companies (Allen and McDermott 1993; Coffee 2006). Following this legislation, the core of the work provided by large accounting firms was established as audit and assurance work. Critically, this work essentially serves those participating in the financial markets—especially investors. The paradox is that accounting firms serve investors but are chosen and paid by those audited—clients.

The American Association of Public Accountants, a predecessor of the American Institute of Certified Public Accountants (AICPA), was established in 1887 (Edwards and Shildneck 1987; Coffee 2006), and in 1917 issued a memorandum on balance sheet audits and acceptable auditing procedures that became a model for the preparation of financial reports (Pichler 1974). Almost two decades later, the US Congress passed the Banking Act of 1933, and the Securities Act of 1933. These security reform legislations were designed to correct the structural problems believed to have contributed to the stock market crash of October 1929 (Carey 1969; McKenna 1995) and prevent a repeat of the 'Kreuger Crash' (Flesher and Flesher 1986; Partnoy 2009), an event similar to Enron, which saw many thousands of Americans lose their life savings. The new legislation required companies to file a balance sheet and profit-and-loss statement 'certified by an independent public or certified accountant' (United States Congress: Schedule A). Previously, company audits had been voluntary. The aim was to provide confidence to investors and bring discipline to corporate accounting.

The Securities Act emphasized the importance of objectivity by defining 'independent' in terms that imposed an absolute arm's-length relationship between practitioner and client (Pichler 1974). The following year, Congress created the Securities and Exchange Commission (SEC) to regulate the financial markets and enforce a more open system of corporate disclosure. The US Congress empowered the new regulatory agency to specify uniform accounting procedures, but by 1937 the SEC had turned over standard setting to the accounting profession (Carey 1969). Nevertheless, the concept of the 'independent' external auditor had become established.

The role of the large accounting firm was integrally linked with, and perhaps even defined by, the role of the 'independent' auditor and watchdog of corporate financial reporting practices. As such, these firms protected the integrity of financial markets. But, as the audit industry matured, accounting firms became more responsive to their clients' requests for advice on various non-assurance business issues. Privy to the details of their clients' businesses and experienced in the managerial context of accounting services, it was a relatively easy step for accountants to persuade their clients that the provision of advice on organizational and managerial issues was a complementary and natural extension of their services. These add-ons, typically referred to as 'management advisory services', covered advice given on activities such as general management, operations research, industrial engineering, organization and personnel, data processing, information technology, and marketing (Montagna 1971). Usually, in the early years of their evolution, these additional services were provided by accountants who had some knowledge of one of these particular areas, which helped accounting firms avoid 'image contamination costs' (Jones 1995). By the end of World War II, the volume and complexity of these additional services merited hiring specialists in general management, engineering, or information technology (i.e. non-accountants) (Watt 1982). The presence of management consultants in large accounting firms was now established.

The leader in the push to provide consulting services, especially information technology services, was Arthur Andersen, which, from its formation, had seen itself more as a provider of business advice than as a mere accounting firm. By the late 1940s and early 1950s, Arthur Andersen saw the spread of mechanization of a wide range of administrative and accounting functions as an opportunity to build what would eventually be an information systems practice. This mechanization of accounting services included the rise of machine accounting, using applications of punched cards for accounting and reporting systems. The drive to mechanization was stimulated after World War II by the many returning servicemen who had learned machine accounting procedures during their military time and understood how machine accounting could speed the production and improve the quality of financial and statistical reports (Arthur Andersen & Co. 1988: 85). The firm's first major project, the installation in 1952 of an electronic information system for General Electric, established Arthur Andersen as information technology consultants (Arthur Andersen & Co. 1988: 85). The distinct emphasis by Arthur Andersen upon the provision of consulting services differentiated it from other accounting firms and contributed to its rapid growth.

However, most accounting firms, to a greater or lesser extent, were foraying into advisory services and many would become significant players within the management consulting industry (Watt 1982). Mechanization would also lead to the emergence of a group of practitioners (consultants) who would not always be in agreement with their accountancy colleagues, *and* there was the nascent risk that the integrity of the 'independent audit' would be perceived as compromised. There is an implicit contradiction between acting as a watchdog for investors, and as an advisor to managers. Early signs of this tension arose in the economically difficult times of the 1970s. Some of the most spectacular losses occurred in companies that had prospered in the 1960s—conglomerates, computer leasing companies, electronics companies, and franchisers. Policymakers and angry investors sought a connection between faulty financial reporting and business collapse, and there was concern that public accountants were insufficiently independent and were becoming 'inside players in the corporate, global business game' (Allen and McDermott 1993: 171). Although this concern about public accountants related more to the fact that accountants get paid by the firms that they provide services to, which sometimes comes at the detriment of shareholders, there was rising concern at this time that perhaps accounting firms were no longer suitably independent, in part because of the myriad of work they were doing inside firms relating to both assurance and non-assurance activities.

Even with the rising public concern, accounting firms were reluctant to pull back from the provision of non-assurance services. Competitive pressures were making the provision of advisory services more, not less, attractive, especially as clients began to request competitive proposals to determine which firms offered the lowest audit fees. Audits, to clients, were a cost to be minimized. These 'beauty contests', as accountants would pejoratively refer to them, were in marked contrast to traditional practices, where the relationships between firms and clients were close and longstanding. Fee-shopping inevitably put downward pressure on returns from audit and assurance services, a trend that accelerated after the AICPA voted in 1972 in favour of competitive bidding and then, in 1979, to allow advertising and solicitation (Weil 2004). In the face of these competitive pressures, audit firms denied any risk to the objectivity and independence of the audit function, insisting that Chinese walls separated assurance and consulting services. And, as consulting services expanded, firms began to hire greater numbers of non-accountants and began the transformation into multidisciplinary practices (MDPs). This transformation came to a head in the late 1970s when accounting firms sought to acquire law firms, butting against the interests of a highly organized and resistant profession (Greenwood and Suddaby 2006). In an attempt to maintain audit independence the SEC proposed a global test that would compare an accounting firm's audit and non-audit fees, and, according to one interpretation, declare a firm 'not independent' of any audit client if it failed the test.

This issue of audit/non-audit services came at a time when the audit universe was shrinking and firms of every size were seeking to broaden their involvement with clients (i.e. cross-selling services) (Arthur Andersen & Co. 1988: 150). By 1987, consulting averaged 21 per cent of the total fees of chargeable hours of the biggest American accounting firms, compared with only 12 per cent a decade earlier. Five of the top ten management consulting firms in the nation were accounting firms, with Arthur Andersen in first place. Arthur Andersen's consulting practice amounted to 33 per cent of the firm's almost $2 billion in worldwide revenues in 1987, and involved primarily the design of computer systems. To put the issue in context, the eight largest accounting firms in 1987 generated aggregate fees of $15.8 billion. Consulting accounted for 20 per cent of that total, with audit and tax providing the balance (Arthur Anderson & Co. 1988: 176).

5.2.2 Structure of the Industry

Three features of the accounting industry from the 1960s onwards are of interest here: growth of an elite group of firms; significant expansion of these firms into the provision of consulting services; and the place of these firms in the consulting sector.

5.2.2.1 *Growth of the Elite*

For the later decades of the twentieth century, the accounting industry was distinguished by an elite group of firms, initially a 'Big Eight'. These firms originated from firms founded in the nineteenth or early twentieth century and are the product of a series of mergers (see Appendix). The Big Eight were noticeably larger than other firms in number of professionals and revenues, and they commanded the market for auditing services. In 1966 one firm alone audited more than 1,000 banks, 700 savings and loan associations, 700 insurance companies, and 1,200 not-for-profit institutions in the US and the UK. Collectively, the Big Eight audited 464 of the 500 largest corporations. The average number of clients for a Big Eight firm in the late 1960s was 10,000, and average annual earnings were approximately $100 million (Montagna 1968, 1971).

It should be noted that Arthur Andersen had a very different origin and structure than the others. The former was a very centralized one-firm firm pushing outward, while most of the latter were federations of largely independent national firms operating under a single brand umbrella. These differences affected their geographic scope. In the 1960s, Arthur Andersen, the least dispersed, operated in twenty-one countries; Peat Marwick and Price Waterhouse, the most dispersed, in fifty-five. Over the next three decades the Big Eight would grow ever more complex and more transnational, partly as a consequence of internally generated growth, and partly the result of mergers with smaller firms. Often, mergers were with non-accounting firms, indicating the push into consulting. For example, in 1985 Price Waterhouse acquired Urwick Orr & Partners in the United Kingdom explicitly to accelerate growth of its consulting activities and access new client segments (Jones 1995: 314–315). The first attempted merger involving two members of the Big Eight occurred in 1984 when Price Waterhouse and Deloitte, Haskins & Sells opened discussions. These firms audited the majority of 'blue chip' companies on the New York Stock Exchange (NYSE) and it was anticipated that a merger would increase their ability to provide and expand management consulting services by leveraging a larger number of audit clients (McKenna 2006). But, although partners in the US approved the merger, those in the UK rejected it and discussions ceased (Wooten, Wolk, and Normand 2003). It was rumoured that disparity in levels of partner compensation was one cause of the failed effort.

Five years later, in 1989, Price Waterhouse again entered discussions with a fellow member of the Big Eight, this time with Andersen Worldwide (the umbrella organization of Arthur Andersen and Andersen Consulting). Had it been successful, the merger would have created the world's largest professional services firm, with revenues approaching $5 billion. However, several issues divided the two firms and discussions were terminated (Allen and McDermott 1993; Wooten, Wolk, and Normand 2003). The failure to consummate the merger was partly attributed to the potential conflict that would have arisen in the proposed larger firm between the provision of auditing and consulting services to the same clients. Andersen's computer consultants had established joint ventures with several of Price Waterhouse's largest clients, including IBM and Hewlett-Packard. Given that accounting firms were prohibited by the SEC from auditing a business partner, the potential loss of consulting revenues may have offset any incremental revenues from the merger (*The Economist* 1989; Stevens 1991).

Other merger discussions proved more successful. Peat Marwick Mitchell & Co. became Klynveld Peat Marwick Goerdeler (KPMG) by merging in 1986 with Klynveld Main Goerdeler (KMG) Main Hurdman. The new firm remained a loose federation and in some countries continued to trade under the name of the legacy firm. Nevertheless, the creation of KPMG demonstrated that a merger between two large international accounting firms could succeed. It also showed that an enlarged firm could gain access to new clients that would not be accessible otherwise, providing enhanced opportunities for consulting work. Further, the economies of scale and resulting efficiencies made the firm a formidable competitor (Berton 1989). In the following three years, KPMG's revenues increased by 44 per cent even though the firm had 127 fewer offices and 510 fewer partners than the 'legacy firms' combined (*Business Week* 1989).

Not surprisingly, other mergers soon followed. Three years after the formation of KPMG, Ernst & Whinney and Arthur Young merged to form Ernst & Young. In the same year, Deloitte Haskins & Sells joined with Touche Ross to create Deloitte & Touche in North America, and Deloitte Ross Tohmatsu (DRT) in parts of Europe and Asia. In the UK, the Deloitte partners voted not to join the merger and DRT used the name of Touche Ross. The 'Big Eight' was thus reduced to the 'Big Six'. Later, in 1998, Price Waterhouse finally achieved a merger—with Coopers & Lybrand—establishing PricewaterhouseCoopers (PwC), and the 'Big Five'.

The reasons behind the wave of mergers are not entirely clear. Several arguments were put forward. One was that large size enables firms to spread the costs involved in the development and deployment of new technologies. For example, large firms recognized that a major presence in the United States would require offices located in the top one hundred cities in the country, and to operate such a network would incur substantial overheads (Scherer 1979/1980; Berton 1989; Stevens 1991). Moreover, technology had become a significant cost factor. Merging with complementary firms thus made sense. It was also suggested that the growing sophistication of clients, especially the increasing number of international and transnational clients, had pushed accounting firms to expand their global coverage (see Rose and Hinings 1999). One way of securing global coverage, in order to mirror the geographical configuration of these clients, was to merge with a firm whose network was complementary in scope. Clients were also pushing their accountancy advisers to develop deeper understanding of their industry. Larger firms were more able to develop the economies of scale and scope necessary to sustain a *portfolio* of substantive industry expertise (Scherer 1979/1980; Berton 1989; Stevens 1991).

A third reason for the spate of mergers was that the firms themselves had become caught up in a struggle to position themselves as number one, or at least as a member of the elite. Smaller members of the elite feared being decoupled from this elite category, which was likely if, and as, mergers within the elite took place. Before their merger, for example, Price Waterhouse and Coopers & Lybrand had slipped behind the other four large firms. Behind this fear of losing the status of being a Big Eight (or Big Six) firm, is the simple fact that such status provides a critical competitive asset (Armbrüster 2006; Rindova et al. 2005). Three benefits have been associated with high reputation: the ability to hire the very best professionals, lower marketing costs because clients actively seek higher status firms, and the ability to charge premiums (Beatty 1989; Podolny 1994; Krishnan and Schauer 2000). Greenwood and colleagues (2005) showed how an accounting firm's status and reputation are significant determinants of its financial performance.

A less publicized reason underlying the merger mania was the increasingly important connection with consulting. Mergers provided accounting firms with access to more clients and thus more opportunities for the delivery of consulting services. Moreover, revenues from consulting were generating a notable proportion of total revenues and were growing significantly faster than those for more conventional accounting services. Arthur Andersen's consulting practice, for example, grew at 15 per cent a year in 1979, nearly four times that of its auditing practice (Allen and McDermott 1993: 188). By the late 1980s, consulting was generating 21 per cent of the total fees of the largest accounting firms, compared to 12 per cent a decade earlier. In all of these firms consulting was not only the fastest growing sector but in some years it was the most profitable. Five of the top ten US management consulting firms were accounting firms, headed by Arthur Andersen. Consulting revenues were growing by an average of 30 per cent annually, almost double the growth of auditing and tax revenues (Allen and McDermott 1993) and, by 1992, revenue from non-audit work ($6.2 billion) surpassed the fees from corporate audits ($5.3 billion) (McKenna 2006: 236).

The above features of the accounting industry are summarized in Table 5.1. It shows the relative dependency of the larger US firms upon consulting revenues, the size and complexity of the largest firms, and the significant gap between the (then) Big Six and the next tier of firms.

5.2.2.2 *Expansion of consulting services*

By the mid-1990s, the worldwide management consulting industry employed at least 100,000 people full time and over the previous decade had grown more than twice as fast as the world economy (Micklethwait and Wooldridge 1997: 47). According to *Consultant's News*, the industry generated $40 billion in revenue in 1996. Accounting firms, especially the very large firms, were integrally involved in, and benefited from, this expansion (Micklethwait and Wooldridge 1997: 47).

Partly, their success arose from demands by clients wishing to upgrade or integrate their information systems (Allen and McDermott 1993; Nanda, Haddad, and Hsieh 2002). Kipping (2002) referred to this period of focus on information technology as the 'third wave' of consulting firms. As the client firms grew and changed, it was necessary for management consulting firms to follow suit and adapt their services as necessary to

Table 5.1 Largest US accounting firms, 1991 ($ million)

Rank	Firm	Revenue	Partners	Professionals	Offices	SEC Clients	MAS* (%)
1	Arthur Andersen & Co.	2,463	1,370	18,586	89	1,738	44
2	Ernst & Young	2,240	1,921	15,869	111	2,559	25
3	Deloitte & Touche	1,952	1,525	11,075	116	2,079	22
4	KPMG Peat Marwick	1,813	1,555	11,445	135	2,201	18
5	Coopers & Lybrand	1,470	1,282	11,419	98	1,455	24
6	Price Waterhouse	1,300	950	8,500	113	1,828	28
7	Grant Thornton	206	209	1,691	52	201	14
8	McGladrey & Pullen	188	362	1,340	70	165	16
9	Kenneth Leventhal & Co.	182	73	776	13	40	36
10	BDO Seidman	181	260	1,201	42	181	7
11	Baird, Kurtz & Dobson	57	115	331	18	20	18
12	Crowe, Chizek & Co.	52	70	550	8	30	37
13	Clifton, Gunderson & Co.	51	105	383	40	4	7
14	Plante & Moran	48	90	395	13	2	12
15	Moss Adams	44	75	330	20	15	11

Source: Public Accounting Report, 15 July 1992.
*MAS—management advisory services

accommodate client preferences. But growth in demand was not restricted to information technology. Clients were open to other forms of advice, such as analysis of their
strategy and assistance in organizational restructuring. In moving into these services,
accounting firms were directly competing with consulting firms, but had the advantage
of relationships established through their audit and assurance work. Accounting firms
could leverage these relationships and 'cross-sell' consulting advice. Given that the selling of intangible services is very dependent upon the relationship between provider and
client, and given that clients are often reluctant to migrate from their current advisors
because of uncertainty over the relative capability of alternative providers, the advantage
provided by an audit-based relationship allowed accounting firms to considerably
expand their consulting practices. A common strategy was to offer the advantage of 'one
stop shopping'.

The growing significance of consulting revenues to the accounting industry is indicated in Figure 5.1, which shows the percentage of revenues derived from management
advisory/consulting services for each of the Big Six (then Five) firms in the US from
1992 to 2008. Two interesting observations stand out. First, for each of the Big Five firms,
consultancy work was a very significant and growing source of revenue. For example,
Arthur Andersen remained successful even after the firm separated into two global business units in 1989—Arthur Andersen and Andersen Consulting. The continued interest
in management advisory services led Arthur Andersen to launch their own business
consulting division and saw consultancy revenues rise from 44 per cent of total revenues
in 1992 to almost 70 per cent by the end of the decade. But *all* of the Big Five firms had

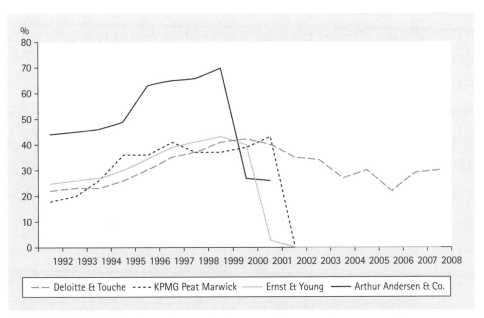

FIGURE 5.1 Percentage revenues from management advisory services, 1992–2008

Source: Public Accounting Report, 30 April 1992–2008.

success in providing these services and *all* were thus dependent upon them. The second observation is the precipitous drop in consulting income at the end of the decade as a consequence of both end of Y2K fears, as well as the fallout from the Enron affair and the resulting legislative changes (see below).

5.2.2.3 *Accounting's place in the consulting industry*

The natural advantages available to the large accounting firms made them formidable competitors and they became significant players in the consulting industry. The zenith of their status, reached in the late 1990s before the regulatory backlash following the Enron affair, is given in Table 5.2. It shows that each of the firms ranked in the top 11 consulting firms. Even the consulting practice of Arthur Andersen, which had separated itself from Andersen Consulting in 1989 (see below), was ranked in the top ten.

The importance of consulting to accounting firms is not only shown by revenue statistics. Firms were increasingly downplaying their roots in accounting and portraying themselves as a different type of advisory firm. The public announcement of the merger that formed PricewaterhouseCoopers, for example, explicitly emphasized the fact that the firm sought to capture increased synergies in management consulting and industry specialization (Middlemiss 1998: 20–27; Wooten, Wolk, and Normand 2003: 25). Moreover, members of the Big Five began relabelling themselves as 'business advisory firms', 'multidisciplinary practices', or 'professional service firms' (Hinings, Greenwood, and Cooper 1999: 136). They sought to legitimate the move towards the MDP as a response to client demands (Greenwood and Suddaby 2006).

Table 5.2 Largest 15 management consulting firms by 1996 revenues ($ million)

Rank	Firm	Revenues
1	Andersen Consulting	4,720
2	EDS/AT Kearney	2,870
3	Computer Sciences Corp (CSC)	2,600
4	Ernst & Young	2,100
5	McKinsey & Co.	2,100
6	Cap Gemini Sogeti	1,444
7	Coopers & Lybrand	1,422
8	KPMG Peat Marwick	1,380
9	Arthur Andersen	1,380
10	Deloitte & Touche	1,303
11	Price Waterhouse	1,200
12	Mercer Consulting Group	1,159
13	Booz Allen Consulting Group	980
14	Towers Perrin	903
15	Sema Group	788

Source: Bourgeois 1997.

Table 5.3 Largest US accounting firms, 2007

Rank	Firm	Rev. $	Partners	Prof. Staff	Offices	SEC Clients	MAS %
1	Deloitte	9,849	2,758	29,725	101	1,264	30
2	PricewaterhouseCoopers	8,362	2,151	22,541	75	1,193	0
3	Ernst & Young	7,561	2,314	20,163	90	1,631	0
4	KPMG	5,357	1,715	15,164	89	1,033	0
5	RSM McGladrey	1,467	728	5,400	100	159	21
6	Grant Thornton	1,195	522	3,916	52	361	17
7	BDO Seidman	659	266	2,140	37	345	11
8	CBIZ & Mayer Hoffman McCann	500	243	2,086	33	27	50
9	Crowe Group	492	143	1,606	23	107	22
10	BKD	353	230	1,323	27	48	19
11	Moss Adams	315	230	1,205	17	67	17
12	Plante & Moran	291	206	1,242	16	24	21
13	UHY	277	146	920	26	67	18
14	Clifton Gunderson	247	208	1,447	17	3	28
15	Reznick Group	224	106	1,051	10	22	23

Source: Public Accounting Report, 31 August 2008.

Despite the optimism and claims of the large firms, muted fears were growing that audit standards were becoming compromised as firms sought to win future consulting contracts. The independence of the audit process was perceived to be at risk because the audit had become secondary to the more profitable consulting projects, and the large firms were overly dependent upon consulting assignments. Moreover, tensions between auditors and consultants were becoming evident (Aharoni 1999) as consultants flexed their status as revenue generators. Managing the evolving multidisciplinary practice was proving problematical. The cuckoo—consulting—was destabilizing the nest.

It would be wrong to draw the conclusion that the actions of the Big Five firms signalled the withdrawal of accounting firms from the consulting industry. Moreover, the Big Five were the *only* firms that felt, for a time, the need to withdraw their consulting services because it was *they* who dominated the assurance and audit industry and thus were more publicly visible and more vulnerable to regulatory challenges. Other firms, with less significant assurance practices, and who were thus less visible, were comparatively unaffected by the Enron fallout and better able to retain their consulting interests. Table 5.3, for example, shows that, in 2007, accounting firms *outside* the (now) Big Four still retained their significant consulting presence. Today, moreover, even the Big Four are moving back into consulting, albeit with much clearer policies about the separation of consulting and assurance work. Post-Enron regulatory requirements and a more circumspect approach from the firms themselves has rearranged the relationship between audit and consulting services, but has hardly checked their enthusiasm for delivering non-assurance advice.

5.3 THE CUCKOO IN THE NEST

5.3.1 The Growing Tension between Accountants and Consultants

Placing more emphasis on management consulting had implications for the organizational arrangements of accounting firms because, by definition, the composition of the workforce became more heterogeneous. For example, Price Waterhouse was being staffed almost entirely by chartered accountants in the 1960s, but by 1990 non-accountants composed approximately two-thirds of the professional workforce. The proportional increases in 'partners' admitted to Price Waterhouse's audit and non-audit practices went from 80/20 in 1960 to 30/70 in 1990 (Allen and McDermott 1993). Technically, non-accountants cannot be equity 'partners' in an accounting firm. Therefore, firms would treat the consulting business either as a 'separate' organization, or use a status other than partner.

The first tension discussed in this section relates to the increasing size and growing heterogeneity that made it ever more difficult to rely upon the collegial arrangements of the traditional partnership format (Greenwood et al. 1993; see Morris, Gardner, and Anand, Chapter 14, this volume). Formalized structures of decision-making and hierarchical mechanisms became necessary, typically layered on top of traditional arrangements (Cooper et al. 1996; Brock 2008; Brock, Powell, and Hinings 1999). Human resource practices moved from the distinctive patterns of up-or-out career progression and lock-step compensation in favour of emphasis upon formal appraisal, non-equity partners, and merit-based compensation. Global knowledge-management systems were introduced. These movements towards greater formalization inevitably changed the firms' cultures, making them less cohesive. Moreover, the governing rules that generally did not permit non-chartered accountants (non-CAs) to be equity partners, led to growing unrest amongst management consultants who perceived that their interests were neither protected nor appropriately recognized.

The history of Arthur Andersen nicely illustrates the growing tension between accountants and consultants. When consulting services grew to 21 per cent of total revenues, Andersen's CEO, Harvey Kapnick, put forward a recommendation at the 1979 annual partners' meeting that consulting and accounting activities be separated into two firms. Kapnick presented the idea as 'turning one great firm into two great firms' (Arthur Andersen & Co. 1988: 150). Kapnick tried to develop support from the partnership by indicating that the SEC would soon require greater structural distancing of audits from consulting, but many partners questioned his interpretation of the SEC's position. They believed there was no need to limit the services a firm could offer its clients. Chinese walls and professional integrity would suffice. In the end, the recommendation to divide the firm was rejected by a slim margin.

Andersen's consultants remained dissatisfied with their low representation on the firm's global board, where they had only five of the sixteen positions, despite contributing approximately 40 per cent of global revenues (Arthur Andersen & Co. 1988). They also chafed under their accountability to local office managing partners, who were almost always accountants. Consultants felt that their status and influence within the firm was inadequately recognized and resented their exclusion from positions of influence. Moreover, accounting partners were compensated on a per-share basis from worldwide profits even though consulting partners, known as 'principals' instead of partners, contributed twice the amount generated by accountants. In effect, consultants were subsidizing accounting partners and yet were not afforded equal status in the management of the firm (Arthur Andersen & Co. 1988).

In 1989, the firm finally separated into two global business units—'Arthur Andersen' and 'Andersen Consulting'—headed by an accountant and a consultant respectively, under the umbrella of 'Andersen Worldwide'. Consultants were promised greater representation on the worldwide governing committee, and a 15 per cent limit was set on the revenues that could be transferred annually from one business unit to another. However, the separation did not fully resolve the tension. Liability would still cross the two units and there remained the potential for a conflict of interest if Arthur Andersen and Andersen Consulting audited and advised the same client (Arthur Andersen & Co. 1988).

For the first few years following reorganization the relationship between Arthur Andersen and Andersen Consulting improved. It helped, for a time, that both business units achieved comparable revenue and profitability growth. But in the mid-1990s consulting again began generating higher revenue growth. Complicating matters, Arthur Andersen and Andersen Consulting found themselves competing with one another for systems integration projects, even though the creation of the two business units had been premised, in part, on the accounting side limiting its consulting activities to modest-sized projects (Walmsley 2000) while Andersen Consulting would deal exclusively with clients and projects with revenues over $175 million. However, by the mid-1990s, market competition and growth had pushed Arthur Andersen to pursue larger clients and the two sides of the firm found themselves in direct competition, sometimes bidding for the same contract. Not surprisingly, this development angered the consultants (Walmsley 2000).

Consulting partners continued to have less representation (one-third membership) on Andersen Worldwide's governing board and continued to be upset with the transfer of profits from Andersen Consulting to Arthur Andersen. In 1997, $173 million was transferred from Andersen Consulting, at a cost of $153,000 per consulting partner (Walmsley 2000). Tensions thus continued to escalate and the consultants sought formal separation from Andersen Worldwide. The dispute was moved to the Chamber of Commerce Court of International Arbitration in Paris, which ruled that Andersen Consulting should provide Arthur Andersen with a $1 billion one-time separation payout (Walmsley 2000). The arbitration payment was disappointing to Arthur Andersen: its partners had hoped to receive about $14.5 billion (Walmsley 2000). The departing consulting group renamed itself Accenture. Ironically, the name change protected the reputation of the departing consulting group from the Enron scandal that dragged Arthur Andersen to its demise. Accenture continues to thrive and was ranked at number one in revenues (US$25,300 billion) in management consulting firms in 2009 (http://www.careers-in-business.com/consulting/consrank09.htm and www.accenture.com).

The remaining Big Five firms were not immune to the growing tension between accounting and management consulting and also reconsidered their relationship with consulting. Ernst & Young sold its management consulting practice to Cap Gemini in 2000 to form Cap Gemini Ernst & Young Consulting. The same year, KPMG divested its consultancy group, renamed as KPMG Consulting. The newly spun-off firm went public and, in 2002, adopted the name BearingPoint. BearingPoint subsequently filed for Chapter 11 bankruptcy in February 2009. IBM Global Services acquired the PricewaterhouseCoopers consultancy business in 2002 for $3.9 billion in cash and stock (after the failure of an earlier attempt by PwC's accounting firm to sell it to Hewlett-Packard). Deloitte initially intended to divest its consulting practice but, in the end, retained it. These structural shifts inevitably changed the position of 'accounting' firms in the industry with only Deloitte ranked in the top ten in 2006 (see Table 5.4).

The tension between Arthur Andersen and Andersen Consulting illustrates our 'cuckoo in the nest' thesis. Consulting, or management advisory services, introduced as a

Table 5.4 Largest 10 management consulting firms by 2006 revenues ($ million)

Rank	Firm	Revenues
1	IBM Global Business Services	13,209
2	Accenture	9,892
3	Deloitte	8,848
4	CSC	7,440
5	Fujitsu	7,091
6	NTT Data	6,803
7	CapGemini	5,434
8	KPMG International	5,280
9	McKinsey & Co.	4,016
10	Lockheed Martin	3,978

Source: Consultants News, 22 June 2007.

way of diversifying and enriching services provided by accountants, outgrew the firm and fundamentally altered the way that services were regarded and provided. Instead of being a supplementary service, consulting became dominant, or at least a sizeable and demanding, one, and it implicitly threatened the integrity of the traditional core service—audit and assurance. Because it leveraged the firms' relationships with clients the shift to consulting had made strategic sense, but it was proving organizationally more difficult than anticipated. The strategy made sense, but only to a point.

As long as consulting services had been provided by accountants diversification had largely proved to be non-problematic. But, once provided by non-accountants, tensions became inevitable. As Rose and Hinings (1999) point out, this tension arose partly because audit is largely a recurring business based upon long-term relationships with clients, whereas management consulting is project-based and more cyclical in nature. Further, accountants and consultants are 'different'; consultants are more 'entrepreneurial, more egotistical, and faster moving' (Black and Chambers 1999: 85). Consulting *is* a different kind of business.

5.3.2 Conflicts of Interest

The second tension that arose from the growth of the MDP resulted from the heightened risk of 'client capture', the ability of consumers to control the activities, timing, and costs of professional work. In effect, the 'consumer becomes sovereign' (Leicht and Fennel 2001: 106). In a similar vein, DeAngelo (1981) argued that when significant revenues are gained from assurance *and* consulting work, the firm's dependence on the client increases, with the result that the integrity of the audit is potentially compromised by the risk of losing lucrative consulting projects. Enron proved to be the epitome of the client capture/independence tension.

There is a tendency to think that the concerns of independence and client capture are new. In fact, both were matters of concern decades before the Enron affair. Soon after World War II, critics were warning that the provision of consulting services could impair the independence of audits. At that time, however, consulting contributed only a small fraction of the industry's revenues and these fears were relatively muted (Coffee 2006). Concerns began to be heard again, however, in the late 1970s and 1980s as the role and purpose of the audit came under serious scrutiny, partly because of growing litigation against accounting firms (Ashbough, LaFond, and Mayhew 2003). Whittington (2007: 442) summarized the situation: 'firms whose main business, in revenue terms, lies outside auditing may come to regard auditing as a "loss leader" which is justified mainly by its ability to generate more lucrative add-on services'. Looking back, *Consultants News* (22 June 2007: 2) put it more bluntly: 'consulting...had become like heroin driving overall firm growth. And like any addiction, the need for a fix brought potential conflicts to the fore.'

Challenges to the MDP also came from another set of actors. In 1997, Ernst & Young established a 'captive' law firm in Toronto, Canada, an event soon followed by announcements that US law firms were targets of acquisition (ABA 2000). This declaration brought the strategic aspirations of the accounting firms to the boundaries of the powerful legal profession. It triggered a hostile response. Both the Canadian and the American Bar Associations announced formal inquiries into MDP and by 1999 all but four US state bar associations had established investigatory committees. In 2000, the American Bar Association (ABA) voted three to one to retain its rule prohibiting lawyers from sharing fees with non-lawyers, a direct rejection of the move by accounting firms to 'acquire' law firms (*The Economist* 2001: 65). Interestingly, Britain and Europe were moving in the *opposite* direction to that of the US and Canada. In March 2001, a report on competition and the professions prepared by the Office of Fair Trading (OFT) in the UK came out in favour of MDPs. In France and Germany, lawyers unsuccessfully resisted the introduction of multidisciplinary firms and accounting firms began setting up their own legal divisions. By 2001, KPMG's law firm, Fidal, employed 1,200 lawyers in France.

The response of the legal profession did not focus upon the independence issue, but it was *the* concern of the SEC. Arthur Levitt, the SEC's chairman, decided that auditors were no longer sufficiently independent from their corporate clients, and, in a speech to the Certified Public Accountant Association stated that the accounting profession is one that:

> ...demands you defend and protect, above all else, the public trust; a franchise that asks you to stand firm—even under the weight of management's pressure to see things their way...The watchword of many in the business is the 'customer is always right'. But in what other profession is it one's duty to tell the customer when he is wrong? (Levitt 2000: 4)

The scale of the problem worrying the SEC can easily be illustrated. The Marriott International Hotel chain paid Arthur Andersen $1 million for its audit services and $30.3 million for 'other' services. Similarly, Motorola paid KPMG $3.9 million for preparing an audit and $62.2 million for other advice (*The Economist* 2001: 65). The SEC's concern was heightened by several high-profile restatements of financial reports. Waste Management Inc. (WMI), which had been audited by Arthur Andersen for more than 30 years, had to restate its annual financial reports for 1993 to 1996 by more than $1.4 billion. WMI had paid Arthur Andersen $7.5 million in audit fees and $11.8million for other services. Arthur Andersen denied any conflict of interest or professional misbehaviour and tried to persuade the SEC that it was not in the public interest to discourage a company from using the broader range of expertise and services of the firm that knew it best—its auditor. The SEC was not convinced and, in June 2001, fined Arthur Andersen $7 million for improper professional conduct. It was the SEC's first such case in more than twenty years (*The Economist* 2001: 65).

Levitt and the SEC failed, however, in their initial attempt to resolve the independence problem. Levitt proposed to the US Congress that accounting firms be banned from providing a wide range of consulting services to their audit clients. He also recommended that accounting and consulting be separated (Coffee 2006; McKenna 2006). The Big Five reacted strongly. Three firms threatened to sue the SEC and Levitt came under intense pressure from lobbyists and politicians (Levitt 2002: 241). And, despite its impressive title and mandate, the position of the SEC vis-à-vis the accounting firms was weak (Becker 2001; Levitt 2002). The general counsel of the SEC illustrates the SEC's difficulty:

> From the outset we were threatened with litigation...At one point the Big Five accounting firms that opposed the rulemaking had retained much of the heart and brains of what turned out to be the Bush election dispute legal team and the Gore election dispute legal team. Our would-be opponents spoke openly about attacking any final rules through legislative action as well. (Becker 2001: 5–6)

It looked, therefore, as if the strategies of the Big Five multidisciplinary practices would succeed. The emerging consensus of opinion was that MDPs would be commonplace in Britain within five years and in the United States within ten years (McKenna 2006). But the success of the Big Five in repelling Levitt and the SEC was short-lived. The collapse of Enron, the financial scandals at WorldCom, Tyco, Global Crossing, and others, and the demise of Arthur Andersen, raised, once again, questions about the independence of auditors in MDPs, dramatically tilted public opinion against the Big Five, and enabled regulatory reform: 'No event made management consulting more visible than the collapse of Enron in 2001' (McKenna 2006: 216).

Enron was one of the world's leading electricity, natural gas, pulp and paper, and communications companies, with claimed revenues of $101 billion. Its collapse began in August 2001, with the announcement that it had overstated its earnings since 1997 by almost US$600 million. Later, Enron also admitted that debts were understated by over

US$600 million. Deals that looked profitable, such as the US$500 million fibre optics contract with Qwest, turned out to be valueless swaps made to inflate revenue figures. Enron's stock fell 99.9 per cent and the company filed for Chapter 11 bankruptcy protection on 20 December 2001, leaving behind $15 billion in debt, worthless shares, and 20,000 workers without employment (Prakash 2007: 5). This occurred despite the corporation using one of the world's largest accounting firms, Arthur Andersen, as its primary auditor.

Investigations revealed that several of Enron's in-house accountants and attorneys had expressed concerns about Enron's accounting practices as early as 1998; but although the concerns were communicated to top management *and* to the company's auditors, they were ignored. When the SEC began to investigate Enron, in January 2002, it found that Arthur Andersen had shredded relevant documents. Three months later, Arthur Andersen was charged with obstruction of justice and convicted. Arthur Andersen surrendered its right to practise and began winding down its US operations. Ironically, but too late to save the firm, on 31 May 2005, the US Supreme Court overturned Andersen's conviction because of flaws in the jury instructions (Prakash 2007: 5).

Enron's bankruptcy damaged the credibility of audit firms and as a result brought criticism of MDPs to light. The involvement of prestigious professional service firms, notably Arthur Andersen and McKinsey, but also elite law firms and investment banks, was heavily reported by the media and there was much talk about the conflict of interest caused by the $27 million in management consulting fees received by Arthur Andersen compared to the $25 million paid for audit work (McKenna 2006: 216). As Macey (2004: 46) put it:

> The exclusive relationship between audit partner and client, upon which the partner's career largely depends, makes the partner particularly susceptible to client capture. Even though Arthur Andersen was deemed 'independent' because Enron accounted for less than 1% of Andersen's total, Enron accounted for all of the billings of the lead partner assigned to Enron and for several members of his audit team. Further, Arthur Andersen's management in Chicago apparently relied solely on the captured audit team for information about the client.

The outcry resulted in the Sarbanes–Oxley Corporate Reform Act, signed into law on 30 July 2002, and considered the most significant change to federal securities laws since Franklin D. Roosevelt's New Deal in the 1930s (Prakash 2007). Among other things, the Act established standards for external auditor independence so that conflicts of interest are averted. In particular, Section 201 states that a registered public accounting firm cannot provide any non-audit service *to an assurance client*, including bookkeeping, financial information systems design and implementation, management functions or human resources, legal counsel, or advice related to appraisals, valuations, internal audit outsourcing, and actuarial reports (Elson and Lynn 2008). In addition, the accounting profession's long history of standard setting and self-regulation was effectively ended by the creation of a new, quasi-public agency, the Public

Company Accounting Oversight Board, to register, regulate, inspect, and discipline accounting firms in their role as auditors of public companies (Kinney and Simunic 2005). Accounting firms have been forced to rethink their service offerings and client relationships. But the Act it did not stop accounting firms from providing consulting services to *non*-audit clients.

Although Arthur Andersen was the scapegoat in the Enron case, it is unlikely that the other large accounting firms were completely innocent. The practices in place at Andersen were to some degree in place at other audit firms and accounting scandals have been alleged against most of the large firms (Grey 2003: 575). Whether conflicts of interest raised by the provision of assurance and consulting to the same client are real or perceived is, perhaps, immaterial. What matters is that the image of accounting firms as guardians of the public interest (or, at least, of the interests of financial investors) was badly compromised by the exposures following the Enron affair. Management consulting, the cuckoo in the nest, had almost destroyed the nest.

5.4 CONCLUSIONS

We have focused on the proliferation of management consulting as the 'cuckoo in the nest' of large accounting firms. Although the provision of management consulting or business advisory services in large accounting firms dates back to the early 1900s, it was the rise of information technology in the 1960s that led to the standardization of accounting services and the lowering of client fees in the 1970s and 1980s, which led, in turn, to diversification by accounting firms in order to 'add value' to audit services. The transformation into multidisciplinary firms allowed management consulting services to become a high growth area within large accounting firms. The growing presence of management consulting services was not unlike the baby cuckoo taking over the nest of its unsuspecting foster family. Two consequences, we argued, followed. Accountants found it problematical to retain their status and 'control' the firm. And there were renewed fears that the integrity of the audit process was being affected as firms fought to win future consulting contracts from their audit clients.

Accounting firms in general have shown themselves to be highly resilient—see, for example, the arguments of Sikka and Wilmott (1995). By reshaping themselves to be more competitive, and by expanding the scale and scope of their product offerings, they have become larger, heterogeneous, and ultimately stronger firms. The Arthur Andersen collapse, however, highlights their nascent vulnerability. For the moment, the increased regulatory attention to auditor independence has made accounting firms more circumspect about the types of businesses in which they might sensibly become involved, and about the nature of the relationship between their audit responsibilities and the provision of business advisory services. Nevertheless, the tensions described in this chapter remain and the consequences of the consulting 'cuckoo' upon the accounting nest are fundamentally unresolved. From a research perspective, there is an increased need to study this rich dataset in order to understand more fully the role of management consulting and accounting in the professional service firm sector.

APPENDIX—'THE BIG EIGHT'

1 Arthur Andersen and Co.

In 1913, Arthur Andersen and Clarence Delaney, both from Price Waterhouse, bought out The Audit Company of Illinois to form Andersen, Delaney & Co. It became Arthur Andersen & Co. in 1918. Andersen Consulting split from the parent in 1989 to become the largest consulting firm in the world. In 2002, Arthur Andersen & Co. voluntarily surrendered its licences to practise as certified public accountants in the US pending the result of prosecution by the Department of Justice over the firm's handling of the auditing of Enron.

2 Arthur Young & Co.

Arthur Young was a Scottish barrister and opened a Chicago office in 1894 to handle the affairs of British investors. The firm merged with Ernst & Whinney in 1989.

3 Coopers & Lybrand

William Cooper opened his London office in 1854. He was joined by three of his brothers to form Cooper Brothers & Co. in 1861. William Lybrand, Adam and Edward Ross, and Robert Montgomery founded their firm in 1898 in Philadelphia. They merged with Cooper Brothers and the Canadian firm McDonald, Currie & Co. in 1956 to form Coopers & Lybrand. Coopers & Lybrand merged with Price Waterhouse in 1998 to become PricewaterhouseCoopers.

4 Deloitte Haskins & Sells

William Deloitte founded his London firm in 1854. Deloitte began collaborating with Haskins & Sells in 1905 and the firms merged in 1978. Deloitte merged with Touche Ross in 1989. Charles Haskins began a New York practice in 1886. He worked with Sells on the Dockery Commission in 1895 (on financial reform of the federal government) and they became partners that same year. Haskins & Sells began collaborating with Deloitte, Plender, Griffiths in 1905 and the firms merged in 1978. DH&S merged with Touche Ross in 1989.

5 Ernst & Whinney

The oldest originating partnership affiliated with Ernst & Whinney originated in 1849 in Britain as Harding and Puellin. That same year the firm was joined by Frederick Whinney. He was made a partner in 1859 and, with his sons in the business, it was renamed Whinney, Smith & Whinney in 1894. The Ernst Brothers formed a partnership in Cleveland in 1903. Ernst & Ernst affiliated with Whinney, Smith & Whinney in 1924 and they merged in 1979. Ernst & Whinney merged with Arthur Young in 1989.

6 Peat Marwick Mitchell & Co.

James Marwick opened an office in Glasgow in 1887 and in New York in 1896. He formed a partnership with Roger Mitchell in 1897. William Peat founded his company in London in 1867 and merged with Marwick Mitchell and Co. in 1911. In 1986, Peat Marwick Mitchell merged with KMG (Klynveld Main Goerdeler) Main Hurdman to form KPMG Peat Marwick.

7 Price Waterhouse & Co.

Samuel Price and Edwin Waterhouse formed a partnership with William Holyland in 1849 in London. In 1890, Price Waterhouse established a permanent New York office as Jones, Caesar & Co. They merged with Coopers & Lybrand in 1998.

8 Touche Ross Bailey & Smart

George Touche formed a partnership with John Niven in 1900 in London; later Touche, Niven, Bailey & Smart, then Touche, Ross, Bailey & Smart, shortened to Touche Ross in 1969. They merged with Deloitte in 1989.

References

Aharoni, Y. (1999). 'Internationalisation of Professional Services: Implications for Accounting Firms.' In D. Brock, M. Powell, and C. R. Hinings (eds), *Restructuring the Professional Organization: Accounting, Healthcare and Law*. London: Routledge, 20–40.

Allen, D. G. and McDermott, K. (1993). *Accounting for Success: A History of Price Waterhouse in America 1890–1990*. Boston: Harvard Business School Press.

ABA (American Bar Association) (2000). 'Constitution and Bylaws: Rules of Procedure House of Delegates'. Chicago: American Bar Association.

Armbrüster, T. (2006). *The Economics and Sociology of Management Consulting*. New York: Cambridge University Press.

Arthur Andersen & Co. (1988). *A Vision of Grandeur*. Chicago: Arthur Andersen & Co.

Ashbough, H., LaFond, R., and Mayhew, B. W. (2003). 'Do Non-Audit Services Compromise Auditor Independence? Further Evidence'. *The Accounting Review*, 78/3, 611–639.

Beatty, R. P. (1989). 'Auditor Reputation and the Pricing of Initial Public Offerings'. *The Accounting Review*, 64/4, 693–709.

Becker, D. M. (2001). 'A Temperate Peace'. Speech by US Securities and Exchange Commission General Counsel, Scottsdale, Arizona, 10 March, 1–15. Available at http://www.sec.gov/news/speech/spch478.htm accessed 1 October 2011.

Berton, L. (1989). 'Peat Experience Shows Why Accountants are Rushing to Merge'. *Wall Street Journal*, 17 July, 1, 7.

Black, J. A. and Chambers, M. (1999). 'The Accountants and Their Law Firms'. *Lexpert*, November, 80–90.

Bourgeois, T. (1997). *The Global Management Consulting Marketplace: Key Data, Forecasts and Trends*. Peterborough, NH: Kennedy Information.

Brock, D. M. (2008). 'The Reconstructed Professional Firm: A Reappraisal of Ackroyd and Muzio'. *Organization Studies*, 29/1, 145–149.

Brock, D. M., Powell, M. J., and Hinings, C. R. (1999). 'The Restructured Professional Organization: Corporates, Cobwebs and Cowboys'. In D. M. Brock, M. J. Powell, and C. R. Hinings (eds), *Restructuring the Professional Organization: Accounting, Health Care and Law*. London: Routledge, 215–229.

Business Week: (1989). 'The New Numbers Game in Accounting', 24 July, 20–21.

Carey, J. L. (1969). *The Rise of the Accounting Profession Volume 1: From Technician to Professional, 1896–1936*. New York: American Institute of Certified Public Accountants.

Coffee Jr, J. C. (2006). *Gatekeepers: The Professions and Corporate Governance*. New York: Oxford University Press.

Cooper, D. J., Hinings, C. R., Greenwood, R., and Brown, J. L. (1996). 'Sedimentation and Transformation in Organizational Change: The Case of Canadian Law Firms'. *Organization Studies*, 17/4, 623–647.

DeAngelo, L. (1981). 'Auditor Independence, "Low Balling", and Disclosure Regulation'. *Journal of Accounting and Economics*, 3, 183–199.

The Economist (1989). 'Price Andersen', 312 (30 September), 84.

The Economist (2001). 'Special Report: Professional-Service Firms', 7 July, 64–66.

Edwards, J. D. and Shildneck, B. J. (1987). 'AICPA's First Century: Highlights from 100 Years of Progress'. *Management Accounting*, 69, 57–61.

Elson, R. J. and Lynn, L. M. (2008). 'The Impact and Effect of the Sarbanes–Oxley Act on the Internal Audit Profession: Chief Executives' Perspectives'. *Academy of Accounting and Financial Studies Journal*, 12/1, 59–66.

Flesher, D. L. and Flesher, T. K. (1986). 'Ivar Kreuger's Contribution to U.S. Financial Reporting'. *Accounting Review*, 61/2, 421–434.

Greenwood, R. and Suddaby, R. (2006). 'Institutional Entrepreneurship in Mature Fields: The Big Five Accounting Firms'. *Academy of Management Journal*, 49/1, 27–48.

Greenwood, R., Cooper, D. L., Hinings, R. C., and Brown, J. L. (1993). 'Biggest is Best? Strategic Assumptions and Actions in the Canadian Audit Industry'. *Canadian Journal of Administrative Science*, 10/4, 308–321.

Greenwood, R., Li, S. X., Prakash, R., and Deephouse, D. L. (2005). 'Reputation, Diversification, and Organizational Explanations of Performance in Professional Service Firms'. *Organization Science*, 16/6, 661–675.

Grey, C. (2003). 'The Real World of Enron's Auditors'. *Organization*, 10/3, 572–576.

Hinings, C. R., Greenwood, R., and Cooper, D. L. (1999). 'The Dynamics of Change in Large Accounting Firms'. In D. M. Brock, M. J. Powell, and C. R. Hinings (eds), *Restructuring the Professional Organization: Accounting, Healthcare and Law*. London: Routledge, 131–153.

Jones, E. 1995. *True and Fair: A History of Price Waterhouse*. London: Hamish Hamilton.

Kinney, W. R. and Simunic, D. A. (2005). 'Twenty-Five Years of Audit Deregulation and Re-Regulation: What Does It Mean for 2005 and Beyond'? *Auditing*, 24, 89–113.

Kipping, M. (2002). 'Trapped in Their Wave: The Evolution of Management Consultancies'. In T. Clark and R. Fincham (eds), *Critical Consulting: New Perspectives on the Management Advice Industry*. Oxford: Blackwell, 28–49.

Krishnan, J. and Schauer, P. C. (2000). 'The Differentiation of Quality Among Auditors: Evidence from the Not-For-Profit Sector'. *Auditing*, 19/2, 9–27.

Leicht, K. T. and Fennel, M. L. (2001). *Professional Work: A Sociological Approach*. New York: Wiley-Blackwell.

Levitt, A. (2000). 'The Public's Profession'. Speech by SEC Chairman to the Fall Council of the American Institute of Certified Public Accountants, Las Vegas, Nevada, 24 October.

Levitt, A. (2002). *Take on the Street*. New York: Pantheon.

Macey, J. (2004). 'Wheel of Justice'. *Forbes*, 173/13 (21 June), 46.

McKenna, C. D. (1995). 'The Origins of Modern Management Consulting'. *Business and Economic History*, 24/1, 51–58.

McKenna, C. D. (2006). *The World's Newest Profession: Management Consulting in the Twentieth Century*. Cambridge: Cambridge University Press.

Micklethwait, J. and Wooldridge, A. (1997). *The Witch Doctors: Making Sense of the Management Gurus*. New York: Times Books.

Middlemiss, J. (1998). 'The Urge to Merge'. *CA Magazine*, 131/8, 20–25.

Montagna, P. D. (1968). 'Professionalization and Bureaucratisation in Large Professional Organizations'. *The American Journal of Sociology*, 74/2, 138–145.

Montagna, P. D. (1971). 'The Public Accounting Profession: Organization, Ideology, and Social Power'. *The American Behavioral Scientist*, 14/4, 475–491.

Nanda, A., Haddad, K., and Hsieh, N. H. (2002). *Consulting by Auditors (A): Independence Compromised or Assured?* Boston: Harvard Business School Press, case no. 9–902-161.

Nayyar, P. R. (1993). 'On the Measurement of Competitive Strategy: Evidence from a Large Multiproduct U.S. Firm'. *Academy of Management Journal*, 36/6, 1652–1669.

Partnoy, F. (2009). *The Match King: Ivar Kreuger, the Financial Genius Behind a Century of Wall Street Scandals*. New York: PublicAffairs.

Pichler, J. A. (1974). 'An Economic Analysis of Accounting Power'. In R. R. Sterling (ed.), *Institutional Issues in Public Accounting*. New York: Scholars Book Co.

Podolny, J. M. (1994). 'Market Uncertainty and the Social Character of Economic Exchange'. *Administrative Science Quarterly*, 39/3, 458–483.

Prakash, R. (2007). 'The Influence of Organizational Forms and Client Relationships in Professional Behaviour: The Case of Enron'. Unpublished Ph.D. dissertation, University of Alberta, Edmonton.

Rindova, V., Williamson, I. O., Petkova, A. P., and Sever, J. M. (2005). 'Being Good or Being Known: An Empirical Examination of the Dimensions, Antecedents, and Consequences of Organizational Reputation'. *Academy of Management Journal*, 48/6, 1033–1059.

Rose, T. and Hinings, C. R. (1999). 'Global Clients' Demands Driving Change in Global Business Advisory Firms'. In D. M. Brock, M. J. Powell, and C. R. Hinings (eds), *Restructuring the Professional Organization: Accounting, Healthcare and Law*. London: Routledge, 20–40.

Scherer, F. M. (1979/1980). 'No Boon in the Merger Boom'. *Business and Society Review*, 32 (winter), 17–23.

Sikka, P. and Willmott, H. (1995). 'The Power of "Independence": Defending and Extending the Jurisdiction of Accounting in the United Kingdom'. *Accounting, Organizations and Society*, 20/6, 547–581.

Stevens, M. (1991). *The Big Six*. New York: Simon & Schuster.

United States Congress (1933). Securities Act of 1933. 15 U.S.C. 77a.

Walmsley, A. (2000). 'The Great Divide'. *R.O.B. Magazine*, November, 54–60.

Watt, M. L. (1982). *The First Seventy-Five Years*. Toronto: Price Waterhouse & Co.

Weil, J. (2004). 'Accounting Board Should Expand its Authority, SEC Official Says'. *Wall Street Journal*, 15 July, C3.

Whittington, G. (2007). *Profitability, Accounting Theory and Methodology: The Selected Essays of Geoffrey Whittington*. London: Routledge.

Woolf, A. H. (1912). *A Short History of Accountants and Accountancy*. London: Gee.

Wooten, C. W., Wolk, C. M., and Normand, C. (2003). 'An Historical Perspective on Mergers and Acquisitions by Major US Accounting Firms'. *Accounting History*, 8/1, 25–60.

CHAPTER 6

IT CONSULTING AND OUTSOURCING FIRMS: EVOLUTION, BUSINESS MODELS, AND FUTURE PROSPECTS

KERIM GALAL

ANSGAR RICHTER

VERA WENDLANDT

6.1 INTRODUCTION

SINCE its emergence about fifty years ago, the IT consulting market has grown at an exponential rate—for many years even outpacing the growth rate of the general management consulting sector (Nolan and Bennigson 2002). Market research shows that the size of the market for IT consulting services now exceeds that for general management consulting services by a considerable margin (Armbrüster and Kipping 2001; Eurostat 2008). In addition, IT consulting and IT outsourcing firms have diversified into related activities, broadening their service bundles.

Despite the impressive development of IT consulting and outsourcing (ITCO), there has been little systematic examination of the evolution of the industry and the business models of its participants. Most of the established literature, both on the history of consulting as well as on the organization and strategy of consulting firms, focuses primarily on general management consulting (GMC), and addresses IT-oriented consulting firms only in passing (Knights and Murray 1994; Wilson and Howcroft 2005). Against this background, the objective of this chapter is to provide a comprehensive overview of the development of the IT consulting and outsourcing industry, and the business models of the firms operating in this sector. In order to sharpen the portrayal of the business models of ITCO firms, the chapter uses the GMC firms as a backdrop.

The structure of the chapter is as follows: in the next section we provide a short overview of the history of IT consulting and outsourcing, the players in this market, and its overall size and structure. The following section analyses the business models of ITCO firms and compares them with those of GMC firms. On this basis, the conclusion develops recommendations for future research in this area.

6.2 THE EVOLUTION OF IT CONSULTING AND OUTSOURCING

This section first describes the emergence and development of IT consulting as an increasingly distinct line of activity. This development is closely interwoven with the rise of the computer industry. Second, it explicates three growth periods of IT consulting and relates them to technological progress in the computer industry. Third, it addresses the development of the outsourcing industry as many of the firms that became involved in outsourcing early on were different from those providing IT consulting services.

6.2.1 The Emergence of IT Consulting

IT consulting and business process outsourcing emerged as part of the 'third wave' of the development of the consulting industry (Kipping 2002). More specifically, IT consulting can be traced back to the introduction of commercially usable computers in the period following World War II. From the beginning of the 1950s, companies began to explore the benefits of using computer technology in their operations (Attewell 1992; Campbell-Kelly and Aspray 2004). In this context, three groups of companies, namely technology companies, accounting and auditing firms, and management consulting companies, began to introduce IT consulting services to the market.

The first group comprises both hardware and software manufacturers (e.g. IBM, CSC, Hewlett-Packard), which provided technical assistance as an add-on to the hardware they offered in order to facilitate the implementation and application of the new technology to customers' organizations. A main technological breakthrough during this period of time was the introduction of the mainframe computer in 1956. IBM dominated the market for IT products during the 1950s and 1960s, as reflected in the expression 'IBM and the seven dwarfs' (Burroughs, Univac, NCR, Control Data, Honeywell, General Electric, and RCA) (Greenwald and van Voorst 1983). The services that these companies provided comprised not only systems engineering and systems implementation, but also personnel education and on-the-job training in using computer technology. In a similar way to software, the advisory services were mostly provided free of charge to clients who invested heavily in information technology (Grad 2002; Pugh 2002; Campbell-Kelly and Aspray 2004).

However, from 1956 onwards, IBM was barred by antitrust regulation from providing IT-related consulting services (see McKenna 2006: 20–23). This decision by the US Department of Justice was accepted by IBM's president at the time, Thomas Watson Jr, in order to settle a longstanding antitrust suit (Watson and Petre 1990; Heller 1994). As the nature of the case was a bilateral one, it did not extend to other IT companies, so they were able to continue in their provision of IT-related consulting services. However, the virtual removal of IBM from the IT consulting market enabled a second group of companies, namely the established auditing and accounting firms such as Arthur Andersen and Price Waterhouse, to push into this emerging market (see McDougald and Greenwood, Chapter 5, this volume). These firms recognized that the rapid development of the computer industry engendered a market opportunity for additional IT-related consulting services. As one of their first services in this field, they began to conduct feasibility studies. In 1953–1954, Arthur Andersen's Joe Glickauf, as a project leader, did a feasibility study for General Electric (GE) with his team. GE sought advice on the feasibility of automating payroll processing and manufacturing at GE's Appliance Park facility near Louisville, Kentucky (Spacek 1989; Moore and Crampton 2000–1; Squires et al. 2003). Arthur Andersen recommended the installation of a Remington Rand UNIVAC I computer and a printer, which marked the start of commercial computers and commercial data processing in the United States (Gray 2001). This project for GE also constituted the first IT consulting engagement of Arthur Andersen (Hawkins and Cohen 2006).

As a third group, existing management consulting firms (e.g. PA Consulting, Urwick, Orr & Partners, and Arthur D. Little) recognized the rising importance of IT consulting and the necessity to acquire specific expertise in this field. They, too, became involved in feasibility studies and data processing in the late 1950s (Ferguson 2002). At the beginning, these assignments related to the application of computer technology and were mostly carried out as part of their general management consulting work. However, by the 1960s, companies such as PA Consulting had already set up dedicated units (e.g. PA's Electronic Data Processing (EDP) division) that specialized in IT in response to the rapid growth in demand for IT consulting services. Urwick developed proficiency in analysing processes within clients' organizations and evaluating the potential for improving these through the use of computer technology (Ferguson 2002). In the 1960s, Arthur D. Little worked in co-operation with IBM, and on behalf of American Airlines, to help develop SABRE, a computerized airline ticket reservation system, and thus became involved in IT consulting (Kahn 1986; Magee 2002).

Despite the involvement of the last group, the first two groups—and in particular the auditing and accounting service providers such as Arthur Andersen—took the lead in IT consulting in the 1950s and early 1960s (McKenna 2006; McDougald and Greenwood, Chapter 5, this volume). In 1958, the total number of computers in the world was below 4,000. Their high procurement costs implied that these mainframe computers were mainly concentrated in public organizations, such as universities and government bureaucracies, and in large firms with strong public sector links, such as aerospace companies (CSC 2008). IBM captured nearly 80 per cent of the computer market and provided many clients with 'implicit' IT-related advisory services, without, however, being allowed to charge for them. The introduction of the minicomputer in the early 1960s reduced the complexity of large-scale mainframes and decreased purchasing costs, thus making computer technologies attractive to a broader range of companies.

The existing general management consulting companies could not develop the specific expertise required by the use of IT within such a short period of time, particularly in a situation where hardware products and software applications were far less standardized than they are today. In order to overcome this challenge, some of the established broad-based consulting firms developed associations with specialist firms, thus combining consulting techniques with IT-related knowledge (Ferguson 2002). The early providers of IT consulting services from all three groups began to provide these services as part of a differentiation strategy to their existing business models. They realized the economic potential inherent in the technological innovations and the need to establish proficiency in their application swiftly.

6.2.2 Three Phases of Market Growth

For much of its history, the growth in the market for IT consulting services has been closely associated with technological innovations in the IT industry and the development of corporate spending on IT. Since its emergence, the IT industry can be characterized by three periods of growth and innovation. The *first phase* of innovation and growth, described above, started in the 1950s and lasted throughout the 1960s. The *second growth period* can be identified with the introduction of the microprocessor and the personal computer from the early 1970s to 1985 (Farhoomand 2005). In 1971, Intel introduced the first microprocessor to the market and commercialized the first silicon computer-on-a-chip. This development marked a new era of computer technology as it allowed manufacturers to produce smaller units of hardware at more affordable prices. This invention paved the way for the personal computer, first introduced by IBM in 1981 (Langlois and Robertson 1995). The market introduction of the personal computer accelerated the adoption of computing by individuals, departments, and small businesses (Farhoomand 2005).

In conjunction with this trend towards smaller, more individualized applications in the 1970s, companies began to change their ways of using computing technology. At the beginning of the 1970s, computers were still mainly used to optimize routine office and business support processes including clerical tasks, data storage, and statistical processes. Increasingly, managers began to use IT to help align internal processes with their organizations' business objectives. The growing use of programming functions for conducting 'what if' scenarios in strategic decision-making points to this alignment of IT and strategy (Jones 1995). These new client demands favoured IT consulting services from management consultants with a background in strategy. Furthermore, IT became recognized as a facilitator of change, especially in terms of integrating existing business operations (Tisdall 1982). New software applications designed especially for business customers, including early integrated financial accounting systems, and, later on, customer relationship management (CRM), supply management solutions, and others were introduced by firms such as SAP (founded in 1972) and Oracle (founded in 1977). IT consultants became more strongly involved in their clients' operations and served as change managers in a large number of companies. Formerly specialized IT consultancies diversified their offerings and developed management consulting approaches. For example, Diebold repositioned itself from its former focus on IT, and began to offer management and technology consulting services in the 1980s (Diebold 1996).

In order to keep pace with the emerging information technologies and to exploit the resulting business opportunities, demand from businesses for IT-related services increased rapidly in the 1970s. This development brought about an equally rapid growth of the IT consulting market. Traditional management consultancies expanded their business models by providing IT consulting services. Others expanded their offerings to include more standardized services; for example, Diebold established early versions of standardized benchmarking procedures to analyse companies' existing IT structures and identify optimization potentials (Diebold 1996). In addition, new technology-based consultancies successfully entered the market (Ferguson 2002). In order to secure their share of this segment of the consulting market, the established computer manufacturers and software service providers began to review their earlier policies of providing IT-related advice free of charge as an add-on service to hardware and software sales. Many believe that IBM's decision in 1969 to unbundle software and services from hardware sales was a pivotal moment in the growth of the business software and IT consulting market (Grad 2002). Although IBM remained barred from setting up a separate IT consulting unit until 1991 (McKenna 2006), many other established manufacturers and software companies had expanded the range of services offered in IT consulting by the mid-1970s and early 1980s (Campbell-Kelly 2003).

The introduction of network computing in the 1990s led to the *third growth and innovation phase*, which lasted until the early years of the new millennium. The early 1990s saw the launch of the first computer networks in a business environment outside of academia and the military. These computer networks were used to connect a limited, defined group of business partners (business-to-business or B2B) as well as businesses and customers (B2C) with one another and facilitated so-called e-solutions (Ferguson 2002). The spread of the Internet from 1994 onwards (Kahn and Cerf 1999), in contrast, provided opportunities for ubiquitous linkages among unlimited numbers of participants of any kind, and fundamentally transformed the nature of commercial transactions. For example, the Internet facilitated the emergence of the concept of on-demand business, where businesses are able to identify customers' needs on a real-time basis and to adjust their services to these (Farhoomand 2005). In addition, it facilitated to a greater extent than had been possible before interactions among parties, including service providers, from remote locations (see Hagel and Armstrong 1997).

The development of e-business engendered the emergence of a host of 'dot.com consultancies' that provided their clients with advice on how to exploit the new business opportunities. Of particular importance among them were the so-called 'Fast Five', which included iXL, MarchFirst, Razorfish, Scient, and Viant, which were founded from the mid-1990s onwards. However, all five of them were short-lived. Their remains were often snapped up by larger IT and media companies. For example, Razorfish (set up in 1995) acquired some of the assets of MarchFirst—a company only founded in 2000 through the merger of systems integrator Whittman-Hart and USWeb/CKS—when MarchFirst filed for bankruptcy in 2001. Razorfish was eventually acquired by SBI Group, as was Scient, which had previously integrated iXL. SBI Group merged all the various assets it had acquired into a unit called Avenue_A/Razorfish, which it sold to aQuantive in 2004. This company, in turn, was acquired by Microsoft in 2007 and sold on to Publicis Groupe in 2009.

The *third phase of the growth* of the IT market differed from the two earlier ones in that it was not primarily driven by the development of new hardware technologies, but rather by new applications and services, including IT consulting services. IT consulting and outsourcing services became increasingly standardized during this period (Farhoomand 2005), leading to rapid commoditization, strong pressure on unit prices, and hence increased affordability. These developments strengthened the competitive positions of newer players with service offerings that were similar to, but cheaper than, those of the established large players. Companies that had been founded earlier but that had hitherto concentrated largely on their domestic or regional markets, now began to offer their services on a global basis. Most prominent among them are Tata Consultancy Services (founded in 1968 as a division of the Tata Group), WIPRO Technologies (founded in 1980), Infosys (founded in 1981), and Satyam (founded in 1987; now part of the Mahindra Group) (see Capur 2006), which are listed in Table 6.1. These new players achieved significant price advantages by leveraging a relatively cheap labour force in the emerging economies, most notably India (Farhoomand 2005).

In recent years, IT services firms (including IT outsourcing providers) have developed in China and other countries, and are expected to make a big impact on the global IT services market over the next ten years (Carmel, Gao, and Zhang 2008). While some have argued that the Chinese market for IT-related services is still fairly fragmented and held back by structural factors such as weak institutions and language barriers (de Filippo, Hou, and Ip 2005; Benni and Peng 2008), others predict that it will rapidly become the largest IT services market in the world (Chan 2005).

6.2.3 The Emergence of Outsourcing

In conjunction with the development of the IT industry, outsourcing emerged as a new IT-related service industry. Outsourcing is a broad concept that refers to the decision by an organization to procure support functions otherwise provided in-house from external parties. These functions may be in areas as diverse as human resources, facilities management, or environmental regulations (Gupta and Gupta 1992). The primary focus here is on information systems outsourcing, which includes the following external services: 'applications development and maintenance, systems operation, network/telecommunications management, end-user computing support, systems planning and

Table 6.1 New players in the IT consulting and outsourcing market

Tata Consultancy Services	WIPRO Technologies	Infosys
■ Founded 1968 in Mumbai, India	■ Founded 1980 in Bengaluru, India	■ Founded 1981 in Pune, India
■ TCS is part of one of India's largest and oldest conglomerates, the Tata Group	■ Leading provider of integrated business, technology, and process solutions on a global delivery platform	■ Multinational information technology services company
■ Considered a pioneer in the Indian IT industry	■ The largest independent R&D services provider in the world	■ Over 63 offices and development centres in the world
■ Asia's largest provider of information technology and business process outsourcing services	■ Among the top 3 offshore BPO service providers in the world	■ Forbes rated Infosys among the 5 best performing companies in the global software and services sector
■ Specialized in IT services, business solutions, and outsourcing	■ No. 2 Indian domestic IT services provider	■ Ranked among the BusinessWeek IT100 companies (2009)
■ Revenues of $6.3bn (fiscal year 2009/10)	■ Revenues of around $5.9bn (fiscal year 2009/10)	■ Revenues of $4.8bn (fiscal year 2009/10)
■ More than 160,000 employees (2010)	■ Over 108,000 employees (2010)	■ More than 114,000 employees (2010)

management, and purchase of application software, but excludes business consulting services, after-sale vendor services, and the lease of telephone lines' (Cheon, Grover, and Teng 1995: 209). Nevertheless, the terminology used in information systems outsourcing is far from clear, with different authors including different aspects in the definition of outsourcing (de Looff 1995).

Outsourcing dates back to the use of mainframe computers from the late 1950s onwards. The high purchasing costs of this equipment made time-sharing—enabling several organizations to process data on the same mainframe computer within a certain time window—economically advantageous. This new concept, first discussed by Bemer (1957), provided a larger number of users with the opportunity to benefit from the advantages of computer technology without making heavy investments. Among the first time-sharing projects were the Compatible Timesharing System (CTSS) and project MAC (short for 'Multiple Access Computers'), both developed at MIT in the early 1960s, which led to the Multics (Multiplexed Information and Computing Service) system in 1965, which was used until 2000 (for a history of the Multics system and its origins, see http://www.multicians.org/ and http://www.multicians.org/history. html; accessed 1 October 2011). Time-sharing can be considered as an early form of IT outsourcing.

As with IT consulting services, established hardware manufacturers took the lead; for example, IBM with its Service Bureau and GE's GEISCO subsidiary (GE's computer business was acquired by Honeywell in 1970). In addition, new players specializing in the provision of data processing services on single mainframes successfully entered the market. Electronic Data Systems (EDS), founded in 1963, is considered one of the first professional specialized IT outsourcing providers (Weinert and Meyer 2005). Another player, Tymshare, was set up in 1966. Computer Software Systems (CSS), which was established in 1966 to provide technical consulting to clients and was renamed 'National CSS' in 1970, bought an IBM mainframe computer in 1968 in order to offer time-sharing to its clients (Feinleib 2005). Throughout the 1970s, the service of time-sharing continued to expand, especially for small and medium-sized client businesses. In the early 1970s, Computer Sciences Corporation (CSC) developed a time-sharing network in association with the US Department of Defense. The so-called '100,000 mile network' allowed hundreds of clients at different locations to run their data procedures on the same mainframe computer unit (CSC 2008). At the time, IT was not considered a strategic differentiator. Consequently, client companies relied heavily on the few large outsourcing providers such as IBM, EDS, National CSS, and CSC.

With the more widespread use of smaller IT products at lower unit costs during the 1970s, companies began to increasingly rely on software, and standard software packages were launched in the market. These standardized products, however, required customization in order to meet the customers' specific demands (Campbell-Kelly 2003). Due to labour market shortages for software programmers, companies began to sign contracts with outsourcing providers who were able to programme, customize, monitor, and run software products (Clott 2004). In the 1980s, managers considered IT more and more as a commodity, which led to rapid growth of the outsourcing industry. Companies preferred to purchase IT and IT-related activities from the market rather than providing them expensively in-house (Weinert and Meyer 2005).

Eastman Kodak's widely publicized decision to outsource the majority of its IT operations to IBM in 1989 is considered to be the starting point of the rapid growth of the outsourcing market during the 1990s (Lacity and Hirschheim 1993a, 1993b). Kodak's trust in IBM's ability to provide most of its IT operations, referred to as 'total solutions outsourcing' (see Lee et al. 2003), paved the way for other large companies to outsource their IT needs. This growth in the IT outsourcing market has continued unabated until today (see the contributions in Carmel and Tjia 2005). In the literature, there is a longstanding and inconclusive debate on whether the diffusion of outsourcing is driven primarily by internal factors (e.g. companies imitating Kodak's deal with IBM), or by external influences amongst different user organizations (Loh and Venkatraman 1992b; see also Clark, Zmud, and McGray 1995). Hu, Saunders, and Gebelt (1997) find that mixed influences are likely to account for the diffusion of information systems outsourcing. Despite the problems that may be associated with outsourcing—client satisfaction rates with outsourcing deals are reported to be low (Gorla and Lau 2010)—IT outsourcing enjoys continued popularity.

The outsourcing market is presently less fragmented than the IT consulting market (and, in particular, the general management consulting market); it is characterized by the presence of both large onshore (US and European-based) outsourcing companies such as IBM, CapGemini, Accenture, and EDS (recently acquired by Hewlett-Packard), and offshore outsourcers such as Tata and WIPRO. Some of these companies have integrated established management consulting firms, or units thereof. This is, for example, the case of Cap Gemini Sogeti, the predecessor organization of CapGemini, which formed Gemini Consulting in 1991 through the integration of two existing management consulting firms: United Research and The MAC Group (Moingeon et al. 2005). However, none of these firms have their primary roots in management consulting. Rather, they usually emerged from hardware producers (for example, IBM, Hewlett-Packard), accounting, and auditing firms, or were new foundations (Tata, WIPRO).

6.3 BUSINESS MODELS OF ITCO COMPANIES

The historical overview provided above has shown that the development of IT consulting and outsourcing has been influenced to a greater extent by technology providers and accounting and auditing firms than by companies active in general management consulting. This development has resulted in a situation where IT consulting and outsourcing and general management consulting can be identified as two distinct segments of the larger consulting market. Today, the majority of firms can be allocated relatively clearly to one or the other of these two groups, as cluster analytical approaches attest (Galal and Richter 2007). Recent years have even witnessed the organizational separation of firms that, for several years, attempted to operate in both segments at the same time. For example, through a management buy-out, A. T. Kearney was taken out of the fold of EDS in 2006.

In order to understand whether companies active in the 'e-space'—to which ITCO firms clearly belong—constitute a distinct form of economic value creation, Amit and Zott (2001) use the notion of the 'business model', which defines the content, structure, and governance of a firm's activities (see also Morris, Schindehutte, and Allen 2005; Zott and Amit 2010). Their discussion of the business model in e-business draws on several strands of the established strategy and organization literature, in that a business model describes the resources a company employs, the value chain—through which these resources are transformed into marketable products or services—and the relationships that govern the transactions taking place along the value chain. In the following, the chapter reviews the existing literature in order to identify the main features of the business model of IT consulting and outsourcing firms.

First, there is the nature of IT consulting and outsourcing services and of the processes involved in their provision. A central variable for the identification of the type of service provided by a consulting firm relates to the extent to which the service is 'standardized' or, to use Maister's (1993) terminology, 'procedural' in nature. With respect to the services typically provided by ITCO firms, there is some disagreement in the literature on whether these services can adequately be described as 'standardized' or not. One group of authors argues that the overall objectives of ITCO projects are usually well defined early on, and that the main steps leading to the achievement of these objectives can generally be defined before or in the beginning stages of the delivery of these projects. For example, Hansen, Nohria, and Tierney (1999) found that consultants in IT-related services are given step-by-step instructions on how to carry out different kinds of assignments. A set of analytical tools and detailed guidelines define the production process (Hansen, Nohria, and Tierney 1999). These factors reduce the influence of the individual consultant on the results of a project and limit the variability of the process. Similarly, Kipping (2002), using Maister's (1993) terminology, describes IT consultancy as procedural in nature. Kipping and Kirkpatrick (2008) speak of a new Taylorism in the delivery of IT-related consulting processes. In his empirical study, Graubner (2006) finds that the representatives of the ITCO firms he interviewed described their services as relatively 'productized', implying either the offering of predefined service 'packages' or 'modules' from which the client could choose, or a clear association between the consulting projects and other services or products bought from the consulting firm or a third party.

With respect to outsourcing services in particular, the literature suggests that these are provided on a multi-year basis through longstanding partnerships between service provider and client (Riemensperger 2004). Outsourcing contracts usually contain detailed service level agreements (SLAs) pertaining to the time at which the services are to be available, the volume of service capacities to be made available by the providing party, expected response time, escalation mechanisms, and so on. In the governance literature, such contractual provisions are seen as risk-reducing devices. There is an extensive literature on the optimal design of such contracts, which has largely been published in IT/information systems-related journals (e.g. *MIS Quarterly, Information Systems Management*). Overall, this literature relies on the intertwined notions that service levels between exchange partners can be specified *ex ante* and evaluated *ex post* (e.g. Singleton, McLean, and Altman 1988). However, others contend that these contracts cannot mitigate the risks in client–vendor relations completely (Bahli and Rivard 2003, 2005; Natovich 2003). Goo, Kishore, and Rao (2009) argue that the use of detailed SLAs complement, rather than substitute for, the use of relational governance mechanisms (such as trust) in IT outsourcing contracts.

Another group of authors, however, has pointed out that there are limits to the explicability and therefore to the standardization of IT-related services. These authors tend to emphasize that IT consulting services, like other services, are social processes involving human interaction. For example, Werr and Stjernberg (2003) find that IT consultancies often provide guidelines for practice, but characterize them as loose. They argue that there is a complementary relationship between tacit and explicit knowledge (Werr and Stjernberg 2003: 882). Similarly, in Alvesson's analysis of a computer consultancy case, interpersonal processes are portrayed as more important for the success (or failure) of a project than technical factors (Alvesson 1993a, 1993b; see also Fincham et al. 2008). According to Robertson, Scarborough, and Swan (2003), in IT development the time spent on communicating the solution can easily exceed the time spent on programming and installing it.

The debate in the literature with respect to the degree of standardization of consulting services can be resolved in part by taking into account the complex nature of such services. IT-related services are usually offered in bundles (Engwall and Eriksson 2005) and IT consulting projects may last for several years. Riemensperger (2004) and Graubner (2006) find them to be significantly longer than GMC projects. They also tend to involve large teams of consultants (Lindvall and Pahlberg 1999). The complex nature of large-scale IT consulting projects is further heightened by the fact that IT-related services often involve the entire organizational system of clients. Therefore, they require co-ordination across multiple functions and hierarchical levels. As Bloomfield and Danieli (1995) have pointed out, socio-political skills and symbolic resources are an inherent part of the construction of IT systems. Therefore, despite a relatively high degree of predictability and standardization in individual project steps or phases, the resulting entire service bundles may involve a large number of interdependencies and expose the service process to internal and external contingencies (see also the case studies in Devos, van Landeghem, and Deschoolmeester 2008). In order to manage this complexity, a set of norms guiding the behaviour of the parties involved is of critical importance (Kern and Blois 2002). The high failure rate of IT consulting projects provides an indicator of this complexity. Freedman's (2005) findings show that 31 per cent of all IT consulting projects are cancelled before project completion. Fincham and colleagues (2008) identify the size of a project and the need to change the consultants involved between different project phases as challenges to the success of such projects. With respect to information systems outsourcing, Sullivan and Ngwenyama (2005) provide an analysis of the risks involved in such projects.

In summary, the business model of ITCO firms is characterized by the provision of large-scale, complex projects. Despite their relatively high degree of standardization, the services provided by ITCO firms rely on processes of interpersonal communication and social interaction. Therefore, client–vendor relationships require well-designed governance mechanisms in order to be effective (Ali and Green 2009).

The differences in the nature of the services sketched out above have implications for the type of resources used by ITCO as opposed to GMC firms. First, ITCO firms are bigger and have significantly greater capital needs and larger office infrastructures than GMC firms (Richter and Schröder 2006, 2008). Moreover, although both ITCO and GMC firms are clearly knowledge-intensive firms, they source different types of knowledge and capabilities from the external labour market. As Richter, Dickman, and Graubner (2008) show, ITCO firms seek to hire recruits with strong commercial and/or technological skills. Often, they specify programming languages or software applications in which they expect applicants to be proficient. They also use a relatively large proportion of independent contractors (Bidwell and Briscoe 2009), attesting to the idea that at least part of the activities involved in the provision of IT-related services are contractually specifiable with some degree of precision. In contrast, GMC firms prefer to hire consultants with broad general skills, ideally combined with an MBA or some other postgraduate qualification in management or related disciplines (Adams and Zanzi 2001; Richter and Schmidt 2008). Other indications for the differences in the type of knowledge resources that the firms in the two segments require can be gleaned from the types of external partners with whom they predominantly co-operate: technical universities versus business schools; hardware, software, and information services providers (with whom ITCO firms often have strong, formal, and long-term relationships) versus market research firms (with which GMC firms usually maintain weaker ties; see Newell 2004).

In his survey of 32 ITCO and 36 GMC firms, Nissen (2007) finds that both groups of firms pursue the same, broadly defined objectives in their knowledge-management (KM) efforts. However, ITCO firms make much greater use of IT-based systems such as groupware, document-sharing systems, and databases containing information on employee know-how, whereas GMC firms rely to a greater extent on catalogue-type information systems containing lists of and access to particular materials such as prior project reports, general frameworks, and market analysis reports. However, Kirk and Vasconcelos (2003) find evidence of convergence between general management consultancies and technology consultancies from a knowledge-management perspective.

Overall, the extant literature portrays ITCO firms as relatively sophisticated in terms of the way in which they manage their central sources of value creation, namely their human and knowledge resources. For example, as and Hansen, Nohria, and Tierney (1999) and Kipping and Amorim (2003) point out, IT consulting firms tend to employ relatively elaborate human resource management systems. In doing so, IT consulting firms bundle individually held resources and turn them into appropriable, organizationally controlled resources or 'structural capital' (McKinlay 2005). Standardization processes abstract knowledge from its context and reduce it to a generalized form that can be easily transferred to other projects. In its application in a specific situation, this knowledge is then again re-localized and adapted to the specific business needs at hand (Hsiao 2008). For this purpose, IT consultancies have invested heavily in codification and 'data ware-housing' and have a well-developed knowledge-management approach (Roslender and Fincham 2003; McKinlay 2005).

Finally, ITCO and GMC firms differ in their approaches to selling and distributing their services in the market. The functional capabilities offered by the services of ITCO firms translate into distinct contractual characteristics (Behrens 2007) and pricing models. Implementation support constitutes a central aspect of their value proposition, as enhanced functional capabilities typically only become visible when the systems or processes to which these functional capabilities pertain are up and running (Armbrüster and Kipping 2003, Liao and Cheung 2003). In fact, large parts of the services provided by ITCO firms do not call for their implementation *post hoc*: they are part of the implementation of strategic or other plans devised by the ITCO firm, its client, or third parties *ex ante*. ITCO firms show a higher propensity for accepting payment by results than is the case among GMC firms. ITCO firms have, more readily than GMC firms, used fixed prices for projects or project modules, indicating their belief that, with proper specification of project outcomes and milestones, they are able to estimate the time at which such results are achieved and the resources needed to do so with some precision (Carr 2003).

The sketch of the business model of ITCO firms as compared to the one of GMC firms has provided a stylized image of these two groups of firms. ITCO firms are not all alike; there is significant variance among them in terms of their strategic orientation, organizational structures and processes, and the specific services they include in their portfolios. However, complementarities among the multiple variables discussed above imply that companies cannot easily adopt 'mix and match' strategies in choosing the configuration of their business models (Roberts 2004). The pressures of a competitive market environment requires both ITCO and GMC firms to adopt service model characteristics that mutually reinforce one another by helping to leverage each other's benefits. To provide just one example, the procedural nature of much of ITCO firms' services and the resulting division of labour allows them to exploit the economies of scale resulting from relatively large upfront investments, which in turn call for longer-term contracts with customers (Clark, Zmud, and McGray 1995; Bahli and Rivard 2003). Such reinforcement effects lead to the recurring 'bundling' of characteristics, which result in the persistent grouping of firms (Armbrüster and Kipping 2003) that share these characteristics, even if there is competition between different groups of firms at the margin (Crossmann and Lee-Kelley 2004).

6.4 Directions for Future Research

This chapter has sketched the development of the IT consulting and outsourcing market. The historical overview was followed by a discussion of the business model (Amit and Zott 2001) of IT consulting and outsourcing firms, focusing in particular on the nature of the services provided by these firms, the resources involved in this provision, and their relationships with clients. The review has shown that the market for IT consulting and outsourcing services, and the business models of the companies active therein, provide a rich ground for investigating strategic and organizational issues. However, important questions in this area have not been sufficiently addressed. There are two interrelated topics that offer particularly fruitful areas for future research.

First, the literature on client–vendor relationships in IT consulting and outsourcing has tended to emphasize transaction-cost economic considerations (Grover, Cheon, and Teng 1996; Wang 2002; Aubert, Rivard, and Patry 2004). Transaction-cost economic factors such as asset specificity and contractual uncertainty are clearly important in clients' decisions to buy IT-related services from external providers. However, the hoped-for benefits of such decisions relate, to a large extent, to savings in production costs (Loh and Venkatraman 1992a, 1992b; Ang and Straub 1998; Currie and Willcocks 1998); in particular when they involve the offshoring of services (Carmel and Tjia 2005). Furthermore, the significant risks involved in IT consulting and outsourcing go beyond transactional difficulties between the parties concerned; they involve, among others, technological and economic factors (Currie 1998; Currie and Willcocks 1998; Barthélemy 2001; Gupta et al. 2007; Gefen, Wyss, and Lichtenstein 2008). The extant literature has yet to provide a generally accepted, integrative framework for evaluating clients' decisions to procure IT consulting and outsourcing services from outside providers. Such a framework would have to differentiate between partial or selective outsourcing and total outsourcing (Barthélemy and Geyer 2004), as the former is found to have higher success rates than the latter (Lacity and Willcocks 1998).

Second, and related to the above, further research is needed regarding the structures governing the relationship between clients and vendors that are best suited to mitigate the risks involved in IT consulting and outsourcing, and to maximize success. Goo, Kishore, and Rao (2009) have argued that in these relationships formal, contractual mechanisms and relational mechanisms complement one another. The latter involve mutual continuity expectations, solidarity and the preparedness for flexible adaptation (Kim and Chung 2003), a high level of co-ordination (Sabherwal 2003), and other mechanisms that enhance partnership quality (Klepper 1995; Lee and Kim 1999; Goo et al. 2009). However, there are a wide variety of IT consulting and outsourcing services, and the field is subject to rapid evolution. It is unlikely that a single governance structure is equally useful for all types of IT consulting and outsourcing relationships. To give one example, client–vendor relationships in cloud computing involve an even greater need for predefining expected service levels and for standardization than is the case in IT consulting projects. It is also well known that the management of IT consulting and outsourcing projects require distinct competencies (Shi, Kunnathur, and Ragu-Nathan 2005) both on the client's and on the vendor's side (Karlsen and Gottschalk 2006). However, the exact nature of these competencies is likely to vary from project to project. The extant literature on governance relationships in IT consulting and outsourcing has not sufficiently taken into account the multifaceted nature of the services provided in this area. Both academic research and managerial practice would greatly benefit from a sound understanding of the optimal matching between governance structure, competency requirements, and IT consulting and outsourcing service types.

In addition to the two topic areas outlined above, there are further research needs, for example, with respect to the role of the IT consulting and outsourcing services sector in local and regional development. As sections 2 and 3 of this chapter have indicated, this sector has become a major source of employment for large numbers of people in India, and other countries (e.g., Russia, China) are also developing significant ITCO sectors. However, little research has investigated the socio-economic opportunities (and potential problems) that this development engenders. Moreover, while it is clear that information technology plays an important role in the growth of developing countries (see the contributions and the foreword by Walsham, Robey, and Sahay (2007) in the special issue of *MIS Quarterly*), there does not seem to be any research on the specific importance of IT consulting and outsourcing services in this context. Further research on these issues is urgently needed.

References

Adams, S. M. and Zanzi, A. (2001). 'Are We Producing Information Age Consultants? Reflections on U.S. Business Schools' Course Offerings'. In A. Buono (ed.), *Research in Management Consulting: Current Trends in Management Consulting*, vol. 1. Greenwich, CT: Information Age Publishing, 189–206.

Ali, S. and Green, P. (2009). 'Effective Information Technology (IT) Governance Mechanisms: An IT Outsourcing Perspective'. *Information Systems Frontiers (ISF), Special Issues in Governance, Risk and Compliance: Applications in Information Systems.* Available at http://dx.doi.org/10.1007/s10796-009-9183-y accessed 1 October 2011.

Alvesson, M. (1993a). 'Organizations as Rhetoric: Knowledge-Intensive Firms and the Struggle with Ambiguity'. *Journal of Management Studies*, 30/6, 997–1015.

Alvesson, M. (1993b). *Management of Knowledge-Intensive Companies*. New York: De Gruyter.

Amit, R. and Zott, C. (2001). 'Value Creation in e-Business'. *Strategic Management Journal*, 22, 493–520.

Ang, S. and Straub, D. W. (1998). 'Production and Transaction Economies and IS Outsourcing: A Study of the U.S. Banking Industry'. *MIS Quarterly*, 22/4, 535–552.

Armbrüster, T. and Kipping, M. (2001). 'Strategic Change in Top Management Consulting: Market Evolution and Current Challenges in a Knowledge-Based Perspective'. Academy of Management Annual Meeting, Washington, DC, August. *Academy of Management Best Paper Proceedings 2001*, Management Consulting Division, A1–A6.

Armbrüster, T. and Kipping, M. (2003). 'Strategy Consulting at the Crossroads'. *International Studies of Management & Organization*, 32/4 (winter), 19–42.

Attewell, P. (1992). 'Technology Diffusion and Organizational Learning: The Case of Business Computing'. *Organization Science*, 3/1, 1–19.

Aubert, B. A., Rivard, S., and Patry, M. (2004). 'A Transaction Cost Model of IT Outsourcing'. *Information and Management*, 41, 921–932.

Bahli, B. and Rivard, S. (2003). 'The Information Technology Outsourcing Risk: A Transaction Cost and Agency Theory-Based Perspective'. *Journal of Information Technology*, 18/3, 211–221.

Bahli, B. and Rivard, S. (2005). 'Validating Measures of Information Technology Outsourcing Risk Factors'. *Omega*, 33/2, 175–187.

Barthélemy, J. (2001). 'The Hidden Costs of IT Outsourcing'. *MIT Sloan Management Review*, 42/3, 60–69.

Barthélemy, J. and Geyer, D. (2004). 'The Determinants of Total IT Outsourcing: An Empirical Investigation of French and German Firms'. *Journal of Computer Information Systems*, 44/3, 91–97.

Behrens, S. (2007). 'Information Systems Outsourcing: Five Essays on Governance and Success'. Ph.D. dissertation, European Business School, Wiesbaden.

Bemer, R. W. (1957). 'How to Consider a Computer'. *Automatic Control Magazine*, 3 (March), 66–69.

Benni, E. and Peng, A. (2008). 'China's Opportunity in Offshore Services'. *McKinsey Quarterly*, 3 (May), 1–2.

Bidwell, M. and Briscoe, F. (2009). 'Who Contracts? Determinants of the Decision to Work as an Independent Contractor Among Information Technology Workers'. *Academy of Management Journal*, 52/6, 1148–1168.

Bloomfield, B. P. and Danieli, A. (1995). 'The Role of Management Consultants in the Development of Information Technology: The Indissoluble Nature of Socio-Political and Technical Skills'. *Journal of Management Studies*, 32/1, 23–46.

Campbell-Kelly, M. (2003). *From Airline Reservations to Sonic the Hedgehog: A History of the Software Industry*. Cambridge, MA: MIT Press.

Campbell-Kelly, M. and Aspray, W. (2004). *Computer: A History of the Information Machine*. 2nd edn. Boulder, CO: Westview Press.

Capur, A. (2006). *Infosys Consulting in 2006: Leading the Next Generation of Business and Information Technology Consulting*. Stanford, CA: Stanford Graduate School of Business, case no. SM-151, 16 May.

Carmel, E. and Tjia, P. (2005). *Offshoring Information Technology: Sourcing and Outsourcing to a Global Workforce*. Cambridge: Cambridge University Press.

Carmel, E., Gao, G., and Zhang, N. (2008). 'The Maturing Chinese Offshore IT Services Industry: It Takes 10 Years to Sharpen a Sword'. *MIS Quarterly Executive*, 7/4, 157–170.

Carr, N. G. (2003). 'IT doesn't Matter'. *Harvard Business Review*, 81/5 (May), 41–49.

Chan, S. S. (2005). *IT Outsourcing in China: How China's Five Emerging Drivers are Changing the Technology Landscape and IT Industry*. China: The Outsourcing Institute. Available at http://www.outsourcing.com/china_trends/index.html accessed 1 October 2011.

Cheon, M. J., Grover, V., and Teng, J. T. C. (1995). 'Theoretical Perspectives on the Outsourcing of Information Systems'. *Journal of Information Technology*, 10, 209–219.

Clark, T., Zmud, R., and McGray, G. (1995). 'The Outsourcing of Information Services: Transforming the Nature of Business in the Information Industry'. *Journal of Information Technology*, 10, 221–237.

Clott, C. (2004). 'Perspectives on Global Outsourcing and the Changing Nature of Work'. *Business and Society Review*, 109/2, 153–170.

Computer Sciences Corporation (CSC) (2008). *The CSC Story*. Falls Church, VA: CSC.

Crossmann, A. and Lee-Kelley, L. (2004). 'Trust, Commitment, and Team Working: The Paradox of Virtual Organizations'. *Global Networks*, 4/4, 375–390.

Currie, W. L. (1998). 'Using Multiple Suppliers to Mitigate the Risk of IT Outsourcing at ICI and Wessex Water'. *Journal of Information Technology*, 13, 169–180.

Currie, W. L. and Willcocks, L. P. (1998). 'Analysing Four Types of IT Sourcing Decisions in the Context of Scale, Client/Supplier Interdependency and Risk Mitigation'. *Information Systems Journal*, 8/2, 119–143.

De Filippo, G., Hou, J., and Ip, C. (2005). 'Can China Compete in IT Services?' *McKinsey Quarterly*, 1, 10–11.

De Looff, A. L. (1995). 'Information Systems Outsourcing Decision-Making: A Framework, Organizational Theories and Case Studies'. *Journal of Information Technology*, 10/4, 281–297.

Devos, J., van Landeghem, H., and Deschoolmeester, D. (2008). 'Outsourced Information Systems Failures in SMEs: A Multiple Case Study'. *The Electronic Journal of Information Systems Evaluation*, 11/2, 73–82.

Diebold (1996). 'Am Puls des Marktes'. *Diebold Management Report*, 2, 6–7.

Engwall, L. and Eriksson, C. B. (2005). 'Doing Deals Despite Distrust'. In S. Furusten and A. Werr (eds), *Dealing With Confidence: The Construction of Need and Trust in Management Advisory Services*. Copenhagen: Copenhagen Business School Press, 149–168.

Eurostat (2008). *Eurostat Regional Yearbook 2008*. Luxembourg: Office for Official Publications of the European Communities.

Farhoomand, A. (2005). *IBM's On Demand Business Strategy*. Hong Kong: Asia Case Research Centre, University of Hong Kong,

Feinleib, H. (2005). *A Technical History of National CSS*. Mountain View, CA: Computer History Museum.

Ferguson, M. (2002). *The Rise of Management Consulting in Britain*. Aldershot: Ashgate.

Fincham, R., Clark, T., Handley, K., and Sturdy, A. (2008). 'Knowledge Narratives and Heterogenity in Management Consultancy and Business Services'. In D. Muzio, S. Ackroyd, and J-F. Chanlat (eds), *Redirections in the Study of Expert Labour*. London: Palgrave Macmillan, 183–203.

Freedman, R. (2005). 'More on Standards-Based IT Consulting'. *Consulting to Management*, 16/2, 43–46.

Galal, K. and Richter, A. (2007). 'Positioning of Consulting Firms: A Segmentation Study of the German Market for Management Consulting Services'. In F. Poulfelt and K. Hoeg (eds), *Client–Consultant Cooperation: Coping with Complexity and Change*. Proceedings of the 3rd International Conference on Management Consulting of the Management Consulting Division of the Academy of Management. Copenhagen Business School, Copenhagen, 39.

Gefen, D., Wyss, S., and Lichtenstein, Y. (2008). 'Business Familiarity as Risk Mitigation in Software Development Outsourcing Contracts'. *MIS Quarterly*, 32/3, 531–551.

Goo, J., Kishore, R., and Rao, H. R. (2009). 'The Role of Service Level Agreements in Relational Management of Information Technology Outsourcing: An Empirical Study'. *MIS Quarterly*, 33/1, 119–145.

Gorla, N. and Lau, M. B. (2010). 'Will Negative Experiences Impact Future IT Outsourcing?' *Journal of Computer Information Systems*, 50/3, 91–101.

Grad, B. (2002). 'A Personal Recollection: IBM's Unbundling of Software and Services'. *IEEE Annals of the History of Computing*, 24/1, 64–71.

Graubner, M. (2006). 'Task, Firm Size, and Organizational Structure in Management Consulting: An Empirical Analysis from a Contingency Perspective'. Ph.D. thesis, European Business School, Wiesbaden.

Gray, G. (2001). 'UNIVAC I: The First Mass-Produced Computer'. *Unisys History Newsletter*, 5/1. Available at http://www.cc.gatech.edu/~randy/folklore/ accessed 1 October 2011.

Greenwald, J. and van Voorst, B. (1983). 'The Colossus that Works'. *Time Magazine*, 122/2 (11 July). Available at http://www.time.com/time/magazine/article/0,9171,949693-5,00.html accessed 1 October 2011.

Grover, V., Cheon, M. J., and Teng, J. T. C. (1996). 'The Effect of Service Quality and Partnership on the Outsourcing of Information Systems Functions'. *Journal of Management Information Systems*, 12/4, 89–116.

Gupta, U. G. and Gupta, A. (1992). 'Outsourcing the IS Function: Is it Necessary for Your Organization?' *Information Systems Management*, 9/3, 44–50.

Gupta, A., Carroll, J., Gatti, P., and Greiner, E. (2007). 'The Perceived Risks of IT Outsourcing: An Exploratory Comparison of Large MNC and SME's'. *Oxford Journal*, 6/1, 60–68.

Hagel III, J. and Armstrong, A. (1997). *Net Gain: Expanding Markets Through Virtual Communities*. Boston: Harvard Business School Press.

Hansen, M. T., Nohria, N., and Tierney, T. (1999). 'What's Your Strategy for Managing Knowledge?' *Harvard Business Review*, 77/2 (March/April), 106–116.

Hawkins, D. F. and Cohen, J. (2006). *Arthur Andersen LLP*. Boston: Harvard Business School Press, case no. 9-103-061.

Heller, R. (1994). *The Fate of IBM*. London: Little Brown.

Hsiao, R-L. (2008). 'Knowledge Sharing in a Global Professional Service Firm'. *MIS Quarterly Executive*, 7/3, 123–137.

Hu, Q., Saunders, C., and Gebelt, M. (1997). 'Research Report: Diffusion of Information Systems Outsourcing: A Reevaluation of Influence Sources'. *Information Systems Research*, 8, 288–301.

Jones, E. (1995). *True and Fair: A History of Price Waterhouse*. London: Hamish Hamilton.

Kahn, E. J. (1986). *The Problem Solvers: A History of Arthur D. Little, Inc*. Boston: Little Brown.

Kahn, R. and Cerf, V. (1999). 'What is the Internet (and What Makes it Work)'. Internet Policy Institute, Aspen. Available at http://www.policyscience.net/cerf.pdf accessed 1 October 2011.

Karlsen, J. P. and Gottschalk, P. (2006). 'Project Manager Roles in IT Outsourcing'. *Engineering Management Journal*, 18/1, 3–9.

Kern, T. and Blois, K. J. (2002). 'Norm Development in Outsourcing Relationships'. *Journal of Information Technology*, 17/1, 33–42.

Kim, S. and Chung, Y-S. (2003). 'Critical Success Factors for IS Outsourcing Implementation from an Interorganizational Relationship Perspective'. *Journal of Computer Information Systems*, 43/4, 81–90.

Kipping, M. (2002). 'Trapped in Their Wave: The Evolution of Management Consultancies'. In T. Clark and R. Fincham (eds), *Critical Consulting: New Perspectives on the Management Advice Industry*. Oxford: Blackwell, 28–49.

Kipping, M. and Amorim, C. (2003). 'Consultancies as Management Schools'. In R. P. Amdam, R. Kvalshaugan, and E. Larsen (eds), *Inside the Business Schools*. Oslo: Abstrakt, 133–154.

Kipping, M. and Kirkpatrick, I. (2008). 'From Taylorism as Product to Taylorism as Process: Knowledge-Intensive Firms in a Historical Perspective'. In D. Muzio, S. Ackroyd, and J-F. Chanlat (eds), *Redirections in the Study of Expert Labour*. London: Palgrave Macmillan, 163–182.

Kirk, J. and Vasconcelos, A. (2003). 'Management Consultancies and Technology Consultancies in a Converging Market: A Knowledge Management Perspective'. *Electronic Journal of Knowledge Management*, 1/1, 33–46.

Klepper, R. (1995). 'The Management of Partnering Development in I/S Outsourcing'. *Journal of Information Technology*, 10, 249–258.

Knights, D. and Murray, F. (1994). *Managers Divided*. Chichester: John Wiley & Sons.

Lacity, M. and Hirschheim, R. (1993a). 'The Information Systems Outsourcing Bandwagon'. *Sloan Management Review*, 3/1, 73–86.

Lacity, M. and Hirschheim, R. (1993b). *Information Systems Outsourcing: Myths, Metaphors and Realities*. Chichester: John Wiley & Sons.

Lacity, M. and Willcocks, L. P. (1998). 'An Empirical Investigation of Information Technology Sourcing Practices: Lessons from Experience'. *MIS Quarterly*, 22/3, 363–408.

Langlois, R. and Robertson, P. (1995). *Firms, Markets, and Economic Change: A Dynamic Theory of Business Institutions*. London: Routledge.

Lee, J-N. and Kim, Y-G. (1999). 'Effect of Partnership Quality on IS Outsourcing Success: Conceptual Framework and Empirical Validation'. *Journal of Management Information Systems*, 15/4, 29–61.

Lee, J-N., Huynh, M. Q., Kwok, R. C-W., and Pi, S-M. (2003). 'IT Outsourcing Evolution: Past, Present, and Future'. *Communications of the ACM*, 46/5, 84–89.

Liao, Z. and Cheung, M. T. (2003). 'Concurrent-Convergent Strategy in IT Consulting'. *Communications of the ACM*, 46/3 (September), 103–104.

Lindvall, J. and Pahlberg, C. (1999). 'SAP/R3 as a Carrier of Management Knowledge'. Paper presented at the SCANCOR workshop 'Carriers of Management Knowledge', Stanford University, 16–17 September.

Loh, L. and Venkatraman, N. (1992a). 'Determinants of Information Technology Outsourcing: A Cross-Sectional Analysis'. *Journal of Management Information Systems*, 9/1, 7–24.

Loh, L. and Venkatraman, N. (1992b). 'Diffusion of Information Technology Outsourcing: Influence Sources and the Kodak Effect'. *Information Systems Research*, 3, 334–358.

Magee, J. (2002). 'Operations Research at Arthur D. Little, Inc.: The Early Years'. *Operations Research*, 50/1, 149–153.

Maister, D. H. (1993). *Managing the Professional Service Firm*. New York: Free Press.

McKenna, C. D. (2006). *The World's Newest Profession: Management Consulting in the Twentieth Century*. New York: Cambridge University Press.

McKinlay, A. (2005). 'Knowledge Management'. In S. Ackroyd, R. Batt, P. Thompson, and P. S. Tolbert (eds), *The Oxford Handbook of Work and Organization*. Oxford: Oxford University Press, 242–262.

Moingeon, B., Nanda, A., Rohrer, L., and Soenen, G. (2005). *CapGemini Ernst & Young: A Global Merger*. Boston: Harvard Business School Press, case no. 9-903-056.

Moore, M. V. and Crampton, J. (2000–1). 'Arthur Andersen, Challenging the Status Quo'. *Journal of Business Leadership*, 11, 71–89.

Morris, M., Schindehutte, M., and Allen, J. (2005). 'The Entrepreneur's Business Model: Toward a Unified Perspective'. *Journal of Business Research*, 58, 726–735.

Natovich, J. (2003). 'Vendor Related Risks in IT Development: A Chronology of an Outsourced Project Failure'. *Technology Analysis and Strategic Management*, 15/4, 409–419.

Newell, S. (2004). 'Enhancing Cross Project Learning'. *Engineering Management Journal*, 16/1, 12–20.

Nissen, V. (2007). 'Wissensmanagement in der Strategischen und IT-orientierten Unternehmensberatung'. Technische Universität Ilmenau, Working paper no. 2007–02.

Nolan, R. and Bennigson, L. (2002). 'Information Technology Consulting'. Harvard Business School, Boston, MA. Working paper no. 03-069.

Pugh, E. (2002). 'Origins of Software Bundling'. *IEEE Annals of the History of Computing*, 24/1, 57–58.

Richter, A. and Schröder, K. (2006). 'The Allocation of Ownership Rights in Management Consulting Firms'. *Journal of Problems and Perspectives in Management*, 4/1, 123–135.

Richter, A. and Schmidt, S. (2008). 'The Effectiveness of University-Level Management Consulting Courses'. *Journal of Management Education*, 32/1, 84–99.

Richter, A. and Schröder, K. (2008). 'Determinants and Performance Effects of the Allocation of Ownership Rights in Consulting Firms'. *Journal of Organizational Behavior*, 29/6, 1049–1074.

Richter, A., Dickmann, M., and Graubner, M. (2008). 'Patterns of Human Resource Management in Consulting Firms'. *Personnel Review*, 37/2, 184–202.

Riemensperger, F. (2004). 'The Third Revolution of Business Value Creation'. In J-P. Thommen and A. Richter (eds), *Management Consulting Today: Strategies for a Challenging Environment*. Wiesbaden: Gabler, 83–97.

Roberts, J. (2004). *The Modern Firm: Organizational Design for Performance and Growth*. New York: Oxford University Press.

Robertson, M., Scarbrough, H., and Swan, J. (2003). 'Knowledge Creation in Professional Service Firms: Institutional Effects'. *Organization Studies*, 24/6, 831–857.

Roslender, R. and Fincham, R. (2003). *The Management of Intellectual Capital and Its Implications for Business Reporting*. Edinburgh: ICAS.

Sabherwal, R. (2003). 'The Evolution of Coordination in Outsourced Software Development Projects: A Comparison of Client and Vendor Perspectives'. *Information and Organization*, 13, 153–202.

Shi, Z., Kunnathur, A. S., and Ragu-Nathan, T. S. (2005). 'IS Outsourcing Management Competence Dimensions: Instrument Development and Relationship Exploration'. *Information and Management*, 42, 901–919.

Singleton, J., McLean, E. R., and Altman, E. N. (1988). 'Measuring Information Systems Performance: Experience with the Management by Results System at Security Pacific Bank'. *MIS Quarterly*, 12/2, 325–337.

Spacek, L. (1989). *The Growth of Arthur Andersen & Co. 1928–1973: An Oral History*. New York: Garland.

Squires, S. E., Smith, C. J., McDougall, L., and Yeack, W. L. (2003). *Inside Arthur Andersen: Shifting Values, Unexpected Consequences*. Upper Saddle River, NJ: Pearson Education.

Sullivan, W. E. and Ngwenyama, O. K. (2005). 'How are Public Sector Organizations Managing IS Outsourcing Risks? An Analysis of Outsourcing Guidelines from Three Jurisdictions'. *Journal of Computer Information Systems*, 45/3, 73–87.

Tisdall, P. (1982). *Agents of Change: The Development and Practice of Management Consultancy*. London: Heinemann.

Walsham, G., Robey, D., and Sahay, S. (2007). 'Foreword: Special Issue on Information Systems in Developing Countries'. *MIS Quarterly*, 31/2, 317–326.

Wang, E. T. G. (2002). 'Transaction Attributes and Software Outsourcing Success: An Empirical Investigation of Transaction Cost Theory'. *Information Systems Journal*, 12, 153–181.

Watson Jr, T. J. and Petre, P. (1990). *Father, Son & Co.: My Life at IBM and Beyond*. New York: Bentham Books.

Weinert, S. and Meyer, K. (2005). 'The Evolution of IT Outsourcing: From its Origins to Current and Future Trends'. University of Wuppertal, Working paper no. 202.

Werr, A. and Stjernberg, T. (2003). 'Exploring Management Consulting Firms as Knowledge Systems'. *Organization Studies*, 24, 881–908.

Wilson, M. and Howcroft, D. (2005). 'Power, Politics and Persuasion in IS Evaluation: A Focus on Relevant Social Groups'. *Journal of Strategic Information Systems*, 14, 17–43.

Zott, C. and Amit, R. (2010). 'Business Model Design: An Activity System Perspective'. *Long Range Planning*, 43, 216–226.

PART 2

DISCIPLINARY AND
THEORETICAL
PERSPECTIVES

CHAPTER 7

··

SOCIOLOGICAL PERSPECTIVES ON MANAGEMENT CONSULTING

··

MICHAEL FAUST

7.1 INTRODUCTION

··

THE purpose of this chapter is to present and discuss the main sociological perspectives on management consulting. The chapter is structured according to two main, broadly defined sociological approaches, which rest upon distinguishable theoretical assumptions and to a considerable degree also imply a specific focus regarding subjects studied and methodologies employed: (i) institutional and cognitive-cultural; and (ii) relational and structural. The first of these addresses most of the issues that relate to what Fincham (1999) has called the 'strategic perspective': the 'symbolic nature' of consultant strategies and consultancy as a 'powerful system of persuasion' (see especially Clark 1995; Clark and Salaman 1996, 1998). Although sociological neo-institutionalism is a key reference in this section, other theoretical perspectives are also relevant here, for example, what Sturdy (2004) termed the 'psychodynamic' and the 'dramaturgical view'. It also integrates the so-called translation perspective from actor-network theory into more traditional diffusion studies (Czarniawska and Sevon 1996). The second approach, referred to as the 'structural' perspective by Fincham (1999), is somewhat akin to embeddedness theory (Armbrüster 2006: 14–18). In addition, power and/or micro-political views from organization studies are of importance, some of which explicitly link back to symbolic resources of power, but in a more relational and structural way and thus more situated and contextualized (Sturdy et al. 2009). Whereas the 'strategic perspective' emphasized the uncertainty of managers who are in need of reassurance, and are vulnerable and insecure (Sturdy 1997), in contrast, the 'structural perspective' clarifies that 'consultants are under similar, if not greater pressures than clients to resolve uncertainty and secure a sense of control over market (including client) environments and personal careers/identities' (Sturdy 1997: 405). As agents of managerial tasks consultants inherit managerial uncertainty 'in heightened form' (Fincham 2003: 68) and are faced with a 'tenuous legitimacy' (ibid.: 67; see also Salaman 2002). The recognition of consultancy uncertainty directs attention to relational and structural perspectives and has spurred research on the client–consultancy relationship (Fincham 1999; Armbrüster 2006: 86–100; Sturdy et al. 2009).

Following this basic distinction, the chapter consists of two main sections. Section 7.2 draws on the accounts of management consultancy in the creation and diffusion (or diffusion-as-translation) of management concepts and ideas, and deals with the question of how the credibility of management consultancy has been explained in institutional and cognitive-cultural perspectives. Section 7.3 explores the specifics of market relations and structures in management consultancy informed by social network theory, and explores network theoretical explanations of 'prominence', 'reputation', and 'social capital', and their potential to correct or complement institutional and cognitive-cultural accounts of 'credibility'. Both sections discuss not only the virtues of these main approaches but also the potential drawbacks, suggesting ways to better integrate them or at least compensate for mutual blind spots in each perspective. These issues will be addressed again in the concluding section.

7.2 Institutional and Cognitive-Cultural Approaches

The 'strategic perspective' in the field of management consulting research, building on 'how a non-codified body of knowledge like "consultancy" could become so apparently influential' (Fincham 1999: 335), emphasizes the uncertainty of managers. This refers both to personal (individual career and identity) and corporate (performance, managerial) control dimensions of the double-control issue of managerial work (Watson 1994). It is the resulting managers' anxiety and uneasiness that management consultants and gurus could address with their offers promising relief (or even salvation) and personal promotion (Clark 1995). In this perspective management consultancies are predominantly perceived as creators and disseminators of the cognitive-cultural material that unsettles and reassures managers (Sturdy 1997). Hence, research on the creation, dissemination, diffusion, and/or translation of management knowledge, often inspired by neo-institutionalism, paved the way to management consulting research.

7.2.1 The Diffusion and/or Translation of Management Knowledge?

Research on management consultancy started with the observation of a considerable 'expansion of management knowledge' (Sahlin-Andersson and Engwall 2002a) for which consultancies were partly responsible. The basic insight of the cognitive-cultural perspective is that the 'travel of ideas' (Czarniawska and Joerges 1996) relies on 'institutional conditions' (Strang and Meyer 1993). The very existence of a comprehensible idea (ranging from categories, world-views, and concepts to recipes, scripts, and techniques) implies theorization whereby the idea is made more abstract and universally applicable (ibid.). What is transferred 'is not practice as such but accounts of this practice' (Sahlin-Andersson and Engwall 2002a: 24).

A major development in understanding the diffusion or expansion of management knowledge is the notion of 'translation' that has frequently been taken up in research on management consulting (Czarniawska and Sevon 1996; Clark and Salaman 1998; Benders and van Veen 2001; Sahlin-Andersson and Engwall 2002a, 2002b; McKenna, Djelic, and Ainamo 2003; Giroux 2006). More or less explicitly, it has been inspired by actor-network theory (Callon 1986; Latour 1987; Legge 2002). In contrast to diffusion, the notion of translation directs attention to the role of actors—among them management consultants—in shaping and reshaping ideas while they travel. While the term diffusion evokes the notion of physical objects or particles moving through liquids or gases remaining unchanged while they flow, the term translation emphasizes changeability during travel. What travels is a textual or linguistic account of a practice, the result of 'theorizing' (Strang and Meyer 1993), which is then subject to further readings and finally recontextualization, except for cases of rejection or non-adoption. Scholars, engaged in management consulting research, valued the notion of translation because of its ability to account for the 'interpretative viability' (Benders and van Veen 2001) or the 'pragmatic ambiguity' (Giroux 2006) of ideas and concepts, allowing for more than one course of action (ibid.: 1,229). A variety of studies proved the value of this perspective by analysing the reception patterns of management concepts such as the balanced scorecard, business process re-engineering (BPR), total quality management (TQM), lean production, and shareholder value (Benders, van den Berg, and van Bijsterveld 1998; Benders and van Bijsterveld 2000; Heusinkveld and Benders 2001; Giroux 2006; Braam, Benders, and Heusinkveld 2007).

They produced a useful counterweight to diffusion studies that emphasized homogenization because they only counted adoption rates based on standardized survey methods that were not able to account for the ambiguity of the concepts, changing meanings in receiving contexts, and the role of actors in redefining these concepts for different local contexts (e.g. Benders, van den Berg, and van Bijsterveld 1998). Even what appears as almost perfect imitation needs an active apprehension of the idea and the political will and skill of some powerful actors in the 'adopting' organization (Sahlin-Andersson 1996). Thus, early neo-institutional diffusion studies have been criticized for neglecting to account for agency (Latour 1987: 266–267; DiMaggio 1988; Stinchcombe 1997). One answer to such criticism can be seen in attempts to incorporate 'carriers' of management knowledge—among them management consultancies—which in conventional diffusion studies are frequently not accounted for (Ruef 2002: 94). By contrast, the translation perspective directs attention to the role of carriers across the overall process of knowledge transformation during the travel of ideas as well as to the role of 'skilled actors' (Fligstein 2001) on the receiving side. The following subsection discusses this perspective in more detail.

7.2.2 Consultancies as 'carriers' of management knowledge

Within neo-institutionalism, several authors have characterized management consultancies as 'carriers' of management knowledge (e.g. Sahlin-Andersson and Engwall 2002a)—a term that emphasizes both the considerable autonomy of the agents and their influence. A carrier should not be regarded only as a reporter 'of what is going on in different places' but rather as 'an activating entity' or a 'reporter with influence' (Sahlin-Andersson and Engwall 2002a: 10). Similarly, according to David and Strang (2006), diffusion processes can be better understood if, besides adopters, 'opinion leaders' and 'gate keepers', such as the mass media, consulting firms, and business schools are also taken into account—similar to Abrahamson's (1996) 'fashion-setting-community'. Meyer (1996: 249) refers to management consultants as 'Others', defined as agents of a 'modern rationalistic and universalistic culture' in which 'true ideas and knowledge about organizational life' are anchored. Sahlin-Andersson and Engwall (2002a) link the term 'carrier' to the notion of 'secondary carriers' of modernization from Berger, Berger, and Kellner (1973), and their definition comes close to Meyer's agents of a modern rationalistic and universalistic culture. These carriers 'can attain considerable autonomy as agents in themselves' (Sahlin-Andersson and Engwall 2002a: 9).

'Globalization amplifies the modern explosion of organizing ideas' (Meyer 1996: 249) and '(i)deas tend to be framed in global and extended ways as a result of their having flowed extensively' (Sahlin-Andersson and Engwall 2002a: 23), which also explains that the carriers of ideas have more standing and an 'interactional advantage' vis-à-vis the carriers of action, that is, responsible actors (Meyer 1996: 248). Carriers such as management consultancies create generalized concepts of organization and management that pretend to be universally applicable across nations, sectors, and fields (Meyer 2002; Ruef 2002; Sahlin-Andersson and Engwall 2002a). Thereby, management itself becomes a 'dominant model in various contexts', for instance, in sectors that were previously ruled by a professional or bureaucratic logic (Sahlin-Andersson and Engwall 2002a: 4). More organizations are perceived as being similar and thus become receptive to similar ideas, which, in turn, enable knowledge to flow (see also Røvik 2002).

Others have also acknowledged that management consultancies as carriers do not only play an active role in coining and circulating knowledge but also in 'experimenting with management and management knowledge' in different contexts (Sahlin-Andersson and Engwall 2002b: 295). This is due to the fact that, in contrast to most other carriers, management consultancies are typically involved in the on-site translation of ideas and hence exposed to a variety of different context-specific editing rules. Therefore, among other carriers (media, business schools) consultancies 'have become a *particular* class of secondary carriers through their direct contact with practice' (emphasis added). Thereby, they 'come to orchestrate the field of management more generally' (Sahlin-Andersson and Engwall 2002a: 18). This view, again, emphasizes the autonomy and influence of this particular class of carriers.

However, neo-institutional accounts invest little effort in exploring *how* management consultancies are involved in translation and 'experimenting' in different settings, and whether and how the exposure to different 'editing rules' (Sahlin-Andersson 1996: 85–88) impacts the coining and circulation of knowledge. Rather the 'self-sustaining processes for the expansion of management knowledge' that 'are formed in the elaborated relations between consultants and their clients' (Sahlin-Andersson and Engwall 2002b: 278) are emphasized. In this view, relationships with clients are foremost an opportunity to redefine locally perceived problems in such a way that they fit with the prefabricated, packaged consultancy solutions, and to create new demand for their services by defining new problem areas, which, in turn, fosters long-lasting and repeated assignments (Ernst and Kieser 2002; Jung and Kieser, Chapter 16, this volume). In this perspective, the fact that consultant–client relations are 'embedded in networks of relationships wherein other carriers play significant roles' (Sahlin-Andersson and Engwall 2002b: 278) is seen to reinforce the self-sustaining process of supply-driven demand, as the expansion of one type of carrier fuels the expansion of others: for example, the rise of elite MBA education among managers is beneficial for consultancy assignments as social and cultural backgrounds and habitus increasingly become the same (Ruef 2002; David, Chapter 4, this volume).

Moreover, 'connectedness' to practice does not seem sufficient as a characterization of management consultancies. Their connectedness is of a specific kind as they are financially rewarded carriers that live from *business* relations with clients. In this respect they are not just disinterested *agents* of a 'modern rationalistic and universalistic culture' (Meyer 1996), but *actors* that pursue their own interests. While Sahlin-Andersson and Engwall (2002b: 294) note that 'carriers are mainly driven by interests in expanding their own activities and ensuring their own survival', the fact that management consultancies are commercially operating and motivated organizations is not examined in detail in neo-institutionalist accounts. How, one has to ask, can management consultants maintain their autonomy and 'interactional advantage' vis-à-vis responsible clients if they are dependent on (repeat) assignments and on appraisals by these clients?

7.2.3 Contestations of Expertise and Experts

Finally, research interested in the translation process of particular ideas and concepts suggests that the expertise of management consultancies and their authority as knowledge providers may be contested by other expert groups. Some studies shed light on the interplay between management consultancies and established professional dynamics. As Scarbrough (2003) has shown for knowledge management (KM), different 'intermediary groups' draw on the ambiguity of fashionable concepts to pursue competitive differentiation through the development of their own interpretations. Their 'collusive interaction' accelerated the diffusion of KM, but it also reduced 'the legitimacy of KM-inspired changes to a narrow technological domain' (ibid.: 87). By contrast, in 'quality management', the TQM-fashion, both driven and deployed by external consultants, made quality a general management issue and somehow by-passed the established professional occupations within firms as Giroux and Sergi (2008) demonstrate. They also suggest that, in other fields, management fashions (often consultancy promoted) could make established professional occupations the real victims, undermining their authority. At the same time, there are also indications that consultants may be faced with a 'host of rival experts' within and around organizations (Bloomfield and Danieli 1995; Fincham 2002: 202) to which they have to constantly stand up.

Besides rivalry between consultants and established professions, different orientations between management consultants and management gurus or between different types of consultants (Alvesson and Johansson 2002) have been considered. This corrects the often conveyed image that these carriers necessarily act as *one* homogenizing agent. For instance, Fincham (2002) pointed at different foundations of management guru and consultant expertise that is differently tested and verified in practice. These different knowledge foundations lead to different orientations with respect to both discourse participation and management interaction. For example, in the BPR discourse management gurus initially had the lead but, when more specialized consultants joined, the contours of the field changed 'from fad to technique' (Fincham 1995; Fincham and Evans 1999). Similarly, in the TQM field David and Strang (2006) observed that in the high fashion period generalist consultancies dominated the discourse, while during the decline of public attention more technically oriented specialist companies, which could comprise both functional and 'sector specialists', prevailed (see also Fincham et al. 2008).

The review of the literature so far has already put into perspective the notion of management consultancies as autonomous creators and disseminators of ideas. In contrast to other secondary carriers, they are connected with management practice and particularly involved in the translation of ideas, including the need to listen to a variety of context-specific voices. At the same time, their expertise may be contested by other expert groups in the respective field. Despite these contestations, many scholars have highlighted the capacity of management consultants to control belief systems (Fincham 1999: 335), their 'increasingly pervasive influence on the behavior of formal organizations' (Ruef 2002: 74), and the '*invincible* character of management consulting rhetorics' (Berglund and Werr 2000: 639–640, emphasis added; see also Deutschmann 1993). The reasons for their rise have been debated quite extensively in the extant literature—a debate summarized in the next subsection.

7.2.4 Neo-Institutional Explanations for the Rise of Consulting

Regarding the emergence of management consulting as an increasingly important carrier of management knowledge, Ruef (2002: 94) argues that this development formalized and ritualized inter-organizational diffusion itself and imbued it with value. As a result, 'the process of hiring *institutionally approved agents*, such as management consultants' is more important for the legitimacy of modern organizations than the content of institutionally approved structural elements, such as organizational forms or management techniques (ibid.: 94–95, emphasis added; see also Røvik 2002; Sahlin-Andersson and Engwall 2002a). According to McKenna, Djelic, and Ainamo (2003) meanwhile, the 'medium', that is, the messenger, 'is the message', which means that scholars should direct more attention to the 'form' of consulting and not so much to content or message.

Some authors go as far as to conclude that contemporary societies can be character-ized as 'consultocracies' (Saint-Martin 1999; also Kipping and Wright, Chapter 8, this volume) and that management consulting has become the hallmark of an epoch. For Thrift (2005: 35) management consultancies are a 'generator and distributor of new knowledge' and an integral part of the 'cultural circuit of capital' in contemporary capi-talism, promoting a neoliberal reform agenda (ibid.: 97). Sennett (2006: 55–56) intro-duces consultants as an excellent case for understanding how 'social distance'—one of the main distinguishing features of present-day capitalism—'operates on the ground'. For him, consultants are servants of managerial power doing 'the painful work of reor-ganizing activities throughout the peripheries of the organization' (ibid.). They are an integral part of the 'culture of a new capitalism', where corporate short-termism, with the stock price in mind, goes along with a 'superficial, quick-strike form of consulting' (ibid.: 98). Similarly, Boltanski and Chiapello (2005: 169) attribute the new 'project-oriented justificatory regime' of present-day capitalism in France mostly to consultant and man-agement guru texts of the early 1990s.

If consultants are indeed so significant, the question arises as to what the bases for their truth claims are (Salaman 2002: 251–252). Put differently, in which respect or in which meaning of the term 'institutional' can we talk of management consultancies as 'institutionally approved agents' (Ruef 2002) that supposedly enhance the legitimacy of managers and organizations they advise? In neo-institutional theory the professions are the main candidate for 'institutional agents' that 'rule by controlling belief systems' (DiMaggio and Powell 1983: 147; Scott 2001: 129). Indeed, neo-institutionalists refer to management consultancies as a new 'category of professionals that has slowly become institutionalized [...] and now exercises an increasingly pervasive influence on the behavior of formal organizations' (Ruef 2002: 74). However, the literature concurs in the conclusion that the widely perceived credibility of management consultancies does not rely on professionalization in the conventional sense of the term—while debating the reason for their failure to professionalize (for a comprehensive discussion, see Kirkpatrick, Muzio, and Ackroyd in Chapter 9, this volume).

Therefore, the question remains—How a non-codified body of knowledge like 'consul-tancy' could become so apparently influential? In answering this question much of the literature has stressed the symbolic nature of consultant strategies and consultancy as a 'powerful system of persuasion' (Fincham 1999: 335). Thereby, emphasis shifts from a col-lective (professional) achievement of credibility to individual and firm-specific efforts and achievements of a 'new would-be professional occupation' (Leicht and Lyman 2006) or 'market professionalism' (Gross and Kieser 2006) that may rest upon or result in firm-specific 'reputation' or personal charisma (see also Kipping 2011). This view is confirmed by Berglund and Werr (2000: 639–640), who state that 'the legitimization of management consulting services is to a large extent about constructing convincing narratives and giving authoritative performance'. The need for 'impression management' and convincing narratives is traced back to basic consultancy service characteristics, particularly intangibility, that makes buyers vulnerable and dependent on unguarded promises of competence, reliability, and loyalty (Clark 1993; Clark and Salaman 1998).

By stressing the 'invincible character of management consulting rhetorics' (Berglund and Werr 2000: 639–640; see also Höner 2008: 285–286) the focus of attention is shifted to immediate interaction with audiences and clients, for example, analyses of 'knowledge legitimation and audience affiliation through storytelling' (Clark and Greatbatch 2002a). In this respect considerable progress, based on methodologically sophisticated studies, has been made in the analysis of 'impression management' as a 'core feature of consultancy work' (Clark and Salaman 1998; see also Alvesson 1993; Bloomfield and Danieli 1995; Clark and Salaman 1996; Kieser 1997, 2002; Berglund and Werr 2000; Clark and Greatbatch 2002a, 2002b). Notable is Clark's (1995) utilization of the 'dramaturgical metaphor', drawing on Kenneth Burke and Erving Goffman. However, it should be noted that 'impression management' is a far more fragile foundation of authority and credibility, and is far more dependent on individual mastery, than the initial neo-institutionalist notion of 'institutionally approved agents'. Legge's (2002: 76) contribution to this debate is of particular interest here as she points at the combined effects of rhetorical mastery and network affiliation to gain credibility: business consultants as both 'rhetoricians *and* networkers'. Empirically, her study addresses networking only in terms of references to former clients ('demonstration projects') that consultants use to back a 'good story'. This links to network theoretical foundations of reputation, but lacks the relational properties of networks to which this chapter returns in the following section.

The review so far conveys the overall picture that the rise of powerful management consultancy is not backed by traditional professionalization but, at least according to some observers, can be traced back to the rise of neo-liberalism and/or a second round of globalization that cuts back state influence, delegitimizes the traditional professional model, celebrates markets and networks, gives rise to the expansion of more managerial settings, and sees the 'entrepreneurial self' as the main identity on offer (Leicht and Lyman 2006: 36–37; also Thrift 2005; Sennett 2006). For instance, Legge (2002: 76) characterizes consultants as a type of knowledge worker 'that create[s] uncertainty [. . .] as an opportunity to achieve competitive advantage via innovation', and relates their emergence to a specific formation of capitalism, 'a post-Fordist world of disorganized capitalism'. However, despite the appeal of such a combined institutional and cultural analysis, several drawbacks and limitations have to be considered.

7.2.5 Limitations of the Institutional and Cognitive-cultural Perspective

Time-specificity of the analyses. Often explicitly, and certainly implicitly, the explanations above refer to the rise of management consulting since the 1980s, the startling boom period that propelled both public and academic attention and concern towards management consulting and that coincided with the rise of neo-liberalism and globalization (Faust 2005). It is this concurrence that makes neo-institutional explanations implausible: Meyer (1996: 249) portrays management consultancies as agents of a *time-invariant* 'modern rationalistic and universalistic culture', while neo-liberalism, to which their rise is linked, is a *time-specific* selection from a broader universe of modern ideas (Campbell and Pedersen 2001). However, it is exactly this time-specificity that renders the explanation incomplete if we consider earlier historic phases of management consulting up-take (Wright and Kipping, Chapter 2, this volume), the early US experience since the 1930s (McKenna 2006; David, Chapter 4, this volume), and the earlier phases of management consulting internationalization to Europe (Kipping 1997, 1999). Resistance against and/or counter movements to neo-liberalism, the resilience or recovery of the authority of the nation-state, and, again, changing patterns of corporate governance and restructuring in the face of the global financial market crisis would at least raise questions regarding the future development of management consultancy if the formerly proposed explanation is to be defended as it so strictly couples the rise of consultancy to a specific set of ideas, that is, neo-liberalism.

Underdeveloped recognition of institutional and cultural diversity. The uneven development of management consulting emergence and expansion directs attention to explanations that consider institutional or cultural variety explicitly. Such approaches prove its relevance till this day in the differently given institutional and cultural 'receptivity' to management consulting expansion across the globe (see Kipping and Wright, Chapter 8, this volume; Faust 2002: 160–163). The emergence of management consulting and its early expansion has been, to a large degree, a US story that, for a considerable time span, had no parallel elsewhere. It can be traced back to specific institutional and cultural conditions in the US (McKenna 1995, 2006; Byrkjeflot 1998, 2002; Ruef 2002; Faust 2005; David, Chapter 4, this volume). Where these or similar conditions were absent and 'functional equivalents' were available (Faust and Schneider forthcoming) management consulting did not emerge. The increasing expansion of this US invention to Western Europe, later Asia, and the newly accessible former Soviet domain (Kostera 1995; Meaney 1995; Gilbert 1998; Kipping 1999), needs carefully drafted, time-sensitive, country-by-country case studies in order to account for the institutional and cultural conditions that helped management consulting institutionalization and internationalization to succeed to quite differing degrees. Especially, 'there is little comparative work or exploration of contexts where consultancy is not highly utilized' (Sturdy et al. 2009: 6; see for exceptions Kipping 2002b; Wright and Kwon 2006). The degree of utilization does not only differ from country to country, but also within national environments, for example, between the corporate sector and family business, which can be traced back to different foundations of managers' or managing owners' authority (Bäcker 2004; Faust 2005). This already highlights the fact that institutional variety is not only a matter of the past but remains important today (see also Kipping and Wright, Chapter 8, this volume).

Selective accounts of actors and scope of explanation. Most accounts within this perspective by and large deal with management consultancy as such, that is, without differentiation, and implicitly refer to the most visible groups: the large, internationally operating consultancies that were appraised as influential 'carriers' of management knowledge, and as creators and disseminators of authoritative knowledge at the same time. The power position of consultancies vis-à-vis (corporate) management, especially, must be assessed quite differently if we talk about smaller consultancies that are not involved in authoritative 'theorization'. They are more likely to be driven by management fashions than be their drivers, and hence are more likely to find themselves as a follower and implementer of managerial agendas than as its co-definers (see also Armbrüster 2006: 91). Apart from differences between different types of consultancies in terms of relative power position, the basic insecurity of consulting work (Sturdy 1997) results in a far more tenuous legitimacy of consultancies (Fincham 2003: 67) than the notion of 'institutionally approved agents' (Ruef 2002) suggests. According to Fincham (1999: 349) there is no fixed dependency in the consulting process, rather, the balance of power 'may be tipped one way or another by contingent factors'. Neo-institutional accounts have been criticized since they underestimate, if not ignore, the relational and interactional episodes involved in the overall process of knowledge flows and tend to overestimate the autonomy and interactional advantages of 'carriers', while the managerial counterparts are portrayed as cultural dupes, gullible victims, or even addicts of influential consultancies (Sturdy 1997; Armbrüster 2006).

Equally, the interactive nature of 'impression management' in ongoing consulting processes has largely not been addressed, and thus the contestation and negotiation of knowledge in 'front-line diffusion' (Sturdy 2002) tends to be disregarded. Scholars that emphasize translation instead of diffusion are better equipped to account for the specifics of management consultancies as carriers and the dynamics of interaction in consulting projects where the outsider or expert status of the consultant cannot just be assumed (Sturdy et al. 2009) and the 'burdens' and not only the 'benefits of otherness' come to the fore (Kipping and Armbrüster 2002). However, most empirical insights into these processes come from other perspectives that pay more attention to knowing and learning-in-organizing (Gherardi and Nicolini 2001; Araujo 2002), local sense-making, locally negotiated orders, or micro-politics (e.g. Fincham 1999, 2003; Sturdy et al. 2009, 2005). Questions of these kinds are better addressed in the relational and structural perspective to which this chapter now turns.

7.3 THE RELATIONAL AND STRUCTURAL PERSPECTIVE

At least at first sight the relational and structural perspective starts from a completely different origin. The initial question is not how a non-codified body of knowledge could become so apparently influential. It is rather the question: why do clients agree to pay in advance for services that appear as unguarded promises? How can we understand the existence of such markets or, put differently, which (sociological) market theory is adequate to understand market relationships and structures in consulting services and the obvious international expansion of these markets over time? These kinds of questions are addressed by network theories of markets, which also lead to different conceptions of credibility and reputation than those in the previous section.

7.3.1 Management Consulting as a (Relational) Market

Neo-institutional accounts of management consulting hardly ever speak of consulting *markets*. Scholars that view management consultants as carriers of management knowledge tend to oversee very basic features of markets that nevertheless apply to consulting: exchange of money for goods or services and competition between producers (service providers), which—in this case—implies competition between knowledge claims and also between a wider set of competence claims, for example, the capability to intervene appropriately in organizations. Relational perspectives on management consulting take the market features serious but distance themselves from the atomistic and undersocialized concepts of market actors and interactions of economics (Granovetter 1985; Fligstein 2001; Saam, Chapter 10, this volume). By using the 'markets-as-networks' metaphor, the relational embeddedness as well as the structural position of management consultancies come to the fore.

A number of authors characterize consulting markets as 'associative', that is, producers and buyers have to come together in order to produce the service, which is typical for project-based activities (Aspers 2006: 431). This feature accords with conventional assumptions about the constitutive criteria of services that include co-production (not only co-presence), and intangibility or incomprehensibility of the 'product' in advance (Clark 1993). Therefore, consulting as a service has been characterized as an 'experience good' (Aspers 2007), because the quality of the service and the confidentiality of the service provider can only be judged *ex post* (Clark 1993; Clark and Salaman 1998; Glückler 2004, 2006; Armbrüster 2006). Moreover, the problems evaluating consulting services are notorious. This is due to the inextricable causal texture of complex organizations preventing the identification of isolated cause-and-effect relationships such as the one between consultancy intervention and changes in performance (March and Sutton 1997; Ernst 2002). Therefore, consulting services are also 'credence goods' (Armbrüster 2006) that cannot be evaluated *ex post* whatever the 'experience' may have been. Hence, evaluation in practice often refers only to some rough measures of client satisfaction—primarily a relationship assessment (Ernst 2002).

Performance and relational risk could, in principle, be overcome or tempered if clients could rely on some kind of 'systemic trust' (Giddens 1990) or 'institutional trust' (Zucker 1986; Clark 1993: 247–249). Most scholars agree that such a trust-generating mechanism is missing, given the absence of a conventional profession (see above). As a surrogate for professional status, three mechanisms to overcome performance and relational risk and to provide competence and goodwill trust have been discussed in the literature (Glückler 2006, 2004). These mechanisms are all rooted in relational and structural network perspectives of markets: (1) personal, experience-based trust; (2) networked reputation; (3) public reputation.

Personal, experience-based trust may operate in the beginning of a business relationship as participants can rely on existing ties to trusted others from various origins. The relevance of experience-based trust that emerges from previous consulting projects is best illustrated by the significance of so-called repeat business, which also provides consultancies with the opportunity to follow their clients to foreign locations. Long-term perspectives are underscored by the fact that consultancies engage in early project development activities together with clients (Heusinkveld and Benders 2005a, 2005b), and by the evidence of 'long-term partnership contracts' (Werr and Styhre 2003) with more emphasis on implementation responsibilities. Moreover, consultants and managers often keep in touch in informal ways while having no contractual relationship (Faust 2002: 156; Sturdy et al. 2005). This underlines the fact that consulting relationships often connect people rather than firms and that senior consultants and senior managers are more continuously involved in 'largely hidden promotion, sharing, and constructions of ideas or perspectives' (Sturdy et al. 2009: 177) than formal assignments can tell (see also Armbrüster 2006: 110–11; Mohe 2008). Maintaining close extra-project ties with high-level members of the client organization over time may imply more personal intimacy and commitment than if contact is simply project-related (Kitay and Wright 2003). However, experience-based trust 'evolves only slowly and its maintenance demands commitment and energy' (Armbrüster 2006: 77). Therefore, it limits the expansion of consulting firms as well as the access of client firms to new, potentially better suited service providers, and thus may result in a problematic 'over-embeddedness'.

The second mechanism is '*networked reputation*' (Glückler and Armbrüster 2003); it is based on word-of-mouth recommendations through the wider network of the market participants and is a powerful means to overcome the restrictions of experience-based trust. Podolny (2006: 577) calls this second mechanism 'focused reputation', which implies an understanding of networks as 'pipes' for the flow of information about actors. Focused reputation is a reputation *for* some kind of behaviour related to the prior experience of trusted others. Its relevance was demonstrated in a variety of studies, often with a focus on internationalization processes (Clark 1993; O'Farrell, Wood, and Zheng 1996; Kipping 1999; Glückler and Armbrüster 2003; Glückler 2004, 2006; Kandrova 2006; Kandrova and Helfen 2006; Birkner, Faust, and Mohe forthcoming; Sanderson and Faust forthcoming).

'*Public reputation*', the third mechanism, in contrast, does not rely on the 'pipes' of the network, but 'has a general, anonymous source and circulates freely in the management arena' (Armbrüster 2006: 76), often disseminated by the media as individual firms' brand images (Kipping 2011). Armbrüster (2006: 76) defines it as a 'perception of a consulting firm's past performance'. However, (public) reputation can also be defined with less emphasis on behaviours or perceptions of their effects. Podolny (2006: 575) contrasts 'focused reputation' with a 'diffuse concept of reputation' reflecting 'past affiliations' rather than past behaviour (ibid.: 577), which links reputation to concepts of social capital (see also Legge 2002). Frequently used synonymous terms for diffuse reputation include 'status', 'prestige', 'identity', or 'legitimacy'. In the diffuse concept of reputation networks act as 'prisms'. 'To whom an actor is (and is not) tied is the critical determinant of other's expectations of that actor' (Podolny 2006: 577). The relevance of accounts of past performance and/or affiliations and the resulting brand images have also been acknowledged by authors cited in the previous section (Ruef 2002; McKenna 2006). The notion of reputation as developed here gives these accounts of credibility an additional network theoretical underpinning.

The emphasis on the relational and structural properties of networks involving both consultancies and clients, puts 'impression management' and symbolic virtuosity (Jackall 1988: 137) into perspective and has led some to question its validity. Thus, for Armbrüster (2006: 95), an argument suggesting that 'consulting growth hinges on client-satisfaction, and assuming that this can be manipulated by information asymmetries and impression management seems to be based on a shaky premise: that clients are naïve, quality-imperceptive victims in the management arena'. In this vein, the relational perspective can also be read as a caution against exaggerated accounts of consultancy power vis-à-vis management (Sturdy 1997; Armbrüster 2006; Sturdy et al. 2009). Even in the case of high-status consulting there are always several promising alternatives on the supplier side, and most large corporations have ongoing relations with more than one senior consultant from different consultancies. While the consulting firm may not necessarily rely on repeat business, their senior managers definitely do so in order to be promoted (Armbrüster 2006).

Additionally, sociological market theory can contribute to analyses of the structure and dynamics of the management consulting industry. Associative markets are likely to be 'status markets' (Aspers 2006, 2005). In status markets differentiation follows stratification according to the status of participants. Here, the hierarchical status order on both sides of the market is the defining social construction, not the socially defined quality standards of the good that is exchanged (Aspers 2007: 434). Hence, if sellers and buyers of high status meet, the traded 'product' becomes valuable. This is reflected in the extraordinarily high fees in the upper stratum of the consulting market and the efforts of high-status consultancies to defend these fees in all instances because they symbolize their position in the social structure (Armbrüster 2006). Consultancies mainly compare themselves to competitors in the same stratum and to potential challengers that try to climb up the ladder of the stratified market. During the 1990s this insight was used to analyse competitive struggles between the incumbent strategy-and-organization consultants and their challengers from IT consulting (Armbrüster 2006; see Galal, Richter, and Wendlandt, Chapter 6, this volume). In consulting markets, status is both attributed to organizations (e.g. the large multinational corporations compared to local family business) and to positions within firms. The first tier of the consulting market comprises those consultancies that have access to the boards of the large corporations whose members represent an important component of the societal elite as well.

Challengers, most prominently IT consultants during the 1990s, may try to rise to the upper tier of the market by defining their specialty as an urgent boardroom topic (Armbrüster and Kipping 2002; Armbrüster 2006) and thus getting access to CEOs. However, in status markets the established status order often proves quite stable, despite attempts to redefine strategic competencies (Aspers 2007). It has been argued that strategy consultancies were more successful in enlarging their competencies than IT consultants were in getting access to the boardroom and lifting their fees to the highs of the incumbent firms (Armbrüster 2006: 136–137). Whether or not (former) IT consultancies are or will be on equal footing with the established strategy-and-organization consultancies or will even get ahead of them, has been assessed differently in the literature (ibid.; Kipping 2002a; Galal, Richter, and Wendlandt, Chapter 6, this volume). The theoretical point here is the question of whether the redefinition of the strategic importance of knowledge claims may supersede or redefine a given status order. Such status-based models of markets have so far hardly been used in management consulting research. However, the basic idea that consultants and gurus use their (proclaimed) affiliation with high-status clients to make their ideas more convincing is a well-reported measure of impression management (see, e.g., Clark and Greatbatch 2002a; Legge 2002).

7.3.2 Social Capital and Elite Formation

Network theory also provides an alternative account and explanation for the existence and reputation of management consulting—a topic already prominent in the institutional perspective. To put it bluntly, the 'institutionally approved agent' from neo-institutionalist accounts (Ruef 2002) is replaced by a network-structure-approved agent.

In general terms, according to Burt (2002: 149) focused reputation (as 'models of contagion') and diffuse reputation (as 'models of prominence') can be subsumed under a broad metaphorical notion of social capital: any 'advantages that individuals or groups have because of their location in the social structure'. 'Brokerage' bridging 'structural holes' in networks is the case in point. It 'creates advantages by increasing the value for cooperation' and it is similar to the role of 'opinion leaders' in early diffusion literature as the agents 'responsible for the spread of new ideas and behaviors' (ibid.: 155). Individuals and groups that span structural holes 'can expect to find themselves synthesizing new understandings as they seem to others to be gifted with creativity' (ibid.: 158). This results in 'control benefits of bridging structural holes' (emphasis added) that can be regarded as entrepreneurial opportunities, in the literal sense of entrepreneurship, which rests upon the ability to bring together separate pieces (ibid.).

The term 'network entrepreneur' takes up the notion of the 'ostensibly entrepreneurial character' of management consultancy (Ruef 2002: 75) from the previous section, but gives it a different theoretical foundation. Consultants 'are considered in the context of technology transfer and bridges of innovation between formerly unconnected actors or firms' (Armbrüster 2006: 30), resulting in a source of power for the network connector vis-à-vis the unconnected or less connected corporate client (ibid.: 89). Implicitly this is consonant with literatures that highlight the virtue of externality, the 'benefits of otherness' (Kipping and Armbrüster 2002), and the broader knowledge base of consultancies that results from being exposed to a variety of realities (Armbrüster 2006: 105), which may help to overcome business myopia on the client side.

The (implicit) assumption in this argument—that the corporate client is less connected than the consultancy—has been questioned (Faust and Schneider forthcoming). Despite the fact that there is no sound empirical evidence of the overall connectedness of, for instance, large, globally acting consultancies as compared to global corporations, the issue that counts is whether the individual consultant or project team is, as consultancies claim, actually able to mobilize the scattered knowledge throughout the organization and to bring it into use for the specific problem of the client. Research on this topic so far casts quite some doubt on this assumption (Robertson and Swan 1998; Werr 2002; Werr and Stjernberg 2003; Heusinkveld and Benders 2005a, 2005b; Armbrüster 2006: 152–177; Kordon and Faust forthcoming). Transnational corporations actually might be able to leverage their own multiple connectedness in order to gain and mobilize 'good ideas' (Burt 2002) and thereby become less dependent on external connecters or brokerage (Faust and Schneider forthcoming). This suggests that brokerage positions are a matter of perception and attribution, which is underscored by the fact that consultancies put a lot of effort into demonstrating their global connectedness (see also Faulconbridge and Jones, Chapter 11; Kipping and Wright, Chapter 8; both this volume).

The theory of structural holes could, moreover, be used in a 'social class perspective on networks of power and influence' (Powell and Smith-Doerr 1994). It 'builds on the arguments of Mills (1956) that social, political, and economic linkages among elite groups create a cohesive power elite' (ibid.: 378). Today, in many countries the highly reputed international management consultants also belong to these 'closely-tied networks of corporate leaders, key policy-making bodies, and elite social groups' (ibid.). Savage and Williams (2008) suggested that network theories of social capital could contribute to a better understanding of *new* types of elites, 'not as fixed, traditional pillars, but as a group of intermediaries whose power rests on being able to forge connections and to bridge gaps' (ibid.: 4, 16–17).

Similarly to the financial intermediaries to which these authors devote their interest, the large and internationally operating consultancies confirm the 'dynamic and "mobile" nature of present day elites' (ibid.: 3) that increasingly bridge national borders and reflect the increasingly transnational character of organizational fields (Arias and Guillén 1998). Quite a lot of case studies reconstructing the advance of mostly US-based, nowadays 'global' consulting, firms in a variety of countries suggest that their dominance in the consulting field and their overall high esteem in the eyes of economic and political elites was based on both kinds of social capital—connectedness and network prominence—that could be translated into symbolic capital (Ainamo and Tienari 2002; Henry 2002; McKenna, Djelic, and Ainamo 2003; Faulconbridge and Jones, Chapter 11, this volume).

7.3.3 The Client–Consultant Relationship in Action

Research in the relational and structural network perspective also emphasizes the relationship between consultancies and clients and their wider connections, thereby complementing insights from institutional and cognitive-cultural perspectives.

However, research in the relational perspective so far mostly deals with the question of how clients select and evaluate consultancies and how consultancies make use of 'relational marketing' activities, while the interaction process between consultants and their clients in ongoing projects is 'still poorly understood' (Engwall and Kipping 2002: 8). Sturdy and colleagues (2009), who made a major contribution to overcome these deficiencies, relate the fact that consultancy is still portrayed as a 'largely effective system of persuasion' (ibid.: 10) to the 'empirical research neglect of management consultancy in action' (ibid.: 172). This criticism also refers to the structural network perspective, where the entrepreneurial opportunities of bridging structural holes and the related 'relative cosmopolitan' character of consultancies 'who can draw on a range of, often privileged, sources, including innovative clients' (ibid.: 11), too readily translates into assumptions about their ability to generate new knowledge and transfer it effectively.

Kipping and Armbrüster (2002) have already directed attention to 'the burden of otherness' potentially resulting in resistance to the consultancy's views and proposals because they fail to communicate meaningfully with clients and to effect lasting change. This is due to the fact that the consultants' knowledge is too new and/or they and the clients lack a shared frame of reference, a common language. Based on a long-term (participant) observation of four consulting projects, Sturdy and colleagues (2009) go further and question the assumption of a fixed outsider role of consultancies. Their perspective is not relational or structural as opposed to cognitive-cultural, but an attempt to integrate the views 'on the ground' in ongoing social practice. They reject 'the still dominant latent identity of consultants as organizational, epistemic and social outsiders' (Sturdy et al. 2005: 36). In their view, '[k]nowledge is not so much outside knowledge as (other) client or shared knowledge' (Sturdy et al. 2009: 15), and rather 'co-produced than transferred like an object from expert consultant to client learner' (ibid.: 172–173). This implies that knowledge flows and learning are not one-sided but (potentially) mutual. In the ongoing interaction, on-site consultants get their knowledge claims tested, confirmed, modified, or rejected, and come across unfamiliar practices and ideas that have the potential to be repackaged for wider use (Faust 2002).

Thus, in many respects, consultants may be better seen as insiders (Sturdy et al. 2005: 37), at least from time to time and to an extent that qualifies for 'legitimate peripheral participation' (Lave and Wenger 1991), allowing for practice-based knowing or 'learning-in-organizing' (Gherardi and Nicolini 2001; see also Araujo 2002). A more intensive involvement in internal affairs may also result from the fact that consultants quite often act as allies of their specific sponsors in contested political arenas (Jackall 1988). Therefore, restrictions to learning may not follow predominantly from them being an epistemic or social outsider but from their selective access to the client organization and their involvement in political games by which other stakeholders are excluded and silenced (Sturdy et al. 2005: 37). These and other aspects of the consultant–client relationship are discussed in more detail in other chapters in this volume (Fincham, Chapter 20; Nikolova and Devinney, Chapter 19; both this volume).

7.3.4 Main Limitations of the Relational and Structural Perspective

In part, the drawbacks and limitations of studies in the structural perspective inversely result from its particular virtues. This is particularly the case where the blind spots are theoretically determined. Thus, network theory complements insights derived from institutional and cognitive-cultural accounts, for example, regarding the expansion of US management consultancies to Europe since the 1960s. This cannot be explained solely by the cultural construction of US management superiority, nor by formal institutional support (e.g. US-sponsored European recovery programmes), but only in connection with the possibility of consultancies to follow US clients to Europe and to make use of their existing wider connectedness (Kipping 1996, 1999; McKenna, Djelic, and Ainamo 2003; McKenna 2006).

The basic drawback of relational and structural accounts based on network theories can be seen in their mirror-inverted neglect of the content of consultancy interventions, and of the wider managerial and societal discourse formation processes to which management consultancies themselves contribute. Network theory has a tendency for 'morphological determinism' (Fourcade 2007). For instance, the theory of structural holes gives the notion of a 'preeminent knowledge broker' (McKenna 2006: 16) a network theoretical underpinning. But the network theoretical explanation of brokerage does not explain why structural holes exist or emerge or why management consultancies are perceived as specifically equipped to act as such a bridge. These questions cannot be answered within a network perspective alone, but need institutional and cultural explanations to account for the emergence of the new actor and its uneven expansion and institutionalization across countries (see Kipping and Wright, Chapter 8, this volume).

Similarly, there is a widely emphasized need for valuable in-depth studies of the client–consultancy relationship, anchored in an understanding and empirical recognition of the political dynamics of the client as well as the consultancy organization (Armbrüster 2006: 152–177; Sturdy et al. 2009). However, one also needs to be aware of the dangers and limitations that often go along with this kind of case study research, namely its neglect to integrate its findings into a broader picture of both discursive and institutional environments. This could partly be overcome if each case study would be more context-sensitive or if one could arrive at a broader research programme that integrates in-depth studies with an explicit comparative perspective (Sturdy et al. 2009: 172–179; see also Nikolova and Devinney, Chapter 19; Fincham, Chapter 20; both this volume).

7.4 Conclusion and Outlook

It should have become obvious that the shortcomings of each of the two perspectives— at least in their pure forms—are mirror-inverted. To put it bluntly, research in the institutional and cognitive-cultural perspective tends to disregard the relational and structural embeddedness of both main groups of actors—consultants and managers—and their impact on the autonomy of management consultancies. Inversely, research in the relational and structural perspective tends to disregard the content of management consultancy interventions and their potential impact as well as the discursive and ideational processes by which the credibility of institutional agents are constructed, which cannot be reduced to mere effects of network morphology (Fourcade 2007).

It is widely acknowledged in the field of management consulting research that these different perspectives as such have contributed substantially to our understanding of the phenomenon (Fincham 1999: 335; see also Armbrüster 2006; Sturdy et al. 2009). However, given the theoretically determined blind spots and the empirically selected main foci of each of the two perspectives several scholars have argued that they should be viewed as 'complementary' (Fincham 1999: 335; Sturdy 2004; Sturdy et al. 2009: 3–8, 23–24), a view that has been tellingly captured by Legge's (2002: 76) description of consultants as both 'rhetoricians and networkers'. This suggests that in the future the two perspectives should be brought into a more systematically organized dialogue in order to better understand management consultancies as 'ambiguity-intensive' organizations (Fincham and Clark 2002: 8) and, thereby, to overcome dichotomous—and probably misleading—images: management consultants as 'puppets brought in to legitimize managerial maneuvers, and as puppet masters who wield unaccountable power behind the scenes' (Fincham 2003: 69). Some efforts have been devoted to this task, for instance, when Armbrüster (2006) contrasts the mutual virtues and drawbacks of embeddedness theory and sociological neo-institutionalism.

It is commonly acknowledged that one of the main deficiencies in the field is the neglect of client–consultancy interaction in the empirical research (see Sturdy et al. 2009). The progress that has been made in this respect clearly shows that the basic insights from embeddedness theory have to be complemented by theories of organizations and interaction that are able to better account for both power/interest constellations and processes of knowing and learning in practice. These shifts partly reflect theoretical 'turns' in the wider field of organization studies, that is, from the 'cognitive turn' (Hirsch and Lounsbury 1997) to the 'practice turn' (e.g. Lave and Wenger 1991; Gherardi and Nicolini 2001). It is still an open question whether it is possible to transform a dialogue of perspectives into an overarching theoretical framework—that is, more than just a reference to some basic concepts from social theory—or whether we will have to live with the incommensurability problem not only with respect to economic and sociological theories but also within the field of sociology (Armbrüster 2006: 32–37; for a promising approach, see Djelic 2004; Beckert 2010). In any case, a more explicit dialogue of different theoretical perspectives would be a good start.

REFERENCES

Abrahamson, E. (1996). 'Management Fashion'. *Academy of Management Review*, 21, 254–285.

Ainamo, A. and Tienari, J. (2002). 'The Rise and Fall of a Local Version of Management Consulting in Finland'. In M. Kipping and L. Engwall (eds), *Management Consulting: Emergence and Dynamics of a Knowledge Industry*. Oxford: Oxford University Press, 70–87.

Alvesson, M. (1993). 'Organizations as Rhetoric: Knowledge Intensive Firms and the Struggle with Ambiguity'. *Journal of Management Studies*, 30/6, 997–1019.

Alvesson, M. and Johansson, A. W. (2002). 'Professionalism and Politics in Management Consultancy Work'. In T. Clark and R. Fincham, R. (eds), *Critical Consulting: New Perspectives on the Management Advice Industry*. Oxford: Blackwell, 228–245.

Araujo, L. (2002). 'Knowing and Learning as Networking'. *Management Learning*, 29/3, 317–336.

Arias, M. E. and Guillén, M. (1998). 'The Transfer of Organizational Techniques Across Borders: Combining Neo-Institutional and Comparative Perspectives'. In J-L. Alvarez (ed.), *The Diffusion and Consumption of Business Knowledge*. London: Macmillan, 110–137.

Armbrüster, T. (2006). *Economics and Sociology of Management Consulting*. Cambridge: Cambridge University Press.

Armbrüster, T. and Kipping, M. (2002). 'Strategy Consulting at the Crossroads: Technical Change and Shifting Market Conditions for Top-Level Advice'. *International Studies of Management & Organization*, 32/4, 19–42.

Aspers, P. (2005). *Markets in Fashion: A Phenomenological Approach*. London: Routledge.

Aspers, P. (2006). 'Markets, Sociology of'. In J. Beckert and M. Zafirovski (eds), *International Encyclopedia of Economic Sociology*. London: Routledge, 427–432.

Aspers, P. (2007). 'Wissen und Bewertung auf Märkten'. *Berliner Journal für Soziologie*, 17/4, 431–449.

Bäcker, E. M. (2004). 'Beratung als Legitimation und Limitation: Barrieren externer Unternehmensberatung in mittelständischen Familienunternehmen'. In R. Schützeichel and T. Brüsemeister (eds), *Die beratene Gesellschaft: Zur gesellschaftlichen Bedeutung von beratung*. Wiesbaden: VS Verlag, 79–94.

Beckert, J. (2010). 'How Do Fields Change? The Interrelation of Networks, Institutions, and Cognition in the Dynamics of Markets'. *Organization Studies*, 31/5, 605–627.

Benders, J. and van Bijsterveld, M. (2000). 'Leaning on Lean: The Reception of a Management Fashion in Germany'. *New Technology, Work and Employment*, 15/1, 50–64.

Benders, J. and van Veen, K. (2001). 'What is in a Fashion: Interpretative Viability and Management Fashions'. *Organization*, 8/1, 33–53.

Benders, J., van den Berg, R-J., and van Bijsterveld, M. (1998). 'Hitch-Hiking on a Hype: Dutch Consultants Engineering Re-Engineering'. *Journal of Organizational Change Management*, 11/3, 201–215.

Berger, P. L., Berger, B., and Kellner, H. (1973). *The Homeless Mind: Modernization and Consciousness*. New York: Vintage Books.

Berglund, J. and Werr, A. (2000). 'The Invincible Character of Management Consulting Rhetorics'. *Organization*, 7/4, 633–655.

Birkner, S., Faust, M., and Mohe, M. (forthcoming). 'International Business of Professional Service Firms in Central and Eastern Europe: Empirical Insights into Management Consulting Firms Going International'. In M. Faust, M. Mohe, and M. Moldaschl (eds), *Internationalization of Consulting—Internationalisierung von Beratung*. Munich: Hampp.

Bloomfield, B. P. and Danieli, A. (1995). 'The Role of Management Consultants in the Development of Information Technology: The Indissoluble Nature of Socio-Political and Technical Skills'. *Journal of Management Studies*, 32/1, 23–46.

Boltanski, L. and Chiapello, E. (2005). 'The New Spirit of Capitalism'. *International Journal of Politics, Culture, and Society*, 18, 161–188.

Braam, G. J. M., Benders, J., and Heusinkveld, S. (2007). 'The Balanced Scorecard in the Netherlands'. *Journal of Organizational Change Management*, 20/6, 866–879.

Burt, R. S. (2002). 'The Social Capital of Structural Holes'. In M. F. Guillén, R. Collins, P. England, and M. Meyer (eds), *The New Economic Sociology: Developments in an Emerging Field*. New York: Sage, 148–190.

Byrkjeflot, H. (1998). 'Management as a System of Knowledge and Authority'. In J.-L. Alvarez (ed.), *The Diffusion and Consumption of Business Knowledge*. London: Macmillan, 58–80.

Byrkjeflot, H. (2002). 'Management Models and Technical Education Systems: Germany and the United States 1870–1930'. In K. Sahlin-Andersson and L. Engwall (eds), *The Expansion of Management Knowledge*. Stanford, CA: Stanford University Press, 212–245.

Callon, M. (1986). 'Some Elements of a Sociology of Translation: Domestication of the Scallops and the Fisherman of St Brieuic Bay'. In J. Law (ed.), *Power, Action, and Belief: A New Sociology of Knowledge*. London: Routledge and Keagan Paul, 196–233.

Campbell, J. L. and Pedersen, O. K. (eds) (2001). *The Rise of Neoliberalism and Institutional Analysis*. Princeton, NJ: Princeton University Press.

Clark, T. (1993). 'The Market Provision of Management Services, Information Asymmetries and Service Quality—Some Market Solutions: An Empirical Example'. *British Journal of Management*, 4, 235–251.

Clark, T. (1995). *Managing Consultants: Consultancy as the Management of Impressions*. Buckingham: Open University Press.

Clark, T. and Greatbatch, D. (2002a). 'Knowledge Legitimation and Audience Affiliation Through Storytelling: The Example of Management Gurus'. In T. Clark and R. Fincham (eds), *Critical Consulting: New Perspectives on the Management Advice Industry*. Oxford: Blackwell, 152–171.

Clark, T. and Greatbatch, D. (2002b). 'Collaborative Relationships in the Creation and Fashioning of Management Ideas: Gurus, Editors, and Managers'. In M. Kipping and L. Engwall (eds), *Management Consulting: Emergence and Dynamics of a Knowledge Industry*. Oxford: Oxford University Press, 129–145.

Clark, T. and Salaman, G. (1996). 'The Management Guru as Organizational Witchdoctor'. *Organization*, 3, 85–107.

Clark, T. and Salaman, G. (1998). 'Telling Tales: Management Gurus' Narratives and the Construction of Managerial Identity'. *Journal of Management Studies*, 35/2, 137–161.

Czarniawska, B. and Joerges, B. (1996). 'Travel of Ideas'. In B. Czarniawska and G. Sevón (eds), *Translating Organizational Change*. Berlin: De Gruyter, 13–48.

Czarniawska, B. and Sevón, G. (eds) (1996). *Translating Organizational Change*. Berlin: De Gruyter.

David, R. J. and Strang, D. (2006). 'When Fashion is Fleeting: Transitory Collective Beliefs and the Dynamics of TQM Consulting'. *Academy of Management Journal*, 49/2, 215–234.

Deutschmann, C. (1993). 'Unternehmensberater: eine neue 'Reflexionselite?' In W. Müller-Jentsch (ed.), *Profitable Ethik—effiziente Kultur: Neue Sinnstiftung durch das Management?* Munich: Hampp, 57–82.

DiMaggio, P. J. (1988). 'Interest and Agency in Institutional Theory'. In L. G. Zucker (ed.), *Institutional Patterns and Organizations: Culture and Environment*. Cambridge, MA: Ballinger, 3–21.

DiMaggio, P. J. and Powell, W. W. (1983). 'The Iron Cage Revisited: Institutional Isomorphism and Collective Rationality in Organizational Fields'. *American Sociological Review*, 48, 147–160.

Djelic, M-L. (2004). 'Social Networks and Country-to-Country Transfer: Dense and Weak Ties in the Diffusion of Knowledge'. *Socio-Economic Review*, 2, 341–370.

Engwall, L. and Kipping, M. (2002). 'Introduction: Management Consulting as a Knowledge Industry'. In M. Kipping and L. Engwall (eds), *Management Consulting. Emergence and Dynamics of a Knowledge Industry*. Oxford: Oxford University Press, 1–16.

Ernst, B. (2002). *Die Evaluation von Beratungsleistungen: Prozesse der Wahrnehmung und Bewertung*. Wiesbaden: DUV.

Ernst, B. and Kieser, A. (2002). 'In Search for Explanations for the Consulting Explosion'. In K. Sahlin-Andersson and L. Engwall (eds), *The Expansion of Management Knowledge: Carriers, Ideas, and Sources*. Stanford, CA: Stanford University Press, 47–73.

Faust, M. (2002). 'Consultancies as Actors in Knowledge Arenas: Evidence from Germany'. In M. Kipping and L. Engwall (eds), *Management Consulting: Emergence and Dynamics of a Knowledge Industry*. Oxford: Oxford University Press, 146–163.

Faust, M. (2005). 'Managementberatung in der Organisationsgesellschaft'. In W. Jäger and U. Schimank (eds), *Organisationsgesellschaft: Facetten und Perspektiven*. Wiesbaden: VS Verlag, 529–588.

Faust, M. and Schneider, K. (forthcoming). 'Functional Equivalents to Management Consulting: A Case Study on a Reluctant German Corporation'. In M. Faust, M. Mohe, and M. Moldaschl (eds), *Intervention und Evaluierung: Zur Begründung und Bewertung von Beratungshandeln*. Munich: Hampp.

Fincham, R. (1995). 'Business Process Reengineering and the Commodification of Managerial Knowledge'. *Journal of Marketing Management*, 11, 707–719.

Fincham, R. (1999). 'The Consultant–Client Relationship: Critical Perspectives on the Management of Organizational Change'. *Journal of Management Studies*, 36/3, 335–351.

Fincham, R. (2002). 'Charisma Versus Technique: Differentiating the Expertise of Management Gurus and Management Consultants'. In T. Clark and R. Fincham (eds), *Critical Consulting: New Perspectives on the Management Advice Industry*. Oxford: Blackwell, 191–205.

Fincham, R. (2003). 'The Agent's Agent: Power, Knowledge, and Uncertainty in Management Consultancy'. *International Studies of Management & Organization*, 32/4, 67–86.

Fincham, R. and T. Clark (2002). 'Introduction: The Emergence of Critical Perspectives'. In T. Clark and R. Fincham (eds), *Critical Consulting: New Perspectives on the Management Advice Industry*. Oxford: Blackwell, 1–18.

Fincham, R. and Evans, M. (1999). 'The Consultants Offensive: Reengineering—From Fad to Technique'. *New Technology and Employment*, 14, 32–44.

Fincham, R., Clark, T., Handley, K., and Sturdy, A. (2008). 'Configuring Expert Knowledge: The Consultant as Sector Specialist'. *Journal of Organizational Behavior*, 29/8, 1145–1160.

Fligstein, N. (2001). *The Architecture of Markets: An Economic Sociology of Twenty-First-Century Capitalist Societies*. Princeton, NJ: Princeton University Press.

Fourcade, M. (2007). 'Theories of Markets and Theories of Society'. *American Behavioral Scientist*, 50, 1015–1034.

Gherardi, S. and Nicolini, D. (2001). 'The Sociological Foundations of Organizational Learning'. In M. Dierkes, A. Berthoin, J. Child, and I. Nonaka (eds), *Handbook of Organizational Learning and Knowledge*. Oxford: Oxford University Press, 35–60.

Giddens, A. (1990). *The Consequences of Modernity*. Stanford, CA: Stanford University Press.

Gilbert, K. (1998). '"Consultancy Fatigue": Epidemiology, Symptoms and Prevention'. *Leadership and Organization Development Journal*, 19/6, 340–346.

Giroux, H. (2006). 'It was Such a Handy Term: Management Fashions and Pragmatic Ambiguity'. *Journal of Management Studies*, 43/6, 1227–1260.

Giroux, H. and Sergi, V. (2008). 'Professionals and Management Fashion: The Case of the Quality Movement'. Paper presented at the 24th EGOS Colloquium, Amsterdam.

Glückler, J. (2004). *Reputationsnetze: Zur Internationalisierung von Unternehmensberatern. Eine Relationale Theorie*. Bielefeld: Transcript Verlag.

Glückler, J. (2006). 'A Relational Assessment of International Market Entry in Management Consulting. *Journal of Economic Geography*, 6/3, 369–393.

Glückler, J. and Armbrüster, T. (2003). 'Bridging Uncertainty in Management Consulting: The Mechanisms of Trust and Networked Reputation'. *Organization Studies*, 24/2, 269–297.

Granovetter, M. (1985). 'Economic Action and Economic Structure: The Problem of Embeddedness'. *American Journal of Sociology*, 91, 481–510.

Gross, C. and Kieser, A. (2006). 'Are Consultants Moving Towards Professionalization?' In R. Greenwood, R. Suddaby, and M. McDougald (eds), *Professional Service Firms, Research in the Sociology of Organizations, Vol. 24*. Bingley: Emerald, 69–100.

Henry, O. (2002). 'The Acquisition of Symbolic Capital by Consultants: The French Case'. In M. Kipping and L. Engwall (eds), *Management Consulting: Emergence and Dynamics of a Knowledge Industry*. Oxford: Oxford University Press, 19–35.

Heusinkveld, S. and Benders, J. (2001). 'Surges and Sediments: Shaping the Reception of Reengineering'. *Information and Management*, 38/4, 239–251.

Heusinkveld, S. and Benders, J. (2005a). 'A Dispersed Repertoire: Exploring Struggles to Knowledge Dissemination within Consultancies'. In A. F. Buono and F. Poulfelt (eds), *Challenges and Issues in Knowledge Management*. Greenwich, CT: IAP, 133–154.

Heusinkveld, S. and Benders, J. (2005b). 'Contested Commodification: Consultancies and their Struggle with New Concept Development'. *Human Relations*, 58/3, 283–310.

Hirsch, P. M. and Lounsbury, M. (1997). 'Ending the Family Quarrel: Towards a Reconciliation of "Old" and "New" Institutionalisms'. *American Behavioral Scientist*, 40/4, 406–418.

Höner, D. (2008). *Die Legitimität von Unternehmensberatung: Zur Professionalisierung und Institutionalisierung der Beratungsbranche*. Marburg: Metropolis.

Jackall, R. (1988). *Moral Mazes: The World of Corporate Managers*. Oxford: Oxford University Press.

Kandrova, D. (2006). *Internationalisierung von beratungsunternehmen: Die bedeutung sozialer netzwerkbeziehung*. Saarbrücken: VDM Verlag Dr Müller.

Kandrova, D. and Helfen, M. (2006). 'Soziale Einbettung und Internationalisierung Deutscher Beratungsunternehmen'. In M. Reihlen and A. Rohde (eds), *Internationalisierung Professioneller Dienstleistungsunternehmen*. Köln: Kölner Wissenschaftsverlag, 107–143.

Kieser, A. (1997). 'Rhetoric and Myth in Management Fashion'. *Organization*, 4, 49–74.

Kieser, A. (2002). 'Managers as Marionettes? Using Fashion Theories to Explain the Success of Consultancies'. In M. Kipping and L. Engwall (eds), *Management Consulting: Emergence and Dynamics of a Knowledge Industry*. Oxford: Oxford University Press, 167–183.

Kipping, M. (1996). 'The U.S. Influence on the Evolution of Management Consultancies in Britain, France, and Germany since 1945'. *Business and Economic History*, 25/1, 112–123.

Kipping, M. (1997). 'Consultancies, Institutions and the Diffusion of Taylorism in Britain, Germany and France, 1920s to 1950s'. *Business History*, 39/4, 67–83.

Kipping, M. (1999). 'American Management Consulting Companies in Western Europe, 1920 to 1990: Products, Reputation, and Relationships'. *Business History Review*, 73/2, 190–220.

Kipping, M. (2002a). 'Trapped in Their Wave: The Evolution of Management Consultancies'. In T. Clark and R. Fincham (eds), *Critical Consulting: New Perspectives on the Management Advice Industry*. Oxford: Blackwell, 28–49.

Kipping, M. (2002b). 'Why Management Consulting Developed So Late in Japan and Does It Matter?' (in Japanese). *Hitotsubashi Business Review*, 50/2, 6–21.

Kipping, M. (2011). 'Hollow from the Start? Image Professionalism in Management Consulting'. *Current Sociology*, 59/4, Monograph 2, forthcoming.

Kipping, M. and Armbrüster, T. (2002). 'The Burden of Otherness: Limits of Consultancy Interventions in Historical Case Studies'. In M. Kipping and L. Engwall (eds), *Management Consulting: Emergence and Dynamics of a Knowledge Industry*. Oxford: Oxford University Press, 203–221.

Kitay, J. and Wright, C. (2003). 'Expertise and Organizational Boundaries: Varying Roles of Australian Management Consultants'. *Asia Pacific Business Review*, 9/3, 21–40.

Kordon, T. and Faust, M. (forthcoming). 'Truly Global? Wie global agiert die Managementberatung?' In M. Faust, M. Mohe, and M. Moldaschl (eds), *Internationalization of Consulting: Internationalisierung von Beratung*. Munich: Hampp.

Kostera, M. (1995). 'The Modern Crusade: The Missionaries of Management Come to Eastern Europe'. *Management Learning*, 26/3, 331–352.

Latour, B. (1987). *Science in Action*. Buckingham: Open University Press.

Lave, G. and Wenger, E. (1991). *Situated Learning: Legitimate Peripheral Participation*. Cambridge: Cambridge University Press.

Legge, K. (2002). 'On Knowledge, Business Consultants and the Selling of Total Quality Management'. In T. Clark and R. Fincham (eds), *Critical Consulting: New Perspectives on the Management Advice Industry*. Oxford: Blackwell, 74–92.

Leicht, K. T. and Lyman, E. C. W. (2006). 'Markets, Institutions, and the Crisis of Professional Practice'. In R. Greenwood, R. Suddaby, and M. McDougald (eds), *Professional Service Firm's Research in the Sociology of Organizations, Vol. 24*. Bingley: Emerald, 17–44.

March, J. G. and Sutton, R. I. (1997). 'Organizational Performance as a Dependent Variable'. *Organization Science*, 8/7, 698–706.

McKenna, C. D. (1995). 'The Origins of Modern Management Consulting'. *Business and Economic History*, 24/1, 51–58.

McKenna, C. D. (2006). *The World's Newest Profession: Management Consulting in the Twentieth Century*. New York: Cambridge University Press.

McKenna, C. D., Djelic, M-L., and Ainamo, A. (2003). 'Message and Medium: The Role of Consulting Firms in Globalization and its Local Interpretation'. In M-L. Djelic and S. Quack (eds), *Globalization and Institutions: Redefining the Rules of the Economic Game*. Cheltenham: Edward Elgar, 83–107.

Meaney, C. (1995). 'Foreign Experts, Capitalists, and Competing Agendas: Privatization in Poland, the Czech Republic, and Hungary'. *Comparative Political Studies*, 28/2, 275–305.

Meyer, J. W. (1996). 'Otherhood: The Promulgation and Transmission of Ideas in the Modern Organizational Environment'. In B. Czarniawska and G. Sevón (eds), *Translating Organizational Change*. Berlin: De Gruyter, 241–252.

Meyer, J. W. (2002). 'Globalization and the Expansion and Standardization of Management'. In K. Sahlin-Andersson and L. Engwall (eds), *The Expansion of Management Knowledge: Carriers, Flows, and Sources*. Stanford, CA: Stanford University Press, 33–44.

Mohe, M. (2008). 'Bridging the Cultural Gap in Management Consulting Research'. *International Journal of Cross Cultural Management*, 8/1, 41–57.

O'Farrell, P. N., Wood, P., and Zheng, J. (1996). 'Internationalisation of Business Services: An Interregional Analysis'. *Regional Studies*, 30/2, 101–118.

Podolny, J. M. (2006). 'Reputation'. In J. Beckert and M. Zafirovski (eds), *International Encyclopedia of Economic Sociology*. London: Routledge, 573–578.

Powell, W. W. and Smith-Doerr, L. (1994). 'Networks and Economic Life'. In N. J. Smelser and R. Swedberg (eds), *The Handbook of Economic Sociology*. Princeton, NJ: Princeton University Press, 368–402.

Robertson, M. and Swan, J. (1998). 'Modes of Organizing in an Expert Consultancy: A Case Study of Knowledge, Power and Egos'. *Organization*, 5/4, 543–564.

Røvik, K. A. (2002). 'The Secrets of the Winners: Management Ideas that Flow'. In K. Sahlin-Andersson and L. Engwall (eds), *The Expansion of Management Knowledge*. Stanford, CA: Stanford University Press, 113–144.

Ruef, M. (2002). 'At the Interstices of Organizations: The Expansion of the Management Consulting Profession, 1933–1997'. In K. Sahlin-Andersson and L. Engwall (eds), *The Expansion of Management Knowledge*. Stanford, CA: Stanford University Press, 74–95.

Sahlin-Andersson, K. (1996). 'Imitating by Editing Success: The Construction of Organizational Fields'. In B. Czarniawska and G. Sevón (eds), *Translating Organizational Change*. Berlin: De Gruyter, 69–92.

Sahlin-Andersson, K. and Engwall, L. (2002a). 'Carriers, Flows, and Sources of Management Knowledge'. In K. Sahlin-Andersson and L. Engwall (eds), *The Expansion of Management Knowledge*. Stanford, CA: Stanford University Press, 3–32.

Sahlin-Andersson, K. and Engwall, L. (2002b). 'The Dynamics of Management Knowledge Expansion'. In K. Sahlin-Andersson and L. Engwall (eds), *The Expansion of Management Knowledge*. Stanford, CA: Stanford University Press, 277–296.

Saint-Martin, D. (1999). 'The New Managerialism and the Policy Influence of Consultants in Government: An Historical-Institutionalist Analysis of Britain, Canada and France'. *Governance*, 11/3, 319–356.

Salaman, G. (2002). 'Understanding Advice: Towards a Sociology of Management Consultancy'. In T. Clark and R. Fincham (ed.), *Critical Consulting: New Perspectives on the Management Advice Industry*. Oxford: Blackwell: 247–259.

Sanderson, J. and Faust, M. (forthcoming). 'Die Internationalisierung der Unternehmensberatung: Der Länderfall Rumänien'. In M. Faust, M. Mohe, and M. Moldaschl (eds), *Internationalization of Consulting: Internationalisierung von Beratung*. Munich: Hampp.

Savage, M. and Williams, K. (2008). 'Elites: Remembered in Capitalism and Forgotten by Social Scientists'. *The Sociological Review*, 58/1, 1–24.

Scarbrough, H. (2003). 'The Role of Intermediary Groups in Shaping Management Fashion: The Case of Knowledge Management'. *International Studies of Management & Organization*, 32/4, 87–103.

Scott, W. R. (2001). *Institutions and Organizations*. 2nd edn. Thousand Oaks, CA: Sage.

Sennett, R. (2006). *The Culture of the New Capitalism*. London: Yale University Press.

Stinchcombe, A. L. (1997). 'On the Virtues of the Old Institutionalism'. *Annual Review of Sociology*, 23, 1–18.

Strang, D. and Meyer, J. W. (1993). 'Institutional Conditions for Diffusion'. *Theory and Society*, 22, 487–511.

Sturdy, A. (1997). 'The Consultancy Process: An Insecure Business'. *Journal of Management Studies*, 34, 389–413.

Sturdy, A. (2002). 'Front-Line Diffusion: The Production and Negotiation of Knowledge through Training Interactions'. In K. Sahlin-Andersson and L. Engwall (eds), *The Expansion of Management Knowledge*. Stanford, CA: Stanford University Press, 130–151.

Sturdy, A. (2004). 'The Adoption of Management Ideas and Practices: Theoretical Perspectives and Possibilities'. *Management Learning*, 35/2, 155–179.

Sturdy, A., Clark, T., Fincham, R., and Handley, K. (2005). 'Both Cosmopolitans and Locals? Multiplicity, Fluidity and Exclusion in Management Consultant–Client Knowledge Relationships'. Evolution of Business Knowledge, Working paper no. 2005/2. Available at http://www.ebkresearch.org/downloads/wp0502_asturdy.pdf

Sturdy, A., Handley, K., Clark, T., and Fincham, R. (2009). *Management Consultancy: Boundaries and Knowledge in Action*. Oxford: Oxford University Press.

Thrift, N. (2005). *Knowing Capitalism*. London: Sage.

Watson, T. J. (1994). 'Management "Flavours of the Month": Their Role in Managers' Lives'. *International Journal of Human Resource Management*, 5/4, 893–909.

Werr, A. (2002). 'The Internal Creation of Consulting Knowledge: A Question of Structuring Experience'. In M. Kipping and L. Engwall (eds), *Management Consulting: Emergence and Dynamics of a Knowledge Industry*. Oxford: Oxford University Press, 91–108.

Werr, A. and Stjernberg, T. (2003). 'Exploring Management Consulting Firms as Knowledge Systems'. *Organization Studies*, 24/6, 881–908.

Werr, A. and Styhre, A. (2003). 'Management Consultants—Friend or Foe? Understanding the Ambiguous Client–Consultant Relationship'. *International Studies of Management and Organization*, 32/4, 43–66.

Wright, C. and Kwon, S-H. (2006). 'Business Crisis and Management Fashion: Korean Companies, Restructuring and Consulting Advice'. *Asia Pacific Business Review*, 12/3, 355–373.

Zucker, L. G. (1986). 'Production of Trust: Institutional Sources of Economic Structures, 1840–1920'. *Research in Organizational Behavior*, 8, 53–111.

CHAPTER 8

....

CONSULTANTS IN CONTEXT: GLOBAL DOMINANCE, SOCIETAL EFFECT, AND THE CAPITALIST SYSTEM

....

MATTHIAS KIPPING
CHRISTOPHER WRIGHT

8.1 INTRODUCTION

ONE of the major debates in the social sciences concerns the balance between forces driving global convergence of national business systems and forces that maintain the existing differences. Some authors see the world becoming 'flat' (e.g. Friedman 2006), while others suggest that the extent of 'globalization' has been greatly exaggerated, or that globalization might even reinforce national and local diversity (e.g. Guillén 2001; Ghemawat 2007). Global differences have been studied by a large number of scholars, from a wide range of perspectives, using labels such as 'national innovation systems', 'societal effect', 'culture', 'national business systems', or 'varieties of capitalism' (for a partial summary, see Redding 2005; Sorge 2005). When it comes to the role of management consultants within this context, a large part of the literature seems to have little doubt that they are agents of globalization, or, at least, 'Americanization'. At the same time, there is a surprising lack of research on the role of consultants in context, be it national or global. While there are studies examining the evolution of consultancy and its role within a given country, these analyses have remained largely descriptive and do little to identify, let alone compare, cross-national differences. The few comparative studies that do exist are usually static—taking a snapshot of different markets—and are often based on questionable data.

The purpose of this chapter is to review the extant research on consultants in global and national contexts in some detail, identify gaps within this research, and make suggestions about how they might be addressed. To structure this review, the chapter uses a framework originally proposed by Smith and Meiksins (1995), which seeks to bridge the broader literatures on convergence and divergence by setting out a model that distinguishes three different effects shaping the outcome of this dichotomy (and their dynamic interaction): a 'system effect' relating to the broad economic system of capitalism, which poses a set of issues that each society has to answer; a 'societal effect', where these answers are developed, institutionalized, and, sometimes, changed; and a global 'dominance effect', which recognizes a (shifting) hierarchy among nations, allowing some of them to influence developments in others. The following section will provide a more detailed overview of this framework and explain why it is useful in examining consultants and their broader context. The remainder of the chapter then summarizes and critically discusses this research along the three dimensions identified in the framework and identifies open questions within each of these dimensions.

8.2 FRAMEWORK

In exploring the development of management consulting in different contexts, it is important to be conscious of the extensive and polarized debate that has developed on globalization and national business systems. The extant literatures often distinguish between the broad trends of convergence of practice and systems, on the one hand, and increasing divergence between national and regional phenomena, on the other (see, for example, Guillén 2001). While different attempts have been made to bridge this convergence/divergence dichotomy (e.g. Hall and Soskice 2001; Sorge 2005), these interpretations are limited in their ability to explain the factors underlying differences and similarities between economies. One of the most useful interventions in this debate has been that of Smith and Meiksins (1995). They provide a multifaceted interpretation of the interrelationship between economic convergence and national/institutional divergence, suggesting that specific patterns of practice are shaped by what they term 'system', 'societal', and 'dominance' effects.

'System effects' refer to the broader economic mode of production, where the same system leads to common practices and relations between different actors. Thus, all capitalist economic systems will share a number of common features such as the centrality of competitive markets, the profit motive, value creation within organizational hierarchies, and the division of labour. Second, while much of world today operates within the broader dynamics of a capitalist economic system, the specific pattern of capitalist relations within societies is shaped by the historical legacies and institutional patterns of different country settings. The specificity of these institutions and their evolution '*encultures* systemic forces with unique qualities' (Smith and Meiksins 1995: 254; emphasis in original). For example, while labour-management relations are part of any capitalist system, the way they are enacted can vary significantly in terms of the legitimacy of organized labour or the degree to which the state might constrain managerial prerogative. Finally, the third dimension of the model stresses the importance of power dynamics within the global economic system and the role of dominant or hegemonic models of rationalization at particular points in time. That is, certain countries and types of practice are seen as more effective or legitimate and become identified as models to be emulated. A key example here might be the dominant model of US managerial capitalism, which has become emblematic of industrial and economic modernization.

Put succinctly, Smith and Meiksins (1995) suggest that the economic system poses the questions to which actors in a given society need to respond. Societal effects condition this response in terms of its necessary 'fit' with the existing institutional and cultural framework within that society, and dominance effects determine from which, if any, other country models might be borrowed, emulated, and adapted. While these system, societal, and dominance effects influence all societies, the degree of influence of each factor will vary between countries and over time.

While originally applied to the issue of work organization across national settings, this framework can also be also helpful in understanding the role and effect of management consultancies in the global economy. Rather than providing a simple comparative snapshot of cross-national economic development, Smith and Meiksins' (1995) model is a dynamic interpretation, which places strong emphasis on the role of history in understanding observed phenomena. In rejecting the primacy of economic *or* social contingencies, the model acknowledges *both* as important, while also emphasizing broader power differentials within the global economy. Most importantly for our purposes in this chapter, however, this framework, when applied to management consultancy, highlights a wider range of issues than has typically been considered within the consulting literature and highlights areas where research is deficient.

While using this framework as its structure, the chapter will address the three effects in reverse order to reflect the focus of the extant consulting literature. There is actually significant research into the role of consultancies as agents of global knowledge diffusion. Moreover, they have been popularly presented as central to the transmission of global 'best practice' (that is, as contributors to broader 'dominance' effects). By comparison, consideration of different societal contexts on the diffusion of consulting knowledge, let alone how such contingencies shape the operation of consultancies themselves as business organizations, is less well understood. When turning to 'system effects', the gap in the extant literature becomes even more pronounced, with surprisingly little consideration of the role of consultancies in the broader economic system. In particular, the question of how management consultancies have become legitimate and influential agents within capitalism is, we suggest, significantly under-researched.

8.3 GLOBAL DOMINANCE: CONSULTANTS AND 'BEST PRACTICE'

8.3.1 Agents of 'Americanization' and 'Globalization'

A large part of the consulting literature stresses the role of consultancies as agents of globalization. Within this process, consultants are seen as important global carriers and promoters of management innovations. In particular, the history and growth of global consulting firms appears to provide a powerful example of a specific form of dominance effect often referred to as 'Americanization'. The United States emerged as the twentieth century's dominant industrial economy, and US industry became the source of key managerial innovations, from scientific management to mass production, to the multidivisional organizational structure.

As a variety of historical studies have highlighted, management consulting as a business activity originated in the US, and the emergence of modern consultancy in other parts of the world occurred through the international expansion of US consultancies, beginning with industrial engineering in the first half of the twentieth century, later through corporate consultants such as McKinsey & Co., and most recently through the large accounting or information technology (IT)-based consultancies (Kipping 2002; see also Wright and Kipping, Chapter 2; David, Chapter 4; Galal, Richter, and Wendlandt, Chapter 6; all this volume). In many cases, these consultancies rode on the coat-tails of US multinationals as they expanded their operations to other parts of the world (Kipping 1999a). While a complex process of localization occurred in these settings through acquisitions of local providers or, more often, spin-offs (an issue discussed in more detail later), management consultancy as a global industry is still dominated by its North American origins, with most of the large firms continuing to have their operational headquarters located in the US. Recently, professional service firms have attempted to become more global (see Fenton and Pettigrew 2003), namely through the institution of geographically dispersed centres of excellence and international human resource and knowledge management. But this process has been all but smooth—with problems apparently in part due to the Anglo-American origins of the consultancies (Boussebaa 2009).

Not only have US-based consultancies dominated the global consulting industry in terms of their size and number, they have also defined the image and identity of consulting as an occupation and activity—largely due to the coverage they have received in the business press and popular management books since the 1960s (e.g. Higdon 1969; O'Shea and Madigan 1997). This effect is not only limited to public perception. As Kipping (1999a: 215) has shown, European consultants tried to mimic the lifestyle and 'look of successful young professionals' of their US counterparts during the 1960s. More recently, the success of global—read US—consultancies in China seems to be largely based on similar branding and reputation effects (Wang 2009).

While much of the extant research and public attention has focused on the largest and most visible consultancies, some scholars also highlight dominance effects when examining small and medium-sized firms. Thus, based on a comparative study of the role of consultants in regional development in Europe, Wood (2002a: 67–68) concludes that 'consultancies are primarily agents of globalizing change'. He argues that even smaller, regionally based consultancies will draw on the knowledge of their multinational clients and therefore, indirectly, on the larger global service providers who tend to dominate this market. He also highlights the potential negative aspects of these developments, since 'sources of intelligence and authority are increasingly remote from traditional corporate culture and also [...] from the social, including employment and community consequences of change'. While Wood sees this development as limited to certain 'core regions' such as southern England, a study of small Italian consultancies suggests that these have similarly acted as 'translators', both in a literal and metaphoric sense, for ideas originally developed by the large, global firms (Crucini and Kipping 2001).

One danger in emphasizing consultants as agents of US or global dominance is to understate the potential for local resistance. There has been growing criticism in the popular press regarding the supposedly superior expertise of global consultancies and increasing doubts about their ulterior motives, which seems to have made managers more sceptical, even hostile towards them (e.g. Macdonald 2006). Moreover, dominance may in itself promote local resistance in reaction to a form of perceived neo-imperialism (Kipping, Engwall, and Üsdiken 2008; see also Frenkel and Shenhav, Chapter 26, this volume; Sturdy 2004). As is discussed later in considering the impact of differing societal contexts, foreign consultants are not always readily accepted in local environments because of their identification with a dominant national identity; they may in fact struggle to gain legitimacy as management experts in locations with different traditions of organizational learning, as well as rival sources of professional expertise.

8.3.2 Transmitters of Management Innovations and 'Fashions'

At the micro-level, there has also been significant research about how consultants contributed to the diffusion of specific ideas around the globe. Probably most extensive in this respect has been the literature on the diffusion of innovation, which has highlighted the part played by consultants as 'transmitters' (Hagedorn 1955), 'conduits' (Morris 2000), 'bridges' (Bessant and Rush 1995), and 'carriers' of managerial innovation (Sahlin-Andersson and Engwall 2002). Unlike the previously discussed literature, here consultants are no longer portrayed as active purveyors of a globally dominant, usually US-based model of management. Instead they are seen to play a largely passive or, at the very least, neutral role as mediums through which innovations in management practice 'flow' to client organizations. Since the content of the innovations remains unaltered, most of these approaches tend to imply that recipients everywhere implement the same ideas—even if some authors also acknowledge the possibility that some 'translation' of these ideas will occur at the receiving end (e.g. Czarniawska and Sevón 1996; see also Faust, Chapter 7, this volume).

A far more agential vision of consultancy is provided by other authors, who suggest that consultancies play an important determining role in choosing new management models, and that this role can be extremely powerful in deciding organizational outcomes. For instance, neo-institutionalist theorists such as DiMaggio and Powell (1983: 152) note how major management consultancies act as a key means of diffusing defined models of organizational structure, which '…like Johnny Appleseeds, spread a few organizational models throughout the land'. In this view, consultancies are seen as key contributors to a broader process of convergence and organizational 'isomorphism', in that managers embrace common consultancy templates in order to increase their legitimacy in the eyes of stakeholders as modern and up-to-date actors (Jackall 1988). This organizational mimicry, neo-institutionalists argue, results in a growing convergence of organizational forms and practices around the world, as other options are neglected in favour of the models defined as desirable by institutionalizing agents such as consultancies.

Building on neo-institutional theory, there has been considerable research on the global diffusion of new management ideas over the last two decades. This literature has highlighted the fashion-like character of this process, with new ideas gaining rapid popularity, but then equally rapidly fading from view only to be replaced by new fashions (Abrahamson 1996). Important from the perspective of this chapter is the role ascribed to consultants in this process as part of a management advice industry (Clark and Fincham 2002) or fashion-setting community (Abrahamson 1991), which also includes management gurus, business schools, and the business press (see Jung and Kieser, Chapter 16; Clark, Bhatanacharoen, and Greatbatch, Chapter 17; Engwall, Chapter 18; all this volume). Implicit within these characterizations is a power dynamic, where these actors determine what constitutes legitimate business knowledge. The result, more implicit than explicit in the literature on management fashions, is a global uniformity or 'commodification' of the ideas disseminated, among others, by consultancies (Fincham 1995). Among the limited empirical examples are those of Benders, van den Berg, and van Bijsterveld (1998), who have shown how consultants quickly jumped on the bandwagon of Business Process Re-engineering (BPR) by developing their own version or, sometimes, simply renaming their slightly modified existing approaches.

Once again, such a view can be overstated. In particular Clark (2004) has criticized the management fashion literature's almost exclusive use of bibliometric analysis, which, he suggests, is more indicative of the way in which business publications and their editors work rather than providing insight into the actual dissemination of these ideas. Moreover, as many studies of the diffusion of management practices have noted, managers will often adopt a pragmatic approach to their application, picking and choosing aspects of the overall model that most appeal or fit their specific circumstances (see below).

8.3.3 Consultancy Practices as Universal Examples

A further aspect of the dominance effect of consultants can be found in a sizeable body of management literature, which uses management consulting organizations as a best practice in and of themselves. Thus, within popular media, consultancies have been presented—sometimes critically—as 'thought leaders', 'business Jesuits', 'witch doctors', or even 'Masters of the Universe' (e.g. Micklethwait and Wooldridge 1996; O'Shea and Madigan 1997; Films of Record 1999). These terms portray consultancies as powerful, influential, and secretive organizations, which fundamentally shape the ideas and actions of other organizations and managers not only through their suggestions, but also through their own example.

Similarly, for many researchers management consultancies are key empirical examples of the so-called 'knowledge-intensive firm' and employers of 'knowledge workers', who are often presented as the future workforce of modern post-industrial economies (Starbuck 1992; Alvesson 1993; see also Alvesson, Chapter 15, this volume). For instance, many studies of 'knowledge management' focus on large global consultancies as the best examples of sophisticated strategies that utilize both information technologies to capture and codify knowledge, as well as more personalized techniques of 'communities of practice' to better share tacit consulting experience on a global scale (Hansen, Nohria, and Tierney 1999; Davenport and Prusak 2005; Haas and Hansen 2005; see also Werr, Chapter 12; Morris, Gardner, and Anand, Chapter 14, both this volume). In the area of human resource management, researchers often focus on large consulting firms such as Accenture and McKinsey & Co. as leading examples of superior human resource practices, from recruitment and selection, through to training and performance management, as well as leading examples of the central role of corporate culture in instilling and reinforcing values and beliefs amongst their workforce (see, for example, Ghoshal and Bartlett 1997; Alvesson and Kärreman 2007).

Here, as above, recent research—and events—suggest caution regarding the alleged superiority and transferability of management models from consulting firms to other organizations. Thus, for instance, Boussebaa (2009) found significant economic conflict and competition between the national subunits of global consultancies. More importantly, the fate of Enron should stand as a strong warning against uncritically mimicking consulting practices and cultures (e.g. Gladwell 2002; McLean and Elkind 2003; Krehmeyer and Freeman, Chapter 24, this volume). The failed Houston-based energy company seemed to be heavily influenced by the ideas of McKinsey & Co., namely the much-hyped concept of the 'war for talent'. Several of Enron's senior managers were former McKinsey consultants and appear to have acted out the consultancy's assumptions regarding business strategy, corporate culture, and performance management in the 'new economy'. The process of influence was probably symbiotic, since at the same time McKinsey celebrated Enron as exemplary in its own publications. The Enron case points to a further mechanism of consultancy dominance: the career transition of former consultants into business enterprises, where they can potentially apply consulting knowledge through their own example and behaviour as practising managers (see Sturdy and Wright 2008).

In summary then, much of the extant literature on consultants focuses on their contribution to an organizational 'dominance effect'. This includes their presentation as agents of globalization and Americanization, and as carriers of management innovations and fashions, in which consultancies contribute to the promotion and spread of 'dominant' models and discourses of management. A further dimension of such a dominance effect can also be seen in the way in which consultancies themselves are often portrayed as 'best practice' examples of various management practices. As noted, these arguments tend to understate the potential for local adaptation, pragmatism, and resistance to such broader models, a theme considered in more depth in the following section.

8.4 SOCIETAL EFFECT

By comparison to the broader literature on management consultancy, research focusing on the role, evolution, and status of consultants in different national settings has remained fairly limited to date. It consists, on the one hand, of market surveys by industry experts or the consultants' own trade associations. On the other hand, there are a growing number of country-based historical studies, which remain however rather atheoretical and usually fail to draw on or contribute to the rich literature on national business systems.

8.4.1 Market Surveys

There are a number of observers and self-declared experts of the consulting industry, which periodically provide surveys of different national markets as well as the global market—usually for a fee. Internationally, probably most well known among them is Kennedy Information, publisher of *Consultants News* and *Management Consultant International* (http://www.kennedyinfo.com/consulting/ accessed 1 October 2011). There are also national services of this kind, for example, Lünendonk in Germany (http://www.luenendonk.de/Management_Beratungs_Markt.php accessed 1 October 2011). These market research firms usually focus on the largest and most well-known consultancies, compiling league tables based on publicly available data, such as consultancy annual reports, and their own estimates. These lists of the largest firms also often find their way into the general business press.

Both more comprehensive and more consequential for academic research have been the statistics compiled by the national trade and professional associations of consultancies. Rather than focusing on individual service providers, the associations usually provide estimates of overall market size, types of services (strategy, IT, etc.), and types of clients (manufacturing, services, public sector, etc.). The data are highly variable, since membership in these associations is not compulsory and criteria for admission as well as actual membership differ significantly from one country to the next. Nevertheless, in the absence of government statistics and the difficulty in collecting their own large-scale datasets, a number of academic studies have used these statistics for both country-specific and comparative studies. For the latter, researchers have relied in particular on the annual reports by the European umbrella association, the Fédération Européenne des Associations de Conseils en Organisation (FEACO), which puts together the statistics from all its member associations.

Many of these studies were actually funded by the European Commission and identified significant differences among the European Union (EU) member countries. Thus, drawing on data from both the European and German consultancies associations, respectively FEACO and the Bundesverband Deutscher Unternehmensberater (BDU), Keeble and Schwalbach (1995) showed that the UK was dominated by large consultancies, while service providers were, on average, much smaller in Germany. Another EU-funded study, also based on FEACO data, reached similar conclusions by looking at concentration ratios (measured in terms of both revenue and employment accounted for by the largest ten and twenty consultancies): the UK ranked highest followed closely by the Netherlands, while Germany could be found at the other extreme (Kipping and Armbrüster 1999). Using survey results from the University of Cambridge's Small Business Research Centre, Keeble and Schwalbach (1995) actually concluded that the 'rapid proliferation' of small consultancies in the UK had driven much of the sector's fast growth during the second half of the 1980s. Several studies conducted by economic geographers have come to similar results for most European countries, stressing namely the contribution of small consultancies to regional development (e.g. Wood 2002b; see also Faulconbridge and Jones, Chapter 11, this volume).

These studies have provided relevant data and interesting, sometimes surprising, insights, but they have done little to explain the differences they identified. Thus, while it has been important to draw attention to small and medium-sized consulting firms, little explanation has been offered as to why they were more vigorous in certain countries. Moreover, since all of these studies usually adopt a static approach based on a single point in time, it is not known whether these national features and differences are a recent phenomenon or have deeper roots and longevity. In this respect, the growing number of historical studies provide more insights.

8.4.2 Historical Developments at a National Level

After several decades of research there is now a substantial literature on the development of the consulting business in most of the core industrial and, increasingly, emerging economies. Among the literature available in English there are, in particular, the contributions in Kipping and Engwall (2002), which provide overviews of the developments in France, the Netherlands, and Australia. There are Ph.D. theses, monographs, (summary) articles, and conference papers on the industry evolution in the United Kingdom (Tisdall 1982; Ferguson 2002), Italy (Crucini 2004), Spain, and Portugal (Amorim and Kipping 1999; Faust and Kordon 2011), as well as the United States (McKenna 2006; see also Wright and Kipping, Chapter 2, David, Chapter 4, McDougald and Greenwood, Chapter 5, Galal, Richter, and Wendlandt, Chapter 6, all this volume). There has also been a growing interest in consulting activities in the emerging economies (for Korea, see Wright and Kwon 2006; for China, Wang 2009; for Brazil, Donadone 2009), and the transition economies in Central and Eastern Europe (Kostera 1995; see also the contributions in Faust, Mohe, and Moldaschl 2011).[1]

Taken together, these studies show that management consulting as a business activity developed earliest in the US, followed closely by the United Kingdom and the Netherlands. By contrast, consultancies were rather late in developing in countries like Germany (where they have become significant since the 1970s), Japan, and South Korea (where they became more important in the 1990s). In the last decade, most of the transition economies in Central and Eastern Europe and the large emerging economies such as China have also witnessed a rapid expansion of their consultancy markets. Whether the timing of development might explain some of the differences in concentration ratios (see above) is a question that remains to be answered. What these studies do reveal is the important role of US service providers in the development of many markets—which gives some credence to the dominance effect. But the US consultancies sometimes became indigenized—usually through spin-offs—and also had to contend with domestic consultancies in most countries.

While these historical studies have provided considerable in-depth evidence, they also have important limitations. First of all, much of this research has focused on the most visible service providers, in particular McKinsey & Co. and, more generally, on the so-called strategy or corporate consultancies. This limited focus reflects the successful self-promotion of these firms (see above) and the interests of historical scholars in the most prominent or heroic actors. Second, and more importantly, these studies neither situate the development of consulting in each country within the broader context of society, political economy, and culture nor do they compare and explain the different national trajectories.

Some efforts in this direction can be found in the work of Kipping (1996), who has compared the role of US consultancies in Britain, Germany, and France after 1945, suggesting that the 'systemic context' influenced the ability of US service providers to enter these countries, with Germany proving particularly difficult due to the need to involve all relevant stakeholders in a consulting project. In a series of subsequent studies (Kipping 1997, 1999b, 2009) he has stressed the role of 'trust' as a determining factor for the development of consulting, arguing that in high-trust business systems, such as Germany or Japan, knowledge exchange took more collective, associative forms, whereas systems with lower levels of trust such as the UK have tended to rely more on consultants. Building on Kipping's work, Faust and his colleagues have recently suggested the use of the concept of 'functional equivalents', when examining the development of consulting markets (Faust and Kordon 2011); that is, the decisions by companies between alternative knowledge providers (Faust and Schneider 2011). These equivalents include alternative and varying sources of management knowledge and advice beyond consultancies, such as internal experts, professional networks, universities, and business academics.

These are promising beginnings, but there is scope for more extensive research. Thus, little has been done so far in linking the development of consulting markets to characteristics of national cultures. A recent article has tried to examine the consulting industry from this perspective (Mohe 2008), but—somewhat surprisingly—the author develops a new multi-level framework of analysis rather than building on (and testing) the established models such as Hofstede's (1980) work-related values or that of the GLOBE Project (House et al. 2004).

8.4.3 Consultants, 'Proximity Institutions', and Clients

While some attempts have been made to link country-level developments with the broader literature on national business systems, much less has been done at the micro-level to examine the relationships of consultants with the different 'proximity institutions', such as trade unions and the government, as well as the financial or education system. For example, little is known about how the industrial relations system in a given national context affected the way in which consultants and industrial engineers interacted with workers and trade unions, and ultimately shaped the outcome of the consulting intervention. The limited available evidence comes from a range of case studies on the introduction of scientific management in different company and country settings (e.g. Littler 1982; Wright 2000). However, broader questions remain unanswered regarding, for example, the influence of different labour market structures, or trade union roles and ideologies, on the use and the effectiveness of consultants. Similarly, one might ask how the education and promotion system of both middle and top managers shaped their attitude towards external consultants.

The influence of corporate governance or the financial system on the development and role of consultants also needs to be explored more systematically (cf. McKenna 2006). Regarding the former, as noted, Kipping (1996) has highlighted the fact that the need to address all stakeholder concerns had slowed the expansion of foreign consultancies into Germany. By the same token, stakeholder power might also encourage the use of consultants as arbiters, power brokers, or scapegoats (Jackall 1988). In terms of the financial systems, one important question is how stock markets 'value' the fact that companies hire consultants—something event studies might be able to address. A more general question might consider their prevalence in financial market-based as compared to bank-based systems. There is some evidence that bankers played an important role in connecting consultants with potential clients in trust-based economies (Kipping 1999a). Moreover, what about ownership structures? Do family firms, for example, have less recourse to consultants, and might this be one of the reasons why the market in Italy has remained rather under-developed (Crucini 2004)? At the same time, case studies suggest that consultants have actually been used in family feuds (Kipping 2000).

Thus, while some evidence is available to address these issues, much more needs to be done to synthesize these findings and relate them to broader (theoretical) debates. One area where there has been a more systematic effort to situate the development of management consulting within its systemic context concerns the so-called 'new public management'. In particular, there is the study by Saint-Martin (2000) on the role of consultants in public sector reform in Britain, France, and Canada. He found that the degree to which the public sector in these countries espoused managerialist ideas was a function of their openness to external advice and, more broadly, the influence and recognition consultants had previously gained in the country. More research needs to be conducted on the role of consultants in other parts of the public sector, such as health care and education, which are a growing consulting market and where managerialist ideas have taken hold over the past decades (O'Shea and Madigan 1997).

Last but not least, there is the question of the extent to which consultants have had to adapt their own organizations and practices to different social systems in the various countries in which they have operated. As noted, the literature has usually treated these firms as exemplars of global practices that introduce and follow uniform standards regardless of the national or local context. However, a case study of the Italian branch of a global consulting firm shows that variation in terms of human resource and knowledge management practices does exist (Crucini 2002; see also Boussebaa 2009; Wang 2009). On the other hand, there is some indication that powerful consultancies actually try to shape their environment. Thus, McKinsey apparently supported the creation of US-type business schools in Europe in the late 1950s and 1960s, since these constituted an important element in its recruitment, legitimation, and networking strategy (Kipping 1999a; Barsoux 2000; see also Engwall, Chapter 18, this volume).

Thus, in terms of Smith and Meiksins' (1995) societal effect, there are many country-level studies that highlight variations in institutional and historical contexts for the development of consultancy. However, systematic cross-national analysis or attempts to theorize variations in the development of consultancy in different societal contexts are under-developed. This section has attempted to identify some potential explanatory variables, including the broader systemic context of national business systems and the role of proximity institutions, such as differing financial systems or patterns of ownership and governance. Importantly, rather than being solely subject to 'societal effects', there is also some evidence that large consultancies seek to shape societies in ways that support their activities. This not only links back to the earlier consideration of consultants as contributors to 'dominance effects' but also raises broader questions about their role within capitalism as a system of economic organization.

8.5 CONSULTANTS IN THE CAPITALIST SYSTEM

There is little doubt that consultants have managed to insert themselves 'in the interstices of organizations' as Ruef (2002) has succinctly put it. They seem to have become almost indispensable for managers—which is all the more surprising as there is no obligation for organizations to hire them (Kieser 2002; Kitay and Wright 2007; Jung and Kieser, Chapter 16, Clark, Bhatanacharoen, and Greatbatch, Chapter 17, both this volume). Moreover, consulting has also become an occupation of choice for many business graduates (Ruef 2002; Engwall, Chapter 18, this volume), who appear to prefer what is widely perceived as a 'sexy' consulting role to the job of manager—a fact lamented by several business commentators (see, for example, Lemann 1999). Consultants also seem to have replaced managers as experts on business issues in the eyes of the media (Faust 2002). Why the capitalist system of production has engendered management consulting as such an important and influential activity is a question that, so far, has found only very limited answers in the extant literature. Some might argue that the role of trusted advisor (or jester) has been a feature of any human organization. However, none of the historical examples has even remotely reached the scale of today's consulting firms nor did they seem primarily based on the profit motive. This section discusses these answers and suggests some avenues for future research to better understand the place and role of consultants in the broader capitalist system.

8.5.1 Addressing Managerial Needs?

Regarding the role of consultants in a capitalist economy, probably the most widely held view in the current literature focuses on the insecurity of managers and their psychological control needs (cf. Faust, Chapter 7; Jung and Kieser, Chapter 16, both this volume). As seen above, Abrahamson (1996) has outlined how management consultancies—along with other groups of fashion setters—promote the merits of new and often transitory management practices amongst managers. A—sometimes implicit—assumption in this literature is that managers cling to these management fashions as a means of appearing in control and up-to-date, reflecting their underlying uncertainties and control needs (e.g. Jackall 1988; Gill and Whittle 1992; Huczynski 1993). Taking this view to a certain extreme, Ernst and Kieser (2002) and Kieser (2002) have argued that consultants not only use fashions to alleviate the managers' fears and provide them with at least the semblance of control, but that they also stoke these fears by continuously inventing and pushing new ideas. By constantly restarting the cycle of fear and—ultimately elusive—control, they make managers 'addicted' to the constant flow of ideas and turn them into 'marionettes on the strings of their fashions'—promoting their own business in the process (Kieser 2002: 176; see also Jung and Kieser, Chapter 16, this volume). This view has not remained without its critics. Thus, some authors have highlighted that such an image of managers as 'gullible victims' of the fashion-setting consultants might be exaggerated (Fincham 1999 and Chapter 20, this volume), and that consultants are equally, if not more, insecure than their clients (Sturdy 1997).

The 'needs' of managers are also at the core of Kipping's (2002) attempt to explain the historical shifts among the dominant consulting firms. He argued 'that the evolution of the consulting industry and of its pre-eminent firms is closely linked to the development of management practice and ideology' (ibid.: 29). In his view, 'consultancy can be understood as a kind of reflection of prevailing managerial problems and definitions' (ibid.). In an embryonic form, this contains a systemic view of the relationship between the development of consulting and the development of capitalism itself. Future research in this direction might attempt to provide a more explicit link between this account and broader narratives about the evolution of managerial capitalism (e.g. Chandler 1990), corporate control (e.g. Fligstein 1990), or managerial ideology (e.g. Barley and Kunda 1992). With regard to corporate control, McKenna (2006) has actually linked the rise of the corporate strategy consultants since the 1930s with regulatory changes in the US, namely the adoption of the Glass–Steagall Act in 1933, which separated commercial from investment banking. This prohibited banks from conducting 'bankers' surveys' and made it possible for McKinsey and others to provide these services either to the banks or directly to the clients. Similarly, McKenna has explored the resilience of these firms despite the regulatory and legal pressure on corporate boards since the 1990s, which has led to boards hiring consultants as a kind of insurance (ibid.). Looking at the relationship between managers and shareholders more generally, Fincham (2002) has argued that consultants exist as an extension of managerial power, and are therefore the 'agent's agent'—given that managers themselves are the agents of the owners of capital.

More broadly, the uneven spread of capitalism as an economic system might also explain—at least to some extent—the differences in the evolution of management consulting around the world, discussed above. Thus, the early development of competitive managerial capitalism in the US (Chandler 1990) might have promoted the growth of management consulting there. By contrast, in both Japan and Korea during their periods of industrialization and modernization, there are strong traditions of firm internal learning and inter-firm collaboration (e.g. Wright and Kwon 2006), which might have slowed the development of home-grown consulting and the penetration of foreign consultancies. The more recent expansion of consulting in these countries could therefore be indicative of a broader shift, where pre-capitalist structures and patterns of behaviour are gradually being replaced by 'pure' market mechanisms. This is even more obvious in the case of the planned economies in Central and Eastern Europe, and in China, where the introduction of market mechanisms was followed very closely by the arrival of Western management consultancies (Kostera 1995; Wang 2009). However, such a link between the emergence and worldwide spread of capitalism and what seems like a parallel development of management consulting remains highly speculative for the time being—subject to confirmation (or not) through further research.

8.5.2 From Handmaidens of Capital to Masters of the Universe?

While the dominance effect suggests that consultants are agents of 'Americanization', they can also be seen more broadly as key representatives of a transnational community with a similar educational and professional background, that is, US-style MBA programmes (Morgan 2001; see also Engwall, Chapter 18, this volume) or a global elite of 'cosmocrats' (Micklethwait and Wooldridge 2003). As such they do share a dominant 'Western' sensibility, but they also define and promote economic globalization and market liberalism or, in other words, capitalism. This has probably been put most succinctly by Thrift (2005: 93) who defines management consultants as 'capitalism's commissars', since they are a central part of the 'cultural circuit of capital [...] able to produce constant discursive-cum-practical change with considerable power to mould the content of people's work lives'.

But consultancies do not seem content to provide knowledge within a capitalist system or to promote and spread capitalism worldwide. They are also attempting to actively shape the nature of the capitalist system itself, beyond their role within specific client organizations, by intervening in public debates and pontificating on economic and social issues. This role has drawn some attention in the business and popular press, but is still awaiting a more rigorous academic treatment. Part of this role can be observed in the magazines and books consultancies now produce, which serve to promote the consultancy brand, but also act more broadly as a form of 'thought-leadership' (Davenport and Prusak 2005). Consultancies have also established research and policy bodies, which promote various public policy agendas. One of the best known in this regard is McKinsey & Co.'s Global Institute, which has been highly active in compiling country reports and analysis that have fed into broader macroeconomic reforms of different countries such as Sweden, France, Germany, South Korea, Brazil, and Russia (McKinsey Global Institute 1995, 1997, 1998; see Engwall, Chapter 18, this volume).

Not surprisingly, these countrywide recommendations have emphasized the need for greater market freedom, foreign direct investment, and the adoption of management 'best practices', which together reinforce the need for consulting services. For example, in Australia, McKinsey & Co. was a key contributor to the reshaping of industry policy and labour market deregulation during the 1980s, which radically altered the traditional patterns of tariff protection and collective bargaining (Wright and Kitay 2004). Moreover, consulting advice and the implementation of efficiency measures often feed into these broader market-driven agendas. For example, as O'Shea and Madigan (1997: 146–182) outline, Boston Consulting Group played a central role in the redesign of US health care during the 1980s and 1990s, through cost-containment measures that shaped the debate around health care reform towards allegedly more efficient market-based alternatives.

Of course, this is not entirely new. Many of the pioneers of scientific management were public figures and advocated the use of their systems not only for client organizations, but for society as a whole. Taylor's efforts in this respect are well documented, but Charles Bedaux also played an important, albeit less well-known, role as a public advocate, by advising various governments (for more details and references, see Wright and Kipping, Chapter 2, this volume). These and other consultancies played similar roles during and after World War II (see David, Chapter 4, this volume). Thus, in all these cases prominent consultants and the firms they represented went beyond the more micro-organizational application of management technique as 'practitioners' and adopted a qualitatively larger role within broader economic and social debates, which most closely approximates Guillén's (1994) idea of the 'management intellectual'. While more research into this broader aspect of consultancy is clearly needed, its potential impact at this level is indeed systemic, linking as it does to changes in the very nature of capital accumulation and the social relations of production.

It is at this third level of 'system effect' that our understanding of consultancy in a global context is at its weakest. The extant literature offers some insight regarding the role of consultants in catering to the psychological needs of managers in a capitalist system, and historians have highlighted the changing functions consultants provide as industries and regulatory structures change. Moreover, as noted, consultants are also contributors to broader systemic changes in our economic system, most notably through their promotion of competitive market economies. However, this is an area in which much greater research is needed, linking consultants and consultancies to the broader dynamics of political economy.

8.6 Conclusions and Outlook

This chapter has summarized research that examines the role of consultants in a broader context using a framework originally proposed by Smith and Meiksins (1995), which distinguishes systemic, societal, and dominance effects. This review shows that it is the latter that has so far commanded most attention in the extant literature, where consultancies are often portrayed as agents of Americanization or globalization, as purveyors of best practice, and as exemplars of knowledge-intensive firms. The dominance of the dominance effect is also visible in the role that neo-institutional theory and the related 'fashion theory' have played in this literature (see also Faust, Chapter 7, this volume). Regarding the societal effect, there have been a growing number of largely historical studies on the development of consulting activities in a wide range of industrialized and, increasingly, emerging economies. These have gone further than the static snapshot-like market surveys conducted by industry associations or self-declared experts. However, they have yet to make more explicit use of, or contributions to, the literature on national business systems at the macro level and regarding specific elements of these systems—with the influence of consultants on the public sector a notable exception (see also Saint-Martin, Chapter 22, this volume). There is even less research on the role of consultants in capitalism as an economic system—and this despite mounting evidence that consultants have not only been able to legitimize their own role as knowledge brokers, but are increasingly contributing to the spread of a 'free market ideology' and, in certain sectors, such as health care, have started to influence the shape of the capitalist system itself.

While there remain many areas to be explored when it comes to the relationship between consultants and the contexts in which they are working, a number of important preliminary steps need to be taken. First, there is a need to develop theoretical alternatives to neo-institutionalism and fashion theory, which have so far dominated this research and fuelled the image of consultants as a mimetic force. Second, to identify societal effects both at a national level and—regarding the different elements of the national business systems—more truly internationally *comparative* research is necessary. Third, given the task at hand, more cooperation is needed between those who provide a significant part of the empirical evidence—historians and market analysts, and those with an ability to synthesize, generalize, and theorize these findings—organization theorists.

Note

1. We have only mentioned selected publications in English here; most of these will include details about additional publications in other languages.

References

Abrahamson, E. (1991). 'Managerial Fads and Fashions: The Diffusion and Rejection of Innovations'. *Academy of Management Review*, 16/3, 586–612.

Abrahamson, E. (1996). 'Management Fashion'. *Academy of Management Review*, 21/1, 254–285.

Alvesson, M. (1993). 'Organizations as Rhetoric: Knowledge Intensive Firms and the Struggle with Ambiguity'. *Journal of Management Studies*, 30/6, 997–1019.

Alvesson, M. and Kärreman, D. (2007). 'Unraveling HRM: Identity, Ceremony, and Control in a Management Consulting Firm'. *Organization Science*, 18/4, 711–723.

Amorim C. and Kipping, M. (1999). 'Selling Consultancy Services: The Portuguese Case in Historical and Comparative Perspective'. *Business and Economic History*, 28/1, 45–56.

Barley, S. R. and Kunda, G. (1992). 'Design and Devotion: Surges of Rational and Normative Ideologies of Control in Managerial Discourse'. *Administrative Science Quarterly*, 37/3, 363–399.

Barsoux, J-L. (2000). *INSEAD: From Intuition to Institution*. Basingstoke: Palgrave Macmillan.

Benders, J., van den Berg, R-J., and van Bijsterveld, M. (1998). 'Hitch-Hiking on a Hype: Dutch Consultants Engineering Re-Engineering'. *Journal of Organizational Change Management*, 11/3, 201–215.

Bessant, J. and Rush, H. (1995). 'Building Bridges for Innovation: The Role of Consultants in Technology Transfer'. *Research Policy*, 24/1, 97–114.

Boussebaa, M. (2009). 'Struggling to Organise Across National Borders: The Case of Global Resource Management in Professional Service Firms'. *Human Relations*, 62/6, 829–850.

Chandler Jr, A. D. (1990). *Scale and Scope: The Dynamics of Industrial Capitalism*. Cambridge, MA: Harvard University Press.

Clark, T. (2004). 'The Fashion of Management Fashion: A Surge Too Far?' *Organization*, 11/2, 297–306.

Clark, T. and Fincham, R. (eds) (2002). *Critical Consulting: New Perspectives on the Management Advice Industry*. Oxford: Blackwell.

Crucini, C. (2002). 'Knowledge Management at the Country Level: A Large Consulting Firm in Italy'. In M. Kipping and L. Engwall (eds), *Management Consulting: Emergence and Dynamics of a Knowledge Industry*. Oxford: Oxford University Press, 109–128.

Crucini, C. (2004). 'The Management Consultancy Business in Italy: Evolution, Structure and Operations'. Unpublished Ph.D. thesis, School of Business, University of Reading.

Crucini, C. and Kipping, M. (2001). 'Management Consultancies as Global Change Agents? Evidence from Italy'. *Journal of Organizational Change Management*, 14/6, 570–589.

Czarniawska, B. and Sevón, G. (eds) (1996). *Translating Organizational Change*. Berlin: De Gruyter.

Davenport, T. and Prusak, L. (2005). 'Knowledge Management in Consulting'. In L. Greiner and F. Poulfelt (eds), *The Contemporary Consultant: Insights From World Experts*. Mason, OH: Thomson South-Western, 305–326.

DiMaggio, P. and Powell, W. (1983). 'The Iron Cage Revisited: Institutional Isomorphism and Collective Rationality in Organizational Fields'. *American Sociological Review*, 48 (April), 147–160.

Donadone, J. C. (2009). 'Brazilian Consulting Cartography and the New Recontextualization and Internationalization of Interchanges and Managerial Contents'. *Corporate Ownership & Control*, 6/4, 302–308.

Ernst, B. and Kieser, A. (2002). 'In Search of Explanations for the Consulting Explosion'. In K. Sahlin-Andersson and L. Engwall (eds), *The Expansion of Management Knowledge: Carriers, Flows, and Sources*. Stanford, CA: Stanford University Press, 47–73.

Faust, M. (2002). 'Consultancies as Actors in Knowledge Arenas: Evidence from Germany'. In M. Kipping and L. Engwall (eds), *Management Consulting: Emergence and Dynamics of a Knowledge Industry*. Oxford: Oxford University Press, 146–163.

Faust, M. and Kordon, T. (2011). 'The Development of Management Consulting in Spain'. In M. Faust, M. Mohe, and M. Moldaschl (eds), *Internationalization of Consulting— Internationalisierung von Beratung*. Munich: Hampp, forthcoming.

Faust, M. and Schneider, K. (2011). 'Functional Equivalents to Management Consulting: A Case Study on a Reluctant German Corporation'. In M. Faust, M. Mohe, and M. Moldaschl (eds), *Intervention und Evaluierung: Zur Begründung und Bewertung von Beratungshandeln*. Munich: Hampp, forthcoming.

Faust, M., Mohe, M., and Moldaschl, M. (eds) (2011). *Internationalization of Consulting— Internationalisierung von Beratung*. Munich: Hampp.

Fenton, E. M. and Pettigrew, A. M. (2003). 'Complementary Change: Towards Global Integration in Four Professional Service Organizations'. In A. M. Pettigrew, R. Whittington, L. Melin, and C. Sanchez-Runde (eds), *Innovative Forms of Organizing*. London: Sage, 208–239.

Ferguson, M. (2002). *The Rise of Management Consulting in Britain*. Aldershot: Ashgate.

Films of Record (1999). *Masters of the Universe*, Channel 4 (UK), London.

Fincham, R. (1995). 'Business Process Reengineering and the Commodification of Managerial Knowledge'. *Journal of Marketing Management*, 11, 707–719.

Fincham, R. (1999). 'The Consultant–Client Relationship: Critical Perspectives on the Management of Organizational Change'. *Journal of Management Studies*, 36/3, 335–351.

Fincham, R. (2002). 'The Agent's Agent: Power, Knowledge, and Uncertainty in Management Consultancy'. *International Studies of Management & Organization*, 32/4, 67–86.

Fligstein, N. (1990). *The Transformation of Corporate Control*. Cambridge, MA: Harvard University Press.

Friedman, T. L. (2006). *The World is Flat: The Globalized World in the Twenty-First Century*. London: Penguin.

Ghemawat, P. (2007). 'Why the World Isn't Flat'. *Foreign Policy*, 159, 54–60.

Ghoshal, S. and Bartlett, C. (1997). *The Individualized Corporation: A Fundamentally New Approach to Management*. New York: HarperCollins.

Gill, J. and Whittle, S. (1992), 'Management by Panacea: Accounting for Transience'. *Journal of Management Studies*, 30/2, 281–295.

Gladwell, M. (2002). 'The Talent Myth'. *The New Yorker*, 22 July, 28–33.

Guillén, M. (1994). *Models of Management: Work, Authority, and Organization in a Comparative Perspective*. Chicago: University of Chicago Press.

Guillén, M. (2001). 'Is Globalization Civilizing, Destructive or Feeble? A Critique of Five Key Debates in the Social-Science Literature'. *Annual Review of Sociology*, 27, 235–260.

Haas, M. and Hansen, M. (2005). 'When Using Knowledge Can Hurt Performance: The Value of Organizational Capabilities in a Management Consulting Company'. *Strategic Management Journal*, 26, 1–24.

Hagedorn, H. (1955). 'The Management Consultant as Transmitter of Business Techniques'. *Explorations in Entrepreneurial History*, February, 164–173.

Hall, P. A. and Soskice, D. (eds) (2001). *Varieties of Capitalism: The Institutional Foundations of Comparative Advantage*. Oxford: Oxford University Press.

Hansen, M. T., Nohria, N., and Tierney, T. (1999). 'What's Your Strategy for Managing Knowledge?' *Harvard Business Review*, 77/2, 106–116.

Higdon, H. (1969). *The Business Healers*. New York: Random House.

Hofstede, G. (1980). *Culture's Consequences: International Differences in Work-Related Values*. Beverly Hills: Sage.

House, R. J., Hanges, P. J., Javidan, M., Dorfman, P. W., and Gupta, V. (eds) (2004). *Culture, Leadership and Organizations: The GLOBE Study in 62 Societies*. Thousand Oaks, CA: Sage.

Huczynski, A. (1993). 'Explaining the Succession of Management Fads'. *International Journal of Human Resource Management*, 4/2, 443–463.

Jackall, R. (1988). *Moral Mazes: The World of Corporate Managers*. New York: Oxford University Press.

Keeble, D. and Schwalbach, J. (1995). 'Management Consultancy in Europe'. ESRC Centre for Business Research, University of Cambridge, Working paper no. 1.

Kieser, A. (2002). 'Managers as Marionettes? Using Fashion Theory to Explain the Success of Consultancies'. In M. Kipping and L. Engwall (eds), *Management Consulting: Emergence and Dynamics of a Knowledge Industry*. Oxford: Oxford University Press, 167–183.

Kipping, M. (1996). 'The U.S. Influence on the Evolution of Management Consultancies in Britain, France and Germany since 1945'. *Business and Economic History*, 25/1, 112–123.

Kipping, M. (1997). 'Consultancies, Institutions and the Diffusion of Taylorism in Britain, Germany and France, 1920s to 1950s'. *Business History*, 39/4, 67–83.

Kipping, M. (1999a). 'American Management Consulting Companies in Western Europe, 1910s to 1990s: Products, Reputation, and Relationships'. *Business History Review*, 73/2, 190–220.

Kipping, M. (1999b). 'British Economic Decline: Blame It on the Consultants?' *Contemporary British History*, 13/3, 23–38.

Kipping, M. (2000). 'Consultancy and Conflicts: Bedaux at Lukens Steel and the Anglo-Iranian Oil Company'. *Entreprises et Histoire*, 25, 9–25.

Kipping, M. (2002). 'Trapped in Their Wave: The Evolution of Management Consultancies'. In T. Clark and R. Fincham (eds), *Critical Consulting: New Perspectives on the Management Advice Industry*. Oxford: Blackwell, 28–49.

Kipping, M. (2009). 'Management Consultancies and Organizational Innovation in Europe'. In P. Fernández Pérez and M. B. Rose (eds), *Innovation and Entrepreneurial Networks in Europe*. London: Routledge, 61–80.

Kipping, M. and Armbrüster, T. (1999). 'The Consultancy Field in Western Europe'. The Creation of European Management Practice (CEMP), University of Reading, Report no. 6.

Kipping, M. and Engwall, L. (eds) (2002). *Management Consulting: Emergence and Dynamics of a Knowledge Industry*. Oxford: Oxford University Press.

Kipping, M., Engwall, L., and Üsdiken, B. (2008). 'The Transfer of Management Knowledge to Peripheral Countries'. *International Studies of Management & Organization*, 38/4, 3–16.

Kitay, J. and Wright, C. (2007). 'From Prophets to Profits: The Occupational Rhetoric of Management Consultants'. *Human Relations*, 60/11, 1613–40.

Kostera, M. (1995). 'The Modern Crusade: The Missionaries of Management Come to Eastern Europe'. *Management Learning*, 26/3, 331–352.

Lemann, N. (1999). 'The Kids in the Conference Room'. *The New Yorker*, 75/31, 209–216.

Littler, C. (1982). *The Development of the Labour Process in Capitalist Societies: A Comparative Analysis of Work Organisation in Britain, the USA, and Japan*. London: Heinemann.

Macdonald, S. (2006). 'From Babes and Sucklings: Management Consultants and Novice Clients'. *European Management Journal*, 24/6, 411–421.

McKenna, C. D. (2006). *The World's Newest Profession: Management Consulting in the Twentieth Century*. Cambridge: Cambridge University Press.

McKinsey Global Institute (1995). 'Sweden's Economic Performance'. McKinsey & Co.

McKinsey Global Institute (1997). 'Removing Barriers to Growth in France and Germany'. McKinsey & Co.

McKinsey Global Institute (1998). 'Productivity-Led Growth for Korea'. McKinsey & Co.

McLean, B. and Elkind, P. (2003). *Smartest Guys in the Room: The Amazing Rise and Scandalous Fall of Enron*. New York: Penguin.

Micklethwait, J. and Wooldridge, A. (1996). *The Witch Doctors: What the Management Gurus Are Saying, Why It Matters and How to Make Sense of It*. London: Heinemann.

Micklethwait, J. and Wooldridge, A. (2003). *A Future Perfect: The Challenge and Promise of Globalization*. New York: Random House.

Mohe, M. (2008). 'Bridging the Cultural Gap in Management Consulting Research'. *International Journal of Cross Cultural Management*, 8/1, 41–57.

Morgan, G. (2001). 'Transnational Communities and Business Systems'. *Global Networks: A Journal of Transnational Affairs*, 1/2, 113–130.

Morris, T. (2000). 'From Key Advice to Execution? Consulting Firms and the Implementation of Strategic Decisions'. In P. C. Flood, T. Dromgoole, S. Carroll, and L. Gorman (eds), *Managing Strategic Implementation: An Organizational Behaviour Perspective*. Oxford: Blackwell, 125–137.

O'Shea, J. and Madigan, C. (1997). *Dangerous Company: The Consulting Powerhouses and the Businesses They Save and Ruin*. New York: Times Business.

Redding, G. (2005). 'The Thick Description and Comparison of Societal Systems of Capitalism'. *Journal of International Business Studies*, 36/2, 123–155.

Ruef, M. (2002). 'The Interstices of Organizations: The Expansion of the Management Consulting Profession, 1933–1997'. In K. Sahlin-Andersson and L. Engwall (eds), *The Expansion of Management Knowledge: Carriers, Flows, and Sources*. Stanford, CA: Stanford University Press, 74–95.

Sahlin-Andersson, K. and Engwall, L. (2002). 'Carriers, Flows, and Sources of Management Knowledge'. In K. Sahlin-Andersson and L. Engwall (eds), *The Expansion of Management Knowledge*. Stanford, CA: Stanford University Press, 3–32.

Saint-Martin, D. (2000). *Building the New Managerialist State: Consultants and the Politics of Public Sector Reform in Comparative Perspective*. Oxford: Oxford University Press.

Smith, C. and Meiksins, P. (1995). 'System, Society and Dominance Effects in Cross-National Organisational Analysis'. *Work, Employment and Society*, 9/2, 241–267.

Sorge, A. (2005). *The Global and the Local: Understanding the Dialectics of Business Systems*. Oxford: Oxford University Press.

Starbuck, W. (1992). 'Learning by Knowledge-Intensive Firms'. *Journal of Management Studies*, 29/6, 713–740.

Sturdy, A. (1997). 'The Consultancy Process: An Insecure Business?' *Journal of Management Studies*, 34/3, 389–413.

Sturdy, A. (2004). 'The Adoption of Management Ideas and Practices: Theoretical Perspectives and Possibilities'. *Management Learning*, 35/2, 153–177.

Sturdy, A. and Wright, C. (2008). 'A Consulting Diaspora? Enterprising Selves as Agents of Enterprise'. *Organization*, 15/3, 427–444.

Thrift, N. (2005). *Knowing Capitalism*. London: Sage.

Tisdall, P. (1982). *Agents of Change: The Development and Practice of Management Consultancy*. London: Heinemann.

Wang, Y. (2009). 'Global Management Consultancy in China'. Unpublished M.Phil dissertation, School of Organization and Management, University of New South Wales.

Wood, P. (2002a). 'The Rise of Consultancy and the Prospect for Regions'. In T. Clark and R. Fincham (eds), *Critical Consulting: New Perspectives on the Management Advice Industry*. Oxford: Blackwell, 50–73.

Wood, P. (ed.) (2002b). *Consultancy and Innovation: The Business Service Revolution in Europe*. London: Routledge.

Wright, C. (2000). 'From Shopfloor to Boardroom: The Historical Evolution of Australian Management Consulting, 1940s to 1980s'. *Business History*, 42/1, 86–106.

Wright, C. and Kitay, J. (2004). 'Spreading the Word: Gurus, Consultants and the Diffusion of the Employee Relations Paradigm in Australia'. *Management Learning*, 35/3, 271–286.

Wright, C. and Kwon, S-H. (2006). 'Business Crisis and Management Fashion: Korean Companies, Restructuring and Consulting Advice'. *Asia Pacific Business Review*, 12/3, 355–373.

CHAPTER 9

PROFESSIONS AND PROFESSIONALISM IN MANAGEMENT CONSULTING

IAN KIRKPATRICK
DANIEL MUZIO
STEPHEN ACKROYD

9.1 INTRODUCTION

IN recent years, the terms profession, professional, and professionalism have become common currency (Fournier 1999). However, professionalism also carries a more specific sociological meaning as a distinctive way of organizing (Johnson 1972) whereby members of an occupation rather than consumers retain control over the definition, performance, and evaluation of their work (Freidson 2001). Such an arrangement is thought to be particularly effective in the context of esoteric, intangible, and individually tailored services where quality is best served by regulating inputs (through the qualification and licensing of producers) rather than outputs (Mintzberg 1979). Also, whatever the alleged benefits for the consumer, professionalism may be advantageous for producers, allowing them to maintain artificial skills scarcity and therefore increase the financial and symbolic value of their expertise (Larson 1977). For these reasons professionalism has historically established itself as the standard if not proper way of organizing the production and delivery of expertise in modern societies.

Given the continued importance of this model of organizing it seems especially pertinent to consider it in relation to management consultants. As we have seen from earlier chapters of this volume, consultancy is one of the fastest growing and arguably most successful occupations in recent decades. Starting from rather modest origins at the beginning of the twentieth century (Kipping 2002; McKenna 2006) consultants have succeeded in embedding themselves in 'the interstices of organizations' (Ruef 2002). Yet, despite these trends questions remain concerning the professional status of management consultants and how this will develop in the future. Addressing this issue is important, not least because many practising consultants identify themselves as being professionals (Kitay and Wright 2007). Public concerns about the quality of consulting advice and the costs of failure have also drawn attention to the relative lack of regulation in this industry and raised the issue of whether a stronger emphasis on professionalism will be required in the future (Kubr 2002).

This chapter aims to explore this matter, focusing on three main themes that have been prominent in the literature. First, is the question of how far, if at all, one should define management consulting as a profession or even an occupation with aspirations to become a profession. To address this, concepts from the sociological literature on professions will be introduced to frame the analysis. A second theme concerns how one should best account for weak professionalism in this sector. Finally, there are debates about the wider consequences of weak professionalism, in particular for clients on the receiving end of consulting services. In the concluding section these themes are reviewed alongside a number of ideas for future research.

9.2 WHAT ARE PROFESSIONS?

Initial work in the sociology of the professions was guided by a taxonomic agenda focusing on the classification of different types of occupations. From this point of view, professions were occupations that shared a set of defining traits (for instance, a systematic body of knowledge, formal training, a deontological code, a professional association, etc.). As a consequence, early studies focused mainly on the development of conclusive checklists, which established professional or semi-professional status. However, the difficulties in producing such authoritative lists soon became apparent, leading Millerson (1964: 15) to conclude that 'of the dozens of writers on this subject few seem able to agree on the real determinants of professional status'. Indeed, it transpired that most lists were based on considerations of what a profession ought to be, grounded in the idealized models provided by the showcase professions of the nineteenth century: law and medicine. Thus, trait theory, in many ways, reproduced the 'mythology of professionalism' (McKinlay 1973: 77) rather than describing its realities. These static, largely ahistorical models bracketed the issue of professional power and failed to capture 'what professions do in everyday life to negotiate and maintain their special occupational position' (Larson 1977: xii).

The 1970s saw the reframing of the sociology of the professions away from the old question 'what is a profession' towards a new set of questions centred on how occupations accomplish and maintain professional status (Hughes 1971). This new approach recasts professionalism not as a specific occupation endowed by certain fixed traits but as a way of organizing and controlling an occupation, one which crucially tends to empower the producer over the consumer (Johnson 1972). In this context, professionalism emerges as a distinct work organization ideology and method, in which an occupation retains a significant degree of control over the definition, execution, and evaluation of its work 'as well as the social and economic methods of organizing and performing this work' (Freidson 1970: 185–186). Crucially, this state of affairs is not viewed as a historical accident nor as something functional to society but as the result of a 'professional project' (Larson 1977): a deliberate, conscious, and co-ordinated attempt by professionals to translate a scarce set of cultural and technical resources into a secure and institutionalized system of social and financial rewards (ibid.). At the heart of such attempts lie processes of occupational closure as professions 'seek to maximize rewards by restricting access to rewards and opportunities to a limited circle of eligibles' (those with the relevant credentials; Parkin 1974: 3). These monopolistic and restrictive claims are rendered more palatable through claims to quality and public interest as professions legitimize their role by presenting themselves as trustees of valuable forms of expertise, which are essential to individual and societal well-being (Brint 1994).

Although the notion of the 'professional project' has been dominant within the sociology of the professions, more recently a growing body of work (Fournier 1999; Anderson-Gough, Grey, and Robson 2000) has emphasized the role of professionalism as a discourse of organizational change and control (Evetts 2006). Appeals to 'professionalism' can be deployed from above by management as a normative instrument to extract commitment for the workforce and re-programme individual subjectivities around new corporate priorities such as: flexibility, client service, and efficiency. Thus, the emphasis shifts from being a professional, a matter of credentials and qualifications, to being professional, a matter of behaviour and attitudes (Anderson-Gough, Grey, and Robson 2000) to be enacted through self-presentation, appearance, and appropriate conduct.

9.3 THE PROFESSIONAL STATUS OF MANAGEMENT CONSULTING

Turning to the specific case of management consultants, the extent to which these sociological models of professionalization apply is debated quite widely in the literature. At one level there are those who claim that consultants are an emerging profession with a distinct 'project' (McKenna 2006). This is justified with the acquisition of some of the key traits of professionalism such as the development of formal professional associations, representing both firms and individuals, and the introduction of ethical codes. In the UK, for instance, Tisdall (1982: 83) notes how the Management Consultancies Association (MCA) dates back to 1956, and the Institute of Management Consulting to 1962. The latter, now renamed the Institute of Consulting (IC), sought to build a 'true profession…based on qualifying the individual' rooted in a shared knowledge and shared code of ethics. Similarly, in the US moves to professionalize began with the foundation of the Association of Consulting Management Engineers (ACME)—later renamed Association of Management Consulting Firms (AMCF)—in 1933. According to McKenna (2007) this association bore many of the hallmarks of a profession. While representing firms as opposed to individuals, ACME espoused a shared code of ethics and strict rules to prohibit advertising.

Others have drawn attention to how efforts to professionalize management consulting also took on an international dimension (Kubr 2002; ICMCI 2008). An example of this is the creation of the International Council of Management Consulting Institutes (ICMCI), an umbrella federation, established in 1987, of forty-four national associations, which is concerned with the creation and promotion of global standards, qualifications, credentials, and best practices for the consultancy profession. The most notable result of the ICMCI is the Certified Management Consultant (CMC) qualification, an internationally recognized benchmark for consultancy excellence, which is awarded on behalf of the Institute to individual practitioners by the various national associations.

A different indicator of professional development, often noted in the literature, would be the introduction of voluntary codes of ethics. O'Mahoney (2010), for example, notes how in the UK the MCA's code stipulates that members shall only accept work which they are qualified to undertake, will act with fairness and integrity towards all people with whom their work is connected, and will reject business practices that might be deemed improper. Gross and Kieser (2006: 84) also draw attention to how some consulting associations have sought to (in theory at least) play a role in quality assurance, judging cases of professional misconduct. Hence, in Germany, the largest association, the Bundesverband Deutscher Unternehmensberater (BDU), operates an 'honorary council' responsible for investigating client complaints against member firms.

However, while these facts point to the existence of a 'professionalization' project, most observers take the view that, at best, this is emergent. A reason often given for this is the low membership of key associations. Figures published by the Institute of Business Consulting (IBC, previously the Institute of Management Consultants or IMC) in the UK, show that total membership stands at only 7,000, or less than 7 per cent of all consultants employed in the sector (given the fact that in the UK anyone can lawfully use the title management consultant, this is, of course, only an estimate of membership density) (Kirkpatrick, Muzio, and Kipping 2008). In the US, despite the larger consulting sector, the equivalent organization, the Institute of Management Consultants USA (IMC USA), has only 1,700 members (ibid.).

As well as low membership, questions have been raised in the extant literature about how far management consultants meet other criteria of established professions. Using data from eighteen countries, Kyrö (1995) notes that almost everywhere consultants lack a common stock of knowledge, formal education, and legal closure. In a similar way Kubr (2002) identifies three features of weak professionalism. First is the fact that in most countries consultants have failed to clearly define their occupation: '[E]ven in sophisticated business cultures, virtually anyone can call himself or herself a management or business consultant and offer services to business clients without any diploma, certificate, license credentials, recommendations or registration' (Kubr 2002: 130–131). Related to this is the fact that management consulting qualifications, like the CMC, are pitched at a fairly general, or even 'elementary' level and 'cannot show whether a consultant is competent for a given task' (ibid.: 133). Finally, while some associations have sought to regulate the behaviour of practitioners—for example, with restrictions on advertising in the UK (Kipping and Saint-Martin 2005)—they have generally been less effective in terms of disciplining cases of professional misconduct. This stems both from the fact that associations infrequently audit their members (Kubr 2002) and the intangible nature of consulting work itself, with no clear standards against which to judge (Clark 1995; Glückler and Armbrüster 2003).

Hence, it is widely argued that management consulting is, at best, 'an emerging profession, a profession in the making, or an industry with significant professional characteristics and ambitions' (Kubr 2002: 131). Returning to the sociological concepts introduced at the start of this chapter, this view holds that management consultants have engaged in a 'professionalization project', albeit one that is still far from complete. However, while most commentators might accept this conclusion, two questions have been raised.

First is the argument that consultants have not really been interested in controlling the supply of qualified labour but in projecting an 'outward appearance of a profession' (McKenna 2006: 248). This is reflected in the values espoused by individual practitioners and the behaviour of leading firms. Drawing on interviews with fifty-eight consultants in Australia, Kitay and Wright (2007) noted a strong identification with 'professional' ideals of independence, integrity, expertise, and experience. Many consulting firms also display what Alvesson and Johansson (2002) describe as 'quasi professionalism'. These organizations, frequently classified as 'professional service firms' in the literature (Brock, Powell, and Hinings 1999; von Nordenflycht 2010), invest heavily in the recruitment and selection of new graduates (or MBAs), the codification of knowledge, and strict 'up or out' career structures similar to those found in law or accounting firms (Galanter and Palay 1991). In some cases, they also deliberately employ discourses and 'images of professionalism' (Kipping 2011). From the 1940s, firms such as McKinsey and Booz Allen, for example, set out to model themselves on law firms and sought to cash in on the growing reputation of the leading MBA programmes from which most staff were recruited (Edersheim 2004; McKenna 2006). Even today some global accounting or IT consultancies continue to label themselves 'partnerships' (Empson and Chapman 2006) and sometimes go to great lengths to foster a 'professional' appearance and 'elite identity' amongst their workforce (Alvesson and Robertson 2006).

In this respect, sociological understandings of 'professionalism' as a discourse or pattern of behaviour would seem to be particularly relevant. While there may be limited enthusiasm for creating strong professional associations this does not mean that consultants (or firms) are entirely disinterested in using notions of professionalism as 'resources to support claims for authority, status and credibility' (Alvesson and Johansson 2002: 228). This is especially important when they seek to present themselves as experts with superior knowledge to clients, but also applies to situations where consultants act as so-called 'traders in trouble' (helping clients to legitimate unpopular change). In the latter case, 'when top management wants to buy political services these services preferably should be constructed in terms of professionalism' (ibid.: 240). Either way, there may be strong incentives for consultants to work hard at creating a 'professional appearance' (Gross and Kieser 2006: 95) even if this does not translate into third party, professional regulation.

A further question concerns the issue of whether recent events in the political economy will provide a window of opportunity for the professional development of consultants in the future. According to McKenna (2007), the Enron debacle and the recent financial crisis have exposed the risks of deregulation and stimulated the appetite for 'new regulative' bargains. The Sarbanes–Oxley Act, in particular, promises to incentivize but also formalize and 'responsibilize' the role of professional oversight in corporate governance (Coffee 2006). This includes management consultants who, in their informal role as certifiers of management decisions and strategies, may come under increasing pressure 'either to abandon their lucrative practices as gatekeepers for strategic decision-making or to finally accept their place among the full professions through the introduction of an explicit system to monitor both institutional and individual malpractice' (McKenna 2007: 215). Implied therefore is that '[p]rofessional culture and responsibility are not dead concepts' (Kubr 2002: 830) and that stronger regulation in future might be favoured not just by regulators and clients, but by many practising consultants themselves.

9.4 ACCOUNTING FOR THE WEAK PROFESSIONAL DEVELOPMENT OF MANAGEMENT CONSULTING

Turning to the next question debated in the literature—of how we should explain the uneven development in management consulting—it is useful to distinguish between two schools of thought. On the one hand are those who stress the obstacles to professionalization, which are either those intrinsic to the work of consultants or of a more institutional nature. On the other hand are those who argue that management consulting represents a distinctly new kind of occupation of 'knowledge workers', which has largely (if not completely) side-stepped the established model of professional closure in favour of alternative 'occupational strategies' (Fincham 2006).

9.4.1 Barriers to Professional Formation

A starting point for many discussions of why management consultants have been slow to professionalize is the view that distinctive characteristics of their knowledge, their relationships with clients, and the nature of the consulting industry itself have stood in the way (Kyrö 1995; Kubr 2002). It is frequently argued, for example, that consultants operate within a 'weak knowledge field' (Alvesson 1994) and that their expertise does 'not amount to a genuine occupational language or body of theory' (Fincham 2006: 20). Consulting knowledge is also distinctive from that of other professions (such as accounting or medicine), being too esoteric, fluid, and changeable to be embedded in portable, transferable, and testable credentials. Hence Reed (1996: 585) suggests that consultants rely on 'a sophisticated combination of theoretical knowledge, analytical tools and tacit judgemental skills that are very difficult [...] to standardize, replicate and incorporate within formalized [...] routines'. Linked to this is the idea is that consulting knowledge is 'relational', developed through a process of co-production and knowledge transfer with clients (Clark 1995; Fincham 1999; Fincham et al. 2007). Whereas the 'expert discourses' of established professions support 'a monopoly of knowledge' and detachment from clients, that of consultants is focused more on 'supporting shared learning' (Fincham 2006: 20).

A related argument is that commercial pressures faced by management consultants generate strong disincentives to formalize and share knowledge (making it a public good). According to Suddaby and Greenwood (2001), the key to success in management consulting is how quickly firms or individuals are able to discover new management fashions, repackage them as commodities, and disseminate them ahead of the competition. In such an environment the objectives of professional associations—to standardize knowledge (creating what O'Mahoney (2010: 272) terms shared 'libraries of best practice')—may run counter to the goal of developing services, human capital, and brands that are 'organizationally specific' (Morris and Empson 1998).

Lastly it is suggested that the fragmented and open nature of the management consulting business itself has represented an obstacle to professional development. According to Kitay and Wright (2007: 1618): 'reviews of the consulting industry highlight variations in functional focus and structure, ranging from large global corporations to medium sized domestic firms, small partnerships, solo practitioners, academic consultants and corporate "internal" consultants'. Such diversity is further exaggerated by the permeable nature of the boundaries between management consulting and other business sectors such as IT, finance, human resources management (HRM), and project management, all with their own professional associations (O'Mahoney 2010). These conditions, it is argued, are hardly conducive to building a shared sense of professional identity (Kyrö 1995). Nor are they likely to support efforts to agree on a standardized body of knowledge and associated credentials that are unique to management consulting. As Gross and Kieser (2006: 89) suggest, 'a more standardized approach to the training of consultants would presuppose more standardized tasks'.

However, while these explanations are useful to a point, there is a risk of overstating the significance of industry fragmentation and weak knowledge. Historically these conditions have not prevented other groups, such as social workers, or even—if one looks back to the late nineteenth century—accountants (MacDonald 1995), from achieving professional closure. The focus on static characteristics of consulting work and knowledge may also lead us to ignore the historical character of professionalization projects, how these develop over time, and the institutional conditions that either help or hinder their progress.

Recently, a number of studies have begun to address these concerns, focusing not just on the intrinsic characteristics of management consulting but also on how professionalization projects have developed over time (Kipping and Saint-Martin 2005; Gross and Kieser 2006; McKenna 2006, 2007; Kirkpatrick, Muzio, and Kipping 2008; Muzio, Kirkpatrick, and Kipping 2011). The strength of these studies is their ability to identify key actors and negotiations within the historical formation of the management consulting industry, revealing how these connect to wider processes of professionalization. Thus, Gross and Kieser (2006) chart the development of the leading professional association in Germany, the BDU, which represents approximately 23 per cent of consultants. In 1997, this body submitted a proposal to the Ministry of Economics for a law giving them sole right (monopoly) to use the title, 'consultant'. As in Austria, where a form of licensing had been established earlier, the aim was to create a public register of consultants, restricting entry to those with a recognized qualification: the CMC. This proposal was, however, subsequently rejected on the grounds that such regulation might limit choice by raising barriers to competition. In part this reflected the commitment of political elites in Germany to increased deregulation, although, importantly, many large consulting firms were also opposed. According to Gross and Kieser (2006: 80), these firms were 'not concerned about the image of the occupation as such, and they are not at all interested in the establishment of a state-regulated title that would make it easier for their employed consultants to become self-employed'.

Very similar observations about the role of large firms and the state in impeding the development of professions can be drawn from the work of McKenna (2006, 2007). Focusing on the US he notes how leading strategy firms—McKinsey and Booz Allen— campaigned hard to prevent individual states from introducing licensing rules (McKenna 2006). At the same time these firms relied heavily on the targeted recruitment of MBAs, in-house training schemes, and strong corporate cultures as alternative forms of socialization and 'implicit certification' (ibid.: 203). Most were also unwilling to allow top partners from their rivals to sit in judgement on their practice, adopting instead a 'unilateral perspective', which emphasized 'the unique status of each firm's supposedly higher professional standing' (McKenna 2007: 213). Hence, as in Gross and Kieser's (2006) account, the focus is on the practices of leading consulting firms and the indifference of government regulators when explaining the failure of management consultants to professionalize. Over time, these conditions 'drew the centre of gravity away from the battle over individual professional status, and instead imbued the professional field with all of the traits of professional standing, but lacking individual status as a true profession' (McKenna 2007: 210).

Finally, parallels with this argument can be found in the work of Kirkpatrick, Muzio, and Kipping (2008), Muzio, Kirkpatrick, and Kipping (2011), and Kipping and Saint-Martin (2005). Focusing on the UK, these authors note how dominant firms tolerated a weak version of professional regulation largely in order to prevent the state from becoming more involved. Alerted by the rapid growth of the industry in the post-war era and complaints about the quality of services, the government prompted the British Institute of Management (BIM), established in 1947/1948, to address these issues. Following its recommendations, the Institute established a register of 'approved' consultants, with firms asked to provide details about the qualifications of their staff, submit client references, and subscribe to a code of conduct. However, the larger firms (then known as the 'Big Four') opposed this initiative and opted instead for their own brand of self-regulation by forming the Management Consultancies Association (MCA) in 1956. While ostensibly a trade association, this body also sought to regulate the professional standards in the industry and, for a long time after, imposed stringent rules of entry on new members. Nevertheless, by establishing itself as a 'quality control mechanism', the MCA effectively 'reduced the rationale for any government intervention' (Kipping and Saint-Martin 2005: 453).

There has therefore been considerable debate regarding the obstacles to professional development in consulting. While many continue to emphasize the characteristics of consulting knowledge, others have preferred to adopt a more inclusive, historical perspective. The latter makes no *a priori* assumptions about the capacity of management consultants (or any other group) to organize themselves, but rather 'allows critics to identify professionalization efforts independent of their success rates' (Gross and Kieser 2006: 93). As such, the focus shifts away from the traits and resources of a given occupation to the broader historical and institutional conditions that have either helped or hindered efforts to achieve professional recognition.

9.4.2 Management Consulting as an Alternative Form of Occupational Development

In marked contrast to the work discussed so far, others have raised more fundamental questions about whether management consultancy represents a distinctive kind of occupation with a quite different 'occupational strategy' (Leicht and Lyman 2006; Muzio, Ackroyd, and Chanlat 2007). Influential here is Reed's (1996) typology of different forms of expert labour, including so-called liberal and entrepreneurial professions (or knowledge workers). Liberal professions, such as lawyers and doctors, he argues, thrive through processes of occupational closure, restricting access to certain tasks and activities through the development of mandatory credentials and qualifications. Historically, these professionals have prioritized occupational over organizational allegiances and are structured around powerful peak associations, which enjoy extensive representative and self-regulatory powers over their jurisdiction. Traditionally, liberal professionals gravitate towards collegial and informal working arrangements where ownership, control, and work execution are tied together. Conversely, knowledge workers, including management consultants, display a more markedly entrepreneurial orientation as they succeed by solving problems, real or imaginary, for their largely corporate clientele. Implied is a pluralist perspective whereby conventional professionalization is just one of several theoretically possible 'occupational strategies'.

Fincham (2006) also takes up this idea, arguing that management consultants, alongside other groups of knowledge workers (for example, in IT), have actively rejected conventional professionalism and may even consider it 'outdated'. In part this is due to the weak knowledge of consultants (see above), forcing them to focus primarily on the 'legitimation of skills' (ibid.: 20). However, he further suggests that these groups have found viable alternatives to the reliance on professional credentials as a way of promoting collective interests. Specifically, management consultants have relied on strategies of 'marketization' focusing on the acquisition of 'in-demand expertise', such as new techniques or management fashions and the use of 'rhetorical strategies' to justify and stimulate new demand (ibid.: 23). In these ways consultants have achieved impressive growth without forming professions and have had little need for or commitment to 'professional self images' (ibid.: 21).

A slightly different spin on this theme of consultants representing a new kind of occupation or 'profession' is found in the work of Alvesson and Johansson (2002). These authors, like those discussed already, draw attention to the ways in which conventional professionalism might be counter-productive for management consultants. For example, professional claims of independence, objectivity, and neutrality sit uncomfortably with the pressure on consultants to satisfy dominant stakeholder interests within client organizations. This need to downplay professionalism is even greater with respect to what they term the 'agents of anxiety and suppliers of security' role. Here, the focus on promoting management fads and fashions is likely to be in tension with professional notions of 'science or validated practice'. Indeed, '[t]he premium of novelty, exaggeration, persuasiveness, crude commercialism and grand claims runs directly against the conservatism and supposedly rational and sober practice of the acknowledged professions' (ibid.: 239). As such, conventional professionalization might be more of a hindrance than help for consultants, preventing 'free and flexible maneuvering' (ibid.: 243).

In developing this idea of management consulting as an alternative kind of occupation, others have focused more on the wider ideological, regulatory, and historical context (Leicht and Lyman 2006; Muzio, Ackroyd, and Chanlat 2007). Leicht and Lyman (2006: 26) suggest that the rise of neo-liberalism, associated with deregulation, increased competition, lowering trade barriers, and public sector privatization generated significant opportunities for management consultants to emerge and prosper. Specifically, consultants have developed the skills to interpret markets, allowing them to exploit the very same 'neo-liberal market-based logic that led to their creation and prosperity in the first place' (ibid.: 38). They have also benefited from a 'reluctance of Western Governments to intervene with additional regulation/coercion', even 'in the wake of questionable professional conduct' (Leicht and Lyman 2006: 35).

Similarly, Muzio, Ackroyd, and Chanlat (2007) link the peculiar development of management consulting to broader changes in what they call the 'allocative regime'. This is constituted by the policies, priorities, and orientations of powerful institutions, such as the state and capital, which define, frame, and regulate social and economic exchange in a specific historical epoch. Following this line of argument, different types of profession, such as those identified in Reed's (1996) typology (see above), owe their distinctiveness to the historical peculiarities of their context of formation. More specifically, these authors argue that different solutions to the organization of expert labour are functional to the broader rules, assumptions, and institutions (allocative regime), which underpin and govern socio-economic exchanges at a given time. In this context, the entrepreneurial orientation and fluid organization of new forms of expert labour such as management consultancy reflect the workings of a new post-Fordist allocative regime, which emphasizes new priorities such as competitiveness, international expansion, innovation, and cost effectiveness. Such conditions mean that new aspiring occupations are less likely to adopt traditional patterns of professionalization, which are expressions of a past allocative regime.

9.5 Exploring the Consequences of Weak Professionalism

Although the question of why management consultants have failed to professionalize has often taken centre stage in the literature, a related debate has focused more on the *consequences* of this. The emphasis here has been on highlighting the risks of management consulting advice and how such risks might, in turn, be exaggerated by the relative lack of professional regulation. However, while some argue that strengthening the profession could offer a solution to this problem, others are far more sceptical in this regard.

9.5.1 The Risks of Hiring Consultants

The risks associated with management consulting advice are well documented. In recent years the management consulting industry has come under attack from politicians, the popular press, academics, and a growing number of disaffected industry insiders for a number of alleged offences (Pinault 2001; Craig and Brooks 2006). These include wasting public money in government contracts, selling fads that don't work, taking advantage of managers to sell unnecessary services, and ignoring conflicts of interest in their dealings with clients. A number of highly publicized consultancy failures such as the extreme cost over-runs arising from the computerization of the NHS (O'Mahoney 2010), the failure of a large IT system designed for the Child Support Agency (Cohen 2005), and the whole Enron debacle (see below; MacDougald and Greenwood, Chapter 5, this volume) has led many to question the practices of the industry and the value that consultants deliver.

These themes are also echoed in the growing critical academic literature on how consultants relate to their clients (Clark and Fincham 2002; Sturdy et al. 2009). Here emphasis is placed on the 'symbolic nature of consultant strategies and consultancy as a powerful system of persuasion' (Fincham 1999: 335). In common with other agents such as gurus, business schools, and mass media organizations, consultants are seen as key players in the manufacture and dissemination of management fashions (Jung and Kieser, Chapter 16, this volume). While these fashions may promise quantum leaps in performance, it is suggested that more often than not they are based on hype-driven and unsubstantiated advice (Sorge and van Witteloostuijn 2004). Indeed, to a greater extent than with other business services professions, consultants are accused of actively generating 'demand for their own services [...] by stirring up managers' fear and greed and by making managers dependent on them' (Kieser 2002: 182). The result is to artificially inflate the uptake of management fads not to mention the costs associated with cynicism and disillusionment when change interventions fail to produce results (Sturdy et al. 2009).

Returning to the main concerns of this chapter it is often argued that these risks associated with management consulting advice flow in large part from the absence of professional regulation (Kipping, Kirkpatrick, and Muzio 2006; McKenna 2007). Unlike other business services—such as law or accounting—there exist no 'institutional clues to distinguish qualified from non qualified consulting providers' (Glückler and Armbrüster 2003: 272–273). Linked to this are risks associated with the lack of any effective means of holding management consultants to account when things go wrong. According to McKenna (2007: 212), '[u]nlike law, medicine or even commercial aviation, there exists no institutionalized system to deal with professional errors in the routine practice of management consulting'. In practice, clients are left with the choice of either litigation through the civil courts or exit, both of which are unsatisfactory. While civil cases on the basis of professional misconduct are not unheard of, they are hard to prove due to the lack of publicly agreed standards against which consulting practice might be judged (Glückler and Armbrüster 2003: 273). Client exit strategies (terminating the relationship with a consulting firm) are equally problematic, especially in situations where contracts have been running for some time and where both the client and supplier have made extensive transaction-specific investments (Werr and Permer 2007).

These risks associated with the lack of regulation are most telling when one looks closely at major scandals involving consultants. Kipping, Kirkpatrick, and Muzio (2006: 161) for example, note that, following the Enron collapse, while McKinsey & Co. had been a key advisor—praising the company for it's 'visionary "asset light" business strategy'—it was Andersen, the accountants and auditors, that took the blame and eventually disappeared as a firm. Importantly, Andersen could be held accountable for breaking their legal and 'professional' obligations as auditors of a public company (see also Coffee 2006). By contrast, McKinsey, which had only offered 'advice', was largely unaffected. Even though 'an article in *Business Week* by John Byrne highlighted the fact that Enron was only the last of a whole string of McKinsey clients to declare bankruptcy [...] this caused only a small dent in the consultancy's reputation and it was soon back to business as usual' (Kipping, Kirkpatrick, and Muzio 2006: 162).

9.5.2 Professional Regulation: Would It Make a Difference?

Notwithstanding these observations about the risks of management consulting advice, there is some disagreement in the literature concerning how much difference strong professional regulation would make. On the one hand is the view that it would be highly beneficial to clients (Kubr 2002). As well as providing external third party standards that might be used to judge quality, there is the possibility that a more established professional body would police its own membership more effectively. It could offer a viable alternative to the court system if things go wrong, especially if exclusion from the profession also meant exclusion from the market (Coffee 2006). In the longer term such regulation might also engender deeper changes in behaviour, perhaps even helping to 'prevent a [...] slide to the lowest common denominator by which some consultancies felt compelled to get too close to their clients in order to prevent their competitors landing lucrative contracts' (O'Mahoney et al. 2008: 37).

Added to this are the benefits for practitioners themselves. Important here is the role professional associations might play in enhancing the reputation and legitimacy of the sector as a whole. In the US for example, Booz Allen Hamilton, McKinsey, and others originally formed the Association of Consulting Management Engineers (ACME) in direct response to what they saw as charlatanism on the part of firms that did not subscribe to their professional model of management consulting (see above). More recently, it has been suggested that in the post-Enron environment, a greater stress on ethics and 'social responsibility' can only be beneficial for consultants (Kubr 2002: 143). This may especially be the case for small firms and self-employed practitioners. Lacking their own distinctive brands, these firms might view membership of professional associations not only as an opportunity for networking, but also as an important source of reputation capital (ibid.).

However, against this, others have raised questions about the feasibility and effectiveness of stronger professional controls. An obvious problem is that, even where established professions are concerned, well-established institutions of voluntary self-regulation are often no guarantee of protection for clients. This can be seen in the case of law, accounting, and even medicine (the archetypal profession), where institutions of self-regulation have recently been found wanting as mechanisms for preventing individual and systemic malpractice (Dent 2007). Taking up this theme, O'Mahoney (2010) argues that professional registration is unlikely to raise standards or offer much protection for clients. Because consultants work in fluid project teams it may be very hard to identify malpractice, and normally firms rather than individuals are held liable. These firms, in turn, are also likely to be more effective than professions when it comes to detecting and punishing malpractice. Indeed, 'a reputation for quality is so valuable to consultancy firms that incompetent employees are unlikely to be tolerated for long [...] in stark contrast to other "professions" in which individuals are rarely removed from the registers' (ibid.: 272).

Linked to this is the argument that professional regulation—even if it could be achieved—would only be of limited use given the indeterminate nature of consulting advice (Clark 1993). Important here is a distinction made by Glückler and Armbrüster (2003: 270) between 'institutional' and 'transactional' uncertainty. The former 'derives from the lack of formal institutional standards such as professionalization, industry boundaries, and product standards'. This exaggerates the problem discussed earlier of clients being unable to differentiate between qualified and unqualified providers. However, management consulting is also characterized by 'transactional uncertainty', which 'derives from confidentiality of information, service-product intangibility, and the interdependent and interactive character of the co-production of consultants and clients' (Glückler and

Armbrüster 2003: 270). This level of uncertainty generates further risks for clients associated with the leakage of commercial information and the intangibility of consulting services. According to Glückler and Armbrüster (2003), while stronger professional regulation might theoretically help to reduce institutional uncertainty it is of little use in dealing with transactional uncertainty, which is inherent to the nature of consultancy as a service. To cope with transactional uncertainty clients rely instead on other mechanisms such as brand or 'networked reputation'. The latter represents a cost-effective way of learning about a given supplier from the direct experience of other client organizations within established networks. By contrast, referrals from professional associations are used hardly at all by clients when making decisions about the purchase of consulting advice.

Such arguments also connect with observations about the growing sophistication of clients in the procurement and evaluation of consulting services (Sturdy et al. 2009; O'Mahoney 2010). In recent years procurement specialists (sometimes recruited from management consulting firms themselves) have become more involved in decision-making, employing new techniques to limit risks to the client. The latter include contingent contracts, framework agreements, reverse auctions, and incentivized or fixed-price payment schemes (Werr and Permer 2007; O'Mahoney et al. 2008). A further development is the growth of new business services, such as 'meta consulting', which focus on enhancing client capabilities to procure and then effectively manage consultants (Mohe 2007). Taken together these changes could imply a shift in the balance of power between clients and consulting firms, arguably reducing the need for third party standards and industry associations. As clients themselves become more 'professional' in their procurement, this, in turn, serves as a proxy for the professional self-regulation of suppliers (Mohe 2005).

Lastly, it has been suggested that clients themselves may, paradoxically, have little interest in greater professional regulation. One reason for this is that enhanced training requirements and licensing could drive up the price of qualified labour and therefore the cost of consulting advice (Muzio, Kirkpatrick, and Kipping 2011). Client organizations may also view third party obligations and claims of impartiality as unnecessary constraints. This is particularly so when consultants are asked to adopt the role of 'traders in trouble', where the focus is on 'a demonstrated ability of a consultant to act in a way that supports the interests of the person paying for the service' (Alvesson and Johansson 2002: 237–238). Hence it is possible that clients will be less than enthusiastic about strong professional regulation and may prefer instead 'soft forms of regulation' (Kipping and Saint-Martin 2005: 461), where the emphasis is on agreeing looser guidelines for ethical practice (O'Mahoney 2010).

9.6 Conclusion

The aim of this chapter has been to explore the question of the professional status and development of management consultants. As we have seen, the literature on this topic is still very much in its infancy, although a number of emerging themes and debates can be identified. First, this concerns the extent to which one might reasonably define management consultants as a profession. Here there is evidence to suggest that while consultants in many countries have tried to organize themselves as professions, this has not been particularly effective in terms of securing occupational closure. Related to this is a second theme concerning how one might account for this relative failure to professionalize—especially given the growing size and profile of management consulting? Finally, attention has focused on the consequences of weak (or non-existent) professional regulation for those who consume or use management consulting advice.

Evident from the literature on both of the latter themes are diametrically opposing viewpoints and conclusions. On the question of why consultants have failed to professionalize, for example, a majority operate within the framework of an 'unwilling and/or unable to' thesis, which emphasizes how a series of functional characteristics of the knowledge-base, work profile, and industry structure makes professionalization unattainable or undesirable. By contrast, others have adopted a more inclusive perspective—drawing on ideas from the sociology of professions—to argue that prevailing institutional conditions (in particular the role of the state and large firms) have been equally if not more important in shaping professional development. Similar divisions are apparent in debates focusing on the consequences of weak professional regulation. While some take the view that stronger professional associations would serve to enhance the reputation and trustworthiness of consultants, others are much more sceptical.

In some respects it is hard to see how further progress might be made in these debates given such radically different starting points. As we have seen, there are, in much of the literature, deeply rooted assumptions about the distinctiveness of management consulting (both as an occupation and as a type of business service). This in turn encourages the view that 'professional' modes of regulation are both unnecessary and undesirable, representing 'archaic and quaint constraints on unfettered and efficient capital markets' (Greenwood, Suddaby, and McDougald 2006). By contrast, if one starts with an alternative view, that management consulting is not particularly distinctive (as an occupation or type of knowledge) then entirely different conclusions are possible. From this perspective the question of whether or not management consultants *could* professionalize and whether doing so would make any difference to clients is far more open ended.

Notwithstanding these obstacles to productive dialogue, there exist a number of useful avenues for further research and debate. First, there is the question of whether recent events in the political economy will provide a window of opportunity for the professional development of consultants. This is something which, in the post-Enron context, has been raised as a distinct possibility in the recent literature, although more empirical research is required to assess this potential development. A second, related, theme regards the consequences of professionalization (or the lack of it) for those who work in the industry. On the one hand it might be argued that management consultants have little need for professions given the fact that they already enjoy high levels of pay and workplace autonomy (Alvesson and Thompson 2005). However, these conditions may not apply to the majority of graduate trainees working in firms that are focused primarily on the delivery of highly standardized, off-the-peg services (Kipping and Kirkpatrick

2007). Where this group is concerned, professional credentials may serve to increase mobility and employability in the 'war for talent'. A stronger sense of professional identity rooted in shared socialization beyond the firm might also serve to counterbalance many of the anxieties and insecurities experienced by consultants in their day-to-day dealings with clients and peers (Whittle 2006; O'Mahoney 2007). But while these outcomes have been hinted at in the literature only very few studies, to date, have investigated this topic in detail.

Lastly, there are questions about how the specific case of management consulting might contribute to our wider understanding of the changing nature and focus of professionalism. Important here is the work of Reed (1996), Fincham (2006), and Leicht and Lyman (2006) on the distinctive occupational strategies of consultants vis-à-vis more established professions. But equally significant is the argument that management consulting also represents a new model of 'corporate professionalism' that is increasingly skewed to the interests and priorities of large firms (Kipping, Kirkpatrick, and Muzio 2006; Kirkpatrick, Muzio, and Kipping 2008; Muzio, Kirkpatrick, and Kipping 2011). This role of firms as 'significant actors and sites for professional regulation' (Suddaby, Cooper, and Greenwood 2007: 356) has been noted elsewhere (for example, in law and accounting), but seems especially marked in the case of management consulting. As we saw, in many countries, leading firms have been instrumental in preventing greater regulation. They have also invested heavily in the development of own brands, mimicking the language and culture of established professions to build reputation and control their workforce (Kipping 2011). In such a hostile environment professional associations themselves have changed their tactics, focusing increasingly on the accreditation of loose competencies and the recruitment of firms, as corporate members, in addition to their traditional constituency of individual practitioners. However, while these trends are noted in the literature our ability to comment in more detail remains limited, thus suggesting another potentially very fruitful line of enquiry in the future.

REFERENCES

Alvesson, M. (1994). 'Organizations as Rhetoric: Knowledge Intensive Firms and the Struggle with Ambiguity'. *Journal of Management Studies*, 30/5, 997–1015.

Alvesson, M. and Johansson, A. W. (2002). 'Professionalism and Politics in Management Consultancy Work'. In T. Clark and R. Fincham (eds), *Critical Consulting: New Perspectives on the Management Advice Industry*. Oxford: Blackwell, 228–246.

Alvesson, M. and Robertson, M. (2006). 'The Best and the Brightest: The Construction, Significance and Effects of Elite Identities in Consulting Firms'. *Organization*, 13/2, 195–224.

Alvesson, M. and Thompson, P. (2005). 'Post-Bureaucracy?' In S. Ackroyd, R. Batt, P. Thompson, and P. S. Tolbert (eds), *The Oxford Handbook of Work and Organization*. Oxford: Oxford University Press, 485–507.

Anderson-Gough, F., Grey, C. and Robson, K. (2000). 'In the Name of the Client: The Service Ethic in Professional Service Firms'. *Human Relations*, 53/9, 1151–1174.

Brint, S. G. (1994). *In an Age of Experts: The Changing Role of Professionals in Politics and Public Life*. Princeton, NJ: Princeton University Press.

Brock, D., Powell, M., and Hinings, C. R. (eds) (1999). *Restructuring the Professional Organization: Accounting, Healthcare, and Law*. London: Routledge.

Clark, T. (1993). 'The Market Provision of Management Services, Information Asymmetries and Service Quality—Some Market Solutions: An Empirical Example'. *British Journal of Management*, 4/4, 235–251.

Clark, T. (1995). *Managing Consultants: Consultancy as the Management of Impressions*. Buckingham: Open University Press.

Clark, T. and Fincham, R. (eds) (2002). *Critical Consulting: New Perspectives on the Management Advice Industry*. Oxford: Blackwell.

Coffee, J. C. (2006). *Gatekeepers: The Professions and Corporate Governance*. Oxford: Oxford University Press.

Cohen, N. (2005). 'Natural Born Billers'. *The Observer*, 19 June. Available at http://www.guardian.co.uk/money/2005/jun/19/comment.publicservices accessed 21 September 2011.

Craig, D. and Brooks, R. (2006). *Plundering the Public Sector*. London: Constable.

Dent, M. (2007). 'Medicine, Nursing and Changing Professional Jurisdictions in the UK'. In D. Muzio, S. Ackroyd, and J-F. Chanlat (eds), *Redirections in the Study of Expert Labour: Established Professions and New Expert Occupations*. Basingstoke: Palgrave Macmillan, 101–117.

Edersheim, E. H. (2004). *McKinsey's Marvin Bower: Vision, Leadership, and the Creation of Management Consulting*. Hoboken, NJ: John Wiley & Sons.

Empson, L. and Chapman, C. S. (2006). 'Partnership Versus Corporation: Implications of Alternative Forms of Governance for Managerial Authority and Organizational Priorities in Professional Service Firms'. *Research in the Sociology of Organizations*, 24, 145–176.

Evetts, J. (2006). 'A Short Note: The Sociology of Professional Groups'. *Current Sociology*, 54/1, 133–143.

Fincham, R. (1999). 'The Consultant–Client Relationship: Critical Perspectives on the Management of Organizational Change'. *Journal of Management Studies*, 36/3, 335–351.

Fincham, R. (2006). 'Knowledge Work as Occupational Strategy: Comparing IT and Management Consulting'. *New Technology, Work and Employment*, 21/1, 16–28.

Fincham, R., Clark, T., Handley, K., and Sturdy, A. (2007). 'Knowledge Narratives and Heterogeneity in Management Consultancy and Business Services'. In D. Muzio, S. Ackroyd, and J-F. Chanlat (eds) *Redirections in the Study of Expert Labour: Established Professions and New Expert Occupations*. Basingstoke: Palgrave Macmillan, 183–203.

Fournier, V. (1999). 'The Appeal to "Professionalism" as a Disciplinary Mechanism'. *Sociological Review*, 47/2, 280–307.

Freidson, E. (1970). *Professional Dominance: The Social Structure of Medical Care*. New York: Atherton Press.

Freidson, E. (2001). *Professionalism: The Third Logic*. Cambridge: Polity.

Galanter, M. and T. Palay (1991). *Tournament of Lawyers: The Transformation of the Big Law Firm*. Chicago: University of Chicago Press.

Glückler, J. and Armbrüster, T. (2003). 'Bridging Uncertainty in Management Consulting: The Mechanisms of Trust and Networked Reputation'. *Organization Studies*, 24/2, 269–297.

Greenwood, R., Suddaby, R., and McDougald, M. (2006). 'Introduction'. *Professional Service Firms: Research in the Sociology of Organizations*, 24, 1–16.

Gross, C. and Kieser, A. (2006). 'Are Consultants Moving Towards Professionalization?' *Research in the Sociology of Organizations*, 24, 69–100.

Hughes, E. C. (1971). *The Sociological Eye: Selected Papers*. Chicago: Aldine-Atherton.

International Council of Management Consulting Institutes (ICMCI) (2008). 'Certified Management Consultant Brochure'. Available at http://static.icmci.org/download/?noGzip=1&id=1797497 accessed 1 October 2011.

Johnson, T. J. (1972). *Professions and Power*. London: Macmillan.

Kieser, A. (2002). 'Managers as Marionettes? Using Fashion Theories to Explain the Success of Consultancies'. In M. Kipping and L. Engwall (eds), *Management Consulting*. Oxford: Oxford University Press, 167–183.

Kipping, M. (2002). 'Trapped in Their Wave: The Evolution of Management Consultancies'. In T. Clark and R. Fincham (eds), *Critical Consulting: New Perspectives on the Management Advice Industry*. Oxford: Blackwell, 28–49.

Kipping, M. (2011). 'Hollow from the Start? Image Professionalism in Management Consulting'. *Current Sociology*, 59/4, 530–550.

Kipping, M. and Kirkpatrick, I. (2007). 'From Taylorism as Product to Taylorism as Process: Knowledge-Intensive Firms in a Historical Perspective'. In D. Muzio, S. Ackroyd, and J-F. Chanlat (eds), *Redirections in the Study of Expert Labour: Established Professions and New Expert Occupations*. Basingstoke: Palgrave Macmillan, 163–182.

Kipping, M. and Saint-Martin, D. (2005). 'Between Regulation, Promotion and Consumption: Government and Management Consultancy in Britain'. *Business History*, 47/3, 449–465.

Kipping, M., Kirkpatrick, I., and Muzio, D. (2006). 'Overly Controlled or Out of Control? Management Consultants and the New Corporate Professionalism'. In J. Craig (ed.), *Production Values: Futures for Professionalism*. London: Demos, 153–165.

Kirkpatrick, I., Muzio, D., and Kipping, M. (2008). 'From Association Led to Corporate-Led Professions: The Case of Management Consulting in the UK'. Paper presented at International Sociological Association conference, Barcelona, September.

Kitay, J. and Wright, C. (2007). 'From Prophets to Profits: The Occupational Rhetoric of Management Consultants'. *Human Relations*, 60/11, 1,613–1,640.

Kubr, M. (2002). *Management Consulting: A Guide to the Profession*. Geneva: International Labour Office.

Kyrö, P. (1995). 'The Management Consulting Industry Described by Using the Concept of "Profession"'. University of Helsinki, Research bulletin no. 87.

Larson, M. S. (1977). *The Rise of Professionalism: A Sociological Analysis*. Berkeley: University of California Press.

Leicht, K. T. and Lyman, E. C. M. (2006). 'Markets, Institutions and the Crisis of Professional Practice'. *Research in the Sociology of Organizations*, 24, 17–44.

MacDonald, K. M. (1995). *The Sociology of the Professions*. London: Sage.

McKenna, C. D. (2006). *The World's Newest Profession: Management Consulting in the Twentieth Century*. New York: Cambridge University Press.

McKenna, C.D. (2007). 'Give Professionalization a Chance! Why Management Consulting May Yet Become a Full Profession'. In D. Muzio, S. Ackroyd, and J-F. Chanlat (eds), *Redirections in the Study of Expert Labour: Established Professions and New Expert Occupations*. Basingstoke: Palgrave Macmillan, 204–216.

McKinlay, J. B. (1973). 'On the Professional Regulation of Change'. In P. Halmos (ed.), *Professionalization and Social Change*. Keele: University of Keele, 61–84.

Mintzberg, H. (1979). *The Structuring of Organizations: A Synthesis of the Research*. London: F. T. Prentice Hall.

Millerson, G. (1964). *The Qualifying Associations: A Study in Professionalization*. London: Routledge and K. Paul.

Mohe, M. (2005). 'Generic Strategies for Managing Consultants: Insights from Client's Companies in Germany'. *Journal of Change Management*, 5/3, 357–365.

Mohe, M. (2007). 'Meta Consulting: Idea, Function and Limitations of a New Business Model in the Consulting Market'. Paper presented at the workshop on 'Innovative Capabilities and the Role of Consultants in the Information Economy', ZEW Mannheim, Germany, November.

Morris, T. and Empson, L. (1998). 'Organization and Expertise: An Exploration of Knowledge Bases and the Management of Accounting and Consulting Firms'. *Accounting, Organizations and Society*, 23/5–6, 609–624.

Muzio, D., Ackroyd, S., and Chanlat, J-F. (eds) (2007). *Redirections in the Study of Expert Labour: Established Professions and New Expert Occupations*. Basingstoke: Palgrave Macmillan.

Muzio, D., Kirkpatrick, I., and Kipping, M. (2011). 'Professions, Organizations and the State: Applying the Sociology of the Professions to the Case of Management Consultancy'. *Current Sociology*, 59/6, 805–824.

O'Mahoney, J. (2007). 'Disrupting Identity: Trust and Angst in Management Consulting'. In S. Bolton (ed.), *Searching for the H in Human Resource Management*. London: Sage, 281–302.

O'Mahoney, J. (2010). *Management Consultancy*. Oxford: Oxford University Press.

O'Mahoney, J., Adams, R., Antonacopoulou, E., and Neely, A. (2008). *A Scoping Study of Contemporary and Future Challenges in the UK Management Consulting Industry*. London: ESRC.

Parkin, F. (1974). *The Social Analysis of Class Structure*. London: Tavistock Publications.

Pinault, L. (2001). *Consulting Demons: Inside the Unscrupulous World of Global Corporate Consulting*. New York: Harper Business.

Reed, M. I. (1996). 'Expert Power and Control in Late Modernity: an Empirical Review and Theoretical Synthesis'. *Organization Studies*, 17/4, 573–597.

Ruef, M. (2002). 'At the Interstices of Organizations: The Expansion of the Management Consulting Profession, 1933–1997'. In K. Sahlin-Andersson and L. Engwall (eds), *The Expansion of Management Knowledge: Carriers, Flows, and Sources*. Stanford, CA: Stanford University Press, 74–95.

Sorge, A. and van Witteloostuijn, A. (2004). 'The (Non)sense of Organizational Change: An Essai About Universal Management Hypes, Sick Consultancy Metaphors, and Healthy Organization Theories'. *Organization Studies*, 25, 1205–1231.

Sturdy, A., Handley, K., Clark, T., and Fincham, R. (2009). *Management Consultancy: Boundaries and Knowledge in Action*. Oxford: Oxford University Press.

Suddaby, R. and Greenwood, R. (2001). 'Colonizing Knowledge: Commodification as a Dynamic of Jurisdictional Expansion in Professional Service Firms'. *Human Relations*, 54/7, 933–953.

Suddaby, R., Cooper, D. J., and Greenwood, R. (2007). 'Transnational Regulation of Professional Services: Governance Dynamics of Field Level Organizational Change'. *Accounting, Organizations and Society*, 32, 333–362.

Tisdall, P. (1982). *Agents of Change: The Development and Practice of Management Consultancy*. London: Heinemann.

Von Nordenflycht, A. (2010). 'What is a Professional Service Firm? Towards a Theory and Taxonomy of Knowledge Intensive Firms'. *Academy of Management Review*, 35/1, 155–174.

Werr, A. and Permer, F. (2007). 'Purchasing Management Consulting Services: From Management Autonomy to Purchasing Involvement'. *Journal of Purchasing and Supply Management*, 13/2, 98–112.

Whittle, A. (2006). 'The Paradoxical Repertoires of Management Consultancy'. *Journal of Organizational Change Management*, 19/4, 424–443.

CHAPTER 10

ECONOMICS APPROACHES TO MANAGEMENT CONSULTING

NICOLE J. SAAM

10.1 INTRODUCTION

THE purpose of this chapter is to provide an overview of the contribution of economics perspectives to our understanding of management consulting. It examines what approaches there are, what we know, and future directions for research in management consulting. Prior to the emergence of new institutional economics, which arose as a response to criticisms of neoclassical economic theory, there was no significant research that focused on management consulting from an economics perspective. Most probably, mainstream economics simply assumed that neoclassical economic theory would apply to any industry and business. Therefore, from the point of view of neoclassical economic theory, there is barely any explicit research on management consulting. This situation changed with the development of the transaction-cost approach, the property rights approach, and agency theory, which have become the major contributions to what is known today as new institutional economics. These approaches have analysed industries and businesses in more detail; in particular, they have sought industries where they could apply their criticism of neoclassical economic theory. One of these turned out to be the management consulting industry.

This chapter will begin with an outline of the evolution of economics and its basic assumptions. It then turns to the contributions from new institutional economics for the understanding of management consulting—specifically, agency theory, transaction-cost economics, and property rights theory—with overviews of the extant literature for each of them. Contributions from another institutional economics school of thought, namely heterodox institutional economics, are presented in the subsequent section, before the chapter turns to other economics approaches, including classical microeconomic theory and behavioural economics. Finally, the present state of affairs will be summarized and assessed, and, most importantly given the current dearth of work from an economics perspective, directions for future research will be outlined.

10.2 AN OVERVIEW OF ECONOMICS AND ITS BASIC ASSUMPTIONS

Neoclassical microeconomic theory is based on methodological individualism, according to which the analysis and explanation of collective phenomena are carried out through assumptions about the actions of actors in particular situations. Actors have at their disposal resources (including restrictions on action), which they can employ to achieve their aims (also known as preferences). To this end they can choose between different alternatives for action. Actors are assumed to choose alternatives that permit the most complete achievement of their aims, taking account of any restrictions on action. Further differentiation of assumptions about restrictions on action and what is meant by 'most complete' (e.g. maximization of utility, maximization of subjectively expected utility, or 'satisficing') leads to different variants of economics.

Utility theory is based on the microeconomic theory of total competition in a world where resources are scarce (see, as an introduction, Frank 1997). It assumes fully informed actors, who confront each other in the market—the actions of one actor having no direct effects on the choices made by other actors. This approach assumes many consumers and large markets, where the actors (households or firms) are obliged to adapt their price to the market rate. Due to the number of competing offers, the chances of influencing the prices of goods and services are minimal. Consumers and producers therefore react only to the market prices, not to the actions of the other participants in the market. The target volumes that the market participants seek to maximize depend entirely on their own choices regarding quantities of sales or consumption of goods and market prices. The expression 'direct effects' also refers to the quality of the products. The products are described as exchange goods, that is, as finished products, with neither the purchaser nor the seller having any influence on their characteristics at the moment of transfer to the client. Within utility theory, optimization calculations come into play.

John von Neumann and Oscar Morgenstern (1947) criticized utility theory, arguing that most economic problems were strategic problems, that is, problems that require market participants to involve the actions of other actors in their choices, for example, when very few firms are competing against each other as suppliers. The problems resulting from such deficiencies in competition can be dealt with adequately only by means of strategic thinking. From these basic ideas game theory has developed (see, as an introduction, Osborne 2004). This is a theory of rational action that assumes that the actions of an actor have direct effects on the choices of other actors (strategic interdependence).

The next stage was the development of so-called new institutional economics (see, as an introduction, Furubotn and Richter 1998), which arose as a response to criticisms of the neoclassical theories of rational action. According to North (1981: 5), '[t]he world with which [neoclassical theory] is concerned is a frictionless one in which institutions do not exist and all change occurs through perfectly operating markets. In short, the costs of acquiring information, uncertainty, and transaction costs do not exist.' Transaction-cost theory, property rights theory, and agency theory all developed in parallel, each abandoning the idea of the completely smooth-running and cost-free interaction between actors. Today, these theoretical positions constitute the different branches of new institutional economics.

Neoclassicism assumes the foundation and use of institutions or organizations by economic actors to be a matter of course and cost-free. Coase (1937) stresses, by contrast, that their foundation and use involves costs, which he calls transaction costs. Transaction costs comprise the costs of provision, maintenance, and use of institutions. In the words of Arrow (1969: 48), they are the running costs of an economic system. The transaction-cost approach explains the existence of non-market institutions, such as organizations (including firms) and the state, as arising out of the aim of rationally acting actors to minimize their transaction costs (Williamson 1975, 1985).

In a world of uncertainty and transaction costs, the question of ownership of property becomes significant, as powerful incentives for the provision and use of economic goods (resources) are attributed to property. The property rights approach (Alchian 1961; Demsetz 1967; Alchian and Demsetz 1972) therefore focuses on property relationships in society. This approach defines property as a bundle comprising four property rights in a good: the right to use the good (usus), the right to earn income from the good (usus fructus), the right to change the substance of the good (abusus), and the right of transfer. Property rights are regulated in contracts (e.g. purchase contracts, employment contracts, or constitutions), which are concluded between actors. According to this approach, the actors also behave in a rational way in relation to their property rights, that is, they 'make the most of' their property rights. Consequently, property rights structures of greater or lesser efficiency can be identified, and statements about the effect of private property and common property can be inferred from them.

At the heart of agency theory (Ross 1973; Jensen and Meckling 1976; Fama 1980) is the institution of the contract and its embodiment in exchange relationships between a principal and an agent. Examples of agency relationships are the relationships between purchaser and seller, employer and employee, and shareholder and manager. The principal delegates certain tasks and decisions to the agent, who receives remuneration for their services. Agency theory assumes that the behaviour of individuals is characterized by individual utility maximization, rationality, and opportunism. It shares the assumptions of utility maximization and rationality with several other economics approaches, such as utility theory and game theory. In these approaches, opportunism represents an additional assumption that goes beyond that of utility maximization. Opportunism assumes that actors make opportunistic use of the behavioural scope offered by, for instance, incomplete contracts, and that they employ cunning in the strategic pursuit of their individual interests (Williamson 1975: 26) and indeed are dishonest in the sense that they conceal their preferences, misrepresent data, and deliberately distort facts (Furubotn and Richter 1998). Williamson (1985) has made it clear that this assumption is not a statement about humans in general, but is merely a behavioural assumption related to the situation, for example when people interact as principal and agent: 'I merely assume that some individuals are opportunistic some of the time and that different trustworthiness is rarely transparent *ex ante*' (ibid.: 64). The possibility of incorrect behaviour is borne in mind when the contract is drawn up. Agency relationships are, moreover, characterized by asymmetric information distribution, uncertainty, and the different risk preferences of the principal and agent. Agency theory analyses typical problems of agency relationships from the perspective of the principal and elaborates solutions to the principal's problems.

10.3 CONTRIBUTIONS FROM NEW INSTITUTIONAL ECONOMICS

10.3.1 The Nature of the Consulting Service

The effort to describe the peculiarities of the market for consultancy services, in particular the market provision and the purchase of consultancy services, has been apparent from the outset of an economic analysis of management consulting (Clark 1993; Mitchell 1994; Kaas and Schade 1995). Authors concur that the market for management consulting services is rather opaque. The consultants' qualifications and the quality of their service are difficult to judge. Moreover, there is often a considerable asymmetry of information between consultants and their clients, and high levels of uncertainty characterize the decision process of the client when choosing a certain consultant. To a large degree, the client is involved in the creation of the consulting product. At the same time the economic repercussions of consulting services for businesses can be momentous. While Clark (1993) and Kaas and Schade (1995) agree on these characteristics, they approach the question of the nature of the consultant's product from different perspectives. Clark (1993) relies on the distinction between goods and services to describe and explain the character of the consultant's product; in contrast, Kaas and Schade (1995) refer to the concepts of exchange good and contracted good.

Thus, Clark (1993) conceptualizes the consultant's product as a service. Services differ from goods in a number of important respects. For example, they cannot be sampled before purchase (intangibility), and there is often no separation between the consumption and production of services (inseparability). Services are difficult to standardize because the client plays an important role in the production of the service (heterogeneity). Additionally, they are perishable since they are destroyed in the process of consumption and cannot be stored. Clark (1993) states that these features create special problems for the market provision of management consulting services, in particular problems of quality assurance. Such problems indicate the importance of formal regulation. In the absence of regulation there is an information asymmetry between client and consultant, which can be further described and analysed by principal-agent theory (Clark 1993). Clark (1995) makes the point that clients are buying no more than a promise.

Kaas and Schade (1995) classify management consulting as a contracted good, which is produced by the joint action of consultant (agent) and client (principal) after the consulting contract has been signed. In this, they follow Schade and Schott (1993), who state that at the moment of purchase, management consulting exists not in the form of a good but in that of a contract including a service commitment. If sales negotiations are understood primarily as an act of purchase—in other words, as an exchange of property rights—some of the key features characterizing the management consulting market are overlooked. Schade and Schott (1993) argue that sales negotiations for management consulting are fundamentally about the negotiation of a contract relating to a co-operative relationship, within which the good is produced after entering into the contract. Both the buyer (client) and the seller (consultant) can have a considerable bearing upon the quality of the good after the conclusion of a contract. Schade and Schott (1993) argue that while some service commitments lend themselves to standardization (e.g. the food offered at franchise restaurants), management consulting represents a non-standardized service commitment. This results in problems of information and uncertainty: the quality of the good cannot be positively determined, neither prior to nor after purchase.

Thus, management consulting is characterized by credence qualities, that is, it is difficult for clients to ascertain the quality even after they have consumed it. By contrast, it is not correctly described as a search good, for example, a product or service with features and characteristics easily evaluated before purchase, nor as an experience good, that is, a product or service where product characteristics such as quality or price are difficult to observe in advance, but can be ascertained upon consumption. Put differently, neither the optimization of the number of search steps leading up to the purchase decision, nor the processes of trial and error after purchase can create certainty about the quality of consulting (Schade and Schott 1993). The purchase frequency is too low for processes of trial and error. Moreover, the cost of management consulting is often so high that clients cannot easily repeat the purchase.

Schade and Schott (1993) also refer to the path dependencies that are created by the first intervention of the consultants. Path dependencies refers to the notion that the set of decisions one faces for any given circumstance is limited by the decisions one has made in the past, even though past circumstances may no longer be relevant. It is virtually impossible to purchase the same consulting package/service for the same problem again. The problem will naturally be somewhat different after the first consulting assignment; if it were to remain the same (i.e. if the solution was not effective), the same consulting service would not be considered for future assignments. In summary, it can be said that, in the case of management consulting, the contract becomes a critical product property, which clearly sets the consultant's product apart from exchange goods (Schade and Schott 1993).

Several empirical studies have collected evidence suggesting that the consultant's product cannot be characterized as an exchange good. In particular, consulting firms do not compete on the basis of the price of their services. Clients do not choose providers on that basis. This result was confirmed for companies in Australia (Dawes, Dowling, and Patterson 1992), the United Kingdom (Clark 1993, 1995; Bryson 1997), Germany (Kaas and Schade 1995; Kohr 2000; Greschuchna 2006), and the United States (Lindahl and Beyers 1999). Instead, evidence suggests that reputation (Dawes, Dowling, and Patterson 1992; Clark 1993; Kaas and Schade 1995; Bryson 1997; Lindahl and Beyer 1999), personal recommendation (Clark 1993; Kaas and Schade 1995), personal knowledge of the consultant, and long-term relationships with the client (Dawes, Dowling, and Patterson 1992; Kaas and Schade 1995; Svensson 2000, 2001), as well as previous experience with the consulting firm (Dawes, Dowling, and Patterson 1992; Bryson 1997), play major roles in the client's decision for either contacting or selecting a certain consultant.

However, two more detailed empirical analyses of German companies assume a stage-by-stage selection process. Whereas Höck and Keuper (2001) propose a two-stage process, with a first and a final stage, Kohr (2000) assumes a three-stage process: gross selection, pre-selection and final selection. They suggest that previous experience, reputation, and personal recommendation play a major role in the first stage, whereas the consultant's qualifications, their understanding of the client's problem, the achievability of the consultant's concept, and the inclusion of the client in the consulting project become the key decision criteria in the final stage (Kohr 2000; Höck and Keuper 2001). Meffert (1990), Wick (2000), and Greschuchna (2006) have introduced trust as a variable that mediates the influence between the aforementioned decision criteria and the choice of a consultant, concluding that trust is the critical criterion. All these mechanisms have been interpreted as institutions that help reduce uncertainty and enable sustained transactions between consultants and clients in an agency framework.

10.3.2 Consulting Seen from Agency Theory

Agency theory has been applied both to explain the institutions that give shape to the relationship between consultants and their clients (e.g. Clark 1993; Kaas and Schade 1995; Saam 2002) and to analyse the behaviour of the client's employees in empirical consulting projects (Weiershäuser 1996).

Clark (1993) was the first to apply a principal-agent framework that relies on the concepts of adverse selection and moral hazard in order to describe and analyse the information asymmetry between client and consultant. Pre-contractual and post-contractual opportunism on the part of the agent (consultant) may lead to quality uncertainty on the side of the principal (client). Clark (1993) considers three institutions that help overcome or circumvent these informational asymmetries: contingent fees, reputation, and regulation. These institutions may be looked upon as trust-producing mechanisms.

These and further institutions have been considered by Saam (2002), who has applied an agency framework that relies on the concepts of hidden characteristics (in the principal-agent framework referred to as adverse selection), as hidden intentions, hidden information, and hidden action (in the principal-agent framework referred to as moral hazard), in order to describe and analyse the information asymmetry between client and consultant. She argues that institutions such as formal selection procedures, bidding conferences, and testing the consultant at small tasks, such as a half-day workshop with the client's staff, constitute screening procedures that may help overcome or circumvent information asymmetries. Codes of ethics offered by the consultant constitute self-selection techniques; reports, meetings, and mixed project teams constitute monitoring systems; the establishment of internal consulting units constitutes vertical integration; the establishment of long-lasting business relations between client and consultant constitute game theory solutions; and the cultural integration of consultants constitutes an identification system. It is not only contractual penalty clauses but also business friendships that constitute bonding (Saam 2002).

Institutions that may be interpreted as a signal of the consultant's quality have received attention from many researchers. The choice of a high-level education by the consultant, the presentation of certificates, and public relations may be interpreted as institutional signals (Saam 2002), as may the distinct selection mechanism of case studies (Armbrüster 2004, 2006), signing a contract (Kaas and Schade 1995), working in an external and not an internal consultancy (Pudack 2004), the high rejection rate in recruitment (Franck and Pudack 2000), the 'up or out' policy of top-tier consultancies (Waldman 1990), and the governance structure of the partnership (Levin and Tadelis 2005; see below). A long list of applicants in consultancy recruitment both attracts and challenges highly qualified graduates, which, on the one hand, constitutes a self-selection technique and, on the other hand, also constitutes a signal of meritocracy (Franck and Pudack 2000).

During a consulting project, the client might face an agency problem regarding a second group of actors: the client's employees. Weiershäuser (1996) has derived solution mechanisms for this kind of agency problem. However, in her empirical study of five cases she finds no evidence for hidden action problems with employees. Instead, she finds considerable evidence of hidden action on the side of the top management, a finding that conflicts with the assumptions of traditional agency theory. For example, project managers stated that there seemed to be no commitment to the project from the perspective of the top management.

10.3.3 Transaction-Cost Economics and Property Rights Theory

Transaction-cost theory and property rights theory have been used to explain why management consultants exist at all, as well as to explain the decision of the client when choosing between in-house and external consultants, the growth of the consulting industry, and the governance structure of consultancies.

Why managers would want to open up, even delegate, important areas such as strategy and re-engineering to outsiders is still not clear. What needs to be explained is why management consultants exist and why managers hire outside experts instead of doing the same work internally. Nor is it obvious why it is more cost effective to hire consultants. Kehrer and Schade (1995) and Canback (1998, 1999) discuss dimensions of the make-or-buy question. Kehrer and Schade (1995) consider the specificity and complexity of the task, the demand intensity for the task, and the similarity of the expected tasks to each other. They argue that the higher the specificity, the demand intensity, and the similarity, the more efficient an in-house solution becomes. The efficiency of external consultants increases with the complexity of the task.

Canback (1998, 1999) picks up the concept of asset specificity, which basically refers to the extent to which a party is 'tied in' to a business relationship. According to transaction-cost theory, the choice for an internal or an external expert hinges on the degree of asset specificity, demand volatility, technological uncertainty, and the frequency of transactions involved. If these factors are insignificant, buying the services in the external market is the better solution. Canback (1998, 1999) argues that human asset specificity stands alone as the most important factor. All other things being equal, external consultants can be expected to work on issues having low human asset specificity, while internal consultants deal with issues highly specific to the client. Richter and Schröder (2006) give a transaction-cost explanation for the limited importance of in-house consulting. In situations where market imperfections are high, clients might be better off internalizing the service, instead of buying it via the market. However, while the transaction costs between a client organization and its consultant can be reduced significantly through the establishment of an in-house consulting unit, the transaction costs between a client-owned management consultancy and its other potential clients become prohibitively high. Clients tend to be reluctant to procure consultancy services from subsidiaries of their own competitors. A client-owned consultancy will most likely generate business only with its owner.

Canback (1998, 1999) has developed an explanation for the growth of management consulting based on transaction-cost theory. He argues that in the US transaction costs have become an increasingly important part of the economy. Between 1870 and 1970 transaction costs increased from 8 to 45 per cent. Today's executives must still manage production costs, but an even greater challenge lies in optimizing transaction costs. Management consultants offer services that reduce transaction costs. Their services in the fields of organizational design, strategic planning, and governance can assist clients in minimizing bureaucratic (internal) transaction costs. Thus, as the transaction aspect of the economy has grown, so has the management consulting industry. Indeed, McKenna (2006: 10–24) has argued that although management consultancy grew as a result of regulatory changes in the US in the 1930s, fundamental client demand for their services is driven by lower external than internal transaction costs. In his view, 'through their intrinsic "economies of knowledge" [...] management consultants provided their clients with a cost-effective means to acquire managerial skills, techniques, and processes at a lower cost than the equivalent internal studies of the same problems.

[...] Consultants, in effect prosper on the razor's edge of the managerial/transaction cost calculus' (ibid.: 13, 14).

The arguments of Kehrer and Schade (1995) and Canback (1998, 1999) are supported by Armbrüster (2006). He argues that there are certain trends that have prompted disparate tasks unique to the client firms, which involved high co-ordination costs within the firm, and which required a different type of knowledge with low human asset specificity. These include the growing involvement of foreign markets and investors in production, finance, and distribution; the shift from inter-industry to intra-industry exchange; the offshoring of production processes, IT services, and business services; the wave of mergers and acquisitions; and the deregulation of industries and privatization of firms (Armbrüster 2006).

Two peculiarities in the governance structure of the consultancy industry have attracted the attention of economics researchers: the predominance of partnerships and the 'up or out' system. While the latter has been a topic for agency theory, the former has been researched within a transaction-cost framework. Why are many management consultancies organized as partnerships, that is, as firms in which a group of senior employees holds the ownership rights? Richter and Schröder (2006) have investigated the transaction and governance costs that may arise if consultancy firms' ownership rights are assigned to external providers of financial capital, to suppliers of intermediate goods and services, to clients, or to employees. They argue that the costs of monitoring consulting firms pose significant obstacles to the assignment of ownership rights to external providers of capital. The intangibility of consulting services, their provision through the close interaction between consultants and clients, and the importance of confidentiality render the monitoring of consulting firms problematic. Contacts established while working with the client may be beneficial to consultants in setting up their own business. Consultants tend to have ample scope for opportunistic behaviour in relation to their own firm. The importance of these factors, which raise the transaction costs between consulting firms and their employees, increases with seniority, since senior consultants work more autonomously and have stronger client relationships than junior consultants. Richter and Schröder (2006) argue that consulting firms reduce the potential for moral hazard by assigning ownership to employees. As the participation of all employees in the ownership would prohibitively raise governance costs, the attribution of property rights is limited to senior consultants, as is typical of partnerships (see Morris, Gardner, and Anand, Chapter 14, this volume).

While Armbrüster (2006) parallels their argument, Levin and Tadelis (2005) give an alternative explanation from an agency perspective. They define partnership as an institution that redistributes profits among partners and interpret partnerships as a signal. Profit sharing in partnerships is a means by which to select employees, not to motivate them. It is a signal for high quality that is of special importance if clients are not themselves able to assess quality. Partnerships select partners with a higher quality than corporations do. As a consequence, they argue, with the increasing standardization of consulting products and better market monitoring by the client, consultancies will more often choose the organizational form of a corporation and hire low-quality workers because they can dispense with the signal.

Chou (2007) investigates why human-capital-intensive firms such as consulting firms merge or separate, thereby contributing another argument to understanding the predominance of partnerships in the consultancy industry. He refers to the explanation of property rights theory, which interprets integration as a concentration of ownership under certain parties. This theory predicts that under certain circumstances, which are analysed using one type of bargaining model, investments with externalities—a cost or benefit, not transmitted through prices—favour integration of firms. However, if a different bargaining model is used this result reverses. Then, investments with externalities favour separation. Chou (2007) advances the critique that this theory defines the firm as a collection of physical assets and that human assets are ignored. Consequently, this theory cannot help us to understand the governance structure of human-capital-intensive firms.

In order to understand integration in human-capital-intensive firms he proposes an alternative explanation, which is based on the observation that if several businesses are integrated in one firm, their individual identities become less observable to outsiders, compared to the case where they are separated as different firms. Because of this information asymmetry across firm boundaries, outsiders may misattribute the value of some parts of a firm's operations to other parts. Chou (2007) therefore defines a firm as a collection of human assets, the owners of which work so closely together that outsiders cannot clearly distinguish one from the other. His theory predicts that, irrespective of the bargaining model used, investments with externalities favour integration of firms. When a relationship between parties includes large potential externalities—as is the case in human-capital-intensive firms—reducing the outside option of each party will be beneficial. Integration provides this reduction by blurring the contribution of individual parties within the firm and thus lowering their independent market value.

Over the past decade several consultancies have transferred to a corporate structure (see also Morris, Gardner, and Anand, Chapter 14, this volume). Armbrüster (2006) argues that the corporate structure facilitates raising large amounts of capital, thereby reducing transaction costs for consultancies. Capital has become important for those consultancies that need expensive equipment which has a high turnover rate, for example, for IT outsourcing contracts.

10.4 Contributions from Heterodox Institutional Economics

Contributions from an heterodox institutional economics perspective, known by some as institutionalist political economy, have put forward the hypothesis that institutions have played a major role in shaping the establishment and evolution of the consultancy industry in different countries. Different institutional arrangements, in particular regulations and the availability of intermediary organizations, explain, to a large extent, the different paths of institutionalization of management consulting in the United States, Britain, Germany, France, and Portugal (see also David, Chapter 4; Kipping and Wright, Chapter 8; both this volume).

The establishment of the consultancy industry in the United States has been explained as a non-intended consequence of institutional reforms in the US's system of banks in the 1930s. With the Glass–Steagall Banking Act, companies turned from bankers to management consultants for organizational advice (McKenna 1995). Market entry into certain consulting-related services was prohibited until the law was changed by antitrust regulation, for example, the move of International Business Machines (IBM) into IT consulting. The Banking Act and the Securities and Exchange Commission prohibited rival professional groups, like lawyers, engineers, and accountants, from continuing to act as consultants (McKenna 2006). In Germany, by contrast, as Kipping (1997, 1999) has argued, trade and professional associations as well as chambers of commerce and other collective actors have provided services that were delivered by consultants in the Anglo-Saxon countries, which hampered and delayed consultancies' establishment in Germany. These intermediary institutions helped managers in establishing quasi-public or associationally constructed networks of business friendships and in exchanging management knowledge independent of consultants.

Consultancies entering a new market have only been successful in establishing long-term trust-based relationships if they included existing intermediary institutions in their strategy (Kipping 1997; Amorim and Kipping 1999). Institutions do not only define arenas and networks in which management knowledge is created, exchanged, validated, modified, and eventually revised, they also define the actors and their legitimacy in these processes. There is an affinity between governance models and the institutionalization of the consultancy industry. Whereas the co-operative and relational governance models of Germany and Japan respectively hampered the institutionalization, the liberal governance model or competitive capitalism in the US and UK has supported it (Faust 2005).

10.5 Contributions from other Economics Approaches

Beyond new institutional economics and heterodox institutional economics there are only a few scattered economics-based studies of management consulting. One discussion centres on the consulting industry benefiting from economies of scale and scope, concepts from classical microeconomic theory. Becker and Schade (1995) argue that economies of scale can only be put to use—and hierarchically organized consulting firms established—if a consultancy succeeds in standardizing its consultancy products (tools) and in passing on this standardized knowledge in the course of further company training to university graduates without specific knowledge. This view is supported by Richter and Lingelbach (2004) and by Armbrüster (2006), who investigated the evolution of IT consulting, when clients started outsourcing IT services (see also Galal, Richter, and Wendlandt, Chapter 6, this volume). They found that in offering these services large accounting firms benefited from economies of scale and scope. However, this required extraordinary investment and called for financial resources, which the traditional partnership structure could no longer provide. Richter and Lingelbach (2004) have demonstrated that the likelihood of adopting outside ownership grows with capital requirements, business risk, firm size, and the standardization of services.

For the analysis of optimal compensation rules for integrated services, for example consulting services, Löbler, Posselt, and Welk (2006) have developed a model with a very general production and cost function, which assumes no uncertainty and perfect information. Integrated services require input from both the service provider and client, and both the provider's input and the client's input can be substituted by each other to some degree. The authors show that input-based compensation characterized by compensation based on work hours or work days is superior to both sales-based and profit-based compensation, because the client can govern the service provider's input using the input-based compensation. In the sales-based and profit-based compensation models, neither party can govern the other party's input. Both end up in a conflict over the share of profit they receive. The authors claim that in the case of uncertainty this result may be even stronger, as uncertainty typically means that generated value cannot be observed.

Hansen and Hughes (2005) investigate the conditions under which either immediate or delayed dissemination of innovations may be optimal from the perspective of the consultant. They assume that the innovation provided by the consultant is a product that may be licensed (e.g. a business methods software) and whose impact on the costs of clients increases after every implementation by the consultant (learning by doing), because errors may be corrected. Therefore, a second implementation is more effective. Hansen and Hughes (2005) find that whether immediate or delayed dissemination is optimal depends both on the consultant's bargaining power and on the magnitude of learning by doing. Concurrent engagements provide for an immediate dissemination of the innovation, but at the loss of deeper cost reduction in the later period from learning by doing. Sequential engagements provide for a delayed dissemination of the innovation, but with deeper cost reductions from learning by doing. When the consultant has very high bargaining power, the sequential engagement's benefit can exceed that of the concurrent engagement.

While Hansen and Hughes (2005) and Löbler, Posselt, and Welk (2006) assume a rational consultant who intends to optimize compensation, following the neoclassical model of homo oeconomicus, Watson, Rodgers, and Dudek (1998) are the first authors to refer to the emerging behavioural economics framework (see, as an introduction, Altman 2006). Such a framework uses social, cognitive, and emotional factors in order to understand the economic decisions of individuals and institutions performing economic functions, and their effects on market prices, returns, and resource allocation. Watson, Rodgers, and Dudek (1998) redirect the attention of an economics perspective to the actual behaviour of the consultant. Put differently, they are no longer interested in the consultant's behaviour in terms of co-operation with the client, but in terms of their judgements and decision-making, when applying their expertise. They describe a consultant whose analysis of the client's problems is based on heuristics, bias, and errors. In their conceptual article, they argue that the insights into human decision-making, for example, representativeness heuristic, confirmation bias, and fundamental attribution error, should be applied to the inferences and decisions made by management consultants. Once any biases, errors, and heuristics influencing consulting have been documented and understood, it becomes possible for attention to turn to research on how to improve the judgement of consultants.

10.6 SUMMARY AND DIRECTIONS FOR FUTURE RESEARCH

Research on management consulting is relatively young. In this field, economics approaches have a marginal position. Problems of scarcity of resources, the focus of economics analysis, are far from essential in understanding management consulting. There has been no affinity between the topics explored by the consulting literature—such as the questions of how the phenomenon of management consulting can be explained, whether consultants really are knowledge brokers, how they gain legitimacy for their knowledge, and how micro-politics shape the behaviour of client and consultant—and economic theory.

The major contribution of economics to the understanding of management consulting comes from new institutional economics, because this perspective explains how institutions, which are peculiar to the consultancy industry, such as long-lasting business relationships, reputation, partnerships, and the 'up-or-out' system, are created and maintained by rational clients and consultants in order to facilitate co-operation under conditions of asymmetrical information and uncertainty. They establish trust between client and consultant by reducing the potential for opportunistic behaviour on the side of the consultant. Neoclassical economics, by contrast, has made only minor contributions to the understanding of management consulting, namely concerning the benefits the consulting industry might derive from economies of scale and scope. However, the micro-analytic models of neoclassical economics suffer from limited applicability; they restrict their analysis to situations that are rather untypical for management consulting—situations where the consultant's product can be characterized as an exchange good, *not* a credence good; where the market is *not* characterized by quality uncertainties with respect to the consultants and their services; and where the client is *not* involved in the production of the service.

A second major contribution of economics to the understanding of management consulting comes from heterodox institutional economics, because this perspective has reconstructed how the complex interaction of various institutions, such as intermediary institutions, states, and regulations, has shaped the establishment and evolution of the consultancy industry in different countries.

Management consulting has been a thorny topic for formal analysis, traditionally the strength of economics approaches. Apart from a few exceptions, the research has been based on the descriptive variants of economics, for example, positive agency theory, transaction-cost economics, and property rights theory. There are neither common research questions nor common formal approaches that can connect the few formal models from a principal-agent perspective and from neoclassical microeconomic perspectives, nor have any noteworthy game theory models been developed.

Key unanswered questions and directions for future research concern conceptual issues, the economics framework, the development of formal models, the empirical testing of hypotheses, and the claim to give theory-based recommendations to the client.

Conceptual issues. While there has been considerable research of the institutions which give shape to the relationship between consultants and their clients, one aspect should be elaborated in more detail—the concept of trust. If the institutions are trust-producing mechanisms, then trust must be reconceptualized as a variable that mediates the influence of these institutions on the decision of the client (Greschuchna 2006). This differs sharply from the concept of reputation. The interrelation of reputation and trust needs to be specified. Furthermore, there is scarcely any research that concentrates on the client from an economics perspective (Buono 2009). For a more balanced analysis of the client–consultant relationship there is a need to investigate the client and the act of co-production (see also Fincham, Chapter 20, this volume).

Choice of framework. A major shortcoming of the neoclassical approach, including the new institutional and the game theory framework, is a very abstract concept of information (and knowledge). In economics, information is captured in the concepts of (in)complete information, (im)perfect information, public or private knowledge, and informational (a)symmetry. These concepts apply to any industry and business. The economic analysis of knowledge industries might benefit from the consideration of social and cognitive factors in a behavioural framework. In this framework, knowledge would have to be captured in hitherto unknown dimensions, including, for example, the use of heuristics by decision-makers both on the side of the consultants and of their clients. A behavioural framework would increase the knowledge of how decisions in businesses actually are made, in particular how biases, errors, and heuristics influence management consulting, and might offer results on the performance of different heuristics (descriptive theory) and on how the judgements of consultants might be improved (prescriptive theory).

Formal models. Principal-agent models and game theory models are most suited to conceptualize client–consultant interaction. However, what is lacking is a description of typical client–consultant interaction situations that go beyond the well-known simple hidden characteristics (adverse selection), hidden intention, hidden information, and hidden action (moral hazard) type of situations. It might be best to first empirically observe client–consultant interaction in more detail and identify specific patterns of interaction, that is, patterns that are not observed in other principal–agent relations and have not yet been conceived of as institutions. Then we might ask for an explanation of these patterns and turn to formal modeling to demonstrate under which conditions these patterns and/or institutions might evolve.

Empirical tests. There is still no research that directly tests alternative explanations of institutions. Recent changes like the establishment and later closure of in-house consultancies or the restructuring of partnerships into corporations would allow testing alternative explanations based on agency theory or transaction-cost economics.

Recommendations for clients. Economics approaches contribute positive as well as normative perspectives, for example agency theory and principal-agent theory. The positive approaches are valued for deriving hypotheses for empirical tests, the normative approaches for allowing prescriptions and policy recommendations. As far as recommendations to clients are concerned, it turns out that mechanisms described in positive theory cannot automatically be transformed into recommendations. This problem can be illustrated with the example of contingency fees. These fees have long been one of the most controversial issues in management consulting. In the past they were banned by professional codes of conduct. Although this ban has been lifted in most countries, a majority of consultancies continue to reject them. There are several serious shortcomings that limit the scope of their use in consulting, for example the difficulty of agreeing on results that can be correctly measured, the difficulty of differentiating between the client firm's results and the consultant's results, the danger that long-term interests are neglected by the consultant, and the importance of external influences such as the business climate. These aspects have to be considered and weighed against the advantages that contingency fees offer. So far, a thorough analysis of all these shortcomings and advantages has been lacking. It seems that economics approaches cannot yet give theory-based recommendations that consider these interdependent effects.

And this is a key question not only in the analysis of contingency fees. Although we might give recommendations only on a case-by-case basis, there is still a need for thorough analyses of the intended and unintended effects of these different mechanisms. This leads back to empirical research as a source of knowledge about unintended effects.

References

Alchian, A. A. (1961). *Some Economics of Property.* Santa Monica, CA: Rand Corporation.

Alchian, A. A. and Demsetz, H. (1972). 'Production, Information Costs and Economic Organization'. *American Economic Review*, 62, 777–795.

Altman, M. (ed.) (2006). *Handbook of Contemporary Behavioral Economics: Foundations and Developments.* Armonk, NY: Sharpe.

Amorim, C. and Kipping, M. (1999). 'Selling Consultancy Services: The Portuguese Case in Historical and Comparative Perspective'. *Business and Economic History*, 28, 45–56.

Armbrüster, T. (2004). 'Rationality and Its Symbols: Signaling Effects and Subjectification in Management Consulting'. *Journal of Management Studies*, 41, 1,247–1,269.

Armbrüster, T. (2006). *The Economics and Sociology of Management Consulting.* Cambridge: Cambridge University Press.

Arrow, K. J. (1969). 'The Organization of Economic Activity: Issues Pertinent to the Choice of Market Versus Nonmarket Allocations'. In W. Patman and W. Proxmire (eds), *The Analysis and Evaluation of Public Expenditures: The PBB-System*, vol. 1. US Joint Economic Committee, 91st Congress, 1st Session. Washington, DC: US Government Printing Office, 47–64.

Becker, U. and C. Schade (1995). 'Betriebsformen der Unternehmensberatung: Eine Erklärung auf der Basis der neuen Institutionenlehre'. *Zeitschrift für betriebswirtschaftliche forschung*, 47, 327–354.

Bryson, J. R. (1997). 'Business Service Firms, Service Space and the Management of Change'. *Entrepreneurship and Regional Development*, 9, 93–111.

Buono, A. F. (2009). 'Management Consulting: Introducing the Client'. *Scandinavian Journal of Management*, 25, 247–312.

Canback, S. (1998). 'The Logic of Management Consulting (Part One)'. *Journal of Management Consulting*, 10/2, 3–11.

Canback, S. (1999). 'The Logic of Management Consulting (Part Two)'. *Journal of Management Consulting*, 10/3, 3–12.

Chou, E. S. (2007). 'The Boundaries of Firms as Information Barriers'. *RAND Journal of Economics*, 38, 733–746.

Clark, T. (1993). 'The Market Provision of Management Services, Information Asymmetries and Service Quality: Some Market Solutions: an Empirical Example'. *British Journal of Management*, 4, 235–251.

Clark, T. (1995). *Managing Consultants: Consultancy as the Management of Impressions*. Buckingham: Open University Press.

Coase, R. H. (1937). 'The Nature of the Firm'. *Econometrica*, 4, 386–405.

Dawes, P., Dowling, G. R., and Patterson, P. G. (1992). 'Criteria Used to Select Management Consultants'. *Industrial Marketing Management*, 21, 187–193.

Demsetz, H. (1967). 'Toward a Theory of Property Rights'. *American Economic Review*, 57, 347–359.

Fama, E. (1980). 'Agency Problems and the Theory of the Firm'. *Journal of Political Economy*, 88, 288–307.

Faust, M. (2005). 'Managementberatung in der Organisationsgesellschaft'. In W. Jäger and U. Schimank (eds), *Organisationsgesellschaft: Facetten und Perspektiven*. Opladen: VS Verlag, 529–588.

Franck, E. and Pudack, T. (2000). 'Unternehmensberatungen und die Selektion von Humankapital: Eine Ökonomische Analyse'. *Die unternehmung*, 54, 145–155.

Frank, R. H. (1997). *Microeconomics and Behavior*. New York: McGraw-Hill.

Furubotn, E. G. and R. Richter (1998). *Institutions and Economic Theory: The Contribution of the New Institutional Economics*. Ann Arbor, MI: University of Michigan Press.

Greschuchna, L. (2006). *Vertrauen in der unternehmensberatung: Einflußfaktoren und Konsequenzen*. Wiesbaden: DUV Gabler.

Hansen, S. C. and Hughes, J. S. (2005). 'The Dissemination of Management Consulting Innovations and the Pace of Technological Improvements'. *Journal of Institutional and Theoretical Economics*, 161: 536–555.

Höck, M. and Keuper, F. (2001). 'Empirische Untersuchung zur Auswahl und Kompetenz von Beratungsgesellschaften'. *Die Betriebswirtschaft*, 61, 427–442.

Jensen, M. and Meckling, W. (1976). 'Theory of the Firm: Managerial Behavior, Agency Costs, and Ownership Structure'. *Journal of Financial Economics*, 3, 305–360.

Kaas, P. and Schade, C. (1995). 'Unternehmensberater im Wettbewerb: Eine Empirische Untersuchung aus der neuen Institutionenlehre'. *Zeitschrift für Betriebswirtschaft*, 65, 1067–1089.

Kehrer, R. and Schade, C. (1995). 'Interne Problemlösung oder Konsultation von Unternehmensberatern? Ein Rahmenkonzept zur Sukzessiven Entscheidungsfindung auf transaktionskosten- und organisationstheoretischer Basis'. *Die Betriebswirtschaft*, 55, 465–480.

Kipping, M. (1997). 'Consultancies, Institutions and the Diffusion of Taylorism in Britain, Germany and France, 1920s to 1950s'. *Business History*, 39/4, 67–83.

Kipping, M. (1999). 'British Economic Decline: Blame It on the Consultants?'. *Contemporary British History*, 13/3, 23–38.

Kohr, J. (2000). *Die Auswahl von Unternehmensberatungen: Klientenverhalten—Beratermarketing*. München: Hampp.

Levin, J. and Tadelis, S. (2005). 'Profit Sharing and the Role of Professional Partnerships'. *Quarterly Journal of Economics*, 120, 131–171.

Lindahl, D. P. and Beyers, W. B. (1999). 'The Creation of Competitive Advantage by Producer Service Establishments'. *Economic Geography*, 75, 1–20.

Löbler, H., Posselt, T., and Welk, M. (2006). 'Optimal Compensation Rules for Integrated Services'. *OR Spectrum*, 28, 355–373.

McKenna, C. D. (1995). 'The Origins of Modern Management Consulting'. *Business and Economic History*, 24, 51–58.

McKenna, C. D. (2006). *The World's Newest Profession: Management Consulting in the Twentieth Century*. Cambridge: Cambridge University Press.

Meffert, H. (1990). 'Unternehmensberatung und Unternehmensführung: Eine empirische Bestandsaufnahme'. *Die Betriebswirtschaft*, 50, 180–197.

Mitchell, V. W. (1994). 'Problems and Risks in the Purchasing of Consultancy Services'. *Service Industries Journal*, 14, 315–339.

North, D. C. (1981). *Structure and Change in Economic History*. New York: Norton.

Osborne, M. J. (2004). *An Introduction to Game Theory*. Oxford: Oxford University Press.

Pudack, T. (2004). *Signale für Humankapital: Die rolle von Unternehmensberatungen beim Berufseinstieg von Hochschulabsolventen*. Wiesbaden: DUV Gabler.

Richter, A. and Lingelbach, K. (2004). 'The Allocation of Ownership Rights in Management Consulting Firms: An Institutional Economics Approach'. European Business School, IMC Working paper, no. 7.

Richter, A. and Schröder, K. (2006). 'The Allocation of Ownership Rights in Management Consulting Firms: An Institutional Economics Approach'. *Problems and Perspectives in Management*, 4, 123–135.

Ross, S. A. (1973). 'The Economic Theory of Agency: The Principal's Problem'. *American Economic Review*, 63, 134–139.

Saam, N. J. (2002). *Prinzipale, Agenten und Macht: Eine Machttheoretische Erweiterung der Agenturtheorie und ihre Anwendung auf Interaktionsstrukturen in der Organisationsberatung*. Tübingen: Mohr Siebeck.

Schade, C. and Schott, E. (1993). 'Kontraktgüter im Marketing'. *Marketing: Zeitschrift for forschung und Praxis*, 15, 15–25.

Svensson, R. (2000). *Success Strategies and Knowledge Transfer in Cross-Border Consulting Operations*. Dordrecht: Kluwer.

Svensson, R. (2001). 'Success Determinants when Tendering for International Consulting Projects'. *International Journal of the Economics of Business*, 8, 101–122.

Von Neumann, J. and Morgenstern, O. (1947). *Theory of Games and Economic Behavior*. Princeton, NJ: Princeton University Press.

Waldman, M. (1990). 'Up-or-Out Contracts: A Signalling Perspective'. *Journal of Labor Economics*, 8, 230–250.

Watson, A., Rodgers, T., and Dudek, D. (1998). 'The Human Nature of Management Consulting: Judgement and Expertise'. *Managerial and Decision Economics*, 19, 495–503.

Weiershäuser, S. (1996). *Der Mitarbeiter im Beratungsprozess: Eine Agenturtheoretische Analyse*. Wiesbaden: Gabler.

Wick, V. (2000). 'Mittelständische Unternehmen und ihre Berater: Ein Netzwerkorientiertes Konzept der Nutzung von externen Beratungsleistungen'. Doctoral dissertation, University of St Gallen.

Williamson, O. E. (1975). *Markets and Hierarchies: Analysis and Antitrust Implications*. New York: Free Press.

Williamson, O. E. (1985). *The Economic Institutions of Capitalism*. New York: Free Press.

CHAPTER 11

THE GEOGRAPHIES OF MANAGEMENT CONSULTANCY FIRMS

JAMES FAULCONBRIDGE
ANDREW JONES

11.1 INTRODUCTION

THIS chapter summarizes the state-of-the-art knowledge about the geographies of management consultancy firms. The approach taken is to, firstly, draw on insights from a range of scholars, and in particular the work of economic geographers, on both the local (i.e., city and regional) and global (i.e., cross-border, international business) geographies of management consultancy. However, the main theme that cuts across our analysis is that, with a few exceptions (Daniels, Leyshon, and Thrift 1987; Jones 2003, 2005; Wood 2006; Glückler 2007), there is little explicit focus on the geographies of management consultancy firms in economic geographers' and others' work. This means the second and complimentary approach is to develop a discussion that reads off the geographies of management consultancy firms from fertile debates in economic geography over the past thirty years about the locational strategies of knowledge-intensive producer services (Daniels 1993).

Stemming from interest in the vertical disintegration of manufacturing corporations and the externalization of the provision of services such as advertising and IT as part of a shift towards what have been variously classified as 'post-Fordist' production methods (on which, see Wood 1991), economic geographers have explored the spatial strategies of a range of producer service firms—that is, firms providing advisory services exclusively to business. Studies have focused on sectors including accountancy (Daniels, Leyshon, and Thrift 1988; Beaverstock 1996), advertising (Clarke and Bradford 1989; Grabher 2001;

Faulconbridge 2006; Faulconbridge et al. 2011), executive search (Faulconbridge, Hall, and Beaverstock 2008; Hall et al. 2009), law (Beaverstock, Smith, and Taylor 1999; Jones 2005; Faulconbridge 2007a) and, albeit to a much lesser extent, management consultancy. The reason for the relative dearth of studies of management consultancy firms is unclear. The implications are, however, much clearer: understanding of the geographies of management consultancy firms requires analysis that takes inspiration from studies of allied industries such as accountancy, advertising, and law. As a result, each of the subsequent sections of the chapter begins by considering the general insights that can be gleaned from studies of a wide range of knowledge-intensive producer services before considering the applicability of the insights to management consultancy firms through relevant literature where available or through identification of key research questions where there is a dearth of industry-specific literature.

The rest of the chapter is structured around two macro-scale classifications that draw attention to the two main theoretical debates relevant to the geographies of management consultancy firms, the importance of place and locality in the production and delivery of services, and the role of globalization and cross-border business in the growth of the largest management consultancy firms. These classifications are used to structure the chapter around four sections. Relating to the theme of place and locality, the next section examines work relating to the activities of management consultancy and producer service firms in *cities* by discussing the agglomeration and localization processes at play in urban economies. It reveals how the nature of consultancy work and producer service work more generally has led to firms developing urban geographies with disproportionate concentrations of firms in a few business centres. Subsequently, and further developing the theme of place and locality, the chapter considers the implications of disproportionate concentrations of firms in a few cities for what can be classified as 'spatial divisions of expertise'. This reveals how an urban locational hierarchy has emerged in terms of the knowledge intensity of management consultancy work. The following section then outlines issues associated with the theme of globalization and cross-border business. It examines the geographies of the globalization strategies of management consultancy firms and the impacts of this globalization on different cities and regions. The discussion reveals the geographical complexities of cross-border business and highlights the key questions raised in existing literatures about how management consultancy firms should respond to these complexities. Finally, the chapter ends by identifying a number of important future research questions and directions that might help enhance understanding of the geographies of management consultancy firms in the twenty-first century.

11.2 CITIES AND PRODUCER SERVICE FIRMS

One of the most influential ways of conceptualizing the geography of producer services firms has been as a form of externalized service provision that has grown in importance as a result of broader changes towards post-Fordist economies and industry practices (see Coffey and Bailly 1991; Goe 1991; Bryson, Daniels, and Warf 2004). This is especially important in the case of management consultancy, which has been shown by a wide range of research to be an industry that grew and globalized as a result of its role in helping manufacturing firms enhance productivity (see Kipping 1999; McKenna 2006; Wright and Kipping, Chapter 2, this volume). In economic geographers' work on the role of producer services in post-Fordist economies, the clients of producer service firms—whether small or large business or government departments—are highlighted as needing the advice of consultants either because of a lack of in-house expertise or, relatedly, because of a desire to focus on the 'core competencies' (Prahalad and Hamel 1990) of the organization. As a result, many years ago Allen (1992) made the insightful prediction that the future of the UK economy lay in business services, and not solely business services provided to manufacturing firms, but services such as management consultancy provided to other service organizations, from government to banks. Such predictions acted as the basis for economic geographers' interest in producer services because of a desire to understand the geographical impacts of any boom in producer service work on national and regional economies.

In particular, the relationship between producer services and cities became the focus of economic geographers' analysis because, as Bryson, Daniels, and Warf (2004: 96–97) report, 93 per cent of US employment in producer services is in cities with a population of over 100,000, with 65 per cent of employment being in cities with a population of over 1 million. Similarly, in the UK, Wood (2006) reports that 83 per cent of UK employment in knowledge-intensive producer services is located in four cities, London (38 per cent), Manchester (16 per cent), Birmingham (13 per cent), and Leeds (16 per cent).

Specifically in relation to management consultancy, such urban geographies are explored by Glückler (2007), who studies management consultancy firms in Germany. He suggests that firms benefit from reputation enhancement when located in major business cities and are more successful at attracting new clients, because of the importance of reputation in clients' decision-making about which consultancy firm to use (see also Glückler and Armbrüster 2003). Glückler (2007) also shows that a presence in key business cities allows consulting firms to benefit from business acquired by intra-city referrals—when one client in the city recommends the firm to another potential client. Keeble and Nachum (2002) also study the role of metropolitan locational strategies for management consultancy firms, but in the UK. They show that firms in London benefit, first, from easy access to a large pool of clients who can easily be served thanks to the benefits of co-location—that is, the ease of meeting clients face to face. Second, Keeble and Nachum (2002) show that London-based firms find it easier to innovate and develop novel lines of consultancy advice because of the benefits of informal interactions with fellow consultants based in the city. This gives London-based firms an advantage over firms based in other, smaller cities, where there are fewer management consultancy firms.

In the rest of this section we consider how we might theorize the empirical explanations offered by Keeble and Nachum (2002) and Glückler (2007) of the city geographies of management consultancy firms. This is done by drawing on economic geographers' work on producer services to make sense of the reputational, client referral, innovation advantages management consultancy firms apparently accrue from locating in major business cities.

11.2.1 Agglomeration and Localization Logics

This intimate relationship between the growth of a post-industrial economy, in which producer services play a central role, and the development of metropolitan service centres has been explained by economic geographers using, in particular, theories of agglomeration and localization (see O'Farrell and Hitchens 1990; Daniels 1993; Sassen 2006; Faulconbridge et al. 2011). At their simplest, theories of agglomeration identify the savings made in relation to the cost of key infrastructures (public transport, information communication technology) when firms co-locate. However, in relation to producer services, co-location benefits are said to refer, in particular, to the need to be close to major clients, something that distinguishes producer services from many of the manufacturing corporations that were studied and were used to develop theory in the 1960s and 1970s (see Daniels 1993; Bryson, Daniels, and Warf 2004). One of the defining features of producer service firms is that services exist in the form of advice designed to meet the very specific needs of a clients.

Empson (2001) and Empson and Chapman (2006) contend that this advice is hard to assess because, reflecting the points made above, clients lack the in-house expertise to complete the task devolved to the chosen producer service and thus also lack the expertise to evaluate the work of the producer service firm employed (see also Clark 1993). Moreover, it is suggested that the services provided by one producer service firm cannot be compared with services provided by other firms because of their contingent, unique, and one-off nature. As a result, Jones (2007) argues that meetings are the most important moments of work in producer service firms. Client meetings allow, at the beginning of a project, the client's needs to be understood and a trusting relationship to be developed between the client and the consultants providing advice. Occasional meetings throughout the life of a project then allow the delivery of advice to clients, clear communication, and the reinforcement of the trusting relationship. As such, face-to-face meetings overcome some of the difficulties associated with the intangibility of the work of producer services, outlined above. Clear communication and trust help mitigate a client's inability to evaluate the advice provided by consultants (Daniels 1993; Keeble and Nachum 2002). Consequently, locating in a city provides a major competitive advantage for producer service firms because a large number of potential clients are co-present and easily accessible for meetings. Combined, the valuable travel time saved when clients are located in the same city and the ability to arrange meetings at short notice is said to be behind the way cities have become *the* sites of producer service work (Daniels 1993).

In addition, the role of cities as the sites at which producer service firms cluster has also been explained through theories of localization (see Pryke 1994; Thrift 1994; Faulconbridge et al. 2011). The main emphasis in theories of localization is on the benefits that co-location brings in terms of industry-specific knowledge, learning, and innovation. Economic geographers, most recently including Grabher (2001), Keeble and Nachum (2002), Faulconbridge (2007b), and Hall (2007), have shown that, for producer services, two city-based knowledge and innovation-related advantages are particularly important. First, the concept of 'buzz' details the way social interactions, which occur when employees from competing producer service firms and clients of firms work and socialize in one city, lead to access to market-related knowledge. Morgan (2004) and Storper and Venables (2004) outline how such buzz relies on face-to-face encounters, trusting and reciprocal relationships, and the development of city-specific industrial languages and codes, which together lead to knowledge spillovers.

In particular, it has been shown that interactions between producer service workers in bars (Thrift 1994), at professional associations (Faulconbridge 2007b), or at formal training and professional development events (Hall and Appleyard 2009) lead to insights being gained into new business opportunities as a result of idle chat and gossip. This is what Grabher (2002) describes as 'buzz', which forms a constant background 'noise' about new business opportunities. Such noise is also said to help clients to assess the work of producer service firms. When clients of multiple producer service firms interact in such social, professional, or educational spaces they share their experiences of working with different firms. The gossip and rumour this generates leads to the construction of a positive reputation for those firms judged by clients to provide the best services and damages the reputation of poor performers. Similar arguments have been developed by Clark (1993, 1995) in relation to the information asymmetries faced by individuals trying to assess the quality of management consultancy services, but the unique contribution of economic geographers is to highlight the role of the city and localization in overcoming such difficulties.

Secondly, the presence of multiple producer service firms in a city is also associated in the existing literature with the development of a pool of expert labour, which acts as another localization advantage. For example, both Grabher (2001) and Ekinsmyth (2002) study London and show that when rival producer service firms are located in the same city, intra-city labour churn provides a competitive advantage as talented individuals can be more easily encouraged to move between firms (see Saxenian (1994) on the analogous process in engineering communities). In addition, Grabher (2001) and Ekinsmyth (2002) show that the increasing reliance on project teams made up of individuals drawn from within but also without the organization's boundaries has rendered cities important strategic sites of work for some producer services.

In producer service firms where each project requires a very different type of expertise, project teams often include freelancers, brought in because of their particular specialism. Cities act as vortexes sucking in freelance workers, who can be drawn on as and when needed to provide expertise that is crucial for a project's success, hence making metropolitan locational strategies even more advantageous. At one level, being in a major business city means that the process of searching for an individual with the required expertise is simplified. As Vinodrai (2006) shows, cities provide an 'ecology' of labour. This ecology is comprised of individual workers, labour market intermediaries, and multiple co-located firms from the same industry. The ecology generates career paths for a cohort of freelance and temporary workers built on multiple short-term contacts, which is advantageous for firms seeking to 'hire in' knowledgeable individuals as and when needed. In addition, and at another level, Sydow and Staber (2002) reveal that city-based pools of freelance labour are valuable for producer service firms, because firms can develop repeat relationships with a subset of individuals, leading to the development of an institutional structure for project work. This institutional structure develops over time as a result of repeat project working and leads to norms (trust, reciprocity, etc.) being shared by both firms hiring freelancers and freelancers themselves, which helps smooth the project management process when individuals are 'hired in'.

Together, the agglomeration and localization advantages described above explain the reputational, referral, and innovation advantages that Keeble and Nachum (2002) and Glückler (2007) suggest management consultancy firms gain by locating in key business cities. It is somewhat problematic, though, that, despite their research, in general it is still necessary to use work with a generic focus on producer services or studies of other industries such as advertising or law to understand the geography of management consultancy firms. This leaves a number of unanswered questions about agglomeration and localization advantages. For example, it might be assumed that awareness of business opportunities and access to freelancers that can contribute to project work are advantages that management consultancy firms might accrue from locating in major business cities. But the state-of-art research at present only provides suggestions of the likely importance of such factors and does not offer conclusive evidence that the manifestations and explanations of agglomeration and localization advantages in the case of management consultancy are always the same as those studied in relation to other producer services. Hence, it seems vital that more research, which can begin to fill this void in existing understanding, is completed; that is, research offering detailed empirical focus on all types of management consultancy firm, from the smallest to the largest, and the operations of firms in a range of different cities, not just the main business centre in any one country. And this is not the only area of research in relation to the role of place and locality in the geographies of management consultancy firms that needs further investigation.

11.3 SPATIAL DIVISIONS OF PRODUCER SERVICE EXPERTISE

Like advertising, law, and other producer services, different types of consultancy work and different projects involve varying degrees of knowledge intensity. For example, the Work Foundation (2009: 43) suggests that up to 23 per cent of all producer service work involves 'little or no knowledge tasks' whilst an additional 37 per cent only involves 'some knowledge tasks'. It is beyond the remit of this chapter to engage in analysis of the knowledge-base and knowledge intensity of different types of producer service and, specifically, consultancy work (although, see Fincham 2006; Muzio, Ackroyd, and Chanlat 2008). Instead the focus here is on the geographical manifestations of such variability in the knowledge intensity of producer service work. Specifically, the focus is on a key geographical trend in the knowledge intensity of management consultancy firms' work, identified by Keeble and Nachum (2002). They show that in 1990 one-third of all management consultancy firms in the UK were based in London and that a disproportionate amount of the large firms operating in the UK are also in London, the regions being characterized by small and medium-sized firms. Keeble and Nachum (2002) also show that there is a significantly higher chance of London-based firms developing innovative new services, with around one in four London-based management consultancy firms being able to demonstrate service innovations compared, for example, with only one in ten firms in East Anglia in the UK. But how might this trend be explained?

Through case studies of the UK in particular (Wood 2006; Massey 2007) but also Norway (Bryson and Rusten 2005) an important debate has developed in economic geography about the spatial divisions of expertise that exist in producer service work. This emerges out of a broader concern in economic geography with uneven development, with studies focusing on the unevenness of producer service work at the national scale and the effects of this on regional development. The main argument, developed by both Wood (2006) and Massey (2007), centres around the apparent dominance of London in the UK in terms of knowledge-intensive work, and the resultant 'back office' function of other cities such as Birmingham and Manchester. For example, Wood (2006) argues that whilst producer services make important contributions in terms of employment and supporting the day-to-day needs of local businesses in cities such as Manchester, Birmingham, and Leeds, much of the work completed is less knowledge-intensive than that completed in London and involves more routine advice. The cause of this trend is said to be related to London's role as an international financial centre. The prestige of the City of London leads clients to associate innovation with London-based firms, thus encouraging them to turn to such firms when advice is required in relation to the most complex management tasks. Consequently, Wood (2006: 354) suggests that

> by far the richest social, economic, and cultural environment for KIBS [knowledge-intensive business services] development in the UK remains London [...] small-medium KIBS there rely more on local clients [...], are also engaged more in international trade because they build on specialized expertise developed with demanding regional clients [...]. They also benefit from a richer supply of spin-off founders from large KIBS and other firms, and more repeat and recommendation-based projects.

A similar story might also be constructed about the effects of New York City on other cities on the east coast of the USA, Paris on cities in France, and so on. There is, however, some disagreement in existing literatures about the validity of such representations of spatial divisions of expertise. Daniel and Bryson (2005) argue, for example, that producer service firms operating outside of London in the UK are just as innovative and do engage in knowledge-intensive work, but work which is tailored to the needs of a different type of market to that present in London. In particular they claim that producer services in cities such as Birmingham, Leeds, and Manchester develop expertise relating to the cultural, economic, political, and social specificities of markets and clients' businesses in 'regional' cities that is vital for driving economic growth.

Bryson and Rusten (2005) develop a similar argument using the case of Norway, showing that whilst there are spatial divisions of expertise, in the case of Norway multiple centres of knowledge-intensive work exist, with firms in each city specializing in particular types of producer service advice. When coupled to the arguments developed by Daniels and Bryson (2005) this suggests that, if one recognizes the heterogeneity and complexity of the knowledge-base and work associated with producer services, such as management consultancy and the many different ways that producer service firms can drive innovation, a more nuanced picture emerges of the *many* cities that act as a home for knowledge-intensive producer service firms, such as management consultancy firms, with each city having firms with specializations relevant to particular 'local' clients.

In sum, research on the uneven spatial divisions of producer service expertise once more reveals the centrality of place in explanations of the geographies of management consultancy firms. But, again, there is a need to apply such ideas more directly to management consultancy firms. Whilst studied by Bryson and Rusten (2005), Daniels and Bryson (2005), and Wood (2006) as part of wider research, there has been little explicit analysis—with the exception of the work of Keeble and Nachum (2002) discussed at the start of the chapter—of how such ideas apply to the contingent work of management consultancy firms. The need to meet the place-specific requirements of clients and the way this creates complex spatial divisions of expertise within consultancy firms and between offices in different cities can be assumed but is in need of empirical analysis. The conclusion of the chapter will return to such questions of future research.

But, it is not just the role of cities that is important when examining the geographies of management consultancy firms. One of the most important geographical phenomena of the past twenty to thirty years has been globalization. And, in contrast to the discussion so far, the globalization of management consultancy firms is a topic that has received a reasonable amount of attention from economic geographers. This chapter therefore now turns to the insights into the geographies of management consultancy firms that can be gleaned from work on the topic of globalization.

11.4 GEOGRAPHICAL APPROACHES TO CORPORATE GLOBALIZATION IN PRODUCER SERVICES

As the wider management literature has explored in some depth, the globalization of management consultancy as an industry has its roots in the early decades of the twentieth century, as US firms began to globalize their operations by entering Western European markets in the 1920s and 1930s (Kipping 1999). However, the development of this globalization in recent decades has become a much more extensive and complex process as the global population of consultancy and other producer service firms has increased, and they have established operations in an increasing number of countries (Daniels 1993; Jones 2003; Bryson, Daniels, and Warf 2004). The degree to which producer service and consultancy firms have undertaken 'organizational globalization', the factors that shape this process, and the nature of the global corporate geographies that have emerged have thus been of particular interest to economic geographers. Two strands of work within economic geography have focused on these issues, concerned respectively with the geographical factors that have shaped the globalization of both business services generally and management consultancy specifically, and the key significance of social networks and interpersonal relations to the globalization of business service activity.

11.4.1 Geographical Factors in the Globalization of Management Consultancy Activity

Geographical thinking has argued that existing theories of firm globalization developed from manufacturing industries are inadequate to understand producer service globalization such as that engaged in by management consultants over the past fifty years or so (Boddewyn, Halbrich, and Perry 1986; Daniels 1993; Bagchi-Sen and Sen 1997; Jones 2003; Faulconbridge, Hall, and Beaverstock 2008). Longer standing theories of firm globalization based around the three dominant elements of firm-specific ownership advantages, location-specific advantages, and internalization advantages, known as the OLI paradigm (e.g. Dunning and Norman 1983), are also said to be problematic when applied to producer service firms (Bagchi-Sen and Sen 1997). The key issues relevant to management consultants that render such theories inappropriate relate to the intangibility, perishability, inseparability and heterogeneity of producer service industries (Clark 1995). Of especial relevance to management consultancy firms is the argument that product specialization and diversification (i.e. economies of scope) are more important as growth strategies for firms than economies of scale because of the immobility of many services (Enderwick 1989). Thus, the literature suggests that the bespoke knowledge-intensive nature of management consultancy 'products' (Boddewyn, Halbrich, and Perry 1986; Kipping 1999) in combination with the heavy reliance on face-to-face interaction in the work process (Jones 2003) mean that conventional models of firm globalization provide only very limited insight into the nature of firm globalization in management consultancy. Two further issues have also been highlighted that reflect a distinctly economic geographical perspective.

First, a number of *impediments* to the globalization of producer services such as management consultancy, which contrast with those identified in work on the international of firms in manufacturing sectors, have been identified (Dicken 2007). At one level, economic geographers have shown how the regional context in which management consultancy firms and other producer service firms operate shapes the kinds of capacities and opportunities they have for globalization. For example, examining management consultancies and other business service firms within different regional economies, O'Farrell, Wood, and Zhiang (1998) show how their ability to globalize is strongly influenced by their embeddedness in a number of regionally constituted factors. These include the contact networks firms can access *within* a given region that then lead to contacts amongst potential clients in overseas markets. There is thus evidence that management consulting firms globalize their businesses via social contact networks that develop in regions or places where they already operate. It is not a question of starting up a new international operation 'cold' but pursuing potential new business overseas by exploiting existing social contact networks in a current operational geography.

At another level, Bagchi-Sen and Sen (1997) suggest that significant hurdles to globalization exist for management consultancy firms in relation to the nature of their products and regulatory issues. They argue that, in terms of products, 'the heterogeneity of the services rendered' by consultancy firms represents a barrier because products that are suited to one national economy are not necessarily suited to another and 'the international diversity in the rules for granting licenses to practice' (ibid.: 1153) for management consultancy means that firms often face a different set of rules in each new national context with which they have to comply. Similarly, in many countries the fact that consultancy firms are partnerships is often a disincentive to invest as there is a potential for 'unlimited liability of the partners'. Other regulatory barriers also include 'restrictions induced by government or professional associations on the use of a firm's name', 'restrictions on trans-border data flow' (which inhibit much of the normal work process of consultancy), 'government regulations limiting the tradability or access to markets', and, of course, 'differences in professional standards' in different countries (ibid.: 1153). Bagchi-Sen and Sen (1997) thus suggest that theories of producer service globalization should focus on what they argue are 'the conditioning, motivating and controlling factors', which help producer service firms to overcome these impediments. The implication of this is that theories of globalization in management consultancy need to examine, in depth, what has enabled some firms to successfully enter overseas markets and the reasons why they have adopted such a strategy when others have either failed or not sought to do so. Kipping (1999), for example, provides a contribution in this respect by examining how reputation and the development of host country client networks have been essential to the success of US management consulting firms' operations in Western Europe.

Second, the geographical literature has examined a number of factors that have *driven* the globalization of producer service firms in general and which are applicable to management consultancies. Foremost, and as other producer service industries including advertising, marketing, and accountancy, management consulting firms have been driven by client-following activities that led firms to globalize their activities to meet the demands of clients (Bagchi-Sen and Sen 1997; Jones 2003, 2005; Faulconbridge, Hall, and Beaverstock 2008). Related, and as discussed Kipping and Wright (Chapter 8, this volume) is the important role played by management consultancy in facilitating the globalization of firms in other industries. Debates about the globalization of management consultancies

themselves are intimately bound into wider debate about the globalization of other industries, which have used management consulting to provide knowledge-based services to
enable corporate globalization to take place (Czerniawska 2001; Jones 2003).

It has further been argued that growing pressure from domestic competition and
domestic market saturation in advanced industrial economies has also led producer
service firms to seek to globalize (Bagchi-Sen and Sen 1997). However, this may be more
relevant to producer service industries such as accountancy that offer more standardized products than the bespoke informational services provided by management and
specialist strategy consultancies, which have seen markets in developed economies such
as the UK grow over recent years (Jones 2003). As a result, in order to understand the
globalization of management consultancy as a producer service, recent economic geographical research has sought to develop a more nuanced theoretical approach that
focuses on the specific attributes of management consultancy products and working
practices. The following subsection turns to these theoretical arguments, which are often
built through empirical study of management consulting.

11.4.2 Globalized Management Consulting Firms and the Significance of Social Networks

A small but growing body of literature has focused specifically on the development of a
globalized management consulting industry. Four key strands of argument that inform
understanding of the emergence of global management consultancies can be identified
in this literature. First, the increasing focus in economic geography on the nature of
social relations in global business activity has led to a so-called 'relational turn' (Bathelt
and Glückler 2003; Yeung 2005) within the sub-discipline, with work seeking to understand how social contact networks at both the inter- and intra-firm level are important
to the operation and competitiveness of global business service firms. Most important
in relation to the aims of this chapter is Glücker and Armbrüster's (2003) already discussed contribution, which is grounded in research into management consulting in
Germany. They find that competition amongst German management consultancy firms
takes place on very different grounds to other services sectors. They argue that trust and
the 'networked reputation' of firms are crucial and, as well as leading to the metropolitan
locational strategies discussed above, this reliance on networked reputation has significant implications for understandings of globalization. It suggests that developing social
contact networks amongst 'local elites' within new foreign markets is essential to market
entry—an argument backed by historical analysis of the evolution of the industry
(Kipping 1999).

Glücker (2007) develops these arguments further by refining economic geographical
critiques of dominant firm globalization theories using research into the global management consulting industry (Bagchi-Sen and Sen 1997). Glückler (2007) argues that a 'relational perspective' on international market entry reveals that management consulting

firms rely heavily on social networks in order to globalize their operations. Furthermore, this applies not only to large management consultancies, but also to small and medium-sized ones. Glückler's (2007) research also provides insight into the difference in globalization strategies between small and large management consulting firms, demonstrating how the impact of this 'relational entry context' is a bigger challenge for small management consultancy firms, which do not have the capacity to cope with the risks of globalizing through merger and acquisition. Thus Glücker's relational approach provides an important socio-economic attempt at understanding the emerging corporate geographies of management consultancies in the globalizing economy, since it provides the means to understand how the complex interaction of social networking capacities, firm size, and firm-specific contexts shape globalization.

Secondly, and closely related, economic geographical work has also provided insight at the firm level into the specific nature of the social contact networks and social interactions in the work process of management consultancy firms. This research reveals how globalizing management consulting firms rely on social contact networks as a central element of gaining but also *undertaking* service work. Both internal and external social contact networks are important (Jones 2003). With respect to the former, as management consultancies increasingly employ workers in disparate locations around the globe, there is a significant need for internal global socialization, which involves strategies designed to facilitate co-presence between employees of the firm located in different offices around the globe. Strategies include global training programmes, conferences, and practice community meetings (Kipping 1999; Jones 2003; see Faulconbridge 2007a for a similar example of such strategies in law firms). The maintenance of internal contact networks in consultancy is a functional necessity in order for global management consulting firms to cross-refer business, develop global project teams, maintain organizational coherence in terms of service standards, and ensure service product consistency.

Equally, regarding external contact networks, the globalization of firms is to a considerable extent reliant on the extensiveness and quality of social networks with key employees in client firms (Jones 2005). Whilst a few of the larger firms have been able to enter new international markets on the basis of their brand images (e.g. McKinsey), the geography of globalizing management consultancy firms is to a considerable extent shaped by the capacity of key (senior) partners or managers to gain business through personal contact with key employees in client firms in different countries or regions. Jones (2003) suggests that these networks of contacts that senior employees maintain, develop, and perpetuate in the global context represent the major deciding element in whether these business service firms gain contracts or not in markets outside of their home country. Meanwhile Hall and colleagues (2009) similarly suggest, using a study of what they call the 'offshoot industry' from management consulting—executive search—that 'iconic individuals' can be important in facilitating the globalization of an industry because of the way individuals legitimate the activity of new arrivals in a country through their contacts. Such findings reinforce the significance of the concentration of management consulting firms in global cities, as discussed earlier, which facilitates and supports more frequent and effective social interaction with client firms.

Third, economic geographical research has engaged critically with debates about how business service and management consulting firms have restructured their organizational form as they seek to globalize. At the firm level, management consultancies have generally globalized by opening up operations in new foreign markets or developing strategic collaboration, rather than by the acquisition of foreign firms (O'Farrell and Wood 1999; Wood 2002). This has produced an ongoing need to develop more effective international corporate forms. Jones (2003) examines how different consulting firms have experimented with developing a *transnational* or *global* model, rather than the multinational model identified amongst manufacturing and extractive firms since the 1970s (Cohen et al. 1979; Dunning 1993). A key argument developed here is that differences in organizational architecture notwithstanding, management consultancy firms have sought in various ways to shift towards organizational forms that represent an extension and deepening of organizational restructuring towards 'corporate globality' (Jones 2005). During the 1990s a number of the larger firms underwent dramatic internal restructuring (Jones 2003), moving away from a geographical to a product-based divisional structure. In essence, this represents a move away from US, UK, or Asian divisions of firms towards global-scale functional divisions based around communities of practice and knowledge/expertise (e.g. a global-scale retail consultancy or utilities practice community).

Thus, management consulting presents a strong contrast to the evolving organizational form of many large manufacturing firms (Johansson and Vahlne 1990; Andersen 1993). These discussions also relate to wider debates in economic geography about the role of mobility and technology and the way in which globalization is transforming the nature of work. This literature demonstrates that despite the globalization of management consulting firms over the last two decades, face-to-face interaction and co-presence remain central and crucial elements of working practices and ultimately of firm success. New information technologies have played an important role in facilitating and enabling the globalization of management consultancy firms, but the nature of the management consulting work process has meant that virtual interactions, for example via video-conferencing, have not become a substitute for the majority of forms of face-to-face interaction (Jones 2003, 2005; see also Sturdy, Schwarz, and Spencer 2006). The key impact of this has been to significantly increase the levels of business travel of employees, with substantial impacts on the working practices undertaken as firms globalize (see Faulconbridge et al. 2009).

Finally, according to the extant literature, the globalization of consulting firms has necessitated a wider shift to 'global working' practices beyond simple conceptions of increased international business travel (Wood 2002; Jones 2003, 2005). This shift has several elements, including a substantial increase in the numbers of foreign 'expatriate' workers moving between different offices in developing global networks; the development of more extensive secondment schemes, where more employees increasingly spend periods of months or years abroad; and a widening of the recruitment base of employees, where the employee profile of the company reflects rising percentages of employees from a larger number of different countries. Thus there has been a blurring and dilution of the 'home economy' component of the workforce within management consultancies, along with a growing prevalence of business travel and a growing numbers of employees living in countries other than their home state (Harvey et al. 1999; Jones 2003).

In sum, the economic geographical literature suggests that the globalization of management consulting firms has been shaped by a number of distinctly geographical factors including the regional strategic context from which consultancy firms seek to globalize, and also the geographical configuration of the social contact networks that are crucial to market entry and the business process in management consultancy. Economic geographers have thus contributed to an understanding of how the development of a global management consulting industry is uneven at both the regional and firm level, and provided conceptual tools to better understand the factors that shape the emerging global corporate geographies of firms.

11.5 Conclusion and Future Research Directions

By reviewing existing work on the geography of management consultancy firms, and in particular studies by economic geographers, this chapter has teased out the multiple spatial influences on the organization of the production and delivery of consultancy advice. In doing this, one of the most important future directions for research that becomes apparent is empirical in focus and involves developing in-depth empirical case studies of the way management consulting firms operate in and through cities across the global economy. Such research is important because it will help reveal, in more depth, the subtleties of the way ideas about producer services, place, and locality, and globalization and cross-border business apply to, or are not relevant to, management consultancies and, in the case of topics already explored through study of management consulting firms, will help deepen understanding of variations in strategies and practices within the industry.

In addition, work on the geographies of management consulting firms might also be developed by conceptually and theoretically drawing on key debates within economic geography and the wider social sciences that have been applied to other producer service firms but not considered in relation to management consulting firms. And this might also allow studies of management consultancies to relate back to and refine such theoretical debates. For example—and we could use many other examples but are selective in our choice here for sake of conciseness—making connections to wider debates about, first, the influence of the varieties of capitalism and national business systems on firms (see, for example, Morgan 2007; Faulconbridge 2008) may prove fruitful. Debates about the varieties of capitalism and national business systems centre around the influence of institutional ensembles, made up of both formal regulations and informal norms, on both the structures of firms and the cultures of workers (see Kipping and Wright, Chapter 8, this volume). For economic geographers the main interest in such debates relates to the way the globalization of producer services such as management consultancy has been affected by national variations in institutional ensembles and the associated varieties of capitalism and business systems (see, for example, the work of Clark, Mansfield, and Tickell 2002).

It would seem important to use such debates as a starting point for explorations of issues of place and locality, and globalization and cross-border business, in the work of management consulting firms. In terms of place and locality, the impact of subnational varieties of capitalism on management consulting firms might be examined, such as the difference between the business systems in northern and southern Italy and the cities in the two distinctive regions. How, for example, do consultancy firms adapt to such variety, and does presence in the cities, *in situ* service production and delivery, and membership of localized economies help in the adaptation process? In relation to globalization and cross-border business, how might the successes and failures of management consulting firms in different countries be explained with reference to, and provide more insight into, the effects of varieties of capitalism and national business systems on global service firms? How have differences in the logic of purchasing advice from consultants in different national markets defined the geographies of management consultancy firms' globalization? To answer such questions would again involve further empirical research but with the intention of developing new theoretical conceptualizations of the international dimensions of management consulting markets, firm structures, and strategies.

Second, future research might also investigate in much greater depth the heterogeneous and firm-specific nature of globalization in management consulting firms. From an economic geographical perspective, this informs a growing theoretical debate about the complexity of socio-economic practices at the firm level in the contemporary global economy. Economic geographers have in recent years become increasingly concerned to better theorize and understand the socio-economic aspects of global corporate development and behaviour (Yeung 2005; Jones and Murphy in press), and, as Glücker's and others' work on social networks and relations demonstrates, this opens up a wider range of potential research avenues in relation to how firm-level practices shape firm performance and evolution within the management consultancy sector.

The few studies discussed in this chapter do provide a basis for conceptualizing the debates about the role of social contact networks, information and communications technology (ICT), new forms of working practice, and mobility in management consultancy. But clearly these general trends conceal a great deal of diversity and complexity. Little is known, for example, about the contrasting strategies deployed by larger management consulting firms in comparison to the important subsector of small consultancies. Equally, different management consulting firms have based their globalization strategies on providing services to specific industries in the global economy, and little is known about how such specialism has produced different impacts in those firms. Similarly, it is unclear how management consultancies fit into the 'born-global' view of new firm formation discussed by management theorists in the 1990s (Madsen and Servais 1997; Bell, McNaughton, and Young 2001), since many smaller firms continue to operate in national-based markets and globalize from that base. This also means that, contrary to common assumptions, not all global management consulting firms are large firms. Many are small and operate globally without multiple offices staffed by several hundred consultants. The differences in the scale of global management consultancies are, then, also another area for future research.

By way of overall conclusion, therefore, it is fair to state that, whilst there is limited existing research on the geography of management consultancy firms, the beginnings of a solid set of foundations for future study do exist. But these foundations should not draw our attention away from the difficulties created by the dearth of in-depth theoretically informed empirical analysis of the key role played by the management consultancy industry in the contemporary global knowledge economy.

References

Allen, J. (1992). 'Services and the UK Space Economy: Regionalization and Economic Dislocation'. *Transactions of the Institute of British Geographers*, 17, 292–305.

Andersen, O. (1993). 'On the Interationalization Process of Firms: A Critical Analysis'. *Journal of International Business Studies*, 24/2 209–231.

Bagchi-Sen, S. and Sen, J. (1997). 'The Current State of Knowledge in International Business in Producer Services'. *Environment and Planning A*, 29, 1153–1174.

Bathelt, H. and Glückler, J. (2003). 'Toward a Relational Economic Geography'. *Journal of Economic Geography*, 3, 117–144.

Beaverstock, J. V. (1996). 'Subcontracting the Accountant! Professional Labour Markets, Migration, and Organisational Networks in the Global Accountancy Industry'. *Environment and Planning A*, 28, 303–326.

Beaverstock, J. V., Smith, R., and Taylor, P. J. (1999). 'The Long Arm of the Law: London's Law Firms in a Globalising World Economy'. *Environment and Planning A*, 13, 1857–1876.

Bell, J., McNaughton, R., and Young, S. (2001) 'Born-Again Global Firms: An Extension to the "Born-Global" Phenomenon'. *Journal of International Management*, 7, 173–189.

Boddewyn, J., Halbrich, M., and Perry, A. (1986). 'Service Multinationals: Conceptualization, Measurement and Theory'. *Journal of International Business Studies*, 17/3, 4–57.

Bryson, J. R. and Rusten, G. (2005). 'Spatial Divisions of Expertise: Knowledge Intensive Business Service Firms and Regional Development in Norway'. *Service Industries Journal*, 25/8, 959–977.

Bryson, J. R., Daniels, P. W., and Warf, B. (2004). *Service Worlds*. London: Routledge.

Clark, T. (1993). 'The Market Provision of Management Services, Information Asymmetries and Service Quality—Some Market Solutions: An Empirical Example'. *British Journal of Management*, 4/4, 235–251.

Clark, T. (1995). *Managing Consultants: Consultancy as the Management of Impressions*. Buckingham: Open University Press

Clarke, D. B. and Bradford, M. G. (1989). 'The Uses of Space by Advertising Agencies within the United Kingdom'. *Geografiska Annaler B: Human Geography*, 71B, 139–151.

Clark, G. L., Mansfield, D., and Tickell, A. (2002). 'Global Finance and the German Model: German Corporations, Market Incentives, and the Management of Employer-Sponsored Pension Institutions'. *Transactions of the Institute of British Geographers NS*, 27, 91–110.

Coffey, W. and Bailly, A. (1991). 'Producer Services and Flexible Production: An Exploratory Analysis'. *Growth and Change*, 22/4, 95–117.

Cohen R. B., Felton, F., Nkosi, M., and van Liere, J. (eds) (1979). *The Multinational Corporation: A Radical Approach: Papers by Stephen Herbert Hymer*. Cambridge: Cambridge University Press.

Czerniawska, F. (2001). *Management Consultancy: What Next? Future Directions*. Basingstoke: Palgrave Macmillan.

Daniels, P. W. (1993). *Service Industries in the World Economy*. Oxford: Blackwell.

Daniels, P. W. and Bryson, J. R. (2005). 'Sustaining Business and Professional Services in a Second City Region'. *Service Industries Journal*, 25/4, 505–524.

Daniels, P. W., Leyshon, A., and Thrift, N. J. (1987). 'Trends in the Growth and Location of Professional Producer Services: UK Property Consultants'. *Tijdschrift voor Economische en Sociale Geografie*, 79/3, 162–174.

Daniels, P. W., Leyshon, A., and Thrift, N. J. (1988). 'Large Accountancy Firms in the UK: Operational Adaptation and Spatial Development'. *Service Industries Journal*, 8/3, 317–346.

Dicken, P. (2007). *Global Shift: Mapping the Changing Contours of the World Economy*. London: Sage.

Dunning, J. (1993). *The Globalization of Business*. London: Routledge.

Dunning, J. and Norman, G. (1983). 'Theory of Multinational Enterprise: An Application to Multinational Office Location'. *Environment and Planning A*, 15/5 675–692.

Ekinsmyth, C. (2002). 'Project Organization, Embeddedness and Risk in Magazine Publishing'. *Regional Studies: The Journal of the Regional Studies Association*, 36/3, 229–243.

Empson, L. (2001). 'Introduction: Knowledge Management in Professional Service Firms'. *Human Relations*, 54/7, 811.

Empson, L. and Chapman, C. (2006). 'Partnership Versus Corporation: Implications of Alternative Governance for Managerial Authority and Organizational Priorities in Professional Service Firms'. *Research in the Sociology of Organizations*, 24, 145–176.

Enderwick, P (1989). *Multinational Service Firms*. London: Routledge.

Faulconbridge, J. R. (2006). 'Stretching Tacit Knowledge Beyond a Local Fix? Global Spaces of Learning in Advertising Professional Service Firms'. *Journal of Economic Geography*, 6, 517–540.

Faulconbridge, J. R. (2007a). 'Relational Spaces of Knowledge Production in Transnational Law Firms'. *Geoforum*, 38/3, 925–940.

Faulconbridge, J. R. (2007b). 'Exploring the Role of Professional Associations in Collective Learning in London and New York's Advertising and Law Professional Service Firm Clusters'. *Environment and Planning A*, 39, 965–984.

Faulconbridge, J. R. (2008). 'Negotiating Cultures of Work in Transnational Law Firms'. *Journal of Economic Geography*, 8/4, 497–517.

Faulconbridge, J. R., Hall, S., and Beaverstock, J. V. (2008). 'New Insights into the Internationalization of Producer Services: Organizational Strategies and Spatial Economies for Global Headhunting Firms'. *Environment and Planning A*, 40/1, 210–234.

Faulconbridge, J. R., Beaverstock, J. V., Derudder, B., and Witlox, F. (2009). 'Corporate Ecologies of Business Travel in Professional Service Firms: Working Towards a Research Agenda'. *European Urban and Regional Studies*, 16/3, 295.

Faulconbridge, J. R., Beaverstock, J. V., Taylor, P. J., and Nativel, C. (2011). *The Globalization of Advertising: Firms, Cities and Innovation*. London: Routledge.

Fincham, R. (2006). 'Knowledge Work as Occupational Strategy: Comparing IT and Management Consulting'. *New Technology, Work and Employment*, 21/1, 16–28.

Glückler, J. (2007). 'Geography and Reputation: The City as the Locus of Business Opportunity'. *Regional Studies*, 41/7, 949–961.

Glückler, J. and Armbrüster, T. (2003). 'Bridging Uncertainty in Management Consulting: The Mechanisms of Trust and Networked Reputation'. *Organization Studies*, 24/2, 269–297.

Goe, W. (1991). 'The Growth of Producer Services Industries: Sorting Through the Externalization Debate'. *Growth and Change*, 22/4, 118–140.

Grabher, G. (2001). 'Ecologies of Creativity: The Village, the Group and the Heterarchic Organisation of the British Advertising Industry'. *Environment and Planning A*, 33, 351–374.

Grabher, G. (2002). 'Cool Projects, Boring Institutions: Temporary Collaboration in Social Context'. *Regional Studies*, 36/3, 205–214.

Hall, S. (2007). ' "Relational Marketplaces" and the Rise of Boutiques in London's Corporate Finance Industry'. *Environment and Planning A*, 39, 1838–1854.

Hall, S. and Appleyard, L. (2009). 'City of London City of Learning? Placing Business Education Within the Geographies of Finance'. *Journal of Economic Geography*, 9/5, 597–617.

Hall, S., Beaverstock, J., Faulconbridge, J., and Hewitson, A. (2009). 'Exploring Cultural Economies of Internationalization: The Role of "Iconic Individuals" and "Brand Leaders" in the Globalization of Headhunting'. *Global Networks*, 9/3, 399–419.

Harvey, M., Speier, C., and Novicevic, M. (1999). 'The Impact of Emerging Markets on Staffing the Global Organization: A Knowledge-Based View'. *Journal of International Management*, 5, 157–186.

Johansson, J. and Vahlne, J. (1990). 'The Mechanism of Internationalization'. *International Marketing Review*, 7/4, 11–24.

Jones, A. (2003). *Management Consultancy and Banking in an Era of Globalization*. Basingstoke: Palgrave Macmillan.

Jones, A. (2005). 'Truly Global Corporations? Theorizing Organizational Globalisation in Advanced Business-Services'. *Journal of Economic Geography*, 5, 177–200.

Jones, A. (2007). 'More than "Managing Across Borders"? The Complex Role of Face-to-Face Interaction in Globalizing Law Firms'. *Journal of Economic Geography*, 7, 223–246.

Jones, A. and Murphy, J. T. (2011). 'Theorizing Practice in Economic Geography: Foundations, Challenges and Possibilities. *Progress in Human Geography*, 35, 366–392.

Keeble, D. and Nachum, L. (2002). 'Why do Business Service Firms Cluster? Small Consultancies, Clustering and Decentralization in London and Southern England'. *Transactions of the Institute of British Geographers*, 27/1, 67–90.

Kipping, M. (1999). 'American Management Consulting Companies in Western Europe, 1920 to 1990: Products, Reputation, and Relationships'. *Business History Review*, 73/2, 190–220.

Madsen, T. and Servais, P. (1997). 'The Internationalization of Born Globals: An Evolutionary Process?' *International Business Review*, 6/6, 561–583.

Massey, D. (2007). *World City*. Cambridge: Polity.

McKenna, C. D. (2006). *The World's Newest Profession: Management Consulting in the Twentieth Century*. Cambridge: Cambridge University Press.

Morgan, G. (2007). 'National Business Systems Research: Progress and Prospects'. *Scandinavian Journal of Management*, 23/2, 127–145.

Morgan, K. (2004). 'The Exaggerated Death of Geography: Learning, Proximity and Territorial Innovation Systems'. *Journal of Economic Geography*, 4/1, 3–21.

Muzio, D., Ackroyd, S., and Chanlat, J-F. (eds) (2008). *Redirections in the Study of Expert Labour: Established Professions and New Expert Occupations*. Basingstoke: Palgrave Macmillan.

O'Farrell, P. N. and Hitchens, D. M. (1990). 'Producer Services and Regional Development: Key Conceptual Issues of Taxonomy and Quality Measurement'. *Regional Studies*, 24/2L, 163–171.

O'Farrell, P. and Wood, P. (1999). 'Formation of Strategic Alliances by Business Service Firms: Towards a New Client-Oriented Conceptual Framework'. *Service Industries Journal*, 19, 133–151.

O'Farrell, P. N., Wood, P., and Zhiang, J. (1998). 'Regional Influences on Foreign Market Development by Business Service Companies: Elements of a Strategic Context Explanation'. *Regional Studies*, 32/1, 31–48.

Prahalad, C. K. and Hamel, G. (1990). 'The Core Competence of the Corporation'. *Harvard Business Review*, May–June, 79–91.

Pryke, M. (1994). Looking Back on the Space of a Boom: (Re)developing Spatial Matrices in the City of London. *Environment and Planning A*, 26, 235–264.

Sassen, S. (2006). *Cities in a World Economy*. 3rd edn. London: Sage.

Saxenian, A. (1994). *Regional Advantage: Culture and Competition in Silicon Valley and Route 128*. London: Harvard University Press.

Storper, M. and Venables, A. J. (2004). 'Buzz: Face-to-Face Contact and the Urban Economy'. *Journal of Economic Geography*, 4, 351–370.

Sturdy, A. J., Schwarz, M., and Spencer A. (2006). 'Guess Who's Coming to Dinner? Structures and Uses of Liminality in Strategic Management Consultancy'. *Human Relations*, 59/7, 929–960.

Sydow, J. and Staber, U. (2002). 'The Institutional Embeddedness of Project Networks: The Case of Content Production in German Television'. *Regional Studies*, 36/3, 215–227.

Thrift, N. (1994). 'On the Social and Cultural Determinants of International Financial Centres: The Case of the City of London'. In S. Corbridge, N. Thrift, and R. Martin (eds), *Money, Power and Space*. Oxford: Blackwell, 375–355.

Vinodrai, T. (2006). 'Reproducing Toronto's Design Ecology: Career Paths, Intermediaries, and Local Labor Markets'. *Economic Geography*, 82/3, 237–263.

Wood, P. A. (1991). 'Flexible Accumulation and the Rise of Business Services'. *Transactions of the Institute of British Geographers*, 16, 160–172.

Wood, P. (2002) 'European Consultancy Growth: Nature, Causes and Consequences'. In P. Wood (ed), *Consultancy and Innovation: The Business Service Revolution in Europe*. London: Routledge, 35–71.

Wood, P. (2006). 'Urban Development and Knowledge-Intensive Business Services: Too Many Unanswered Questions?' *Growth and Change*, 37/3, 335–361.

Work Foundation (2009). *Knowledge Workers and Knowledge Work*. London: The Work Foundation.

Yeung, H. W-C. (2005). 'Rethinking Relational Economic Geography'. *Transactions of the Institute of British Geographers NS*, 30, 37–51.

PART 3

CONSULTING AS A KNOWLEDGE BUSINESS

CHAPTER 12

....

KNOWLEDGE MANAGEMENT AND MANAGEMENT CONSULTING

....

ANDREAS WERR

12.1 INTRODUCTION

....

THE role and handling of knowledge in management consulting firms has been a strong area of focus within research on management consulting. Ever since the early 1990s management consulting firms have provided an empirical context for what was perceived as a new and important management challenge—knowledge management (KM). On the basis of the argument that management consultancies compete primarily on their knowledge, they have been portrayed and studied as pioneers of KM. As Hansen, Nohria, and Tierney (1999: 107) note, '[b]ecause knowledge is the core asset of consultancies, they were among the first businesses to pay attention to—and make heavy investments in—the management of knowledge'.

This has made management consultancies a popular object of study as exemplars of KM for other industries. Being archetypical 'knowledge businesses', lessons learned from management consultants were viewed as potentially applicable to other sectors with a high knowledge content (Hansen, Nohria, and Tierney 1999; Empson 2001a; Løwendahl, Revang, and Fosstenløkken 2001; Weeks 2004). Research on KM in management consulting firms has thus been carried out both as a way of increasing our understanding of the activity of management consulting, but also with a claim of wider relevance for organizations in the 'knowledge society', in which knowledge is increasingly becoming a key source of competitive advantage.

This chapter presents a systematic review of the literature on KM within management consulting. It will first provide a brief overview of KM in management consulting and its definition(s). The chapter will then review the extant literature, which has focused on four main—primarily empirical—issues, each of which will be addressed in turn in the remainder of the chapter. These are: (1) What is the nature of knowledge in management consulting? (2) How is knowledge shared and transferred within the consulting firm? (3) What are the effects of KM? and (4) How is new knowledge created? These four themes and the order in which they are presented reflect a crude and overlapping timeline of the overall evolution of research on KM (Rolland, Guilhon, and Trepo 2005). The chapter concludes with some suggestions for the directions of future research.

12.2 Definitions of Knowledge Management in Consulting

The general concept of 'knowledge management' began to emerge in the literature in the early 1990s, and reached its peak in popularity in the late 1990s and early 2000s (Scarbrough and Swan 2003). In general management practice, the concept has had a consistently high usage during the 2000s. In a survey among organizations all over the world conducted by Bain & Co., about 60 per cent of organizations claimed to apply 'knowledge management' throughout the 2000s, with a slight drop in 2008 (Rigby and Bilodeau 2010). The emergence and proliferation of KM as a management discourse has been driven by three main themes, reflecting contemporary management challenges as well as theoretical and practical developments (Scarbrough and Swan 2003). These include an increasing focus on the 'knowledge society', identifying knowledge (rather than labour) as the key source of competitiveness. Theoretically, the emergence of the resource-based view of the firm (e.g. Nahapiet and Ghoshal 1998) has been an important source in motivating the need to start 'managing knowledge' (Alvesson and Kärreman 2001). Finally, technological developments regarding information and communication technology (ICT) played an important enabling role in facilitating the processing, storage, and access of knowledge across spatial and temporal boundaries (Alvesson and Kärreman 2001; Ofek and Sarvary 2001).

Underlying much of the literature on KM in management consulting is an assumption that knowledge is a strategic asset to management consulting firms and that KM is the way to capitalize on this asset. Hargadon (1998) describes the brokering of knowledge between firms as an important role of management consulting firms. Through their assignments with clients, consultants gain access to both problems and solutions in different contexts. This gives them a unique position to transfer knowledge between different actors but also to combine this knowledge in new ways or move it to new places and thereby support innovation. By leveraging knowledge and experience from client projects, management consulting firms have the potential to create not only efficiency gains but a leap in the quality of their offerings (Ofek and Sarvary 2001). The management consulting firm's reliance on client projects as a main source of knowledge creates a specific kind of competitive dynamic where knowledge-based economies of scale can be created through KM activities (Sarvary 1999; Løwendahl, Revang, and Fosstenløkken 2001).

Definitions of KM in management consulting reflect a number of common themes. First, they focus on the sharing and dissemination of knowledge, that is, making sure that the individual knowledge of organizational members is made available to the entire organization. Second, they link KM to competitive advantage and business results. Third, KM is described as a business process consisting of a number of sub-activities including organizational learning/capturing knowledge, knowledge production/codification, and knowledge distribution/transfer (see also Kakabadse, Kakabadse, and Kouzmin 2003). Two fundamental assumptions underpin most of the KM literature—that people are willing to share their knowledge with others and that they are naturally willing to learn and seek new knowledge. These assumptions are, however, questionable (Morris 2001; Husted, Gammelgaard, and Michailova 2005), and this will be discussed further later in this chapter.

Beyond these common themes, definitions of KM and associated approaches also differ in important dimensions. One such dimension is the breadth of the concept, where some definitions become rather all-encompassing, viewing KM as an integrated part of all management activities (e.g. Davenport and Prusak 2000). However, this risks making KM about everything and nothing, thus limiting its value as a specific management concept (Alvesson and Kärreman 2001; Rolland, Guilhon, and Trepo 2005). Such broad definitions of KM also make the task of this chapter—to review the research focusing on KM in management consulting—rather challenging, as it would make the entire literature on organizing and managing management consulting organizations relevant (see Morris, Gardner, and Anand, Chapter 14, this volume). The current review thus applies a pragmatic delimitation to the systematic literature review. It focuses on the literature labelled by its authors as dealing with 'knowledge management'. The large majority of the research identified on this basis falls within the more limited definition of KM as a set of business processes aimed at creating, storing, and transferring knowledge in order to create a competitive advantage.

A second dimension in which definitions and approaches to KM differ is in relation to how knowledge is viewed. The KM literature is, in general, rather vague when it comes to defining what is meant by 'knowledge'. However, two underlying positions can be identified. One views knowledge as a 'possession' that can be objectified (captured, codified, and transferred) within the organization. Another (less common) position views knowledge as 'socially embedded' and thus linked to individuals and activated in relation to a specific situation (Hansen, Nohria, and Tierney 1999; Empson 2001a; Schwartz and Clark 2010). Consequently, the next section will examine the related debates in the management consulting specific literature.

12.3 THE NATURE OF KNOWLEDGE IN MANAGEMENT CONSULTING

The nature of knowledge in organizations in general as well as in consulting specifically is a much-debated issue that has produced a wide array of typologies of different kinds of knowledge. Most of these typologies, in one form or another, build on a juxtaposition of two opposing epistemological stances. Newell (2005) labels these two positions as 'knowledge as possession' versus 'knowledge as socially embedded' (see also Empson 2001a).

From the 'knowledge as possession' stance, knowledge is viewed as an objectively definable commodity, which can be easily moved from one place to another. It is assumed that it is possible to articulate and store knowledge in databases for transfer and future use. Such a view of knowledge has been driving many KM initiatives in practice, where the focus has been on building and maintaining ICT-supported 'knowledge management systems' (Ruggles 1998). Common conceptualizations of KM as consisting of capturing, codifying, and distributing knowledge follow naturally from a view of 'knowledge as possession' (e.g. Deng 2008). Central challenges in this context relate to what content to add to these knowledge repositories and how to structure the repositories (e.g. Griggs, Wild, and Li 2002) as well as how to motivate individuals in organizations to contribute and use the knowledge available within these systems.

The 'knowledge as socially embedded' stance, by contrast, focuses on the tacit and socially embedded nature of knowledge. From this perspective, knowledge is viewed as situation specific, embedded in practice, and difficult to articulate. It is about acting knowingly in the specific situation rather than applying generic approaches or methodologies from KM systems. Visscher (2006: 248), for example, in the specific context of management consulting, concludes that 'instead of following phase-models, consultants appear to be improvising bricoleurs, tailoring their ways of working to specific situations, and using broad, heterogeneous and partly implicit repertoires, which are built mainly through action-learning' (see also Werr and Stjernberg 2003). From this perspective, the sharing and transfer of knowledge among consultants requires interaction in relation to a specific problem. Rather than accumulating knowledge in organizational databases, accumulation implies the continual development of shared understandings among a group of actors sharing a practice. As argued by Fincham and colleagues (2008), an important dimension of knowledge in this context is the business sector or industry with which the consultants engage. Central challenges from the socially embedded perspective of knowledge include understanding the social and interactive formation and application of knowledge in practice and in a specific social context.

While these two positions—with a focus on either explicit knowledge or tacit knowledge—and their related KM strategies have often been presented as opposing (e.g. Hansen, Nohria, and Tierney 1999), it has also been suggested that they may be viewed as complementary, with tacit and explicit knowledge being different but co-existing forms of knowledge (Robertson and Swan 1998; Newell 2005; Hislop 2008). One way of conceptualizing such a complementary relationship between tacit and explicit forms of knowledge is the SECI (Socialization, Externalization, Combination, Internalization) model by Nonaka and Takeuchi (1995). Although not specifically developed in a management consulting context, it deserves mention as it is frequently cited in the literature on KM in management consulting. The basic notion of this model is that knowledge creation and sharing takes place in recurring transformations between tacit and explicit knowledge. The model describes four such transformations—socialization (from tacit to tacit knowledge through, for example, collaborating and acting together), externalization (from tacit to explicit knowledge through, for example, formulating methods and tools based on experiences), combination (from explicit to explicit knowledge through, for example, combining insights from different documents), and finally internalization (from explicit to tacit knowledge through applying, for example, explicit methodologies in a specific case).

A second conceptualization of the relationship between tacit and explicit forms of knowledge developed specifically in a consulting context is provided by Werr and Stjernberg (2003), who focus on the complementarity of these knowledge forms rather than the transformations between them. They argue that consulting firms may be understood as knowledge systems composed of three different kinds of knowledge: (1) the (tacit) experiences of consultants; (2) explicit and general methodologies available in the consulting organization; and (3) explicit and specific material related to specific client cases. The tacit experiences of consultants are argued to be central to the application of the explicit knowledge stored in the company databases as they provide the basis for the adaptation of the latter knowledge to the specific situation at hand. However, the explicit knowledge in the form of methods and tools and cases is also important. The methods and tools provide a common language that enables consultants to share and apply their tacit experiences in joint action as well as access and understand other consultants' client cases in the databases. The explicit cases finally have a role in the knowledge system as examples of practice in specific situations. Unlike the methods and tools, they are not decontextualized and thus provide insights into specific practices in particular situations. Rather than focusing on either explicit knowledge and databases or tacit knowledge and interaction, this approach highlights the fact that it is the interaction of both that makes up knowledge in management consulting (Werr and Stjernberg 2003).

Within the domain of management consulting, one can also identify a third conceptualization of knowledge, which could be labelled 'knowledge as symbol'. This view of knowledge is rooted in the epistemological position of 'knowledge as socially embedded', and elaborates on the idea that knowledge cannot be objectively defined and managed. Instead the focus is shifted to the performative aspects of knowledge and KM in management consulting. This literature claims that the knowledge of consultants is vague and ambiguous as it lacks a clearly defined body of specialist knowledge (Alvesson 1993, 2001; Clark 1995; Jones 2003). Rather than asking how knowledge is generated and transferred in organizations these authors ask how knowledge is rhetorically constructed—both in the eyes of fellow consultants and in those of the client—and how such knowledge claims are used by managers and organizations. This stream of research highlights the importance of 'impression management' (Clark 1995) and rhetoric (Bloomfield and Best 1992; Bloomfield and Danieli 1995; Legge 2002) in creating impressions of knowledge, and draws attention to political aspects of consulting knowledge (Sturdy et al. 2009). From this perspective KM becomes at best a management fad and resource in the construction of credible knowledge claims (Alvesson 2001; Swan and Scarbrough 2001). Based on such a view of knowledge as fluid, vague, and person-bound, the notion of KM has been critiqued for being oxymoronic as the notion of management, involving order and control, is in direct contrast with such characteristics of knowledge (Alvesson 2001; Styhre 2003).

The current understanding of knowledge in management consulting and, consequently, how it may be managed, is thus multifaceted, ranging from a view of knowledge as mainly explicit and thus easily stored and transferred, to more complex conceptualizations viewing knowledge as tacit and embedded in a social context, which makes the task of 'managing' knowledge more complex or even futile, reducing it to mere legitimacy-creating symbolic acts. While conceptualizations of knowledge underlying research on KM in management consulting have increased in complexity and level of articulation, the majority of research still builds on rather unarticulated and one-dimensional conceptualizations, often with an implicit foundation in the 'knowledge as asset' approach. Few conceptualizations of knowledge go beyond a discussion of tacit versus explicit knowledge, creating a tendency to oversimplify and over-stabilize the analysis of knowledge (Robertson and Swan 1998).

Further research could thus contribute to more multidimensional conceptualizations of knowledge in management consulting. Recent efforts in this direction regarding professional knowledge more generally suggest some promising avenues in linking professional knowledge and identity (e.g. Ibarra 1999; Sandberg and Pinnington 2009).

12.4 Knowledge Sharing and Transfer

The second focal issue in research on KM in management consulting is the transfer and sharing of knowledge, which represents the bulk of the publications in this area. Research on this topic is typically based on qualitative case studies of a single consultancy and rooted in a 'knowledge as asset' epistemological position. From early on, this research acknowledged the limits to the codification of knowledge, which consequently called for combinations of initiatives focusing on the formulation and transfer of explicit knowledge through, for example, databases and the creation of opportunities for the exchange of tacit knowledge through social interaction.

Two approaches to the sharing and transfer of knowledge are generally identified, which relate to the two epistemological positions noted previously. In Hansen, Nohria, and Tierney's (1999) much cited version these two approaches are labelled 'codification' and 'personalization' respectively. The codification approach focuses on making knowledge explicit and transferring it by means of databases, thus reflecting a 'knowledge as asset' epistemology. The personalization strategy, on the other hand, focuses on transferring tacit knowledge between individuals and thus emphasizes mechanisms for creating connections and facilitating interactions between individuals, which reflects more of a 'knowledge as socially embedded' epistemology. These two approaches are viewed as mutually exclusive and the suitability of each approach is portrayed as contingent upon the level of standardization and maturity of the service offered as well as the nature of the knowledge-base that underlies the service (Morris and Empson 1998; Hansen, Nohria, and Tierney 1999).

While Hansen, Nohria, and Tierney (1999) present codification and personalization as two alternative strategies, other authors often find a mix of different forms of both tacit and explicit knowledge and associated KM mechanisms. In line with this, research also points to a combination of structural and technical factors and cultural and social factors as central enablers of the sharing and transfer of knowledge. In the following, the central organizational enablers of KM in management consulting as identified in the literature are reviewed. These enablers have been identified both from a 'knowledge as asset' perspective, focusing on explicit knowledge, and a knowledge as socially embedded perspective, focusing on tacit knowledge. However, the way in which the enablers support knowledge sharing and transfer differs depending on the underlying conceptualization of knowledge (for a summary, see Table 12.1).

IT systems. While IT systems and their design have been a focus of the general KM literature (Scarbrough and Swan 2003), this has not been a strong focus in the literature on KM in management consulting. Still, some kind of IT support is generally involved in KM initiatives (Apostolou and Mentzas 1999b; Chait 1999), most often based on different kinds of Internet technology applications, including e-mail (Kim and Trimi 2007). IT systems may serve both as a vehicle for storing and transferring explicit knowledge and as a way of enhancing networking, communication, and interaction in order to share tacit knowledge. The design of the IT-based KM systems used is seldom discussed beyond examples of specific cases (e.g. Baladi 1999; Griggs, Wild, and Li 2002). Olivera (2000) discusses the perceived effectiveness of different memory systems where IT-based knowledge repositories are one example. He highlights five factors contributing to effectiveness: (1) relevance and specificity of the system's content; (2) effectiveness of the system's indexing; (3) extent to which the content has been filtered by experts; (4) extent to which the system's content is updated; and (5) ease of accessing the system. The most common reference to the role of IT in KM in the extant literature, however, is the advice not to overemphasize IT. The implementation of IT-based KM systems needs to be accompanied by other changes in the organization. Without such changes, the implementation of IT-based KM systems may fail or even become counter-productive (Robertson, Sørensen, and Swan 2001; Deng 2008). This downplaying of the role of IT is related to observed challenges in relation to ensuring both input into the systems as well as their use to find information.

Reward structures/incentive system. A common finding in studies on knowledge sharing is that sharing and reusing knowledge (regardless of its form as tacit or explicit) does not come naturally. Barriers such as time pressures (Henriksen 2005), fear of losing a key asset (Morris and Empson 1998; Morris 2001), concerns that knowledge that is shared is misused (Ejenäs and Werr 2005), and so on create barriers towards sharing knowledge. Similarly, although not as well studied, reusing knowledge is met by resistance originating from, for example, the difficulties of finding relevant knowledge or professional pride (Dunford 2000; Robertson, Sørensen, and Swan 2001). To overcome these barriers the incentive system, including both rewards and

Table 12.1 Organizational enablers of knowledge transfer and sharing

Enabler	Knowledge as asset approach (focus on explicit knowledge)	Knowledge as socially embedded approach (focus on tacit knowledge)
IT systems	Repository of knowledge; enabler of knowledge storage and dissemination	Enabler of networking (identifying the right people) and communication
Reward structures/incentive systems	Affects willingness to engage in updating and consulting databases	Affects willingness to support colleagues on projects, respond to questions, and the preferred media of communication
Business processes	Encourages interaction with knowledge systems as a natural part of the process	Initiates and legitimates interaction and knowledge exchange through organizational and process structures
Roles and structures	Formal KM roles ensure and enforce quality and use of knowledge repositories	Communities of practice create spaces for interaction and knowledge sharing and creation
Organizational culture	Provides a basis for trust, which influences the willingness to share and reuse knowledge from repositories	Provides a basis for trust, which encourages the sharing of failures and creates commitment and openness among consultants
Common language	Provides a structure for knowledge that enables access and reuse across cultural and other boundaries	Facilitates collaboration and learning as well as face-to-face sharing of knowledge
Power and politics	Fear to lose status and power may reduce willingness to codify knowledge	Fear to lose out in internal career competition limits individual knowledge sharing and seeking
Management support	Successful integration of KM systems requires that they are part of the strategic agenda and that top management demonstrates desirable behaviour	Social mechanisms for knowledge sharing are difficult to control. Research focuses on the consultants and their work rather than managerial initiatives

career, is identified as critical (e.g. Morris and Empson 1998; Apostolou and Mentzas 1999b; Lahti and Beyerlein 2000; Weeks 2004; Henriksen 2005; Kaplan and Thomson-Reed 2007; Deng 2008). As argued by Robertson, Sørensen, and Swan (2001), the way in which (formal and informal) rewards are distributed affects not only to what extent knowledge is shared but also in what ways. Furthermore, the common focus on billable hours as a central basis for evaluation in management consulting firms is seen as a barrier to sharing both explicit and tacit knowledge, since it discourages spending time on non-client-related tasks such as synthesizing experiences, answering questions from colleagues, or acquiring and testing new knowledge (Bang 2005; Chao 2005). Studies thus point out that the incentive system needs to be aligned to the KM system. Few studies, however, explicitly discuss how incentive systems encouraging different kinds of knowledge sharing could be designed. In this context, cultural variation in multinational settings also needs to be taken into account (Paik and Choi 2005).

Business processes. In order to overcome some of the barriers to knowledge sharing discussed above, several studies point out that specific KM activities need to be incorporated in the natural workflow in order to become 'part of the way people do business' (Kaplan and Thomson-Reed 2007: 221). Activities related to the capture, transfer, and reuse of practices (primarily explicit knowledge) need to be simple enough to become an integrated part of the way of working in order not to be perceived as just an extra administrative burden (Weeks 2004; Kaplan and Thomson-Reed 2007: 221; Ambos and Schlegelmilch 2009). Also, some slack and room for reflection built into the business processes are identified as enablers of knowledge sharing (Apostolou and Mentzas 1999a). Furthermore, the design of the business processes in service delivery is pointed out to be important as this enables participation and collaboration and thereby social mechanisms for (tacit) knowledge sharing. Chao (2005), for example, shows how the peripheral participation of young consultants in project work enables them to acquire central competencies, including a professional identity (see also Morris, Gardner, and Anand, Chapter 14, this volume). The detailed connections between the design and organization of consulting work and the sharing of knowledge between consultants, however, remain to be explored in greater detail.

KM roles and structures. It is further argued that knowledge sharing and transfer activities require a clear structure of roles, related to especially the maintenance and use of IT-based KM systems (Baladi 1999; Weeks 2004; Henriksen 2005). These roles could be specialized, with dedicated incumbents, or temporary, so that active consultants could rotate in and out of the roles. Depending on the kind of service delivered, firms were found to have different strategies regarding the extent to which KM was handled by specialists as opposed to regular consultants (Apostolou and Mentzas 1999b). Another structural intervention related to KM (although from a 'knowledge as socially embedded' position) is the creation of communities of practice, groupings of people that share a specific practice and thus knowledge domain (Kohlbacher and Mukai 2007). Communities of practice in consulting firms may either emerge naturally from informal networks or be formed top down, developed as a part of the business strategy. A study by

Pastoors (2007) found that consultants preferred the naturally formed communities as they were closer to their members' interests and thus were perceived as being more valuable.

Organizational culture. The attitudes and values making up the culture of the consulting organization are recurrently mentioned as enablers of sharing and transferring both tacit and explicit knowledge (e.g. Morris and Empson 1998; Apostolou and Mentzas 1999b; Baladi 1999; Chait 1999; Henriksen 2005; Deng 2008). Exactly what constitutes a 'knowledge-sharing culture'—beyond that it makes it legitimate to share and reuse knowledge—is, however, unclear. Trust is one aspect, which is mentioned repeatedly. Thus, sharing knowledge on an individual basis, or even through IT-based systems, involves showing openness and vulnerability, and individuals need to trust their co-workers to do so (Ejenäs and Werr 2005; Henriksen 2005). Trust is also believed to bind people and their companies together, which discourages self-serving behaviour and encourages knowledge sharing (Morris and Empson 1998; Deng 2008). An additional aspect of a culture supporting knowledge sharing is a tolerance for making mistakes (Henriksen 2005). In forming knowledge-sharing cultures, structural means such as organizational structures, business process-related interventions, and the incentive system are identified as key tools (Apostolou and Mentzas 1999b). Robertson, Scarbrough, and Swan (2003) also argue that in cases where the consulting service is based on a strong profession, professional norms of knowledge sharing and seeking may be mobilized for corporate ends.

Common language. It has further been argued that the sharing of knowledge among consultants can be facilitated by the existence of common frameworks and vocabularies (Apostolou and Mentzas 1999a; Lahti and Beyerlein 2000; Werr and Stjernberg 2003; Ejenäs and Werr 2005; Kaplan and Thomson-Reed 2007). In order to share knowledge over geographical, cultural, and educational boundaries, as is often the case in large management consultancies, a common language that can be used for the exchange of both tacit and explicit knowledge is needed. As suggested by Werr and Stjernberg (2003), this common language may be provided by structured methodologies, which supply both conceptual frameworks and detailed concepts of how to approach certain tasks. These frameworks and concepts facilitate both communication and collaboration between consultants.

Power and politics. Knowledge, as a key asset in the management consulting firm, is closely linked to power on both an individual and group level (Robertson and Swan 1998; Morris 2001). A key issue discussed by Morris (2001) is the tension between the individual's expert knowledge as a prerequisite for reward and promotion within the firm and the firm's desire to appropriate that knowledge by codifying it and transmitting it throughout the firm. The risk of losing expert-based power is frequently referred to as an impediment for consultants to share knowledge. Morris (2001), however, shows that this risk in codification projects is often exaggerated due to limitations of what knowledge it is actually possible to articulate (see also Werr and Stjernberg 2003; Visscher 2006). Studies have also shown that concerns with status and identity on a group level may influence the sharing of knowledge. Sharing as well as reusing knowledge from groups with perceived status differences has been found to be difficult. This has been highlighted specifically in merger contexts, where Empson (2001b) found that individuals resist knowledge transfer if they perceive fundamental differences in the forms of the knowledge-bases and the images of the combining firms. Similar intergroup power dynamics were found between regional offices in multinational consulting firms (Paik and Choi 2005; Donnelly 2008). Taken together, however, there are surprisingly few studies that focus on power and politics in relation to knowledge transfer.

Management behaviour/support. In their search for success factors for KM initiatives the literature, especially the literature viewing 'knowledge as an asset', repeatedly comes back to the behaviour and support of management. Key roles for top management are to make the KM strategy part of the overall strategy (Kaplan and Thomson-Reed 2007), to show commitment and support (Deng 2008), and to 'walk the talk' (Baladi 1999). This advice reflects an underlying assumption in much of the literature that KM initiatives represent large-scale change programmes that need to be managed from the top (cf. Kaplan and Thomson-Reed 2007). The literature taking a 'knowledge as socially embedded' position is more interested in the local social interactions through which knowledge is shared and enacted and thus has less faith in the actions of top management.

In addition to the enablers of KM discussed above—which mainly relate to the organizational level—a limited number of studies have focused on the drivers of individual behaviour when it comes to knowledge sharing and reuse. Focusing on the demand side, Sussman and Siegal (2003) have investigated factors such as the usefulness of advice, the perceived quality of the argument, the credibility of the source, and the expertise and involvement of the recipient in the topic. On the supply side, Hansen and Haas (2001) have examined the strategies suppliers of electronic documents have used in order to gain the attention of users. They found that suppliers with a selective and concentrated strategy gained most attention as they developed a reputation for quality and focus (Hansen and Haas 2001).

While the question of how knowledge within management consulting organizations can be shared and transferred has attracted significant attention, this review still points to the need for further research on some aspects. First, there is a need for comparative studies that can shed more light on the contingencies behind the choices and effects of different ways of approaching the sharing and transfer of knowledge in consulting firms. Several studies show that the sharing and transfer of knowledge is dealt with differently in different firms. Understanding these differences beyond simple dichotomies, as well as the antecedents and effects of these differences, merits further research. Second, some of the enablers identified in the literature are in need of further elaboration. This is especially true for the concept of 'culture'. Current studies say little about the nature of a 'knowledge-sharing culture' and what the key elements of such a culture may be. Also, the incentive system and work processes merit further research to establish how their design influences knowledge sharing and transfer in different contexts.

Third, the review has identified power and related status and identity issues as central barriers to knowledge sharing and transfer. These issues have, however, received a rather limited attention in the KM literature. Further investigations into the power context of different kinds of consultancies may thus create important insights. Fourth, KM has been presented as a strategic enabler of the large, global consulting firm (Sarvary 1999). However, the multinational context and the challenges this may create in terms of language, status, culture and other barriers is little studied. The few studies that take this outlook (e.g. Crucini 2002; Paik and Choi 2005; Donnelly 2008) find a need for substantial adaptations of KM practices across cultural contexts. Finally, the role and effects of social networks as a vehicle for knowledge sharing and transfer remain unexplored. While the importance of personal relations is pointed out occasionally (e.g Henriksen 2005), the detailed constitution of social networks and their effects on the sharing and transfer of knowledge has not been studied to any larger extent. Studies of social networks in consulting firms may further our understanding of the nature and enablers of knowledge sharing.

12.5 THE EFFECTS OF KNOWLEDGE MANAGEMENT

In research focusing on the sharing and transfer of knowledge, the (positive) effects of KM are generally taken for granted. The basic premise for most of the literature reviewed in the previous section is 'the more knowledge sharing and exchange, the better'. A third theme in the literature on KM in management consulting focuses on the relation between KM and performance, and this research gives reason to moderate this assumption. Research within this third theme is dominated by quantitative methodologies.

While the investments of large management consulting firms into KM initiatives have been considerable, few efforts have been made to actually follow up the return on such investments. In an effort to do so, the multinational consulting firm, Accenture, conducted a survey in which consultants were asked to estimate time savings related to the use of the IT-based KM system (Aaron 2009). The results showed a considerable increase in productivity related to the KM system and a return on investment of about 1:18. However, looking at time savings only captures one aspect of the potential benefits of KM. Ofek and Sarvary (2001) argue for, and model, two potential effects of KM—increasing efficiency (time savings) and increasing quality (offering more robust and innovative services). In a competitive setting, with sufficient potential for economies of scale, they argue, consulting firms will focus on building KM systems aimed at delivering higher quality services to customers rather than increasing efficiency. Haas and Hansen (2005, 2007) elaborate on this idea and investigate the effects of different KM initiatives on the efficiency and quality of consulting services. Their findings suggest that different kinds of knowledge and knowledge sharing have different effects in different settings and that using more knowledge does not always benefit performance.

With the increasing possibilities for networking provided by ICT, consultants also have the possibility to go beyond their co-workers to obtain knowledge. In a study of consultants in an IT and management consulting firm, Teigland and Wasko (2003) found a positive relationship between boundary-spanning communication and creativity and general performance, and a negative relationship between a reliance on co-located co-workers and creativity. Taken together, the small number of studies that have examined the effects of KM activities show a differentiated picture where more KM is not always better and where different kinds of knowledge and knowledge sources have different effects in different situations. These findings call for more research that shows awareness of both the context in which KM is performed and the effects KM activities generate in specific contexts.

12.6 THE CREATION OF NEW KNOWLEDGE

Finally, a fourth theme in the literature on KM in management consulting is concerned with the creation of new knowledge (see also Heusinkveld and Benders, Chapter 13, this volume). In the research focusing on knowledge sharing and transfer, the creation of knowledge is regarded as unproblematic. It is continuously created in client projects and the challenge is to share and transfer these constant improvements in practice (Werr and Stjernberg 2003). Research in this fourth theme instead focuses on the creation of more radically new knowledge and how it emerges and becomes accepted as new concepts and practices. Research within this theme is dominated by qualitative methodologies.

Innovative activities within consultancies are often carried out under the label of 'thought leadership' (Davenport and Prusak 2005) and linked to experiences with clients, although the closeness of different thought-leadership activities to ongoing projects and client relations may vary (Morris and Empson 1998; Anand, Gardner, and Morris 2007). As argued by Hargadon (1998), the innovation potential in management consulting derives from consultancies' potential role as knowledge brokers. Consultants' diverse experiences create a potential for innovative solutions based on existing knowledge, which is connected through analogical reasoning. This is enabled through intensive face-to-face communication around client problems. Robertson, Scarbrough, and Swan (2003) further discuss how the process of knowledge creation is shaped by the institutional context and professional norms. In a comparison of science consultants and law consultants, differences in the relative work autonomy of professional groups, the nature of the knowledge-base, and the social identity formation of professional practitioners were found to create observable differences in the way in which knowledge was created and legitimated. These differences were reflected with varying emphasis on experimentation versus interpretation, different forms of personal networking, and differences in the importance of codifying knowledge. This indicates a need to link the analysis of different kinds of knowledge creation processes to the institutional context in general and to professional norms in particular (Robertson, Scarbrough, and Swan 2003).

Based on the claim that knowledge development in consulting is driven by client engagements (Løwendahl, Revang, and Fosstenløkken 2001), the characteristics of client engagements that support knowledge development have also attracted some attention, highlighting factors such as novel tasks that require the development of customized knowledge, working in multidisciplinary assignment teams, time pressure in the assignment, the size of the assignment, the knowledge and ability of the client, and opportunities for face-to-face interaction with client representatives (Løwendahl, Revang, and Fosstenløkken 2001; Fosstenløkken, Løwendahl, and Revang 2003; Skjølsvik et al. 2007). The accumulated and ongoing experiences with clients within a management consultancy firm are thus seen as a key source of new knowledge creation. The translation of these experiences into new concepts and practices is, however, a challenging process that may take different forms and involve a multitude of challenges. However, they will not be reviewed further here as they are dealt with in detail in other chapters of this book, particularly Chapter 13 by Heusinkveld and Benders.

12.7 Emerging Directions and Future Research

The bulk of the studies identified as a basis for this review dealt with the issue of knowledge sharing and transfer in management consulting, and did so most often from a 'knowledge as asset' perspective. However, based on the discussions in the literature on the nature of knowledge in consulting, this perspective has its limits and may miss out on important aspects that would follow from alternative epistemological positions such as viewing 'knowledge as socially embedded' (Hislop 2008; Hicks, Nair, and Wilderom 2009). There is, however, a relative lack of studies that address issues of KM from this perspective, pointing to a need for elaboration in future research. Mechanisms such as communities of practice and social networks have gained considerable interest outside the empirical context of management consulting. Applying such concepts in the context of management consulting holds the potential of developing interesting new insights both when it comes to management consulting and KM more generally.

Questions that should be asked include: How are networks in consulting firms built and maintained? How do different network structures shape knowledge application? What is their role in sharing and transferring knowledge? Can such networks be managed? What are the forces forming and enabling the creation of networks and communities of practice? In this context, emerging new technologies in the area of social networking (Facebook, etc.) in combination with a new generation of consultants and clients accustomed to new interaction patterns may provide entirely new ways of setting up KM systems in globalized organizations that may extend even across firm boundaries to clients. Studying these possibilities as well as their consequences provides an interesting avenue for future research.

Also within the 'knowledge as asset' perspective there is potential for further research in opening up and elaborating some of the continuing black boxes. We have shown that research here has come some way in identifying the important factors (such as culture, work processes, KM structure, etc.). However, some of these factors still have the character of 'black boxes'. We know that culture is important, but less about the detailed characteristics of this culture. Lingering questions include: What is the character and what are the mechanisms behind a 'knowledge-sharing culture'? What is the nature of a work process that encourages and supports knowledge sharing? In order to answer these questions in a way that can guide action in practice, more attention also needs to be given to contextual factors, as different conditions most likely lead to different answers to these questions. This calls for studies that enable the comparison of different contexts and their effects on KM structures and processes.

Furthermore, the interplay between the different aspects enabling KM deserves additional attention. As this review has indicated, KM is intertwined with ongoing work in client projects, the strategy process, organizational structure, HR practices, and so forth. This implies that KM systems need to be understood in relation to the activities that they support and the contexts within which these activities are carried out. The kinds of services offered, the expectations of clients, the motivational set-up of the employed consultants, their networks, and so on are all potentially important contextual factors. Which factors are important in which context and how they may impact the set-up of KM systems and procedures are fruitful areas for further research.

The few existing studies on the effects of KM activities also indicate a potential for further studies in this area. KM has often been treated as a 'universal good'. Closer investigations into the consequences of knowledge sharing are needed to modify this picture and show under what conditions sharing and creating new knowledge is beneficial to different stakeholders, including the firm, individual consultants, or the client. Little is known about the potential risks or downsides of KM activities. However, they most probably exist. The formalization and dissemination of knowledge may increase the risk that important knowledge may get into the hands of competitors. KM activities aimed at formalizing and articulating consultants' knowledge may also create a deskilling of consulting work, reducing the motivation of individual consultants but also turning the consulting service into a commodity, which may lead to a downward pressure on consulting fees. There is thus room for further critical examinations of KM initiatives. Such investigations should also pay more attention to the power and politics involved in KM, looking closer at the winners and losers of knowledge sharing and creation and how they are created.

Additional areas for future research may also be derived from the empirical limitations of previous research, including its focus on large firms, which are treated as homogeneous systems. However, the bulk of consulting work is carried out in small and medium-sized firms (Doucet and Barefield 1999). Further research is thus needed to show how these firms may leverage and develop their consultants' collective experience, as the mechanisms applied in large firms are not necessarily feasible or suitable in small or mid-sized consulting organizations. This may also include the study of personal and organizational networks across firm boundaries as vehicles for knowledge sharing and development. In the context of multinational consultancies, studies also point out a need for more attention to local variations and adaptations. Questions to address include: What is the role of cultural and other kinds of boundaries for knowledge sharing and creation?

Finally, recent developments in the consulting industry and the context of management consulting open up new avenues for research. The knowledge environment of management consulting is changing. Knowledge development is increasing in speed and is increasingly global, clients are getting more demanding and expect their consultants to possess both state-of-the-art problem-solving skills as well as functional and industry expertise. Additionally, cost pressures will increase (Poulfelt, Greiner, and Bhambri 2005). Taken together this will increase the pressure on management consulting organizations to leverage their collective competencies through different KM activities (Davenport and Prusak 2005). While KM activities are more important than ever for management consulting organizations, consulting firms are also increasingly put under economic pressure to run operations more efficiently. This has created a trend to offshore, or even outsource, parts of KM activities. The consequences of these initiatives and the challenges they create for consultancies are, however, largely unstudied. Questions such as what kinds of KM activities may be offshored or outsourced, and what activities need to be carried out closer to the core operations, merit further research.

References

Aaron, B. (2009). 'Determining the Business Impact of Knowledge Management'. *Performance Improvement*, 48/4, 35–45.

Alvesson, M. (1993). 'Organizations as Rhetoric: Knowledge-Intensive Firms and the Struggle with Ambiguity'. *Journal of Management Studies*, 30/6, 997–1015.

Alvesson, M. (2001). 'Knowledge Work: Ambiguity, Image and Identity'. *Human Relations*, 54/7, 863–886.

Alvesson, M. and Kärreman, D. (2001). 'Odd Couple: Making Sense of the Curious Concept of Knowledge Management'. *Journal of Management Studies*, 38/7, 995–1017.

Ambos, T. C. and Schlegelmilch, B. (2009). 'Managing Knowledge in International Consulting Firms'. *Journal of Knowledge Management*, 13/6, 491–508.

Anand, N., Gardner, H. K., and Morris, T. (2007). 'Knowledge-Based Innovation: Emergence and Embedding of New Practice Areas in Management Consulting Firms'. *Academy of Management Journal*, 50/2, 406–428.

Apostolou, D. and Mentzas, G. (1999a). 'Managing Corporate Knowledge: A Comparative Analysis of Experiences in Consulting Firms. Part 1'. *Knowledge and Process Management*, 6/3, 129–138.

Apostolou, D. and Mentzas, G. (1999b). 'Managing Corporate Knowledge: A Comparative Analysis of Experiences in Consulting Firms. Part 2'. *Knowledge and Process Management*, 6/4, 238–254.

Baladi, P. (1999). 'Knowledge and Competence Management: Ericsson Business Consulting'. *Business Strategy Review*, 10/4, 20–28.

Bang, A. (2005). 'Knowledge Management in Practice: Examining Knowledge as Modes of Production'. In A. Buono and F. Poulfelt (eds), *Challenges and Issues in Knowledge Managmenent*. Greenwich, CT: Information Age Publishing, 23–50.

Bloomfield, B. P. and Best, A. (1992). 'Management Consultants: Systems Development, Power and the Translation of Problems'. *The Sociological Review*, 40/3, 533–560.

Bloomfield, B. P. and Danieli, A. (1995). 'The Role of Management Consultants in the Development of Information Technology: The Indissoluble Nature of Socio-Political and Technical Skills'. *Journal of Management Studies*, 32/1, 23–46.

Chait, L. P. (1999). 'Creating a Successful Knowledge Management System'. *The Journal of Business Strategy*, 20/2, 23–26.

Chao, C. (2005). 'Toward Full Participation in Management Consulting Practice: Experiences of Recent College Graduates'. *Education and Training*, 47/1, 18–30.

Clark, T. (1995). *Managing Consultants: Consultancy as Impression Management*. Buckingham, UK: Open University Press.

Crucini, C. (2002). 'Knowledge Management at the Country Level: A Large Consulting Firm in Italy'. In M. Kipping and L. Engwall (eds), *Management Consulting: Emergence and Dynamics of a Knowledge Industry*. Oxford: Oxford University Press, 109–128.

Davenport, T. H. and Prusak, L. (2000). *Working Knowledge*. Boston: Harvard Business School Press.

Davenport, T. H. and Prusak, L. (2005). 'Knowledge Management in Consulting'. In L. Greiner and F. Poulfelt (eds), *The Contemporary Consultant*. Mason, OH: Thomson South-Western, 305–326.

Deng, P-S. (2008). 'Applying a Market-Based Approach to the Development of a Sharing-Enabled KM Model for Knowledge-Intensive Small Firms'. *Information Systems Management*, 25/2, 174–187.

Donnelly, R. (2008). 'The Management of Consultancy Knowledge: An Internationally Comparative Analysis'. *Journal of Knowledge Management*, 12/3, 71–83.

Doucet, T. A. and Barefield, R. M. (1999). 'Client Base Valuation: The Case of a Professional Service Firm'. *Journal of Business Research*, 44, 127–133.

Dunford, R. (2000). 'Key Challenges in the Search for the Effective Management of Knowledge in Management Consulting Firms'. *Journal of Knowledge Management*, 4/4, 295–302.

Ejenäs, M. and Werr, A. (2005). 'Merging Knowledge: A Study of Knowledge Management in a Consulting-Firm Merger'. In A. Buono and F. Poulfelt (eds), *Challenges and Issues in Knowledge Management (Research in Management Consulting, Volume 5)*. Greenwich, CT: Information Age Publishing, 179–207.

Empson, L. (2001a). 'Introduction: Knowledge Management in Professional Service Firms'. *Human Relations*, 54/7, 811–817.

Empson, L. (2001b). 'Fear of Exploitation and Fear of Contamination: Impediments to Knowledge Transfer in Mergers between Professional Service Firms'. *Human Relations*, 54/7, 839–862.

Fincham, R., Clark, T., Handley, K., and Sturdy, A. (2008). 'Configuring Expert Knowledge: The Consultant as Sector Specialist'. *Journal of Organizational Behavior*, 29/8, 1145–1160.

Fosstenløkken, S. M., Løwendahl, B. R., and Revang, Ø. (2003). 'Knowledge Development through Client Interaction: A Comparative Study'. *Organization Studies*, 24/6, 859–879.

Griggs, K. A., Wild, R. H., and Li, E. Y. (2002). 'A Web-Based Knowledge Management Environment for Consulting and Research Organizations'. *Journal of Computer Information Systems*, 42/5, 110–118.

Haas, M. R. and Hansen, M. T. (2005). 'When Using Knowledge Can Hurt Performance: The Value of Organizational Capabilities in a Management Consulting Company'. *Strategic Management Journal*, 26/1, 1–24.

Haas, M. R. and Hansen, M. T. (2007). 'Different Knowledge, Different Benefits: Toward a Productivity Perspective on Knowledge Sharing in Organizations'. *Strategic Management Journal*, 28/11, 1133–1153.

Hansen, M. T. and Haas, M. R. (2001). 'Competing for Attention in Knowledge Markets: Electronic Document Dissemination in a Management Consulting Company'. *Administrative Science Quarterly*, 46, 1–28.

Hansen, M. T., Nohria, N., and Tierney, T. (1999). 'What's Your Strategy for Managing Knowledge?' *Harvard Business Review*, 77/2 (March–April), 106–116.

Hargadon, A. B. (1998). 'Firms as Knowledge Brokers: Lessons in Pursuing Continuous Innovation'. *California Management Review*, 40/3, 209–227.

Henriksen, L. (2005). 'In Search of Knowledge Sharing in Practice'. In A. Buono and F. Poulfelt (eds), *Challenges and Issues in Knowledge Management*. Greenwich, CT: Information Age Publishing, 155–178.

Hicks, J., Nair, P., and Wilderom, C. (2009). 'What If We Shifted the Basis of Consulting from Knowledge to Knowing?' *Management Learning*, 40/3, 289–310.

Hislop, D. (2008). 'Conceptualizing Knowledge Work Utilizing Skill and Knowledge-Based Concepts: The Case of Some Consultants and Service Engineers'. *Management Learning*, 39/5, 579–596.

Husted, K., Gammelgaard, J., and Michailova, S. (2005). 'Knowledge-Sharing Behaviour and Post-Acquisition Integration Failure'. In A. Buono and F. Poulfelt (eds), *Challenges and Issues in Knowledge Management (Research in Management Consulting, Volume 5)*. Greenwich, CT: Information Age Publishing, 209–226.

Ibarra, H. (1999). 'Provisional Selves: Experimenting with Image and Identity in Professional Adaptation'. *Administrative Science Quarterly*, 44, 764–791.

Jones, M. (2003). 'The Expert System: Constructing Expertise in an It/Management Consultancy'. *Information and Organization*, 13, 257–284.

Kakabadse, N. K., Kakabadse, A., and Kouzmin, A. (2003). 'Reviewing the Knowledge Management Literature: Towards a Taxonomy'. *Journal of Knowledge Management*, 7/4, 75–91.

Kaplan, W. S. and Thomson-Reed, A. F. (2007). 'KM: From Concept to Theory to Practice'. *VINE*, 37/2, 219–232.

Kim, S. and Trimi, S. (2007). 'IT for KM in the Management Consulting Industry'. *Journal of Knowledge Management*, 11/3, 145–155.

Kohlbacher, F. and Mukai, K. (2007). 'Japan's Learning Communities in Hewlett-Packard Consulting and Integration: Challenging One-Size Fits All Solutions'. *The Learning Organization*, 14/1, 8–20.

Lahti, R. K. and Beyerlein, M. M. (2000). 'Knowledge Transfer and Management Consulting: A Look at "The Firm"'. *Business Horizons*, 43/1, 65–75.

Legge, K. (2002). 'On Knowledge, Business Consultants and the Selling of Total Quality Management'. In T. Clark and R. Fincham (eds), *Critical Consulting: New Perspectives on the Management Advice Industry*. Oxford: Blackwell, 74–90.

Løwendahl, B. R., Revang, Ö., and Fosstenløkken, S. M. (2001). 'Knowledge and Value Creation in Professional Service Firms: A Framework for Analysis'. *Human Relations*, 54/7, 911–931.

Morris, T. (2001). 'Asserting Property Rights: Knowledge Codification in the Professional Service Firm'. *Human Relations*, 54/7, 819–838.

Morris, T. and Empson, L. (1998). 'Organization and Expertise: An Exploration of Knowledge Bases and the Management of Accounting and Consulting Firms'. *Accounting, Organizations and Society*, 23/5–6, 609–624.

Nahapiet, J. and Ghoshal, S. (1998). 'Social Capital, Intellectual Capital, and the Organizational Advantage'. *Academy of Management Review*, 23/2, 242–266.

Newell, S. (2005). 'The Fallacy of Simplistic Notions of the Transfer of "Best Practice"'. In A. Buono and F. Poulfelt (eds), *Challenges and Issues in Knowledge Management*. Greenwich, CT: Information Age Publishing, 51–68.

Nonaka, I. and Takeuchi, H. (1995). *The Knowledge Creating Company*. New York: Oxford University Press.

Ofek, E. and Sarvary, M. (2001). 'Leveraging the Customer Base: Creating Competitive Advantage through Knowledge Management'. *Management Science*, 47, 1441–1457.

Olivera, F. (2000). 'Memory Systems in Organizations: An Empirical Investigation of Mechanisms for Knowledge Collection, Storage and Access'. *Journal of Management Studies*, 37/6, 811–832.

Paik, Y. and Choi, D. Y. (2005). 'The Shortcomings of a Standardized Global Knowledge Management System: The Case Study of Accenture'. *Academy of Management Executive*, 19/2, 81–84.

Pastoors, K. (2007). 'Consultants: Love–Hate Relationships with Communities of Practice'. *The Learning Organization*, 14/1, 21–33.

Poulfelt, F., Greiner, L., and Bhambri, A. (2005). 'The Changing Global Consulting Industry'. In L. Greiner and F. Poulfelt (eds), *The Contemporary Consultant*. Mason, OH: Thomson South-Western, 3–22.

Rigby, D. and Bilodeau, B. (2010). *Management Tools and Trends 2009*. Boston: Bain & Co.

Robertson, M. and Swan, J. (1998). 'Modes of Organizing in an Expert Consultancy: A Case Study of Knowledge, Power and Egos'. *Organization*, 5/4, 543–564.

Robertson, M., Sørensen, C., and Swan, J. (2001). 'Survival of the Leanest: Intensive Knowledge Work and Groupware Adaptation'. *Information Technology and People*, 14/4, 334–353.

Robertson, M., Scarbrough, H., and Swan, J. (2003). 'Knowledge Creation in Professional Service Firms: Institutional Effects'. *Organization Studies*, 24/6, 831–857.

Rolland, N., Guilhon, A., and Trepo, G. (2005). 'Ten Years of Knowledge Management: Ramifications for Consultants'. In A. Buono and F. Poulfelt (eds), *Challenges and Issues in Knowledge Management (Research in Management Consulting, Volume 5)*. Greenwich, CT: Information Age Publishing, 317–336.

Ruggles, R. (1998). 'The State of the Notion: Knowledge Management in Practice'. *California Management Review*, 40/3, 80–89.

Sandberg, J. and Pinnington, A. H. (2009). 'Professional Competence as Ways of Being: An Existential Ontological Perspective'. *Journal of Management Studies*, 46/7, 1138–1170.

Sarvary, M. (1999). 'Knowledge Management and Competition in the Consulting Industry'. *California Management Review*, 41/2, 95–107.

Scarbrough, H. and Swan, J. (2003). 'Discourses of Knowledge Management and the Learning Organization: Their Production and Consumption'. In M. Easterby-Smith and M. A. Lyles (eds), *The Blackwell Handbook of Organizational Learning and Knowledge Management*. Oxford: Blackwell, 495–512.

Schwartz, M. and Clark, T. (2010). 'Clients' Different Moves in Managing the Client–Consultant Relationship'. In A Buono and F. Poulfeldt (eds), *Research in Management Consulting: Client–Consultant Cooperation*. Greenwich: CT: Information Age Publishing, 3–28.

Skjølsvik, T., Løwendahl, B. R., Kvålshaugen, R., and Fosstenløkken, S. M. (2007). 'Choosing to Learn and Learning to Choose: Strategies for Client Co-Production and Knowledge Development'. *California Management Review*, 49/3, 110–127.

Sturdy, A., Clark, T., Fincham, R., and Handley, K. (2009). 'Between Innovation and Legitimation: Boundaries and Knowledge Flow in Management Consultancy'. *Organization*, 16/5, 627–653.

Styhre, A. (2003). *Understanding Knowledge Management: Critical and Postmordern Perspectives*. Malmö, Sweden: Liber.

Sussman, S. W. and Siegal, W. S. (2003). 'Informational Influence in Organizations: An Integrated Approach to Knowledge Adoption'. *Information Systems Research*, 14/1, 47–65.

Swan, J. and Scarbrough, H. (2001). 'Editorial. Knowledge Management: Concepts and Controversies'. *Journal of Management Studies*, 38/7, 913–921.

Teigland, R. and Wasko, M. M. (2003). 'Integrating Knowledge through Information Trading: Examining the Relationship between Boundary Spanning Communication and Individual Performance'. *Decision Sciences*, 34/2, 261–287.

Visscher, K. (2006). 'Capturing the Competence of Management Consulting Work'. *Journal of Workplace Learning*, 18/4, 248–260.

Weeks, M. (2004). 'Knowledge Management in the Wild'. *Business Horizons*, 47/6, 15–24.

Werr, A. and Stjernberg, T. (2003). 'Exploring Management Consulting Firms as Knowledge Systems'. *Organization Studies*, 24/6, 881–908.

CHAPTER 13

CONSULTANTS AND ORGANIZATION CONCEPTS

STEFAN HEUSINKVELD
JOS BENDERS

13.1 INTRODUCTION

ORGANIZATION concepts have always played a fundamental role in the way consultancies have legitimized their existence, created their business, and intervened in organizations (Guillén 1994; Kipping 1999; Wright 2002). For instance, various scientific management techniques and the Bedaux system of work measurement are regarded as important determinants in the expansion of pioneering management consultancies in the 1920s and 1930s (Kipping 2002; see Wright and Kipping, Chapter 2, this volume). During the 1960s, a firm like McKinsey extensively encouraged the dissemination of the multidivisional model of organization across European countries (McKenna 2006). A few years later, consultants from the Boston Consulting Group became widely renowned for their portfolio matrix. More recently, David and Strang (2006) demonstrated how consultancies went into the market for Total Quality Management (TQM) when this concept was becoming fashionable in the early 1980s. Not surprisingly, therefore, consultants are increasingly regarded as important suppliers of popular management ideas (Abrahamson 1996; Kieser 1997; Suddaby and Greenwood 2001; Faust 2002; Jung and Kieser, Chapter 16, this volume). However, despite the generally recognized significance of these concepts in management consulting work, the literature on this topic shows an important divergence about whether the development process is mainly supply or demand driven. More specifically, while more traditional approaches emphasize the fact that consultants may develop concepts to help clients and client organizations (Greiner and Metzger 1983; Holtz 1983), more critical perspectives consider the potential financial gains as the key driver for consultants to develop new concepts (e.g. Kieser 2002).

Against the backgrounds of these debates, there is a growing body of research that examines how consultants develop new concepts and disseminate their ideas. Some authors argue that consultants are particularly involved in 'productivizing' (Huczynski 1993: 217) or 'commodifying' management knowledge into a sellable form that is expected to meet the needs for managerial solutions (Fincham 1995; Suddaby and Greenwood 2001; Collins 2003; see Clark, Bhatanacharoen, and Greatbatch, Chapter 17, this volume). However, others show that consultants do not only play an important role in the production and dissemination of these concepts but are also widely involved in their application within organizations (Wright and Kitay 2004). The implementation of these concepts by consultants may have significant consequences for the functioning of client organizations (O'Shea and Madigan 1997; Knights and McCabe 1998). This would mean that the development of new concepts by consultants also has some notable implications beyond a concept's market launch, that is, on the demand side of the market for management solutions.

This chapter examines how the literature has addressed the role of organization concepts in management consulting work so far, and what additional research could be conducted in the future. In our discussion of the current literature we distinguish between supply-side and demand-side perspectives, each of which provide important insights into some key drivers behind the way consultants deal with organization concepts. The first part of this chapter elaborates on various approaches that focus on the supply side. Here, we review the literature that regards consultants as important 'knowledge entrepreneurs' within the market for management solutions. Within this context, a growing body of literature discusses the development of ideas within consultancies—a process often referred to as 'new concept development' (Heusinkveld and Benders 2002). In the second part, we concentrate on the demand side of the concept development process. In this section, we review the extant literature that examines how concepts are used by consultants in a variety of different client contexts and discuss the possible organizational consequences that are associated with these concepts. In the conclusion, we stress that, according to the extant literature, the development and application of new concepts is neither a homogeneous nor a straightforward matter for consultancies. We therefore believe that future research should pay more attention to the interaction between the supply and demand sides of the market for management solutions, and provide some specific suggestions in this respect.

13.2 SUPPLY-SIDE PERSPECTIVES

In this section, we will discuss some important supply-side views on the role of organization concepts in management consulting work, and point to their limitations and possibilities for further research. First of all, we briefly discuss the literature on management consultants as 'knowledge entrepreneurs' (Clark 2004). An important stream of literature considers consultants as key suppliers of organization concepts in the market for management solutions. These 'market-level' views of the way consultants deal with concepts is the first approach that can be distinguished in the literature. A second and emerging body of literature that can be distinguished within the supply-side perspectives on consultants and organization concepts focuses on the way these ideas are developed within consultancies. These 'intra-organizational' views provide important insights into how consultancies organize the process of 'new concept development', and point to a number of important elements that may encourage or inhibit this process.

13.2.1 Market-level Approaches

Market-level approaches present consultants as key suppliers of new concepts in the market for management solutions (Abrahamson 1996; Kieser 1997; Fincham and Evans 1999; Suddaby and Greenwood 2001). This perception is mainly related to their large-scale involvement in the propagation of new concepts (Guillén 1994; Fincham and Evans 1999; Wright and Kitay 2004; Braam, Benders, and Heusinkveld 2007). Faust (2002) even argues that consultants' general influence on management thinking is gradually increasing.

Many authors emphasize that a key driver for the supply of innovative concepts lies in the fact that they support consultants in convincing potential clients of the value of their expertise and in generating legitimacy for their services (Alvesson 1993; Clark 1995; Sturdy 1997; Wright 2002; Glückler and Armbrüster 2003). Indeed, various studies indicate that new organization concepts generally act as an important vehicle for selling a consultant's expertise and generating business (Fincham and Evans 1999; Kieser 2002). For instance, CSC Index, as one of the initial propagators of Business Process Re-engineering (BPR), was able to expand their revenues from US$30 million in 1988 to US$150 million in 1993 (Jackson 1996: 576). Similarly, Gemini Consulting generated considerable revenues from the sales of their 'Business Transformation' concept (O'Shea and Madigan 1997), and McKinsey not only significantly increased its profits in the 1960s by 'supplying' the multidivisional model (Kipping 1999), it was also able to re-emerge as 'the preeminent management consulting firm' through its popularization of its 7S-model and 'corporate culture' concepts in the 1980s (McKenna 2006: 214). Thus, presenting themselves as skilful and innovative 'thought leaders' (Wright and Kitay 2004), provides consultancies with significant business opportunities.

In addition to discussing the value of organization concepts for consultants, various empirical and conceptual studies provide important insights into *how* consultants disseminate new concepts in the market and seek to gain attention for their expertise. These studies emphasize the importance of the rhetorical techniques used by these knowledge entrepreneurs (Kieser 1997; Benders and van Veen 2001; Jackson 2001; Røvik 2002). According to these authors, an important rhetorical element that is used by consultants is that they seek to present a new concept as the most efficient and innovative solution to contemporary problems. Thus, Benders and van Veen (2001) identified some key elements of this rhetoric such as promises of performance improvements; referring to well-known and successful users; stressing universal applicability; and presenting the concept as easily understandable, innovative, and 'interpretatively viable', that is, leaving room for different interpretations (see also Suddaby and Greenwood 2001). A second element, highlighted by Berglund and Werr (2000), is that consultants not only present their knowledge products as objectified and universal, but also tend to emphasize the importance of an elaborate experience base in applying the concept. In this way consultants position themselves as 'obligatory passage points' (Berglund and Werr 2000: 650) in the application of the concepts they promote (see also Braam, Benders, and Heusinkveld 2007). This means that consultants not only use rhetorical techniques to gain legitimacy for their solutions, but to present themselves as indispensable in the effective implementation of their particular concepts.

The role of consultants as important suppliers of organization concepts on the market for management solutions has also generated a number of notable criticisms. A first critique is that by being involved in the supply of management ideas, consultants seek to talk problems into organizations in order to sell their predefined solutions and increase their business (O'Shea and Madigan 1997; Pinault 2000; Kieser 2002; Craig 2005). For instance, O'Shea and Madigan (1997: 189) emphasize that the consulting industry is renowned for its 'propensity for presenting fads as solution to problems'. Kieser (2002: 180) even argues that 'consultants who compile a new management concept also construct the business problem for which the offered solution fits'. In this view, consultants take advantage of clients by shaping the perception of problems and playing upon managers' anxiety in various ways (Grint and Case 1998). As a result, the constant introduction of new concepts forces clients to remain in tune with the latest management ideas, thereby making them permanently receptive to consultancy services.

A second critique is that consultants' behaviour in relation to organization concepts is considered to play an important role in reinforcing recurrent transient cycles in the supply of management solutions. For instance, Gill and Whittle (1993: 292) talk about 'the cyclical and non-cumulative nature of much of what passes for consulting approaches to organizational change'. Suddaby and Greenwood (2001) explain this by arguing that the commodification of management knowledge by consultants intensifies the supply of new concepts in the management knowledge market. One important implication discussed in the literature relates to the fact that the constant introduction and abandonment of these concepts may reinforce a persistent lack of knowledge accumulation within the system of knowledge supply (Lammers 1988). This has prompted some scholars to warn against the danger of reinventing the wheel and the under-utilization of current organizational knowledge (Lammers 1988; Brunsson and Olsen 1997). Brunsson and Olsen (1997: 42) even see 'forgetfulness' as a key competence of management consultants, thereby suggesting that the persistent introduction of new ideas by these consultants permits the repeating of previous mistakes and inhibits organizations from learning.

In sum, the extant market-level literature about consultants and organization concepts provides important insights into the importance of this actor in the management knowledge market, and into the rhetorical techniques consultants use to sell their solutions. In addition, this literature offers several critical perspectives on the effects of consultants' typical behaviour on this market. However, with a few exceptions, little empirical work has been conducted beyond analysing media declarations of consultants or tracing the use of popular labels (see also Clark 2004). Moreover, there has been scant attention paid to how consultants seek to influence the managerial discourse on a fashionable concept, and what different corporate and personal strategies they employ to gain reputation through the media (Nijholt 2010). Therefore, a fruitful direction for future research would involve further study of the consultants' role in broader processes of influencing public opinion on the market for management ideas. Further research in this area may draw from theories of agenda setting (Kingdon 1995; Dutton et al. 2001), directing the attention of managers to specific new concepts and getting them to commit to projects that aim to implement these concepts. This may involve creating a deeper understanding of how consultants employ different issue-selling moves, which can shape top management's attention. This may generate more insight into the question 'how does an idea's time come?' (Kingdon 1995: 1), and how consultants influence this process beyond the use of the print media. This may also shed further light on differences between consultants' media tactics (Nijholt 2010) and the specific strategies that they employ in attracting the attention of (potential) clients—an issue that so far has received little attention in the relevant literature.

13.2.2 Intra-organizational Approaches

As detailed above, consultancies are viewed as major actors in the dissemination of organization concepts within the market for management knowledge. But what does the literature say about the way these ideas are developed within consultancies? In answering these questions, various intra-organizational approaches provide important insights into the process of 'new concept development'. Three streams of research can be distinguished in this literature. A first approach conceptualizes the development of new concepts as a series of distinct phases, resulting in a commodity that can be 'sold' into the market for management solutions. A second, emerging stream of research concentrates on the factors that may enhance or impede the process of new concept development. Third, another emerging body of work examines the involvement of the market in the development process and points to mechanisms that are crucial in adapting the consulting capabilities to market needs.

13.2.2.1 *Activity stages in concept development*

An important strand of work describes the generation and construction of new concepts by knowledge entrepreneurs as a series of distinct phases. Focusing on the firm level, Heusinkveld and Benders (2002) and Anand, Gardner, and Morris (2007) identify a number of key activities through which a concept proceeds within a consultancy. This literature suggests that a first constellation of activities is related to the initiation of innovative ventures by organizational members. A second central activity in the development process concerns the formation and facilitation of a group of people who are involved in a concept development effort. A final cluster of activities entails the construction of a 'repertoire' to support the commercialization and implementation of a concept, and the dissemination of this repertoire throughout the consultancy (Heusinkveld and Benders 2002).

At the same time, various studies have revealed that consultancies are not particularly uniform in their concept development efforts and in the way in which the underlying repertoire is managed (Morris and Empson 1998; Hansen, Nohria, and Tienery 1999; Heusinkveld and Benders 2002; Anand, Gardner, and Morris 2007). In these studies, it is argued that while concept development ventures may share some general activities, the way these activities are carried out varies considerably between different consulting firms. The work of Morris and Empson (1998) and Hansen, Nohria, and Tienery (1999) relates the differences in development process and knowledge-bases to the structural characteristics of the firm, which become apparent in distinct 'business models' and related value propositions. Other authors link the variations in new concept development efforts to the way in which relevant activities are interpreted and carried out within different consultancies (Heusinkveld and Benders 2002; Anand, Gardner, and Morris 2007). They suggest that concept development ventures may diverge between distinct 'structural forms' or 'pathways'.

One typical development form identified in the literature is driven largely by the professional interests and initiatives of individual consultants and fuelled by their interactions with clients. The initiation of this 'expertise-based pathway' (Anand, Gardner, and Morris 2007) is marked by the continuous emergence of local development ventures, each driven by the efforts of one or several consultants (Heusinkveld and Benders 2002; Anand, Gardner, and Morris 2007). Here, concept development efforts are characterized by an incremental trajectory in which a repertoire is shaped and fed by the assignments a consultant is able to obtain. In another typical form, concept development is primarily driven by corporate efforts to systematically facilitate the exploration of a complete repertoire that is disseminated throughout the entire consultancy (Heusinkveld and Benders 2002). Here, only a few promising ideas are initiated and receive corporate support. This form is dubbed the 'support-based pathway' by Anand, Gardner, and Morris (2007), referring to the explicit involvement of a consulting firm's top management.

Scholars of management consulting have also revealed important differences in the way consultancies seek to stimulate concept development within their firm either by creating focus or by enhancing entrepreneurship. For instance, a study by Heusinkveld and Benders (2002) shows that consultancies may seek to enhance focus in their concept development ventures by transforming successful local practices into corporate efforts. Other consultancies seek to create focus by providing funding for only a selected number of consultants, who submit plans for developing new concepts. This allows consultants to reserve time for development activities without being dependent on the availability of client projects in a certain area. In addition, to enhance entrepreneurship among their present staff of consultants, various consultancies follow a highly structured firm-wide iterative processes, involving going back and forth between, on the one hand, locally generated market signals and, on the other hand, corporate decisions about which themes are turned into development activities. Other consultancies may deploy a system that allows consultants to participate in the development process of a concept by adapting the repertoire to the needs of specific clients or sectors (Fincham et al. 2008).

In sum, the extant literature has provided important insights into the key activities related to concept development. In addition, recent studies have shown that consultancies are not uniform in the way they perform these development activities. But while this literature has revealed some important routes through which new concepts are developed within consultancies, there is still a need to place greater emphasis on the differences among the actors on the supply side of the management knowledge market. Therefore, future research might benefit from drawing on the innovation literature to gain further insight into the differences between consultancies' development processes and their antecedent conditions (e.g. Cooper 1983; Benghozi 1990; Lewis et al. 2002). More specifically, scholars of innovation have identified a range of different intra-organizational elements, such as project management and leadership style, organizational size and maturity, structural configuration, and communication patterns, that may influence the way innovation processes are performed (Dougherty and Hardy 1996; Tidd, Bessant, and Pavitt 1997; Lewis et al. 2002). Gaining more insight into how these elements might work in consultancies is of particular relevance given the highly differentiated consulting industry (Clark 1995), which includes a variety of different firms providing a 'bewildering range of services' (Clark and Fincham 2002: 4).

13.2.2.2 *Impediments to concept development*

Recent research also highlights the fact that developing new ideas is not necessarily unproblematic within consultancies (Heusinkveld and Benders 2005; Gardner, Anand, and Morris 2008). Rather than seeing concept development as a straightforward process that results in a concept that can be sold to potential clients, this research presents a view in which the development of new ideas in consulting organizations is often highly contested and generally encounters substantial resistance. This literature suggests that concept development does not involve merely moving through a series of logical phases and does not easily generate support within a consultancy.

According to some authors, the impediments to concept development are related to their internal legitimacy, that is, the degree of acceptance of new ideas or practices within a consultancy (Gardner, Anand, and Morris 2008; Heusinkveld and Reijers 2009). Various studies show that concept development efforts do not necessarily meet with a favourable response within consultancies, and suggest the importance of internal legitimation efforts before the market launch (Heusinkveld and Benders 2005; Gardner, Anand, and Morris 2008; Heusinkveld and Reijers 2009). These struggles become apparent in internal criticism and disbelief about the value of a new idea, and shape obstructions in the realization of a concept-in-development. This literature indicates the importance of considering the process by which management ideas gain 'good currency' within the system of knowledge supply. Moreover, using both qualitative surveys and case study approaches, this research provides an important understanding of the internal elements that may inhibit or encourage the development of new organization concepts. Empirical evidence suggests that the supply of management solutions is preceded by important processes where consultants have to sell their new 'products' first internally, in order to be able to then sell them on the knowledge market. The extant literature identifies the different drivers of the legitimacy struggles inherent in concept development.

First, several empirical studies show that one key driver of legitimacy problems lies in the (in)ability of consultants to link these concept development efforts to their organization (Heusinkveld and Benders 2005; Anand, Gardner, and Morris 2007). These studies suggest that a lack of fit between the new concept and the present ideas and practices may increase criticism and disbelief within a consultancy and reduce the likelihood of new concepts being accepted as legitimate practices in a consultancy. Although product innovation normally implies novelty, the extant research indicates that firm-wide appreciation of new concepts actually favours compatibility and familiarity with existing standards and practices (Heusinkveld and Reijers 2009). The incompatibility of a new concept with the current product range of a consultancy is considered highly problematic, and a major reason for criticism, irrespective of its intrinsic merits. This means that within a consultancy, elements such as established and institutionalized consulting practices, perceived inconsistency of an innovation with the image of a firm, and possibility of cannibalization violating an established practice area or territory of a specific group within a consultancy may constitute considerable barriers to the emergence and development of new concepts (Heusinkveld and Benders 2005; Gardner, Anand, and Morris 2008).

Second, another driver identified in the literature concerns the lack of agency and involvement of a consultancy's management and of other organizational members. This entails that the appreciation of its underlying repertoire throughout a consultancy is regarded as essential for a new concept to become established in that firm. As various empirical studies have shown, development efforts may suffer from an absence of internal support and collaboration—factors that, according to various scholars, play an important role in the realization of a new knowledge product (Anand, Gardner, and Morris 2007; Heusinkveld and Reijers 2009). The recent literature shows that while consultancy firms may be eager to present themselves as innovative suppliers of management knowledge, a consultancy's management is not necessarily supportive of new concept development efforts. The same literature also suggests that different consultants within a firm do not automatically understand the value of a new concept (see also Morris 2001). Thus, the codification of knowledge in a new concept does not necessarily mean that the peers of the pioneering consultant are able and willing to apply it in practice during their assignments. Although consultants may be working in the same firm and share similar professional interests, this does not necessarily guarantee co-operation in new concept development ventures.

In terms of future research, these current insights into the complexities and struggles inherent in the development of new concepts can probably be further enhanced by drawing on the innovation literature. Innovation theorists (e.g. van de Ven 1986;

Dougherty and Heller 1994; Benders and Vermeulen 2002) have persistently emphasized the fact that the development of novelty in organizations is unavoidably a source of problems, and point to important elements that may enhance or inhibit the development of new products. They point to a number of basic problems that confront managers in translating an idea into a viable innovation. For instance, van de Ven (1986) emphasizes that issues such as gaining the attention of relevant intra-organizational and external stakeholders, managing the socio-political process, and dealing with multiple functions and disciplines should be the guiding focus in innovation research. In line with this, Dougherty (1996) argues that innovation activities involve various tensions such as those emerging from market-technology linking. A fruitful avenue for future research may lie in identifying the key problems and tensions in concept development and in examining how consultancies seek to restore balance despite these tensions. This is of particular interest given the fact that, unlike substantive innovations, new organization concepts lack a material component (Benders and van Veen 2001). Also, the professional and knowledge-intensive work associated with consultancies (Alvesson 1993; Morris 2001) may have important implications for the nature of development efforts and their typical issues and tensions.

13.2.2.3 *Market orientation in concept development*

A third and final issue that is raised by the present literature on new concept development is related to their market orientation, that is, the involvement of 'the market' in the development process (Fosstenløkken, Løwendahl, and Revang 2003; Gardner, Anand, and Morris 2008; Heusinkveld, Benders, and van den Berg 2009). Various authors in this emerging area emphasize the importance of the interaction between 'innovator' and consumer (Clark and Salaman 1998; Fosstenløkken, Løwendahl, and Revang 2003; ten Bos and Heusinkveld 2007; Heusinkveld, Benders, and van den Berg 2009). Earlier work in this area (e.g. Abrahamson 1996; Suddaby and Greenwood 2001) pointed to the importance of 'sensing incipient preferences' in the development of new concepts, an issue that implies a good 'nose' for new marketable products at the start of a development project.

Drawing on elaborate case study research into the practice of concept development, Gardner, Anand, and Morris (2008) and Heusinkveld, Benders, and van den Berg (2009) extend this argument by highlighting the importance of continuous interaction between internal and external constituencies. They argue that translating client information into new concepts within consultancies involves two crucial elements: (1) continuously performing market information-processing activities throughout the entire concept development process; and (2) internal organizational capabilities that enable learning about clients. First of all, this research shows that market sensing is not regarded as a distinct or separate activity, but considered an integral element of every phase of the concept development process. Moreover, the way this takes shape depends on the specific development stage. In early phases, market sensing is understood as generating information in talks with a small group of clients in a consultant's own network and involves more general information about the market needs. Later phases of market sensing are related to the information generated from the performance of assignments within client organizations and the reactions from larger scale communication events, which involve more specific and detailed ideas.

Second, this research also stresses the role of senior management and interdepartmental dynamics as key elements shaping the market sensing process of the concept-in-development (Heusinkveld, Benders, and van den Berg 2009). Specifically, in the early phases, market information not only serves as an input for the development process, but is mainly used to internally legitimate new forms of expertise by convincing the consultancy's top management and the management of the different sector groups, and by creating awareness among peers. This may pave the way for a 'champion' to further develop a piece of expertise and commercialize it on the market. It is only during later phases that consultants use market information to shape the content of a new practice in more detail, that is, particularly during its dissemination and application. These studies by Gardner, Anand, and Morris (2008) and Heusinkveld, Benders, and van den Berg (2009) provide important evidence that market sensing is considered a critical activity for consultants to obtain client interest for a 'new' concept. Moreover, the studies detail the organizational capacities involved in translating the knowledge towards practical needs, and the potential barriers involved in this process (see also Heusinkveld and Reijers 2009).

However, even if this emerging research has provided a first step into this area, the issue of market sensing still receives little attention in current discussions about new concept development within management consultancies. Further research can extend present insights by drawing from the literature on how organizations deal with market-technology linking in relation to new product development. Innovation theorists consider various boundary-spanning mechanisms as critical in the successful development of new products and the ability to 'learn' from customers (Tidd, Bessant, and Pavitt 1997). Research into this area has shown that there are significant organizational learning barriers that may influence the acquisition, internal dissemination, and use of relevant market information (Deshpande and Zaltman 1982; Adams, Day, and Dougherty 1998). Future research into new concept development could provide more insight into how these learning barriers take shape within different consultancies and what antecedent conditions are related to market orientation (Kohli and Jaworski 1990; Day 1994; Brown and Ennew 1995). Also, future research may shed some more light on the involvement of users in concept development ventures, an important issue in the innovation literature (see, for example, von Hippel 1978; Kok, Hillebrand and Biemans 2003), which has received scant attention in relation to the development of new concepts in consultancies.

13.3 DEMAND-SIDE PERSPECTIVES

Another important, albeit less elaborate, strand of literature in the field of consultants and organization concepts indicates that consultants are not only important propagators of concepts on 'public display' (Furusten 1999; Faust 2002), but are also often deeply involved in actual change projects that are induced by or associated with these concepts (Bloomfield and Danieli 1995; O'Shea and Madigan 1997; Visscher 2001). This is relevant because the development of a new concept is considered an ongoing activity since it cannot be separated from its application (Suddaby and Greenwood 2001). As Morris (2001) indicates, the construction of a codified repertoire can be seen only as part of a concept development effort. Thus, according to Heusinkveld and Benders (2002: 118), concept development is finalized within the client organization 'because these ventures also include a consultant's own input'. Various accounts discussing this topic provide some important insights into how concepts are used by consultants in concrete projects and in direct interaction with their client organizations. For instance, a study by Wright and Kitay (2004) shows how consultants were not only involved in the large-scale proliferation of the employee relations model on a market level, but also drew on this concept in their day-to-day work with clients, that is, at the level of a consulting project. This suggests that a new and 'legitimate' concept may constitute a useful starting point for developing a client–consultant relationship. In the current literature, this demand side is viewed from different perspectives.

First, more functionally oriented project-level approaches stress that a concept's application by consultants may lead to an enhanced performance level of client organizations (e.g. Greiner and Metzger 1983). This is often presented through different 'success stories', emphasizing a number of key points that have been crucial in the successful implementation of a concept. Typically, these perspectives on a concept's application by consultants can be found in professional magazines and management books. For instance, the study by Braam, Benders, and Heusinkveld (2007) shows that consultants wrote a lot of the case descriptions about the implementation of the Balanced Scorecard in the professional journals. Although these accounts of a concept's implementation by consultants provide a 'window on praxis', critical approaches suggest that these represent a selective image of the way organizations deploy a new concept, since difficulties in implementation or contentious issues are potentially glossed over—as might be suggested by these texts (Kieser 1997; Furusten 1999; Røvik 2002).

Second, other critical accounts emphasize that the application of new concepts by consultants often involves substantial negative consequences for employees (O'Shea and Madigan 1997; Knights and McCabe 1998; Craig 2005). For example, O'Shea and Madigan (1997) draw on cases of the implementation of the 'Transformation' concept by Gemini Consulting. They show how the consultants' application of their concept had substantial consequences for the client organization: 'these efforts involved sweeping change and left their share of victims in their wakes, the displaced middle managers at Cigna, the nurses and staff and middle managers at Montgomery General who saw their jobs disappear' (ibid.: 198). At the same time these authors show that the consultancy generated not only substantial revenues from these projects but also valuable experiences, which they could sell to other clients in the same sector: 'The smart companies walk away not only with fat checks, but with something that is much more valuable over the long run, experience in a particular industry' (ibid.: 204).

Third, while the previous approaches mainly concentrate on one side of the coin, that is, either the positive or the negative side, practice-based views on the use of concepts in client–consultant relationships typically present consultants as pragmatic and flexible in the translation of these concepts to the specific problem situation (Benders, van den Berg, and van Bijsterveld 1998; Benders and van Veen 2001; Visscher 2001). It is indicated that using legitimate rhetoric helps a consultant to obtain a position in a project, while a concept's interpretative space creates the possibility to adapt the general ideas that are associated with that concept to the specific client situation (Werr, Stjernberg, and Doucherty 1997). As Benders, van den Berg, and van Bijsterveld (1998: 212) suggest, consultants handle a concept 'highly pragmatically and tend to go along with customer demands and interpretations'. In other words, while establishing a common framework, these concepts allow for the creative and pragmatic application of different approaches and techniques by individual consultancies (Benders, van den Berg, and van Bijsterveld 1998; Visscher 2001; Werr and Stjernberg 2003) and enable consultants to deal with unexpected circumstances in a consultancy project. In line with this, Heusinkveld and Visscher (2006) have identified various elements that shape the interpretation of a concept by a consultant in a concrete project. It is also emphasized in this literature that concepts do not directly shape the actions of consultants; rather it is 'improvisation' on these concepts that characterizes consultancy work (Morris 2001; Visscher 2001). Improvisation on concepts is necessary to develop tailor-made solutions for the client organization.

An important limitation of the current demand-side research is that there is still little empirical work on how these concepts are actually applied in organizational praxis (Benders, van den Berg, and van Bijsterveld 1998). Although the sweeping rhetoric on management fashions leads one to believe that organization concepts have considerable consequences for organizations and employees, the issue has scarcely been studied systematically. Suddaby and Greenwood (2001) emphasize that a final element of the knowledge production concerns the 'translation' of the abstracted repertoire into action. However, it should be stressed here that the current research still remains unclear about how consultants actually apply these concepts in organizational praxis (see also Benders and van Veen 2001; Clark 2004; Heusinkveld, Sturdy, and Werr 2011). Or, as Werr (2002: 104) states, 'the application of this knowledge is hardly discussed'. Further research into this area might beneficially draw from theories of translation (Bijker 1990; Czarniawska and Sévon 1996; Sahlin and Wedlin 2008) or the sociology of consumption (Heusinkveld, Sturdy, and Werr 2011) in order to better understand how different consultants use the interpretative space of a concept in their work (Benders and van Veen 2001; Giroux 2006) and how this may lead to a variety of different adaptations. This would shed further light on questions such as how consultants use popular concepts in their assignments within client organizations; to what extent these concepts determine the way in which the problem-solving process takes shape (Fincham 1999); and what elements shape the impacts of these concepts in different consulting projects.

13.4 CONCLUSIONS AND FUTURE DIRECTIONS

The current literature has provided important insights into the supply- and demand-side drivers that underpin the way consultants deal with organization concepts. Concerning the supply side, the literature clearly emphasizes the importance of consultants in the dissemination of organization concepts. In addition, the extant research provides some important insights into the intra-organizational development processes within consultancies, and the different managerial problems that are associated with it. Although the demand-side perspectives are still considered significantly under-researched, various studies provide some important clues about the way consultants apply these concepts in their projects.

Having reviewed the literature on consultants and organization concepts it can be concluded that this area of research has both important limitations and rewarding research possibilities. A central issue emerging from this review is that there is little overlap between the supply-side views and demand-side approaches. More specifically, those researchers who focus on market-level and intra-organizational development processes within consulting firms, remain relatively separate from authors who study the application of new concepts within client organizations. The previous sections have presented some fruitful research directions for these separate topics. However, a further important future research direction would be to strengthen the link between these relatively separate, but highly related, streams of research. Further enhancing such a synthesis between supply- and demand-related approaches can be done by addressing a number of key unanswered questions.

First, there is the issue of how clients influence the process of new concept development. The current research highlights the importance of the adequate use of market and client information in the development process. In addition, the extant literature suggests that a consultancy may increase the likelihood of acquiring new assignments when client needs are systematically translated into a piece of expertise to support future client interactions. However, as discussed above, more research is needed to uncover the antecedents and consequences of market orientation in concept development.

Second, there is the issue of how the application of new organization concepts takes shape within client organizations, and to what extent these concepts play a role in client–consultant interactions. There is still a lot of emphasis on the supply side and situations are often viewed from the consultant's perspective. The discussion in the previous sections has indicated that a fruitful avenue for future research would be to pay more attention to how management consultancies deal with management ideas during their assignments, and what factors and conditions play a role in the consumption of these ideas (Heusinkveld, Sturdy, and Werr 2011).

Finally, there is the issue of how the emergence of organization concepts within consultancies may co-evolve in relation to managerial discourse and client demand (Nijholt and Benders 2007), and to what extent consultancies develop any activities that increase the likelihood of knowledge entrenchment (Zeitz, Mittal, and McAulay 1999). Although the process of concept development is often related to the managerial discourse, the extant literature still presents a static view of new concept development and hardly pays attention to the issue of how the popular managerial discourse relates to changes in the internal repertoire of consultancies. Therefore, future research could provide important insights into how new concepts evolve beyond their creation and establishment within a single consultancy.

References

Abrahamson, E. (1996). 'Management Fashion'. *Academy of Management Review*, 21/1, 254–285.

Adams, M., Day, G., and Dougherty, D. (1998). 'Enhancing New Product Development Performance: An Organizational Learning Perspective'. *Journal of Product Innovation Management*, 15/3, 403–422.

Alvesson, M. (1993). 'Organizations as Rhetoric: Knowledge-Intensive Firms and the Struggle with Ambiguity'. *Journal of Management Studies*, 30/6, 997–1015.

Anand, N., Gardner, H., and Morris, T. (2007). 'Knowledge-Based Innovation: Emergence and Embedding of New Practice Areas in Management Consulting Firms'. *Academy of Management Journal*, 50/2, 406–428.

Benders, J. and van Veen, K. (2001). 'What's in a Fashion? Interpretative Viability and Management Fashion'. *Organization*, 8/1, 33–53.

Benders, J. and Vermeulen, P. (2002). 'Too Many Tools? On Problem Solving in NPD Projects'. *International Journal of Innovation Management*, 6/2, 163–185.

Benders, J., van den Berg, R-J., and van Bijsterveld, M. (1998). 'Hitch-Hiking on a Hype: Dutch Consultants Engineering Re-Engineering'. *Journal of Organizational Change Management*, 11/3, 201–215.

Benghozi, P. J. (1990). 'Managing Innovation: From Ad Hoc to Routine in French Telecom'. *Organization Studies*, 11/4, 531–554.

Berglund, J. and Werr, A. (2000). 'The Invincible Character of Management Consulting Rhetoric: How One Blends Incommensurates while Keeping Them Apart'. *Organization*, 7/4, 633–655.

Bijker, W. (1990). *The Social Construction of Technology*. Enschede: Alfa.

Bloomfield, B. and Danieli, A. (1995). 'The Role of Management Consultants in the Development of Information Technology: The Indissoluble Nature of Socio-Political and Technical Skills'. *Journal of Management Studies*, 32/1, 23–46.

Braam, G., Benders, J., and Heusinkveld, S. (2007). 'The Balanced Scorecard in the Netherlands: An Analysis of its Evolution Using Print-Media Indicators'. *Journal of Organizational Change Management*, 20/6, 866–879.

Brown, A. and Ennew, C. (1995). 'Market Research and the Politics of New Product Development'. *Journal of Marketing Management*, 11/4, 339–354.

Brunsson, N. and Olsen, J. (1997). *The Reforming Organization*. Bergen: Fagbokforlaget.

Clark, T. (1995). *Managing Consultants: Consultancy as the Management of Impressions*. Buckingham: Open University Press.

Clark, T. (2004). 'The Fashion of Management Fashion: A Surge too Far?' *Organization*, 11/2, 297–306.

Clark, T. and Fincham, R. (2002). *Critical Consulting: New Perspectives on the Management Advice Industry*. Oxford: Blackwell.

Clark, T. and Salaman, G. (1998). 'Telling Tales: Management Gurus' Narratives and the Construction of Managerial Identity'. *Journal of Management Studies*, 35/2, 137–161.

Collins, D. (2003). 'The Branding of Management Knowledge: Rethinking Management Fads'. *Journal of Organizational Change Management*, 16/2, 186–204.

Cooper, R. (1983). 'The New Production Process: An Empirically Based Classification Scheme'. *R & D Management*, 13/3, 1–13.

Craig, D. (2005). *Rip-Off! The Scandalous Inside Story of the Management Consulting Money Machine*. London: The Original Book Company.

Czarniawska, B. and Sévon, G. (1996). *Translating Organizational Change*. Berlin: De Gruyter.

David, R. and Strang, D. (2006). 'When Fashion is Fleeting: Transitory Collective Beliefs and the Dynamics of TQM Consulting'. *Academy of Management Journal*, 49/2, 215–233.

Day, G. (1994). 'The Capabilities of Market-Driven Organizations'. *Journal of Marketing*, 58/4, 37–52.

Deshpande, R. and Zaltman, G. (1982). 'Factors Affecting the Use of Market Research Information: A Path Analysis'. *Journal of Marketing Research*, 19/1, 14–31.

Dougherty, D. (1996). 'Organizing for Innovation'. In S. R. Clegg, C. Hardy, and W. R. Nord (eds), *Handbook of Organization Studies*. London: Sage, 424–439.

Dougherty, D. and Hardy, C. (1996). 'Sustained Product Innovations in Large Mature Organizations: Overcoming Innovation-to-Organization Problems'. *Academy of Management Journal*, 39/5, 1120–1153.

Dougherty, D. and Heller, T. (1994). 'The Illegitimacy of Successful Product Innovation in Established Firms'. *Organization Science*, 5/2, 200–218.

Dutton, J., Ashford, S., O'Neill, R., and Lawrence, K. (2001). 'Moves that Matter: Issue Selling and Organizational Change'. *Academy of Management Journal*, 44/4, 716–736.

Faust, M. (2002). 'Consultancies as Actors in Knowledge Arenas: Evidence from Germany'. In M. Kipping and L. Engwall (eds), *Management Consulting*. Oxford: Oxford University Press, 146–163.

Fincham, R. (1995). 'Business Process Reengineering and the Commodification of Management Knowledge'. *Journal of Marketing Management*, 11/7, 707–719.

Fincham, R. (1999). 'The Consultant–Client Relationship: Critical Perspectives on the Management of Organizational Change'. *Journal of Management Studies*, 36/3, 335–351.

Fincham, R. and Evans, M. (1999). 'The Consultants' Offensive: Reengineering—From Fad to Technique'. *New Technology, Work and Employment*, 14/1, 32–44.

Fincham, R., Clark, T., Handley, K., and Sturdy, A. (2008). 'Configuring Expert Knowledge: The Consultant as a Sector Specialist'. *Journal of Organizational Behavior*, 29/8, 1145–1160.

Fosstenløkken, S., Løwendahl, B., and Revang, O. (2003). 'Knowledge Development through Client Interaction: A Comparative Study'. *Organization Studies*, 24/6, 859–879.

Furusten, S. (1999). *Popular Management Books: How They are Made and What They Mean for Organizations*. London: Routledge.

Gardner, H., Anand, N., and Morris, T. (2008). 'Chartering New Territory: Diversification, Legitimacy, and Practice Area Creation in Professional Service Firms'. *Journal of Organizational Behavior*, 29/8, 1101–1122.

Gill, J. and Whittle, S. (1993). 'Management by Panacea: Accounting for Transience'. *Journal of Management Studies*, 30/2, 281–295.

Giroux, H. (2006). 'It Was Such a Handy Term: Management Fashions and Pragmatic Ambiguity'. *Journal of Management Studies*, 43/6, 1227–1260.

Glückler, J. and Armbrüster, T. (2003). 'Bridging Uncertainty in Management Consulting: The Mechanisms of Trust and Networked Reputation'. *Organization Studies*, 24/2, 269–297.

Greiner, L. and Metzger, R., (1983). *Consulting to Management*. Englewood Cliffs, NJ: F. T. Prentice Hall.

Grint, K. and Case, P. (1998). 'The Violent Rhetoric of Re-Engineering: Management Consultancy on the Offensive'. *Journal of Management Studies*, 35/5, 557–577.

Guillén, M. (1994). *Models of Management: Work, Authority and Organization in a Comparative Perspective*. Chicago: University of Chicago Press.

Hansen, M., Nohria, N., and Tienery, T. (1999). 'What's Your Strategy for Managing Knowledge?' *Harvard Business Review*, 77/2, 106–116.

Heusinkveld, S. and Benders, J. (2002). 'Between Professional Dedication and Corporate Design: Exploring Forms of New Concept Development in Consultancies'. *International Studies of Management & Organization*, 32/4, 104–122.

Heusinkveld, S. and Benders, J. (2005). 'Contested Commodification: Consultancies and their Struggle with New Concept Development'. *Human Relations*, 58/3, 283–310.

Heusinkveld, S. and Reijers, H. (2009). 'Reflections on a Reflective Cycle: Building Legitimacy in Design Knowledge Development'. *Organization Studies*, 30/8, 865–886.

Heusinkveld, S. and Visscher, K. (2006). 'On the Construction of Problems and Solutions in the Client–Consultant Relationship'. Best Papers Proceedings, Academy of Management Conference, Atlanta.

Heusinkveld, S., Benders, J., and van den Berg, R. (2009). 'From Market Sensing to New Concept Development in Consultancies: The Role of Information Processing and Organizational Capabilities'. *Technovation*, 29/8, 509–516.

Heusinkveld, S., Sturdy, A., and Werr, A. (2011). 'The Co-consumption of Management Ideas and Practices'. *Management Learning*, 42/2, 139–147.

Holtz, H. (1983). *How to Succeed as an Independent Consultant*. New York: John Wiley & Sons.

Huczynski, A. (1993). *Management Gurus: What Makes Them and How to Become One*. London: Routledge.

Jackson, B. (1996). 'Re-Engineering the Sense of Self: The Manager and the Management Guru'. *Journal of Management Studies*, 33/5, 571–590.

Jackson, B. (2001). *Management Gurus and Management Fashions: A Dramatistic Inquiry*. London: Routledge.

Kieser, A. (1997). 'Rhetoric and Myth in Management Fashion'. *Organization*, 4/1, 49–74.

Kieser, A. (2002). 'Managers as Marionettes? Using Fashion Theories to Explain the Success of Consultancies'. In M. Kipping and L. Engwall (eds), *Management Consulting*. Oxford: Oxford University Press, 167–183.

Kingdon, J. (1995). *Agendas, Alternatives and Public Policies*. New York: Longman.

Kipping, M. (1999). 'American Management Consulting Companies in Western Europe, 1920s to 1990s: Products, Reputation and Relationships'. *Business History Review*, 73/2, 190–220.

Kipping, M. (2002). 'Trapped in Their Wave: The Evolution of Management Consultancies'. In T. Clark and R. Fincham (eds), *Critical Consulting: New Perspectives on the Management Advice Industry*. Oxford: Blackwell, 28–49.

Knights, D. and McCabe, D. (1998). 'What Happens when the Phone goes Wild? Staff, Stress and Spaces for Escape in a BPR Telephone Banking Work Regime'. *Journal of Management Studies*, 35/2, 163–194.

Kohli, A. and Jaworski, B., (1990). 'Market Orientation: The Construct, Research Propositions, and Managerial Implications'. *Journal of Marketing*, 54/2, 1–18.

Kok, R., Hillebrand, B., and Biemans, W. (2003). 'What Makes Product Development Market Oriented? Towards a Conceptual Framework'. *International Journal of Innovation Management*, 7/2, 137–162.

Lammers, C. (1988). 'Transience and Persistence of Ideal Types in Organization Theory'. In N. DiTomaso and S. Bacharach (eds), *Research in the Sociology of Organizations*. Greenwich, CT: JAI Press, 203–224.

Lewis, M., Welsh, M., Dehler, G., and Green, S. (2002). 'Product Development Tensions: Exploring Contrasting Styles of Project Management'. *Academy of Management Journal*, 45/3, 546–564.

McKenna, C. (2006). *The World's Newest Profession: Management Consulting in the Twentieth Century*. New York: Cambridge University Press.

Morris, T. (2001). 'Asserting Property Rights: Knowledge Codification in the Professional Service Firm'. *Human Relations*, 54/7, 819–838.

Morris, T. and Empson, L. (1998). 'Organization and Expertise: An Exploration of Knowledge Bases and the Management of Accounting and Consulting Firms'. *Accounting, Organizations and Society*, 23/5–6, 609–624.

Nijholt, J. (2010). 'The Role of Print Media in Management Fashions'. Ph.D. thesis, Radboud University, Nijmegen.

Nijholt, J. and Benders, J. (2007). 'Coevolution in Management Fashions: The Case of Self-Managed Teams in the Netherlands'. *Group & Organization Management*, 32/6, 628–652.

O'Shea, J. and Madigan, C. (1997). *Dangerous Company: The Consulting Powerhouses and the Businesses they Save and Ruin*. London: Nicholas Brealey.

Pinault, L. (2000). *Consulting Demons: Inside the Unscrupulous World of Global Corporate Consulting*. Chichester: John Wiley & Sons.

Røvik, K-A. (2002). 'The Secrets of the Winners: Management Ideas that Flow'. In K. Sahlin-Andersson and L. Engwall (eds), *The Expansion of Management Knowledge: Carriers, Ideas and Sources*. Thousand Oaks, CA: Stanford University Press, 113–144.

Sahlin, K. and Wedlin, L. (2008). 'Circulating Ideas: Imitating, Translating and Editing'. In R. Greenwood, C. Oliver, K. Sahlin, and R. Suddaby (eds), *The Sage Handbook of Organizational Institutionalism*. Los Angeles: Sage, 218–242.

Sahlin-Andersson, K. and Engwall, L. (2002). *The Expansion of Management Knowledge: Carriers, Ideas and Sources*. Thousand Oaks, CA: Stanford University Press.

Sturdy, A. (1997). 'The Consultancy Process: An Insecure Business?' *Journal of Management Studies*, 34/3, 389–413.

Suddaby, R. and Greenwood, R. (2001). 'Colonizing Knowledge: Commodification as a Dynamic of Jurisdictional Expansion in Professional Service Firms'. *Human Relations*, 54/7, 933–953.

Ten Bos, R. and Heusinkveld, S. (2007). 'The Gurus' Gusto: Management Fashion, Performance and Taste'. *Journal of Organizational Change Management*, 20/3, 304–325.

Tidd, J., Bessant, J., and Pavitt, K. (1997). *Managing Innovation: Integrating Technological, Market and Organizational Change*. Chichester: John Wiley & Sons.

Van de Ven, A. (1986). 'Central Problems in the Management of Innovation'. *Management Science*, 32/5, 590–607.

Visscher, K. (2001). *Design Methodology in Management Consulting*. Enschede: University of Twente.

Von Hippel, E. (1978). 'Successful Industrial Products from Customer Ideas'. *Journal of Marketing*, 42/1, 39–49.

Werr, A. (2002). 'The Internal Creation of Consulting Knowledge: A Question of Structuring Experience'. In M. Kipping and L. Engwall (eds), *Management Consulting*. Oxford: Oxford University Press, 91–108.

Werr, A. and Stjernberg, T. (2003). 'Exploring Management Consulting Firms as Knowledge Systems'. *Organization Studies*, 24/6, 881–908.

Werr, A., Stjernberg, T., and Docherty, P. (1997). 'The Functions of Methods of Change in Management Consulting'. *Journal of Organizational Change Management*, 10/4, 288–307.

Wright, C. (2002). 'Promoting Demand, Gaining Legitimacy and Broadening Expertise: The Evolution of Consultancy–Client Relationships in Australia'. In M. Kipping and L. Engwall (eds), *Management Consulting*. Oxford: Oxford University Press, 184–202.

Wright, C. and Kitay, J. (2004). 'Spreading the Word: Gurus, Consultants and the Diffusion of the Employee Relations Paradigm in Australia'. *Management Learning*, 35/3, 271–286.

Zeitz, G., Mittal, V., and McAulay, B. (1999). 'Distinguishing Adoption and Entrenchment of Management Practices: A Framework for Analysis'. *Organization Studies*, 20/5, 741–776.

CHAPTER 14

STRUCTURING CONSULTING FIRMS

TIMOTHY MORRIS
HEIDI GARDNER
N. ANAND

14.1 INTRODUCTION

THE purpose of this chapter is to present an overview of the extant research on the structural characteristics of consulting firms, outlining the explanations for these characteristics and their relationship to the organizational dynamics of these firms. There is little discussion in the literature on the structure of consulting firms specifically, but they are generally seen as one form of the professional service firm. The chapter therefore draws on the literature on professional service firms to provide some of the overview of consulting firms' structural arrangements and implications. The underlying assumption in the literature is that consulting firms, like other types of professional service firms, are a distinctive type of organization and that this distinctiveness influences structural arrangements. Their distinctiveness relates to the nature of their staff, whose professional norms influence their goals and the structures of their employing organizations (Hall 1968; Greenwood, Hinings, and Brown 1990; Kirkpatrick, Muzio, and Ackroyd, Chpater 9, this volume). Consulting and other professional service firms are also said to be distinctive organizations because of the extensive use of the partnership form of ownership and governance (Greenwood and Empson 2003; von Nordenflycht 2010). The partnership form has been shown to have implications for the microstructuring of professional work in teams of consultants, as will be shown below.

The chapter proceeds as follows. The first section briefly summarizes the core literature on organization structure and elaborates the central features of this concept. The second section outlines the literature on the structures of professional service firms in general and consulting firms in particular, examining the basis of their distinctive structural features and their validity with respect to consulting firms. The literature on structure in professional firms addresses two interrelated but discrete levels of analysis, microstructural and macrostructural forms, and in the third and fourth sections these will be discussed. Thus, the third section focuses on how the literature links the organizing process of consulting firms with structuring decisions at the micro-level of the consulting *team*. Section 4 then considers the literature at the macro-level of structure, where decisions about how to organize expertise also occur, principally through units called practices. Here, the focus is on the debate about the nature of international structures in consulting firms and how they are managed. The section then addresses the literature on the process of structural change that links the dynamics of growth and diversification to structural choices. The sixth section outlines some of the future directions for research on the structure of these firms before concluding.

14.2 THE CONCEPT OF ORGANIZATIONAL STRUCTURE

Scholarly interest in organization structure developed in the 1960s (e.g. Burns and Stalker 1961; Hall 1963; March 1965) when aspects of formal and more informal dimensions of organization design (a synonym for organization structure) were central to the field of organization theory (Thompson 1967). The fact that all but the smallest organizations displayed evidence of complexity, that is, substantial variety in the number of subparts and in the way these subparts fit together, spurred interest in both the categorization and explanation for organization structure and form. Much theorizing about structure developed from the concept of organizations as open systems, that is, systems of activities that were influenced by the environment in which they were located (Burns and Stalker 1961; Lawrence and Lorsch 1967) and which explained differences between organizations in their overall structural arrangements and between individual parts of their internal structure, such as departments or offices.

This chapter deals with two core aspects of structural complexity, namely *horizontal differentiation* and *vertical differentiation* or hierarchy. The comparative study of organizations in different industries by Lawrence and Lorsch (1967) explored horizontal differentiation, that is, between subunits, such as departments, with regard to the ways in which they were organized and operated. By differentiation they meant that different departments or subunits develop distinctive attributes and modes of operating to meet specific environmental demands, which also have an impact upon the attitudes and behaviours of people working in these departments. Because the study compared firms in the same industry and across three different industries, they could show differences between departments in the same organization and between industries. By comparing the same type of department, such as sales or production, across firms in the same industry they could also show similarity in structure and attitudes and behaviours. They explained these results in terms of the varying environmental pressures upon each unit and upon firms in different industries.

Their work also considered how firms achieved *integration*, which is the counterpart of differentiation. Integration is 'the quality of the state of collaboration that exists among departments that are required to achieve unity of effort by the demands of the environment' (Lawrence and Lorsch 1967: 47). Thus, the generic organizational challenge in terms of designing the structural architecture of an organization is to select the basis (or bases) on which differentiation will occur and then to select the mechanisms, structural or otherwise, by which the integration of different subunits can be achieved. Organizational structuring within management consulting firms therefore encompasses choices about the basis of dividing up the component parts (or subunits such as practices, departments, or work teams) of a consulting firm and the ways in which they are integrated with each other.

Some subsequent work has taken a broader definition of structure, particularly that of Miller and Friesen (1984), whose work on the concept of configurations suggests that design choices include the systems of accountability and responsibility that exist to implement strategic goals, including the allocation of human resources, information processes, and control systems. Following this, organization structure in management consulting also includes decisions about the allocation of people and resources to particular work groups and to practice areas, the core unit of the consulting firm (Kubr 2002). It also includes the supporting systems and policies that enable structures, including human resources policies, to select, monitor, reward, and promote professionals, and functions such as business development and information systems to underpin management control.

Analysis of organization structure also derives from the literature on bureaucracy, particularly drawing on Weber's (1947) ideal-type analysis. Bureaucratic organizations are characterized by formal hierarchies of authority and by a clear division of labour in which roles are filled by technically competent individuals and undertaken according to detailed procedures, and in which the office or specific position is separate from the individual office holder. Hall (1963, 1968) shows that, in practice, organizations vary from Weber's ideal-type formulation, although virtually all organizations of any size display elements of the bureaucratic model, which is designed for the efficient replication of activities in conditions of relative environmental stability (Mintzberg 1979). Subsequent research on structure has drawn heavily on aspects of the bureaucratic model, in particular by examining vertical hierarchy, formalization of rules and procedures, and the linked concept of centralization of authority, particularly with regard to decision-making (e.g. Pugh, Hickson, and Hinings 1969).

Structural choices are also said to be important because they logically follow from strategic goals and underpin the implementation of strategic decisions or, in Chandler's terms, *structure follows strategy* (Chandler 1962; Foss 1997). In consulting firms, strategic decisions concern both the positioning of the firm in the labour (input) market and client (product or output) market in which it operates, and how the firm chooses to develop and deploy its resources to create competitive advantage (Maister 1993; Løwendahl 2000). It is argued that this concern with the supply side of the equation occurs because consulting firms have few fixed assets and compete on the basis of intangible resources, notably their professional staff, firm-specific know-how, and reputation (Kipping 2002; Greenwood et al. 2005). Firms must therefore attract and retain employees of appropriate quality to execute assignments by both carrying out the core technical task (Morris and Pinnington 1998) and by creating the right impressions as they interact with clients (Alvesson 1995; Clark 1995). Damaging labour turnover occurs if employees leave and take with them their knowledge and their connections to the client market (Broschak 2004; Greenwood et al. 2005; Broschak and Niehans 2006).

These distinctive characteristics of consulting and other professional service firms drive an imperative to grow in order to offer career opportunities for staff, and therefore a reason for them to stay and work hard (Galanter and Palay 1991; Maister 1993; Malhotra, Morris, and Smets 2010). Explanations of structural choice in consulting firms are therefore based both on managing the demand side, that is, client market pressures or opportunities (how best to serve clients and maximize the opportunities they present), *and* managing pressures from the supply side, that is, from professional staff's aspirations (Anand, Gardner, and Morris 2007).

14.3 SOURCES OF DISTINCTIVENESS IN ORGANIZATIONAL STRUCTURE IN CONSULTING AND OTHER PROFESSIONAL SERVICE FIRMS

As noted above, there are relatively few studies of the internal structures of consulting firms, but because they are seen as a type of professional service firm (von Nordenflycht 2010; Kirkpatrick, Muzio, and Ackroyd, Chapter 9, this volume) this section proceeds by considering the broader literature on the structure of professional service firms. It then shows that as newer forms of professions such as consulting have emerged, this has raised questions in the literature about the generalizability of professional organization concepts and structural features. The section draws attention to areas where research has suggested that consulting differs from other types of professions, and looks at how this affects consulting firms' structures.

Research interest in the structure of organizations in which professionals worked was first prompted by the growth of employment among members of formal or collegial professions (Muzio, Ackroyd, and Chanlat 2008) within organizational settings (Gouldner 1957; Abbott 1988) and the increasing size and scale of these organizations (Wright Mills 1951). Studies of different types of professional organizations, such as hospitals and accounting firms, focused on a hybrid form of organization, termed professional bureaucracy, which blended centralized managerial decision-making with professional task autonomy and the sharing of administrative tasks among core professional staff (Litwak 1961; Smigel 1964). Thus, the typical professional organization was distinctive in structural terms from the predominantly bureaucratic organizations it served. Scholars concluded that this hybrid form was able successfully to blend these different forms of organizing, combining bureaucratic control of process and output, with professional control through input standardization achieved through professional training (Hall 1968; Hastings and Hinings 1970). Mintzberg (1979, 1993) subsequently detailed the distinctive features of the design and workings of the professional bureaucracy, emphasizing the strength of the operating core of professionals functioning in a relatively autonomous manner and often with informal co-ordination between each other (i.e. there was high decentralization of decision-making over day-to-day operating matters). Control was primarily achieved by the standardization of professionals' skills in their training as well as the inculcation of the appropriate work values.

Research on the structure of professional organizations gave way to a concern with the deprofessionalization of work in the 1970s but returned in the late 1980s, when a more dynamic focus on the way these organizations were managed began to develop among organization and management scholars (Malhotra, Morris, and Hinings 2006). One reason for this renewed focus on the structure of professional organizations was a growing interest in a broader set of occupations than the formal professions, which embraced management consulting and focused around terms such as knowledge workers and knowledge-intensive work (e.g. Alvesson 1995). Another reason for the renewed interest in structure was the trend by some professions, notably led by the largest accounting firms, to diversify into contiguous occupations like consulting—which intensified jurisdictional competition (Suddaby and Greenwood 2001).

Research on organizational structure was framed around detailed examination of the archetypal organization form in accounting firms—as an exemplar of the professional service firm—how this archetype form was changing and proliferating, and the underlying forces for change (Hinings, Brown, and Greenwood 1991; Brock 2006). For Greenwood, Hinings, and Brown (1990) archetype structures express an interpretive scheme, that is, an underlying set of ideas about how best to organize or what is most appropriate as an organization structure. In other words, structures and systems are infused with the values, meanings, and preferences held by its dominant members rather than being purely functionally determined to achieve a set of goals. In the case of professional firms this interpretive scheme reflects values associated with professionalism and partnership.

Greenwood, Hinings, and Brown (1990) argued that what they called the 'professional partnership' or P² archetype was the dominant form among professional organizations, embodying these partnership and professional values in the interpretive scheme. Professional service firms were therefore distinct from other organizations in structural and management terms because of these values. Partnership meant that senior professionals owned and governed the firm as well as being the core producers (and even where partnership forms of ownership did not exist, as, for example, among some strategy consulting firms, a number mimicked the organizational form and attributes of a partnership (McKenna 2006)). Professionalism encompassed beliefs that professional knowledge is central to the firm, control and evaluation is exercised by peers, authority is widely distributed across partners and senior professionals, decision-making consensus is important, and work responsibility is indivisible. Structurally, the implications of this interpretive scheme are that the archetypical professional firm is characterized by a low degree of vertical differentiation (minimal hierarchy) but more pronounced horizontal differentiation, with specialities built around individual preferences rather than formal departments. Limited use of formal integrating devices between departments occurs. Centralization varies across several dimensions with high central control of financial performance and low central control of the day-to-day working of the operating core of professionals or of strategic decision-making (Greenwood, Hinings, and Brown 1990).

As noted above, archetypes are ideal typifications of organizations and, empirically, variation will be observable among a population of consulting or other professional service firms. However, the importance of the concept is that it seeks to explain how and why these sorts of firms are likely to be structurally distinctive from others.

Some scholars have subsequently examined the validity of the P^2 archetype. First, they have asked to what extent can this structural form be observed empirically and what areas of variation exist around the core model? Findings among samples of firms in formal professional settings showed evidence of structural change: they were becoming more bureaucratic with managerial methods becoming more prominent. Firms adopted strategic plans, hired professional support staff with expertise in marketing, finance, and human resources, developed formal monitoring of professionals' performance, and instituted clearer lines of internal differentiation into practices and departments and more formal integrating devices such as client-relationship partners (Morris and Pinnington 1999; Rose and Hinings 1999). Some saw this as evidence of a new archetype, termed the Managed Professional Business (MPB) (Cooper et al. 1996; Brock, Powell, and Hinings 1999), although other studies have pointed to the persistence of features of the original P^2 form, in particular in the continuing control of senior professionals over strategic decision-making and client relationships in formal professions such as architecture (e.g. Pinnington and Morris 2002). Others have argued for a process of archetype proliferation, with novel forms such as the global professional network emerging as the giant business service firms diversified from accounting into consulting and other activities and built international structures around loose networks of local partnerships grouped under a one-firm brand—a theme returned to below (Koza and Lewin 1999; Rose and Hinings 1999; Aharoni and Nachum 2000).

A second line of critique of the P^2 archetype is focused more on its applicability to consulting firms and other entrepreneurial professions (Reed 1996), that is, occupations where the nature of the claim to professional status and jurisdiction is different from the traditional collegial model of medicine and law, for instance (McKenna 1996; Muzio, Ackroyd, and Chanlat 2008). In particular, scholars have argued that the notion of professional autonomy via high decentralization of operating decisions is contestable. For instance, Kärreman and Alvesson (2004) have argued that there is evidence of substantial bureaucratic control over day-to-day activities, including close monitoring of consultants' daily activities, effort levels, and practices. Others have also noted the expansion of systems such as codified knowledge-bases, which prescribe the methods of work analysis and task execution among teams in large consulting firms (e.g. Hansen, Nohria, and Tierney 1999; Haas and Hansen 2001; Morris 2001; Werr, Chapter 12, this volume). Malhotra and Morris (2009) have also argued that the predominant knowledge-base of the profession will affect the organizational structure of firms within that profession. Using Halliday's (1987) typology (normative, syncretic, or technical), they propose normative professions such as law are more likely to adhere to the traditional archetype and professions with syncretic or technical knowledge-bases such as engineering consulting are more likely to have bureaucratic structures. More broadly, Faulconbridge and Muzio (2008) argue that the structures of firms in newer professions are replete with managerial/bureaucratic systems and even if there are vestiges of the professional archetype these are more for symbolic reasons than as signifiers of a substantive structural model.

A historical critique of the notion of a distinctive professional archetype and its applicability to consulting has been developed by Kipping and Kirkpatrick (2008). These authors segment the historical development of the consulting industry into three separate stages, suggesting that each is characterized by different forms of organizational structure. In the first, dominated by the application of scientific management, any control and co-ordination of consultants' work is limited and high reliance is placed on the prior work experience and expertise of the consultants as engineers in applying the principles of Taylorism. In the second phase, dominated by firms focused on strategic and structural projects, there are residual elements of the professional model, supported by bureaucratic features such as committee co-ordination and systems of employee monitoring such as performance appraisal. High emphasis on integration via corporate culture complements a structure in which consultants are permitted some autonomy over their work. Horizontal differentiation exists but is not pronounced.

The third phase is dominated by large-scale information and communication consulting firms in which bureaucratic features are more explicit. Vertical hierarchy is formalized and extended, career paths are also formalized and planned, work is highly structured around codified 'methodologies' and techniques, and performance monitoring becomes highly developed, facilitating centralized control of employees' performance. Horizontal differentiation is also extended, as a complex matrix structure based on expertise, client or market sector, product, and geography is developed. The largest business service firms that have grown out of their accounting base, and information and communication firms such as IBM and Accenture, exemplify this third stage. In short, the literature suggests that the structures of the large consulting firms are more managerial and bureaucratic than the traditional archetype would imply and that this is also increasingly the case with other types of professions.

14.4 KEY ORGANIZATIONAL PROCESSES AND THE MICRO-STRUCTURE OF CONSULTING FIRMS

This section focuses on the microstructural arrangements of consulting firms. These are built on an organizing process based upon leverage and teamwork and these concepts will be discussed in relation to the literature on consulting firms. The organizing process transforms inputs (the expertise of individuals and the firm's know-how) into outputs (complex, customized solutions for clients in which there is a degree of interaction between consultant and client) (Maister 1993; Grey 1994; Morris and Empson 1998; McKenna 2006). This transformation is undertaken by teams of professional staff, operating with a basic division of professional labour into two groups, partners and associates (Galanter and Palay 1991; Haas and Hansen 2001). Underpinning the team structure are choices about how to enact what is called leverage (Maister 1993).

Leveraging knowledge and the labour power of juniors sustains the basic division of labour in a professional firm and underpins its profitability (Maister 1993; Sherer 1995; Malos and Campion 2000; Hitt et al. 2001). To meet clients' demands, partners and associates need appropriate skills, experience, and training. Associates acquire these skills and knowledge by serving a long apprenticeship before being assessed for partnership. Partners, the senior members of the firm, 'lend' their personal expertise or that codified by the consulting firm to the juniors who carry out professional tasks under their supervision, and this is leverage (Gilson and Mnookin 1989). Exempt from other responsibilities, associates develop their professional competence by working on client assignments while partners seek out further client work. Complementing the leverage model are billing arrangements through which time and expertise are monetized. Billing models vary from fixed fees to time-based fees (Kor and Leblebici 2005). Fixed fees are the norm in consulting (Malhotra and Morris 2009). Success at meeting billing targets is an important factor in promotion decisions (Landers, Rebitzer, and Taylor 1996). Billing targets are thus a central feature of consulting firms' monitoring and incentive systems.

In structural terms, the characteristic mode of organization to enact client engagements and secure leverage by deploying knowledge is the project or assignment team (Haas and Hansen 2001; Werr and Stjernberg 2003). This knowledge may be codified as methods and cases, or it may remain relatively tacit in the form of personal or team-based experiences (Morris and Empson 1998; Hansen, Nohria, and Tierney 1999; Morris 2001). The corollary of task delegation to associates on client projects is that partners and more senior associates devote time to supervision and knowledge transfer by working alongside juniors. Decisions about team structure involve customizing the mix of partners and associates (of varying experience levels) on a project or transaction, and the internal distribution of tasks (Maister 1993; Werr and Stjernberg 2003).

Effective leverage of associates' labour power therefore calls for decisions about the appropriate team structure for executing a client task. To manage leverage effectively, consulting firms form pools of labour that can be deployed on several projects simultaneously (Armbrüster 2006). For the firm, pooling provides the flexibility to adjust to different levels of demand as well as the opportunity to achieve profitable levels of staff utilization. For associates, pooling offers opportunities to build human capital through on-the-job learning in the course of client engagements, as long as they can access suitable projects. More senior personnel progressively specialize and can deploy their experience and expertise to address more complex client problems, but the cost of specialization for the firm is that it has to continue to source appropriate assignments to keep its associates busy and committed or risk unanticipated 'quits' (Gilson and Mnookin 1989).

The translation of leverage into profit for the consulting firm therefore influences hiring, promotion, and the structure of teams. In turn these relate to the sort of consulting model in which the firm is engaged. Kipping (2002) has argued that the type of consulting projects which predominated in his first and second waves were typically 'brains' and 'grey-hair' assignments respectively (Maister 1993), in which leverage was relatively low (he mentions a ratio of 1:6 in McKinsey & Co. as an example) and in which the experience gap between partners and associates was less significant. The importance of this experience to the project placed a limit on the standardization and routinization of work practices and meant that through some transfer of experience to associates the leverage of the partner's personal know-how took place. In the third wave, where assignments are typically characterized by 'procedure', by contrast, leverage is much higher—Kipping mentions a ratio of 1:20—and routinization of work is more pronounced. Consultants become 'implementation specialists' (2002: 39). In this sort of assignment, teams are much larger, the hierarchical mix differs from the grey-hair model, and the skills acquired by the consultant are from codified data bases, although, as Werr and Stjernberg (2003) note, there is still some opportunity to deploy tacit knowledge to expedite assignments.

Teams are therefore the basic organizational unit of work in consulting, embodying different vertical levels of hierarchy through which different models of leverage and know-how are enacted (Haas and Hansen 2001). Assignment teams are also the key integrating device through which horizontally differentiated parts of the firm are brought together.

14.5 DIVERSIFICATION AND THE MACRO-STRUCTURE OF CONSULTING FIRMS

At the macro-level, it is typical to find mature consulting firms organized around a set of practices and, as was noted above, this division is a form of horizontal differentiation. Kubr (2002: 769) notes that 'most consulting firms [...] structure their operating core—the professional staff—in more or less permanent home units (called practice groups in some professions)'. Characteristically, practices are differentiated on expertise (however that term is defined within the firm and in the wider professional community). However, consulting firms typically seek to balance organization around technical expertise with organization around a market-based category like industry, sector, or client group. It is common for large firms, such as strategy consulting firms or IT-based firms like Accenture and IBM, to create practices focusing on sectors like consumer goods, financial services, retailing, and the public sector. Many of the large consulting firms add the dimension of *market-* or *sector-based expertise* to technical expertise in a matrix structure (Greenwood et al. 2010).

A third dimension of horizontal differentiation is based on the geographical diversification of consulting firms. One explanation for the internationalization of consulting firms is that they have followed their multinational clients. For example, Kipping (1999) shows that McKinsey moved into Europe in the 1960s both because it had exhausted its home territory market and saw opportunities to advise European clients (its first one was Shell) and because its core clients, US multinationals, offered consulting opportunities in their overseas operations (see also McKenna 2006). Often, international expansion was accomplished by entrepreneurial individuals, working for their own clients and with little central co-ordination from headquarters. Consulting firms therefore allowed individual partners to build national subsidiaries to follow clients, and ran relatively decentralized international structures. Subsequently, they formalized an organization structure more based on geographic regions in an effort to integrate their subsidiaries more completely and to transfer or build their capabilities, notably knowledge and individuals (e.g. Armbrüster 2006).

The debate in the literature that follows from this internationalization of consulting firms concerns the nature of the relationships between different parts of the organization and the extent to which these firms operate as an integrated whole. Put another way, how far and in what ways do firms achieve integration across their differentiated structures? Boussebaa (2009) notes that the evidence on consulting firms is limited but he suggests that consulting and other professional service firms have 'often been touted as the paragons of the globally integrated network (GIN) [...] requiring as they do organizational structures that can facilitate both decentralization and integration' (ibid.: 830). Such network arrangements allow firms to share resources such as knowledge and people when necessary, perhaps on a quasi-market basis without recourse to strong central fiat, as per the orthodox multinational corporation (Ferner, Edwards, and Sisson 1995; Rose and Hinings 1999). Using data drawn from studies in four large consulting firms, Boussebaa (2009: 844) concludes that while the firms under study had 'institutionalized resource management systems that were transnational in scope [...] the process of resource management was subject to conflicts and tensions that continually undermined its raison d'être'.

A slightly different conclusion is reached by Greenwood and colleagues (2010). Recognizing the extreme degree of structural differentiation operating simultaneously among the largest business advisory firms (which they term multiplex organizations), they argue that a set of integrating devices are in place to cope with these. First, they argue that the differentiation via multiple axes of structure also acts as an integrating device by connecting professionals across a latticework of communities within the larger organization. In other words, professionals play multiple roles simultaneously in overlapping communities, creating a dense network of connections with few intermediaries. Second, they argue that the prioritization of client management systems and the teams that drive these systems within these firms also ensure that these communities function. Third, they suggest that integration is underpinned by what they term cultures of reciprocity, which encourage the fusing of these elements of the consulting firm.

14.6 STRUCTURAL CHANGE AND PRACTICE AREA CREATION

Structural *change* occurs as firms seek to diversify or grow, or indeed to shed practices and refocus. The literature deals with structural change by analysing the motivation of consulting firms to pursue growth and the limits of growth possibilities as well as the process by which growth is said to proceed. On the motivation for growth, Suddaby and Greenwood (2001) argue, for example, that as expert knowledge commodifies over time professional firms seek to 'colonize' new territories, provoking jurisdictional disputes with other professional communities such as consulting firms (see also Heuskinveld and Benders (2005); Heuskinveld and Benders, Chapter 13, this volume, for an account of the consequences of knowledge commodification in consulting firms). Greenwood and Suddaby's account of the expansion of the Big Five accounting firms into broader business advisory services also highlights the central role of claims to legitimacy, that is, efforts to legitimize a firm's own expertise and to delegitimize its competitors through the process of diversification (Suddaby and Greenwood 2005; Greenwood and Suddaby 2006). In reputational terms, firms diversify in order to exploit their reputations, either by selling more services to existing clients or by finding new clients. The result is growth through diversification based on new products or on new client markets (Armbrüster 2006). We should also note that Kipping's (2002) evolutionary model of the industry in three stages suggests that there are structural and cultural limits to growth among consulting firms: his argument is that, regardless of motivation, firms cannot easily change from one model of consulting (such as the low-leverage grey-hair model) to another (such as the high-leverage procedural model).

These macro-level explanations for the structural forms that consulting firms may adopt emphasize the link between the choice of structure and the challenge of growth and diversification, but say less about how the process of structural development occurs. Gardner, Anand, and Morris (2008) fill this gap with a process explanation of how firms adapt to new opportunities while providing the scope for ambitious professionals to build their reputations. Central to this process is the creation of new practices. New and internally differentiated practice areas are squarely implicated in consulting and other professional firms' innovation and diversification efforts (Heuskinveld and Benders 2005; see also Chapter 13, this volume). New practice creation occurs largely through initiatives from the periphery of the consulting firm rather than through charters directed from the centre, as the novel expertise on which new practices are based tends to come from constant interaction with clients (Fosstenløkken, Løwendahl, and Revang 2003). The process by which new practices are created illuminates the relationship between structural diversification and knowledge-based innovation, and provides a link between the micro- and macro-levels of structural change in consulting firms.

Gardner, Anand, and Morris (2008) show that new practices are relatively commonplace in consulting firms, but that only around 50 per cent of a sample of new practice initiatives led to a sustainable independent practice. Their model combines structural features and skilful agency and requires that four crucial ingredients— (i) social agency, (ii) expertise development, (iii) 'turf' or the establishment of clear territorial boundaries, and (iv) organizational support—merge in one of three possible sequences. During the combinatory process, astute actions by individual actors or groups can resolve political challenges and secure the necessary resources. Thus, new practice creation is rarely easy and is inherently political, because it requires the garnering and deployment of valued resources and because, like other forms of innovation, it demands legitimization by powerful groups such as clients, as Glückler and Armbrüster's (2003) study of the management consulting sector shows. Likewise, Heuskinveld and Benders (2005) have argued that new concept development in consulting firms relies on innovators' ability to get round internal resistance (see also Heunsinkveld and Benders Chapter 13, this volume).

Anand, Gardner, and Morris (2007) show that all four ingredients mentioned above are necessary to build a new practice and the absence of one cannot be compensated for by amplifying any of the others. They must also be combined effectively via a two-stage process in which the agent, or champion, combines with one of the other three ingredients in the *Emergence Step*. For example, they may develop a specific form of expertise that is valued by clients and seen as sufficiently different from the expertise residing in other practices. This means that two of the ingredients have combined. In the second stage, the *Embedding Step*, the other two ingredients are successfully introduced. For example, this embedding step could involve establishing organizational 'turf', usually by building on existing client relationships—thereby showing others in the firm that the nascent practice has internal and external legitimacy—and by obtaining sufficient support from the rest of the organization, in the form of people, budget, and recommendations to clients that bring in a flow of work, for the practice to survive and flourish.

This account of how consulting firms' structures develop acknowledges the relatively decentralized nature of authority to pursue innovation in these settings. Structures do not come into being by executive fiat, and individual partners enjoy considerable power by virtue of their reputations and client contacts (Morris and Empson 1998; Gardner, Anand, and Morris 2008). Viewing consulting firms as a constellation of practices in which structural variation via practice creation occurs as a political process is consistent with coalitional models of the organization (Cyert and March 1963).

14.7 FURTHER WORK

While structure is important for understanding consulting firms, because it is the means by which core resources, people, knowledge, and reputation can be deployed and developed it has only received limited attention in the literature. For this reason this chapter has drawn on the literature on the broader professional service firms as well as that on consulting firms. For both theoretical and practical reasons research focused on the outcomes of structure are important, and studies of the relationship between structure and performance outcomes across a sample of consulting firms would be valuable. This requires careful design to take account of confounding variables and multiple measures of performance, by perhaps including client-based measures, such as achievement of transactional objectives, and professional-staff-based measures, such as commitment.

Second, the chapter has noted that archetype concepts crystallized a great deal of work on the distinctive structures of professional organizations but subsequent research shows that the distinctiveness of consulting and other professional firms has diminished as they acquire features of the corporation in the ways they are managed and organized. A criticism of this stream of research is that it has largely been focused on small numbers of organizations and on particular sectors or industries (Morris and Pinnington 1999). More broadly, recent work on the nature of professions has challenged the generalizability of the professional archetype—particularly in relation to newer, entrepreneurial professions—and its historical veracity, given the evolution of the consulting industry (e.g. Brock, Powell, and Hinings 1999; Kipping and Kirkpatrick 2008; Muzio, Ackroyd, and Chanlat 2008). If it is to progress fruitfully, further research on the professional archetype should be based on larger samples and be more rigorously comparative in order to understand the contours of structural similarity and difference within and across sectors. Comparing consulting firms with another more formally professionalized sector like law might, for instance, illuminate theoretical accounts of the influence of professional values on structure. Archetype work can also progress conceptually by generating propositions about the causes of change and development of new archetypes, possibly by incorporating explanatory models from theoretical domains such as institutional theory. For instance, Greenwood and Suddaby's (2006) notion of contradictions triggering institutional change could usefully be applied to the question of archetype change.

Third, research needs to clarify through granular studies how structure actually works in consulting firms. As noted above, extensive work on the structures of professional service firms has been done but relatively little of it has, as yet, focused on consulting. Research in this arena is likely to be processual and sensitive to the relationship between formal, macro-level policies, for example on the structure of the practice portfolio, and more informal, micro-level activities, which enact structure on the ground. One important area where further work is required concerns the enactment of structures at their most complex, that is, in the arena of complex international assignments. A focus on the core mechanism of integration, the client management system and how this works across a range of assignments with differing outcomes, would extend existing theory by providing insight into the working of the international organization and potentially link structure to action and performance.

A fourth area of research that is needed concerns the relationship of structure and innovation in consulting and other professional firms because understanding how innovation is fostered is seen to be so important to firms' survival and success (see Heuskinveld and Benders, Chapter 13, this volume). Much work has considered how firms achieve the exploitation of existing assets and the simultaneous exploration for new ways of competing with different organizational forms (March 1991). In consulting, however, innovation often emerges from ongoing work (Dougherty 2004). The tight coupling of exploratory activities with the core work of such firms suggests that more research is needed to assess how, structurally, this concurrent exploitation and exploration is achieved.

14.8 CONCLUSIONS

Understanding the structures of consulting firms has several important and related aspects. First, structure viewed broadly, or organization design, is distinctive in these firms because of the nature of the work, staff, and clients. Whether consultants are viewed as professionals or not, many firms have characteristics typical of the professional organization. While it appears that the largest firms have taken on corporate forms of management and become more like the corporations they serve, control of the client relationship largely remains in the hands of front-line professionals, and this mitigates the development of a uniformly bureaucratic model.

Second, structural differentiation occurs at the micro-level of the everyday consulting task and the macro-level of the firm's portfolio of practices. Structural differentiation at the macro-level has proliferated in the form of practices based on sector, expertise, and geography, and co-ordinated by complex matrices. Balancing this differentiation is the project team, the microstructural form characteristic of all consulting firms and their primary integrating device. This microstructure is also the means by which leverage is enacted. The macrostructure provides a platform for locating different types of expertise and the microstructure is a platform for integrating multiple forms of expertise in work assignments.

Third, structural choices about the portfolio of practices must be viewed in light of the growth dynamics of the firm. These are driven partly by client opportunities but also by the need to provide careers for professional staff. Growth via diversification is one route by which consulting firms seek to mitigate the risks of knowledge commoditization, although there appear to be structural and cultural limits to such growth ambitions. Growth is, in turn, linked to expertise-based innovations that take the form of new practices. In short, understanding changes in the structure of a consulting firm requires an understanding of the process whereby new practices are created.

At the macro-level, a consulting firm's strategy is embodied in its portfolio of practices and how they interact, such as cross-selling or sharing resources of staff and expert knowledge. Practices constitute the firm's organizational bedrock. Though usually defined in terms of technical expertise, practices are often overlaid with market-facing structures based on sector or client type, and in the largest firms with geographic units as well. As a result, large consulting firms are typically structurally complex and managed via matrix systems. The portfolio of practices that constitutes a firm is not exclusively the result of top-down decisions. Rainmakers and partners with valued connections to clients can influence choices about resource allocation and support for innovations. Furthermore, competing claims to expertise can affect patterns of growth. Understanding how practices are created and destroyed thus offers insight into patterns of structural development in consulting firms.

REFERENCES

Abbott, A. (1988). *The System of Professions*. Chicago: University of Chicago Press.

Ahroni, Y. and Nachum, L. (2000). *Globalization of Services: Some Implications for Theory and Practice*. London: Routledge.

Alvesson, M. (1995). *Management of Knowledge-Intensive Companies*. Berlin: De Gruyter.

Anand, N., Gardner, H., and Morris, T. (2007). 'Knowledge-Based Innovation: Emergence and Embedding of New Practice Areas in Management Consulting Firms'. *Academy of Management Journal*, 50/6, 1554–1557.

Armbrüster, T. (2006). *The Economics and Sociology of Management Consulting*. Cambridge: Cambridge University Press.

Boussebaa, M. (2009). 'Struggling to Organize across National Borders: The Case of Global Resource Management in Professional Service Firms'. *Human Relations*, 62/6, 829–850.

Brock, D. M. (2006). 'The Changing Professional Organization: A Review of Competing Archetypes'. *International Journal of Management Review*, 8/3, 157–174.

Brock, D. M., Powell, M., and Hinings, C. R. (eds) (1999). *Restructuring the Professional Organization: Accounting, Health Care and Law*. London: Routledge.

Broschak, J. P. (2004). 'Managers' Mobility and Market Interface: The Effect of Managers' Careers on the Dissolution of Market Ties'. *Administrative Science Quarterly*, 49, 608–640.

Broschak, J. P. and Niehaus, K. (2006). 'Social Structure, Employee Mobility and the Circulation of Client Ties'. In R. Greenwood and R. Suddaby (eds), *Research in the Sociology of Organizations: Professional Service Firms*, vol. 24. Oxford: JAI Press, 369–401.

Burns, T. and Stalker, G. (1961). *The Management of Innovation*. Oxford: Oxford University Press.

Chandler, A. (1962). *Strategy and Structure*. Cambridge, MA: MIT Press.

Clark, T. (1995). *Managing Consultants: Consultancy as the Management of Impressions*. Buckingham: Open University Press.

Cooper, D. J., Hinings, C. R., Greenwood, R., and Brown, J. L. (1996). 'Sedimentation and Transformation in Organizational Change: The Case of Canadian Law Firms'. *Organization Studies*, 17/4, 623–647.

Cyert, R. M. and March, J. G. (1963). *A Behavioral Theory of the Firm*. Englewood Cliffs, NJ: F. T. Prentice Hall.

Dougherty, D. (2004). 'Organizing Practice in Services to Capture Knowledge for Innovation'. *Strategic Organization*, 2, 35–64.

Faulconbridge, J. and Muzio, D. (2008). 'Organizational Professionalism in Globalizing Law Firms'. *Work Employment and Society*, 22/1, 7–25.

Ferner, A., Edwards, P., and Sisson, K. (1995). 'Coming Unstuck? In Search of the "Corporate Glue" in an International Professional Service Firm'. *Human Resource Management*, 34/3, 343–361.

Foss, N. (1997). *Resources and Strategy: A Reader*. Oxford: Oxford University Press.

Fosstenløkken, S., Løwendahl, B., and Revang, O. (2003). 'Knowledge Development through Client Interaction: A Comparative Study'. *Organization Studies*, 24, 859–879.

Galanter, M. and Palay, T. (1991). *Tournament of Lawyers: The Transformation of the Big Law Firm*. Chicago: University of Chicago Press.

Gardner, H., Anand, N., and Morris, T. (2008). 'Chartering New Territory: Diversification, Legitimacy and Practice Area Creation in Professional Service Firms'. *Journal of Organizational Behavior*, 29, 1101–1121.

Gilson, R. and Mnookin, R. H. (1989). 'Coming of Age in a Corporate Law Firm: The Economics of Associate Career Patterns'. *Stanford Law Review*, 41, 567–595.

Glückler, J. and Armbrüster, T. (2003). 'Bridging Uncertainty in Management Consulting: The Mechanisms of Trust and Networked Reputation'. *Organization Studies*, 24, 269–297.

Gouldner, A. W. (1957). 'Cosmopolitans and Locals: Toward an Analysis of Latent Social Roles'. *Administrative Science Quarterly*, 2, 281–306.

Greenwood, R. and Empson, L. (2003). 'The Professional Partnership: Relic or Exemplary Form of Governance?' *Organization Studies*, 24/6, 909–933.

Greenwood, R. and Suddaby, R. (2006). 'Institutional Entrepreneurship in Mature Fields: The Big Five Accounting Firms'. *Academy of Management Journal*, 49/1, 27–48.

Greenwood, R., Hinings, C. R., and Brown, J. L. (1990). 'P² Form Strategic Management: Corporate Practices in Professional Partnership'. *Academy of Management Journal*, 33, 725–755.

Greenwood, R., Li, X., Prakash, R., and Deephouse, D. (2005). 'Reputation, Diversification, and Organizational Explanations of Performance in Professional Service Firms'. *Organization Science*, 16/6, 661–673.

Greenwood, R., Morris, T., Fairclough, S., and Boussebaa, M. (2010). 'The Organizational Design of Transnational Professional Service Firms'. *Organization Dynamics*, 39/2, 173–183.

Grey, C. (1994). 'Career as a Project of the Self and Labour Process Discipline'. *Sociology*, 28/2, 479–497.

Haas, M. and Hansen, M. T. (2001). 'Competing for Attention in Knowledge Markets: Electronic Document Dissemination in a Management Consulting Company'. *Administrative Science Quarterly*, 46, 1–28.

Hall, R. (1963). 'The Concept of Bureaucracy'. *American Journal of Sociology*, 69, 32–40.

Hall, R. (1968). 'Professionalization and Bureaucratization'. *American Sociological Review*, 33, 92–104.

Halliday, T. (1987). 'Knowledge Mandates: Collective Influence by Scientific, Normative and Syncretic Professions'. *British Journal of Sociology*, 36, 421–447.

Hansen, M. T., Nohria, N., and Tierney, T. (1999). 'What's Your Strategy for Managing Knowledge?' *Harvard Business Review*, 77/2, 106–116.

Hastings, H. and Hinings, C. (1970). 'Role Relations and Value Adaptation: A Study of the Professional Accountant in Industry'. *Sociology*, 4/3, 353–366.

Heuskinveld, S. and Benders, J. (2005). 'Contested Commodification: Consultancies and their Struggle with New Concept Development'. *Human Relations*, 58, 283–310.

Hinings, C. R., Brown, J. L., and Greenwood, R. (1991). 'Change in an Autonomous Professional Service Firm'. *Journal of Management Studies*, 24, 373–395.

Hitt, M., Bierman, L., Shimizu, K., and Kochlar, R. (2001). 'Direct and Moderating Effects of Human Capital on Strategy and Performance in Professional Service Firms: A Resource-Based Perspective'. *Academy of Management Journal*, 44, 13–28.

Kärreman, D. and Alvesson, M. (2004). 'Cages in Tandem: Management Control, Social Identity, and Identification in a Knowledge-Intensive Firm'. *Organization*, 11/1, 149–175.

Kipping, M. (1999). 'American Management Consulting Companies in Western Europe, 1920 to 1990: Products, Reputation and Relationships'. *Business History Review*, 73/2, 190–220.

Kipping, M. (2002). 'Trapped in Their Wave: The Evolution of Management Consultancies'. In T. Clark and R. Fincham (eds), *Critical Consulting: New Perspectives on the Management Advice Industry*. Oxford: Blackwell, 28–49.

Kipping, M. and Kirkpatrick, I. (2008). 'From Taylorism as Product to Taylorism as Process: Knowledge-Intensive Firms in a Historical Perspective'. In D. Muzio, S. Ackroyd, and J-F. Chanlat (eds), *Redirections in the Study of Expert Labour*. Basingstoke: Palgrave Macmillan, 163–182.

Kor, Y. and Leblebici, H. (2005). 'How Do Interdependencies among Human-Capital Deployment, Development, and Diversification Strategies Affect Firms' Financial Performance?' *Strategic Management Journal*, 26, 967–995.

Koza, M. and Lewin, K. (1999). 'The Coevolution of Network Alliances: A Longitudinal Analysis of an International Professional Service Network'. *Organization Science*, 10/5, 638–653.

Kubr, M. (2002). *Management Consulting: A Guide to the Profession*. Geneva: International Labour Office.

Landers, R., Rebitzer J., and Taylor, L. (1996). 'Rat Race Redux: Adverse Selection in the Determination of Work Hours in Law Firms'. *American Economic Review*, 86/3, 329–338.

Lawrence, P. R. and J. W. Lorsch (1967). *Organization and Environment*. Cambridge, MA: Harvard University Press.

Litwak, E. (1961). 'Models of Bureacracy which Permit Conflict'. *American Journal of Sociology*, 67, 177–184.

Løwendahl, B. (2000). *Strategic Management of Professional Service Firms*. Copenhagen: Copenhagen Business School Press.

Maister, D. H. (1993). *Managing the Professional Services Firm*. New York: Free Press.

Malhotra, N. and Morris, T. (2009). 'Heterogeneity in Professional Firms'. *Journal of Management Studies*, 46/6, 895–922.

Malhotra, N., Morris, T., and Hinings, C. R. (2006). 'Variation in Organizational Form among Professional Service Organizations'. In R. Greenwood and R. Suddaby (eds), *Research in the Sociology of Organizations: Organizations and Professions*. Greenwich, CT: JAI Press, 171–202.

Malhotra, N., Morris, T., and Smets, M. (2010). 'New Career Models in UK Professional Service Firms: From Up-or-Out to Up-and-Going Nowhere?' *International Journal of Human Resource Management*, 21/9, 1396–1413.

Malos, S. and Campion, M. (2000). 'Human Resource Strategy and Career Mobility in Professional Service Firms: Test of an Options-Based Model'. *Academy of Management Journal*, 43, 749–760.

March, J. G. (1965). *Handbook of Organizations*. Chicago: Rand McNally.

March, J. G. (1991). 'Exploration and Exploitation in Organizational Learning'. *Organization Science*, 2, 71–87.

McKenna, C. (2006). *The World's Newest Profession: Management Consulting in the Twentieth Century*. New York: Cambridge University Press.

Miller, D. and P. Friesen (1984). *Organizations: A Quantum View*. Englewood Cliffs, NJ: F. T. Prentice Hall.

Mintzberg, H. (1979). *The Structuring of Organizations: A Synthesis of the Research*. Englewood Cliffs, NJ: F. T. Prentice Hall.

Mintzberg, H. (1993). *Structure in Fives: Designing Effective Organizations*. Englewood Cliffs, NJ: F. T. Prentice Hall.

Morris, T. (2001). 'Asserting Property Rights: Knowledge Codification in the Professional Service Firm'. *Human Relations*, 54/7, 819–838.

Morris, T. and Empson, L. (1998). 'Organization and Expertise: An Exploration of Knowledge Management in Accounting and Consulting Firms'. *Accounting, Organizations and Society*, 23/5–6, 609–624.

Morris, T. and Pinnington, A. (1998). 'Promotion to Partner in Professional Service Firms'. *Human Relations*, 51/1, 3–24.

Morris, T. and Pinnington, A. (1999). 'Continuity and Change in Professional Organizations: Evidence from British Law Firms'. In D. Brock, C. R. Hinings, and M. Powell (eds), *Restructuring the Professional Organization: Accounting, Health Care and Law*. New York: Routledge, 200–214.

Muzio, D., Ackroyd, S., and Chanlat, J-F. (2008). 'Introduction: Lawyers, Doctors and Business Consultants'. In D. Muzio, S. Ackroyd, and J-F. Chanlat (eds), *Redirections in the Study of Expert Labour*. Basingstoke: Palgrave Macmillan, 1–28.

Pinnington, A. and Morris, T. (2002). 'Transforming the Architect: Ownership Form and Archetype Change'. *Organization Studies*, 23, 189–210.

Pugh, D., Hickson, D., and Hinings, C. R. (1969). 'An Empirical Taxonomy of Work Organizations'. *Administrative Science Quarterly*, 14, 115–126.

Reed, M. I. (1996). 'Expert Power and Control in Late Modernity: An Empirical Review and Theoretical Synthesis'. *Organization Studies*, 17/4, 573–597.

Rose, T. and Hinings, C.R. (1999). 'Global Clients' Demands Driving Change in Global Business Advisory Firms'. In D. Brock, M. Powell, and C. R. Hinings (eds), *Restructuring the Professional Organization*. London: Routledge, 41–67.

Sherer, P. (1995). 'Leveraging Human Assets in Law Firms: Human Capital Structures and Organizational Capabilities'. *Industrial and Labor Relations Review*, 48, 671–691.

Smigel, E. (1964). *The Wall Street Lawyer: Professional Organization Man?* New York: Free Press.

Suddaby, R. and Greenwood, R. (2001). 'Colonizing Knowledge: Commodification as a Dynamic of Jurisdictional Expansion in Professional Service Firms'. *Human Relations*, 54, 933–953.

Suddaby, R. and Greenwood, R. (2005). 'Rhetorical Strategies of Legitimacy'. *Administrative Science Quarterly*, 50, 35–67.

Thompson, J. D. (1967). *Organizations in Action*. New York: McGraw-Hill.

Von Nordenflycht, A. (2010). 'What is a Professional Service Firm? Towards a Theory and Taxonomy of Knowledge-Intensive Firms'. *Academy of Management Review*, 35/1, 155–174.

Weber, M. (1947). *The Theory of Social and Economic Organization*. New York: Free Press.

Werr, A. and Stjernberg, T. (2003). 'Exploring Management Consulting Firms as Knowledge Systems'. *Organization Studies*, 24/6, 881–908.

Wright Mills, C. (1951). *White Collar: The American Middle Classes*. New York: Oxford University Press.

CHAPTER 15

....

MANAGING CONSULTANTS: CONTROL AND IDENTITY

....

MATS ALVESSON

15.1 INTRODUCTION

....

A lot of management consultancy is exercised by people working on their own, in small companies or in loose networks, sometimes under the same formal umbrella. Sometimes the 'organization' means little more than a shared office and mailbox. In these cases, issues around the management and organization of consultants as constraints and/or supports are not relevant. But many and perhaps an increasing number of consultants work in medium and large-sized firms, and this motivates an interest in how they are managed and how organizational conditions—structures as well as cultures and to some extent leadership—provide a mix of control, guidance, and support. This is the topic of this chapter, which provides a review of research on the management of consultants.

Management consultancy is sometimes hard to distinguish from other areas of advice and/or qualified external resource support. Psychologists, IT suppliers, legal advisors, engineers, communication specialists, and many others can sometimes be seen as part of an overall category of management consultants—'management' is a broad and vague field (see Galal, Richter, and Wendlandt, Chapter 6, this volume). Therefore, the chapter will occasionally invoke studies and literatures that cast a broader net, addressing knowledge-intensive and professional service firms and workers (see also Werr, Chapter 12; Kirkpatrick, Muzio, and Ackroyd, Chapter 9, both this volume), even if the relevance for management consultants remains the guideline for their inclusion. The chapter starts with a brief summary of various views on the nature of consultancy work and then highlights some key characteristics of the work situation of consultants, as identified in the extant literature, before addressing problems and possibilities for future research on managing consultants. Here the interplay between internal management and client control—clients are directly and indirectly central in the management of consulting—is emphasized. The subsequent section deals with identity, addressing the individual as well as organizational levels, followed by a brief conclusion with suggestions for future research.

15.2 CONSULTANCY WORK: SOME BASIC POSITIONS OF UNDERSTANDING

This is of course not the place for an ambitious review of approaches to the overall understanding of management consultancy, but two basic aspects on how to approach key themes in the literature are worth bringing forward to illustrate various ways of framing the preconditions for the management of consultants (see also Werr, Chapter 12, this volume).

Many *functionalist* authors assume a certain level of rationality and 'value-creation' as a key element in 'normal' consultancy and other knowledge-intensive work. This assumption may be implicit. The wealth of studies focusing on knowledge in management consultancy and other professional service firms often displays an impression of actors capable of delivering something valuable through rational interventions based on sophisticated knowledge. Consultants are assumed to create value through esoteric expertise and the use of knowledge systems, to solve problems, and to act as knowledge brokers (for example, Løwendahl 1997; Sarvary 1999; Schein 2002; Werr and Stjernberg 2003). The rapid expansion of the consultancy business is sometimes viewed as evidence that it makes important contributions to client organizations and society (Poulfelt 1999). Management issues here seem fairly straightforward: recruit and develop qualified people; develop and apply knowledge; get the right culture, identity, and structure in place; and work to improve structures and mechanisms so that a high-quality consultancy service, to which the market is likely to respond positively, will be delivered. Good consultancy service leads to good outcomes—for clients and consultants alike. In addition, management is, of course, very much a matter of getting clients and maintaining and developing client relations. However, the focus of this chapter is on managing consultants, that is, the internal side.

What can be labeled an *agnostic–sceptical* position draws attention to the high level of ambiguity involved. Here the 'market knows best' argument is questioned. Sharma (1997) makes the point that the market is highly inefficient with regards to professional services—the quality of service is not easy to assess and there is seldom any systematic and comprehensive communication between clients about the outcomes they experienced, so it is difficult for the market to react 'rationally'. Reputation (from gossip and personal impressions), image, and personal relations may matter more than the 'objective' quality of services (Clark 1995). Sceptics emphasize the ambiguity of work and performances

(Engwall and Kipping 2002; Alvesson 2004) and highlight the uncertainty surrounding what clients actually get from consultants (Ernst and Kieser 2003). Some even point at negative contributions by stressing the political issues salient in consultancy (Bloomfield and Danieli 1995; Alvesson and Johansson 2002).

Increasingly, authors (e.g. Sturdy 1997; Czarniawska and Mazza 2003; Alvesson 2004) also emphasize the uncertainty and anxiety of consultants in complex and uncertain work situations. Kitay and Wright (2004: 3) suggest that 'the image of the confident consultant/gullible manager may be balanced by the alternative of tough client/vulnerable consultant'. According to Jackall (1988: 141) the management consultancy industry 'fuels executive anxiety with a never-ending barrage of newly packaged schemes, all highly rational, most amelioristic'. Other authors also take this aspect seriously, particularly with respect to perceptions of fundamental changes, turbulence, and a repeated and high-voiced bombardment of calls for radical changes in managerial values and skills (Clark and Salaman 1996; Sturdy 1997; Jung and Kieser, Chapter 16, this volume).

A study of a consulting project where consultants as well as client representatives were interviewed indicated a wide variation of experiences concerning what was, if anything, actually accomplished, if the project was successful or not, and who was to be blamed/credited for the results—or the lack thereof. Interestingly, hardly any of the claims by each group about their own work and contributions were backed up by the other side (Alvesson and Sveningsson 2011). Consultants and client managers provided very different accounts, about themselves as well as the others. The—according to themselves—effective and focused consultants were viewed by the managers of the client firm as slick traders in sales and symbolism. The consultants were portrayed as superficial and greedy, more interested in additional sales than delivering, better at producing smoke-screens through mysterious concepts and overuse of overheads than really understanding and improving the client's business. Client managers saw themselves as substantive, robust, and delivery-focused, but according to the consultants they were spoiled, cautious, and incapable of providing leadership.

As emphasized, one important aspect of consultants is their situation in the middle or at the boundary of the client organization, creating a position as the 'other' (Kipping and Armbrüster 2002; Kitay and Wright 2004). As Deetz (1998: 157) writes, 'the largely fluid nature of anything external to interactional accomplishments provides for very active symbolic labour'. Varied and unstable social relations in work domains of high ambiguity, where competence and contribution sometimes are contested by significant others, lead to the need to secure a stable and positive sense of identity. This has important implications for the management of such organizations, as it needs to work with culture and identity in order to cope with uncertainty and vulnerability and give a clearer sense of direction.

This chapter reviews work based on the two approaches, but gives more emphasis to the second, as the high ambiguity of management consultancy needs to be taken seriously.

15.3 DIFFICULTIES IN MANAGING KNOWLEDGE WORKERS

The literature on managing consultants emphasizes that consultants—like (other) professionals—are difficult to manage. It is often claimed that models for the management of manufacturing and mass service companies have limited, if any, relevance for consultancy firms (Löwendahl 1997; Alvesson 2004). The high level of ambiguity associated with complex interactions, intangible work, political dilemmas, and often contested knowledge claims are important here, and the issue of complex work making professional knowledge and situation adaptation critical, also adds significantly to this.

A basic idea of management, at least as conventionally understood, is that of a separation between the planning and execution of a task. This is hardly a key feature of knowledge-intensive firms (KIFs), including consultancy firms. KIFs in this sense are, by definition, 'non-managerial' in vital respects, or are strongly characterized by informal management. Even though there is a trend towards strengthening managerialism and bureaucracy, in particularly in the large and expanding firms (Hinings, Brown, and Greenwood 1991; Greenwood and Empson 2003; Kipping and Kirkpatrick 2008), formal organization and management is still weak and partial compared to most other organizations. The more it makes sense to talk about knowledge-intensive activity, the less it makes sense to employ a (conventional) management model of thinking. Alvesson and Kärreman (2001) refer to knowledge management as an oxymoron. Operative authority, integration of planning and execution, the reliance on professional authority and judgement rather than bureaucratic position means a marginalization of management. Still, there are activities and functions that the concept of management illuminates productively. As the degree of knowledge intensity is not always particularly high in many KIFs—especially those which rely on organizational resources for the application of ready-made solutions—there is sometimes space for top management to also put its imprint on the organization (Maister 1993; Løwendahl 1997; Hansen, Noria, and Tierney 1999). There are, of course, different views on this; some researchers espousing the functionalist view emphasize options for rational forms of management while ambiguity-oriented researchers emphasize the limits to such forms.

Irrespective of exact views on this, there is some agreement that management in most KIFs is strongly affected by the nature of the tasks and qualifications of the employees—both of which tend to weaken the significance and positional power of top management. In PSFs (professional service firms), based on partnerships, there are frequently tensions between collegial decision-making, exercised by the partner peer group, and positional power, exercised by managing partners (Greenwood, Hinings, and Brown 1990; Hinings, Brown, and Greenwood 1991). As Greenwood, Hinings, and Brown (1990: 750) highlight, in the professional partnership 'strategic direction is weak, and the strategic process is one of negotiation, consensus building, and iteration. Implementing a strategic decision depends on widespread acceptance and professional conviction rather than on corporate manipulation of resources, rewards, and sanctions'.

Even though only 17 per cent of the world's largest management consultancy firms are partnerships (Greenwood and Empson 2003), broadly similar characteristics can be found in many other firms in the field. Leadership in the context of strategic and other broad organizational issues is frequently not salient in KIFs. Management tends to be loose and informal (von Nordenflycht 2010). Due to the complexity of work senior managers frequently do not understand what actually goes on and cannot rely on simple, indirect, quantified performance indicators to manage the process. To be innovative and adaptive, the whole organization must balance the tension between determination and emergence, that is, provide and enforce guidelines securing direction but give much space and support for ad hoc modes of working and individual initiatives.

Frequently, the managing partner in a partnership-based firm has limited influence, while, in non-partner-based consulting firms, the CEO and division manager may work more with administration than strategic decision-making. There is a change of professional service organizations in the direction of greater managerialism, that is, departing from pure models of partnerships towards strengthening management and strategy and creating an integrated firm (Greenwood, Hinings, and Brown 1990; Morris and Molhotra 2002; McDougald and Greenwood, Chapter 5, this volume). But, as several studies show, sometimes this is difficult. Even a law firm that developed strategic plans and management systems, and was trying to concentrate power in the hands of a managing partner was still seen by people in the company as similar to a fashionable store: 'a flash brand on the outside with a lot of franchises on the inside' (Morris and Molhotra 2002: 16). Löwendahl (1997: 63) refers to managers regarding the management of professional service firms as like 'herding wild cats' or 'making ten or twenty racing horses pull a cart together'. This calls for talent in negotiation and persuasion, but as most KIFs are capable of tolerating a fair degree of diversity, not all the horses have to pull the same cart or exactly in the same direction. There is, however, as will be explored below, the matter of counteracting too much diversity.

In some cases, however, there are one or two central actors, often the founder(s) of the firm, that have a guru status, and this person(s) may have considerable impact within a KIF (e.g. Alvesson 1995; Empson 1998; Robertson 1999). In established firms the founder is often gone, but the myth lives on and the influence continues through cultural meanings. This reflects the person-bound nature of consulting work. Strong persistence and persuasive powers may be needed, as people in the organization are used to acting and thinking comparatively independently and the possibilities of using formal authority and imposing sanctions are thus limited. This means that some kind of consensus—or at least a large majority support—around any change must be achieved. In large consultancies characterized by the up-or-out system, hierarchical differentiation combined with careful scrutiny and evaluation of the large number of junior employees contributes to the creation of discipline and the compliance of the personnel, reducing or even eliminating the possibility of 'herding wild cats' in at least parts of the organization (Alvesson and Kärreman 2007; Kärreman and Alvesson 2009).

The need for strategies and the regulating of constraints for employees are less strong in professional service firms (PSFs) than in many other organizations. As Løwendahl (1997: 63) writes, PSFs 'evolve through processes in which the flexibility of adding new clients, services and competent professionals is absolutely crucial'. Strategies are typically less deliberate (planned and centrally controlled decisions followed by implementation as distinctive steps) and more emergent (spontaneous), an outcome of the actions of various actors, acting and deciding almost simultaneously (Mintzberg and Waters 1985; Alvesson 1995). However, some direction is needed in terms of critical issues such as recruitment of new professionals and the portfolio of projects and clients served. To utilize, build upon, and expand the competence is vital and it is risky if this is totally ad hoc and opportunity-driven. Strategic management here becomes more like setting broad parameters and counteracting too much variety than commander-like (Mintzberg and Waters 1985) and involves the development and communication of a consensus-based vision, broad objectives, and a set of priorities (Løwendahl 1997).

Even though many management issues around making strategic decisions, exercising detailed control over subordinates, and making large bureaucratic machinery work are less important for top managers in most KIFs than in many other organizations, there are some management tasks that are significant in KIFs such as management consulting organizations (Løwendahl 1997; Newell et al. 2002; Alvesson 2004). These may include

- creating social integration within the company through managing borders and creating the feeling of a common purpose and community around an organizational identity;
- working with indirect forms of control, that is, normative control, through strengthening common beliefs and values; for example, trying to influence, maintain, and develop organizational culture and corporate identity;
- working towards the client orientation of employees and the satisfaction of important clients. This includes the nurturing of relationships, management of expectations, and perceived quality of important clients. This is most critical in PSFs and in some product-focused KIFs offering tailor-made systems and products;
- working with the development and reproduction of a corporate image and a shared feeling of organizational identity, providing a support for ongoing image management carried out by all employees;
- recruitment, motivation, retention, and mobilization of employees;
- improving the use of knowledge by encouraging employees to build upon existing resources, through knowledge sharing and co-operation across the organization;
- stimulation of innovativeness through development projects and the combination of various competences (knowledge management).

Many of these points can be seen as being contingent upon the high level of ambiguity and need for consistent effort and support to stabilize a sense of the corporate world and its external relations.

It is often believed that 'knowledge work is best conducted in "organic" and informal settings, with egalitarian cultures and where horizontal, as opposed to vertical, communication dominates' (Newell et al. 2002: 98). Although researchers tend to agree about knowledge work often thriving best in such contexts there are strong empirical indications suggesting a significant degree of diversity, to be elaborated in the next section. Some of the largest consulting firms have rather strong bureaucratic features, with hierarchical differentiation and elaborated systems, structures, and procedures for such activities as human resources management (HRM) (Alvesson and Kärreman 2007, 2011; Kipping and Kirkpatrick 2007). Here management style is a combination of strong normative and technocratic control (Kärreman and Alvesson 2004).

To sum up, managing consultants is affected by much of the work calling for operative authority, that is, those doing the job need to have considerable discretion and authority over how the work is actually done. Like other professionals, consultants expect autonomy and collegiality rather than strict hierarchy. Knowledge hierarchies may be inconsistent with organizational hierarchies. Ambiguities also undermine hierarchical control. Important managerial tasks include dealing with expectations and image, negotiating reality claims, dealing with flexible but not too weak boundaries, tying personnel to the employing firm, and so forth.

15.4 FORMS OF CONTROL

15.4.1 In-house Control

Management—in general as well as in KIFs—may involve a multitude of different forms of control. Varying modes are used, ranging from hierarchical and bureaucratic modes of control such as the monitoring of behaviour to rewards such as pay and promotion, to non-pecuniary rewards such as confirmation, status, and the assignment to appealing tasks.

Most organizations use the entire spectrum, but in very different ways. Some KIFs have relatively strong hierarchical and bureaucratic features (Akehurst 1994; Covaleski et al. 1998; Kärreman and Alvesson 2004), others, and probably most, exhibit the opposite qualities (Alvesson 1995; Morris and Empson 1998; Starbuck 1992). The former tendency is partly related to size. Also, firms working a lot with the reuse and implementation of known solutions and not doing much innovative work can sometimes deviate quite a lot from the organic organizational form (cf. Mintzberg's (1983) concept of professional bureaucracy). A partnership system—at least when the ratio of partners/non-partners is high—also seems to fuel hierarchy through making the steps between partners and others significant (Maister 1993). The recruitment of large numbers of graduates working as assistants or in other junior positions for some years is central for the differentiation. Sometimes junior people feel strongly subordinated and exploited as they are exposed to strong pressure to work long weeks and deliver on time (Costas and Fleming 2009;

Kärreman and Alvesson 2009). Apparently, there has been a change over the years from consultancies mainly recruiting and being populated by experienced people to, more recently, in some cases, mainly recruiting graduates and then relying on structures, differentiation, and control to develop and supervise them (Kipping and Kirkpatrick 2008; also Engwall, Chapter 18, this volume).

Studies have shown considerable differences between KIFs in terms of hierarchy and leverage—in particular, in large organizations with rather large projects structured and supported by methodologies and procedures, junior people under supervision can carry out a large portion of the work (Maister 1993). Maister has introduced the concept of 'leverage' to refer to the hierarchical competence structure of work done by a combination of senior and junior professionals. In project teams firms try to leverage the skills of senior people with the efforts of junior people. Through the supervision and support of the senior person the juniors can contribute above their competence level. Since firms also charge quite a lot for the service of the junior professionals compared to their pay, this surplus, in combination with the often large number of juniors compared to seniors, means that juniors are quite profitable and that firms often try to use work models and relationships where as many junior professionals as possible work together with one or a few seniors and perhaps a couple of 'medium-experienced' professionals. In certain industries, including law and accounting, hierarchy is typically weaker and frequently the ratio of partners/non-partners is lower, although there is also variation within industries (Greenwood, Hinings, and Brown 1990), partly depending on whether the firm is using a personalized or codified knowledge strategy, the former meaning that there is a higher ratio of senior to junior consultants (Maister 1993; Hansen, Noria, and Tierney 1999). Still, however, within the fairly large partner group collegial orientations prevail to a higher degree than in companies where the CEO and the board of directors are often clearly above the others.

Despite the variations, control targeted at the values, ideas, beliefs, emotions, and identifications of people, characterize much management in knowledge-intensive firms. Organizational culture, identity, and branding have been found to be areas of significance for management in consultancies (Wilkins and Ouchi 1983; Alvesson 1995; Kärreman and Rylander 2008). Some of this normative influence may be similar across firms, as part of broader industrial–professional cultures, so this does not necessarily imply the existence of unique organizational cultures. Similar efforts and ambitions to manage or engineer culture can characterize many firms. Elements in industrial and occupational cultures may influence how managers try to shape the values and ideas of other people at the organizational level. Some follow a fairly strict 'up-or-out' logic—either people clearly improve and get promoted or are expected to leave the firm. It is impossible to continue at the same hierarchical level for long. This encourages strong career orientations, which exercise a high degree of disciplinary power over people eager to be assessed positively. Extensive HRM systems, with feedback, appraisals, competence-development possibilities, the ranking of employees within a group or unit, and much time and energy going into promotion decisions strengthen 'improvement' and performance-focused subjectivities. Even though it is difficult to make such systems work according to plan—ambiguities and deviations from blueprints tend to creep in—they nevertheless appear to have a strong symbolic significance that imprints on organizational cultures, and are key ingredients in organizational control in some firms (Alvesson and Kärreman 2007). Other firms are almost the opposite, with emphasis on informality and community, shared values, and a downplaying of instrumental rewards like promotion, titles, and strong wage differentiation (as in up-or-out firms) (Alvesson and Robertson 2006).

In some cases 'alternative incentive mechanisms' are being used to reward and retain people. These are not based on short-term performances—often difficult to assess—but on long-term contributions to, and value for, the firm. The partnership system, and also stock options, and collegial control rather than outside ownership are often central here (von Nordenflycht 2010). But here, too, research has found considerable variation as different firms work with a mix of long-term incentive ingredients (Greenwood and Empson 2003).

Despite the variation and the presence of a fair amount of hierarchy and bureaucracy in many large consultancy firms at least, and especially in those built on up-or-out logics, it is fair to say that a considerable amount of self-organization is necessary within management consultancies, which calls for some degree of influence over cultural orientations and identity to make people inclined to voluntarily (that is, in the absence of monitoring) do what is considered to be the 'right thing'. But, as the extant literature suggests, the management and control of consultants are only partially conducted through management and organizational arrangements of the consulting firm. Equally important is the role of the client (see also Fincham, Chapter 20, this volume).

15.4.2 'Outsourcing' Control: Management through Clients

In a consultancy working directly for a customer/client, client control has been identified as a significant part of the overall control structure. More generally, customers are increasingly used as a source of control in business (du Gay and Salaman 1992). Gabriel (2005) views the contemporary organization as a glass cage—rather than a Weberian iron cage—where transparency and visibility from a variety of angles and agents are part of the control. Management is then bringing forward the customer/client as an evaluator of performances and the employee is encouraged to satisfy the customer rather than be so attentive to, or controlled by, the supervisor, risking sanctions if there are indicators of not accomplishing this.

Client control can be exercised in three ways (Alvesson 2004). The most obvious one is when the client makes explicit demands, referring to a contract or demands not formally regulated. The client then acts like a manager, supervising the service/product supplier. A second is when the consulting firm internally emphasizes client orientation and views making the client happy as a major objective for work. The client is not directly exercising control, but the explicit focus on satisfying the client becomes a major element of control. Sometimes this is accomplished through the use of client satisfaction surveys—the client is interviewed by senior people from the PSF and the (dis)satisfaction noted is reported back to the project manager and/or stored in the corporate memory and plays a role in wage setting and future promotion decisions.

A third version of client control concerns the more abstract constructions of the client and how the mobilization of employee attention and motivation is accomplished through the general notion of 'client orientation' and beliefs about what means rather than specific input or reactions of specific clients. Client orientation then is part of the organizational culture and as such guides people as a general value and guideline without necessarily including very much of a reality check in the form of the open-minded testing of the specific client and the demands and wants expressed by him or her. It is the idea or even 'fantasy' about the client that exercises governance. Assumptions and anticipations are important here, meaning that the 'outsourcing' of control also has a strong internal element through internal stories and other constructions of the client, producing and reproducing the ideology of 'client orientation'. Deetz (1997) reports from a case study of an IT group, AIMS, in which the personnel subordinated themselves to very demanding clients:

> In this surrogate management situation, not only did AIMS employees lack normal worker rights since they complied voluntarily to meet the client's needs, but they were also expected to placate clients and maintain friendly, supportive relations. (ibid.: 198–199)

Andersson-Gough, Grey, and Robson (2000) add to Deetz' study by showing how trainees in a large accounting firm do not only respond to specific clients or rely for their judgements on empirical tests—real-life encounters—but instead invent ideas of the client which then become true, at least in terms of control effects. Apart from the client having a concrete expression in the shape of people met and premises visited during work assignments, this notion also had 'an abstract and symbolic significance when invoked to justify general requirements of behaviour' (ibid.: 1171). A complication in client control is that the client is hardly a monolith. In client organizations there is typically a plurality of clients, with different interests and different relationships to the consultants. As Alvesson and colleagues (2009) therefore suggest, the client is not a given but needs to be constructed and reconstructed, as various client configurations may be more or less relevant at various stages during the process and for various representatives of the consulting firm as well. This, of course, adds to the complexity and ambiguity of the work of consultants, calling for flexibility in adaptation and relationship handling, including responsiveness to various control efforts.

In sum, research shows considerable variation between consultancies in terms of hierarchies and level of bureaucracy, although these forms of control tend to be softer and more flexible than in most other firms. Management often aims at influencing the values, ideas, beliefs, emotions, and identifications of people, leading to a focus on organizational culture, identity, and branding. As boundaries between consulting organizations and client organizations are weak and fluctuating in terms of work, control is, to a considerable degree, 'outsourced' to clients—as supervisors, referees, and/or 'images'.

15.5 Attracting, Retaining, and Motivating Consultants

Of course, all organizations need both human capital and human processes in order to work (Boxall and Steeneveld 1999). But as resources are not endless, the two elements may be prioritized differently. One extreme is the effort to exclusively go for the best and the brightest, another is to be satisfied with those sufficiently good—as good as possible, given the allocated money for wages—and put a lot of resources into optimal systems and procedures. These different approaches resemble personalized versus codified strategies for managing personnel and knowledge, in that the emphasis is either on very qualified personnel or databases for carrying out the work (Hansen, Noria, and Tierney 1999). The employment of the best people is often more viable in up-market kinds of consultancy work and in certain advanced R&D projects. In firms characterized by less unique and more routine work, in which previously used solutions can be drawn upon, a greater interest in trying to improve and control human processes makes more sense than employing and retaining highly qualified individuals. Most such firms have, by definition, limited resources for recruiting and retaining (those perceived as) very good people, and lack the reputation and/or the kind of tasks needed for being seen as a really attractive employer by these people. A particular problem for many knowledge-intensive firms, especially in service industries like management consultancy, is not only to recruit but also to retain their key personnel, therefore commitment and loyalty are significant issues that need to be carefully managed (Alvesson 1995; Løwendahl 1997; Davenport and Prusak 1998; Deetz 1998). While it is a standard problem for all firms to attract, retain, and develop competent personnel, this theme is amplified in many KIFs due to two circumstances:

- People are by far the most significant—sometimes the only significant—'resource' of the company. Capital and equipment are normally not of great importance in consulting firms, although the need for capital is increasing somewhat as mergers and acquisitions and internationalization are becoming more common. Still, highly qualified personnel are of greater significance in consultancy than in almost any other type of organization.
- In many cases, an established company may risk entire groups leaving the organization and forming new firms, trying to take 'their' clients with them, thus emptying the former firms not only of important personnel but also of clients.

As Maister (1982) highlights, PSFs compete in two markets simultaneously, the 'output' market for its services and the 'input' market for attracting and keeping the professional workforce. These markets are closely related: a loss in one may affect the other. When a qualified consultant (or a group) leaves a firm, sometimes his/her clients may also be lost. In addition, professionals generally expect a great deal of autonomy and although consultants often reject formal professionalization (Alexius 2007; see also Kirkpatrick, Muzio, and Ackroyd, Chapter 9, this volume) they are seen by many researchers as part of a broader set of professional service or knowledge-intensive organizations, and the autonomy norm puts its imprint on the expectations of the consultants and others. Due to the consulting firm's dependence on qualified labour, including networks of experienced people, the bargaining power of qualified consultants is often strong (von Nordenflycht 2010). Similarly, Drucker emphasizes the dependence of these organizations on their personnel, and the strong bargaining power and relative independence of large groups of knowledge workers. He stresses that in knowledge work, the means of production are now owned by the knowledge worker. They are mobile and can work anywhere. They keep their résumés in their bottom drawer. Consequently, they must be managed as 'volunteers', not as employees. Only the unskilled need the employer more than the employer needs them (summarized in Kreiner and Mouritsen 2003: 233).

This may exaggerate the power of the individual knowledge worker, in particular in large consultancies. While their consultants greatly benefit from organizational belonging and the resources of the organization, the firms still tends to be highly dependent on qualified personnel, making human resources a key issue. To address this challenge, consulting firms work with a set of models for attracting personnel, from highly instrumental reward packages, including ownership (partnership), to emphasizing specific organizational cultures and trying to offer stimulating work (Alvesson and Kärreman 2011). One of the crucial mechanisms for loyalty and commitment, identified in the relevant literature, has been to construct distinct organizational identities and make employees identify with the organization. These findings will be discussed in some detail in the next section.

15.6 IDENTITY IN CONSULTING FIRMS AND WORK

15.6.1 The Importance of Identity

In organizations and occupations where formal rules regulating behaviour are of marginal relevance and effectiveness and simple output measurement only gives a very partial indication of what is being done and accomplished, normative control is central. This is the case in consulting firms and other KIFs (Perrow 1979; Ouchi 1980). Here, organizational culture is a key area (Alvesson 2002). Partly overlapping but also addressing somewhat different aspects are organizational and individual identities (Hatch and Schultz 2002; Alvesson and Empson 2008). These in turn are paralleled and reinforced by image and branding (Alvesson 2004; Kärreman and Rylander 2008). For reasons of space and in order to connect to the theme of anxiety and the difficulties of coping with work indicated above, this section concentrates on identity. However, identity needs to be considered in its cultural context—culture frames how identity constructions are being made. Identity is of particular relevance to consider in the context of KIFs for a variety of reasons, including (i) accomplishing organizational control, (ii) creating an internal, organizational basis for image management, (iii) securing loyalty and retention, and (iv) counteracting existential uncertainty and building self-confidence and self-esteem at work (Alvesson 2004; Alvesson and Robertson 2006).

Perhaps the most significant theme, from a managerial point of view, is that identity—like culture—is a central dimension of control in work that provides considerable space for employees to act based on their own understanding of work. Themes such as knowledge sharing, client orientation in PSFs, and a focus on commercially useful work in knowledge-based companies are highly contingent upon how knowledge workers define themselves, within the context of how they define their organization and their relationship to (identification with) it. When hierarchical and technical means cannot prescribe behaviour in detail due to the complexity and organic nature of the work tasks, the self-image and social group(s) through which the worker defines him/herself become of great significance. Identity (especially regarding its construction and activation process) is therefore a theme of great relevance for understanding the management and working life of consulting firms (Alvesson and Empson 2008; Costas and Fleming 2009; Kärreman and Alvesson 2009). It is somewhat connected to the organizational culture theme as it relates to the realm of how people think, feel, and value. Culture is an important aspect of what shapes identity. Identity, however, goes beyond culture, indicating how people define themselves, which involves individual issues, while culture refers to socially shared meanings and ideas. Most aspects of culture have only indirect consequences for identity constructions, as they do not primarily refer to people's identities, but to all sorts of meanings around the environment, work, time, structure, and so forth (Alvesson 2002).

A second theme identified in the literature concerns the importance of supporting and living the image (or corporate brand) through a set of orientations that ensure people are able to communicate the image both in specific, image-selling situations such as presentations, which are highly crucial in consulting work (Clark 1995), and in everyday work situations (Alvesson 2004; Kärreman and Rylander 2008). It is not necessary, nor perhaps profitable, to produce identities that perfectly match the aspired image, but if the discrepancy is too strong, the image may be undermined by employee behaviour that deviates from the norm. Appearance is vital and this is typically partly an outcome of identity, a key resource for impression management.

A third theme is related to the presence of multiple, competing identities and the significant negative consequences of the potential lack of loyalty of employees towards KIFs. Issues of social identification are, in general, of great importance as they relate to the emotions, thinking, and behaviour of people (Turner 1984; Ashforth and Mael 1989). However, in knowledge-intensive work, competition and ambiguities around this topic become even more significant than in many other workplace contexts. Client relationships are often long-term and complex, which makes the chance of identifying with the client—and possibly changing employment or giving priority to the client's interest—far from insignificant. Consultants in long-term projects sometimes say that they know the client's organization better than their own (Alvesson 1995). In an IT consultancy unit, some people occasionally under-reported the (chargeable) time they worked for clients, for example, when they felt that they had not worked particularly effectively, thus favouring the client at the expense of the employing organization (Deetz 1995). Certain versions of 'client orientation' can thus undermine loyalty to the employer, for example, if the interest of the client to minimize costs is taken too seriously. The profession/occupation is often a very strong source of social identity, even though consultants typically reject formal professionalization (see Kirkpatrick, Muzio, and Ackroyd, Chapter 9, this volume). Managers of KIFs, in particular PSFs, often try to encourage a strong identification with the company, even though there are other routes to loyalty than through identity, such as those through money and ownership (Alvesson 2000).

A fourth theme follows from the significance of work identity for people in knowledge-intensive occupations in combination with the ambiguities of a lot of knowledge-intensive work. In many other jobs, where people view the job mostly as a way of providing an income, work identity is less crucial for the self. But for most people in KIFs much is at stake. In many KIFs there is a blurring of boundaries between self and work/organization (Costas and Fleming 2009; Kärreman and Alvesson 2009). In KIFs, where work and organizational contexts are weak on 'substance' and where frequent assessment of work quality is difficult, some vital sources for the stabilization and reinforcement of identity that work well in other job contexts are only modestly helpful. These include, for example, practical mastery of physical objects, direct feedback from people receiving the service, and a stable social environment. Instead, in many KIFs in general and perhaps consultancies in particular, there are the following sources of identity problems: instability of work and relations (teams, clients, work contexts), questioning and scepticism from significant parts of the environment hostile to management consulting, multiple identifications associated with employer, occupation, and client as well as liminality (on the last point, see Czarniawska and Mazza 2003; see also Chapter 21, this volume). Several ingredients thus add to the ambiguities and vulnerabilities of identity in many KIFs.

Identity at work is often targeted by management through encouraging identification with the organization and what this is perceived to stand for, leading us to the topic of organizational identity.

15.6.2 Organizational Identity

Identity is often defined in terms of its key characteristics: distinctiveness, endurance, and centrality (Albert and Whetten 1985), although critics remark that contemporary organizations and individuals may be more fragmented and malleable than this would suggest—particularly in a dynamic world (Gioia, Schultz, and Corley 2000; Brown 2006). For organizational identity to make sense, organizational members must broadly agree that the organization has certain distinctive features, that it differs from others in certain respects, and that its distinctive features characterize the organization in different situations and across various themes, such as decisions, actions, and policies.

Not all organizations are seen as particularly original or easy to portray in terms of a few key characteristics and some are not likely to attract much positive sentiment from their employees. Clearly, there is a strong variation between groups of people in these respects and it is important to consider this (Humphreys and Brown 2002). Arguably, not many people define themselves primarily through identification with their organization (Alvesson 2003). On the other hand, few people are totally decoupled from workplace group membership and there is frequently some positive affiliation with the organization; the perceived characteristics of at least some (valued) organizations inform the efforts of their employees in determining who they are (Ashforth and Mael 1989, 1996; Dutton, Dukerich, and Harquail 1994).

As research has shown, organizational identity can provide a focus for member identification in an insecure employment context; it can foster group cohesion within a diffuse authority structure; it can provide the basis for a tangible 'external' identity to counteract the intangibility and ambiguity of the service being offered; and it can represent a formal means of managerial control within an ambiguous work context (Empson 2004). All these qualities are potentially characteristic for consulting firms. Consultants have no physical product or clearly defined service and are often exposed to questioning and doubt and used as scapegoats (O'Shea and Madigan 1997; Alvesson and Sveningsson 2011). It therefore becomes important for them to have a clear sense of who they are and what they stand for as a source of support in work. These ideas are also central to the marketing of professional services, which depends on the self-confidence and persuasive style of the professionals (Alvesson 2004).

Research on consultancies indicates some variation in the key themes that people use in these kinds of organizations to construct an idea of what characterizes them (Alvesson and Empson 2008; Alvesson and Robertson 2006). In some organizations people emphasize specific versions of what they know (e.g. intellect, education), others of what they do (e.g. processes, methods), or how the organization is managed or controlled (e.g. through a unique corporate culture). For some it is the link between organization and employees that is key, whereas others emphasize how they share a certain distinct orientation, or how they believe others broadly see them, or how they differ from competitors.

Alvesson and Empson (2008) have shown that organizational members draw upon their powers of fantasy to reconstruct externally imposed pejorative metaphors. Rather than rejecting criticisms, organizational members can reframe and turn these metaphors into defensive, but more positively loaded, organizational identity constructions. Their research reports that in one firm people used 'the McDonald's of consulting' metaphor to draw attention to efficiency, reliability, value for money, and the worldwide success of the McDonalds. In another organization, the consultants, who could simply have accepted their position as a second-tier competitor of McKinsey, chose instead to present themselves as 'as clever as McKinsey but more interesting'. The consultants of a third firm recognized that they were often seen as 'plumbers' rather than 'architects' but at least they were 'first-rate plumbers'. A similar tactic was used by the managing director of a fourth firm, when turning the absence of an organizational identity focus to the firm's advantage: being perceived as anarchistic was interpreted as praise.

The technique used by these firms is not to reject fully the sceptical ascriptions of identity, but to reconstruct them and give them a more positive meaning. Other consulting firms provide more examples of modes through which firms can use different themes in order to construct a distinct, coherent, and appealing identity. One firm emphasizes having a progressive and unique management style and organizational culture (structured around 'fun and profit' as key values). Another focuses on being exceptionally good in selecting, developing, and promoting people. A third allows discretion and time for employees and thus being highly innovative and appealing from a work content and self-actualization point of view. A fourth underscores elite status through status symbolism (Alvesson and Robertson 2006). In these firms, identity constructions and specific packages of rewards and other material advantages go together in varied but distinctive ways.

Many consulting firms are eager to try to construct a self-view as elite, not necessary in all respects, but in certain key areas that are portrayed as particularly significant (Alvesson and Robertson 2006; Alvesson and Empson 2008). A construction of organizational identity that provides a basis for identification means that guidelines for action are offered as well as a means by which the fragmentation problems of consulting organizations—associated with people working autonomously in a variety of different assignments, at different locations, and for a variety of clients—are counteracted. In addition, a valued organizational identity facilitates self-esteem and a sense of stabilized self that counteracts the potentially problematic experiences associated with the need to adapt to a variety of groups, subordinate oneself to powerful individuals (and thus not insist on professional integrity), and face scepticism in an ambiguous and varied social world. In these respects, organizational and self-identity themes are a significant part of the operation of the management consulting business and key concerns for management to address (Alvesson and Empson 2008).

To sum up, the review of the literature in this section suggests that identity, identification, and organizational identity are important targets and vehicles for management control in consulting firms and other KIFs. Given the absence of a physical product or a service that can easily be described and the ambiguous and potentially fragmented nature of consultancy organizations, a construction of what the firm and its employees do represent becomes important. This is also significant when dealing with image management, loyalty, and existential security.

15.7 CONCLUSION

This review has indicated that management consulting firms are characterized, to a high degree, by operative autonomy, expectation of collegiality, and fairly loose management control. The nature of the work as well as professional norms and the bargaining powers of at least senior employees partly account for this. Informal means of control associated with culture and identity play a significant role. Another often used source of control is the client, either directly or through values such as client orientation or facilitating subordination to a real or imagined client. In many cases traditional control forms like formal structure, hierarchy, differentiation, and supervision also matter.

According to the extant literature, the reliance on fairly flexible or soft forms of bureaucracy seems to be expanding; this is associated to a degree with the increasing size of many consultancies. Partly related is the increasing practice of recruiting, training, and promoting young, inexperienced graduates, which calls for clear and elaborated structures and systems for support and control, and fairly fine-grained social differentiation and hierarchy. As consultancy work is difficult to control directly and there are strains on subjectivity following from fluid work relations, a liminal position between employer and client, frequent exposure to questioning from client personnel as well as from the public, ambiguous work results, and sometimes demands for very long work hours, identity regulation for control as well as support is important. Management control is then often focused on organizational identity and standards for self-identity. The significance of communicating the right image also matters here, as this needs back-up in the form of a clear and convincing sense of self. For these reasons consultancy firms tend to emphasize constructions and communication of organizational identity, and conduct identity regulation (of junior employees in particular) as an important part of management control.

Despite a fair bit of research on the management of consultants there are many areas that have not been studied in very much in detail. Thus, further research to explore the way the client is central in defining and controlling consulting work and how the interplay between 'in-house' and 'client control' affects consultants, seems necessary. The degree to which this effectively controls consultants or whether there is still much space for autonomy also appears as an important topic for more research. Generally, in-depth studies of consultancy work and how it is managed/supervised both inside a project and by senior managers monitoring the work are lacking. Another area of interest for further research concerns the regulation of the (dis)continuation of employment. A core principle for partnerships and some other organizations is the up-or-out principle. Control is then exercised through 'aspirational control'—playing on employees' eagerness to do well in order to stay and be promoted—although this also calls for 'exit management', that is, encouraging people to leave but in a 'soft' way so that they can remain part of the network and thus be useful resources for the organization.

References

Akehurst, G. (1994). 'Brownloaf-MacTaggart: Control and Power in a Management Consultancy'. In D. Adam-Smith and A. Peacock (eds), *Cases in Organizational Behaviour*. London: Pitman.

Albert, S. and Whetten, D. (1985). 'Organizational Identity'. In L. L. Cummings and B. M. Staw (eds), *Research in Organizational Behaviour*, vol. 7. Greenwich: JAI Press, 263–295.

Alexius, S. (2007). *Regelmotståndarna*. Stockholm: EFI.

Alvesson, M. (1995). *Management of Knowledge-Intensive Companies*. Berlin: De Gruyter.

Alvesson, M. (2000). 'Social Identity and the Problem of Loyalty in Knowledge-Intensive Companies'. *Journal of Management Studies*, 37/8, 1101–1123.

Alvesson, M. (2002). *Understanding Organizational Culture*. London: Sage.

Alvesson, M. (2003). 'Interpretive Unpacking: Moderately Destabilizing Identities and Images in Organization Studies'. In E. A. Locke (ed.), *Post Modernism and Management (Research in the Sociology of Organizations, 21)*. Amsterdam: Elsevier, 3–27.

Alvesson, M. (2004). *Knowledge Work and Knowledge-Intensive Firms*. Oxford: Oxford University Press.

Alvesson, M. and Empson, L. (2008). 'The Construction of Organizational Identity: Comparative Case Studies of Consulting Firms'. *Scandinavian Journal of Management*, 24/1, 1–16.

Alvesson, M. and Johansson, A. (2002). 'Professionalism and Politics in Management Consultancy Work'. In T. Clark and R. Fincham (eds), *Critical Consulting: New Perspectives on the Management Advice Industry*. Oxford: Blackwell, 228–246.

Alvesson, M. and Kärreman, D. (2001). 'Odd Couple: Making Sense of the Curious Concept of Knowledge Management'. *Journal of Management Studies*, 38/7, 995–1018.

Alvesson, M. and Kärreman, D. (2007). 'Unravelling HRM: Identity, Ceremony, and Control in a Management Consultancy Firm'. *Organization Science*, 18, 711–723.

Alvesson, M. and Kärreman, D. (2011). 'Meritocracy vs Sociocracy: Personnel Concepts and HR Themes in Two IT/Management Consulting Firms'. In S. Clegg, M. Harris and H. Höpl (eds), *Managing Modernity: Beyond Bureaucracy*. Oxford: Oxford University Press, 154–175.

Alvesson, M. and Robertson, M. (2006). 'The Brightest and the Best: The Role of Elite Identity in Knowledge Intensive Companies'. *Organization*, 13/2, 195–224.

Alvesson, M. and Sveningsson, S. (2011) 'Identity Work in Consultancy Projects: Ambiguity and Distribution of Credit and Blame'. In C. Candlin and J. Crichton (eds), *Discourses of Deficit*. London: Palgrave Macmillan, 159–174.

Alvesson, M., Kärreman, D., Sturdy, A., and Handley, K. (2009). 'Unpacking the Client(s): Constructions, Positions and Client–Consultant Dynamics'. *Scandinavian Journal of Management*, 25, 253–263.

Andersson-Gough, F., Grey, C., and Robson, K. (2000). 'In the Name of the Client: The Service Ethic in Two Professional Service Firms'. *Human Relations*, 53/9, 1151–1173.

Ashforth, B. and Mael, F. (1989). 'Social Identity Theory and the Organization'. *Academy of Management Review*, 14, 20–39.

Ashforth, B. and Mael, F. (1996). 'Organizational Identity and Strategy as a Context for the Individual'. *Advances in Strategic Management*, 13, 19–64.

Bloomfield, B. and Danieli, A. (1995). 'The Role of Management Consultants in the Development of Information Technology: The Indissoluble Nature of Socio-political and Technical Skills'. *Journal of Management Studies*, 32/1, 23–46.

Boxall, P. and Steeneveld, M. (1999). 'Human Resource Strategy and Competitive Advantage: A Longitudinal Study of Engineering Consultants'. *Journal of Management Studies*, 36/4, 443–463.

Brown, A. (2006). 'A Narrative Approach to Collective Identities'. *Journal of Management Studies*, 43/4, 731–754.

Clark, T. (1995). *Managing Consultants: Consultancy as the Management of Impressions*. Buckingham: Open University Press.

Clark, T. and Salaman, G. (1996). 'The Management Gurus as Organizational Witchdoctors'. *Organization*, 3/1, 85–107.

Costas, J. and Fleming, P. (2009). 'Beyond Dis-identification: A Discursive Approach to Self-Alienation in Contemporary Organizations'. *Human Relations*, 62/3, 353–378.

Covaleski, M., Dirsmith, M., Helan, J., and Samuel, S. (1998). 'The Calculated and the Avowed: Techniques of Discipline and Struggles over Identity in Big Six Public Accounting Firms'. *Administrative Science Quarterly*, 43, 293–327.

Czarniawska, B. and Mazza, C. (2003). 'Consulting as a Liminal Space'. *Human Relations*, 56/3, 267–290.

Davenport, T. and Prusak, L. (1998). *Working Knowledge*. Cambridge, MA: Harvard Business School Press.

Deetz, S. (1995). *Transforming Communication, Transforming Business: Building Responsive and Responsible Workplaces*. Cresskill, NJ: Hampton Press.

Deetz, S. (1997). 'The Business Concept and Managerial Control in Knowledge-Intensive Work: A Case Study of Discursive Power'. In B. D. Sypher (ed.), *Case Studies in Organizational Communication: Perspectives on Contemporary Work Life*. New York: Guilford, 183–212.

Deetz, S. (1998). 'Discursive Formations, Strategized Subordination, and Self-Surveillance'. In A. McKinley and K. Starkey (eds), *Foucault, Management and Organization Theory*. London: Sage, 151–172.

Du Gay, P. and Salaman, G. (1992). 'The Cult(ure) of the Customer'. *Journal of Management Studies*, 29/5, 615–633.

Dutton, J., Dukerich, J., and Harquail, C. (1994). 'Organizational Images and Member Identification'. *Administrative Science Quarterly*, 39, 239–263.

Empson, L. (1998). 'Mergers between Professional Service Firms: How the Distinctive Organizational Characteristics Influence the Process of Value Creation'. Ph.D. dissertation, London Business School.

Empson, L. (2004). 'Organizational Identity Change: Managerial Regulation and Member Identification in an Accounting Firm Acquisition'. *Accounting, Organizations and Society*, 29, 759–781.

Engwall, L. and Kipping, M. (2002). 'Introduction'. In M. Kipping and L. Engwall (eds), *Management Consulting: Emergence and Dynamics of a Knowledge Industry*. Oxford: Oxford University Press, 1–16.

Ernst, B. and Kieser, A. (2003). 'Do Practitioners Know What They are Getting from Consultants?' Faculty of Business Administration, University of Mannheim, Working paper.

Gabriel, Y. (2005). 'Class Cages and Glass Palaces: Images of Organizations in Image-Conscious Times'. *Organization*, 12/1, 9–27.

Gioia, D., Schultz, M., and Corley, K. (2000). 'Organizational Identity, Image and Adaptive Instability'. *Academy of Management Review*, 25/1, 63–81.

Greenwood, R. and Empson, L. (2003). 'The Professional Partnership: Relic or Exemplary Form of Governance?' *Organization Studies*, 24/6, 909–933.

Greenwood, R., Hinings, C. R., and Brown, J. L. (1990). 'P2-Form Strategic Management: Corporate Practices in Professional Partnerships'. *Academy of Management Journal*, 33/4, 725–755.

Hansen, M. T., Noria, N., and Tierney, T. (1999). 'What's your Strategy for Managing Knowledge?' *Harvard Business Review*, 72/2, 106–116.

Hatch, M. J. and Schultz, M. (2002). 'The Dynamics of Organizational Identity'. *Human Relations*, 55, 989–1018.

Hinings, C. R., Brown, J. L., and Greenwood, R. (1991). 'Change in an Autonomous Professional Organization'. *Journal of Management Studies*, 28, 375–389.

Humphreys, M. and Brown A. D. (2002). 'Narrative of Organizational Identity and Identification: A Case Study of Hegemony and Resistance'. *Organization Studies*, 23/3, 421–447.

Jackall, R. (1988). *Moral Mazes: The World of Corporate Managers*. Cambridge, MA: Oxford University Press.

Kärreman, D. and Alvesson, M. (2004). 'Cages in Tandem: Management Control, Social Identity, and Identification in a Knowledge-Intensive Firm'. *Organization*, 11/1, 149–175.

Kärreman, D. and Alvesson, M. (2009). 'Resistance to Resistance: Counter-Resistance, Consent and Compliance in a Consultancy Firm'. *Human Relations*, 62, 1115–1144.

Kärreman, D. and Rylander, A. (2008). 'Managing Meaning through Branding: The Case of a Consulting Firm'. *Organization Studies*, 29/1, 103–125.

Kipping, M. and Armbrüster, T. (2002). 'The Burden of Otherness: Limits of Consultancy Interventions in Historical Case Studies'. In M. Kipping and L. Engwall (eds), *Management Consulting: Emergence and Dynamics of a Knowledge Industry*. Oxford: Oxford University Press, 203–221.

Kipping, M. and Kirkpatrick, I. (2008). 'From Taylorism as Product to Taylorism as Process: Knowledge Intensive Firms in a Historical Perspective'. In D. Muzio, S. Ackroyd, and J-F. Chanlat (eds), *Redirections in the Study of Expert Labour: Established Professions and New Expert Occupations*. London: Palgrave Macmillan, 163–182.

Kitay, J. and Wright, C. (2004). 'Take the Money and Run? Organizational Boundaries and Consultants' Roles'. *Service Industries Journal*, 24/3, 1–19.

Kreiner, K. and Mouritsen, J. (2003). 'Knowledge Management as Technology: Making Knowledge Manageable'. In B. Czarniawska and G. Sevón (eds), *The Northern Lights: Organization Theory in Scandinavia*. Malmö, Oslo and Copenhagen: Liber, Abstrakt and Copenhagen Business School Press, 223–247.

Løwendahl, B. (1997). *Strategic Management in Professional Service Firms*. Copenhagen: Copenhagen Business School Press.

Maister, D. (1982). 'Balancing the Professional Service Firm'. *Sloan Management Review*, 24/1 (autumn), 15–29.

Maister, D. (1993). *Managing the Professional Service Firm*. New York: Free Press.

Mintzberg, H. (1983). *Structure in Fives: Designing Effective Organizations*. Englewood Cliffs, NJ: F. T. Prentice Hall.

Mintzberg, H. and Waters, J. A. (1985). 'Of Strategies, Deliberate and Emergent'. *Strategic Management Journal*, 6/3, 257–272.

Morris, T. and Empson, L. (1998). 'Organization and Expertise: An Exploration of Knowledge Bases and the Management of Accounting and Consulting Firms'. *Accounting, Organizations and Society*, 23/5–6, 609–624.

Morris, T. and Malhotra, N. (2002). 'Towards Managerialism: Analysing the Process of Change in Professional Service Organizations'. Paper presented at the 4th Biannual Workshop on Professional Service Firms, Alberta, August.

Newell, S., Robertson, M., Scarbrough, H., and Swan, J. (2002). *Managing Knowledge Work*. Basingstoke: Palgrave Macmillan.

O'Shea, J., and Madigan, C. (1997). *Dangerous Company: Management Consultants and the Businesses They Save and Ruin*. New York: Penguin Business.

Ouchi, W. G. (1980). 'Markets, Bureaucracies and Clans'. *Administrative Science Quarterly*, 25, 129–141.

Perrow, C. (1979). *Organization Theory: A Critical Perspective.* 2nd edn. Glenview, IL: Scott, Foreman and Co.

Poulfelt, F. (1999). 'Konsulentrollens Anatomi'. *Nordiske Organisasjons Studier,* 1/1, 25–48.

Robertson, M. (1999). 'Sustaining Knowledge Creation within Knowledge-Intensive Firms'. Ph.D. dissertation, Warwick Business School.

Sarvary, M. (1999). 'Knowledge Management and Competition in the Consulting Industry'. *California Management Review,* 41/2, 95–107.

Schein, E. (2002). 'Consulting: What Should It Mean?' In T. Clark and R. Fincham (eds), *Critical Consulting: New Perspectives on the Management Advice Industry.* Oxford: Blackwell, 21–27.

Sharma, A. (1997). 'Professional as Agent: Knowledge Asymmetry in Agency Exchange'. *Academy of Management Review,* 22, 758–798.

Starbuck, W. (1992). 'Learning by Knowledge-Intensive Firms'. *Journal of Management Studies,* 29/6, 713–740.

Sturdy, A. (1997). 'The Consultancy Process: An Insecure Business'. *Journal of Management Studies,* 34/3, 389–413.

Turner, J. (1984). 'Social Identification and Psychological Group Formation'. In H. Tajfel (ed.), *The Social Dimension,* vol. 2. Cambridge: Cambridge University Press, 518–539.

Von Nordenflycht, A. (2010). 'What is a Professional Service Firm? Towards a Theory and Taxonomy of Knowledge Intensive Firms'. *Academy of Management Review,* 35/1, 155–174.

Werr, A. and Stjernberg, T. (2003). 'Exploring Management Consulting Firms as Knowledge Systems'. *Organization Studies,* 24/6, 881–908.

Wilkins, A. and Ouchi, W. (1983). 'Efficient Cultures: Exploring the Relationship between Culture and Organizational Performance'. *Administrative Science Quarterly,* 28, 468–481.

PART 4

CONSULTANTS AND
MANAGEMENT
FASHION

··

CHAPTER 16

CONSULTANTS IN THE MANAGEMENT FASHION ARENA

··

NICOLE JUNG

ALFRED KIESER

16.1 INTRODUCTION

··

THE change in tastes and convictions as a reaction to past tastes and convictions has been called 'fashion' (Blumer 1969). Fashion is ubiquitous. No area of social life is immune to it. Fashion denotes artefacts that are in accordance with the ruling taste or with ruling convictions. Kawamura (2005: 4) proposes that fashion provides 'extra added value [. . .], but the additional value exists only in peoples' imaginations and beliefs', thus implying that following the crowd offers some—if subjective—advantages over deciding independently on the acquisition of clothes or other items. One advantage is that, according to Czarniawska (2008: 849), 'fashion is one of the ways of introducing order and uniformity into what might seem like an overwhelming variety of possibilities' (see also Esposito 2004). At the same time, fashion, to some extent at least, fosters innovation: individuals imitate approaches that appear to be attractive, which 'leads them to translate management ideas, objects, and practices for their own use. This translation changes what is translated and those who translate' (Czarniawska 2008: 851). Thus, fashion is paradoxical: individuals follow fashions to demonstrate their uniqueness (Esposito 2004). Fashion combines the orientation towards generally accepted examples with the need for distinction (Simmel 1957). Often, fashions are not necessarily reasonable at first sight (Veblen 1949: 115). To drive an off-road vehicle off-road is not necessarily fashionable. To drive it in a city, perhaps is.

Management knowledge is a field in which fashions are highly relevant phenomena. If one takes a look at the field of management over the past decades, one will notice that large fashion waves such as corporate culture, total quality management (TQM), or business process re-engineering (BPR) rolled over it and left some traces. Each of them was the focus of attention for some years, then faded from the management discourse either because they became matter of course—a practice generally implemented—or because they turned out to be flops. To speak about management without speaking about fashions seems to be as impossible as it is to speak about fashions without speaking about the consulting industry and its tremendous growth (see Part I of this Handbook). Not only are the names of consultants such as Tom Peters or James Champy closely linked to the creation of some of these fashionable concepts, consultancies also play a major role in the dissemination and local adaptation of management fashions. But how can consultants as 'rational experts' in a seemingly rational business world create and foster fashions whose implementation is not only paradoxical, but perhaps might not even be reasonable to some extent?

The existence and mode of operation of management fashions and the particular role(s) consultants play in this context will be the focus of this chapter, which will give an overview of the existing literature on the topic and conclude with some further thoughts on the future of fashions and consultants. In the following, the chapter will first describe some characteristics of management fashions as identified in the extant literature. The next section will present the different actors in the 'management fashion arena', as discussed in the literature, and ideas that have been proposed to highlight how different circumstances and particularities of fashions and consulting services collude to create a 'vicious circle' that leads to an ever new demand of consulting services and management fashions. Subsequently, the chapter will discuss the nature of the rhetoric that has been identified in the literature as helping consultants to establish management concepts as cure-alls and fashions. Drawing on the research about the relationship between consultants as producers and disseminators of a fashion and managers as its consumers, the chapter will then deal with a critical examination of current developments on the part of clients and their potential influence on the effectiveness and power of the consultants' strategies discussed so far. The last section will point out new directions for future research on management fashions and consultants.

16.2 Defining Management Fashions

Abrahamson (1996: 257) characterizes management fashion as 'a relatively transitory collective belief, disseminated by management fashion setters, that a management technique leads to rational management progress' (see also Carson et al. 2000). Whereas this definition suggests that a management fashion is triggered by an increasing number of people being convinced that a specific management technique increases performance, for other definitions it is the discourse around a management concept that constitutes a management fashion. The management concept is vague and usually gets vaguer during the discourse as different consultancies develop variants and other actors contribute interpretations. In this vein, Benders and van Veen (2001: 40) define fashions as 'patterns of production and consumption of temporarily intensive management discourse, and the organizational changes induced by and associated with this discourse'. Such a definition is in line with Kawamura's (2005: 78) definition of fashion in clothes, according to which fashion 'emanates from many sources and diffuses in various ways to different publics'. Actors in this system are fashion forecasters, fashion editors, department store buyers, fashion magazines, and periodicals. In the management fashion system—or arena—different actors play an important role, too, as will be discussed in the next section.

That a management fashion is rather the discourse around a concept than the actual changes triggered by it is also reflected in its measurement. Usually, a fashion is measured through the publications or citations that refer to it. However, bibliometric measures of this kind do not necessarily reflect a high rate of adoption and vice versa (Clark and Greatbatch 2004; see also Nijholt and Benders 2007). Of course, a management fashion as a discourse can nourish the strong collective belief in the rationality and potential for success of the underlying technique mentioned by Abrahamson (1996: 257). Changes induced by a management fashion discourse may become institutionalized and thus persist long after the respective discourse has come to an end (Perkmann and Spicer 2008). It is also perceivable that the organizational changes triggered by a fashion discourse are only of a peripheral nature and might even get revoked, or that a fashion discourse triggers changes that misrepresent the discourse. As Benders, van den Berg, and van Bijsterveld (1998) point out, it is not uncommon for consultants to interpret the contents of a management fashion like re-engineering differently, according to their customers' expectations or cultural backgrounds (see, e.g., Woywode 2002). In other words, it may be advisable to decouple a management fashion from the traces it leaves in organizations (Vastag and Whybarl 2003). Thus, a definition of management fashions as *management concepts that relatively speedily gain large shares in the public management discourse* seems to find broad acceptance.

But what is a management concept? Management concepts are 'fairly stable bodies of knowledge about what managers ought to do' and consist of 'a system of assumptions, accepted principles and rules of procedure' (Birkinshaw, Hamel, and Mol 2008: 828). Usually, a management concept starts with a text. A book or an article describes a new approach to solving a management problem or a bundle of problems. This text triggers comments, other articles, reports of applications of the concept, and so on. Sooner or later a label like 'TQM', 'lean production', or 'scientific management' is assigned to a new concept that is about to gain popularity. It is difficult to find out retrospectively which was first, the practice or the buzzword. Usually, an organization or a group of organizations that apply a certain practice become the object of a broader interest because this practice seems to solve a problem that many organizations are struggling with (Nicolai, Schulz, and Thomas 2010). The following two sections will take a closer look at the issues that define management fashions.

16.3 The Management Fashions Arena
and Its Participants

The literature suggests that the participants of a discourse around a management fashion can be seen as acting in an arena—the arena of the respective management fashion (Kieser 1997; Faust 2002; Clark 2004a; Green 2004; Parush 2008; see Figure 16.1). These actors include consultants, gurus, management scholars, editors of management magazines, commercial seminar organizers, and managers (see also Abrahamson 1996: 264). All these actors except managers are united in their goal to increase their profit or the profit of their organizations by increasing the discourse arena through luring further participants into it. Consultants, publishers, and seminar organizers can increase the sales and profit of their organization if managers or other interested people buy management books on the fashion, subscribe to management magazines that publish articles on the fashion, and attend and commission seminars. For academics, a fashion opens a field for publications—be they critical or supportive—and for occasional paid lectures.

Consultants, including academic consultants like Porter, Kaplan, or Norton, are seen by many authors (e.g. Abrahamson 1996; Fincham and Evans 1999; Faust 2002; Clark 2004a; David and Strang 2006) as creators of the majority of management fashions. They not only label a practice with a buzzword, but also feed the fashion discourse with the basic goals, principles, and advantages of a fashionable concept, and market this concept as a frame for potential consulting projects. Successful fashions like BPR meant projects of more than US$7 billion worldwide (Jackson 1996). The consultancy business

FIGURE 16.1 The arena of a management fashion

of James Champy, CSC Index, increased its turnover from US$30 million in 1988—that is before his co-authored book *Reengineering the Corporation* appeared—to US$150 million in 1993 (Jackson 1996: 576).

Another group of actors in the fashion arena are *management gurus* (see also Clark, Bhatanacharoen, and Greatbatch, Chapter 17, this volume). Gurus and consultants are sometimes difficult to distinguish and are often used interchangeably in the literature (Fincham 2002). Gurus are different from consultants insofar as they usually are not aiming in their public communication at generating consulting contracts, but rather at selling books and seminars in which they appear as stars (Huczynski 1993; Clark and Salaman 1996; ten Bos 2000; Jackson 2001; Greatbatch and Clark 2005). The guru seeks 'ideas suitable for mass appeal' (Fincham 2002: 203); he (with very few exceptions gurus are men) is a master of tastes and activates emotions (ten Bos and Heusinkveld 2007), whereas the consultant looks for techniques that he or she sells on the basis of rational arguments (Fincham 2002). Gurus primarily celebrate basic values and ideologies—values and ideologies that are not controversial among managers (for a study on the relationship between ideology and management fashion see Parush 2008). They transport these values and ideologies through gripping stories, many of which are hero stories (Greatbatch and Clark 2005; Collins 2007). Collective laughter triggered through jokes by the guru performer creates the impression of easiness and group cohesion (Greatbatch and Clark 2003). However, as ten Bos (2000: 21) emphasizes, 'it is virtually impossible to become a management guru without being a consultant'. But he also maintains that 'while it must be granted that many gurus are consultants, only a few consultants will become gurus' (ibid.: 21).

Management scholars are not suppliers of management fashions unless they fall into the category of 'scholar-consultants' (Adler and Beer 2008: 552; Werr and Greiner 2008: 94). Critically reflecting on management fashions and thus transferring them into the scholarly discourse is typical for management scholars, as Barley, Meyer, and Gash (1988) show with regard to the concept of organizational culture. Management science and consulting, it is suggested, follow different logics with the effect that not only the complexity of scientists' knowledge is higher than that of consultants, but that management science's overall structure of communication is more complex as well (Kieser and Wellstein 2007; Kieser and Leiner 2009). The consequence is that it is extremely difficult to transfer scientific management knowledge into practical problem-solving knowledge (Kelemen and Bansal 2002; Nicolai 2004). Nevertheless, communication in the management science arena can stimulate communication in the fashion arena (Astley and Zammuto 1992). Moreover, by theorizing popular management concepts (Colwyn-Jones and Dugdale 2002; Greenwood, Suddaby, and Hinings 2002; Scarbrough, Robertson, and Swan 2005)—even if in a critical, and sceptical manner (see as an example of a critical assessment of organizational culture, Alvesson 2002)—academics contribute to the legitimization of the respective management fashions. Sometimes consultants and gurus enlist academics as legitimators. Thus, in their bestselling management book, Peters and Waterman (1983) refer to, among others, Chester Barnard, Herbert Simon, and Karl Weick as providers of insights relevant for their work.

As a consequence of the different logics of management and academia, *popular media*, especially management books and professional journals—not scientific media—are seen as the main mediators of management fashions (Mazza 1998; Spell 2001). Publishers and editors provide a forum for the presentation of attractive management concepts— as sensationalistic as possible—and for their discussion from different perspectives, above all from the perspective of managers who have implemented them. Thereby, publishers and editors not only increase the interest in the fashion and the number of actors, but the sales of management books and magazine subscriptions. Thus, in this phase they are the consultants' allies. However, in a fashion's downswing they could as well become its enemies if they come to the conclusion that denouncing the fashion raises more interest than its continued support.

Professional groups also play a more active role in the dissemination of management fashions than scholars (Doorewaard and van Bijsterveld 2001; Scarbrough 2003; Fincham and Roslender 2004; Scarbrough, Robertson, and Swan 2005). Professional groups such as accountants or IT experts have been identified as gatekeepers for fashions and often have a substantial voice in assuring their adoption. In order to maintain legitimacy, professional groups feel called upon to develop an independent view of concepts that are propagated by consultancies. In this role, they often question the packaged solution of consultancies that leave little room for their participation in implementation processes (Heusinkveld and Benders 2005). As Scarbrough, Robertson, and Swan (2005) point out, the professionals' reinterpretations often lead to specific variants of a management fashion.

Moreover, *shareholders and analysts* have a role in the fashion arena. While Staw and Epstein (2000) found that companies which were reported to have implemented management fashions did *not* achieve higher economic performance, these companies nevertheless received more positive coverage in the press than their competitors and were perceived to be more innovative and better managed. Thus, following management fashions can generally contribute to a company's legitimacy. Last but not least, there are a number of other fashion intermediaries in the arena such as companies *offering training to managers* or *conference organizers* who also profit by making a concept more fashionable and a management fashion even more accessible and fashionable.

Besides the groups just mentioned, *managers* are important and often overlooked players in the management fashion arena. On the one hand, they are held up as the creators of some management fashions (Clark 2004a). For example, TQM emerged out of US companies' efforts in the 1980s to improve quality in response to the market losses to Japanese companies offering better quality (Cole 1999). Government initiatives like the foundation of the Baldrige Award in 1987 supported this movement of companies and of industry associations that resulted in the TQM fashion (Zbaracki 1998). Benchmarking is said to have been invented by Xerox managers (Camp 1995) and Six Sigma by managers from Motorola and General Electric (Pande, Neumann, and Cavenagh 2000). However, in these cases, the discourse seems to be fed mainly by consultants, including the inventing managers who increasingly take on the roles of consultants.

More importance is assigned to managers by the literature in their role as *consumers* of management fashions—the fashion arena would not exist without them. But why are managers attracted to fashions? One factor is that first movers, that is, managers who adopt a practice before it turns into a fashion, might be able to achieve a first mover advantage. However, since the advantage of a fashion is extremely hard to support empirically, managers often implement a fashion or a management concept as it emerges as a fashion simply because innovations are expected of them: 'The ideology of good management [...] associates managers with the introduction of new ideas, new organizational forms, new techniques, new products, or new moods' (March 1981: 573). What Simmel (1957: 548) wrote in 1904 about fashion in general still applies to managers: '[T]he individual derives the satisfaction of knowing that as adopted by him it [the fashion] still presents something special and striking, while at the same time he feels inwardly supported by a set of persons who are striving for the same thing [...].'

Following this logic, by adopting a management fashion, managers appear innovative while, at the same time, they feel safe since many others have already implemented the concept and many more will follow. In an increasingly complex and dynamic and thus rather uncontrollable inner and outer environment, the adoption of management fashions provides both an enhancement of (felt) control by the managers and legitimacy for the organization. According to the neo-institutional theory, this isomorphic behaviour is not an outflow of irrationality; rather, it can be interpreted as 'collective rationality' (DiMaggio and Powell 1983). What several other organizations do cannot be wrong; if one does not achieve an advantage by also doing it, one at least does not suffer a disadvantage with regard to others, because these others are also doing it, that is, they are also spending comparable amounts of money on the same measure. As Kant (2006: § 71) formulated: '[I]t is always better... to be a fool in fashion than a fool out of fashion.'

Managers are also seen to find management fashions attractive because they provide an ideological framing of restructuring programmes. For example, empowerment programmes (Ezzamel and Willmott 1994) as well as programmes for the implementation of internal markets (Eccles and White 1988), which are sold under the labels of decentralization and self-co-ordination, can in reality serve to make hierarchical control more effective. And by offering 'packaged solutions'—commodified instruments (Fincham 1995; Abrahamson 1996; Suddaby and Greenwood 2001; Heusinkveld and Benders 2005)—consultants legitimize projects and relieve the managers of a detailed reasoning and implementation design. Moreover, the management fashion delivers a pattern of argumentation that helps to interpret a complex restructuring project as worthwhile and successful—a matter in which initiators of the restructuring process typically have an elementary interest.

A proper evaluation of such projects, most authors agree, is not possible mainly because too many factors within the organization and its environment have changed during its progress, because the implemented concept is, to a large extent, an intangible product, and because many consequences of the project will only become evident some time in the future (Alvesson 1993; Meyer 1994; Clark 1995; Ernst and Kieser 2002). In such a situation, a fashion delivers 'ideas, metaphors, models, and words that impose order on a confusing world, thus reconstructing our appreciation of experience' (March 1991: 29). This is illustrated by Brunsson and Olsen's (1993) analysis of several large restructuring processes in the public sector. In several of these projects they found that next to nothing had changed at the level of operations—predominantly the communication about some management processes had changed—but management nevertheless expressed satisfaction with the results. In this way, management fashions facilitate reaching consensus that a reform was successful without having to prove that on the basis of empirical evidence. With the help of consultants the organization introduced a practice that everybody labels a 'best' or at least an appropriate practice.

However, as Ernst and Kieser (2002) argue, because there is an abundance of management concepts that all promise simplification, complexity actually increases. Moreover, the wave of projects along the current fashion is likely to intensify competition with regard to criteria that are at the centre of a fashion. Most competitors have, for example, improved quality, reduced personnel costs, sped up processes, or increased their customer orientation. Ultimately, insecurity has not only not been reduced, it has probably risen. In this situation, Ernst and Kieser (2002) suggest that receptivity towards a new management fashion tends to increase again. And managers who were not able to deal with previous fashions without the help of consultants are highly likely to call on consultants again. They have gained the impression that consultants are necessary to keep up with competitors that increasingly engage consultants. They are caught in a 'vicious circle'.

In this logic, consultants and managers are seen as the key actors in the fashion arena. Consultants generate fashions because fashions create demand for their services. With fashions, they simultaneously create certainty and uncertainty with clients. Uncertain clients often feel dependent on consultants. Here, a basic motivation of managers to follow fashions is that they can initiate innovations without having to take the risks that are usually connected to innovations.

16.4 COMMUNICATION IN THE FASHION ARENA

Several authors (Kieser 1997; Furusten 1999; Kelemen 2000; Røvik 2002; Green 2004) point out that whether a management concept turns into a fashion or not is, to a large extent, dependent on the rhetoric that the consultancy and other creators and intermediaries apply in propagating it. The literature sees the *buzzword* or *label* that arouses attention as a first important ingredient of this rhetoric (Swanson and Ramiller 1997; Furusten 1998). Good buzzwords are metaphors. *Re-engineering*, for example, implies more than a repair of the organization, it calls for a total redesign, while, at the same time, creating the impression that the organization can be engineered in a rational engineer-like manner. The *Balanced Scorecard* (Kaplan and Norton 1996) triggers associations with sports events, fitness, and championships.

Exemplification, personification, and dramatization are additional rhetorical ingredients regarded as important in the extant literature. Fashion setters, it is pointed out, should not present new management concepts as their own creations but as the condensed master plans of ingenious practitioners. Peters and Waterman, for example, do no more than explain *Lessons from America's Best-Run Companies*, as the subtitle of their book implies (Peters and Waterman 1983). Lean production is presented as being the masterful discovery of the 'young Japanese engineer' Eiji Toyoda and his 'production genius' Taichi Ohno (Womack, Jones, and Ross 1990: 53). As pointed out by, for example, Collins (2007) as well as by Greatbatch and Clark (2005), stories are easier to remember and to communicate than abstract principles or numerical data.

The core of a management concept is identified as a *vision* or *Leitbild* that consists of a number of goals and principles (Christenson and Walker 2004; van den Steen 2005). Visions that communicate management concepts fulfil, as Ramiller and Swanson (2003) explain, three basic functions: *interpretation, legitimization, and mobilization*. The vision provides a focus for interpretation efforts. On the basis of a vision, managers can reinterpret problems within their companies and initiate discourses that attract the attention of colleagues and subordinates. Legitimization can be derived from the cases of best practices that 'prove' the validity and power of the concept. The higher the reputation of early adopting companies, the higher the degree of legitimization that managers can derive from the management fashion. The values that a *Leitbild* conveys motivate—and mobilize—the addressees.

The literature further suggests that management concepts appear particularly attractive if they suggest simple solutions for solving problems that appear highly complex (Huczynski 1993; Furusten 1999; Collins 2000). Fashion setters achieve *simplification* in several ways, for example by concentrating on only one factor that is identified as being the most crucial factor for success, such as organizational culture (Peters and Waterman 1983), quality, leanness (Womack, Jones, and Ross 1990), intrapreneurship (Pinchot 1985), or virtuality (Chesbrough and Teece 1996). It also helps that the labels are most often metaphors: internal entrepreneurs are much more effective than powerful bureaucrats (Pinchot 1985), tent organizations more flexible than palace organizations, network organizations more adaptable than centralized conglomerates (Peters 1992), and boundaryless and virtual organizations are the most flexible of all. As has been highlighted by several authors, such strategies also result in a *vagueness* of the concept (Alvesson 1993; Fincham and Roslender 2004; Graham and Williams 2005; Giroux 2006) or, as Benders and van Veen (2001) term it, an 'interpretative viability', which is fostered by the discourse itself. Different actors, especially different consultancies, publish variations. The managers who follow the discourse interpret these variants as possible options and as design latitude. Such ambiguity is not only unavoidable but functional, as it, for example, permits managers to project the problems they perceive in their companies into the concept and this evokes the impression that the help of consultants is needed to concretize and implement a fashion.

Indeed this vagueness, the literature points out, requires that a management fashion is adapted into specific contexts (see, for example, Benders, van den Berg, and van Bijsterveld 1998; Woywode 2002; Fiss and Zajac 2004; Boxenbaum and Battilana 2005; Morris and Lancaster 2006; Rolfsen and Knutstad 2007; Sanders and Tuschke

2007). The fashion discourse itself describes a management fashion only vaguely so that the implementation process is not covered in any detail (Benders and van Veen 2001). The institutionalization of management fashions needs political, technical, and cultural work for adapting the concept and preparing the receiving organization (Perkmann and Spicer 2008). Here, an intra-organizational fashion arena is seen to build up, encompassing several actors and resembling the 'big' fashion arena. For instance, professionals and consultants who specialize in certain industries and countries assume important roles, adapting broad concepts into company-specific solutions. David and Strang (2006) show that, as a management fashion loses popularity and impact, generalist consultancies with weak links to the technical foundations of the fashion are increasingly replaced by specialist consultancies focusing on technical aspects.

In sum, since, as the literature has shown, the performance of a fashion's implementation is hardly assessable, a fashion's success—that is, the number of client organizations following the fashion and the volume of their investments into it—depends very much on the rhetoric with which the fashion is communicated. The fashion is communicated through a *Leitbild* or vision whose main characteristics are simplicity and vagueness. Simplicity increases the fashion's plausibility and vagueness permits the linking of the fashion with specific organizational problems.

16.5 RECENT CHANGES: WHITHER MANAGEMENT FASHIONS?

As the extant literature suggests, the success and effects of management fashions and the profits these yield for consultants largely depend on the consultants' abilities to stimulate the clients' needs with the help of processes such as those examined in the two previous sections. But while the critical literature has traditionally portrayed the client as very trusting towards consultants and as a 'victim' or 'marionette' of consultants' rhetoric, manipulation, and impression management (Clark 1995; see also Clark and Salaman 1996; Kieser 2002; Kipping and Armbrüster 2002), this notion is increasingly being questioned (Sturdy 1997a; Sturdy 1997b; Hislop 2002; Czarniawska and Mazza 2003). The distribution of power and control between clients and consultants today is regarded more and more as dynamic and dependent on situational characteristics, such as the competence and sophistication of the client in dealing with consulting projects (Sturdy 1997a; Sturdy 1997b; Fincham 1999; Werr and Styhre 2003).

In this context, recent empirical evidence suggests that clients have started to replace their hitherto rather informal, individual, and unsystematic approaches towards consulting projects and their 'lack of emphasis on outcomes' (McGivern 1983: 381; see also Stock and Zinszer 1987; Dawes, Dowling, and Patterson 1992; Wright and Kitay 2002) with more professional, sophisticated, and control-oriented ways of managing consultants (Bäcklund and Werr 2005; Lindberg and Furusten 2005; Mohe 2005; Werr and Pemer 2005; Werr and Pemer 2007). Clients, it is suggested, tend to increasingly formalize, centralize, and rationalize their management of consulting projects and show themselves to be quite critical and distrustful with respect to the consulting industry; they treat consultants and the 'buzzwords' they bring along more matter of factly or even cynically (Sturdy 1997a, 1997b; Engwall and Eriksson 2005; Jung 2008). Such developments might have consequences for future trends with regard to both the power of fashions in general and consultants' role in their creation and distribution more specifically.

Whereas, for example, a few years ago the IT sector was a breeding ground for important fashions such as ERP (Benders, Batenburg, and van der Blonk 2006), e-commerce, or the dot.com hype at the beginning of the millennium (see also Bloomfield and Coombs 1992; Bloomfield and Danieli 1995), Jung's (2008, 2010) qualitative study in eight client companies suggests that it is no longer sufficient that an (IT) solution is regarded and propagated as up to date for managers to have a detailed justification for its introduction (e.g. Ramiller and Swanson 2003). Instead, formalized project applications and cost-benefit analyses that demonstrate the business value of each investment are required to start a consulting project, and the consultants' performance is said to be increasingly evaluated *ex post* (see also Haferkamp and Drescher 2006). Moreover, the personal ties between managers and consultants are being intentionally broken more and more often (Bäcklund and Werr 2005) by involving purchasing departments as central gatekeepers in the selection and buying process (Lindberg and Furusten 2005; Jung 2008). Such arrangements could make it more difficult for consultants to sell their concepts to clients on the basis of their personal relationships with specific managers or by directly addressing managers' personal needs without offering real fundamental and verifiable improvements for the company as a whole.

Moreover, the individual managers themselves also seem to be eager to develop strategic aspects and the big picture by themselves and to only bring in consultants later on (Jung 2008, 2010) as well as to achieve tangible outcomes rather than only a concept on paper that is in danger of disappearing into a drawer (Richter 2004; Richter and Niewiem 2006). This also reflects the relative decline of strategy consultants indicated by Kipping (2002). Moreover, the clients in Jung's (2010) study increasingly attach importance to concepts or ideas that have already been successfully introduced in other companies. It seems difficult to impress them with the kind of dramatized stories of outstanding managers or companies described in the previous sections. They rather look for proof that the solution is used in companies 'within reach', that is, companies of the same industry or size and/or those that are known to the clients and where experiences with the solution can be sought. In this context, Nikolova, Reihlen, and Schlapfner (2009: 295) recently report a tendency in consultants' rhetoric to focus on tangible reference projects: 'Clients were not only presented with success stories, which were common to all other consulting companies, but also got to see "empirical evidence" as a support for the presented story.'

However, the latest academic research also reveals that some of the clients' developments towards a more sophisticated and tightly controlled management of consultants are predominantly rhetoric (Werr and Styhre 2003) or façades of rationality and organizational hypocrisy respectively (for these concepts, see Nystrom and Starbuck 1984; Brunsson 2002; see also Meyer and Rowan 1977). Thus, many of the measures introduced in the course of 'professionalizing' the purchase and management of consultancy services were not adhered to in everyday organizational life (Bäcklund and Werr 2005; Lindberg and Furusten 2005; Jung 2008). Often, many organizational members, including top managers, are not really interested in completely giving up their valued and trusted long-term relationships with their consultants and their freedom to select the consultants and projects they assume to be the best (see also Höner and Mohe 2009). However, in a business climate characterized by reproaches such as the uncontrolled growth of consultants within client companies (Mohe 2005) and the public denouncement of the consultants' tricks and misconduct, clients must increasingly and 'demonstrably' justify the use of consultants to shareholders and stakeholders.

The literature also points out that the (organizational) benefits and effects calculated in the run up to projects are very seldom re-audited and followed up on (Jung 2008; see also Grant et al. 2006). In many cases, it seems to be sufficient that any presentable and communicable result is achieved at all—for example, the error-free running of the information technology—even if the intended organizational changes were not realized. Moreover, if there are formalized *ex post* evaluations of the consultants' performance they still seem to be very subjective. In Jung's (2008) study, for example, these evaluations turned out to be short questionnaires to be completed by one person, for example the project manager, and contained subjective assessments rather than measurable results of the project's effectiveness and the consultants' contribution. Lindberg and Furusten (2005: 170) found similar evidence: 'There are even cases when the evaluation criteria included in the contract document are developed together with a specific consultant so as to fit that consultant perfectly.' Moreover, even if some clients apparently increasingly want to determine the cornerstones of their projects and strategies themselves, only bringing in consultants later on in the projects, this does not mean that consultants no longer influence idea generation or problem recognition. They still play an important role in shaping decision-makers' imagination of what is possible with the help of fashionable concepts, and through (informal) dialogues or regular workshops (Jung 2010).

Thus, while the more recent literature hints at potential restrictions in the future power of fashionable concepts and consultants' use of them, it also highlights the fact that there continues to be a place for management fashions, and that these fashions do not really have to deliver what they promise. These and other developments and issues discussed throughout the chapter, as well as their relationships, open up new directions for future research on the role of consultants and management fashions. The conclusion will point out some of the more important ones.

16.6 New Directions for Research

A first important direction for future research concerns the way management fashions are presented. Consultants and other participants in the management fashion arena might generally have to adjust their *rhetoric* in the future, moving away from the very broad visions and nowadays often critically viewed all-embracing 'buzzwords' as well as the universal validity of concepts towards more 'tangible', implementation-oriented rhetorical elements, as some of Nikolova, Reihlen, and Schlapfner's (2009) results suggest. Rhetoric that aims at exemplification might perhaps put a stronger focus on stories of 'successful' adoptions of management concepts in companies that are known to clients or similar to their own companies and where experiences can be exchanged, rather than on success stories of famous, outstanding companies. In this context, it might be interesting to take a look at the future *form and structure* of fashions. It may, for example, be small or local fashions, or variations of large ones, which are promoted and sold under different labels adjusted to a specific clientele, that gain in importance—concepts that do not create the impression that one merely follows a 'real' fashion.

Furthermore, it might be asked whether consultants will continue to play one of the most significant roles in the fashion arena and to what extent *actors* other than consultants could become more important. For instance, it is up to future research to gain a more comprehensive insight into whether clients' current efforts to 'professionalize' their approach towards consulting projects will erode consultants' impact and legitimation or whether the present changes might even rebuild the power of the consultants. For instance, if Jung (2008, 2010) is correct in thinking that clients' new formal, half-hearted evaluations of consulting projects are not necessarily more valid or comprehensive than the informal ones that had been carried out before, these evaluations will not help to break the 'vicious circle' of creating demand as depicted above. Rather, they might foster it. If these evaluations—which are still very subjective, easily manipulable, and thus seldom really negative—are taken as official, reliable, and objective assessments of the consultant's performance, they become 'proof' of the success of the consulting project. Thus, when insecurity rises again after some time, the cycle might continue with an even higher receptivity of managers towards a new management fashion. Carried to extremes, one might wonder whether being critical, evaluating, controlling, planning, and railing against consultants is just another fashion itself (Clark 2004b).

Furthermore, hitherto largely neglected participants in the management fashion arena and their interrelationship with consultants deserve a closer investigation. For projects, for example, where it is important to be innovative and up to date, Jung (2008, 2010) found that managers had more trust in the expert knowledge of software houses than in the consultancies, and believed the software providers to be more capable of real innovations; however, they also feared the software houses' biases and self-interests in assessing clients' situations and needs. Therefore, occasionally different—and thus more instead of fewer—external advisors were called in, with consultancies being used to review the concepts proposed by the software houses. In other areas of knowledge, it would be interesting to know whether financial analysts might perhaps gain importance as some kind of more trustworthy, 'independent' supra-experts and to what extent they might sanction clients' reliance on fashionable concepts. Do companies that explicitly distinguish themselves as followers of specific fashions like TQM or BPR impress analysts and investors and thereby increase shareholder value (Nicolai, Schulz, and Thomas 2010)?

Last but not least, a group scarcely explored not only in the literature on fashions but also on consulting per se are former consultants. Client managers with a background in consulting often seem to have 'created a more knowledgeable and potentially sceptical clientele for consultancy services' (Kitay and Wright 2003: 35). On the other hand, many consultancies establish and cultivate large and powerful networks with their former members (e.g. Byrne and McWilliams 1993; Wright 2002). Moreover, Sturdy and Wright's (2008) empirical results reveal former consultants' difficulties in identifying with their new employers. One might thus wonder what influence the growing linkages between clients and consultants, resulting from the consultants' diaspora, are going to have on future decisions with respect to consultants and management fashions, and to what extent clients might further develop their role not only as consumers, but also as producers of management fashions. Thus, much remains to be done in terms of future research on consultants in the management fashion arena.

References

Abrahamson, E. (1996). 'Management Fashion'. *Academy of Management Review*, 21, 254–285.

Adler, N. and Beer, M. (2008). 'Collaborative R&D in Management: The Practical Experience of FENIX and TruePoint in Bridging the Divide between Scientific and Managerial Goals'. In A. B. R. Shani, S. A. Mohrman, B. Stymne, and N. Adler (eds), *Handbook of Collaborative Management Research*. Los Angeles: Sage, 545–565.

Alvesson, M. (1993). 'Organization as Rhetoric: Knowledge-Intensive Firms and the Struggle with Ambiguity'. *Journal of Management Studies*, 30, 997–1015.

Alvesson, M. (2002). *Understanding Organizational Culture*. London: Sage.

Astley, W. G. and Zammuto, R. F. (1992). 'Organization Science, Managers, and Language Games'. *Organization Science*, 3, 443–460.

Bäcklund, J. and Werr, A. (2005). 'Breaking the Personal Tie: On the Formalization of the Procurement of Management Consulting Services'. In S. Furusten and A. Werr (eds), *Dealing With Confidence: The Construction of Need and Trust in Management Advisory Services*. Copenhagen: Copenhagen Business School Press, 184–200.

Barley, S. R., Meyer, G. W., and Gash, D. C. (1988). 'Cultures of Culture: Academics, Practitioners and the Pragmatics of Normative Control'. *Administrative Science Quarterly*, 33, 24–64.

Benders, J. and van Veen, K. (2001). 'What's in a Fashion: Interpretative Viability and Management Fashions'. *Organization*, 8, 33–53.

Benders, J., van den Berg, R.-J., and van Bijsterveld, M. (1998). 'Hitch-Hiking on a Hype: Dutch Consultants Engineering Re-Engineering'. *Journal of Product Innovation Management*, 11, 201–215.

Benders, J., Batenburg, R., and van der Blonk, H. (2006). 'Sticking to Standards: Technical and Other Isomorphic Pressures in Deploying ERP-Systems'. *Information and Management*, 43, 194–203.

Birkinshaw, J., Hamel, G., and Mol, M. J. (2008). 'Management Innovation'. *Academy of Management Review*, 33, 825–845.

Bloomfield, B. and Coombs, R. (1992). 'Information Technology, Control and Power: The Centralization and Decentralization Debate Revisited'. *Journal of Management Studies*, 29, 459–484.

Bloomfield, B. P. and Danieli, A. (1995). 'The Role of Management Consultants in the Development of Information Technology: The Indissoluble Nature of Socio-Political and Technical Skills'. *Journal of Management Studies*, 33, 27–46.

Blumer, H. (1969). 'Fashion: From Class Differentiation to Collective Selection'. *Sociological Quarterly*, 10, 275–291.

Boxenbaum, E. and Battilana, J. (2005). 'Importation as Innovation: Transposing Managerial Practices across Fields'. *Strategic Organization*, 3/4, 355–383.

Brunsson, N. (2002). *The Organization of Hypocrisy: Talk, Decisions and Actions in Organizations*. Copenhagen: Copenhagen Business School Press.

Brunsson, N. and Olsen, J. P. (1993). *The Reforming Organization*. London: Routledge.

Byrne, J. A. and McWilliams, G. (1993). 'The Alumni Club to End All Alumni Clubs'. *Business Week*, 20/9, 41.

Camp, R. C. (1995). *Benchmarking: The Search for Industry Best Practices that Lead to Superior Performance*. New York: ASQC Quality Press.

Carson, P. P., Lanier, P. A., Carson, K. D., and Guidry, B. N. (2000). 'Clearing a Path through the Management Fashion Jungle: Some Preliminary Trailblazing'. *Organization Science*, 43, 1143–1158.

Chesbrough, H. W. and Teece, D. J. (1996). 'When Is Virtual Virtuous? Organizing for Innovation'. *Harvard Business Review*, 74 (January–February), 65–73.

Christenson, D. and Walker, D. H. T. (2004). 'Understanding the Role of "Vision" in Project Success'. *Project Management Journal*, 35/3, 39–52.

Clark, T. (1995). *Managing Consultants: Consultancy as the Management of Impressions*. Buckingham: Open University Press.

Clark, T. (2004a). 'Strategy Viewed From a Management Fashion Perspective'. *European Management Review*, 1, 105–111.

Clark, T. (2004b). 'The Fashion of Management Fashion: A Surge too Far'. *Organization*, 11, 271–280.

Clark, T. and Greatbatch, D. (2004). 'Management Fashion as Image-Spectacle: The Production of Best-Selling Books'. *Management Communication Quarterly*, 17, 396–424.

Clark, T. and Salaman, G. (1996). 'The Management Guru as Organizational Witchdoctor'. *Organization*, 3, 85–108.

Cole, R. E. (1999). *Managing Quality Fads*. New York: Oxford University Press.

Collins, D. (2000). *Management Fads and Buzzwords: Critical-Practical Perspectives*. London: Routledge.

Collins, D. (2007). *Narrating the Management Guru: In Search of Tom Peters*. London: Routledge.

Colwyn-Jones, T. and Dugdale, D. (2002). 'The ABC Bandwagon and the Juggernaut of Modernity'. *Accounting, Organizations and Society*, 27/1–2, 121–163.

Czarniawska, B. (2008). 'Management Fashions and Fads'. In S. R. Clegg and J. R. Bailey (eds), *International Encyclopedia of Organization Studies 3*. London: Sage, 849–855.

Czarniawska, B. and Mazza, C. (2003). 'Consulting as Liminal Space'. *Human Relations*, 56/3, 267–290.

David, R. and Strang, D. (2006). 'When Fashion Is Fleeting: Transitory Collective Beliefs and the Dynamics of TQM Consulting'. *Academy of Management Journal*, 49, 215–233.

Dawes, P. L., Dowling, G. R., and Patterson, P. G. (1992). 'Criteria Used to Select Management Consultants'. *Industrial Marketing Management*, 21, 187–193.

DiMaggio, P. J. and Powell, W. W. (1983). 'The Iron Cage Revisited: Institutional Isomorphism and Collective Rationality in Organizational Fields'. *American Sociological Review*, 48, 147–160.

Doorewaard, H. and van Bijsterveld, M. (2001). 'The Osmosis of Ideas: An Analysis of the Integrated Approach to IT Management from a Translation Theory Perspective'. *Organization*, 8, 55–76.

Eccles, R. and White, H. (1988). 'Price and Authority in Inter-Profit Center Transactions'. *American Journal of Sociology*, 94 (supplement), 17–49.

Engwall, L. and Eriksson, C. B. (2005). 'Doing Deals Despite Distrust'. In S. Furusten and A. Werr (eds), *Dealing with Confidence: The Construction of Need and Trust in Management Advisory Services*. Copenhagen: Copenhagen Business School Press, 149–168.

Ernst, B. and Kieser, A. (2002). 'In Search of Explanations for the Consulting Explosion'. In K. Sahlin-Andersson and L. Engwall (eds), *The Expansion of Management Knowledge: Carriers, Flows, and Sources*. Stanford, CA: Stanford University Press, 47–73.

Esposito, E. (2004). *Die Verbindlichkeit des Vorübergehenden: Paradoxien der Mode*. Frankfurt am Main: Suhrkamp.

Ezzamel, M. and Willmott, H. (1994). 'New Management Thinking'. *European Management Journal*, 12, 454–461.

Faust, M. (2002). 'Consultancies as Actors in Knowledge Arenas: Evidence from Germany'. In M. Kipping and L. Engwall (eds), *Management Consulting: Emergence and Dynamics of a Knowledge Industry*. Oxford: Oxford University Press, 146–166.

Fincham, R. (1995). 'Business Process Re-Engineering and the Commodification of Management Knowledge'. *Journal of Marketing Management*, 11, 707–720.

Fincham, R. (1999). 'The Consultant–Client Relationship: Critical Perspectives on the Management of Organizational Change'. *Journal of Management Studies*, 36, 335–351.

Fincham, R. (2002). 'Charisma versus Technique: Differentiating the Expertise of Management Gurus and Management Consultants'. In T. Clark and R. Fincham (eds), *Critical Consulting: New Perspectives on the Management Advice Industry*. Oxford: Blackwell, 191–205.

Fincham, R. and Evans, M. (1999). 'The Consultants' Offensive: Reengineering—From Fad to Technique'. *New Technology, Work and Employment*, 14/1, 50–63.

Fincham, R. and Roslender, R. (2004). 'Rethinking the Dissemination of Management Fashion: Accounting for Intellectual Capital in UK Case Firms'. *Management Learning*, 35/3, 321–336.

Fiss, P. C. and Zajac, E. J. (2004). 'The Diffusion of Ideas Over Contested Terrain: The (Non) Adoption of a Shareholder Value Orientation Among German Firms'. *Administrative Science Quarterly*, 49/4, 501–434.

Furusten, S. (1998). 'The Creation of Popular Management Texts'. In J. L. Alvarez (ed.), *The Diffusion and Consumption of Business Knowledge*. London: Macmillan, 141–163.

Furusten, S. (1999). *Popular Management Books: How They Are Made and What They Mean for Organisations*. London: Routledge.

Giroux, H. (2006). ' "It Was Such a Handy Term": Management Fashions and Pragmatic ambiguity'. *Journal of Management Studies*, 43, 1227–1260.

Graham, I. and Williams, R. (2005). 'The Use of Management Texts: Hammer's Reengineering'. *Scandinavian Journal of Management*, 21/2, 159–175.

Grant, D., Hall, R., Wailes, N., and Wright, C. (2006). 'The False Promise of Technological Determinism: The Case of Enterprise Resource Planning Systems'. *New Technology, Work and Employment*, 21/1, 2–15.

Greatbatch, D. and Clark, T. (2003). 'Displaying Group Cohesiveness: Humour and Laughter in the Public Lectures of Management Gurus'. *Human Relations*, 56/12, 1515–1544.

Greatbatch, D. and Clark, T. (2005). *Management Speak: Why We Listen to What Management Gurus Tell Us*. London: Routledge.

Green Jr, S. E. (2004). 'A Rhetorical Theory of Diffusion'. *Academy of Management Review*, 29, 653–669.

Greenwood, R., Suddaby, R., and Hinings, C. R. (2002). 'Theorizing Change: The Role of Professional Associations in the Transformation of Institutionalized Fields'. *Academy of Management Journal*, 45/1, 58–80.

Haferkamp, S. and Drescher, S. (2006). 'Client Professionalization: Proposed Approach for the Knowledge-Centered Management of Consulting Projects'. In T. Deelmann and M. Mohe (eds), *Selection and Evaluation of Consultants*. München and Mering: Hampp, 123–137.

Heusinkveld, S. and Benders, J. (2005). 'Contested Commodification: Consultancies and their Struggle with New Concept Development'. *Human Relations*, 58/3, 283–310.

Hislop, D. (2002). 'The Client Role in Consultancy Relations during the Appropriation of Technical Innovations'. *Research Policy*, 31, 657–671.

Höner, D. and Mohe, M. (2009). 'Behind Clients' Doors: What Hinders Client Firms from "Professionally" Dealing With Consultancy?' *Scandinavian Journal of Management*, 25/3, 299–312.

Huczynski, A. (1993). *Management Gurus*. London: Routledge.

Jackson, B. (1996). 'Re-Engineering the Sense of Self: The Manager and the Management Guru'. *Journal of Management Studies*, 33, 571–590.

Jackson, B. (2001). *Management Gurus and Management Fashions*. London: Routledge.

Jung, N. (2008). 'Do Clients Really Become More Professional? Analyzing Clients' New Ways of Managing Consultants'. Paper presented at the Annual Meeting of the Academy of Management, Anaheim, 8–13 August. Available at http://ssrn.com/abstract=1440684

Jung, N. (2010). *Fakten und Fiktionen der Kientenprofessionalisierung: Eine Kritische Analyse des Umgangs mit Beratungsleistungen*. Wiesbaden: Gabler.

Kant, I. (2006). *Anthropology from a Pragmatic Point of View*. Trans. and ed. R. B. Louden. Cambridge: Cambridge University Press.

Kaplan, R. and Norton, D. P. (1996). *The Balanced Scorecard: Translating Strategy into Action*. Boston: Harvard Business School Press.

Kawamura, Y. (2005). *Fashion-ology: An Introduction to Fashion Studies*. Oxford: Berg.

Kelemen, M. (2000). 'Too Much or too Little Ambiguity: The Language of Total Quality Management'. *Journal of Management Studies*, 37, 483–498.

Kelemen, M. and Bansal, P. (2002). 'The Conventions of Management Research and their Relevance to Management Practice'. *British Journal of Management*, 13, 97–108.

Kieser, A. (1997). 'Myth and Rhetoric in Management Fashion'. *Organization*, 4/1, 49–74.

Kieser, A. (2002). 'On Communication Barriers between Management Science, Consultancies and Business Companies'. In T. Clark and R. Fincham (eds), *Critical Consulting: New Perpectives on the Management Advice Industry*. Oxford: Blackwell, 206–227.

Kieser, A. and Wellstein, B. (2007). 'Do Activities of Consultants and Management Scientists Affect Decision Making by Managers?' In W. H. Starbuck and G. P. Hodgkinson (eds),

The Oxford Handbook of Organizational Decision Making. Oxford: Oxford University Press, 495–516.

Kieser, A. and Leiner, L. (2009). 'Why the Rigour-Relevance Gap in Management Research is Unbridgeable'. *Journal of Management Studies*, 46/3, 516–533.

Kipping, M. (2002). 'Trapped in Their Wave: The Evolution of Management Consultancies'. In T. Clark and R. Fincham (eds), *Critical Consulting: New Perspectives on the Management Advice Industry*. Oxford: Blackwell, 28–49.

Kipping, M. and Armbrüster, T. (2002). 'The Burden of Otherness: Limits of Consultancy Interventions in Historical Case Studies'. In M. Kipping and L. Engwall (eds), *Management Consulting: Emergence and Dynamics of a Knowledge Industry*. Oxford: Oxford University Press, 203–221.

Kitay, J. and Wright, C. (2003). 'Expertise and Organizational Boundaries: The Varying Roles of Australian Management Consultants'. *Asia Pacific Business Review*, 9/3, 21–40.

Lindberg, N. and Furusten, S. (2005). 'Breaking Laws—Making Deals: Procurement of Management Consultants in the Public Sector'. In S. Furusten and A. Werr (eds), *Dealing with Confidence: The Construction of Need and Trust in Management Advisory Services*. Copenhagen: Copenhagen Business School Press, 169–183.

McGivern, C. (1983). 'Some Facets of the Relationship between Consultants and Clients in Organizations'. *Journal of Management Studies*, 20, 367–386.

March, J. G. (1981). 'Footnotes to Organizational Change'. *Administrative Science Quarterly*, 26, 563–577.

March, J. G. (1991). 'Organizational Consultants and Organizational Research'. *Journal of Applied Communication Research*, 19, 20–31.

Mazza, C. (1998). 'The Popularization of Business Knowledge Diffusion: From Academic Knowledge to Popular Culture?' In J. L. Alvarez (ed.), *The Diffusion and Consumption of Business Knowledge*. London: Macmillan, 164–181.

Meyer, T. W. (1994). 'Measuring Performance in Economic Organizations'. In N. J. Smelser and R. Swedberg (eds), *Handbook of Economic Sociology*. Princeton, NJ: Princeton University Press, 556–588.

Meyer, J. W. and Rowan, B. (1977). 'Institutional Organizations: Formal Structure as Myth and Ceremony'. *American Journal of Sociology*, 83, 340–363.

Mohe, M. (2005). 'Generic Strategies for Managing Consultants: Insights from Clients' Companies in Germany'. *Journal of Change Management*, 5, 357–365.

Morris, T. and Lancaster, Z. (2006). 'Translating Management Ideas'. *Organization Studies*, 27, 207–233.

Nicolai, A. T. (2004). 'The Bridge to the Real "World": Applied Science Fiction or a "Schizophrenic Tour de Force"?' *Journal of Management Studies*, 41, 951–976.

Nicolai, A. T., Schulz, A-C., and Thomas, T. W. (2010). 'What Wall Street Wants: Exploring the Role of Security Analysts in the Evolution and Spread of Management Concepts'. *Journal of Management Studies*, 46, 162–189.

Nijholt, J. J. and Benders, J. (2007). 'Coevolution in Management Fashions'. *Group & Organization Management*, 32/6, 628–652.

Nikolova, N., Reihlen, M., and Schlapfner, J-F. (2009). 'Client–Consultant Interaction: Capturing Social Practices of Professional Service Production'. *Scandinavian Journal of Management*, 25/3, 289–298.

Nystrom, P. C. and Starbuck, W. H. (1984). 'Managing Beliefs in Organizations'. *Journal of Applied Behavioral Science*, 20, 277–287.

Pande, P. S., Neumann, R. P., and Cavenagh, R. R. (2000). *The Six Sigma Way: How GE, Motorola, and Other Top Companies Are Honing their Performance Imprint*. New York: McGraw-Hill.

Parush, T. (2008). 'From "Management Ideology" to "Management Fashion": A Comparative Analysis of Two Key Concepts in the Sociology of Management Knowledge'. *International Studies of Management & Organization*, 38/1, 48–70.

Perkmann, M. and Spicer, A. (2008). 'How Are Management Fashions Institutionalized? The Role of Institutional Work'. *Human Relations*, 61, 811–844.

Peters, T. (1992). *Liberation Management: Necessary Disorganization for the Nanosecond Nineties*. London: Macmillan.

Peters, T. J. and Waterman, R. H. (1983). *In Search of Excellence: Lessons from America's Best-Run Companies*. New York: Harper & Row.

Pinchot, G. (1985). *Intrapreneuring*. New York: Harper & Row.

Ramiller, N. C. and Swanson, B. E. (2003). 'Organizing Visions for Information Technology and the Information Systems Executive Response'. *Journal of Management Information Systems*, 20, 13–50.

Richter, A. (2004). 'The Changing Balance of Power in the Consulting Market and Its Effects on Consulting Firms'. In J-P. Thommen and A. Richter (eds), *Management Consulting Today: Strategies for a Challenging Environment*. Wiesbaden: Gabler, 111–129.

Richter, A. and Niewiem, S. (2006). 'The Relationship between Clients and Management Consultants: An Empirical Analysis'. *Academy of Management Best Paper Proceedings*, MC, C1–C6.

Rolfsen, M. and Knutstad, G. (2007). 'Transforming Management Fashions into Praxis: Action Research Project in AutoParts'. *Action Research*, 5, 341–357.

Røvik, K. A. (2002). 'The Secrets of the Winners: Management Ideas that Flow'. In K. Sahlin-Andersson and L. Engwall (eds), *The Expansion of Management Knowledge: Carriers, Ideas and Sources*. Stanford, CA: Stanford University Press, 113–144.

Sanders, W. M. G. and Tuschke, A. (2007). 'The Adoption of Institutionally Contested Organizational Practices: The Emergence of Stock Option Pay in Germany'. *Academy of Management Journal*, 50/1, 33–56.

Scarbrough, H. (2003). 'The Role of Intermediary Groups in Shaping Management Fashion'. *International Studies of Management & Organization*, 32/4, 87–103.

Scarbrough, H., Robertson, M., and Swan, J. (2005). 'Professional Media and Management Fashion: The Case of Knowledge Management'. *Scandinavian Journal of Management*, 21, 197–208.

Simmel, G. (1957). 'Fashion'. *American Journal of Sociology*, 62, 541–558.

Spell, C. S. (2001). 'Management Fashions: Where Do They Come From, and Are They Old Wine in New Bottles?' *Journal of Management Inquiry*, 10, 358–373.

Staw, B. M. and Epstein, L. D. (2000). 'What Bandwagons Bring: Effects of Popular Management Techniques on Corporate Performance, Reputation, and CEO Pay'. *Administrative Science Quarterly*, 45, 523–556.

Stock, J. R. and Zinszer, P. H. (1987). 'The Industrial Purchase Decision for Professional Services'. *Journal of Business Research*, 15, 1–16.

Sturdy, A. (1997a). 'The Consultancy Process: An Insecure Business'. *Journal of Management Studies*, 34, 389–413.

Sturdy, A. (1997b). 'The Dialectics of Consultancy'. *Critical Perspectives on Accounting*, 8, 511–535.

Sturdy, A. and Wright, C. (2008). 'A Consulting Diaspora? Enterprising Selves as Agents of Enterprise'. *Organization*, 15/3, 427–444.

Suddaby, R. and Greenwood, R. (2001). 'Colonizing Knowledge: Commodification as a Dynamic of Jurisdictional Expansion in Professional Service Firms'. *Human Relations*, 54, 933–954.

Swanson, B. E. and Ramiller, N. C. (1997). 'The Organizing Vision in Information Systems Innovation'. *Organization Science*, 8, 458–474.

Ten Bos, R. (2000). *Fashion and Utopia in Management Thinking*. Amsterdam: John Benjamins.

Ten Bos, R. and Heusinkveld, S. (2007). 'The Guru's Gusto: Management Fashion, Performance and Taste'. *Journal of Organizational Change Management*, 20, 304–325.

Van den Steen, E. (2005). 'Organizational Beliefs and Managerial Vision'. *Journal of Law, Economics and Organization*, 21, 256–283.

Vastag, G. and Whybarl, D. C. (2003). 'Is Anybody Listening? An Investigation into Popular Advice and Actual Practices'. *International Journal of Production Economics*, 81/82, 115–128.

Veblen, T. (1949). *The Theory of the Leisure Class: An Economic Study of Institutions*. London: George Allen & Unwin.

Werr, A. and Greiner, L. (2008). 'Collaboration and the Production of Management Knowledge in Research, Consulting, and Management Practice'. In A. B. R. Shani, S. A. Mohrman, B. Stymne, and N. Adler (eds), *Handbook of Collaborative Management Research*. Los Angeles: Sage, 93–117.

Werr, A. and Pemer, F. (2005). 'Purchasing Management Consultants: From Personal Ties to Organizational Procedures'. *Academy of Management Best Paper Proceedings*, B1–B6.

Werr, A. and Pemer, F. (2007). 'Purchasing Management Consulting Services: From Management Autonomy to Purchasing Involvement'. *Journal of Purchasing and Supply Management*, 13/2, 98–112.

Werr, A. and Styhre, A. (2003). 'Management Consultants: Friend or Foe? Understanding the Ambiguous Client–Consultant Relationship'. *International Studies of Management & Organization*, 32/4, 43–66.

Womack, J. P., Jones, D. T., and Ross, D. (1990). *The Machine that Changed the World*. New York: Rawson Associates.

Woywode, M. (2002). 'Global Manufacturing Concepts and Local Adaptation: Working Groups in the French and German Car Manufacturing Industry'. *Organization Studies*, 23, 497–524.

Wright, C. (2002). 'Promoting Demand, Gaining Legitimacy, and Broadening Expertise: The Evolution of Consultancy–Client Relationships in Australia'. In M. Kipping and L. Engwall (eds), *Management Consulting: Emergence and Dynamics of a Knowledge Industry*. Oxford: Oxford University Press, 184–202.

Wright, J. and Kitay, J. (2002). '"But Does It Work?" Perceptions of the Impact of Management Consulting'. *Strategic Change*, 11/8, 271–278.

Zbaracki, M. J. (1998). 'The Rhetoric and Reality of Total Quality Management'. *Administrative Science Quarterly*, 43, 602–636.

CHAPTER 17

....

MANAGEMENT GURUS AS CELEBRITY CONSULTANTS

....

TIMOTHY CLARK
POJANATH BHATANACHAROEN
DAVID GREATBATCH*

17.1 INTRODUCTION

UNLIKE the majority of chapters in this Handbook this one is concerned with a group of individuals—management gurus—that are not immediately thought of as management consultants in that they do not appear to engage in conventional work with clients. Rather, they are often viewed as lone celebrity organizational thinkers, whose focus is on broadcasting their ideas by writing books and giving presentations. Although many individuals who are ascribed guru status emanate from well-known management consultancies and some run their own consultancies, and their ideas can be packaged and sold by many consultancies, their personal renown overshadows any particular organizational affiliation. Their profile is therefore driven not by their consulting activities but by the level of media attention they and their ideas garner on the basis of the success of their books and public performances. For example, Tom Peters is associated with 'Excellence', Michael Hammer and James Champy with 'business process re-engineering' (BPR), and Peter Senge with the learning organization. In this respect they are celebrity consultants whose public status emerges from a process of celebrification that focuses on the increasing visibility of their ideas (Guthey, Clark, and Jackson 2009).

In the last twenty years there have been a number of overviews of the literature on management gurus (Huczynski 1993; Clark and Salaman 1998; Jackson 2001). Following these, the subsequent empirical literature has primarily sought to explain the impact and popularity of the ideas they generate in terms of specific features associated with the modes of dissemination they use (i.e., books and live presentations), which heighten the managerial audiences' awareness and receptivity to guru ideas. This chapter will provide a review of the extant literature on gurus albeit with a specific focus on their relationship with consulting. This aspect of the guru phenomenon has been discussed indirectly in that the ideas gurus develop and actively proselytize have fed demand for consultancy services as clients seek access to the latest blockbuster ideas. Ernst and Kieser (2002) have suggested that the guru-led ideas are to some extent the fuel that has powered the almost uninterrupted growth of the consulting industry over the past fifty years. They argue that popular/fashionable ideas increase the demand for consultancy services since the churning of ideas exacerbates endemic uncertainties about which ideas are the most effective, with the consequence that managers employ consultants to both help select ideas and implement them within their organizations (ibid.: 59–61). As Micklethwait and Wooldridge (1996) have highlighted, guru ideas can also directly impact on the reputation and revenues of a particular consultancy. The 'Portfolio Matrix', for instance, is associated with the Boston Consulting Group (BCG); BPR led to a fivefold increase in the revenues of CSC Index, where one of its progenitors James Champy worked (Jackson 1996). The success of Peters and Waterman's book had a significant impact on McKinsey where they both worked at the time of writing *In Search of Excellence*.

To address more precisely the (dis)similarities between management gurus as celebrity consultants and the conventional corporate consultants as well as their relationships and interactions, the chapter adopts a fivefold structure. The first section examines the nature of management gurus as celebrity consultants, identifying three different aspects of their role: (i) apostles of management fashion; (ii) authors of bestselling books; and (iii) accomplished orators. The following three sections then detail the characteristics of these three types of management gurus and try to identify gaps in the respective literatures. On this basis, the fifth and final section proposes a number of potentially fruitful avenues for future research.

17.2 DEFINITIONS OF GURUS AND CONSULTANTS

As noted above, the term 'guru' has become the label of choice when media commentators discuss influential and popular management thinkers and proselytizers regardless of the background of the particular individual. In the first academic study of management gurus, Huczynski (1993) argues that, over the course of the twentieth century, management thinking had developed through a series of distinct 'idea families', namely 'bureaucracy', 'scientific management', 'administrative management', 'human relations', 'neo-human relations', and, finally, 'guru theory'—a term he coined for the collection of popular management ideas that emerged in the last forty years of the twentieth century. Huczynski is thus using the term 'guru theory' not to theorize about gurus as knowledge producers, but as a label for a loose collection of management ideas that have become popular in part as a result of the activities of management gurus. By implication, it is the extent and renown of the ideas for which they are known that underpins whether individuals achieve the eminence of guru status.

Regarding the relationship between gurus and these ideas, according to Huczynski (1993: 38), each idea 'relies for its authorization upon the individual who developed and popularized it'. That is, there is an individual, or individuals in the case of co-authors, clearly associated with either originating or popularizing the idea. This is not necessarily a unique feature of 'guru theory' in that Frederick Taylor is identified as the father of scientific management and Elton Mayo with human relations, two earlier idea families (see Wright and Kipping, Chapter 2; Trahair and Bruce, Chapter 3; both this volume). Although gurus are associated with ideas within an idea family rather than with the overall emergence of a single 'idea family', the literature suggests that this disparate collection of ideas and techniques that comprise 'guru theory' share at least two key characteristics that differentiate them from previous 'idea families' (Huczynski 1993; Clark and Salaman 1998; Jackson 2001). First, they are inherently fashion-like in that they are characterized by rapid swings of enthusiasm and disenchantment (see below; also Jung and Kieser, Chapter 16, this volume). Second, these ideas attempt to contribute to the understanding of the problems faced by management and organizations by focusing on a factor or technique that the guru claims has the potential to make a transformational impact. As Clark and Salaman (1998: 138) write, guru theory

> involves the presentation of ambitious claims to transform managerial practice, organizational structures and cultures and, crucially, organizational performance, through the recommendation of an almost magical cure that rejects the past, and reinvents the organization, its employees, their relationships, attitudes and behaviour.

When it comes to identifying individual management gurus, most commentators draw on Huczynski's (1993: 38, 40) point that '[t]he authorization of a management idea stems from the author's position, which can be based upon academic research, experience of consultancy or experience of management'. In this respect, the ideas which propel them from the position of would-be guru to guru, are derived from a range of working experiences and sources. Building on this argument, Huczynski identifies three types of management gurus: (1) 'academic gurus'; (2) 'consultant gurus'; and (3) 'hero managers'. The first group are generally located within a small number of world-renowned business schools (London, Harvard/HBS, MIT/Sloan, Stanford, and so forth) and are exemplified by people such as Charles Handy, Gary Hamel, Rosabeth Moss Kanter, Michael Porter, and Peter Senge (see also Engwall, Chapter 18, this volume). The second group is composed of independent advisors, writers, and commentators and includes the likes of Stephen Covey, Daniel Goleman, Michael Hammer, and Tom Peters. The final group is comprised of successful leaders with a strong public profile who have written an autobiography or 'how to' book that focuses on their experiences of managing often a high-profile organization and the management approach and techniques they adopted. Notable examples include John Harvey Jones (*Making it Happen: Reflections on Leadership*), Lee Iacocca (*Iacocca: An Autobiography*), Alfred P. Sloan (*My Years with*

General Motors), Richard Branson (*Losing My Virginity: The Autobiography*), and Jack Welch (*Jack: Straight from the Gut*).

Whether management gurus can be classified so unambiguously is doubtful. In part this arises because gurus have varying and multiple career trajectories. Thus, some start their careers working at a university or business school and then leave to become a consultant (e.g. Tom Peters). Others continue working at a university or business school and combine this with consulting work (e.g. Rosabeth Moss Kanter). Some combine consultancy work with academia (e.g. Gary Hamel). There is also a group of individuals who are identified as management gurus, who come from very different backgrounds to those already stated. These people are authors of bestselling books that have captured the attention of a large management audience but their background is in training, personal development, or more tangential areas such as poetry and entertainment (Farnham 1996). Consequently, the background and nature of gurus are more blurred and diverse than Huczynski and others have suggested.

To complicate the matter further, questions arise when attempting to conceptualize these celebrity gurus as *consultants*, which is also a term referring to another group of agents within the management consultancy industry, namely the consultants working for conventional consultancy firms. Fincham (2002) has argued that, in the field of management fashion diffusion, there has been a tendency to conflate the roles of gurus with those of corporate consultants. These two groups of agents share some similarities and overlaps as both groups are concerned with impacting on managerial practices in organizations by selling their concepts and ideas. In fact, as Fincham and Clark (2002: 3) pointed out, 'many gurus are, or were at one time, successful management consultants. Similarly, many gurus either operate as individual "star" consultants or own their own consultancies.'

Despite these conflations, however, the two groups differ in one significant way: they employ different modes of diffusion to spread their ideas and techniques. Clark and Greatbatch (2002) proffer that the gurus typically disseminate their ideas through the use of the print media and live presentations (i.e., public lectures) as a way to convert their audiences' beliefs, attitudes, and feelings. In this respect Clark and Salaman (1998) view the archetypical guru as a 'star', or, as Farnham (1996: 80) puts it, 'Academics gone Hollywood'. Conventional consultants, by contrast, work closely with clients on individual projects. It is paramount for consultancies' survival that they build and maintain a continuous and strong relationship with their clients to secure future contracts. Overall, Fincham (2002) suggests that gurus rely on their personal charisma to gain authority whereas consultants depend on their techniques.

Unlike Fincham and Clark (2002: 3) however, this chapter does not apply the term 'consultant' exclusively to those working as conventional consultants. As has been noted above but will be shown in more detail below, those individuals who are recognized as gurus sometimes have backgrounds in conventional consultancy or run consultancies after having attained celebrity status. Their ideas are also packaged, marketed, and sold by their own and other consultancies. Moreover, gurus act as consultants by offering advice through books and oral presentations. Their heightened profile and the focus on them by the media and client organizations mean that management gurus are 'celebrity consultants'. We therefore use a loose definition of a management guru as someone who is ascribed that status by commentators primarily on the basis of their authorship of a successful book and/or oratorical ability on the management lecture circuit, whatever their background. As the review of the literature that follows indicates, the achievement of gurudom is the outcome of the activities of a complex network of intersecting players and practices that produce gurus as management fashion celebrities (Guthey, Clark, and Jackson 2009).

Building on this definition of management gurus, in the next section we discuss the role of management gurus in relation to management fashion. The subsequent sections then discuss the literature relating to their books before turning to that on their public performances.

17.3 'Apostles' of Management Fashions

Gurus' celebrity status is founded on their ability to create and disseminate fashionable management ideas. Therefore, discussions of their activities necessarily relate to the management fashion literature. A key strand of this literature identifies successful management ideas and their life cycles. Jung and Kieser (Chapter 16, this volume) outline the role of different agents in the management fashion arena. This section focuses solely on the role of management gurus in producing ideas that are inherently fashion-like, and can be used by consultants—be it the gurus themselves or existing consulting firms. In an early article on the topic, Gill and Whittle (1993) note that popular ideas wax and wane as they evolve through a series of discrete stages: birth, adolescence, maturity, and decline. Building on the core idea that there is a common bell-shaped trajectory through which popular management ideas pass, Abrahamson (1996) developed a comprehensive and systematic theory of management fashion in an article that has become highly influential. In brief, his key idea was that management fashions are 'the product of a management-fashion-setting *process* involving particular management fashion setters— organizations and individuals who dedicate themselves to producing and disseminating management knowledge' (ibid.: 256, emphasis in the original).

For Abrahamson (1996), management gurus are therefore part of a management knowledge arena, the other members of which are typically identified as consulting firms, business schools, and management academics and publishers (see also Ernst and Kieser 2002; Jung and Kieser, Chapter 16, this volume). He argues that these different agents compete for the attention of the managerial audience. For their ideas to become prominent each agent needs to persuasively articulate at any point in time what they consider to be the key organizational/managerial priorities and why their particular method or technique offers the best means to address these. Their ideas therefore need to capture the zeitgeist or spirit of the times so that the solutions and techniques they propose are perceived as being the most relevant and likely to meet the critical concerns of the managerial audience (see also Barley and Kunda 1992; Grint 1994; Kieser 1997).

Although Abrahamson identified the importance of the members of the management fashion-setting community in the creation, selection, processing, and dissemination of management ideas to the target audience (Hirsch 1972), he did not discuss the relative roles of the various actors at different points in the life cycle of a management idea. Consequently, from Abrahamson's model the role of management gurus (and business academics and management consultants) in the production of fashionable management ideas is not clear. Suddaby and Greenwood (2001) subsequently developed a more detailed model of the knowledge production process within the management fashion-setting community. Although they note (ibid.: 940) that 'events [are] most likely occur contemporaneously', they elaborate a sequential movement of knowledge production through a cycle commencing with legitimation by gurus before its commodification by consultants, colonization by professional service firms (PSFs), and finally analysis and refinement by business schools. A key implication arising from this model is that management gurus are critical in initially identifying the importance of an idea. Without their 'authorization' and communication skills, it is unlikely that it would become popular and fashionable. In turn their own prominence as respected management commentators is tied to the continuing popularity of the ideas with which they are associated.

Following the publication of Abrahamson's theory, a series of empirical studies examined the diffusion patterns of a range of fashionable guru-led discourses within the print media (Abrahamson and Fairchild 1999; Spell 1999, 2001; Benders and van Veen 2001; Gibson and Tesone 2001). Using citation analysis these studies counted and plotted the number of references to a particular term in a sequence of years in order to identify the life cycle of a fashionable management idea. Overall, the results of these studies demonstrate that the life cycles of a number of fashionable management ideas are characterized by an initial period in which the frequency of citations increases, peaks, and then declines; although the shapes of the curves for different ideas are not necessarily identical nor symmetrical (i.e., they do not necessarily increase at the same rate they decline), and vary over time, and between countries.

As Clark (2004) has highlighted, however, citation analysis is not without serious problems. Unless each article is read it cannot indicate whether the idea is central or peripheral to the main topic or whether it is referred to positively or negatively. Citation analysis is limited to the counts of references to an idea in selected sections of the print media, mainly leading academic journals, semi-academic journals, and the popular management press. Such a method cannot determine the degree to which ideas are 'adopted' by organizations. Nevertheless, there is a tendency in the literature to assume that there is a symbiotic relationship between the pattern in the volume of discourse and trends in the adoption and rejection of ideas by organizations. Moreover, although these macro-level studies help us establish the life cycles and identity of successful management fashion ideas, they do not tell us much about the role of the gurus who, after all, are the disseminators/popularizers of these ideas. The next sections will elaborate in more detail the features that have been examined and discussed in the extant literature which underpin the emergence of an individual as a management guru and celebrity consultant.

17.4 Attaining Celebrity Status through Print Media

From Huczynski (1993) onwards it has been repeatedly noted that management gurus are the authors of bestselling management books that afford the gurus their celebrity status. As Clark and Salaman (1998: 140) write, '[t]he traditional way in which gurus and would-be gurus launch themselves and their ideas is by writing a seminal management text'. More recently, with the increasing digitization of media and rise of the internet they also populate all the key services (Facebook, Twitter, etc.) that ensure they develop and maintain a direct and strong connection with their audience. For Furusten (1999) these books are important because they form a discursive realm in which myths, meanings, and symbols of management and organizational life are represented to a wide audience of organizations, industries, and societies. Their success is therefore founded on their ability to convey 'symbolic issues of great pertinence and salience to senior managers: managers' own roles, skills and identities within the "new" organizations' (Clark and Salaman 1998: 149). These writers argue that, by defining the nature and role of the new executive within a remodelled organization in attractive terms, management gurus secure both their own status and the appeal of these books. Similarly, Watson (1994: 896) in a study of UK managers notes that guru writings play a part in helping managers to make sense of their lives, their role and 'their place in the scheme of things'.

These books have perhaps been the publishing phenomenon of the 1980s and 1990s. Prior to the publication of *In Search of Excellence*, management books—although some titles sold in large quantities—did not compete for a place at the top of bestseller lists. The sales generated by the management bestsellers of the 1980s and 1990s were of a different scale to these earlier books—millions rather than tens or hundreds of thousands of copies (see Clark and Salaman 1998: 140). The success of *In Search of Excellence*, and subsequently a number of other titles such as *Re-engineering the Corporation* (Hammer and Champy 1993) or *The Fifth Discipline* (Senge 1990), raised the profile of the genre as a whole and resulted in management books enjoying a more prominent position in bookshops, occupying positions at the top of bestseller lists, and gaining a broader readership.

The significance of these books in terms of their sales and therefore assumed impact on management thinking, as well as their crucial role in launching a number of major management fashions that permeated the management consulting industry in the 1980s and 1990s led to a series of studies aimed at examining the factors that accounted for their popularity and the ideas they sought to project. The key question driving these studies was what makes them a bestseller. In answering this question, some commentators have focused on what Grint (1994) termed the 'internalist' approach. That is, the book's success is seen to be due in large part to the use of a series of conventions and structures, which enhance the understanding and applicability of the ideas for the managerial audience. As Clark and Salaman (1998: 142) note, these presentational forms are necessary since 'gurus" ideas appeal because they are 'formulated in ways that are inherently attractive to and easily accessible by managers in terms of their work-developed preferences for the nature and format of information […] a focus on doing, on tangible, concrete activities, and on the immediate'. Similarly, Huczynski (1993) argues that these books are designed to satisfy deep-seated psychological needs related to a lack of control and social esteem.

Building on Huczynski's (1993) arguments, Newstrom and Pierce (1993) seek to identify the structural features of these books that were attractive to the managerial audience and therefore made them popular. In doing so, they emphasize such features as a book's distinctiveness. For them '[t]he best business books will present something new, creative, and distinctive. They will pull readers into a new era' (ibid.: 27). In Abrahamson's (1996) terms, these books display a strong sense of a 'progressive norm'. Another element is readability in that a book 'must grab and hold the reader's interest […]. Does it flow naturally and yet engage the reader's mind?' (Newstrom and Pierce 1993: 26). A further critical ingredient is practicality—'are the ideas readily transferable to the workplace, in such a way that the typical reader could be expected to know what to do with them a few days later at work?' (ibid.: 27).

The idea that bestselling management books contain a number of key features that heighten their chances of success, because they resonate with the intended audience, is echoed in research undertaken by Clark and Greatbatch (2002, 2003). Their research shows that the writing of these books is a collaborative endeavour in that book editors have a significant, if largely unseen, impact on the shaping of management ideas in book form. These editors work closely with authors, helping them mould their ideas prior to publication to produce books in accordance with general rules or conventions about what has, or appears to have, been successful in the past. Consistent with the depiction of managers presented by the earlier authors, they report that editors 'view managers as being extremely busy with a focus on the tangible and immediate and a tendency towards superficiality and short attention spans' (Clark and Greatbatch 2003: 411). Given this perception of their target audience, they therefore aim to present the ideas in accessible forms that have two characteristics: (1) they are easy to read, and (2) they emphasize and demonstrate the practical relevance of the gurus' ideas. In this way, editors and publishers seek to publish a book that emphasizes a number of features so that the ideas are presented in such a way that they resonate with the expectations and needs of the managerial audience and, in doing so, the book has every chance of becoming a bestseller.

Pagel and Westerfelhaus (2005) also highlight the importance of these features based on a series of interviews seeking to understand managers' reading preferences. Similar to Clark and Greatbatch (2003), their findings suggest that managers prefer short books with a simple writing style and grammatical structure that highlight the key points so that they 'stand out', and have examples to show how the ideas can be applied. Building on the latter point, Lischinsky (2008) examines the use of examples in over one hundred bestselling management books. He argues that the power of examples derives from their ability to 'make a claim *factual*, by linking a general proposition to a real-world instance where it is held true' (ibid.: 253, italics in the original). Examples not only make the gurus' ideas more concrete, they also bolster the credibility of the author by portraying them as a successful consultant who is able to obtain privileged access to prestigious organizations. An interesting finding in this study is that the precise meaning of the examples was more frequently left implicit, with the consequence that readers of these books have to generate their own understandings of their importance. Lischinsky (2008) argues that this makes a text more attractive since it creates a deeper engagement with the book as each reader is required to develop their own interpretations of the meaning of the different examples. In this way the authors create what Benders and van Veen (2001: 37–39) have termed 'interpretative viability'. That is, although the very selection of examples by the author may funnel the reader's focus, there is a degree of ambiguity that permits flexible interpretation and therefore applicability to a whole range of contexts. Thus, rather than decreasing the attractiveness of a book by being overly vague in terms of what the author means, these implicit examples are a key factor accounting for their broad appeal.

Another set of writers have also identified a number of common themes and textual elements in bestselling management books (Kieser 1997; Furusten 1999; Røvik 2002: 142–143; Cullen 2009). These include: a focus on a single factor; the contrasting of old ideas with the new such that the latter are presented as qualitatively better and superior; the creation of a sense of urgency such that the introduction of the ideas is presented as pressing and unavoidable; an emphasis on the need for readers to reflect and change their practice; an individualistic focus in that readers are portrayed as having a moral responsibility and capacity for the improvement of themselves and/or their organizations; the linkage of the ideas to highly treasured management values; case studies of outstanding success; and a stress on the universal applicability of ideas. In a similar vein Jackson (2001, 2002) studied the rhetorical appeal of three management ideas that were popular in the 1990s: effectiveness, the learning organization, and re-engineering. Drawing on Bormann's (1972) Fantasy Theme Analysis his research identified specific rhetorical elements—rhetorical visions, setting, character and action themes, fantasy types, master analogues—that underpinned the popularity of each of these fashionable ideas. The nature of these elements varied across the three ideas with the consequence that while 'there is no doubt considerable overlap between the rhetorical communities that have coalesced around these visions' (Jackson 2001: 184) their appeal varied with the consequence that they enrolled 'quite different communities in terms of membership and the degree and levels of commitment they inspire' (ibid.).

However, imbuing a book with the elements identified in the preceding paragraphs does not guarantee its success. Many books are carefully designed to contain all of these features but do not become sales successes. There is therefore considerable uncertainty as to why one book is successful and another not. As some commentators of the creative industries note, it is a general principle that nobody really knows what is going to be successful because not all elements can be controlled (Caves 2000). A critical area of ambiguity noted in the management fashion literature is whether ideas resonate with the socio-economic and cultural context within which they emerge. As we noted earlier, Abrahamson (1996) emphasized that to obtain traction with an audience fashionable guru-led ideas need to chime with the spirit of the times. *The Economist* (1994: 80) reinforced this point when it noted that every successful management guru must possess a 'nose for the *zeitgeist*'. Therefore, as Kieser (1997: 61) writes, all the conventions identified in the previous paragraph 'are useless if the timing is not perfect'.

Drawing on this notion, other commentators have adopted what Grint (1994: 192) has termed an 'externalist' approach by seeking to determine '*why* the package is effective in its particular envelope of space and time' (emphasis in original). From this perspective, the key question is why do particular ideas become popular and connect with the managerial audience at certain moments in time whilst at the same time other ideas fail to gain traction? In answering this question, the popularity and success of a set of ideas is 'related to their ability to (re)frame their analyses of contemporary management problems and solutions in such a way that they resonate with and are in harmony with the expectations and understandings of their target audience' (Clark and Salaman 1998: 144). To conclude, the scholarship on guru books offers varied explanations for the reasons for these books and therefore the gurus' success. Some authors such as Newstrom and Pierce (1993), Kieser (1997), Clark and Greatbatch (2002), Røvik (2002), and Lischinsky (2008) have elaborated on the rhetorical and textual conventions that are present in these books, the role of management gurus themselves, and their social interactions with other actors involved in the production of management fashion books. Others, such as Grint (1994), Barley and Kunda (1992), and Abrahamson (1996) have attributed the success of an idea to its harmony with broader socio-economic factors. The chapter now turns to consider the live performances of management gurus.

17.5 ATTAINING CELEBRITY STATUS THROUGH LIVE PRESENTATIONS

In addition to writing bestselling management books, management gurus disseminate their ideas through live presentations on the international management lecture circuit. As perhaps the highest profile group of management speakers in the world, they use their lectures to build their personal reputations with audiences of managers. Many gain reputations as powerful orators and subsequently market recordings of their talks as part of management training packages. Commentators have consistently argued that the gurus' public performances are critical to their popularity and success, and help promote and sustain the visibility of their ideas.

The very term 'management guru' has clear religious connotations, as has been highlighted by Jackson (2001). These spill over into discussions and characterizations of their live performances. To date, the literature has overwhelmingly tended to view these as quasi-religious events. They are therefore characterized as exercises in persuasive communication where the purpose is to transform the understandings of the audience members to the guru's way of thinking (Huczynski 1993; Clark and Salaman 1996, 1998;

Jackson 2001, 2002; Carlone 2006). Huczynski (1993: 250) argues that to change audience members' ways of thinking the guru has to 'unhook them from their existing view or beliefs, convert them to his thinking, and then reinforce his ideas so that they are sustained in his absence'. To illustrate how this is achieved Huczynski adopts Lewin's (1951) three-phase change model to argue that these lectures are broadly characterized by three key interlinked stages: unfreezing, changing, and refreezing.

Carlone (2006: 94) has similarly identified a three-stage process through which these presentations pass. Drawing on the work of Turner (1984), and before him van Gennep (1909), he argues that these events are similar to rites of passage in that they begin with 'divestiture', proceed to a 'liminal (i.e., transitional) condition' and end with 'investiture'. However, drawing on an analysis of a performance given by Stephen R. Covey, the author of *The Seven Habits of Highly Effective People*, Carlone (2006), unlike Huczynski (1993), does not argue that the phases are necessarily completed. Rather, he argues that Covey's message about becoming more effective results in a continuous process of self-improvement, which may never be achieved since further improvements can always be made. A person is never fully and always effective. As a consequence, Carlone (2006: 94–95) argues '[w]ith respect to content, the performance advocates ongoing work on the self, delaying any final move from ineffective to effective […]. In form, the performance lacks the reintegration stage.' The audience is therefore left in a permanent state of transition since the end point is never quite, or cannot be, achieved (for a textual analysis of *The Seven Habits of Highly Effective People*, see Cullen 2009).

Huczynski's (1993) description of the unfolding nature of gurus' live performances and the reasons for their potential impact on audience members has been highly influential (see Jackson 2001; ten Bos and Heusinkveld 2007). Indeed, it is reflected in the great majority of descriptions of these events, with the consequence that their quasi-religious status is reinforced. For example, Caulkin (1997: 14) describes Tom Peters' style of lecturing in the following way: 'He rants, sweats, stomps up and down and manipulates the emotions of his middle-management audience with the skill of an old-time evangelist' (see also Baur 1994; Krohe 2004). Summarizing this broad depiction of management gurus' lecturing style, Greatbatch and Clark (2005: 21–22) note that 'gurus' live lectures are repeatedly portrayed as equivalent to evangelical religious revivalist meetings'. In this respect they are seen as modern day management evangelists who draw on the heritage of well-known evangelical preachers such as Billy Graham and Martin Luther King (Sargant 1997).

However, Greatbatch and Clark (2003, 2005) argue that, without detailed analyses of the gurus' live lectures, assumptions relating to the oratorical style gurus actually use, the nature of speaker–audience interaction, and the forms of audience response remain speculative. To address this issue they conducted a series of fine-grained analyses of video recordings of a number of gurus' lectures in order to both reveal and examine tacit—'seen but unnoticed' (Garfinkel 1967)—aspects of speaker–audience conduct in these settings. Their findings show that management gurus are skilled at using a range of presentational practices that generate collective audience laughter during their lectures. This is important, because laughter is not a spontaneous response to inherently humorous remarks but rather has to be invited and therefore signalled as relevant by a speaker. In order to orchestrate a collective response so that individuals are not left with the potentially embarrassing experience of being the only person to laugh, a large number of audience members have to be clear that and when it is relevant to laugh. Greatbatch and Clark's research found that the gurus regularly deployed a range of non-verbal and, less commonly, verbal cues to indicate that they intended their remarks as humorous.

Critically, the management gurus generally provide opportunities for audiences to affiliate with them through laughter without audience members being required to pub-licly affiliate with the values (standards of judgement) embodied in their core ideas and visions—values that characterize familiar organizational practices as inappropriate, unacceptable, and outmoded. One of the ways in which they do this is by investing their messages with multiple sources of humour (deriving from their use of metaphorical imagery, mimicry, facial expressions, exaggerated expressions of emotion, and the like). Another is by identifying unusual and incongruous by-products of the organizational practices they are recommending or criticizing (Greatbatch and Clark 2003: 1535, 1537). This enables them to 'vary the extent to which audience laughter is open to interpre-tation as an unvarnished expression of support for their core management ideas' (ibid.: 1538). They conclude that even though the audience members may not be demon-strating their unambiguous agreement with the gurus' ideas, these techniques play an important role with respect to the maintenance of rapport and group cohesion at these lectures. When audience members respond to the invitation to laugh from the guru they confirm at that moment that they are members of an in-group.

Furthermore, the research by Clark and Greatbatch (2003) shows that in addition to orchestrating expressions of group cohesion and solidarity with audience members, the evocation of collective audience laughter enables them to enhance the entertainment value of their lectures, making gurus' messages more memorable and the audience members more receptive to the gurus' recommendations. Greatbatch and Clark (2003: 1539) conclude by suggesting that '[g]iven that speakers are unlikely to persuade audi-ences to empathize with their positions unless they sustain the attentiveness of audience members, it seems likely that humour is one means through which gurus and other pub-lic speakers create the conditions necessary to win and retain converts'.

More recently, Clark and Greatbatch (2011) have examined whether those manage-ment gurus, who are characterized as charismatic or non-charismatic by audience mem-bers, differ in their use of techniques that have been identified as underpinning charismatic oratory. Conducting a detailed analysis of speeches given by seven gurus, they found that when the speeches are taken as a whole the speakers rated as charismatic differ significantly from their non-charismatic counterparts only in terms of delivery. Analysis of the comments of audience members indicates that they feel charismatic speakers supply greater levels of emphasis, rhythm, and spacing between points. Those speakers rated as non-charismatic have a flatter style that makes differentiating different points more difficult. When the sections of the speeches that contained key points were examined, delivery continued to be significant but, in addition, the speakers rated as charismatic used a higher proportion of the rhetorical techniques associated with persuasive oratory (see also Atkinson 1984; Heritage and Greatbatch 1986). Clark and Greatbatch (2011) conclude that what differentiates charismatic from non-charismatic speakers in this context is the variations in the verbal and non-verbal practices used to package and deliver their messages rather than the content of their speeches.

The importance of these features of speech are further emphasized in a study that Greatbatch and Clark (2010) conducted of Daniel Goleman, the author of *Emotional Intelligence* (1996), telling an almost identical story on two separate occasions. They showed that although the wording was very similar on each occasion, the manner in which the story was told and the audience response differed in significant respects. This arose because Goleman's vocal and non-vocal actions changed the emphasis on different elements of the story at each telling—with the consequence that he 'invited collective laughter in response to different components in the two storytelling episodes' (Greatbatch and Clark 2010: 116). Thus elements that generated collective laughter in one telling did not provoke a similar response when the story was repeated and vice versa. This had important implications for how the audience understood the key message being conveyed through the story. As the authors write, the audience's 'differing interpretive frameworks and reactions [...] [rest] on the storyteller's use of different paralinguistic and visual cues' (ibid.: 117).

In sum, the literature on gurus' live performances has developed from non-empirically based assertions of the gurus as management preachers to a more nuanced understanding of these lectures as co-productions between the gurus and their audiences, with the gurus building affiliation and cohesion through the deployment of a variety of verbal and non-verbal techniques.

17.6 CONCLUSION AND DIRECTIONS FOR FUTURE RESEARCH

Some of the momentum to the growth of the consulting industry over the last thirty years has been supplied by the ideas and activities of management gurus, which have created considerable client demand for particular techniques and consultancy services (see also Jung and Kieser, Chapter 16, this volume). Management gurus disseminate their ideas and offer consultancy advice through the printed media and live presentations to gain mass appeal and heighten their visibility. The guru's high media profile means that they can be conceptualized as 'celebrity consultants'.

Research into management gurus has identified a range of features that apparently contribute to heightening the visibility and mass appeal of their ideas and thereby facilitating their potential take-up by management consultancies. On the one hand, studies of the production process have pointed to the importance of the rhetorical appeal and universal applicability of ideas. On the other hand, studies on the dissemination of the ideas conclude that their appeal derives from the gurus' ability to market and promote them as well as build and sustain a following through books and live presentations. Whilst the literature has exposed management gurus and their ideas to detailed empirical scrutiny, the environment in which they now operate is very different from that in which they flourished in the 1980s and 1990s. As a consequence, three areas stand out as fertile ones for future research into the role and celebrification of management gurus.

First, given the growth of the Internet and lack of information on the size and shifting dynamics of the management book market, it is unclear to what extent books remain important to the launch of a blockbuster idea and to the emergence of gurus. Comparative research on the use of digital communication technologies versus more traditional methods of publishing would help pinpoint the media through which aspiring gurus disseminate their ideas most effectively today.

Second, it would help to establish the various sources of legitimacy and authorization, which may have changed due to the emergence of new media such as the expanded use of the Internet, including blogging and social networks. Although the term management guru is still used, no gurus of the stature of Peters, Kanter, and Hamel have emerged in recent years. It is unclear why this is the case. Has the nature of management gurus changed? In addressing this issue it would be helpful to ascertain how the use of the term management guru and, therefore, how the nature of our conception of gurus has evolved over time. In essence, this new stream of research should seek to identify the changing characteristics of people who are ascribed guru status and to assess the extent to which the processes by which gurus emerge have evolved.

Third, if gurus like Peters, Kanter, and Hamel did indeed render the impetus for the growth of management consulting possible, will the current absence of the emergence of gurus of a similar stature affect the future growth of management consultancy sector? What is required is a detailed appraisal of the linkages between guru-led ideas and the mechanisms consultancies use in relation to new concept development (see Heusinkveld and Benders, Chapter 13, this volume). It remains to be seen how the changing landscape of management gurus impacts on the processes through which consultancies adopt and market management ideas.

NOTE

* The authors acknowledge the financial support of the Leverhulme Trust for the project entitled 'Tipping Points: Mathematics, Metaphors and Meanings'. They are grateful to Matthias Kipping and Stefan Heusinkveld for their comments on an earlier draft of this chapter.

REFERENCES

Abrahamson, E. (1996). 'Management Fashion'. *Academy of Management Review*, 5/1, 254–285.
Abrahamson, E. and Fairchild, G. (1999). 'Management Fashion: Lifecycles, Triggers, and Collective Processes'. *Administrative Science Quarterly*, 44, 708–740.

Atkinson, M. (1984). *Our Masters' Voices: The Language and Body Language of Politics*. London: Routledge.

Barley, S. R. and Kunda, G. (1992). 'Design and Devotion: Surges in Rational and Normative Ideologies of Control in Managerial Discourse'. *Administrative Science Quarterly*, 37, 363–399.

Baur, C. (1994). 'Management Evangelists in Showbiz Arena'. *Sunday Times*, 19 June.

Benders, J. and van Veen, K. (2001). 'What's a Fashion? Interpretative Viability and Management Fashions'. *Organization*, 8, 33–53.

Bormann, E. G. (1972). 'Fantasy and Rhetorical Vision: The Rhetorical Criticism of Social Reality'. *Quarterly Journal of Speech*, 58, 396–407.

Branson, R. (1999). *Losing my Virginity: The Autobiography*. London: Virgin Books.

Carlone, D. (2006). 'The Ambiguous Nature of a Management Guru Lecture': Providing Answers While Deepening Uncertainty'. *Journal of Business Communication*, 43/2, 89–112.

Caulkin, S. (1997). 'Quirky Common Sense at $95,000 a Day'. *Observer* (Business section), 13 April, 14.

Caves, R. (2000). *Creative Industries: Contracts between Art and Business*. Cambridge, MA: Harvard University Press.

Clark, T. (2004). 'The Fashion of Management Fashion: A Surge too Far?' *Organization*, 11/2, 297–306.

Clark, T. and Greatbatch, D. (2002). 'Collaborative Relationships in the Creation and Fashioning of Management Ideas: Gurus, Editors and Managers'. In M. Kipping and L. Engwall (eds), *Management Consulting: Emergence and Dynamics of a Knowledge Industry*. Oxford: Oxford University Press, 129–145.

Clark, T. and Greatbatch, D. (2003). 'Management Fashion as Image-Spectacle: The Production of Management Best-Sellers'. *Management Communication Quarterly*, 17/4, 396–424.

Clark, T. and Greatbatch, D. (2011). 'Audience Perceptions of Charismatic and Non Charismatic Oratory: The Case of Management Gurus'. *Leadership Quarterly*, 22, 22–32.

Clark, T. and Salaman, G. (1996). 'The Management Guru as Organizational Witchdoctor'. *Organization*, 3/1, 85–107.

Clark, T. and Salaman, G. (1998). 'Telling Tales: Management Gurus' Narratives and the Construction of Managerial Identity'. *Journal of Management Studies*, 35/2, 137–161.

Covey, S. R. (1989). *The Seven Habits of Highly Effective People: Powerful Lessons in Personal Change*. New York: Simon & Schuster.

Cullen, J. G. (2009). 'How to Sell Your Soul and Still Get Into Heaven: Steven Covey's Epiphany-Inducing Technology of Effective Selfhood'. *Human Relations*, 62/8, 1231–1254.

The Economist (1994). 'Re-Engineering Reviewed', 2 July, 80.

Ernst, B. and Kieser, A. (2002). 'In Search of Explanations for the Consulting Explosion'. In K. Sahlin-Andersson and L. Engwall (eds), *The Expansion of Management Knowledge: Carriers, Flows and Sources*. Stanford, CA: Stanford University Press, 47–73.

Farnham, A. (1996). 'In Search of Suckers'. *Fortune*, 14 October, 79–85.

Fincham, R. (2002). 'Charisma Versus Technique: Differentiating the Expertise of Management Gurus and Management Consultants'. In T. Clark and R. Fincham (eds), *Critical Consulting: New Perspectives on the Management Advice Industry*. Oxford: Blackwell, 191–205.

Fincham, R. and Clark, T. (2002). 'Introduction: The Emergence of Critical Perspectives on Consulting'. In T. Clark and R. Fincham (eds), *Critical Consulting: New Perspectives on the Management Advice Industry*. Oxford: Blackwell, 1–18.

Furusten, S. (1999). *Popular Management Books*. London: Routledge.

Garfinkel, E. (1967). *Studies in Ethnomethodology*. Cambridge: Polity.

Gibson, J. W. and Tesone, D. V. (2001). 'Management Fads: Emergence, Evolution, and Implications for Managers'. *Academy of Management Review*, 15/4, 122–133.

Gill, J. and Whittle, S. (1993). 'Management by Panacea: Accounting for Transience'. *Journal of Management Studies*, 30, 281–295.

Goleman, D. (1996). *Emotional Intelligence: Why it Can Matter More than IQ*. London: Bloomsbury.

Greatbatch, D. and Clark, T. (2003). 'Displaying Group Cohesiveness: Humour and Laughter in the Public Lectures of Management Gurus'. *Human Relations*, 56/12, 1515–1544.

Greatbatch, D. and Clark, T. (2005). *Management Speak: Why We Listen to What the Management Gurus Tell Us*. London: Routledge.

Greatbatch, D. and Clark, T. (2010). 'The Interactive Construction of Stories: The Case of Management Guru Lectures'. In N. Llewllyn and J. Hindmarsh (eds), *Organisations, Interaction and Practice: Studies in Real Time Work and Organising*. Cambridge: Cambridge University Press, 96–118.

Grint, K. (1994). 'Reengineering History: Social Resonances and Business Process Reengineering'. *Organization*, 1, 179–201.

Guthey, E., Clark, T., and Jackson, B. (2009). *Demystifying Business Celebrities*. London: Routledge.

Hammer, M. and Champy, R. (1993). *Reengineering the Corporation: A Manifesto for Business Revolution*. London: Nicholas Brealey.

Harvey Jones, J. (1988). *Making it Happen: Reflections on Leadership*. London: Fontana.

Heritage, J. and Greatbatch, D. (1986) 'Generating Applause: A Study of Rhetoric and Response at Party Political Conferences'. *American Journal of Sociology*, 92, 110–157.

Hirsch, P. M. (1972). 'Processing Fads and Fashions: An Organization Set Analysis of Cultural Industry Systems'. *American Journal of Sociology*, 38, 593–627.

Huczynski, A. (1993). *Management Gurus: What Makes Them and How to Become One*. London: Routledge.

Iacocca, L. (1986). *Iacocca: An Autobiography*. New York: Bantam Books.

Jackson, B. G. (1996). 'Reengineering the Sense of Self: The Manager and the Management Guru'. *Journal of Management Studies*, 33/5, 571–589.

Jackson, B. (2001). *Management Gurus and Management Fashions: A Dramatistic Inquiry*. London: Routledge.

Jackson, B. (2002). 'A Fantasy Theme Analysis of Three Guru-Led Management Fashions'. In T. Clark and R. Fincham (eds), *Critical consulting: New Perspectives on the Management Advice Industry*. Oxford: Blackwell, 172–188.

Kieser, A. (1997). 'Rhetoric and Myth in Management Fashion'. *Organization*, 4/1, 49–74.

Krohe, J. (2004). 'Look Who's Talking'. *Across the Board*, 41/4, 1–7.

Lewin, K. (1951). *Field Theory in Social Science*. New York: Harper.

Lischinsky, A. (2008). 'Examples as Persuasive Argument in Popular Management Literature'. *Discourse and Communication*, 2/3, 249–263.

Micklethwait, J. and Wooldridge, A. (1996). *The Witch Doctors: What Management Gurus are Saying, Why it Matters and How to Make Sense of It*. London: Heineman.

Newstrom, J. W. and Pierce, J. L. (1993). 'An Analytic Framework for Assessing Popular Business Books'. *Journal of Management Development*, 12/4, 20–28.

Pagel, S. and Westerfelhaus, R. (2005). 'Charting Managerial Reading Preferences in Relation to Popular Management Theory Book: A Semiotic Analysis'. *Journal of Business Communication*, 42/4, 420–448.

Peters, T. and Waterman R. (1982). *In Search of Excellence*. New York: Harper & Row.

Røvik, K. A. (2002). 'The Secrets of the Winners: Management Ideas that Flow'. In K. Sahlin-Andersson and L. Engwall (eds), *The Expansion of Management Knowledge: Carriers, Flows and Sources*. Stanford, CA: Stanford University Press, 113–144.

Sargant, W. (1997 [1957]). *Battle for the Mind*. Cambridge: Malor.

Senge, P. (1990). *The Fifth Discipline: The Art and Practice of the Learning Organization*. New York: Doubleday.

Sloan, A. P. (1965). *My Years with General Motors*. London: Sidgwick & Johnson.

Spell, C. (1999). 'Where do Management Fashions Come From, and How Long Do They Stay For?' *Journal of Management History*, 5, 334–348.

Spell, C. (2001). 'Management Fashions: Where Do They Come From, and Are They Old Wine in New Bottles?' *Journal of Management Inquiry*, 10, 358–373.

Suddaby, R. and Greenwood, R. (2001). 'Colonizing Knowledge: Commodification as a Dynamic and Jurisdictional Expansion in Professional Service Firms'. *Human Relations*, 54/7, 933–953.

Ten Bos, R. and Heusinkveld, S. (2007). 'The Gurus' Gusto: Management Fashion, Performance and Taste'. *Journal of Organizational Change Management*, 20/3, 304–325.

Turner, V. (1984). 'Liminality and the Performative Genres'. In J. J. MacAloon (ed.), *Rite, Drama, Festival, Spectacle: Rehearsals Toward a Theory of Cultural Performance*. Philadelphia: Institute for the Study of Human Issues, 19–41.

Van Gennep, A. (1909). *The Rites of Passage*. London: Routledge and Kegan Paul.

Watson, T. (1994). 'Management "Flavours of the Month": Their Role in Managers Lives'. *International Journal of Human Resource Management*, 5, 893–909.

Welch, J. (2001). *Jack: Straight from the Gut*. New York: Warner.

CHAPTER 18

....

BUSINESS SCHOOLS AND CONSULTANCIES: THE BLURRING OF BOUNDARIES

....

LARS ENGWALL

18.1 INTRODUCTION

....

THE early consultants were mostly men of practice—with a few women, such as Lillian Gilbreth (Lancaster 2004), as notable exceptions. This means that they tended to have considerable work experience, sometimes distinguished careers in other sectors of the economy, before becoming consultants. This is true for the engineers, who created the first 'wave' of major development of the consulting industry, which was linked to 'scientific management' (see Kipping 2002; Wright and Kipping, Chapter 2, this volume). And it is also true for many of the firms that eventually came to embody the second wave, focusing on corporate strategy and organization (Kipping 2002; McKenna 2006; David, Chapter 4, this volume). James O. McKinsey, for instance, who founded his firm in 1926, initially tended to hire experienced businessmen, who then administered his 'general survey' to client firms (Wolf 1978).

This only changed in the 1950s under the stewardship of Marvin Bower, who re-founded McKinsey's consultancy after the latter's untimely death in 1937. From then on, McKinsey tended to hire graduates, who had only limited prior work experience, from the growing number of two-year programmes leading to a Master in Business Administration (MBA) (Bhidé 1995; Edersheim 2004). This practice was emulated by other strategy consultancies and continues today. Normally, those who have not attended business school undertake an internal 'mini-MBA', usually taught by business school faculty. More recently, many of the largest consultancies, often specializing in outsourcing and large-scale reorganizations, usually involving IT, have hired people with close to no practical experience, immediately after they have received their undergraduate degree in IT, business, or other disciplines (Kipping and Kirkpatrick 2007).

There has yet to be a comprehensive and systematic examination of this evolving relationship between the consulting firms and academia in general, and the business schools in particular. In the extant limited literature we can first note that Kipping and Amorim (2003) suggest that consultancies originally acted as a kind of substitute for business schools, due to their absence in many countries, then came to work in 'symbiosis' in terms of recruitment and reputation, before turning into competitors by also offering management training. Second, David (2001, Chapter 4, this volume) argues that the significant increase in business school graduates since World War II provided an important precondition for the growth of strategy consulting in the United States. Third, an in-depth statistical study by Ruef (2002) demonstrates the growing importance of consultancies as a destination for business school graduates. All three studies are in concord about the growing interaction between business schools and consulting during the second half of the twentieth century.

Based on these specific studies as well as other work where the relationship is explored more tangentially, and supplemented by some limited additional research when necessary, this chapter will discuss three aspects in the relationship between business schools and consulting firms. It will focus in particular on strategy consultancies, where this relationship seems closest and most 'symbiotic' (Kipping and Amorim 2003; Edersheim 2004; McKenna 2006). First of all, as noted, among others, by Ruef (2002) and David (Chapter 4, this volume), a large number of business school graduates join (strategy) consultancies. The corresponding section examines the consequences of this career pattern for both business schools and consulting firms. A second issue concerns the fact that some faculty members from leading business schools provide competition to consultants through their status as 'management gurus' or 'celebrity consultants' (Clark, Bhatanacharoen, and Greatbatch, Chapter 17, this volume), with some of them even founding their own consulting firms. Finally, business schools have become role models for consulting firms, which is manifested by the latter's adoption of attributes and practices normally associated with academic institutions.

Taken together, all three developments are indicative of a blurring of the boundaries between business schools and consultancies (Engwall and Kipping 2006), with consequences that have yet to be examined by researchers. Before addressing each of these issues in turn, the next section will provide a brief overview of how business schools themselves became the fundamental institutions linking academia and practice (Khurana 2007; Engwall 2009; Engwall, Kipping, and Üsdiken 2010)—a process that was far from smooth, since both business people and university scholars were initially very sceptical towards proposals to introduce academic business studies.

18.2 THE CONTESTED EMERGENCE OF ACADEMIC BUSINESS STUDIES

Before being able to provide management consultancies with human resources and legitimacy, business schools first needed to establish themselves within an academic context. They did this in a long, complex, and contested process from the late nineteenth century onwards (Engwall, Kipping, and Üsdiken 2010). Thus, at the outset, business people questioned the need for academic studies as a proper preparation for business careers, stressing instead the significance of practical experience (e.g. Kirkland 1956: 86–87). In addition, in the nineteenth century there were already a considerable number of non-academic commercial schools. As we know from the extant literature, many of them had become the recruitment base for business (see Engwall and Zamagni 1998). It was therefore questioned why preparations for business would need to be more complicated than that. Moreover, in many countries where members of business elites held an academic degree, they had usually graduated in fields like engineering and law (Engwall, Gunnarsson, and Wallerstedt 1996; Joly 1996; Shenhav 1999). However, at the same time, prominent representatives of business elites, such as Gustav von Mevissen in Cologne, Knut Wallenberg in Stockholm, and Joseph Wharton in Philadelphia, were eager to promote academic business studies in order to raise the status of the business community (Sass 1982: 20; Gunnarsson 1988: 234; Meyer 1998: 21).

The resistance of the established academic community against the inclusion of business studies into universities was even stronger. For example, just after World War I Thorstein Veblen (1918: 210) argued that '[a college of commerce] belongs in the corporation of learning no more than a department of athletics'. In Europe, academia was even more reluctant to embrace business studies and outside pressures had little effect, due to a long established tradition of universities with academic self-governance, which remained relatively impervious to the demands of external stakeholders. Consequently, in contrast to the United States, European business schools were founded outside universities (Engwall, Kipping, and Üsdiken 2010).

But business studies eventually overcame this kind of reluctance and resistance and became a significant part of today's universities. An important role in their redemption was played by measures taken since the 1950s in the United States in response to reports by the Carnegie Corporation and the Ford Foundation on the standards of business education (Gordon and Howell 1959; Pierson et al. 1959). Their authors advocated improvement of the academic standards of US business education. As a result, US business schools started to hire faculty with a background in political science, psychology, sociology, and statistics. In this way, the ground was paved for the later development of increased publishing in academic journals and the more recent focus on impact factors, citations, and so on. This ultimately led to a tension between practice and academia, chronicled, among others, by Daniel (1998), a discussion about the balance between rigour and relevance (cf., e.g., Vermeulen 2005; Tushman et al. 2007; Clinebell and Clinebell 2008), as well as a broad and lasting critique of management education in general, and the MBA in particular as too academic and not 'professional' enough in the traditional sense of the word (e.g. Porter and McKibbin 1988; Locke 1996; Pfeffer and Fong 2002, 2004; Mintzberg 2004; Ghoshal 2005; Khurana 2007; Starkey and Tiratsoo 2007).

This debate, while taking place largely inside academe, is of particular significance for the question addressed in this chapter, that is, the relationship between consulting (which aims at solving practical problems) and academia (with its emphasis on scientific standards). As two of the subsequent sections will discuss in some detail, the move of business schools towards the latter, sometimes referred to as 'academic drift' (Neave 1979), in order to gain legitimacy inside universities, has opened opportunities to provide the missing link to: (a) some business school professors (offering scientifically grounded advice); and (b) consulting firms (offering practice-oriented research). Before turning to these two scenarios, the next section will address the most obvious connection in terms of the recruitment of business school graduates by management consultancies.

18.3 BUSINESS SCHOOLS AS PROVIDERS OF TALENT

As mentioned above, business schools have come to play a significant role in relation to the recruitment of consultancies. One estimate suggests that by the mid-1990s 'almost a third of those who gained an MBA went into consulting' (Wooldridge 1997a: 3). According to Ruef (2002: 85–87), who surveyed 'all living alumni from a large graduate business school in the western United States', the share had increased dramatically from almost zero in the mid-1960s to 30 per cent in the mid-1990s.

When identifying the reasons for the attractiveness of consulting as a destination for MBA (and other) graduates, observers have often highlighted the benefits of business schools in terms of career progression. For example, according to Crainer and Dearlove (1999: 157), 'no fewer than a quarter of the directors of the Fortune 500 companies are Harvard alumni'. This holds also for the European-based INSEAD, whose alumni can be found in 120 countries, and 36 per cent of whom are company chairmen or CEOs (ibid.: 159). Joining a consulting firm might well accelerate access to the top, as suggested by Mintzberg (1996: 66), who characterizes the global consultancies as 'the graduate graduate school of business'.

Like Mintzberg, Wooldridge (1997a: 5) mentions a work period with a consultancy as 'the standard route to membership of a new global elite', which may lead to top positions in various types of companies. He points out that 'former McKinsey men [sic!] run organizations as disparate as IBM, American Express and in the investment arm of SBC Warburg'. Gross and Kieser (2006: 91) also put a spotlight on McKinsey, since the consultancy claims 'to pick only the most talented alumni of the top universities to build a consulting elite'. As Armbrüster (2004) has highlighted, this feeling of belonging to such an elite is, if not created, then at least reinforced by the recruitment process, which identifies those with the best cultural fit among the top graduates. The extant literature suggests that this 'elitism', grounded in the recruitment from the top business schools, helps the (strategy) consultancies in at least two ways: projecting an image of quality and professionalism towards their clients and facilitating control of their own staff, given the similarity of background and socialization (Kärremann and Alvesson 2004; Gross and Kieser 2006; Kipping 2011). As the literature also points out, a particularly close relationship appears to have developed between Harvard Business School and McKinsey since the 1950s (cf. Bhidé 1995; Edersheim 2004; McKenna 2006: 157–158).

The nature of consultancies as 'graduate graduate schools of business' is not only reflected in the possible acceleration of careers and access to a global business elite, but also in the notion of 'alumni'. This is grounded in a basic principal of the personnel policy of most (strategy) consultancies: 'the up-or-out system', which has been discussed quite extensively in the literature (e.g. Maister 1993: 185; Armbrüster 2004; McKenna 2006; Alvesson, Chapter 15, this volume). It means that only a few make it to the top and become partners, and many leave the consultancy firm after some time for other jobs. This high turnover of personnel would be highly problematic in other companies, since it means that recruits have to be trained repeatedly. However, for consultancies there are also positive sides to it. First, incentives are very strong to perform well in order to stay. Second, those who leave become part of a considerable network of former colleagues who may eventually be customers. It is the latter that has prompted many consultancies to copy academic institutions by creating alumni networks. In the case of McKinsey its alumni network is described in the following way:

> Our alumni number nearly 23,000 and work in virtually every business sector in 120 countries. Through formal events and informal networking, former McKinsey consultants make and sustain professional relationships. This dynamic network is a lasting benefit of a McKinsey career. (http://www.mckinsey.com/en/Alumni.aspx accessed 9 April 2011)

Other strategy firms such as Bain & Company, Boston Consulting Group (BCG), or Booz & Co. boast about their alumni in a similar way on their websites. Logically, the idea of networking and personal contacts is also cultivated in recruiting employees. BCG and Bain & Co. thus inform their job applicants at various educational institutions about their alumni.

In sum, the extant literature has shown that business schools constitute significant providers of talent to consultancies, particularly strategy consultants. In this way, these two types of actors live in a 'symbiosis' in the interest of both as suggested by Kipping and Amorim (2003). In addition to mutually beneficial reputation effects, both types of actors generate additional advantages from the relationship. Consultancies get assistance from business schools to screen people through their admission and grading systems as well as giving them basic knowledge about business concepts and models.

As Armbrüster (2004) has pointed out, business schools using the case study method even train their students for job interviews with consultancies, since the case study is a predominant tool for personnel selection in the consulting industry (Mintzberg 2004: 62). Business schools get their graduates out on the job market at relatively high starting salaries, a circumstance which is very important in the ranking of business schools (Wedlin 2006: 72–77). It is also to the advantage of business schools that consultancies function, to a certain extent, as 'graduate graduate schools', thereby paving the way for their graduates to move into top management positions as and when a relatively large proportion of junior consultants move to work for client organizations.

In relation to this mobility, the practice of consultancies to create alumni networks has been noted as a way they take advantage of their previous employees. It is also a way in which they emulate business schools, which points to two areas where the interaction between the two might be less symbiotic and more competitive. These issues will be dealt with in the next two sections.

18.4 BUSINESS SCHOOL FACULTY AS COMPETITORS

Business schools are not only important for consultants by providing them with junior consultants; they also compete with them through faculty members. As research on the history of management education has shown, it was very common in the early years of business schools for professors to also consult. This is not surprising, since many of them had a background in practice. For example, the initial contract of the first Swedish professor at the Stockholm School of Economics (SSE), Oskar Sillén, actually stipulated that he should both be a faculty member and the head of a consulting organization within the Swedish Federation of Industries (Engwall, Furusten, and Wallerstedt 2002). As a result, he became an important bridge between academia and practice in two ways: he could bring practical problems to his students and had good contacts in companies in order to help his graduates to find jobs.

Business school professors continue to occupy a prominent place among 'management gurus' today. For example, in 2002 the consulting firm Accenture compiled a list of the fifty 'most sought after business gurus and management experts', defined as 'business intellectuals [...] providing the latest and best business thinking', and ranked according to three criteria: (1) hits on the Google search engine; (2) citations in the ISI Social Sciences Citation Index; and (3) mentions in the media data base LexisNexis (http://www.all-rankings.com/business-and-finance-advertising-and-marketing/r-7b333c4368/accenture-top-50-management-guru-list accessed 9 April 2011; for similar evidence, see Crainer and Dearlove 1999: 65). Among the fifty gurus as many as two-thirds had an affiliation with an academic institution. As Table 18.1 shows, Harvard, MIT, and Stanford were the three institutions with the largest number of gurus.

Table 18.1 Academic management gurus at three academic institutions (overall rank)

Harvard	MIT	Stanford
Michael E. Porter (1)	Lester Thurow (13)	Jeffrey Pfeffer (20)
Rosabeth Moss Kanter (11)	Michael Hammer (16)	Myron S. Scholes (42)
Robert C. Merton (22)	Edgar Schein (41)	James March (43)
Chris Argyris (29)		
Robert Kaplan (30)		
John Kotter (34)		
Alfred Chandler (38)		
Clayton Christensen (46)		

Note: Chandler died, aged 88, in 2007.

The extensive literature on these management gurus or 'celebrity consultants' has been examined elsewhere in this volume (see Clark, Bhatanacharoen, and Greatbatch, Chapter 17, this volume). This chapter therefore limits itself to discuss, first, the way some of these gurus are literally sitting on the fence between academia and consulting, and then if and how they contribute to knowledge production.

18.4.1 Academic Gurus, Business Schools, and Consultancies

There is some similarity between the relationship of the business schools with their 'star' professors and the one with the consultants. Both are mutually beneficial or 'symbiotic', even if the former is internal, while the latter is external. The academic gurus, without doubt, benefit from the prestige of their institution, as do the consultants with respect to their graduates. In the other direction, the business schools benefit from having these 'celebrity consultants' on their faculty, since, through their personal prestige, they add to the prestige of the institutions. Not surprisingly therefore, the institutions 'celebrate' the consulting activities of these star professors quite extensively, as can be seen, for example, from the following excerpts of the web pages relating to the two top gurus at the Harvard Business School:

Michael E. Porter: 'Professor Porter has served as a strategy advisor to top management in numerous leading U.S. and international companies, among them Caterpillar, DuPont, Procter & Gamble, Royal Dutch Shell, Scotts Miracle-Gro, SYSCO, and Taiwan Semiconductor Manufacturing Company. [...He] is actively involved in assisting governments in the United States and abroad. He plays an active role in U.S. economic policy with the Executive Branch, Congress, and international organizations.' (http://drfd. hbs.edu/fit/public/facultyInfo.do?facInfo=bio&facId=6532 accessed 9 April 2011).

Rosabeth Moss Kanter: 'Through Goodmeasure Inc., the consulting group she co-founded, she has partnered with IBM on applying her leadership tools from business to other sectors; she is a Senior Advisor for IBM's Global Citizenship portfolio. She advises CEOs of large and small companies, has served on numerous business and non-profit boards [...] and national or regional commissions including the Governor's Council of Economic Advisors. She speaks widely, often sharing the platform with Presidents, Prime Ministers, and CEOs at national and international events, such as the World Economic Forum in Davos, Switzerland.' (http://drfd.hbs.edu/fit/public/facultyInfo.do?facInfo=bio&facId=6486 accessed 9 April 2011).

Publications of popular management books and articles in management-oriented journals like the *Harvard Business Review* further underline the symbiosis of academic work and consulting. Michael Porter, for example, gained acknowledgement, reputation, and consulting assignments through his books *Competitive Strategy* (Porter 1980) and *Competitive Advantage* (Porter 1985), which, in April 2011, according to the HBS website, were in their 63rd and 38th printing, respectively. In addition, he has published numerous articles in the *Harvard Business Review* (e.g. Porter 1979, 1996).

In fact, Michael Porter constitutes a particularly interesting case of symbiosis between a business school and the consulting activities of a faculty member. In 1983, he founded, together with five colleagues with relations to Harvard Business School, the consulting firm Monitor. In 2011, it was ranked fifth in terms of its reputation as a management consultancy among graduates (see http://www.vault.com/wps/portal/usa/rankings/individual?rankingId1=248&rankingId2=-1&rankings=1&regionId=0&rankingYear=2012 accessed 26 September 2011). The consultancy explicitly uses the link with the Harvard Business School and the academic achievements of its founder members in its marketing. Thus, its website points out that 'some of the most influential business strategy books of the last twenty-five years have been written by Monitor authors', making explicit references to the following texts (http://www.monitor.com/AboutUs/WhoWeAre/HistoryandFacts/tabid/116/L/en-US/Default.aspx accessed 9 April 2011):

- Argyris, C. (1990). *Overcoming Organizational Defenses*. Boston: Allyn & Bacon.
- Copeland, T. and Antikarov, V. (2001). *Real Options: A Practitioner's Guide*. London: Texere.
- Jensen, M. C. (2000). *The Theory of the Firm: Governance, Residual Claims, and Organizational Forms*. Cambridge, MA: Harvard University Press.
- Meyer, C. and Davis, S. (1998). *Blur: The Speed of Change in the Connected Ecocnomy*. Reading, MA: Addison-Wesley.
- Nagle, T. and Hogan, J. E. (2006). *The Strategy and Tactics of Pricing: A Guide to Growing More Profitably*. 4th edn. Upper Saddle River, NJ: Pearson Prentice Hall (earlier editions with other author constellations).
- Porter, M. E. (1980). *Competitive Strategy: Techniques for Analyzing Industries and Competitors*. New York: Free Press.
- Porter, M. E. (1985). *Competitive Advantage*. New York: Free Press.
- Schwartz, P. (1991). *The Art of the Long View*. New York: Doubleday.
- Schwartz, P. (2003). *Inevitable Surprises: A Survival Guide in the 21st Century*. New York: Penguin.

The website also stresses the publication record of the same professors-cum-consultants in academic journals: 'We have published scores of articles in the world's leading business journals, including more than 80 articles in *Harvard Business Review*' (ibid.). Similar evidence can easily be found for other academic gurus, including Rosabeth Moss Kanter, who has written several bestsellers (e.g. Kanter 1989, 1993) and was the editor of the *Harvard Business Review* between 1989 and 1992; or their colleague John Kotter, whose 'articles in *The Harvard Business Review* over the past twenty years have sold more reprints than any of the hundreds of distinguished authors who have written for that publication during the same time period' (http://drfd.hbs.edu/fit/public/facultyInfo.do ?facInfo=bio&facEmId=jkotter%40hbs.edu accessed 9 April 2011).

While business schools benefit from these activities, they have nevertheless taken steps to ensure that their faculty members maintain some balance between teaching, research, and consulting. In terms of teaching, one can surmise some pressure from students to interact with the stars and not just read their texts, particularly in schools with high tuition fees—an issue that would certainly merit an in-depth study. In terms of consulting, most top business schools therefore have restrictions on the amount of consulting permitted, often to one day a week. At the University of California, for example, faculty members on a nine-month per year contract can use a total of thirty-nine days for such purposes, while those on twelve-month contracts have forty-eight days (http:// www.ucop.edu/acadadv/acadpers/apm/section1.pdf accessed 9 April 2011). As Bok (2006: 32) highlights, however, many faculty members do not consult at all and very few reach the limit of one day per week—which goes to show that the number of academics competing with consultancies is limited to a small number of 'star professors'. In terms of research, there has been some debate in the literature whether their work can still be considered 'scientific' given its highly practical nature—a debate that will be summarized in the following subsection.

18.4.2 Academic Gurus and the Purpose of Scientific Work

The practice-oriented publications and the consulting activities of the academic gurus clearly highlight a tension between academia and practice, particularly at a time when publishing in scientific journals of high standard has become a key dimension in the evaluation of faculty members (cf., e.g., Moed 2005). More broadly, it raises an issue concerning the purpose of scientific work and the difference between knowledge created and disseminated by academics and by consultants. This issue has been debated by a number of different authors, representing a broad range of opinion.

While not directly addressing the issue of academics-cum-consultants, Habermas (1968) has provided a framework that distinguishes different scientific fields based on their kind of knowledge interest. Thus, he characterizes the natural sciences as having a technical interest of knowledge with a focus on verification and falsification, while he associates the humanities and its interpretive mode with a hermeneutical interest of knowledge. In contrast to the natural sciences and the humanities, the social sciences should, according to Habermas, be critical with an emancipatory interest of knowledge. In other words, he argues that, while the natural scientists try to confirm or reject their theories and their colleagues in the humanities try to understand their study objects, social scientists should try to create change. When it comes to academic gurus and their consulting activities, this change-oriented view of social science research, can and has been interpreted in different ways.

On the one hand, it relates to a research tradition in the social sciences referred to as 'action research', implying that research should lead to change (cf., e.g., Clark 1972; French and Bell 1978; McNiff 1998; Somekh 2006; Trahair and Bruce, Chapter 3, this volume). Some of the management professors offering consulting services have actually defended these activities by stressing the need for business academics to remain in touch with practice. For example, the late Eric Rhenman, a Swedish management professor and founder of the consulting firm SIAR, argued that management professors, like their colleagues in medicine, need to have 'patients', making it possible for them to do 'clinical research' (Engwall, Furusten, and Wallerstedt 2002: 42–48). In consulting itself and in the earlier literature on consulting, there is also a clear and related link with 'organizational development'. This has been discussed in some detail by Fincham and Clark (2002: 5–6) with reference to, among others, MIT's Edgar Schein (1969) and Harvard's Chris Argyris (1970)—both among the leading academic 'celebrity consultants' discussed earlier (see above).

The consulting orientation of business school faculty is also consistent with more recent arguments in the sociology of science regarding 'Mode II research' (Gibbons et al. 1994; Nowotny, Scott, and Gibbons 2001) and the 'Triple Helix' (Etzkowitz and Leydesdorff 1997). In terms of the former it is argued that modern researchers have to interact with society rather than work in isolation, while the latter is more precise regarding this interaction by pleading for a collaboration between scientific institutions, industry, and society. On the other hand, there are also scholars like March (1991) and Kieser (2002b), who have pointed out the difficulties of transferring knowledge between the two systems due to their differences (see also Czarniawska and Mazza, Chapter 21, this volume).

In sum, certain business school faculty, the 'star professors' or 'academic gurus', operate partially in the consulting field. They can do so based on their expertise, in a number of cases promoted by the publication of popular management books. As noted above, some, like Michael Porter and Rosabeth Moss Kanter, have even founded their own consulting firms, Monitor and Goodmeasure, respectively. These activities are mutually beneficial, since the gurus can draw on the reputation (and resources) of the institution, while the latter can enhance its visibility and image through the former. The close connection between academia and business practice—through these consulting activities— has prompted some debate, where some see them as a kind of 'action research', while others are more sceptical, even condemning consulting by academics as a departure from the critical and emancipatory purpose of the social sciences.

However, the boundary between academia and consulting is not only crossed by a number of business school professors. Many consultants and consultancies, in particular those focusing on strategy and organization, also pursue activities and adopt practices and postures that are traditionally associated with academic institutions. Many of these have yet to be researched in detail. The subsequent section will summarize what is known so far.

18.5 BUSINESS SCHOOLS AS ROLE MODELS FOR CONSULTANCIES

According to the extant literature, there has thus also been a tendency for consultancies to adopt academic attributes, thereby mimicking business schools in a number of respects. The rationale seems related to the prestige of academia in general as producing valuable and objective knowledge through its research (Whitley 2000). In addition, similarities are sought with the more established and most prestigious institutions, such as the Harvard Business School, founded in 1908, which itself benefited from the reputation of Harvard University, established in 1636 (Cole 2009: 14). The limited extant literature has identified three major ways in which consultancies have emulated business schools: (i) research-based but highly practice-related publications; (ii) the establishment of research institutes or think tanks; and (iii) the provision of education to managers.

18.5.1 Publications

Publishing by consultants is not a recent phenomenon—suffice to look at Frederick Taylor's books (1903, 1911). However, as Furusten (1999) has suggested, there was a growing interest in popular management knowledge in the 1980s, which eventually prompted consultancies to publish books resembling, at least superficially, research monographs. A kind of starting point seems to have been the successful publication of *In Search of Excellence* in 1982 by the McKinsey consultants Thomas J. Peters and Robert H. Waterman, which in its first fifteen years sold 5 million copies worldwide (ibid.; Wooldridge 1997b: 9; Crainer and Dearlove 1999: 60; McKenna 2006: 192–193; Jung and Kieser, Chapter 16, this volume). At the time McKinsey sponsored two other bestsellers—Pascale and Athos' *The Art of Japanese Management* (1982) and Deal and Kennedy's *Corporate Cultures* (1982) (McKenna 2006: 193–194)—and has sponsored many more since then (more recently, e.g., Fubini, Price, and Zollo 2006; Hexter and Woetzel 2007; Riesenbeck and Perrey 2008).

Apparently encouraged by this success, other consultancies promoted similar publications, including Arthur Anderson (Hiebeler, Kelly, and Ketteman 1998), Ernst & Young (McGee and Prusak 1993), PriceWaterhouseCoopers (Redwood, Goldwasser, and Street 1999), Mercer Management Consulting (Slywotsky et al. 1999), BCG (de Brabandere 2005), Booz & Co. (Moeller and Moeller 2008), and Bain & Co. (Zook

2009). For all these publications, the authors and the consultancies seem to have been interested in seeing high circulation figures, since these constitute a kind of proxy for the popularity and widespread acceptance of these ideas, and promote the advice business. This has led to at least one scandal, when it was revealed that Treacy and Wiersema (1995) had bought a large number of copies of their own book in order to increase circulation figures (Wooldridge 1997c: 18; see also Starkey and Tiratsoo 2007: 126).

In addition to publishing monographs, consultancies promote their business through articles in academic journals or business-oriented newspapers. The former might even constitute the early steps of a bestselling book—according to O'Shea and Madigan (1997 198): 'The recipe: Get an article in the Harvard Business Review, pump it up into a book, pray for a best-seller, then market the idea for all it is worth through a consulting company.' Articles by consultants in business newspapers or magazines clearly have less academic aspirations, even if they often refer to 'studies' or 'research' carried out by the consultancy. These 'studies' and their findings are also increasingly used by journalists in their own articles (Grey 2008). According to research conducted by Faust (2002), in Germany consultants have indeed surpassed academics and even managers as the leading experts on management in the business press.

A third communications strategy of the consultancies is the publishing of their own journals, thereby following the practice in academia. McKinsey was one of the earliest, by starting the *McKinsey Quarterly* in 1964. Since 1995, Booz & Co. has published the magazine *strategy+business* (formerly *Strategy & Business*) and occasionally packages its articles into books (e.g. Bernstein 2008), in the same way that the *Harvard Business Review* puts together previously published articles into monographs. While not publishing specific journals, other consultancies also offer periodic publications (now usually online). For instance, the BCG has a service called BCG Publications. Likewise Bain & Co. circulates *Bain Insights*. All of these publications and their attempt to mimic academic outlets deserve more in-depth research.

18.5.2 Research by Consultancies

In a few cases, the mimicry of academia has gone even a step further through the creation of research institutes. The first in this respect were the Japanese, with the creation of research institutes or think tanks, often by the different business groups—the Nomura Research Institute, established in 1965, and the Mitsubishi Research Institute (MRI), founded in 1970, are probably the most well known. According to Kipping (2002), who has provided one of few academic studies of consulting in Japan, these 'think tanks' constitute a specifically Japanese form of 'collective' consulting since they tend to carry out research projects for several—often competing—client firms. Among the Western, aka US consultancies, as in so many respects (see above) McKinsey was the pioneer, with the creation of the McKinsey Global Institute (MGI)—an organization that the consultancy itself describes as follows:

The McKinsey Global Institute (MGI), the business and economics research arm of McKinsey & Company, was established in 1990 to develop a deeper understanding of the evolving global economy. MGI's mission is to provide leaders in the commercial, public, and social sectors with the facts and insights on which to base management and policy decisions. (http://www.mckinsey.com/mgi/perspective/accessed 26 September 2011)

In relation to the above discussion about the blurring of boundaries between consulting and academia, it is particularly noteworthy that MGI uses academic advisors. Sometimes it also collaborates in joint research teams with business school faculty. Among its former advisors are Olivier Blanchard and Robert Solow, Professors of Economics at MIT; Sergio Rebelo, Professor of International Finance at Northwestern University; Dani Rodrik, Professor of International Political Economy at Harvard University; and Paul Romer, Senior Fellow in the Stanford Center for International Development (http://www.mckinsey.com/mgi/perspective/advisors/index.asp accessed 9 April 2011). Most other consultancies have so far refrained from establishing their own research institutes. Some rely on the existing research infrastructures of business schools instead. For example, according to Crainer and Dearlove (1999: 64), Booz Allen & Hamilton used to have a research alliance with INSEAD, with the consultancy sponsoring 'a major research program through the Center for Integrated Manufacturing and Service Operations at INSEAD'.

The reasons for McKinsey and, to a much lesser extent, other consultancies conducting this kind of macro-level research need to be explored in depth. One reason could be to generate publicity. Findings from MGI studies are indeed reported frequently in the business press (Grey 2008). As Kipping and Wright (Chapter 8, this volume) suggest, these efforts might potentially have a 'systemic' impact, aiming at 'changes in the very nature of capital accumulation and the social relations of production'. Whatever the reason(s), only additional academic studies can elucidate them.

18.5.3 Consultants as Management Educators

Finally, consultancies have been and are involved in the other main role of business schools in addition to research, that is, education. Probably the most well-known historical example of a consultant teaching in business schools is Frederick W. Taylor, who lectured once a year at Harvard Business School from its foundation in 1909 until his death in 1915 (Warner 1996). Today, consultants from the larger firms do not seem to have similar teaching commitments—apart from the occasional guest lecture or recruitment presentations. However, individual consultants sometimes hold positions as adjunct professors or sessional lecturers at business schools—an example once again of the mutual benefit to both the consultant and the institution: the former can use the reputation of the latter (and academia in general) for legitimacy purposes, the latter gains fairly inexpensive teaching resources, appreciated by the students due to their practical knowledge. This arrangement—much like the myriad individual, small, and medium-sized consultancies as a whole—has yet to be examined more systematically by academic research (Kubr 2002; Kipping and Wright, Chapter 8, this volume).

Looking at institutions rather than individuals, Kipping and Amorim (2003: 154), have suggested three phases in terms of the development of the educational relationship within the European context. First, before business schools established themselves, consultancies were, to an extent, 'substitutes', providing training for both their own consultants and their clients. In a second phase, consultancies helped set up business schools in Europe and 'outsourced' training to these. By contrast, in a third phase leading up to the present, Kipping and Amorim suggest that the subcontracting of consultants' training 'to graduate business schools seems definitely passed'. While McKinsey and other strategy firms continue to recruit MBA graduates, the larger consultancies such as Accenture resort to hiring large numbers of undergraduates—not necessarily with business degrees—and provide them with significant additional training in their own in-house 'universities' (Kipping and Kirkpatrick 2007).

Moreover, there are indications that the strategy consultancies, while recruiting MBAs, are starting to compete with them elsewhere. Parts of many consultancy projects tend to contain courses and training of managers in client organizations, thereby creating a blurring of boundaries with respect to executive education, which has become instrumental for the funding of many business schools (Crainer and Dearlove 1999). In a survey conducted by *Business Week* in 1999, companies actually thought that consultants were more effective at providing executive education (Mintzberg 2004: 217). As a result, some foresee a further blurring of the boundaries between the different fields of management. Crainer and Dearlove (1999: 231), for example, envisaged that Harvard Business School and McKinsey could come to an agreement to create an HBS–McKinsey MBA.

Overall, it can be concluded that consultancies, like business schools, operate, at least partially, on the blurred boundaries between them. To a larger or lesser extent, they are conducting activities similar to business schools in terms of publishing, research, and education. While in some instances they do so in collaboration, in others they compete with the schools.

18.6 CONCLUSIONS AND DIRECTIONS FOR FUTURE RESEARCH

This chapter has provided an overview of the research examining the relationship between business schools and management consultancies based on the—rather limited—extant literature. This literature has addressed three broad issues: (i) the recruitment of business school graduates by consultancies, in particular by those focusing on strategy and organization, which have, as has been shown, become a kind of 'graduate graduate schools'—with even their own alumni networks; (ii) the consulting activities of what might be termed 'celebrity professors' or 'guru academics', who not only write popular management books and give speeches, but consult with organizations and sometimes establish their own consulting firms—as illustrated by the cases of Harvard's Michael Porter and Rosabeth Moss Kanter; and (iii) the adoption of certain attributes of business schools by management consultancies, including the publication of research-based monographs or articles—sometimes in collaboration with academics—as well as, in a few cases, the establishment of their own journals, and the educational activities of individual consultants and consulting firms.

More research is needed on all of these issues—along avenues that have been proposed throughout the chapter. At the more general level, it would be interesting to know how the changes in both the business school field as well as the consulting industry have affected the relationship between the two in the past and will affect it in the future. Thus, for example, will the continuing critique of business schools in terms of their relevance drive more professors towards greater involvement in practice through consulting activities and their institutions to ever closer relationships with management consultancies, including the possibility of joint MBA programmes suggested by some? Or will the recurrent corporate fraud and economic crises—where both business schools and consultants have been implicated (see Freeman and Krehmeyer, Chapter 24, this volume)—prompt the former to adopt a more critical stance towards the latter, as is hoped by some (Kieser 2002a; Jung and Kieser, Chapter 16, Czarniawska and Mazza, Chapter 21, both this volume)? Put differently, from the perspective of the business schools, will they return to their vocational origins (Engwall, Kipping, and Üsdiken 2010) or their professional ambitions (Khurana 2007)—and what place might there be for management consultancies in either scenario?

In terms of the evolution of management consulting, the above overview has shown that the relationship of strategy consultancies with business schools has been particularly close (Ruef 2002; David, Chapter 4, this volume). These consultancies no longer dominate the industry as they did several decades ago (Kipping 2002; Armbrüster and Kipping 2003). The newly dominant firms based in accounting and IT (see respectively McDougald and Greenwood, Chapter 5; Galal, Richter, and Wendlandt, Chapter 6; both this volume) seem to rely more on their own brand and reputation and less on the legitimizing role of the business schools (Kipping 2011); they also tend to hire undergraduate students, not MBAs, and train them in their own internal 'universities'. This opens several interesting questions for future research regarding the actual training provided in corporate universities (Crainer and Dearlove 1999: 193–205), and the impact these developments might have on the educational efforts of the business schools, possibly leading to a resurgence of undergraduate education in business—in addition to or as a substitution of MBA programmes.

Last but not least, there is also a need to conceptualize and theorize the relationship between business schools and management consulting more specifically in addition to the broader discussion of the composition and role of the 'management fashion industry' or 'arena' (Abrahamson 1991; Micklethwait and Wooldridge 1997; Faust 2002; Jung and Kieser, Chapter 16, this volume). In this respect, Suddaby and Greenwood (2001) have proposed an interesting sequential model. In their view, business schools offer due diligence and innovation, while gurus inside and outside business schools provide legitimation, ultimately paving the way for the commodification of new ideas by large consultancies and the colonization of management knowledge by the major accounting- and IT-based professional service firms. Building on the research from a large European project (http://www.fek.uu.se/CEMP/ accessed 1 October 2011), Engwall and Kipping (2006) have stressed the increasingly blurred boundaries between, in particular, business schools and management consulting, which has also been a common theme of much of the research reported above. At the same time, they also stressed the need to 're-conceptualize the role of the management knowledge industry beyond the diffusion of labels and ideas' (ibid.: 102), suggesting in particular the importance of business school and academia in general as a 'scrutinizer', not only by selecting students eventually hired by consultants and others, but also through 'the questioning of widely diffused management ideas, which have been successful as a result of strong promotion, for example by consultancies' (ibid.).

These conceptualizations, like the empirical research summarized in this chapter, are promising beginnings. But they need to be critically examined and extended by future work.

References

Abrahamson, E. (1991). 'Managerial Fads and Fashion: The Diffusion and Rejection of Innovations'. *Academy of Management Review*, 16/3, 586–612.

Argyris, C. (1970). *Intervention Theory and Method: A Behavioral Science View*. Reading, MA: Addison-Wesley.

Argyris, C. (1990). *Overcoming Organizational Defenses*. Boston: Allyn & Bacon.

Armbrüster, T. (2004). 'Rationality and Its Symbols: Signalling Effects and Subjectification in Management Consulting'. *Journal of Management Studies*, 41/8, 1247–1269.

Armbrüster, T. and Kipping, M. (2003). 'Strategy Consulting at the Crossroads: Technical Change and Shifting Market Conditions for Top-Level Advice'. *International Studies in Management & Organization*, 32/4, 19–42.

Bernstein, A. (ed.) (2008). *Reinventing Service: New Approaches to Meet New Demands*. New York: Booz & Co.

Bhidé, A. V. (1995). 'Building the Professional Firm: McKinsey & Co. 1939–1968'. Harvard Business School, Working Paper No. 95-010.

Bok, D. (2006). *Our Underachieving Colleges: A Candid Look at How Much Students Learn and Why They Should Be Learning More*. Princeton, NJ: Princeton University Press.

Clark, P. (1972). *Action Research and Organizational Change*. London: Harper & Row.

Clinebell, S. K. and Clinebell, J. M. (2008). 'The Tension in Business Education between Academic Rigor and Real-World Relevance: The Role of Executive Professors'. *Academy of Management Learning & Education*, 7/1, 99–107.

Cole, J. R. (2009). *The Great American University: Its Rise to Preeminence, Its Indispensible National Role, Why it Must be Protected*. New York: Public Affairs.

Copeland, T. and Antikarov, V. (2001). *Real Options: A Practitioner's Guide*. London: Texere.

Crainer, S. and Dearlove, D. (1999). *Gravy Training: Inside the Business of Business Schools*. San Francisco: Jossey-Bass.

Daniel, C. A. (1998). *MBA: The First Century*. Cranbury, NJ: Associated University Presses.

David, R. J. (2001). 'The Emergence and Evolution of an "Expert" Field: The Origins, Growth, and Competitive Dynamics of the Management Consulting Industry'. Unpublished Ph.D. dissertation, Cornell University.

Deal, T. E. and Kennedy, A. A. (1982). *Corporate Cultures: The Rites and Rituals of Corporate Life*. Reading, MA: Addison-Wesley.

De Brabandere, L. (2005). *The Forgotten Half of Change: Achieving Greater Creativity through Changes in Perception*. New York: Kaplan.

Edersheim, E. H. (2004). *McKinsey's Marvin Bower: Vision, Leadership, and the Creation of Management Consulting*. New York: John Wiley & Sons.

Engwall, L. (2009 [1992]). *Mercury Meets Minerva*. 2nd edn. Stockholm: EFI.

Engwall, L. and Kipping, M. (2006). 'Management Education, Media and Consulting and the Creation of European Management Practice'. *Innovation: The European Journal of Social Science Research*, 19/1, 93–104.

Engwall L. and Zamagni, V. (eds) (1998). *Management Education in Historical Perspective*. Manchester: Manchester University Press.

Engwall, L., Gunnarsson, E., and Wallerstedt, E. (1996). 'Mercury's Messengers: Swedish Business Graduates in Practice'. In R. P. Amdam (ed.), *Management Education and Competitiveness: Europe, Japan and the United States*. London: Routledge, 194–211.

Engwall, L., Furusten, S., and Wallerstedt, E. (2002). 'The Changing Relationship between Management Consulting and Academia: Evidence from Sweden'. In M. Kipping and L. Engwall (eds), *Management Consulting: The Emergence and Dynamics of a Knowledge Industry*. Oxford: Oxford University Press, 36–51.

Engwall, L., Kipping, M., and Üsdiken, B. (2010). 'Public Science Systems, Higher Education and the Trajectory of Academic Disciplines: Business Studies in the United States and Europe'. In R. Whitley, J. Gläser, and L. Engwall (eds), *Reconfiguring Knowledge Production*. Oxford: Oxford University Press, 325–353.

Etzkowitz, H. and Leydesdorff, L. (eds) (1997). *Universities and the Global Knowledge Economy: A Triple Helix of University–Industry–Government Relations*. London: Pinter.

Faust, M. (2002). 'Consultancies as Actors in Knowledge Arenas: Evidence from Germany'. In M. Kipping and L. Engwall (eds), *Management Consulting: The Emergence and Dynamics of a Knowledge Industry*. Oxford: Oxford University Press, 146–163.

Fincham, R. and Clark, T. (2002). 'Introduction: The Emergence of Critical Perspectives on Consulting'. In T. Clark and R. Fincham (eds), *Critical Consulting: New Perspectives on the Management Advice Industry*. Oxford: Blackwell, 1–20.

French, W. L. and Bell Jr, C. H. (1978). *Organization Development: Behavioral Science Interventions for Organization Improvement*. Englewood Cliffs, NJ: F. T. Prentice Hall.

Fubini, D., Price, C., and Zollo, M. (2006). *Mergers: Leadership, Performance and Corporate Health*. Basingstoke: Palgrave Macmillan.

Furusten, S. (1999). *Popular Management Books: How They Are Made and What They Mean for Organisations*. London: Routledge.

Ghoshal, S. (2005). 'Bad Management Theories are Destroying Good Management Practices'. *Academy of Management Learning & Education*, 4/1, 75–91.

Gibbons, M., Limoges, C., Nowotny, H., Schwartzman, S., Scott, P., and Trow, M. (1994). *The New Production of Knowledge: The Dynamics of Science and Research in Contemporary Societies*. London: Sage.

Gordon, R. A. and Howell, J. E. (1959). *Higher Education for Business*. New York: Columbia University Press.

Grey, A. (2008). 'Marketing Response to Crisis by Consultants: A Case Study of the Reaction from the Enron Demise'. MBA student paper, Schulich School of Business, York University, Toronto, Canada.

Gross, C. and A. Kieser (2006). 'Consultants on the Way to Professionalization?' In R. Greenwood and R. Suddaby (eds), *Research in the Sociology of Organizations*, 24, 69–100.

Gunnarsson, E. (1988). *Från Hansa till handelshögskola: Svensk ekonomundervisning fram till 1909*. Doctoral dissertation, Acta Universitatis Upsaliensis, Studia Oeconomiae Negotiorum 29. Stockholm: Almqvist & Wiksell International.

Habermas, J. (1968). *Erkenntnis und Interesse*. Frankfurt am Main: Suhrkamp.

Hexter, J. and Woetzel, J. (2007). *Operation China: From Strategy to Execution*. Boston: Harvard Business School Press.

Hiebeler, R., Kelly, T. B., and Ketteman, C. (1998). *Best Practices: Building Your Business with Customer-Focused Solutions*. London: Simon & Schuster.

Jensen, M. C. (2000). *The Theory of the Firm: Governance, Residual Claims, and Organizational Forms*. Cambridge, MA: Harvard University Press.

Joly, H. (1996). *Patrons d'Allemagne: Sociologie d'une élite industrielle 1933–1989*. Paris: Presses de Sciences Po.

Kanter, R. M. (1989). *When Giants Learn to Dance: Mastering the Challenges of Strategy, Management, and Careers in the 1990*. New York: Simon & Schuster.

Kanter, R. M. (1993). *Men and Women of the Corporation*. New York: Basic Books.

Kärremann, D. and Alvesson, M. (2004). 'Cages in Tandem: Management Control, Social Identity, and Identification in a Knowledge-Intensive Firm'. *Organization*, 11/1, 149–175.

Khurana, R. (2007). *From Higher Aims to Hired Hands: The Social Transformation of American Business Schools and the Unfulfilled Promise of Management as a Profession*. Princeton, NJ: Princeton University Press.

Kieser, A. (2002a). 'Managers as Marionettes? Using Fashion Theories to Explain the Success of Consultancies'. In M. Kipping and L. Engwall (eds), *Management Consulting: Emergence and Dynamics of a Knowledge Industry*. Oxford: Oxford University Press, 167–183.

Kieser, A. (2002b). 'On Communication Barriers between Management Science, Consultancies and Business Organizations'. In T. Clark and R. Fincham (eds), *Critical Consulting: New Perspectives on the Management Advice Industry*. Oxford: Blackwell, 206–227.

Kipping, M. (2002). 'Trapped in the Third Wave: The Evolution of Management Consultants'. In T. Clark and R. Fincham (eds), *Critical Consulting: New Perspectives on the Management Advice Industry*. Oxford: Blackwell, 28–49.

Kipping, M. (2011). 'Hollow from the Start? Image Professionalism in Management Consulting'. *Current Sociology*, 59/4 (monograph 2), 530–550

Kipping, M. and Amorim, C. (2003). 'Consultancies as Management Schools'. In R. P. Amdam, R. Kvålshaugen, and E. Larsen (eds), *Inside the Business Schools: The Content of European Business Education*. Oslo: Abstrakt, 133–154.

Kipping, M. and. Kirkpatrick, I. (2007). 'From Taylorism as Product to Taylorism as Process: Knowledge Intensive Firms in a Historical Perspective'. In D. Muzio, S. Ackroyd, and F. Chalant (eds), *Redirections in the Study of Expert Labour: Law, Medicine and Management Consultancy*. London: Palgrave Macmillan, 163–182.

Kirkland, E. C. (1956). *Dream and Thought in the Business Community, 1860–1900*. New York: Cornell University Press.

Kubr, M. (ed.) (2002). *Management Consulting: A Guide to the Profession*. Geneva: International Labour Office.

Lancaster, J. (2004). *Making Time: Lillian Moller Gilbreth: A Life Beyond 'Cheaper by the Dozen'*. Boston: Northeastern University Press.

Locke, R. R. (1996). *The Collapse of the American Management Mystique*. Oxford: Oxford University Press.

Maister, D. H. (1993). *Managing the Professional Service Firm*. New York: Free Press.

McGee, J. and Prusak, L. (1993). *Managing Information Strategically: Increase Your Company's Competitiveness and Efficiency by Using Information as a Strategic Tool*. New York: John Wiley & Sons.

McKenna, C. D. (2006). *The World's Newest Profession: Management Consulting in the Twentieth Century*. New York: Cambridge University Press.

McNiff, J. (1998). *Action Research: Principles and Practice*. Basingstoke: Macmillan.

Meyer, H-D. (1998). 'The German Handelshochschulen, 1898–1933: A New Departure in Management Education and Why it Failed'. In L. Engwall and V. Zamagni (eds), *Management Education in Historical Perspective*. Manchester: Manchester University Press, 19–33.

Meyer, C. and Davis, S. (1998). *Blur: The Speed of Change in the Connected Economy*. Reading, MA: Addison-Wesley.

Micklethwait, J. and Wooldridge, A. (1997). *The Witch Doctors: What the Management Gurus are Saying, Why it Matters and How to Make Sense of It*. London: Heinemann.

Mintzberg, H. (1996). 'Musings on Management'. *Harvard Business Review*, 74 (July–August), 61–67.

Mintzberg, H. (2004). *Managers not MBAs: A Hard Look at the Soft Practice of Managing and Management Development*. San Francisco: Berrett-Koehler.

Moed, H. F. (2005). *Citation Analysis in Research Evaluation*. Dordrecht, Netherlands: Springer.

Moeller, L. and Moeller, E. L. (2008). *The Four Pillars of Profit-Driven Marketing: How to Maximize Creativity, Accountability, and ROI*. New York: McGraw-Hill.

Nagle, T. and Hogan, J. E. (2006). *The Strategy and Tactics of Pricing: A Guide to Growing More Profitably*. 4th edn. Upper Saddle River, NJ: Pearson Prentice Hall.

Neave, G. (1979). 'Academic Drift: Some Views from Europe'. *Studies in Higher Education*, 4/2, 143–159.

Nowotny, H., Scott, P., and Gibbons, M. (2001). *Re-Thinking Science: Knowledge and the Public in an Age of Uncertainty*. Cambridge: Polity.

O'Shea J. and Madigan, C. (1997). *Dangerous Company: Management Consultants and the Businesses They Save and Ruin*. New York: Times Books.

Pascale, R. T. and Athos, A. G. (1982). *The Art of Japanese Management: Applications for American Executives*. New York: Warner.

Peters, T. J. and Waterman Jr, R. H. (1982). *In Search of Excellence: Lessons from American Best-Run Companies*. New York: Harper & Row.

Pfeffer, J. and Fong, C. T. (2002). 'The End of Business Schools: Less Success than Meets the Eye'. *Academy of Management Learning & Education*, 1, 78–95.

Pfeffer, J. and Fong, C. T. (2004). 'The Business School "Business": Some Lessons from the US Experience'. *Journal of Management Studies*, 41, 1501–1520.

Pierson, F. C. et al. (eds) (1959). *The Education of American Businessmen*. New York: McGraw-Hill.

Porter, M. E. (1979). 'How Competitive Forces Shape Strategy'. *Harvard Business Review*, 57/2, 137–145.

Porter, L. W. and McKibbin, L. E. (1988). *Management Education and Development: Drift of Thrust into the 21st Century?* New York: McGraw-Hill.

Porter, M. E. (1980). *Competitive Strategy: Techniques for Analyzing Industries and Competitors*. New York: Free Press.

Porter, M. E. (1985). *Competitive Advantage*. New York: Free Press.

Porter, M. E. (1996). 'What Is Strategy?' *Harvard Business Review*, 74/6, 61–78.

Redwood, S., Goldwasser, C., and Street, S. (1999). *Action Management: Practical Strategies for Making Your Corporate Transformation a Success*. New York: John Wiley & Sons.

Riesenbeck, H. and Perrey, J. (2008). *Power Brands: Measuring, Making and Managing Brand Success*. New York: John Wiley & Sons.

Ruef, M. (2002). 'At the Interstices of Organizations: The Expansion of the Management Consulting Profession, 1933–1997'. In K. Sahlin-Andersson and L. Engwall (eds), *The Expansion of Management Knowledge: Carriers, Flows and Sources*. Stanford, CA: Stanford Business Books, 74–95.

Sass, S. A. (1982). *The Pragmatic Imagination: A History of the Wharton School 1881–1981*. Philadelphia: University of Pennsylvania Press.

Schein, E. (1969). *Process Consultation: Its Role in Organization Development*. Reading, MA: Addison-Wesley.

Schwartz, P. (1991). *The Art of the Long View*. New York: Doubleday.

Schwartz, P. (2003). *Inevitable Surprises: A Survival Guide in the 21st Century*. New York: Penguin.

Shenhav, Y. A. (1999). *Manufacturing Rationality: The Engineering Foundations of the Managerial Revolution*. Oxford: Oxford University Press.

Slywotsky, A. J., Morrison, D. J., Moser, T., Mundt, K. A., and Quella, J. A. (1999). *Profit Patterns: 30 Ways to Anticipate and Profit from Strategic Forces Reshaping Your Business*. New York: Times Books.

Somekh, B. (2006). *Action Research: A Methodology for Change and Development*. Maidenhead: Open University Press.

Starkey, K. and Tiratsoo, N. (2007). *The Business School and the Bottom Line*. Cambridge: Cambridge University Press.

Suddaby, R. and Greenwood, R. (2001). 'Colonizing Knowledge: Commodification as a Dynamic of Jurisdictional Expansion in Professional Service Firms'. *Human Relations*, 54/7, 933–953.

Taylor, F. W. (1903). *Shop Management*. New York: Harper Brothers.

Taylor, F. W. (1911). *The Principles of Scientific Management*. New York: Norton.

Treacy, M. and Wiersema, F. (1995). *The Discipline of Market Leaders: Choose Your Customers, Narrow Your Focus, Dominate Your Market*. Reading, MA: Addison-Wesley.

Tushman, M. L., O'Reilly, C. A., Fenelossa, A., Kleinbaum, A. M., and McGrath, D. (2007). 'Relevance and Rigor: Executive Education as a Lever in Shaping Practice and Research'. *Academy of Management Learning & Education*, 6/3, 345–362.

Veblen, T. (1918). *The Higher Learning in America*. New York: B. W. Huebsch.

Vermeulen, F. (2005). 'On Rigor and Relevance: Fostering Dialectic Progress in Management Research'. *Academy of Management Journal*, 48/6, 978–982.

Warner, M. (1996). 'Taylor, Frederick Winslow (1856–1915)'. In M. Warner (ed.), *International Encyclopedia of Business and Management*. London: Routledge, 4,782–4,786.

Wedlin, L. (2006). *Ranking Business Schools: Forming Fields, Identities and Boundaries in International Management Education*. Cheltenham: Edward Elgar.

Whitley, R. (2000 [1984]). *The Intellectual and Social Organization of the Sciences*. Oxford: Oxford University Press.

Wolf, W. B. (1978). *Management and Consulting: An Introduction to James O. McKinsey*. Ithaca: Cornell University.

Wooldridge, A. (1997a). 'The Advice Business'. *The Economist*, 342/8009, 3–5.

Wooldridge, A. (1997b). 'In Praise of One-Man Bands'. *The Economist*, 342/8009, 9.

Wooldridge, A. (1997c). 'Consultant, Heal Thyself'. *The Economist*, 342/8009, 17–18.

Zook, C. (2009). *A Return to Profit from the Core: How to Manage your Business in Turbulent Times*. Boston: Harvard Business Press.

PART 5

CONSULTANTS AND
THEIR CLIENTS

CHAPTER 19

THE NATURE OF CLIENT– CONSULTANT INTERACTION: A CRITICAL REVIEW

NATALIA NIKOLOVA
TIMOTHY DEVINNEY

19.1 INTRODUCTION

THE literature on consulting is characterized by substantive controversy regarding the nature of consulting and the value of consultants' contributions (Armbrüster 2006). On the one hand, consultants have been seen as 'substantial contributors, in their own right, to our collective store of management knowledge' (Suddaby and Greenwood 2001: 934) and as important change agents who introduce new perspectives and frames of reference into client organizations (Ginsberg and Abrahamson 1991), contributing to 'significant economic growth in many industrialized countries' (Poulfelt, Greiner, and Bhambri 2005: 3). On the other hand, both clients (e.g. Shapiro, Eccles, and Soske 1993) and researchers (e.g. Alvesson 1993, 2001; Clark 1995; Clark and Salaman 1996a, 1996b; Kieser 1997, 2002) have questioned this perspective by arguing that the real value of consulting is very difficult to ascertain and, hence, consulting is concerned mainly with creating an impression of value. Critics argue that consultants are 'pushing standardized solutions rather than really listening to the issues [of clients] and being guided accordingly' (Ashford 1998: xvi) or, even worse, creating solutions for 'manufactured problems' associated with the latest 'thought leadership' fad, to the extreme where clients become 'marionettes' in the hands of consultants (Kieser 2002).

These contrasting viewpoints are well documented in the academic literature. On one side is the 'functionalist' position, which stresses the knowledge-based and helping nature of the relationship, while an opposite 'critical' perspective focuses on the faddish and symbolic nature of consulting (Werr and Styhre 2002/3; Armbrüster 2006; Schwarz and Clark 2009). A close look at the 'functionalist' literature shows that it can be divided in two quite different sub-perspectives, which we call the expert model and the social learning model. Each of these sub-perspectives implies a different understanding of consulting, as well as of consulting practice. According to the first sub-perspective, the *expert model*, which dates back to the start of academic interest in consulting, consultants are providers of technical expertise for, or on behalf of, a client (Kubr 1996; Mulligan and Barber 1998). The client–consultant relationship is described as a client–*expert* interaction (Gallessich 1982; Greiner and Metzer 1983; Wilkinson 1995; Aharoni 1997), implying that consultants as experts have the necessary knowledge to solve clients' problems. The second sub-perspective, originating in the behavioural sciences, emerged in the 1970s. It represents a more participative approach to consulting, with consultants' main role being to assist clients in solving their problems by engaging them in a joint learning process (Kubr 1996; Mulligan and Barber 1998). This view of consulting, which we call the *social learning model*, offers a more *balanced* perspective of the client–consultant relationship, emphasizing that both clients and consultants contribute valuable knowledge and ideas to a project (McGivern 1983; McGivern and Fineman 1983; Schön 1983; Schein 1999, 2002).[1]

What is common to both these views is that they implicitly assume that clients are convinced of the value consultants provide (Fincham and Clark 2002). In contrast, a third, more recent, view of consulting, stresses the need for consultants to persuade clients of the value they provide. This view takes a critical stance regarding the real value of consulting, and we call it the *critical model*. It stresses the *symbolic* character of consulting and regards consultants as impression managers seeking to make their clients dependent on the management fads they produce (Alvesson 1993, 2001; Clark 1995; Clark and Salaman 1998a, 1998b; Kieser 2002).

While these three main models stress important features of the client–consultant interaction, several researchers have suggested that they do not take sufficient account of its complex and multidimensional character (e.g. Engwall and Kipping 2002; Fosstenløkken, Løwendahl, and Revang 2003). Consequently, there is a need for further investigation into the nature of client–consultant interaction and the role clients and consultants play in consulting projects. This chapter therefore not only seeks to describe the contributions of the existing models to our understanding of client–consultant interaction, but also their shortcomings, as well as the possible need for more complex and nuanced models to better represent the nature of the client–consultant relationship. In terms of the detailed picture of the different models of the client–consultant relationship, the chapter examines their assumptions in regard to three interrelated areas: (i) the nature of consulting; (ii) the nature of the client–consultant interaction, including the role of both clients and consultants; and (iii) power relations. From a sociological point of view, any socio-economic relationship is characterized by common features, including the nature of the relationship, the nature of activities performed within the relationship, the actors' roles, and their power relations. This chapter shows that each of the models offers a different interpretation regarding these dimensions. By comparing the models across these dimensions it outlines differences between

Table 19.1 Models of the client–consulting relationship: A summary of their main assumptions

	The Expert Model	The Social Learning Model	The Critical Model
Key Works	Aharoni (1997); Gallessich (1982); Greiner and Metzer (1983); Wilkinson (1995).	Blake and Mouton (1983); McGivern (1983); McGivern and Fineman (1983); Schein (1987, 1988, 1999, 2002); Schön (1983, 1987).	Alvesson (1993, 1995, 2001); Clark (1995); Clark and Salaman (1996a, 1996b, 1998a, 1998b); Jackson (2001); Kieser (1997, 2002).
Metaphors	The consultant as 'seller of expertise' (Aharoni 1997) and a 'doctor' (Gallessich 1982).	The consultant as 'helper' (Schein 1999) and 'reflective practitioner' (Schön 1983, 1987).	The consultant as rhetorician (Alvesson 1993, 1995); 'impression manager' and 'storyteller' (Clark 1995; Clark and Salaman 1996b); creator of management fads (Jackson 2001; Kieser 1997, 2002); and management's ally (Jackall 1988).
Nature of Consulting	Consulting is about solving clients' problems by transferring consultants' knowledge to the client organization.	Consulting is about assisting clients to solve their own problems by combining consultants' expertise with clients' deep knowledge of their company in a process of framing and negotiating different perspectives and views.	Consulting is about creating the impression that clients are buying something of value; it also involves the creation and dissemination of management fads and fashions.
Nature of Knowledge	Consulting knowledge is decontextualized, objective, and rational.	Consulting knowledge is 'constructed' through clients' and consultants' actions and interactions and is embedded in a client-specific context.	Consulting knowledge is ambiguous and idiosyncratic; images, stories, and symbols serve as 'rationality-surrogates'.
Knowledge Asymmetry	Consultants as experts have the capacity to solve clients' problems; the client is a lay persona and is more or less excluded from the problem-solving process (unidirectional knowledge asymmetry).	Client and consultant both possess knowledge important for the problem solution (mutual knowledge asymmetry).	Due to the intangible and interactive character of the consulting work, clients have difficulties in evaluating consultants' knowledge and the provided service prior and after it has been delivered (unidirectional 'knowledge' asymmetry).

continued

Table 19.1 Continued

	The Expert Model	The Social Learning Model	The Critical Model
Nature of Interaction	The interaction consists of the transfer of information from client to consultant and the reciprocal transfer of solutions; the nature of communications channels, characteristics of messages, and motivation and absorptive capacity of the involved individuals determine its success.	Client–consultant interaction is a joint learning process: it is the reciprocal exploration, testing, and negotiation of clients' and consultants' positions, interpretations, and experiences.	The interaction consists in consultants creating impressions, images, and stories whereas clients act as the audience; rhetorical skills and acts are important aspects of the interaction process.
Power Relations	Consultants as experts determine the problem solution on the basis of their expertise and professional judgement. The client is dependent on the knowledge of the expert and accepts consultants' authority (consulting-centric view).	Both consultant and client are powerful and interdependent because both parties possess relevant knowledge and make important contributions to the problem-solving process (a balanced relationship).	Consultants are powerful and persuasive actors; they use rhetoric, stories, and symbols to impress clients and sell management fads. The client is dependent on consultants and the management fads they create (consulting-centric view); the consultant's power is seen as an extension of top management's hierarchical power.

the models as well as their main contributions and shortcomings. Based on the comparison of the main views on the client–consultant relationships, the conclusion outlines directions for future research.

19.2 MODELS OF THE CLIENT–CONSULTANT INTERACTION

19.2.1 The Expert Model

The expert model represents the earliest (Blake and Mouton 1983; Czerniawska 2003) and perhaps most 'stereotyped' (Garratt 1981) view on consulting: characterizing consultants as transmitters of business knowledge and techniques to client organizations

(Gallessich 1982; Greiner and Metzer 1983; Wilkinson 1995; Aharoni 1997). Research shows that this model has been applied in situations involving complex, highly uncertain, and innovative problems, as is the case in strategy consulting, as well as in the case of familiar and routine tasks such as contractor-style consulting (Kitay and Wright 2003).

19.2.1.1 *Overview of key features*

In terms of the *nature of consulting*, according to this model, what differentiates management consultancies and all professional service providers from traditional manufacturing companies is that they create value through their contribution of expertise and experience in solving client problems (Gallessich 1982; Aharoni 1997). Consulting expertise is described as based partly on an abstract body of knowledge, which is normally maintained through professionals or professional associations (Abbott 1988), and partly on methods and concepts developed during consulting practice (Gallessich 1982). It is seen as a reflection of truth, rationality, and wisdom (Fournier 1999), and the result of long experience (McGivern and Fineman 1983). Both the 'ownership' of truth and the respect conveyed by experience legitimize the powerful and protected position of consultants and are the reasons why advocates of the model implicitly assume that there is a knowledge asymmetry between consultants and clients. Hence, the (arrogant) belief held by many consultants that they know better than their client what services the client really needs (Walsh 2001).

According to this model, the *nature of the client–consultant interaction* consists of the client hiring the consultant and transferring information about the issue at hand as required by the consultant, and the consultant diagnosing the problem and providing recommendations for its solution based on an existing classification system of problems (Tilles 1961; Bell and Nadler 1979; Blake and Mouton 1983; Biswas and Twitchell 1999; Semadeni 2001). Thus, consultants are seen as knowledge brokers who solve organizational issues 'not through their innovative solutions to unusual questions, but rather through the application and reformulation of existing knowledge to known problems' (McKenna 2006: 13). This view of the problem-solving process is in line with the assumed unidirectional knowledge asymmetry between clients and consultants. The consultant's role is to generate the 'right' problem solution with the client's role being limited to the delivery of information and the implementation of the proposed solution. 'Once the information is obtained from the client/customer, the [consultant] can proceed directly to employ the discretion and knowledge inherent in the task' (Mills, Chase, and Margulies 1983: 303). Therefore, successful knowledge transfer and creation is mostly dependent on the problem-solving abilities or judgement of the consultants, and to a lesser degree on the clients' motivation to co-operate with the consultants (Kubr 1996; Mills, Chase, and Margulies 1983), clients' possession of related knowledge, and their ability to absorb knowledge (e.g. Abbott 1988).

Regarding *power relations*, a key assumption of the expert model is the autonomy and power of the consultant (Haug and Sussman 1969; Sharma 1997; Kubr 1996; Mills and Moshavi 1999), resulting from the assumed knowledge asymmetry. Whereas clients deliver the raw information, only the consultants are believed to possess the necessary expertise to solve the problem: 'consultants, like other specialists, occupy positions of relative power, as they are often the sole authorities on certain technical problems and their implications' (Gallessich 1982: 381). The expert diagnoses the problem and pre-scribes solutions unilaterally, whereas the 'client is left unaware of what has been going on and is, thus, in a weak position when it comes to having an influence on the outcome' (McGivern and Fineman 1983: 435). Therefore, consultants see clients as dependent on the credibility their expertise provides (Walsh 2001). Some authors even argue that an equalized relationship between clients and consultants is counter-productive due to a 'reduction of rationality in the decision-making process' (Mills and Moshavi 1999: 53). Such a relationship, they conclude, will alter its fundamental nature from a superior–subordinate alliance to peer interaction.

19.2.1.2 *Review of the model*

The implicit assumption behind the expert model is that professionals' expertise in their field alone makes them successful service providers (Walsh 2001). Knowledge is assumed to be a 'decontextualized' asset or resource, an 'objectively definable commodity' (Empson 2001) that retains its meaning while being transferred across individuals and organiza-tions (Alvesson and Kärreman 2001; Werr and Stjernberg 2003). Consultants are seen as experts who give 'the right advice, in the right way, to the right person and at the right time. They are said to be in a position to make an unbiased assessment of any situation, tell the truth and recommend frankly and objectively what the client organization needs to do without having any second thoughts on how this might affect his or her interests' (Alvesson and Johansson 2002: 230; also Sturdy, Werr, and Buono 2009). Accordingly, consultants are seen as having an external 'God's-eye view of the world' (Boland et al. 2001: 396).

In line with this argument, the client–consultant interaction is seen as a process of message sending and message receiving (Boland and Tenkasi 1995). It is implicitly assumed that both client and consultant know how to use the exchanged information, which means that they understand its true meaning. Thus, problem solving is viewed as a consequence of the successful transfer of information (Tilles 1961) and becomes a process of implementing procedures for encoding and decoding messages (Boland and Tenkasi 1995). Interactional problems are attributed either to an insufficient motivation and absorptive capacity or to inadequate transmission channels. Furthermore, due to the assumed knowledge asymmetry, learning is seen as a unidirectional process: the implicit tone is that 'as experts, consultants should not look at their clients as potential teachers' (Walsh 2001: 35). When consultants learn something, it is regarded as the result of their individual abilities.

Several authors who study knowledge transfer between individuals from different per-sonal and cultural backgrounds empirically suggest that the view of knowledge as con-textually and situationally independent is highly limited and problematic (e.g. Winter 1987; Bechky 2003). Thus, in order to understand the process of knowledge creation and transfer, one needs to study knowledge in the context within which it is created and applied (Tsoukas and Vladimirou 2001; Bechky 2003). In addition, recent research on consulting projects has shown that consulting knowledge is not always external and concrete (Sturdy et al. 2009). Often, a major part of consultants' knowledge is made up of what these authors refer to as 'sector knowledge', which is neither external, as clients possess it too, nor concrete, as it is constantly negotiated and constructed by a number of actors, including clients, consultants, business journalists, and academics. Thus, external actors, including clients, often take part in the knowledge development within client–consultant teams (Hislop 2002; Fosstenløkken, Løwendahl, and Revang 2003).

Furthermore, it has been argued that the problem-solving process as proposed by the expert model works only in the case of well-defined routine problems, which are previously known to the problem solvers, and where the client lacks the ability or will to deal with the issue themselves (Schön 1983; Czerniawska 2003; Nikolova, Reihlen, and Schlapfner 2009). In such cases, the client only wants to acquire special technical knowledge, which makes the 'expert' form of interaction economically advantageous for all the involved actors (see Tilles 1961; Kubr 1996). Examples include large-scale problems or issues where extensive quantitative data on large populations is required such as recruitment, remuneration, training, process mapping, and outplacement (McGivern and Fineman 1983; Kitay and Wright 2003). In contrast, the nature of new and complex problems is, by definition, unclear and ambiguous. In this case, successful problem solving is not an error-free process of information exchange but rather a 'reflective', 'non-technical' process of problem naming and framing, which requires the intensive involvement of the client, as stressed by advocates of the social learning model (Schön 1983; also McGivern and Fineman 1983). The expert model downplays this relative pluralism of knowledge and, in particular, the importance and legitimacy of clients' knowledge (also Sturdy et al. 2009).

These weaknesses of the expert model are confirmed by empirical research, showing that little learning between clients and consultants takes place within expert forms of consulting (McGivern and Fineman 1983; Pellegrinelli 2002; Kitay and Wright 2003). Moreover, the absence of understanding and reflection between clients and consultants leads to increased uncertainty as to the exact nature of the problem and what the client expects from the consultant and, consequently, to the unidirectional dependency on the part of the client (Schön 1983). Empirical findings show that the greater the consultant's power and autonomy in the problem-solving process, the lower would be the scale of customization of the solution (Hislop 2002). In such cases, clients get standardized problem solutions, which often do not fit the specific and locally oriented client situation and which are in most cases not implemented successfully. Due to the absence of intensive interaction and knowledge transfer, the client–consultant relationship is not effective and it often ends with frustration on both sides. This criticism is one of the reasons for the emergence of the social learning model, which suggests a different form of interaction between clients and consultants, taking into account the complex nature of client issues.

Finally, the expert model does not discuss how consultants persuade clients that they are the experts for particular types of problems given the intangible character of consulting services (e.g. Clark 1995). How do they legitimize their work? How do they build up their reputation as experts (also Armbrüster 2006)? As we will discuss later, these issues are the main concern of the critical model on consulting.

19.2.2 The Social Learning Model

In contrast to the expert model, the social learning model emphasizes the fact that clients share 'centre stage' with the consultants and are active players in the diagnosis and problem-solving process (e.g. Garratt 1981; McGivern 1983; Schön 1983; Schein 1999, 2002).[2] This approach to consulting is rooted in the behavioural sciences, including literature on organizational development (OD), action research, and organizational learning (see McGivern and Fineman 1983). Its major characteristic, which makes it vastly different from the orthodox, expert model, is its emphasis on a balanced relationship between clients and consultants and the 'demystification' of expertise (McGivern and Fineman 1983). Thus, the shift from the expert mode of consulting towards a model that involves intensive interaction between clients and consultants in the form of a participative learning process arose partly because of increasing dissatisfaction with the outcomes of the expert consulting model (Schön 1983) and partly because of the development of new insights regarding motivation, leadership, team-work, and learning (Gallessich 1982).

19.2.2.1 *Overview of key features*

In terms of the *nature of consulting*, according to this model, consulting is about assisting clients to solve their own problems by combining consultants' expertise with clients' deep knowledge of their company in a process of framing and negotiating different perspectives and views (Blake and Mouton 1983; Schön 1983; Schein 1999, 2002; Czerniawska 2003). Consulting is, therefore, about facilitating clients' problem solving and training them in using diagnostic and problem-solving skills where necessary, that is, it is about changing clients' behaviour (Schein 1987, 1988). Furthermore, advocates of this model stress the need for consultants to accept clients' views as a legitimate frame of reference to work within. Consultants have to accept that they too need to learn and be influenced by the client (Schein 2002). Therefore, clients have an active role in the client–consultant relationship because only they have access to 'hidden cultural, political, and personal factors', which are important for the problem-solving process (Schein 1987: 30; also McGivern 1983). Consequently, consulting becomes a process of 'mutual helping' (Schein 2002: 27) in which consulting knowledge is 'constructed' through individual actions embedded in the client-specific context rather than existent prior to action, as stated in the expert model (Blake and Mouton 1983; McGivern and Fineman 1983; Schön 1987).

Regarding the *nature of client–consultant interaction*, according to the social learning model, it is open and 'minimally defensive', with both client and consultant committed to having their positions and interpretations confronted and tested and with both being open to the reciprocal exploration of risky ideas (Schön 1983). Furthermore, problem solving does not involve consultants trying to apply a standardized solution to a new situation, as suggested by the expert model. Rather, it requires a reflective inquiry into the causes of a problem and the exploration of new options (Blake and Mouton 1983; Schön 1983; Czerniawska 2003). If consultants engage in such an inquiry without sharing their underlying assumptions with the client, their expertise remains a black box, a 'mysterious artistry' for the client (Schön 1983: 243; also McGivern and Fineman 1983). Therefore, clients have to be involved to a much higher degree in the problem-solving process in order to gain access to this 'reflective conversation'. Following this, consultants' and clients' roles consist in helping each other in a process of mutual influence and learning (Schön 1983; Schein 2002). However, because this reflective inquiry poses different demands on clients' and consultants' skills and is very time-consuming, some advocates of this model argue that it should be applied only in cases where the client's problem is of sufficient importance. In emergent or routine situations, a more restricted interaction, as proposed by the expert model, is considered more appropriate and efficient (e.g. Blake and Mouton 1983; McGivern and Fineman 1983; Schön 1983; Czerniawska 2003).

In the social learning model the *power relations* between client and consultant are balanced and based on the demystification of expertise and on mutual exploration (McGivern and Fineman 1983). Both consultants and clients are interdependent as both parties make valuable contributions to the problem-solving process (McGivern 1983; Schön 1983). Consultants are now expected to reflect on their expertise in the presence of clients, thus making themselves confrontable by their clients rather than keeping their expertise private and mysterious, as is the case in the expert model (Schön 1983; Schein 2002). This new type of interaction is only possible if consultants abdicate their unquestioned authority and the comfort of relative invulnerability. On the other side of the relationship, clients have to agree to join the consultant in the problem-solving process and to work to make their knowledge and experience clear to themselves and to the consultants. As a result, so the argument goes, the relationship becomes balanced and free of power issues (Blake and Mouton 1983; Schön 1983; Schein 2002).

19.2.2.2 *Review of the model*

Compared to the expert model, the social learning model provides a more comprehensive view of the interaction process in client–consultant teams. It makes the following important contributions to our understanding of the client–consultant relationship. First, client problems are not regarded as 'fixed' and independent of the actors involved in their solution, as postulated by the expert model, but as constructed in the interaction process between clients and consultants. Second, consulting knowledge is not described as objective and independent of the context in which it is applied but as one particular way of looking at and interpreting topics, which was constructed in a particular context and can be reconstructed in another. In this process, clients play an active role as they also possess valuable contextual knowledge. Therefore, thirdly, the model stresses the need for clients and consultants to reflect on their interpretations and frames, and share them with each other if they are to work effectively together. Fourth, in order to successfully address complex problems, clients and consultants need to engage in a reflective inquiry and create new knowledge instead of relying on standardized 'recipes-in-use' as suggested by the expert model.

However, the social learning model also has some limitations. First, there is a danger of over-emphasizing the relevance of learning as a process of participating while dismissing the importance of learning through analysing and justifying. Research on cognition has shown that 'people learn by being told as well as by "participant observation" and by doing' (Lakomski 2004: S93). In other words, clients do not always need to participate in the problem-solving process for learning to take place. Second, advocates of the model seem to overestimate the relevance of 'otherness' between clients and consultants, that is, the degree to which clients' and consultants' knowledge, work methods, and language differ (Kipping and Armbrüster 2002). Recent research has shown that consultants are often insiders with established relationships with their client organizations, which can make their interaction less problematic than claimed by the advocates of the social learning model (Sturdy et al. 2009). Third, even in cases when clients' and consultants' interpretations vary and 'may not be objectively resolvable', advocates of the model do not offer a solution for how these differences can be overcome. Schön, for example, is aware that the suggestion for an open and intensive communication between clients and consultants is not specific enough to enhance the co-operation within client–consultant teams: the 'resolution of such differences depends on the *little-understood* ability of inquirers to enter into one another's appreciative systems and to make reciprocal translations from one to the other' (1983: 273, emphasis added; see also McGivern and Fineman 1983).

Thus, the model fails to explain the process of translation and show how clients and consultants can improve their interaction. Furthermore, questions regarding the power aspects of the relationship, like whose perspective will build the basis for the problem solution and whether it is necessary that one of the parties dominates the problem-solving process, which have high practical relevance (e.g. Nikolova and Devinney 2009), remain unanswered, as it is assumed that there are no real power issues in a balanced client–consultant relationship where clients and consultants have agreed to an open and constructive confrontation. Finally, given that the model stresses the importance of consultants' (and clients') *subjective* impressions and interpretations, it does not address an important implication of this insight: how the interaction between clients and consultants is altered due to the difficulty that clients have in assessing the validity and value of recommendations based on subjective insights (Czerniawska 2003).

In sum, the social learning model appears less one-dimensional than the expert model, since it pictures a balanced relationship between clients and consultants. However, the model does not address important aspects of the relationship, such as the resolution of differences in clients' and consultants' views, the political nature of consulting knowledge, and the uncertain value of knowledge that is socially constructed.

19.2.3 The Critical Model

During the 1980s a growing number of researchers engaged in the study of client–advisory interactions developed an extreme scepticism about the value of consulting knowledge (e.g. Alvesson 1993, 2001; Clark 1995; Clark and Salaman 1996a, 1996b;

Kieser 1997, 2002; Jackson 2001). From this emerged an alternative critical approach to consultancy that regards consultants as impression managers, the interaction process between client and consultant as a form of symbolic interaction (Fincham and Clark 2002), and consultancies as 'systems of persuasion' (Alvesson 1993: 1011).

19.2.3.1 *Overview of key features*

Regarding the *nature of consulting*, according to the critical model, due to the ambiguous character of consulting knowledge clients do not automatically perceive the value of consulting services, as assumed by the expert and the social learning model. Therefore, consultants need to persuade and impress their clients of the value of their work. In other words, it is not knowledge transfer but impression management that lies at the heart of consulting. For example, Clark and Salaman (1998a: 147) argue that consulting knowledge is not 'a set of expert solutions', as pictured in the expert model, but 'a language for representing mutually acceptable ways of knowing and defining and talking about management, managers and organizations'. It is developed in interaction with the clients through translation, where translation is defined as the process of actors convincing other actors that their interests coincide. Thus, what differentiates management consultancies, and all knowledge-intensive firms from other kinds of organizations is not the possession of an authoritative professional knowledge but the 'degree of elaboration of the language through which one describes oneself and one's organization, regulates client orientations and engages in identity work' (Alvesson 2001: 871). This view of knowledge as language has its origins in social constructivism and the 'linguistic turn', emphasizing knowledge's ambiguous, metaphorical, and context-dependent nature (Clark 1995; Alvesson and Kärreman 2000; Alvesson 2001; Czarniawska and Mazza, Chapter 21, this volume). Consequently, consulting knowledge is seen as a matter of beliefs, impression management, and negotiation of meaning (Alvesson 1993, 2001).

In terms of the *nature of the client–consultant interaction*, advocates of the critical model argue that consultants do not transfer expertise; rather, they create and deliver images, impressions, and rhetorical acts that become substitutes for the ambiguities of their knowledge (Jackall 1988; Alvesson 1993, 2001), create value impressions in the eyes of their clients (Greatbach and Clark 2002), and define problems and problem solutions in the form of organizational myths and fashions (Clark and Salaman 1998a). In this way, consultants legitimize their existence and work (Fincham 1999). Additionally, advocates of this approach claim that consultants' stories reflect 'managers' innate need for "dramatic" impulses, a need to dramatize events in order to ascribe meaning and sift out the significant from the mundane' (Fincham and Clark 2002: 9). As Clark and Salaman (1998b: 25) write, '[c]onsultants seek to create and sustain a reality that persuades clients of their value in the same way that actors seek to create a *theatrical reality*' (emphasis added). Thus, client–consultant interaction is a performance in which clients act as actors and as audience: 'The audience is the performance or at least the means of the performance, its accomplice and its measurement' (Clark and Salaman 1996b: 170). Consequently, impression management is regarded as crucial for the success of client–consultant projects and for the survival of consulting companies in general.

As for *power relations*, according to the critical model, clients are involved to a much higher extent in the client–consultant interaction than suggested by the expert model. Thereby, consultants do not just impose meanings on clients, they do not 'autocratically and manipulatingly produce', and clients do not 'docilely consume' (Clark and Salaman 1998a: 152). It is rather a situation of negotiation where consultants reflect and modify client's meanings together with the client. This does not imply, however, that there is an equalized relationship between clients and consultants as seen by the social learning model. Rather, it is emphasized that consultants 'define the managerial role' and 'must seem to be authoritative, must behave confidently, must be in command' if they are to impress the client and be successful (Clark and Salaman 1998a: 147). Consultants' work is described as producing a 'series of narratives which constitute, make up' clients' reality. Thus, 'their seemingly knowledgeable descriptions of organizational structures, processes and purposes become authoritative exercises of power' (Clark and Salaman 1996a: 179). Stories, symbols, and metaphors are power instruments that help consultants to exercise control and manipulate interpretations and problem solving (Armbrüster 2006). They are 'means of creating legitimacy [...] with regard to [consulting] actions and outcomes' (Alvesson 2001: 882). In other words, consultants' power is the result of consultants' persuasions and manipulations of meaning. Consequently, and similarly to the expert model, the prevalent view within the critical model is that consultants are the dominant and powerful actor in client–consultant teams, whereas clients are in a dependent situation. This position is especially manifested in works that concentrate on the creation and role of consulting fads and fashions (e.g. Kieser 2002), where it is argued that consultants legitimize their work by constructing the problems that clients experience in a way that makes them indispensable (Fincham 1999). By strategically criticizing existing management concepts and constantly introducing new ones, consultancies fuel managers' uncertainty, which creates an environment in which clients experience an increasing fear of loss of control and become dependent on consultants who promise to help them regain that control. In this way, consultancies justify their very existence and have made clients 'marionettes on the strings of their fashions' (Kieser 2002: 176).

Another group of advocates of the critical perspective on consulting argues that top managers use consultants' image and rhetoric as an instrument to further their own objectives by involving consultants in the micro-political games of client organizations (Jackall 1988; Kipping 2000; Alvesson and Johansson 2002). These works picture consultants and top managers as allies: 'each group fuels the other's needs and self-images in an occupational drama where the needs of organizations get subordinated to the maintenance of professional identities' (Jackall 1988: 144). In a sense, consultants are represented as agents of agents (Fincham 2002; also Kipping and Armbrüster 2002), and consultants' dominance vis-à-vis members of the client organization as an extension of top managers' hierarchical power.

19.2.3.2 *Review of the model*

In contrast to the first two models, the critical model emphasizes the ambiguous, metaphorical, context-dependent, and active nature of consulting (Alvesson and

Kärreman 2000). Hence, proponents of the model argue that it is crucially important for consulting companies to find ways to persuade clients of the value of their services. This is achieved with the help of symbolic mechanisms such as consulting stories, metaphors, rhetoric, and images, which are regarded as powerful persuasion instruments that consultants use in order to impress clients and to sell new management concepts and models (Heracleous and Barrett 2001). Consequently, the model stresses that a consultant's dominance does not originate in their expertise, as held by the expert model, but arises during the client–consultant interaction as a result of the consultant's rhetorical and impression skills. In addition, some supporters of the critical view emphasize that top managers often use consultants to advance their own interests vis-à-vis other members of the client organization. This brings in considerations of power as a strategy. Accordingly, consultants exercise influence over clients by constructing the meaning of what clients experience and by producing and disseminating new management fashions. Thus, by acknowledging the evolving and strategic character of power, the model provides a more sophisticated understanding of the power processes within client–consultant teams, insights that are ignored within the expert and the social learning models.

At the same time, the critical approach to consulting has several important weaknesses. Firstly, it implies that all consulting knowledge is ambiguous and idiosyncratic and ignores forms of knowledge such as technical expertise that are less intangible and ambiguous. Thus, the model does not explain those types of consulting that are characterized by the transfer of specific, technical knowledge from consultants to clients, such as, for example, when consultants are engaged to develop a new production layout for a factory or to implement a clearly specified IT solution where technical considerations play the critical role for successful problem solving (also Fincham 1999). It can be argued that rhetoric and impression management are not equally important for all kinds of consulting projects (e.g. Nikolova, Reihlen, and Schlapfner 2009). In general, when the client's problem is relatively familiar, it is easier for clients to define the service they require and to evaluate the presented solution. Interaction ambiguity is high only in situations where clients and consultants have to deal with innovative, complex problems. Thus, the critical model ignores the existence of different types of client problems and, as such, does not account for the complex nature of the client–consultant relationship, ignoring the possibility that there are different motives for clients engaging consultants. Although the model pays attention to one important aspect of successful consulting—the creation of image and positive client expectations, issues that are left out in the expert and the social learning model—because of its restricted assumptions regarding the nature of consulting, it downplays the fact that the co-operation of both parties generates some tangible, valuable, and rational outputs in addition to symbolic and emotional results (see also Pellegrin-Boucher 2006/7).

Additionally, the model ignores the fact that an increasing number of client managers have management education or were previously consultants (Poulfelt, Greiner, and Bhambri 2005; Armbrüster and Glückler 2007), which implies that they share consulting-specific meanings and interpretation schemata to some degree and speak the 'consulting language' (Sturdy et al. 2009). Such clients have fewer difficulties in evaluating consulting expertise and recommendations (see also Armbrüster 2006; Sturdy, Werr, and Buono 2009). For example, in this model it is not recognized that 'sector knowledge', which represents the shared knowledge of a practice community operating in the same functional and client area, represents a much less ambiguous and contested knowledge and provides a shared language for clients and consultants (Sturdy et al. 2009). Finally, as Armbrüster (2006: 6) suggests, in a highly competitive market such as the management consulting industry, it is possible that 'social ties and reputation effects preclude opportunistic action by consultants' (see also Armbrüster and Glückler 2007).

As Huczynski (1993: 60) points out, the use of stories and rhetoric by consultants can enhance their communication with managers: '[Managers] have difficulty understanding excessively technical language; have a short span of attention; a limited span of memory and judgement; and tend to be more convinced by certain modes of communication than others. Popular management ideas take this limitation into account.' Others have stressed the importance of symbolic and dramatic elements for knowledge creation during problem-solving processes. Kanter (2002), for example, argues that a symbolic form of knowledge production is necessary in order to enhance the creativity of the involved individuals, to give free flow to imagination, and, as a result, to enable innovation. Similarly, Clark and Mangham (2004) propose that the use of drama and performance can stimulate the creation of new insights out of the participants' contributions (also Sturdy et al. 2004). Finally, as Wright and Kitay (2004: 283) stress, consultants may use stories, rhetoric, and images to impress clients and sell their services; this, however, does not equate consulting with the mere selling of drama and rhetoric (see also Pellegrin-Boucher 2006/7).

Although advocates of the critical model stress that consultants' power does not originate in their expertise, as held by the expert model, but develops during the client–consultant interaction, they assume that this power originates in consultants' rhetorical elaboration or in their position as top management's advocates and is totally unrelated to consultants' expertise. This is problematic because, as Fincham (1999: 350) suggests, 'the reputational and proprietary knowledge of the consultant versus the organizational and operational knowledge of managers defines the limits of the political process'. In other words, the level of dependency between clients and consultants depends on the interplay between their knowledge-bases, their rhetorical and impression skills, and their access to hierarchical/managerial power. Furthermore, advocates of the critical model fail to integrate their different views on power in client–consultant teams and they fail to acknowledge that client–consultant teams consist of three main groups of actors characterized by different types of power relations: client's managers who select and 'pay' the consultants (the project sponsors); client's employees who participate in consulting projects (the problem owners); and the consultants (Garratt 1981; Nikolova and Devinney 2009). Taking into account differences in the knowledge-bases, power relations, and rhetorical skills of these groups of actors makes it clear that the client–consultant relationship has an interactive, dialectic nature and is characterized by mutual dependence, the outcome of which depends on the specifics of any one consulting project (Sturdy 1997a, 1997b; Kipping and Armbrüster 2002; Werr and Styhre 2002/3 Nikolova and Devinney 2009).

Last but not least, the critical model is based on the implicit assumption that management fashions created and disseminated through consulting fulfil, in the best case, only symbolic functions. It is assumed that they do little to improve organizations' performances and, in the worst case, even harm organizations by either facilitating the adoption of technically inefficient administrative technologies or processes, or rejecting efficient ones (Abrahamson 1991; Jung and Kieser, Chapter 16, this volume). In contrast, Abrahamson (1991) argues that management fashions may play a vital function in drawing attention to problems and solutions that have long remained overlooked. Furthermore, organizations that appear innovative or ethical because of the adoption of a new management concept may gain some economic benefits, such as an easier access to capital or higher attraction to customers. Therefore, management fashions may have some positive influence on organizations and, in this way, consultants might be contributing to clients' improved performance.

To sum up, the critical view oversimplifies the process of social construction during the client–consultant interaction and underplays the role of clients, one consequence of which is the greater focus on the tools and techniques used by consultants to impress the client. As in the case of the expert model, this approach suggests a consulting-centric view of the client–consultant relationship. Although the model offers a view of consulting that seems to explain clients' dissatisfaction with consulting services, its assumptions are not valid for all types of consulting projects and do not account for the multifaceted nature of consulting (Nikolova, Reihlen, and Schlapfner 2009).

19.3 SUMMARY AND DIRECTIONS FOR FUTURE RESEARCH

This chapter has summarized and compared the three main models conceptualizing the client–consultant interaction and has pointed out their differences and contributions. By referring to these models, it has outlined aspects of the client–consultant relationship that each of the models could and could not explain, and in this way has provided a more encompassing view of the relationship (see Armbrüster 2006 for a similar approach). One could argue that each of the models 'illuminates' certain aspects of the interaction between clients and consultants in a way that the other models cannot achieve:

- The expert model provides important insights into the interaction process between clients and consultants in the case of *routine* problems when 'clients know exactly what they are doing when they hire consultants' (Armbrüster 2006: 6) and when the efficiency and/or legitimacy of the outcome rather than its innovativeness are regarded as the main success factor (Nikolova, Reihlen, and Schlapfner 2009; also Carlile 2002).

- The social learning model provides valuable insights into the intensive interaction between clients and consultants when dealing with *complex* and/or *innovative* issues.
- The critical model contributes to a better understanding of the symbolic and persuasive aspects of the interaction between clients and consultants, which becomes critical when clients have difficulty assessing the value of the consulting knowledge and work (Nikolova, Reihlen, and Schlapfner 2009).

Maybe it is too simplistic to regard consultants as only experts, helpers/facilitators, or impression managers. Possibly, consultants slip in and out of these roles depending on the problem situation, the project phase, the client's qualities as a partner, and the client's goals when engaging consultants (Nikolova, Reihlen, and Schlapfner 2009). Consultants might, for example, use symbolic interaction in order to open meanings to new interpretations while simultaneously managing the flow of shifting perspectives in order to secure their legitimacy and to guarantee the generation of a problem solution. Therefore, problem solving can be at the same time strategic and symbolic (also Crozier 2003).

Although such a contingency approach can contribute to a more precise picture of the client–consultant interaction, another and more ambitious alternative might be to synthesize the insights of the models into a completely new model (i.e. adopting a dialectic approach; see Morgan 1983 for detailed discussion of these approaches). Developing such a new model is a major contribution that future research can make to the existing literature, namely by paying special attention to the following areas.

First, more research is needed into the *micro* processes of solution generation, negotiation, and knowledge dissemination that take place within client–consultant teams in order to show the origins of clients' trust in consultants and consultants' reputation. In this regard, research should pay special attention to the dynamic and shifting nature of knowledge boundaries in client–consultant teams as recently discussed by Sturdy and colleagues (2009).

Second, by acknowledging the existence of cognitive pluralism and the importance of both the consultant's and the client's interpretations, research should recognize the existence of a mutual dependency between clients and consultants and their shifting dominance. Power relations in consulting projects should be regarded as only incompletely predetermined by existing structures and management fads, as suggested by proponents of the expert and the critical model. It should be recognized that power also develops during the client–consultant interaction out of clients' and consultants' conversations and negotiations over problems and solutions (Sturdy 1997a, 1997b; Nikolova and Devinney 2009). From this perspective, the power of an actor is dependent on the relevance and importance of their knowledge and on their ongoing ability to enforce their perspective and persuade other actors of the superiority of their knowledge (Foucault 1972; Clegg 1989; Fox 2000). Consequently, further theoretical and empirical research is needed that investigates the interplay of power, knowledge, and rhetorical acts within client–consultant teams and how this interplay influences the outcome of consulting projects.

Third, future research should provide an in-depth understanding of the different activities taking place during client–consultant interactions, including the practices, strategies, and roles employed by clients and consultants and the way they unfold (e.g. Schwarz and Clark 2009). This will provide a dynamic picture of the interaction phases and episodes and will illuminate the evolution of client–consultant relationships. Fourth, we need to better understand how external actors, that is, clients and consultants who are not involved, the government, the media, and the community, influence the interaction between involved clients and consultants (see various other chapters in this volume).

Notes

1. Several authors suggest that there are a number of consulting roles that fall between the two extremes of an expert and a facilitator (e.g. Lippitt and Lippitt 1978; Blake and Mouton 1983). For the purpose of a clear analytical differentiation, this chapter concentrates on discussing the two 'extreme' points on this continuum.
2. Almost every one of the advocates of a participative and balanced consulting approach has given it a different name. Because this review summarizes their suggestions and arguments, we have chosen to give this model another name altogether, which, in our view, represents well the main idea behind the cited works.

References

Abbott, A. (1988). *The System of Professions*. Chicago: University of Chicago Press.

Abrahamson, E. (1991). 'Managerial Fads and Fashions: The Diffusion and Rejection of Innovations'. *Academy of Management Review*, 16/3, 586–612.

Aharoni, Y. (1997). 'Management Consulting'. In Y. Aharoni (ed.), *Changing Roles of State Intervention in Services in an Era of Open International Markets*. Albany, NY: The State University of New York Press, 153–179.

Alvesson, M. (1993). 'Organizations as Rhetoric: Knowledge-Intensive Firms and the Struggle with Ambiguity'. *Journal of Management Studies*, 30/6, 997–1015.

Alvesson, M. (2001). 'Knowledge Work: Ambiguity, Image and Identity'. *Human Relations*, 54/7, 863–886.

Alvesson, M. and Johansson, A. (2002). 'Professionalism and Politics in Management Consultancy Work'. In T. Clark and R. Fincham (eds), *Critical Consulting: New Perspectives on the Management Advice Industry*. Oxford: Blackwell, 228–246.

Alvesson, M. and Kärreman, D. (2000). 'Taking the Linguistic Turn in Organizational Research'. *Journal of Applied Behavioral Science*, 36/2, 136–158.

Alvesson, M. and Kärreman, D. (2001). 'Odd Couple: Making Sense of the Curious Concept of Knowledge Management'. *Journal of Management Studies*, 38/7, 995–1,018.

Armbrüster, T. (2006). *The Economics and Sociology of Management Consulting*. Cambridge: Cambridge University Press.

Armbrüster, T. and Glückler, J. (2007). 'Organizational Change and the Economics of Management Consulting: A Response to Sorge and Witteloostuijn'. *Organization Studies*, 28/12, 1873–1885.

Ashford, M. (1998). *Con Tricks: The Shadowy World of Management Consultancy and How to Make it Work for You.* London: Simon & Schuster.

Bechky, B. (2003). 'Sharing Meaning across Occupational Communities: The Transformation of Understanding on a Production Floor'. *Organization Science*, 14/3, 312–330.

Bell, C. and Nadler, L. (1979). *The Client–Consultant Handbook.* Houston: Gulf Publishing Company.

Biswas, S. and Twitchell, D. (1999). *Management Consulting: A Complete Guide to the Industry.* New York: John Wiley & Sons.

Blake, R. and Mouton, J. (1983). *Consultation: A Handbook for Individual and Organizational Development.* Reading, MA: Addison-Wesley.

Boland, R. and Tenkasi, R. (1995). 'Perspective Making and Perspective Taking in Communities of Knowing'. *Organization Science*, 6/4, 350–372.

Boland, R., Singh, J., Salipante, P., Aram, J., Fay, S., and Kanawattanachai, P. (2001). 'Knowledge Representations and Knowledge Transfer'. *Academy of Management Journal*, 44/2, 393–417.

Carlile, P. (2002). 'A Pragmatic View of Knowledge and Boundaries: Boundary Objects in New Product Development'. *Organization Science*, 13/4, 442–455.

Clark, T. (1995). *Managing Consultants: Consultancy as the Management of Impressions.* Buckingham, UK: Open University Press.

Clark, T. and Mangham, I. (2004). 'From Dramaturgy to Theatre as Technology: The Case of Corporate Theatre'. *Journal of Management Studies*, 41/1, 37–59.

Clark, T. and Salaman, G. (1996a). 'Telling Tales: Management Consultancy as the Art of Story Telling'. In C. Oswick and D. Grant (eds), *Metaphor and Organizations*. London: Sage, 166–184.

Clark, T. and Salaman, G. (1996b). 'The Use of Metaphor in the Client–Consultant Relationship: A Study of Management Consultants'. In C. Oswick and D. Grant (eds), *Organization Development: Metaphorical Explorations*. London: Pitman, 154–174.

Clark, T. and Salaman, G. (1998a). 'Telling Tales: Management Gurus' Narratives and the Construction of Managerial Identity'. *Journal of Management Studies*, 35/2, 137–161.

Clark, T. and Salaman, G. (1998b). 'Creating the "Right" Impression: Towards a Dramaturgy of Management Consultancy'. *Service Industries Journal*, 18/1, 18–38.

Clegg, S. (1989). *Frameworks of Power.* London: Sage.

Crozier, M. (2003). 'Theatres of Innovation: Political Communication and Contemporary Public Policy'. Paper presented at the International Political Science Association 2003 Conference on Innovation, Institutions and Public Policy in a Global Context, Washington, DC, 22–24 May.

Czerniawska, F. (2003). *Management Consultancy in the 21st Century.* Basingstoke: Macmillan.

Empson, L. (2001). 'Introduction: Knowledge Management in Professional Service Firms'. *Human Relations*, 54/7, 811–817.

Engwall, L. and Kipping, M. (2002). 'Introduction: Management Consulting as a Knowledge Industry'. In M. Kipping and L. Engwall (eds), *Management Consulting: Emergence and Dynamics of a Knowledge Industry*. Oxford: Oxford University Press, 1–18.

Fincham, R. (1999). 'The Consultant–Client Relationship: Critical Perspectives on the Management of Organizational Change'. *Journal of Management Studies*, 36/3, 335–351.

Fincham, R. (2002/3). 'The Agent's Agent'. *International Studies of Management & Organization*, 32/4, 67–86.

Fincham, R. and Clark, T. (2002). 'Introduction: The Emergence of Critical Perspectives on Consulting'. In T. Clark and R. Fincham (eds), *Critical Consulting: New Perspectives on the Management Advice Industry*. Oxford: Blackwell, 1–20.

Fosstenløkken, S., Løwendahl, B., and Revang, Ø. (2003). 'Knowledge Development through Client Interaction: A Comparative Study'. *Organization Studies*, 24/6, 859–879.

Foucault, M. (1972). *The Archaeology of Knowledge*. London: Tavistock.

Fournier, V. (1999). 'The Appeal to "Professionalism" as a Disciplinary Mechanism'. *The Sociological Review*, 47/2, 280–307.

Fox, S. (2000). 'Communities of Practice, Foucault and Actor-Network Theory'. *Journal of Management Studies*, 37/6, 853–867.

Gallessich, J. (1982). *The Profession and Practice of Consultation*. San Francisco: Jossey-Bass.

Garratt, R. (1981). 'From Expertise to Contingency: Changes in the Nature of Consulting'. *Management Education and Development*, 12/2, 95–101.

Ginsberg, A. and Abrahamson, E. (1991). 'Champions of Change and Strategic Shifts: The Role of Internal and External Change Advocates'. *Journal of Management Studies* 28/2, 173–190.

Greatbach, D. and Clark, T. (2002). 'Laughing with the Gurus'. *Business Strategy Review*, 13/3, 10–18.

Greiner, L. and Metzer, R. (1983). *Consulting to Management*. New York: F. T. Prentice Hall.

Haug, M. and Sussman, M. (1969). 'Professional Autonomy and the Revolt of the Client'. *Social Problems*, 17/2, 153–161.

Heracleous, L. and Barrett, M. (2001). 'Organizational Change as Discourse: Communicative Actions and Deep Structures in the Context of Information Technology Implementation'. *Academy of Management Journal*, 44/4, 755–778.

Hislop, D. (2002). 'The Client Role in Consultancy Relations during the Appropriation of Technological Innovations'. *Research Policy*, 31/5, 657–671.

Huczynski, A. (1993). *Management Gurus*. London: Routledge.

Jackall, R. (1988). *Moral Mazes: The World of Corporate Managers*. New York: Oxford University Press.

Jackson, B. (2001). *Management Gurus and Management Fashions: A Dramatistic Inquiry*. New York: Routledge.

Kanter, R. (2002). 'Strategy as Improvizational Theater'. *Sloan Management Review*, 43/2, 76–81.

Kieser, A. (1997). 'Rhetoric and Myth in Management Fashion'. *Organization*, 4/1, 49–74.

Kieser, A. (2002). 'Managers as Marionettes? Using Fashion Theories to Explain the Success of Consultancies'. In M. Kipping and L. Engwall (eds), *Management Consulting: Emergence and Dynamics of a Knowledge Industry*. Oxford: Oxford University Press, 167–183.

Kipping, M. (2000). 'Consultancy and Conflicts: Bedaux at Lukens Steel and the Anglo-Iranian Oil Company'. *Enterprises et histoire*, 25, 9–25.

Kipping, M. and Armbrüster, T. (2002). 'The Burden of Otherness: Limits of Consultancy Interventions in Historical Case Studies'. In M. Kipping and L. Engwall (eds), *Management Consulting: Emergence and Dynamics of a Knowledge Industry*. Oxford: Oxford University Press, 203–221.

Kitay, J. and Wright, C. (2003). 'Expertise and Organizational Boundaries: The Varying Roles of Australian Management Consultants'. *Asia Pacific Business Review*, 9/3, 21–40.

Kubr, M. (1996). *Management Consulting: A Guide to the Profession*. Geneva: International Labour Office.

Lakomski, G. (2004). 'On Knowing in Context'. *British Journal of Management*, 15, S89–S95.

Lippitt, G. L. and Lippitt, R. (1978) *The Consulting Process in Action*. San Diego: University Associates.

McGivern, C. (1983). 'Some Facets of the Relationship between Consultants and Clients in Organizations'. *Journal of Management Studies*, 20/3, 367–386.

McGivern, C. and Fineman, S. (1983). 'Research and Consultancy: Towards a Conceptual Synthesis'. *Journal of Management Studies*, 20/4, 425–439.

McKenna, C. (2006). *The World's Newest Profession: Management Consulting in the Twentieth Century*. Cambridge: Cambridge University Press.

Mills, P. and Moshavi, D. (1999). 'Professional Concern: Managing Knowledge-Based Service Relationships'. *International Journal of Service Industry Management*, 10/1, 43–67.

Mills, P., Chase, R., and Margulies, N. (1983). 'Motivating the Client/Employee System as a Service Production Strategy'. *Academy of Management Review*, 8/2, 301–310.

Morgan, G. (1983). *Beyond Method*. Beverly Hills: Sage.

Mulligan, J. and Barber, P. (1998). 'The Client–Consultant Relationship'. In P. Sadler (ed.), *Management Consultancy: A Handbook of Best Practice*. London: Kogan Page, 66–85.

Nikolova, N. and Devinney, T. (2009). 'Influence and Power Dynamics in Client-Consulting Teams'. *Journal of Strategy and Management*, 2/1, 31–55.

Nikolova, N., Reihlen, M., and Schlapfner, J-F. (2009). 'Client–Consultant Interaction: Capturing Social Practices of Professional Service Production'. *Scandinavian Journal of Management*, 25/3, 289–298.

Pellegrin-Boucher, E. (2006/7). 'Symbolic Functions of Consultants'. *Journal of General Management*, 32/2, 1–16.

Pellegrinelli, S. (2002). 'Managing the Interplay and Tensions of Consulting Interventions: The Consultant–Client Relationship as Mediation and Reconciliation'. *Journal of Management Development*, 21/5–6, 343–365.

Poulfelt, F., Greiner, L., and Bhambri, A. (2005). 'The Changing Global Consulting Industry'. In L. Greiner and F. Poulfelt (eds), *The Contemporary Consultant*. Mason, OH: Thomson South-Western, 3–22.

Schein, E. (1987). *Process Consultation: Lessons for Managers and Consultants*. Reading, MA: Addison-Wesley.

Schein, E. (1988). *Process Consultation: Its Role in Organization Development*. Reading, MA: Addison-Wesley.

Schein, E. (1999). *Process Consultation Revisited*. Reading, MA: Addison-Wesley.

Schein, E. (2002). 'Consulting: What Should it Mean?' In T. Clark and R. Fincham (eds), *Critical Consulting: New Perspectives on the Management Advice Industry*. Oxford: Blackwell, 21–27.

Schön, D. (1983). *The Reflective Practitioner: How Professionals Think in Action*. New York: Basic Books.

Schön, D. (1987). *Educating the Reflective Practitioner*. San Francisco: Jossey-Bass.

Schwarz, M. and Clark, T. (2009). 'Clients' Different Moves in Managing the Client–Consultant Relationship'. In A. Buono and F. Poulfelt (eds), *Client–Consultant Collaboration: Coping with Complexity and Change*. Charlotte, NC: Information Age Publishing, 3–28.

Semadeni, M. (2001). 'Toward a Theory of Knowledge Arbitrage: Examining Management Consultants as Knowledge Arbiters and Arbitragers'. In A. Buono (ed.), *Current Trends in Management Consulting*. New York: Information Age Publishing, 43–67.

Shapiro, E., Eccles, R., and Soske, T. (1993). 'Consulting: Has the Solution become Part of the Problem?' *Sloan Management Review*, 34/4, 89–95.

Sharma, A. (1997). 'Professional as Agent: Knowledge Asymmetry in Agency Exchange'. *Academy of Management Review*, 22/3, 758–798.

Sturdy, A. (1997a). 'The Consultancy Process: An Insecure Business?' *Journal of Management Studies*, 34/3, 389–413.

Sturdy, A. (1997b). 'The Dialectics of Consultancy'. *Critical Perspectives on Accounting*, 8, 511–535.

Sturdy, A., Werr, A., and Buono, A. (2009). 'Editorial: The Client in Management Consultancy Research: Mapping the Territory'. *Scandinavian Journal of Management*, 25/3, 247–252.

Sturdy, A., Clark, T., Fincham, R., and Handley, K. (2004). 'Silence, Procrustes and Colonization'. *Management Learning*, 35/3, 337–340.

Sturdy, A., Handley, K., Clark, T., and Fincham, R. (2009). *Management Consultancy: Boundaries and Knowledge in Action*. Oxford: Oxford University Press.

Suddaby, R. and Greenwood, R. (2001). 'Colonizing Knowledge: Commodification as a Dynamic of Jurisdictional Expansion in Professional Service Firms'. *Human Relations*, 54/7, 933–953.

Tilles, S. (1961). 'Understanding the Consultant's Role'. *Harvard Business Review*, 39/6, 87–100.

Tsoukas, H. and Vladimirou, E. (2001). 'What is Organizational Knowledge'. *Journal of Management Studies*, 38/7, 973–993.

Walsh, K. (2001). 'The Role of Relational Expertise in Professional Service Delivery'. In A. Buono (ed.), *Current Trends in Management Consulting*. New York: Information Age Publishing, 23–42.

Werr, A. and Stjernberg, T. (2003). 'Exploring Management Consulting Firms as Knowledge Systems'. *Organization Studies*, 24/6, 881–908.

Werr, A. and Styhre, A. (2002/3). 'Management Consultants: Friend or Foe?' *International Studies of Management & Organization*, 32/4, 43–66.

Wilkinson, J. (1995). 'What is Management Consulting?' In S. Barcus III and J. Wilkinson (eds), *Handbook of Management Consulting Services*. 2nd edn. New York: McGraw-Hill, 3–16.

Winter, S. (1987). 'Knowledge and Competence as Strategic Assets'. In D. Teece (ed.), *The Competitive Challenge: Strategies for Industrial Innovation and Renewal*. New York: Ballinger, 159–184.

Wright, C. and Kitay, J. (2004). 'Spreading the Word: Gurus, Consultants and the Diffusion of the Employee Relations Paradigm in Australia'. *Management Learning*, 35/3, 271–286.

CHAPTER 20

THE CLIENT IN THE CLIENT–CONSULTANT RELATIONSHIP

ROBIN FINCHAM

20.1 INTRODUCTION

THE client-related and client-focused nature of management consultancy work remains one of its defining features. The act of taking on the client's problem, seeking to resolve it and present solutions to the client's satisfaction lies at the heart of consultant occupational identity and in many respects constitutes how 'good consulting' is defined (Fosstenløkken, Løwendahl, and Revang 2003; Nikolova and Devinney, Chapter 19, this volume). Yet interpretations of the client relationship have been ambiguous and shifting and, indeed, some aspects of research on consultancy have been so dominated by the supply side of the consulting input they have almost eclipsed the client in studies. This chapter seeks to redress the balance and consider how the client perspective has been intertwined with continuing debates on management consultancy and how clients figure in the activity systems and change processes associated with consulting.

As numerous writers have pointed out, our understanding of management consultancy and consulting work has been advanced in recent years in part by the development of what is broadly seen as a critical strand of research (Clark and Fincham 2002: 4; Werr 2002; Armbrüster 2006: 2). Calling any school of thought 'critical' is contentious, not least because it sets up oppositions and divisions that are always out of sympathy with some of the developments in a field. But a concern with issues of conflict and power and a questioning of automatic assumptions about the functional intent of consultancy have increasingly infused analysis (Bloomfield and Danieli 1995; Clark 1995; Sturdy 1997a; Fincham 1999). These approaches have been seen as a reaction to a more prescriptive and practitioner-oriented approach, which was more straightforwardly about consultants bringing new expert knowledge to organizations and creating value for clients. Yet, somewhat ironically, it was probably the shift towards the critical study of consultancy that brought about, at least initially, a tendency to overlook the client role. As Sturdy and colleagues (2009: 18) point out, prescriptive approaches to consultancy such as process consulting and organizational development paid close attention to the client viewpoint. In many respects this literature developed from the concern of writers for models of better consulting, defined in terms of solutions tailored to client problems and supportive client relations.

In contrast, more critical research has been shaped by at least two factors that have mediated against an interest in clients. The first has been a pervasive sense of the growing influence of consultancy, which has exhibited a corresponding neglect of client activity. The rapid growth of the industry and increasing numbers of managers who experience consultancy interventions (Ernst and Kieser 2002; Armbrüster 2006: 41), a perception of growing strategic power over corporate and public sectors, and consultants' role as disseminators of new management knowledge or even harbingers of new forms of capitalism (Sahlin-Andersson and Engwall 2002; McKenna 2006) are all supply-side factors stressing consultants as supreme knowledge brokers. They have exaggerated a sense of power asymmetry between client and consultant that has almost had the effect of blotting out the client as an independent agent. Secondly, established research on related occupational areas, particularly the professions, has also shown clients as having a diminished role. The research directions foreshadowed in studies of the professions have tended to concentrate on how expert groups gain legitimacy, how they establish occupational control, and how they construct their knowledge-base (Abbott 1988; Strang and Meyer 1993; Kirkpatrick, Muzio, and Ackroyd, Chapter 9, this volume). Indeed, in classic models of the liberal professions and corporate professional groups an ability to incorporate clients' distinctive interests in the professional field was seen early on as a defining professional feature (Wilensky 1964). This occupation-centric emphasis may have influenced views of consultancy and may have even acted as a kind of unconscious template for how consultancy research has been conducted.

However, studies of consultancy also exhibit counter movements, and any tendency to exclude the client has been matched by pressures to notice their role and bring them back into analysis. For this we probably need look no further than the obvious, namely the simple fact of consulting as interactive work and the product of working relations with clients (Sturdy 1997a; Fincham 1999). Even on an anecdotal level, the experience anyone has when doing research on consultants demonstrates the importance they attribute to understanding the wishes of clients and attending to client demands. Developing a rapport is a constant preoccupation and reflects the role of clients as the recipients of consultants' impression-management activities (Clark 1995). The client perspective raises interesting questions not least because of the vantage point it provides. When the focus shifts to interaction between client firm managers and consultants working in joint teams, much 'consultant activity' turns out to be performed by clients too, or at least in close conjunction with them, which raises questions about consultants' expertise claims (and, of course, the perennial question about what value consultants actually add). There are certain areas where management consultants have special techniques and expertise, but seemingly just as often they have no well-defined monopoly of knowledge; ultimately it is only 'management knowledge' in the broadest sense that consultants possess and transfer, the same basic knowledge that clients have. So, while the image of consultants as 'outside experts' may legitimize their advice, and suggest knowledge categories broader than clients possess, there are no rigid boundaries between knowledge formations inside and outside the organization. Forms of knowledge circulate widely: the consultant outsider can possess inside knowledge of the client firm, through repeated contacts, while client insiders invariably have knowledge of their own sectors and markets (Fincham et al. 2008; Sturdy et al. 2009). 'Consultant knowledge' is as likely to be dependent on particular clients and sector experience as it is to reflect abstract skills and techniques (Fosstenløkken, Løwendahl, and Revang 2003).

Thus, rather than being conceived at face value, as an expert project carried out on behalf of the client, bringing the client into the analysis reveals or helps to reveal new perspectives on the extent of their influence over change-oriented knowledge (e.g. Clark and Salaman 1995; Armbrüster and Kipping 2002). Such an approach explores questions of shared agency between client and consultant, and queries assumptions about consultancy's ability to create dependency and its role as a powerful diffuser of new management ideas. Consideration of the client also opens up analysis to holistic and diverse possibilities. In order to understand consulting episodes, different kinds of 'clients' from inside the client firm as well as other managerial groups may need to be considered. A potentially varied and contingent set of groups and events that might encompass historically embedded organizational politics may play a part in an unfolding narrative (Hislop 2002; Armbrüster 2006). In contrast to an occupation-centric approach to issues of knowledge formation and legitimacy building, the client perspective emphasizes wider contexts in which consulting work is carried out.

In the chapter a number of these issues around the central question of interaction between client and consultant, and what this tells us about the nature of consulting work, will be discussed. First, the active contribution of clients in developing the consultant knowledge-base reveals much about the nature of this knowledge and the distinctiveness of consultancy. Here, a number of researchers have highlighted the subjective and contingent rather than purely cognitive elements of knowledge, reinforcing the differences between consulting and more 'professional' forms of knowledge. Second, because knowledge and power are closely related, issues of power asymmetry and dependency and possible conflict in the client–consultant relationship also arise. While the balance of power between client and consultant tends not to feature in functional models of consulting, more critical approaches that include the client perspective take into account possibilities of conflict and knowledge contested between the parties. And, third, there are complicating factors in the dispersal of both client and consultant interests across teams, hierarchies, and groups of people. This highlights the complexity and uncertainty of client–consultant dynamics, interaction, and dependency, and it corrects simplifying tendencies to assume that client and consultant are monolithic interests.

20.2 CLIENT KNOWLEDGE AND
CONSULTANT KNOWLEDGE

The creation of a knowledge-base has been seen as more or less synonymous with the development of expert occupations—as the cornerstone of occupational identity, legitimacy building, and working capability. Among many expert groups and professions, bodies of knowledge are always ultimately constructed by studying clients' problems. However, this knowledge is not unmediated but goes through long processes of institutionalization and theorizing by expert groups (Abbott 1988; Strang and Meyer 1993; Kirkpatrick, Muzio, and Ackroyd, Chapter 9, this volume). Consultants too independently consolidate the knowledge they obtain from client interaction (Heusinkveld and Benders, Chapter 13; Werr, Chapter 12; both this volume). The know-how that consultants build up from their experience in client firms is frequently generalized and accumulated across projects. As Werr and Stjernberg (2003) point out, consultancies, particularly the large-scale ones, are very effective ideas factories. As a creative force generating new management knowledge, many consultant firms have in place well-developed policies and structures for gathering and grading consultants' work experiences, to make it available as methods for future projects. They have data depositories where project histories are written up and stored and specialist units for sifting this information and applying quality criteria from which the firm gets a flow of new tools. This kind of proprietary knowledge generation represents a large part of the appeal to the client and greatly enhances consultants' ability to intervene in change (Fincham and Evans 1999; Armbrüster and Kipping 2002).

However, in other respects, it has been suggested that management consulting as a distinctive knowledge industry shares few of the traits of the established professions (Fincham 2006; Kirkpatrick, Muzio, and Ackroyd, Chapter 9, this volume). More situated and practice-based learning is deeply implicated in knowledge creation in consultancy and in the consequent nature of its knowledge-base. A number of researchers have argued that the co-production and co-consumption of knowledge in client–consultant groups means that ideas are not simply produced by consultants and consumed by clients. The business of 'consulting' is not about expert diagnosis and treatment but is carried out within processes of interaction and joint accommodation (Fosstenløkken, Løwendahl, and Revang 2003; Bogenrieder and Nooteboom 2004; Nikolova and Devinney, Chapter 19, this volume). Such 'learning spaces' are good at dissolving different kinds of organizational and knowledge boundaries, so that knowledge development can take place across expert groups and help bring about co-ordination of effort and joint problem solving. Various models of learning for consultancy work suggest that the risks of knowledge sharing are minimized, and the chances of people engaging in practical activity improved, in the project group context (Czarniawska and Mazza 2003; Scarbrough et al. 2004).

Thus, the balance between knowledge being generalized versus the affinities with its ultimate source in client organizations seems distinctive for consultancy as an expert grouping. The sheer strength of the client bond suggests that the knowledge component gained from learning in project teams remains extremely important. Here Fosstenløkken, Løwendahl, and Revang (2003) have shown that client interaction is perceived in business service firms like consultancies as the single most important factor promoting knowledge development. These researchers found that consultants saw 'learning through project work' (ibid.: 868) as the most important source of knowledge development, and contrasted it with formal training opportunities, course attendance, and other chances to acquire mainly cognitive or theoretical knowledge. These opportunities and chances were regarded as more limited and narrow, whereas direct client contact and meetings with clients were regarded as very much better learning experiences. Interacting with the right kind of clients enhanced learning—'good clients' were demanding clients often centrally positioned in their industrial marketplace, and experiencing first-hand the pressures of satisfying them was deemed the highest kind of attainment. The nature of the knowledge being acquired and used thus reflects the importance of direct client involvement and learning. Skills such as having an understanding of projects within a wider experience, divining what the client's deep needs are, the ability to revise and adjust solutions, and reporting solutions in ways that gain recognition and are appreciated by clients are all crucial forms of expertise (Anderson-Gough, Grey, and Robson 2000; Werr 2002). This view is at variance with any notion of the expert simply transferring external knowledge to the client (Nikolova and Devinney, Chapter 19, this volume).

But while the co-production of consulting knowledge challenges simple ideas about the expertise consultants bring to client problems, it does not necessarily undermine a basic sense of the value consultancy adds. The scope of management knowledge is complex enough and the dynamics of organizational change are difficult enough to accommodate many possibilities for the co-production of knowledge. As Armbrüster and Kipping (2002) argue, differences between client and consultant 'knowledge' do exist but are more about orientation and the activity systems they are embedded in, rather than overt domain differences; client managers are oriented to the regulation of an existing operation, while consultants are oriented to change in terms of analysing problems and getting people onside in new business processes. Their central interest is to 'transform [the client's] general and regulation-oriented knowledge into change-oriented knowledge to render it usable for them' (ibid.: 104). Perhaps therefore we should not expect any simple answer to the question of what the consultant adds that the client cannot. Even without possessing unique technical knowledge, consultants can bring special capacities and inputs to client problems by contributing fresh market intelligence and authority of purpose to a problem. Thus, consideration of the client helps to provide a view of 'consultant knowledge' that hopefully neither over nor underestimates it, and also helps to identify fertile directions for research in areas such as the significance for consultancy work of powerful and influential clients, the formation of distinctive knowledge within consultant firms, and learning within the web of relations between project teams and client and consultant organizations.

20.3 POWER AND DEPENDENCY

As already indicated, the early stage of critical research on management consultancy distanced itself from practitioner perspectives and, in the process, tended to exclude clients from consideration as active agents. In particular, a concern that almost by default suggested that the consultant dominated the relationship with the client was the development of critical interest in the occupational 'rhetoric' of consultants (Kieser 1997; Berglund and Werr 2000). The development of this approach was a means of exploring and understanding through language the consultancy occupation and how consultants construct identity (for example, Fincham and Evans 1999; Kitay and Wright 2007; Alvesson, Chapter 15, this volume). But, for a number of authors, the interest in 'rhetoric' also stressed the role of fashionable ideas and techniques in the dramatic rise of the consulting industry, and they pictured consulting as a 'system of persuasion' (Alvesson 1993). This approach shared concerns with related research on management gurus as a similar type of powerful change agent. The rise of management gurus as celebrity consultants was seen as a parallel development occurring at the level of discourse and the spread of management ideas (Jung and Kieser, Chapter 16, Clark, Batanacharoen, and Greatbatch, Chapter 17, this volume; also Fincham 2002; Clark et al. 2009), and often, though not exclusively, these influences were revealed in methods that were exclusive of clients, such as the analysis of guru books or the observation of gurus and consultants in action at presentations and workshops.

Social constructionist approaches in particular stress clients as passive victims of rhetorical strategies and tend to assume that the realities of consultant dominance are actually being constructed (Czarniawska and Mazza, Chapter 21, this volume). In a sense word became fact—the inherent insecurities of the managerial role (heightened and intensified in post-modern conditions of uncertainty) created the demand for outside solutions, while it was the consultant genius who simultaneously reinforced and fed off managerial anxiety (Jung and Kieser, Chapter 16, this volume). For example, Bloomfield and Danieli (1995) stressed consultants' power to create gatekeeper roles for themselves positioned between the client and the desired solution. This underscored their ability to provide the assurance that managers craved, while the client–consultant relationship was pictured as being 'between the indispensable and the dependent' (ibid.: 27).

However, what amounted to the airbrushing out of clients and client firm managers was also challenged within an alternative literature strand. Notably Sturdy (1997a, 1997b) pointed out that the picture of consult dominance was derived from quite limited research (often interviews only with consultants) and that studies which focus just on consultants' active role in promoting images of themselves fail to see broader *interaction* between the supply and demand sides of management advice. He queried what evidence there was to prove that managers are actually persuaded to take on consultant ideas and pointed to clients' widespread suspicion of, and resistance to, consultants. Consultancy itself is an 'insecure business' and there is no reason to suppose it is immune from the existential anxieties that afflict the wider management structure. More recently, Armbrüster (2006: 98) similarly refers to abundant anecdotal evidence of consultancy as a stressful occupation (the long hours, always at the client's beck and call), supporting a view of consultancy as essentially a buyer's market. This emphasized client discretion over the demand for consultant techniques and fashionable ideas, which Armbrüster interestingly relates to evidence of fluctuations in worldwide growth rates of consultancy and the links to economic expansion and contraction. These wider economic relationships suggest that client firms go to consultants in the good times, when they are reorganizing and seeking new approaches and techniques; they do not seek out consultants in times of retrenchment and recession (ibid.: 94). The only situation that may change this is when there are economy-wide crises and crazes, such as the 'millennium bug' before the turn of the twenty-first century, which sparked a rise in consultancy growth and revenues.

Others have differed about which way power dependency relationships may be skewed but still questioned whether consulting firms create demand autonomously or promote their skills independent of client constraints. With regard to this, Fincham (1999) stressed consulting as 'relational work' and argued against seeing the client–consultant relationship in terms of fixed dependencies—either the indispensable consultant and the dependent client, or an insecure consultancy business in thrall to client choice. In individual cases consultants with sufficient expertise and reputation may indeed make their solutions into obligatory pathways for clients. But there may be just as many examples of powerful clients able to impose their own demands and definitions of the problem. There may also be examples nearer to true interdependency (and joint learning) where the client has to go to the marketplace for special skills but the consultancy too needs a customer for its product. Fincham argued for a broadly contingent model of power dispersal between client and consultant that would cause us to be critical of power dependency relationships skewed either to the consultant or the client, and stressed 'the range of the consultant–client relationship [and the fact that] consultancy is being seen not as a fixed relationship or a special kind of occupation, but as a market relation between different managerial groupings' (ibid.: 347). Elsewhere Fincham (2002/3) suggests another view of the problematic client–consultant couple, regarding it as a possible agency relationship. This reinforces the point that what may appear as a straightforward intervention—the functional provision of a service by a paid professional—is rarely so simple. The potential differences of orientation and interest between the principal (the client) and the agent (the consultant) effectively add another layer of complexity and uncertainty to the wider managerial function.

Debate has thus fluctuated from an earlier focus on the symbolic agenda of consultancy, and notions of consultancy firms' power to promote expert knowledge and create demand autonomously, towards a more explicit focus on the interaction between client and consultant and what this implies for images of the client role.

20.4 POWER AND KNOWLEDGE

Another approach that originally started from the premise of consultants having a dominant position in the modern economy concerns their role in the diffusion of new management ideas (Jung and Kieser, Chapter 16, this volume). The global proliferation of
techniques of better management in the shape of industry best practices, new organizational forms, and fashionable methods has been seen as a powerful force of corporate and
economic change. It allows organizations to import the strategic knowledge they need
and is behind the spread of design logics and rationalizing trends that shape organizations worldwide (Hansen, Nohria, and Tierney 1999; Meyer 2002; Werr, Chapter 12, this
volume). Consultancy as a component of an 'advice industry' that is both the source and
carrier of management ideas across nations and continents (Kipping and Engwall 2002;
Sahlin-Andersson and Engwall 2002), and the changes introduced by consultancy, are
then seen as a particular instance of the general process of the diffusion of innovations.

However, once again there are debates about agency and the input of client firms into
projects; pure diffusionist approaches have been widely condemned for having a limited
concern with issues of implementation and the adoption stages of innovation. Critics
have argued that to see the 'travel of ideas' as a simple linear process means that receptor
groups are denied an active role, and variations in the idea or technology being diffused
are overlooked (Gammelsaeter 2002; Faust 2002). More nuanced theories of the diffusion of management ideas allow that innovation is not purely a 'diffusion' effect but the
result of interplays between diffusion and localization (Ernst and Kieser 2002; Røvik
2002). Hence, in considering consultancy as a knowledge-diffusing industry it is important not to stress supply over demand. The client influence and possible variations from
client firm to client firm should not be overshadowed. For example, Hislop (2002: 658)
found, in case studies of technological innovation, that clients 'were by no means passively following ideas permeated by consultants'. An active client role was expressed at
various stages and consulting relationships were embedded in pre-existing links between
parties. This constraint from the consultant point of view was frequently the price paid
for the stability of repeat business, but clients also, almost always, actively selected consultants on the basis of some kind of past experience. Hislop found consultants were
often known to the client firm and (more importantly) used accordingly. Distinctive
past experiences formed quite fixed behavioural recipes and preferences in client firms.
There was, for example, a category of 'reluctant clients' who hire a consultant they have
had a poor experience with in the past on the basis of better the devil you know or
because they are still deemed the best available. The important point is that past failure
would define the client's approach to managing the project and the autonomy granted to
the consultant.

In this vein various researchers have pointed out the frequently embedded and socially
shaped aspect of consultancy and client–consultant relations that go beyond the merely
economic and help to overcome uncertainties for both parties (Kitay and Wright 2004;

Sturdy 1997b). It is through concepts of embeddedness and relational contracting that the client role is brought more into the picture and client–consultant relations are seen as constrained and complex. The significance of implementation in these processes often means considerable reshaping and variation of ideas as they travel between initiating groups and organizations, a variability that is substantially accounted for by the client role. Hislop's (2002) case studies mentioned above, for example, involved just such embedded implementation. They were of enterprise resource planning (ERP) systems, and he found that the operating practices surrounding the systems and sometimes their basic functionality were customized and adapted according to the trust and scope given to consultants. As Armbrüster (2006: 14) also points out, because consulting represents a type of contractual relationship, transactions in existing networks of ties with consultants shape the logic behind client decision-making; it means managerial clients do not necessarily follow simple or preconceived notions of what is efficient or cost-effective. Project uncertainty and clients' inability to know in advance whether they will get value for money all shift risk in the client's direction. This means that the symbolic capital inherent in prior ties (reputation, trust, familiarity) disproportionately influences decisions. Relational contracting and a long-term association with a consultant can bring decisive guarantees— the security of repeat business for the consultant and the benefit of overcoming consultants' opportunistic behaviour for the client—and these relationships and networks represent a crucial asset for both parties (see Amorim and Kipping 1999).

However, there may be further steps in understanding the nuances of client–consultant relations. It has frequently been stressed (e.g. Clark 1995) that the basic client perception of consultants is one of ambiguity—the holding of apparently conflicting views that combine wariness and even hostility towards consultants with a recognition of their uses and apparent willingness to use them again and again. Kipping and Armbrüster (2002) suggest this derives from the consultant's outsider status: if consultants lack experience of the client firm, or lack relevant sector experience, as external agents they carry a 'burden of otherness' and are less able to interact with clients or modify their routines. Considerations of embeddedness and relational contracting show that consultants are usually not strangers to the client, but still, Kipping and Armbrüster suggest they invariably remain outsiders and always carry that burden to a degree. However, this may only apply to certain kinds of consulting, albeit those which are probably the majority of cases. These consulting projects fall into what we might refer to as an 'implementation category' where some definite change project is being implemented, or a technology installed. However, consulting is nothing if not varied, and in other types of exercise—if clients are specifically seeking a disinterested view or perhaps some special new methodology—'otherness' and distance from the consultant might be exactly what the clients' want.

Richter and Niewiem (2009), for example, surveyed a wide range of projects—those classified as routine, projects requiring detailed internal knowledge, confidential/ sensitive projects, and projects requiring conceptual or methodological consultant skills. These researchers also made careful distinctions around the extent of relational contracting, contrasting internal consultants, external consultants who were known in varying degrees, and finally consultants who were unknown to the client. What clients perceived as the most *relevant* consultant knowledge varied from project to project. Projects that required firm-specific knowledge did favour consultants with an established relationship to the client firm; often these involved an implementation stage so that a consultant with detailed knowledge of internal operations held a balance of advantages. But where mainly conceptual or methodological knowledge was required—projects that imported some distinctive new approach or were about the generation of ideas—consultants with loose or no established relationships were often sought. For this kind of project these skills would be sought from a specialist consultant firm. Projects involving commercially sensitive activities or confidential knowledge were particularly interesting. This category included the archetype in popular imagery of the consultant brought in to do management's dirty work—unpopular cuts, redundancies, and so on—and here the extreme choices of the internal (and hence wholly familiar) consultant and the consultant unknown to the client were excluded. Neither was trusted with this kind of information, but consultants with a close or loose relationship were both used.

Thus, emphasis on the different kinds of consultancy and the interplay between strong and weak ties helps to restore the importance of the client role by stressing a view of consultancy processes and episodes that is often overlooked in research. The prevailing focus on actual consultancy work has, perhaps not surprisingly, emphasized the consultant project and intervention, whereas decisions taken at some distance from this central stage or at an earlier point have been somewhat less studied. Clients frequently have to balance priorities pulling in different directions when choosing a consultant, and prior selection decisions shape and constrain ensuing project work in ways that remain invisible if only implementation is studied (e.g. Dawes, Dowling and Patterson 1992; Hislop 2003). Among the directions in which research might go in the future are studies of these kinds of embedded relations, which often deviate from simple 'economic' rationales and can only be fathomed by studying the deeper context of client–consultant relations, how clients might initially structure projects, and what they are seeking from the consultants they hire.

20.5 CLIENT (AND CONSULTANT) DIVERSITY

As indicated above, the trend towards including the client perspective has emerged in parallel with a degree of methodological progress in studying consultancy, going beyond single cases or interviews only with consultants (e.g. Richter and Niewiem 2009; Sturdy et al. 2009). In comparing examples of power dependency, in particular, studies of a spectrum of client–consultant relationships are very useful as it is important to have some notion of comparing like with like. Social-capital hierarchies of reputation and experience exist in both consultant and client firms and any assumptions about dependency in the client–consultant relationship ought to take into account wider power distributions across firms and industries, together with some notion of matching and comparing levels.

For example, Sturdy and colleagues (2009) describe consulting episodes that ranged from situations where it was possible to see definite areas of outside expertise to cases where clients were continually challenging consultants' knowledge claims. One case represented perhaps the peak of client power. It involved an assignment conducted by one of the top strategy consulting firms—but the client was a multinational that more than matched the consultant in terms of reputational power and symbolic capital. Client managers conceded nothing to the consultant; consultant knowledge was constantly under test and consultants were used in a strategic planning round that was definitely controlled internally. Compared with this case, other cases in the research involved client organizations and managers with lesser amounts of symbolic and knowledge capital, while the consultants involved claimed more definite areas of expertise. These included industries that were not global (public sector, financial services) and projects characterized by fairly well-defined forms of expertise (including labour procurement, project management, and IT) where consultants with recognized skills worked jointly with internal departments. Clients who conceded ownership of the problem to consultants, instances of the co-production of knowledge and interdependency in the client–consultant relationship were all normal here.

These differences of influence between client and consultant point the way to a more general diversity. Indeed, the underlying assumption that, when bringing 'the client' into the analysis, we are including some monolithic interest or single focus of activity has started to be questioned. For the client to be a single individual, the client firm would probably need to be relatively small so that the consultant selected for a specific job would report only to the unique client. But the situated nature of client–consultant relations and the complicated narratives often attached to particular cases are reflected in degrees of client (and consultant) diversity. More often, a plurality of individuals and groups in the client organization play different roles and are involved to a greater or lesser extent with projects. Schein (1997), for instance, distinguished the main or commissioning client from intermediate clients, usually managers who are co-opted to work with consultants (though whether these groups always feel like 'clients' is another matter). Sturdy and colleagues (2009: 57) pointed out that client involvement is often structured by the management hierarchy; this can go from the more senior levels, where consultants are clearly 'working for' the client, to progressively junior levels that shift more to modes of 'working with' clients. Also, Kipping (2000) examined the impact of consultant interventions on the managerial structure as a whole, adopting a politically complex stakeholder view of the managerial client. Consultant interventions then become part of the managerial power game.

Some have suggested the term 'client system' to indicate the involvement of groups of actors with dynamic knowledge and accountability boundaries (Kieser 2002; Kitay and Wright 2004). Under this view, consultants may collaborate with different groups during the course of projects, obtaining information from some, working with others, advising groups that may be affected, and so on. Among the more centrally involved, different client relations will exist, while more peripheral groups, though still members of the client organization, would hardly be called clients at all. There will also be a parallel 'consultancy system' encompassing different external roles. On the consulting side there is probably more coherence but still diversity and the possibility of tension. Consultants will have reporting links back to their head office and links with senior partners and directors who have their own layer of relations with client firms. It is probably fair to say that these networks have been studied even less, though research has alluded to some interesting project dynamics within the consultancy system. The recent study by Sturdy and colleagues (2009), for instance, identified some consultants who occupied special 'mediating' roles between consultant and client rather than being wholly in the consultant system, while other consultants were deemed to have crossed over to the client side and 'gone native' (ibid.: 81).

Indeed, the notion of a 'system' may suggest too much in the way of coherence. Alvesson and colleagues (2009) prefer to explore a variety of client 'positions' defined by the circumstances of the particular project. These researchers argue that there is a basic client position, which has to be interpreted in terms of some level of collaborative engagement with the consultant, implying a common objective or shared goal. While this does not preclude tensions and conflicts between client and consultant, it does narrow down the conception of the client. In part the purpose is, in a sense, to go beyond the client as a vehicle for studying consulting actions and to consider people, who are members of the client organization but whose interests are distant from the project or may even be damaged by it. Giving a voice and visibility to people who may be the object of consultant actions or whose jobs are blighted or destroyed is to include people and groups whose interests consultants may be conceived of as 'working against' rather than working for or working with. This is not to say that organizational members are necessarily powerless victims of consultancy; they may resist its impact (resistance to controlling Taylorist systems, for example, is well documented) (see Kipping and Armbrüster 2002). Alvesson and colleagues (2009: 256) emphasize fluidity in 'the division of labour within client work and associated positions, the relations within the client system, and the different logics of perceiving, valuing and reasoning within groups of client people'.

In this way consideration of client (and consultant) diversity opens up, for future research, a number of new paradigms in which to frame management consultancy. These mostly challenge the idea of client and consultant as simple partners in a service provision, and stress instead their role as stakeholders in wider organizational life, moving between roles, experiencing ambivalence between them, and possibly changing allegiances during project interactions.

20.6 CONCLUSION

The client perspective helps in understanding consultancy in many ways. It has shed new light on the nature of co-produced and co-consumed management knowledge; it has helped to determine how we conceive of power relations in the client–consultant relationship and the capacity of expert groups like consultants to create demand for their skills; last but not least, diversity and differentiation in the roles of organizational clients has revealed the complexity of project dynamics. In sum, many emerging conceptual themes in consultancy research have involved consideration of the client role, implicitly or explicitly.

We saw how 'bringing the client in' can detract from the distinctiveness of consultant knowledge but clarify the boundaries of consultancy and reinforce differences from other forms of expert labour. This especially applies to the other main category of client-related work, the professions (see also Kirkpatrick, Muzio, and Ackroyd, Chapter 9, this volume). Classic models of the liberal professions and corporate professional groups certainly accept the importance of subjective and pragmatic knowledge in taking account of client preferences. But a focus on the abstract theorizing of knowledge and a degree of dominance over the client base is, in some ways, more typical of the professions. In contrast, emphasizing the client as an active agent, and the importance of client-based knowledge over cognitive knowledge, is more typical of consultancy. Direct (rather than mediated or institutionalized) learning from clients suggests that 'consultant knowledge' combines holistic skills across a range of tacit, explicit, and political forms. Consistent with such a view of knowledge, the debate around dependency relations has retreated somewhat from images of consultants as powerful (and possibly dangerous) persuaders, and emphasized more the service buyers' power to shape and define projects. The impact of consultants as change agents has been modified by an emphasis on relational contracting and the client firm role in the localization of ideas.

Finally, growing awareness of the variability of consulting projects, of which the client perspective is an element, has revealed plural interests dispersed across collaborating groups. Acknowledging client and consultant diversity helps in understanding how projects unfold and how tensions and knowledge boundaries between client and consultancy groupings affect the changing relationship.

References

Abbott, A. (1988). *The System of Professions*. Chicago: University of Chicago Press.

Alvesson, M. (1993). 'Organization as Rhetoric: Knowledge-Intensive Firms and the Struggle with Ambiguity'. *Journal of Management Studies*, 30/5, 997–1015.

Alvesson, M., Kärreman, D., Sturdy, A., and Handley K. (2009). 'Unpacking the Client(s): Constructions, Positions and Client–Consultant Dynamics'. *Scandinavian Journal of Management*, 25/3, 253–263.

Amorim, C. and Kipping, M. (1999). 'Selling Consultancy Services: The Portuguese Case in Historical and Comparative Perspective'. *Business and Economic History*, 28/2, 45–56.

Anderson-Gough, F., Grey, C., and Robson, K. (2000). 'In the Name of the Client: The Service Ethic in Two Professional Service Firms'. *Human Relations*, 53/9, 1151–1173.

Armbrüster, T. (2006). *The Economics and Sociology of Management Consulting*. Cambridge: Cambridge University Press.

Armbrüster, T. and Kipping, M. (2002). 'Types of Knowledge and the Client–Consultant Interaction'. In K. Sahlin-Andersson and L. Engwall (eds), *The Expansion of Management Knowledge: Carriers, Ideas and Sources*. Stanford, CA: Stanford University Press, 96–110.

Berglund, J. and Werr, A. (2000). 'The Invincible Character of Management Consulting Rhetoric: How One Blends Incommensurates While Keeping Them Apart'. *Organization*, 7, 633–655.

Bloomfield, B. and Danieli A. (1995). 'The Role of Management Consultants in the Development of Information Technology: The Indissoluble Nature of Socio-Political and Technical Skills'. *Journal of Management Studies*, 33/1, 27–46.

Bogenrieder, I. and Nooteboom, B. (2004). 'Learning Groups: What Types are There? A Theoretical Analysis and an Empirical Study in a Consultancy Firm'. *Organization Studies*, 25/2, 287–313.

Clark, T. (1995). *Management Consultants: Consultancy as the Management of Impressions*. Buckingham: Open University Press.

Clark, T. and Fincham, R. (eds) (2002). *Critical Consulting: New Perspectives on the Management Advice Industry*. Oxford: Blackwell.

Clark, T. and Salaman, G. (1995). 'The Use of Metaphor in the Client–Consultant Relationship: A Study of Management Consultants'. In C. Oswick and D. Grant (eds), *Organization Development: Metaphorical Explanations*. London: Pitman, 154–174.

Clark, T., Guthey, E., and Jackson, B. (2009). *Demystifying Business Celebrities*. London: Routledge.

Czarniawska, B. and Mazza, C. (2003) 'Consulting as Liminal Space'. *Human Relations*, 56/3, 267–290.

Dawes, P. L., Dowling, G. R., and Patterson, P. G. (1992). 'Criteria Used to Select Management Consultants'. *Industrial Marketing Management*, 21, 187–193.

Ernst, B. and Kieser, A. (2002). 'In Search of Explanations for the Consulting Explosion'. In K. Sahlin-Andersson and L. Engwall (eds), *The Expansion of Management Knowledge: Carriers, Ideas and Sources*. Stanford, CA: Stanford University Press, 47–73.

Faust, M. (2002). 'Consultancies as Actors in Knowledge Arenas: Evidence from Germany', in M. Kipping and L. Engwall (eds.), *Management Consulting: Emergence and Dynamics of a Knowledge Industry*. Oxford: Oxford University Press, 146–163.

Fincham, R. (1999). 'The Consultant–Client Relationship: Critical Perspectives on the Management of Organizational Change'. *Journal of Management Studies*, 36/3, 335–352.

Fincham, R. (2002). 'Charisma versus Technique: Differentiating the Expertise of Management Gurus and Management Consultants'. In T. Clark and R. Fincham (eds), *Critical Consulting: New Perspectives on the Management Advice Industry*. Oxford: Blackwell, 191–205.

Fincham, R. (2002/3). 'The Agent's Agent: Power, Knowledge and Uncertainty in Management Consultancy'. *International Studies of Management and Organization*, 32/4, 67–86.

Fincham, R. (2006). 'Knowledge Work as Occupational Strategy: Comparing IT and Management Consulting'. *New Technology, Work and Employment*, 21/1, 16–28.

Fincham, R. and Evans, M. (1999). 'The Consultants' Offensive: Reengineering—from Fad to Technique'. *New Technology, Work and Employment*, 14/1, 32–44.

Fincham, R., Clark T., Handley, K., and Sturdy A. (2008). 'Configuring Expert Knowledge: The Consultant as Sector Specialist'. *Journal of Organizational Behavior*, 29/6, 1145–1160.

Fosstenløkken, M., Løwendahl, B. R., and Revang, O. (2003). 'Knowledge Development through Client Interaction: A Comparative Study'. *Organization Studies*, 24/6, 859–879.

Gammelsaeter, H. (2002). 'Managers and Consultants as Embedded Actors: Evidence from Norway', in M. Kipping and L. Engwall (eds.), Management Consulting: Emergence and Dynamics of a Knowledge Industry. Oxford: Oxford University Press, 222–237.

Hansen, M. T., Nohria, N., and Tierney, T. (1999). 'What's Your Strategy for Managing Knowledge?' Harvard Business Review, 77/2, 106–116.

Hislop D. (2002). 'The Client Role in Consultancy Relations during the Appropriation of Technological Innovations'. Research Policy, 31, 657–671.

Kieser, A. (1997). 'Rhetoric and Myth in Management Fashion'. Organization, 4, 49–74.

Kieser, A. (2002). 'On Communication Barriers between Management Science, Consultancies and Business Organizations'. In T. Clark and R. Fincham (eds), Critical Consulting: New Perspectives on the Management Advice Industry. Oxford: Blackwell, 206–227.

Kipping, M. (2000). 'Consultancy and Conflicts: Bedaux at Lukens Steel and the Anglo-Iranian Oil Company'. Enterprises et Histoire, 25, 9–25.

Kipping, M. and Armbrüster, T. (2002). 'The Burden of Otherness: Limits of Consultancy Interventions in Historical Case Studies'. In M. Kipping and L. Engwall (eds), Management Consulting: Emergence and Dynamics of a Knowledge Industry. Oxford: Oxford University Press, 203–221.

Kipping, M. and Engwall, L. (eds) (2002). Management Consulting: Emergence and Dynamics of a Knowledge Industry. Oxford: Oxford University Press.

Kitay, J. and Wright, C. (2004). 'Take the Money and Run: Organizational Boundaries and Consultants' Roles'. Service Industries Journal, 24/3, 1–19.

Kitay, J. and Wright, C. (2007). 'From Prophets to Profits: The Occupational Rhetoric of Management Consultants'. Human Relations, 60/11, 1613–1640.

McKenna, C. (2006). The World's Newest Profession: Management Consulting in the Twentieth Century. Cambridge: Cambridge University Press.

Meyer, J. (2002). 'Globalization and the Expansion and Standardization of Management'. In K. Sahlin-Andersson and L. Engwall (eds), The Expansion of Management Knowledge: Carriers, Ideas and Sources. Stanford, CA: Stanford University Press, 33–44.

Richter, A. and Niewiem, S. (2009). 'Knowledge Transfer across Permeable Boundaries: An Empirical Study of Clients' Decisions to Involve Management Consultants'. Scandinavian Journal of Management, 25/3, 275–288.

Røvik, K. A. (2002). 'The Secrets of the Winners: Management Ideas that Flow'. In K. Sahlin-Andersson and L. Engwall (eds), The Expansion of Management Knowledge: Carriers, Ideas and Sources. Stanford, CA: Stanford University Press, 113–144.

Sahlin-Andersson, K. and Engwall, L. (eds) (2002). The Expansion of Management Knowledge: Carriers, Ideas and Sources. Stanford, CA: Stanford University Press.

Scarbrough, H., Swan, J., Laurent, S., Bresnan, M., and Newell, S. (2004). 'Project-Based Learning and the Role of Learning Boundaries'. Organization Studies, 25/9, 1579–1600.

Schein E. H. (1997). 'The Concept of "Client" from a Process Consultation Perspective: A Guide for Change Agents'. Journal of Organizational Change Management, 10/3, 202–216.

Strang, D. and Meyer J. W. (1993). 'Institutional Conditions for Diffusion'. Theory and Society, 22, 487–511.

Sturdy, A. (1997a). 'The Dialectics of Consultancy'. Critical Perspectives on Accounting, 8, 511–535.

Sturdy, A. (1997b). 'The Consultancy Process: An Insecure Business'. Journal of Management Studies, 34/3, 389–413.

Sturdy, A., Clark, T., Handley K., and Fincham R. (2009). Management Consultancy in Action: Knowledge Boundaries and Flows. Oxford: Oxford University Press.

Werr, A. (2002). 'The Internal Creation of Consulting Knowledge: A Question of Structuring Experience'. In M. Kipping and L. Engwall (eds), *Management Consulting: Emergence and Dynamics of a Knowledge Industry*. Oxford: Oxford University Press, 92–108.

Werr, A. and Stjernberg, T. (2003). 'Exploring Management Consulting Firms as Knowledge Systems'. *Organization Studies*, 24, 881–908.

Wilensky, H. (1964). 'The Professionalization of Everyone?' *The American Journal of Sociology*, 70, 137–157.

CHAPTER 21

CONSULTANTS AND CLIENTS FROM CONSTRUCTIVIST PERSPECTIVES

BARBARA CZARNIAWSKA
CARMELO MAZZA

21.1 INTRODUCTION

THE purpose of this chapter is to provide an overview of what has, to date, been a marginal issue in the relevant academic literature: (social) constructivist perspectives on management consulting. Yet, the constructivist perspective may provide answers to a central question for many scholarly approaches to management consulting (see the contributions in Clark and Fincham 2002; Kipping and Engwall 2002; Sahlin-Andersson and Engwall 2002): Are management consultants really helping their clients? And if so, how?

As Nikolova and Devinney show in Chapter 19 in this volume, most scholars address this question under the assumption that an interaction exists between consultants and their clients—an interaction based on learning or an exchange of knowledge. One of the best known of these scholars, Schein (1999), has argued that consultants help clients by constructing usable knowledge during their interactions. This usable knowledge is situated or dependent upon context, and is shaped by the consultant–client relationship rather than being derived from a knowledge-base or experience. The constructivist perspective provides an alternative view of the consultant–client relationship, by questioning its very character. Schein's view implies that help is developed in a dialogue between the consultants and the clients, which takes for granted the possibility of communication and mutual exchange.

The same taken-for-granted possibility stands at the core of the idea that consultants contribute to clients' knowledge by providing them with technical expertise. This assumption of communication and mutual exchange is implicit in the argument that consultants and clients engage in a joint learning project (Kubr 1996; Mulligan and Barber 1998). The symbolic view of consultant–client relationship, as represented by many critical theorists (Clark and Salaman 1998; Alvesson 2001; Clark and Fincham 2002), questions these assumptions. This critical approach implies that asymmetry in communication and mutual exchange may emerge. In particular, management fads and fashions may create asymmetry because consultants act as fashion setters, contributing to the definition of clients' perceptions and the needs of management practices (Engwall and Kipping 2002; Jung and Kieser, Chapter 16, this volume).

Yet all these scholars agree that communication and mutual exchange are possible, if at times complex. What if consultants see 'the reality' in a different way than their clients do, however? Is a common reality among consultants and clients even possible? Constructivist scholars try to address these questions and, in doing so, reframe the consultant–client relationship.

As the term 'constructivism' acquires popularity (Czarniawska 2003), its meanings begin to differ widely. The chapter begins, therefore, by explaining our premises in a brief historical overview of constructivism, followed by our definition of the constructivist perspective. The next section shows how constructivism may contribute to an understanding of the consultant–client relationship, beginning with Niklas Luhmann's (2005) radical view on consulting. Luhmann criticized the received view of consulting as an application of science, noting the impossibility of communication between consultants and the people representing the system the consultants claim to improve. The same section then describes another radical constructivist perspective, portraying consultants as 'parasites' (Clegg, Kornberger, and Rhodes 2004a). The chapter then moves on to less radical approaches looking at consultants as co-constructors of managerial words, including, in particular, as 'merchants of meaning' (Czarniawska-Joerges 1990). The following section explores recent developments of the constructivist approach to consulting, focusing on the concept of 'liminality' (Van Gennep 1960), defined as a transitional stage in which usual prerogatives are suspended. The chapter ends with the suggestion that a constructivist perspective can reveal many complex and poorly understood aspects of management consulting.

21.2 VARIETIES OF CONSTRUCTIVISM

The concept of constructivism has received much attention in social sciences. Nevertheless, the concept has been interpreted in several ways. This section aims to give an introductory outline of the several nuances of constructivism to which the literature on management consulting refers.

As early as 1928, the British psychologist Fredrick C. Bartlett wrote about 'social constructiveness', by which he meant

> a characteristic reaction towards imported elements of culture adopted inevitably by all strong and vigorous groups. It means that imported elements suffer change both in the direction of existing culture and along the general line of development of the receptive group. It means that while it may well be the case that the stimulus to social change comes in the main from social contacts, important social forms may genuinely grow up within the group. (1928: 391)

At the time, psychology was much closer to anthropology than it is today, which explains the obvious connection of Bartlett's text to the then-fierce diffusion versus evolution controversy in anthropology (see Czarniawska 2001b for more on this debate). And, although the present social constructivism in the social sciences has a different genealogy, Bartlett's definition may be worth reconsidering, especially in the context of consulting. A stimulus to change may come from outside, but an everyday construction of organizational realities may itself produce change.

Usually, however, the roots of 'social constructivism' are found not in psychology but in the Russian (Soviet) architecture and art movement called *konstruktivizm*, articulated in the 1920s in the 'Realist Manifesto' by Antoine Pevsner and Naum Gabo, and carried into the 1930s and to the rest of Europe by El Lissitzky and László Moholy-Nagy (Benn 1990). This movement trickled across to Russian poetry, where the constructivists appropriated the futurists' credo *Words are things*, but its proponents decided to construct rather than destroy with words (Chicherin and Selvinsky 1923; Shore 2006). Consequently, art critics, but also psychologists and social scientists, embraced the idea that worlds are not a given, but are constantly made and remade—that actions are driven in part by human agency but always in interaction with other humans and non-humans. Whereas Jean Piaget and other psychologists turned their attention to individual constructions of the world (see Holzner 1968), Jürgen Habermas, among others, noted that individual world-views both produce and are products of *social* constraints by means of language and communication (Habermas 1981).

The classic social science text cited in reference to social constructivism is Peter Berger and Thomas Luckmann's *The Social Construction of Reality* (1967). Their approach can be seen as an outcome of the fruitful encounter between European phenomenology (Alfred Schütz was their teacher) and US pragmatism (primarily George Herbert Mead), being a close relative of symbolic interactionism and ethnomethodology. Although Berger and Luckmann's version of constructivism is usually interpreted as being connected to the views of philosopher Wilhelm Dilthey (1833–1911), according to which only humans construct the world, using language as their construction tools, numerous examples in the book go beyond these boundaries, quoting non-linguistic constructions and describing non-human constructors, such as machines (see, for example, Berger and Luckmann 1966: 149–150).

Berger and Luckmann's claim that reality is socially constructed stimulated further reflections, and a variety of constructivist and constructionist approaches emerged (for a review, see Knorr Cetina 1993, 1994; and Sismondo 1993). The voluntaristic idea, according to which the social construction of reality means that individuals are free to construct their own reality, attracted strong criticism (see Ashmore, Edwards, and Potter 1994 for a review). From a different angle, the sociologists of science and technology (Latour and Woolgar 1979; Knorr Cetina 1981; Latour 1988) have claimed that constructivism can help to reveal how worlds are materially produced in heterogeneous (not merely in human) *networks*. Latour's discontent with the dominant version of constructivism made him plead for the abandonment of the term 'constructing' in favour of 'assembling' (Latour 2005). Although the terms are synonymous, the latter is not heavily ideology-laden. This chapter maintains the conventional terms, although Latour's plea is worth considering.

This overview of the (social) constructivist approach leads us to the stance proposed by Niklas Luhmann who, according to Knorr Cetina (1993), developed the most radical constructivist view and applied it to management consulting. Luhmann's central contribution to the constructivist approach is his theory of social systems, built around the concept of autopoiesis, which was, in turn, developed by Chilean biologists Humberto Maturana and Francisco Varela (Seidl 2005: 19–51). Autopoietic systems contain a prescription for their own reproduction—DNA, for example. Luhmann argued that this idea could be fruitfully applied to a large number of non-biological systems. Social systems, then, can be conceptualized as reproducing their own elements on the basis of their own elements, thus constructing and reconstructing themselves. These elements are neither persons nor actions, as in traditional sociology, but are *communicative events*.

The overview on the (social) constructivist approach in social sciences allows us to move forward to apply constructivism to the analysis of management consulting. The next section will explore the most radical stances of Luhmann, while the remaining parts of this chapter discuss the more symbolic approaches.

21.3 Applying Radical Constructivism to Consultant–Client Relations

Luhmann was among the first of the constructivists to pay attention to the phenomenon of consulting, in trying to address the issues of the consultant–client relationship and the possibility of their common reality. Applying his theoretical device of autopoiesis, Luhmann strongly questioned the possibility of a successful communication between consultants and their clients, as their acts of communication form two distinct and closed systems (Luhmann 2005).[1] A communicative event, according to Luhmann, consists of information, utterance, and meaning. Whereas the information transmitted and received may be identical, and although all parties may perceive the fact of the utterance, the meaning is produced within the system. And, within a system, communications can refer only to what belongs to the system itself. Thus autopoietic systems are intrinsically idiosyncratic, and direct communication among different systems is impossible. Any communication crossing the boundary of a system would become 'different' when processed within the meanings developed by the other system (Luhmann 2005). The systems can shout to each other, as it were, but what reaches them is but a reflection of their own voices.

What do consultants do, in such cases? Traditionally, according to Luhmann, consultants were supposed to offer their clients 'an applied science'. They were expected to communicate the accessible results of science in such a way that their clients could put them to practice. As Luhmann noted, however, a successful communication would mean either that science is completely understandable (and thus there is no need for consultants) or that consultants speak exactly the same language as their clients (which means that there is no difference between them).

> That a group of consultants [...] cannot communicate itself completely (but is nonetheless capable of communicating internally about this impossibility of external communication) is due to the fact that communication is the operation by means of which the group carries its own autopoiesis, and thus the means by which it regenerates its own unity, as well as the difference between this unity and its environment. (Luhmann 2005: 355)

Thus, from the Luhmannian perspective, consultants cannot communicate successfully with their clients. One could almost wonder, within the same radical perspective, if consultants are *willing* to communicate successfully. After all, successful communication could imply that there is no difference between consultants and clients—so consulting is useless—or that their 'science' can be fully understood even without consulting interventions. From this radical viewpoint, clients and consultants are unable to understand one another. They live in two worlds, and will never meet. They do try to communicate, however, and with increasing frequency, but not so much with one another as with their own wider system, including those organizations and institutions that shape their worldviews: institutionalized practices, communities of practices, and taken-for-granted norms and values, for instance. Although autopoietic, the two systems interact and frame responses to the institutional alignment pressures coming from the external environment in similar ways (Oliver 1991).[2]

Building on Luhmann's ideas, but connecting it to the institutional theory of organizations, Kieser (2002: 216) has noted that this all happens because organizations are able to react 'only to the environmental changes as they are recorded and interpreted by the system', and act only according to their own logic—by the means of organizational routines and codes embedding these memories and interpretations—even while trying to change. If this is so, why does consulting exist and prosper? Luhmann has offered an explanation for and justification of the existence of management consultants. In his view, the attempts at communication produced by management consultants serve as an irritant to the client system. Left to themselves, clients would be enacting their own visions of the world (Weick 1988), perhaps until some serious crisis stopped them. Thus, even if consultants cannot communicate their different vision of the world to their clients, their very attempts to communicate may provoke client reaction in a way that is similar to the external jolts that Greenwood, Suddaby, and Hinings (2002) have described as change triggers.

From Luhmann's perspective, consultants can hardly be seen as economic actors providing 'cost effective means to acquire managerial skills, techniques and processes' (McKenna 2006: 13). Kieser (2002) not only agreed with Luhmann, but went even further, by suggesting that due to intentional and unintentional communication barriers, the knowledge of researchers, consultants, and practitioners is and will remain decoupled. Assuming such a standpoint implies, therefore, that there is more than asymmetry in the consultant–client relationship; it is a permanently failing relationship, and a common reality for consultants and clients is impossible.

Another approach within the radical constructivist perspective rejects the idea that consultants help their clients (Clegg, Kornberger, and Rhodes 2004a, 2004b). Proponents of this view do not believe that this problem exists because of a lack of feasible communication between consultants and clients, as suggested by Luhmann. Rather, they claim that consultants do not increase clients' performativity. According to this perspective, consultants merely acquire practical knowledge from their interactions with clients, and then repackage it in the form of effective toolboxes to be sold elsewhere. Clegg, Kornberger, and Rhodes (2004a) use the word 'parasites'—a term borrowed from Michel Serres—to describe the role of consultants in their relationships with clients:

> Consulting may be conceived as a process of tension, oscillating between order and disorder and de- and reconstruction. It can deconstruct organizational routines and taken-for-granted convictions in order to open up a space to the other voices, different perspectives, and differing opinions that operate within it—producing dissensus, searching for instabilities, gaps and divisions, building creative dissonance into practice, even if it challenges the core values of the organization. (2004a: 38)

In the Clegg, Kornberger, and Rhodes conceptualization, 'parasitic consultants' are able to disturb a system because 'they are in between, neither here nor there but in the middle' (2004a: 39). This suggestion does resonate with Luhmann's concept of consultants as 'external irritants', who produce changes not by directly relating to clients, but by stimulating (from outside) the client's social system. Consultants explore the space between order and chaos, both disrupting and reconstructing the existing practices. This activity can hardly serve as a ground for any argument linking consulting to the improvement of clients' performance. To the contrary, Clegg, Kornberger, and Rhodes (2004a) claim that consultants enjoy a condition of privilege, as they are not responsible for the results that clients obtain by following the consultant's advice.

Such a critical view of the consultant–client relationship has itself become the object of criticism. As Sturdy and colleagues (2004) have pointed out, there is evidence of exchanges occurring in the consultant–client relationship—exchanges that are also beneficial for the client, who gains legitimacy as well as interpretative skills. These interactions create opportunities for both consultants and clients to perform their tasks.

Moreover, such interactions—not only such formal interactions as official report presentations, but also informal interactions such as dinners and at the workplace—are the very basis of the co-construction of a reality by consultants and clients (Sturdy, Schwarz, and Spicer 2006).

The next section explores more moderate applications of constructivism to the analysis of management consulting.

21.4 A MODERATE CONSTRUCTIVISM VIEW OF CONSULTING

Reactions to Luhmannian approaches have led to the emergence of more moderate interpretations of the consultant–client relationship within the constructivist perspective. In the attempt to by-pass Luhmann's radical stance, many scholars espousing constructivism chose to ignore the philosophical issue of the possibility or impossibility of communication. In this section, we review such pragmatist (Rorty 1982) approaches to consulting; they all portray management consultants as co-constructors of managerial worlds.

One of the most prominent among them is the 'merchant of meaning' metaphor developed by Czarniawska-Joerges (1990). In this view, consultants relate to clients (managers) in order to reconstruct their managerial tasks and roles by reframing them with the help of linguistic artefacts (images, labels, metaphors). In this way, consultants contribute to sense-making activity, by providing managers with quasi-objects such as reports and models, to be used in the construction of organizational realities in which all managers necessarily engage in order to perform their daily task of organizing (Weick 1995). Consultants are therefore conceptualized as carriers of ideas, vocabularies, and interpretative templates. Next, the section discusses the similarity between the role of consultants and the role aspired to by many social scientists, delving into explorations of various misunderstandings that may arise from such proximity. There is, in particular, the approach developed by Bloomfield and Vurdubakis (1994), who focus their attention on the material artefacts that consultants produce (reports, texts, drawings) and the role of these artefacts in shaping the way clients see their own reality. From this angle, consultants are active co-constructors of managerial reality, shaping its perception with the aid of the material artefacts they produce.

21.4.1 Consultants as 'Merchants of Meaning'

The role played by consultants in framing discourse has raised the interest of several researchers within the constructivist domain. Berglund and Werr (2000) have placed rhetoric at the core of consulting success. In a similar vein, Meriläinen and colleagues

(2004) demonstrate how management consulting talk framed the 'ideal' consultant. This research stream has an antecedent in Czarniawska-Joerges and Joerges (1988, 1990) work on consultants as producers of language artefacts. They noted that an important building block of reality construction consists of three types of linguistic artefacts: a) *labels*, which tell *what* things are—classification tools; b) *metaphors*, which say *how* things are—tools of familiarization, but also tools of estrangement, and therefore able to incite interest; and c) *platitudes*, which standardize and establish *what is normal*.

Such linguistic artefacts are constantly produced and applied inside organizations. But, like any other artefact, they are often bought from external suppliers, that is, management consultants, who are their most prolific producers but who are also processors of raw materials and half-products, which they find in both research results and popular culture. It turned out that consultants spoke of their activity as consisting of product development, idea selling (this was before the word 'concept' had established itself as dominant in the field), and direct versus indirect selling techniques. Articles, panel discussions, interviews with leading consultants, and other notes in the *Journal of Management Consulting*, analysed by Czarniawska-Joerges and Joerges, confirmed that the main products were labels, metaphors, and platitudes. Labels and metaphors were often called *insights, ideas, images*. Speaking about their clients' problems or about themselves, the authors who published in the *Journal* multiplied metaphors infinitely. One company advised a *cookie cutter* approach to consulting; another claimed that business strategy was a large chess game. A CEO of a consulting firm said in an interview that hiring MBAs is like *buying wine*, and another confessed that his first assignment was like *taking a girlfriend for a walk across a minefield* without knowing it.

This ongoing process of creating metaphors and labels helps to provide managerial action with meaning. Therefore, Czarniawska-Joerges (1990) suggested the metaphor 'merchants of meaning', which alluded to the then-dominant metaphor of leadership as 'management of meaning' (Smircich and Morgan 1982). This idea seems to be crucial for understanding the role of consultants as providers of control tools. To quote Brown (1978: 376), 'making decisions' is not the most important exercise of organizational power. Instead, this power is most strategically deployed in the design and imposition of paradigmatic frameworks within which the very meaning of such actions as "making decisions" is defined. The paradigmatic frameworks mentioned by Brown are the means provided by consultants to make sense of managerial actions. Following Weick (1995), it could be said that consultants are called upon for help when an organizational situation no longer makes sense, or does not make the desired sense, and the established ways of sense-making are of no use. Consultants then offer more than just a set of linguistic control tools, however well packaged; they offer *interpretative templates* (Czarniawska 2008).

An interpretative template is a collection of tools that is connected and interdependent. It offers a label, which can also be seen as an indication of what Brown called 'a paradigmatic framework', and that Weick, after Goffman (1974), called 'a frame'—what a narratologist may call a genre. A label such as 'This is a crisis' severely limits further steps of sense-making (one does not celebrate a crisis or reward people for a crisis, for example). A gallery of characters exists within such a framework: the villains, the saviours, and the victims. Again, within such a framework, there are ways of describing the environment (mostly metaphorical) that are appropriate for such a structure. Finally, an interpretative template also contains a plot, which is the final element of sense-making, as it prescribes actions based upon previous actions and events. A crisis caused by a competitor calls for one set of actions and a crisis caused by internal conflict calls for another. Imprisoned in their earlier interpretative templates, which no longer make sense, clients look to consultants for new templates.

In sum, according to this view management consultants could probably be best called the merchants of sense-making tools. Not all such tools are appreciated, however; unsuccessful communication may still be successful consulting, but unsuccessful consulting also exists. Before discussing these cases, the section will consider consultants' other, more direct ways of sense-making, based on an extended range of tools offered by the consultants, which have been identified in further studies.

21.4.2 The Inscriptions of Consulting

Bloomfield and Vurdubakis (1994) noted that consultants contribute to the construction of an organizational reality by selling both linguistic and material artefacts: texts and graphics. The texts they scrutinized were reports on the possible strategic uses of information technology, delivered by management consultants. The purpose of their study was 'to situate IT strategy reports within the broader category of textual and graphical constructs—inscriptions—which in various fields of inquiry and application, discipline and practice, are used to represent reality in order to act on it, control or dominate it, as well as to secure the compliance of others in that domination' (ibid.: 456).

If the linguistic artefacts are meant as tools for controlling the human elements of those heterogeneous networks that form during the process of every collective activity, these textual artefacts were designed to control the non-human ingredients. Both concepts reflect the reasoning typical for actor-network theory, in which organizing is a collective action performed by a network of actants posing as a macro-actor.[3] In Bloomfield and Vurdubakis's view, the IT reports contained a prescription for a 'strategic alignment' between technology and organization. Such documents and such alignments reveal interesting aspects of consulting activities. The declared goal of such activities is always change, but, as noted by Brunsson and Olsen (1993), the most visible effect is the reconfirmation of the status quo. By stressing the need for alignment between technology and organization, however, the consultants studied by Bloomfield and Vurdubakis confirmed the separate existence of the two realms. In doing so, consultants resembled the social scientists, who, as noted by Latour (1993), first separate what is, in fact, unified (social and technical, nature and culture), and then proudly demonstrate their efforts to build a bridge between the elements. According to Latour (1993), this manoeuvre permits social scientists to take the role of intermediaries, linking knowledge domains after having separated them under the form of distinct disciplines. In the same way, consultants build their role by setting separations among domains that are supposed to be unified, often through the creation of categories and taxonomies as well as specific management practice typifications.

Bloomfield and Vurdubakis (1994) detected some specific traits of consultants' reports: traits that make them useful elements in reality construction. One major requirement is that such texts must attempt to limit the potential variety of their readings: 'The condition for a report's success is the extent it is able to produce the reader it requires' (ibid.: 458). Thus the reports set the scene for communication between consultants and clients. Communication is possible not because consultants and clients speak the same language (as the expert approach may hold), but because consultants shape the readers' interpretations of the text, and therefore of the situation. If everything goes as planned, the clients adopt the consultants' framework and language. Bloomfield and Vurdubakis' (1994) concluded their rhetorical analysis of consultants' reports by situating them between two other genres: that of a scientific paper and that of a social scientific paper. A consultant's report cannot muster the authority of a scientific paper, as it has no rules of scientific methodology to evoke. Consultants do try to steer their reports away from the polysemy of social scientific reports, however—at least those reports that invite multiple interpretations and the cultivation of doubt rather than imitating natural sciences rhetorically (on this technique of *scientification*, see also McCloskey 1985).

In this aspect, the consultants' reports differed greatly from the self-descriptions of their activities as published in the *Journal of Management Consulting*. Several textual strategies were employed for limiting the variety of readings: a) an *executive summary*, signalling economy in communication (*just plain facts*); b) *bullet points* (*going straight to the heart of the matter*, ibid.: 460); and c) *numbering* sections and paragraphs (which suggests their equal weight; nothing can be omitted), for instance. Bloomfield and Vurdubakis's study is important not only because it demonstrated in detail how consultants contribute to a construction of organizational reality, but also because it threw light on an uneasy closeness between consultants' reports and social scientific papers (Collins 2004, 2005).

As reported in other chapters in this volume, many approaches define the consultant–client relationship as instrumental. Consultants *help* clients by providing them with knowledge and expertise to perform their task more effectively. As discussed previously, the constructivist approaches that assume the possibility of a co-construction of a reality among consultants and clients concur that instrumentality does provide a ground for the relationship. In particular, as the literature reported in this section has outlined, consultants 'help' clients by providing linguistic and material artefacts, shaping the perception of the reality that clients assume to be the object of their actions and decisions. The next section will explore an alternative, recently proposed framework to look at consultant–client relationships, which is rooted in an anthropologic view of consulting.

21.5 CONSULTING AS A STATE OF LIMINALITY

All the approaches within the constructivist domain share the view that the consultant–client interaction is a special type of interaction—or rather interactions—under a specific condition. Attempting to define this condition, German anthropologist Richard Rottenburg (2005, 2009) concluded, based on many years of observing management consultants in development projects, that a willingly accepted illusion—of a common reality, of a common language, and of a shared meaning—can accomplish a great deal in pragmatic terms. Under what condition can such an illusion be created and maintained? In the last example of a constructivist view on consulting, we draw on a recent approach that suggests characterizing this condition as a state of 'liminality'.

The term 'liminality' was introduced to anthropology by Arnold van Gennep (1909), to denote rituals accompanying the passage from one social status to another, and has been adopted by anthropologists who gave it a variety of meanings. Yet in most variations it is assumed that liminality exists in both time and space—a peculiar condition under which people are perceived to have temporary attributes. As Turner (1982: 24) wrote, '[t]he ritual subjects pass through a period and an area of ambiguity, a sort of social limbo which has few [...] of the attributes of either the preceding or subsequent profane social statuses or cultural states'. He also suggested that the liminal space has a sacred nature, in which existing duties and privileges are suspended and new ones are acquired. Freedom and room for creativity may emerge. Nevertheless, Turner was against applying the notion of liminality to modern societies, and suggested the 'liminoid' condition instead. Many of his insights are directly applicable to the activity of consulting, however. He noted that whereas separation may be characterized by a sharp symbolic inversion of social attributes, the blurring and merging of distinctions characterize liminality. People who find themselves in a liminal phase are 'temporarily undefined, beyond the normative social structure. This weakens them, since they have no rights over others. But it also liberates them from structural obligations' (Turner 1982: 27). The phase is characteristically accompanied by ritual symbols of either effacement or ambiguity and paradox.

Van Gennep distinguished three phases of a rite of passage: separation (divestiture), transition (liminality), and incorporation (investiture). Czarniawska and Mazza (2003) extended the idea of consulting as liminality creation to all three, as consultants are active both in separation and, although less actively, in incorporation. Thus, they described consultancy events and action in terms of *consultancy rites*. In originally applying the concept of liminality to consulting, with the intention of describing the occupational conditions of consultants, they were close to Kipping and Armbrüster (2002), who suggested that the consultants carry 'the burden of otherness'. But this burden is only one constituent of the state of liminality. If it were the very process of consulting, which can be fruitfully described as the creation of a state of liminality, consultants could be even seen as witch doctors (Clark and Salaman 1996; Micklethwait and Wooldridge 1996) by being defined as those who provide a state of liminality for others. Yet, by this very fact, they are condemning themselves to remain in this state—as long as they are occupied with consulting.

Thus, according to Czarniawska and Mazza (2003), the liminal space in which consultancy occurs is that of a *liminal organization*, as perceived by consultants and their clients. It can be argued, however, that the actual place occupied by the liminal organization is the same as that which for many other people is a non-liminal place—a place of stable identities and everyday work. A liminal organization shares its legal boundaries and physical environment with a proper work organization, but it forms a virtual space, which is likely to be experienced differently by consultants and regular employees. Whereas other organizational rites of passage, like the managerial training described by Eriksson-Zetterquist (2002), may occur in a different locality or at least at a time other than that accorded to regular organizing, consulting happens primarily at the same time and place but in a different space. This view has been analysed by Sturdy, Schwarz, and Spicer (2006), who examined such liminal situations as dinners for consultants and their clients. They concluded that the rules and rituals of a workplace have been simply replaced at such times by the rules and rituals of dining. While, both the study and the argument of Sturdy, Schwarz, and Spicer are convincing, it could be questioned whether the situations they studied were conducive to the state of liminality *stricto sensu*.

Most consultants also belong to a non-liminal world, usually a university or a consulting company—somebody else's or their own. Unlike participants in rites of passage, however, consultants do not leave it to re-enter later after a completed transition. They travel back and forth, in and out of the liminal spaces. While within such space, they abdicate control over their time. A consultant's time is an item in the client's budget and is managed like all other budget items. Consultants are controlled through the measurement of their workdays, and their output is calculated in person-per-day units. The time of a given consultant is then checked according to the number of persons-per-day allocated to a given project. The external locus of action control is even more obvious than time control. The consultants must not have their own objectives; their role consists of internalizing those of the client. They are supposed to perceive the world, interpret it, and act on it in a way that best serves their clients' interests (Czarniawska and Mazza, 2003). There is, of course, a possibility that their clients do not perceive their interests correctly—at least according to the consultants—but even correcting misperceptions is part of acting in their clients' interests. In many cases, a consultant cannot decide that, for the good of humanity, the client had better perish, and, although the temptation may exist, such an alternative means taking leave, perhaps permanently, from the role of a consultant condition.

Metaphors are, by definition, short of analogies, and have their obvious limitations. One can point out, for instance, that although the function of rites of passage was to change the novices and keep the community as it was, the function of consulting is to change the community and keep the consultants as they are. But, as Turner (1982) has noted, liminality fosters deviation and creativity, and a new generation of novices may be the ones that will organize a mutiny, or at least renew the community. Even though liminal, consultants are not expected to change. Consultants are not summoned to organizations to undergo rites of passage, but to organize them. Their task is to turn a regular organization into a liminal one—temporarily. Czarniawska and Mazza (2003), however, have observed two parallel and causally connected rites of passage occurring when client organizations involved many employees in the consulting projects: those for consultants and those for employees (where the actual clients—the managers—may or may not be involved). According to their findings, the temporal organization of the two is inverted. The start-up meeting is an investiture for consultants and a divestiture for employees. The presentation of the report is an investiture for employees and the divestiture of consultants. In the phase of transition, the status of both is fluid, and can change dramatically with circumstances. The main difference between the condition of the consultants and that of employees is that the consultants organize rituals for the employees, but collaborate with the clients (usually, the management) in staging their own rituals.

Although it might appear as an extra-ordinary stage, it can be postulated that, surprisingly enough, the state of liminality is becoming more and more permanent in contemporary societies. Rottenburg (2000), who analysed a condition of liminality created in a bar on the Polish–German border, mentioned 'the aporia given by the contradiction between the impossibility of true classifications and the unavoidability of classifying' (ibid.: 98). Labels offered by consultants may appear to be the proper names of things in the world, but only on the first use. All that is said about liminality and aporia suggests a temporary state that may be painful (for example, like purgatory, a state of limbo for Catholics) or even enjoyable, but of limited duration. Some customers of the bar that Rottenburg observed seemed to enjoy their prolonged visits there just because it was limbo. Having separated themselves from whatever was behind and before, they were in no hurry to be incorporated into something new. Perhaps there was nothing new to be incorporated into; perhaps they had to stay in limbo until the new heaven was constructed.

As van Gennep and Turner had already realized, this line of reasoning suggests that liminality can offer a sense of freedom, the possibility of creation, and a special sense of community with others in limbo. When aporia prevails, the exits are open and so, peculiar to our time and place, are the entrances. Although liminality-inducing situations may become regulated and ritualized in time, as noted by Sturdy, Schwarz, and Spicer (2006), it is important to document and analyse their emergence. Furthermore, if a state of liminality is indeed on the increase, it makes even less sense to search for 'the essence of reality'. It makes much more sense to try to see how those, whose vocation and profession is to advise the constructors of organizational worlds, go about their work. Liminality is not the only concept that may be useful in this endeavour. What is important, however, is to remember the precepts of the original constructivists: that words are things, and can be used to build and to destroy; that reality is always different from plans and designs; and that the world, no matter how stable it looks, is under a continuous construction, with a great many constructors whose actions may conflict.

21.6 CONCLUSIONS AND DIRECTIONS FOR FURTHER RESEARCH

This chapter has offered a review of and a reflection on constructionist views of the consultant–client relationship, intending to show how studies of consulting may benefit from a constructivist approach. We summarized the extant literature, which had analysed the consultant–client relationship with different constructivist lenses, and addressed questions concerning the type of help consultants may give to clients, as well as the existence of a common reality among consultants and clients. The chapter first explored the most radical views, in particular the one proposed by Luhmann, who holds that no relationship or common reality is possible. Next, it surveyed more moderate constructivist approaches that allow for the possibility of consultant–client relationships and converge in their understanding of this by viewing relationships as the co-construction of a reality that shapes the way organizational tasks are performed.

The final section outlined a subject matter, where a constructivist view of consulting may be especially relevant: the liminal condition. The concept of liminality, although certainly not the only viewpoint worthy of interest, may prove fruitful for understanding various states of transitions that people are currently experiencing—including the condition of being a consultant. In the liminal space, the (usually distinct) borders between the sacred and the profane are blurred. In organizational vocabulary, one could say that the borders between theory and practice are opened. One way of describing what happens when a liminal space is created in an organization is to see it as a theatre of images, activated during the time of consultancy. After all, according to all constructivist approaches, ideas that the consultants carry are (often literally) images; the metaphors sold by the merchants of meaning are images too. Consultants are expected to help their clients to create a new repertoire of representation(s)—representations that make sense. This new repertoire may be used as a blueprint for forming a new or different work organization, but will most certainly be used directly in an unchanged form as a collection of images to be presented to outside spectators.

Building on these approaches, a potentially fruitful area for future research could be an investigation into the possibility of a constructivist consultant, explored in a preliminary way by Czarniawska (2001a). Her argument was that such consultants do exist, and that they help their clients by offering them reflections on how their present way of constructing and sense-making proceeds, leaving them with a choice of changing it or not—as Argyris (2000) also suggested—rather than suggesting how to construct a (more desirable) reality. However, the constructivist consulting challenges a fundamental belief of most clients: that there is only one objective reality—an objective reality that can have only one correct representation. Power came to the same conclusion by observing researchers who wished to study the construction of the practitioners' 'common sense': 'This is an intellectually attractive programme at the same time as it is a source of irritation to practitioners' (Power 1997: 8). If constructivism remains a marginal view, it is because there exists and has always existed a strong belief in what Tuchman (1978) called *a pregiven world*—a world existing independently of human cognition—and an almost equally common belief that this world can be represented in *one* correct way.

Moreover, another future research domain, which constructivist approaches to consulting may open, concerns the process of the co-construction of organizational reality. There are three types of logic involved in co-construction: the logic of theory, the logic of practice (Bourdieu 1990), and the logic of representation (Czarniawska 2001a). The logic of theory highlights relationships among abstract entities, and it has some claims to the use of formal logic. It hides its rhetorical accomplishments, and applies methodological criteria of truth. This is the logic of the scientific papers to which Bloomfield and Vurdubakis (1994) referred, and it makes efficient use of labels. The logic of practice depicts relationships among concrete entities situated in time and place. It is often discursively incomplete, as it relies on tacit knowledge. It frequently employs narrative knowledge (Clark and Salaman 1996), but the narratives are incomplete and not stylized. Platitudes are welcome, as they stabilize and comfort. The logic of representation follows the axioms of formal rationality superficially, in the sense that it uses dualistic differentiation between nouns, it employs ostensive definitions, and it aims at discovering mechanical connections among attributes (as in contingency theory). In those ways it resembles the logic of theory, but it differs in that it is rhetorically accomplished and explicit about it (the logic of theory hides its rhetorical accomplishments; see McCloskey 1985), and, like logic of practice, uses its narrative knowledge with gusto.

Thus the logic of representation borrows from both the logic of practice and the logic of theory, but is distinct from both (see also van Maanen 1988; and Bloomfield and Vurdubakis 1994). A piece of advice or a consultation may be in perfect accordance with the recognized logic of practice, but will be refused because of its incongruence with the logic of representation, which is assumed to be a proper logic for advice and consultations. A literal presentation of the logic of practice does not guarantee acceptance from outside listeners; the long supremacy of theory has led to a paradoxical situation in which the account most likely to gain acceptance is formulated through normative theory (the state of affairs as wished by the mandators), decorated with fragments of logic of the practice for credibility. Thus the constructivist consultants engage in the logic of practice, helping to develop it without ever stating it explicitly. They also help to formulate representative statements, which mask the logic of practice—according to the rules of representation sanctioned by a given social order. Co-construction of organizational realities emerges from this daily consulting effort to mix the three logics mentioned above to provide a representation of organizational realities that the client should, finally, agree upon.

NOTES

1. Autopoietic systems are open as energy systems, but not as communication systems.
2. Luhmann, who was interested in the thought of Gabriel Tarde before the present 'Tardomania' started (see, e.g., Candea 2010), pointed out that Tarde's theory of imitation

explained how order can be possible without cognition. By the same token, consultants and clients can act similarly without succeeding in communicating with each other.

3. An 'actant' is a term borrowed by ANT scholars from Greimasian semiology; it is any entity that acts or is acted upon. For a review of applications of ANT in organization theory, see Czarniawska and Hernes (2005).

References

Alvesson, M. (2001). 'Knowledge Work: Ambiguity, Image and Identity'. *Human Relations*, 54, 863–886.

Argyris, C. (2000). *Flawed Advice and the Management Trap*. New York: Oxford University Press.

Ashmore, M., Edwards, D., and Potter, J. (1994). 'The Bottom Line: The Rhetoric of Reality Demonstrations'. *Configurations*, 2/1, 1–14.

Bartlett, F. C. (1928). 'Social Constructiveness'. *British Journal of Psychology*, 18, 388–391.

Benn, S. (ed.) (1990). *The Tradition of Constructivism*. Cambridge, MA: Da Capo.

Berger, P. L. and Luckmann, T. (1971 [1966]). *The Social Construction of Reality*. Harmondsworth: Penguin.

Berglund, J. and Werr, A. (2000). 'The Invincible Character of Management Consulting Rhetoric: How One Blends Incommensurates While Keeping Them Apart'. *Organization*, 7, 633–655.

Bloomfield, B. P. and Vurdubakis, T. (1994). 'Re-presenting Technology: IT Consultancy Reports as Textual Reality Constructions'. *Sociology*, 28, 455–477.

Bourdieu, P. (1990). *The Logic of Practice*. Cambridge: Polity.

Brown, R. H. (1978). 'Bureaucracy as Praxis: Toward a Political Phenomenology of Formal Organizations'. *Administrative Science Quarterly*, 23, 365–382.

Brunsson, N. and Olsen, J. (eds) (1993). *The Reforming Organization*. London: Routledge.

Candea, M. (ed.) (2010). *The Social after Gabriel Tarde*. London: Routledge.

Chicherin, A. and Selvinsky, E. (1923). *Znayem (We Know: Declaration of Constructivist Poets)*. Moscow: K. P.

Clark, T. and Fincham, R. (eds) (2002). *Critical Consulting: New Perspectives on the Management Advice Industry*. Oxford: Blackwell.

Clark, T. and Salaman, G. (1998). 'Telling Tales: Management Gurus' Narratives and the Construction of Managerial Identity'. *Journal of Management Studies*, 35/2, 137–161.

Clegg, S. R., Kornberger, M., and Rhodes, C. (2004a). 'Noise, Parasites and Translation: Theory and Practice in Management Consulting'. *Management Learning*, 35, 31–44.

Clegg, S. R., Kornberger, M., and Rhodes, C. (2004b). 'When the Saints Go Marching In: A Reply to Sturdy, Clark, Fincham and Handley'. *Management Learning*, 35, 341–344.

Collins, D. (2004). 'Who Put the Con in Consultancy? Fads, Recipes and "Vodka Margarine"'. *Human Relations*, 57, 553–572.

Collins, D. (2005). 'Pyramid Schemes and Programmatic Management: Critical Reflections on the "Guru Industry"'. *Culture and Organization*, 11, 33–44.

Czarniawska, B. (2001a). 'Is it Possible to be a Constructionist Consultant?' *Management Learning*, 32, 253–272.

Czarniawska, B. (2001b). 'Anthropology and Organizational Learning'. In M. Dierkes, A. Berthoin Antal, J. Child, and I. Nonaka (eds), *Handbook of Organizational Learning and Knowledge*. Oxford: Oxford University Press, 118–136.

Czarniawska, B. (2003). 'Social Constructionism and Organization Studies'. In R. Westwood and S. Clegg (eds), *Debating Organization: Point-Counterpoint in Organization Studies*. Melbourne: Blackwell, 128–139.

Czarniawska, B. (2008). *A Theory of Organizing*. Cheltenham: Edward Elgar.

Czarniawska, B. and Mazza, C. (2003). 'Consulting as a Liminal Space'. *Human Relations*, 56, 267–290.

Czarniawska, B. and Hernes, T. (eds) (2005). *ANT and Organization Theory*. Malmö and Copenhagen: Liber and CBS Press.

Czarniawska-Joerges, B. (1990). 'Merchants of Meaning: Management Consulting in the Swedish Public Sector'. In B. A. Turner (ed.), *Organizational Symbolism*. Berlin: De Gruyter, 139–150.

Czarniawska-Joerges, B. and Joerges, B. (1988). 'How to Control Things with Words: Organizational Talk and Control'. *Management Communication Quarterly*, 2, 170–193.

Czarniawska-Joerges, B. and Joerges, B. (1990). 'Linguistic Artefacts at Service of Organizational Control'. In P. Gagliardi (ed.), *Symbols and Artefacts: Views of the Corporate Landscape*. Berlin: De Gruyter, 339–364.

Engwall, L. and Kipping, M. (2002). 'Introduction: Management Consulting as a Knowledge Industry'. In M. Kipping and L. Engwall (eds), *Management Consulting: Emergence and Dynamics of a Knowledge Industry*. Oxford: Oxford University Press, 1–18.

Eriksson-Zetterquist, U. (2002). 'Gender Construction in Corporations'. In B. Czarniawska and H. Höpfl (eds), *Casting the Other: Production and Maintenance of Inequality in Organizations*. London: Routledge, 89–103.

Goffman, E. (1974). *Frame Analysis*. New York: Harper & Row.

Greenwood, R., Suddaby, R., and Hinings, C. R. (2002). 'Theorizing Change: The Role of Professional Associations in the Transformation of Institutionalized Fields'. *Academy of Management Journal*, 45, 58–80.

Habermas, J. (1981). *Theorie des Kommunikativen Handelns*. Frankfurt am Main: Suhrkamp.

Holzner, B. (1968). *Reality Construction in Society*. Cambridge, MA: Schenkman.

Kieser, A. (2002). 'On Communication Barriers between Management Science, Consultancies and Business Companies'. In T. Clark and R. Fincham (eds), *Critical Consulting: New Perspectives on the Management Advice Industry*. Oxford: Blackwell, 206–227.

Kipping, M. and Armbrüster, T. (2002). 'The Burden of Otherness: Limits of Consultancy Interventions in Historical Case Studies'. In M. Kipping and L. Engwall (eds), *Management Consulting: Emergence and Dynamics of a Knowledge Industry*. Oxford: Oxford University Press, 203–221.

Kipping, M. and Engwall, L. (eds) (2002). *Management Consulting: Emergence and Dynamics of a Knowledge Industry*. Oxford: Oxford University Press.

Knorr Cetina, K. (1981). *The Manufacture of Knowledge*. Oxford: Pergamon.

Knorr Cetina, K. (1993). 'Strong Constructivism—From a Sociologist's Point of View: A Personal Addendum to Sismondo's Paper'. *Social Studies of Science*, 23, 555–563.

Knorr Cetina, K. (1994). 'Primitive Classification and Postmodernity: Towards a Sociological Notion of Fiction'. *Theory, Culture and Society*, 11/2, 1–22.

Kubr, M. (1996). *Management Consulting: A Guide to the Profession*. Geneva: International Labour Office.

Latour, B. (1988). 'The Politics of Explanation. An Alternative'. In S. Woolgar (ed.), *Knowledge and Reflexivity: New Frontiers in the Sociology of Knowledge*. London: Sage, 155–176.

Latour, B. (1993). *We Have Never Been Modern*. Cambridge, MA: Harvard University Press.

Latour, B. (2005). *Reassembling the Social: An Introduction to Actor-Network Theory*. Oxford: Oxford University Press.

Latour, B. and Woolgar, S. (1986 [1979]). *Laboratory Life: The Construction of Scientific Facts*. Princeton, NJ: Princeton University Press.

Luhmann, N. (2005 [1989]). 'Communication Barriers in Management Consulting'. In D. Seidl and K. H. Becker (eds), *Niklas Luhmann and Organization Studies*. Malmö and Copenhagen: Liber and CBS Press, 351–364.

McCloskey, D. N. (1985). *The Rhetoric of Economics*. Madison, WI: University of Wisconsin Press.

McKenna, C. (2006). *The World's Newest Profession: Management Consulting in the Twentieth Century*. Cambridge: Cambridge University Press.

Meriläinen, S., Tienari, J., Thomas, R., and Davies, A. (2004). 'Management Consultant Talk: A Cross-Cultural Comparison of Normalizing Discourse and Resistance'. *Organization*, 11, 539–564.

Micklethwait, J. and Wooldridge, A. (1996). *The 'Witch Doctors': What the Management Gurus are Saying, Why it Matters and How to Make Sense of It*. London: Heinemann.

Mulligan, J. and Barber, P. (1998). 'The Client–Consultant Relationship'. In P. Sadler (ed.), *Management Consultancy: A Handbook of Best Practice*. London: Kogan Page, 66–85.

Oliver, C. (1991). 'Strategic Responses to Institutional Processes'. *Academy of Management Review*, 16, 145–179.

Power, M. (1997). *The Audit Society: Rituals of Verification*. Cambridge, MA: Harvard University Press.

Rorty, R. (1982). *Consequences of Pragmatism*. Cambridge: Cambridge University Press.

Rottenburg, R. (2000). 'Sitting in a Bar'. *Studies in Cultures, Organizations and Societies*, 6, 87–100.

Rottenburg, R. (2005). 'Code-Switching, or Why a Metacode is Good to Have'. In B. Czarniawska and G. Sevón (eds), *Global Ideas: How Ideas, Objects and Practices Travel in the Global Economy*. Malmö and Copenhagen: Liber and CBS Press, 259–276.

Rottenburg, R. (2009). *Far-Fetched Facts*. Cambridge, MA: MIT Press.

Sahlin-Andersson, K. and Engwall, L. (eds) (2002). *The Expansion of Management Knowledge*. Stanford, CA: Stanford University Press.

Schein, E. H. (1999). *Process Consultation Revisited: Building the Helping Relationship*. Reading, MA: Addison-Wesley.

Seidl, D. (2005). 'The Basic Concepts of Luhmann's Theory of Social Systems'. In D. Seidl and K. H. Becker (eds), *Niklas Luhmann and Organization Studies*. Malmö and Copenhagen: Liber and CBS Press, 21–53.

Shore, M. (2006). *Caviar and Ashes: A Warsaw Generation's Life and Death in Marxism, 1918–1968*. New Haven, NJ: Yale University Press.

Sismondo, S. (1993). 'Some Social Constructions'. *Social Studies of Science*, 23/3, 515–553.

Smircich, L. and Morgan, G. (1982). 'Leadership: The Management of Meaning'. *The Journal of Applied Behavioral Science*, 18/3, 257–273.

Sturdy, A., Clark, T., Fincham, R., and Handley, K. (2004). 'Silence, Procrustes and Colonization: A Response to Clegg et al.'s "Noise, Parasites and Translation: Theory and Practice in Management Consulting"'. *Management Learning*, 35, 337–340.

Sturdy, A., Schwarz, M., and Spicer, A. (2006). 'Guess Who is Coming to Dinner? Structures and Uses of Liminality in Strategic Management Consultancy'. *Human Relations*, 59, 929–960.

Tuchman, G. (1978). *Making News: A Study in the Construction of Reality*. New York: Free Press.

Turner, V. (1982). *From Ritual to Theatre: The Human Seriousness at Play*. New York: Performing Arts Journal.

Van Gennep, A. (1960 [1909]). *Rites of Passage*. London: Routledge and Kegan Paul.

Van Maanen, J. (1988). *Tales of the Field*. Chicago: University of Chicago Press.

Weick, K. E. (1988). 'Enacted Sensemaking in Crisis Situations'. *Journal of Management Studies*, 25, 305–317.

Weick, K. E. (1995). *Sensemaking in Organizations*. Thousand Oaks, CA: Sage.

CHAPTER 22

....

GOVERNMENTS AND
MANAGEMENT CONSULTANTS:
SUPPLY, DEMAND, AND
EFFECTIVENESS

....

DENIS SAINT-MARTIN

22.1 INTRODUCTION

MANAGEMENT consultants have become increasingly visible players in the process of government restructuring over the past three decades. According to some estimates, the public sector now accounts for over 30 per cent of the global consulting market (*The Economist* 2005). But there is significant national variation. In Europe for example, of an estimated public sector expenditure on consulting of €11 billion in 2007, the UK alone accounted for €4 billion, which according to the same study, constitutes 'twice the turn-over [i.e. spend] of the German public sector, 3 times that of the Spanish public sector and 7 times that of the French' (FEACO 2007: 20). Historically, governments have used consultants since at least the 1960s with the development of the Planning, Programming and Budgeting System (PPBS) movement. Growth accelerated in the 1980s with the 'audit explosion' (Power 1997) and, more recently, with the move towards eGovernment (Böhlen et al. 2005). Much of the growth in the use of consultants over the past thirty years has taken place in central or national governments (HoC 2007), which will also be the focus of this chapter. Local governments—with fewer resources, a smaller civil service, and weaker management and policy capacities—have often relied more on consultants for policy advice. But as they also have more limited financial resources, in total they spend less on external consulting services than central governments (Abiker 1996; Deakins and Dillon 2006).

In the relevant literature there has been an extensive debate about the reasons for the growing presence of management consultants in government. Thus, there are those arguing that it is the result of politicians, who want to broaden their sources of policy advice. Others have attributed it to the (lobbying) efforts of consulting firms seeking to expand their activities in the public sector. Following the approach used in the study of the British case by Schlegelmilch, Diamantopoulos, and Moore (1992), this chapter will examine the role of consultants in public service reforms in various European and North American countries, looking first at the demand for consultants and then at the supply side. The last section then presents the findings of extant research about the effects of the growing use of consultants in the public sector on the government and the consulting industry. A brief conclusion suggests directions for future research.

22.2 THE DEMAND FOR MANAGEMENT CONSULTANCY IN GOVERNMENT

Management consultancy is an industry largely dominated by US-based firms. The United States continues to represent more than half of the world market for consulting services (Kennedy Information 2007). And, as the available evidence suggests, consultants have always been more actively involved in the policy-making process in Washington than in any other national capital in the developed world (Guttman and Willner 1976; GAO 1992; Heinz et al. 1993). These are two basic facts that cannot be ignored in any discussion of the role of consultants in government. Taken together, they also go far in explaining the widely discussed 'Americanization' of both public and business management practices (e.g. Djelic 1998; Kipping and Bjarnar 1998; Zeitlin and Herrigel 2000; Bissessar 2002).

Various observers have underlined, for instance, the impact of *In Search of Excellence* by Peters and Waterman—two McKinsey consultants at the time—on public sector reform in various countries (e.g. Aucoin 1990); or the influence of *Reinventing Government* by Osborne and Gaebler (1992), described in the British press as the 'two management "fixers", who have achieved cult status in the United States and whose ideas could help transform Britain's public sector' (Holman 1997: 9). As Pollitt (1996: 84–85) notes, 'management consultants have contributed important ideas' to British public service reform, but, as he also highlights, the traffic has been largely one way: '[I]t is American management ideas and American management gurus that have seized the attention of U.K. politicians and public officials.' Before looking at how consultants attracted the attention of public officials, the remainder of this section examines two factors that are seen to have driven the demand for management consultancy in government: the size of the public sector and the organization of the policy advisory system. It then looks at how politics has impacted the way decision-makers have framed the use of consultants in government.

22.2.1 Factors Driving Public Sector Demand: Size and Openness

All things being equal, it would seem likely that a larger public sector would consume more consulting services than a smaller one. While size in itself does not automatically generate demand, it has generally been correlated to organizational complexity and issues of co-ordination and control, all of which are seen to exercise pressure on managers to seek help in finding appropriate solutions (e.g. Kipping and Engwall 2002). This is also the explanation that policy-makers provided in the 1960s, arguing that outside expertise was needed to help public managers face the new organizational challenges created by the growth of the modern welfare state (Fry 1993). A larger public sector also provides more opportunities for suppliers of consulting services as there are more 'doors' on which consultants can knock when trying to promote and sell their products.

However, as the extant literature has shown, this view is only partially supported by the available empirical evidence. As Saint-Martin (2004) has shown in his comparative study of France, Britain, and Canada, the demand for consulting services, as measured by the revenues coming from public sector work, is not automatically higher in countries that have a larger state sector. There is a positive relation between the two variables in the case of Canada, while France and Britain represent two radically opposite scenarios. The former has a large public sector, but relatively small consulting revenues from government, while the latter has a smaller public sector generating a significantly larger share of consulting revenues. There is no comparable data for the American consulting industry in terms of public sector revenues, but other available evidence suggests a situation not unlike that of Britain (Gross and Poor 2008). These studies would actually suggest that the reverse logic is at least as likely, that is, that a smaller public sector consumes more consulting services because more work is contracted-out to private sector suppliers, whereas a larger public sector will tend to rely more on in-house staff. But whatever the direction of the causal connection, the link between public sector size and the demand for consulting services is not as simple as one might have expected. This suggests a need for additional empirical research on this question.

Concerning the second factor, openness, which makes politicians rely heavily on the advice of experts (Hall 1989), in some states this advice comes primarily from an echelon of permanent civil servants who have a virtual monopoly on access both to official information and to the ultimate decision-makers. In others, a new administration can bring its own advisers and consult widely with outside experts. This is the case in the US, where the practice of recruiting 'inners and outers' (MacKenzie 1987) allows each newly elected president to appoint a large number of outsiders to senior civil service positions (Heclo 1977). Not surprisingly therefore, as the extant research has shown, one of the key factors driving the demand for management consulting services in government is largely institutional in nature: the organization of the policy advisory system.

Thus, in the US the greater openness of the policy advisory system has given birth to a wide range of external sources of advice in Washington: private foundations, non-profit research organizations, think tanks, management consulting firms, and various professional associations. By contrast, in parliamentary systems, policy advisory systems have traditionally been much less open than in the US (Plowden 1987). In such systems, recruitment into government is generally less flexible, governed by strict guidelines emphasizing conformity to established civil service norms (Campbell and Wilson 1995). The consequence of this is that the demand for external sources of advice has, traditionally, been more limited, thus making management consultants much less present in the policy process (Saint-Martin 2004).

22.2.2 Framing the Role of Outsiders: The Effect of Politics

In his comparative analysis of policy advice and the public service, John Halligan noted that in many countries, there has been, over the years, 'a tendency to bring in more outsiders' (1995: 146). This tendency—which has contributed to the demand for consultancy in government—is largely a political creation, in the sense that it is politicians who have decided to transform policy-making institutions and make them more open to outside sources of advice. As the following will show, the extant literature has identified three different ways in which policy-makers since the 1960s have framed the use of consultants in government: (i) as rational planners; (ii) as apostles of New Public Management (NPM) with a focus on cost-cutting; and, (iii) as partners in governance.

22.2.2.1 *Rational planning and technocratic politics in the 1960s*

In the 1960s, at a time when Keynesianism was still influential and faith in the capacity of the social sciences to help solve public problems was high, decision-makers in government were looking for new ways to strengthen and rationalize the interventions of the state in society and the economy. This was the era of 'rational management' (Aucoin 1986), of the PPBS, and of the beginning of the so-called 'policy analysis industry' (Pal 1992: 66). The goal was to make the management of the modern welfare state more 'scientific' and professional (Fischer 1990). The requirement to evaluate policy more systematically, which came out of the new budget cycle imposed by PPBS, has been shown to open a lucrative market for management consulting firms (Pattenaude 1979). In the early 1970s, it was estimated that the American government was spending 'billions of dollars' in subcontracting to consulting firms work 'concerned with policy formation, organizational models and even the recruitment of Federal executives' (Nader 1976: x). The title of a book published in 1976 by two American lawyers is highly telling in this respect: *The Shadow Government: The Government's Multi-Billion Dollar Giveaway of its Decision-Making Powers to Private Management Consultants, 'Experts', and Think Tanks* (Guttman and Willner 1976).

In parliamentary regimes, the growing demand for evaluation and policy analysis generated by PPBS or similar types of rational management systems led to the creation, within government, of small policy units, often located at the centre of the executive machinery (Prince 1983). These units, such as the Central Policy Review Staff

(CPRS) in Britain or the Priority Review Staff (PRS) known as the 'policy think tank' created by Australian Prime Minister Gough Whitlam in 1973 (Hawker, Smith, and Weller 1979: 116), were generally staffed by a mix of civil servants, academics, and management consultants (Plowden 1991: 229). This practice became sufficiently widespread for analysts to begin to talk about the 'presidentialization' of the executive in parliamentary systems, in reference to both the American practice of recruiting 'inners and outers', and the growing centralization of power around the prime minister (Jones 1991).

Thus, already by the mid-1970s, the policy advisory systems of governments in many countries became more open than before. One indication of such openness was the growth of think tanks (Stone 1996). 'Once regarded as a peculiarly American phenomenon', Halligan (1995: 153) states, 'the think tank was taken up in other countries' in the 1970s and 1980s. A second indication is that there was, as one observer noted, 'an exponential growth in the use of consultants by the public sector and a concomitant growth in the size of the consulting industry' (Pattenaude 1979: 203).

22.2.2.2 *New public management and 'conviction politics' in the 1980s*

In the 1970s, as governments were consolidating their own, internal, policy-making capacities, and as the fiscal crisis led to cutbacks in public expenditures, the use of consultants in the public sector became less important than it had been in the previous years (Wilding 1976: 69). But, as recent research has shown, that changed in the 1980s when, as a result of the influence of public choice theory and the rise of the New Right, governments, seeking to improve efficiency, increased their reliance on outside consultants as a way to transfer business management ideas and practices into the public sector (Saint-Martin 2004).

Thus, in Britain, the government spent about £6 million on consulting services in the year following Margaret Thatcher's election in 1979. By the end of her tenure as prime minister in 1990, this amount had grown to £246 million. In Canada, when the Conservative government was in power, spending on consultancy went from $56 million in 1984 to almost $190 million in 1993 (Saint-Martin 2004). In Australia, during the Hawke–Keating Labor government, expenditure on consultancies rose from $91 million in 1987 to $342 million in 1993 (Howard 1996: 70). In Australia, the increase was so significant that it led to an inquiry by a parliamentary committee on the engagement of consultants by government departments (Parliament of the Commonwealth of Australia 1990). Growth in expenditures on consultants in New Zealand also led to an investigation by the comptroller and auditor general in 1994 (Audit Office 1994). In that same year, the Efficiency Unit in Britain issued a study on the use of external consultants, which showed that government spending on external consultancy increased 'nearly fourfold' between 1985 and 1990 (Efficiency Unit 1994: 46). This study and its findings created a political backlash as civil service unions, the media, and Labour MPs denounced what they saw as too cosy a relationship between consultants and the Tories (Willman 1994). The academic literature has subsequently echoed these criticisms. For instance, according to Beale (1994: 13), 'the era of Conservative government since 1979 has certainly been the age of management consultancy'. Similarly, Smith and Young (1996: 137) have suggested that 'the rise of management consultants was one of the distinctive features of the Thatcher years'.

But one has to be careful to attribute the growth of public sector consulting exclusively to the political right. In the case of Britain, there was indeed a connection between the rise of consultants in government and the fact that the Tories were in power throughout the 1980s and until the mid-1990s. It is also true that, one year after the election of New Labour, the Management Consultancies Association (MCA), the trade association that represents the interests of the consulting industry in Britain, reported the end of the 'dramatic rise in public sector revenues' of the past fifteen years (MCA 1998: 3). But after a lull of a few years, the Labour government started once again to rely more on external consultants—even if with a somewhat different focus (Kipping and Saint-Martin 2005; see also below). Moreover, the most important—albeit partially temporary—reduction in spending came under the Tories in 1995, suggesting a close link to the 1994 Efficiency Unit report, which was described in the press as evidence of a 'waste of resources' (Willman 1994). Thus, while governments on the right seem potentially (and ideologically) more inclined to hire external consultants, this question deserves more empirical research, which should also look at the interaction of political orientation with other demand-side (and possibly supply-side) factors.

22.2.2.3 Governance and the politics of pragmatism in the new millennium

Starting in the mid-1990s, after almost two decades of focusing on reforming the *management* of government, decision-makers began to worry more about the *policy* side of the governing process (Peters 1996). After coming to power, the Blair government in Britain issued a White Paper on *Modernising Government* (1999). The document argued that whereas earlier management reforms brought improved productivity and better value for money, they paid little attention to the policy process. It underlined in particular the problem of ensuring that policies are devised and delivered in a consistent and effective way across institutional boundaries to address issues that cannot be tackled on a departmental basis—the need for what came to be called 'joined-up' policies—against a background of increasing separation between policy and delivery, and more diverse and decentralized delivery arrangements (Williams 1999: 452). Similarly, in Canada, once the government had solved its deficit problem, the focus of reform in the mid-1990s shifted to building policy capacity and horizontal management (Bakvis 1997).

Largely inspired by the new politics of the 'third way' developed by Clinton in the US, Blair in the UK, Schröder in Germany, and other leaders located at the centre-left of the political spectrum, these reforms were designed to make government more 'intelligent' and better able to meet the needs of the people (Giddens 1998). Whereas the political right of the 1980s was anti-statist or anti-bureaucratic, the politics of the *Neue Mitte* in the late 1990s was more pragmatic and less inclined to denigrate the role of the public sector (Newman 2001). The new focus was on 'partnerships' with either the private or voluntary sectors. As Williams (1999: 456) observed in the case of Britain, modernizing the policy process has meant that there is a 'greater role for outsiders' as a way to ensure that a wider range of viewpoints, knowledge, and experience is brought to bear on policy. It is in this context that management consultants redefined themselves in the late 1990s as 'partners in governance'. Being a partner meant that consultancy was no longer simply about providing advice to a client organization that was then solely responsible for subsequently deciding whether to implement the consultants' recommendations. Now, consultants had to be more involved in service delivery and less detached from their clients than in the past.

In practice, in the public sector—very much like in the private sector—this has translated into a significant growth in 'outsourcing consultancy', where whole businesses or administrative functions were assigned to a consulting firm (Tewksbury 1999). In Britain, for example, a number of Ministries and public agencies have signed long-term outsourcing contracts with consultancies, such as the six-year contract between PricewaterhouseCoopers and the UK Ministry of Defence or the ten-year contract with the Home Office covering immigration programmes and services (Huntington 2001). Again, similar to the private sector, outsourcing is especially strong in the field of information technology (Galal, Richter, and Wendlandt, Chapter 6, this volume). Thus, many consulting firms have become increasingly active in the development of eGovernment, promoting the use of IT as a tool to transcend organizational boundaries and make government more 'joined up' (Fountain 2001). Some have described eGovernment as the 'new paradigm' of public sector reform (Accenture).

In Europe, the eEurope Action Plan first adopted by the European Union (EU) in 2000 has been driving the demand for information technologies in the public sector. Research indicates that eGovernment spending by governments in Western Europe was around US$2.3 billion in 2002 (IDC 2002). And, according to a recent McKinsey study, the US is expected to spend more than $71 billion on IT, of which an estimated 10 per cent is related to eGovernment (Baumgarten and Chui 2009). Moreover, in the US, the use of IT in government has taken a new, more security-oriented direction following the events of 11 September 2001 and the creation of the Homeland Security Department. Consulting firms in Washington are now involved in providing the technology that could help, in the words of the Head of the Public Sector Branch of BearingPoint (formerly KPMG Consulting), 'mitigate the risk of exposing valuable information to our enemies' (BearingPoint 2002). Consultants see the global war against terrorism as a growing market where governments across the world are expected to spend an estimate $550 billion on homeland security (Reuters 2003).

According to Dunleavy and Margetts (2000: 1), eGovernment has 'overtaken and superseded' NPM whose time, they argue, is now 'over'. Whether eGovernment is different from NPM is still an open question and can only be clarified by further research. But, like NPM, whose emergence in the 1980s increased public spending on consulting services, eGovernment has without doubt become a fast growing market for management consultancies.

22.3 SUPPLYING CONSULTING SERVICES TO GOVERNMENTS

From rational planners and technocrats, to advocates of NPM, to partners in governance and in the global fight against terrorism, what stands out from the above overview is that management consultants are highly adaptable creatures, able to transform themselves to seize the opportunities opened by the political context of the moment (see also David, Chapter 4, this volume). In this sense, management consultancy, as a business, is more opportunistic than ideological. Formally, it is decision-makers in government that are seeking the help of consultants in changing the way the public sector is managed. But they would not be likely to do this if management consultancy, as a field of activity, was non-existent or only weakly developed. Obviously, the mere existence, degree of development, and reputation of management consultancy is likely to affect the extent to which states can use the services of management consultants in reforming their bureaucracies (Villette 2003). Moreover, there is also some limited research looking at the active strategies deployed by consultants to win over government clients. It covers two main aspects, the creation of public sector-specific management ideas, or fashions and efforts to build networks with policy-makers in government.

22.3.1 Fashions for the Public Sector

The role of management consultants as fashion setters has been discussed extensively in the extant literature (for an overview, see Jung and Kieser, Chapter 16, this volume). What is less well known and largely under-researched is that consultancies also try to sell their ideas and fashions to the public sector. Thus, for large consultancies such as McKinsey, Booz Allen, and Gemini, one of the key instruments for disseminating ideas is the publication of articles or books, which has become a favoured marketing tactic in the firms' attempts to increase their share of the market (Dwyer and Harding 1996). The book is a tool of the consultant. As one can read in a 'how to' manual on management consulting, 'a book can create wide exposure, immediate credibility and generate revenue' (Blumberg 1994: 46). As the following examples will show, it can also do so with respect to government clients—often with little, if any, adaptation of the underlying ideas to the specificities of the public sector.

It is estimated that McKinsey spends $50 to $100 million a year on research. McKinsey also publishes a review, *The McKinsey Quarterly*, and has produced fifty-four books on management since 1980 (*The Economist* 1995: 57). The most famous book produced by two consultants from McKinsey is the bestselling *In Search of Excellence* by Peters and Waterman (1982), which sold more than 5 million copies. Despite being based on cases exclusively from the private sector, the book has been described by at least one observer as one of the 'most influential' sources of ideas in the development of NPM (Aucoin 1990: 117).

Others have gone further in producing books specifically for government, even if their content has a striking similarity with ideas developed for the private sector. For example, in 1991 Coopers & Lybrand published *Excellence in Government*, which advocated the application of Total Quality Management (TQM) in government (Carr and Littman 1991). In order to popularize the book, its ideas, and its services among government officials, the company used a practice, which had become quite commonplace at the time—passing it along to potential clients as a 'gift'. The introduction gives an idea of how wide they were casting their net (ibid.: 1):

> We hope this book will help promote TQM in government, because we see it as the best way to improve public services [...] To this end we are giving copies of *Excellence in Government* to Members of Congress, the President, federal cabinet secretaries, the heads of major independent agencies, and the governors of all states [...] We address the last chapter of the book to them: they must lead the way to government excellence.

Yet others managed to go a step further in successfully promoting their ideas, not by handing out free copies, but by obtaining an endorsement, not from any public official but from the President of the United States. Thus, on the front cover of Osborne and Gaebler's (1992) book *Reinventing Government*, a bestseller written by two management consultants, there is a quotation from Bill Clinton saying that this book 'should be read by every elected official in America'. Not surprisingly then, *Reinventing Government* has been a major source of NPM ideas across the world in the 1990s, with Osborne and Gaebler giving speeches to senior government officials in places such as Australia, Britain, Canada, Italy, Japan, and Turkey (Saint-Martin 2001: 587).

These are but a few isolated examples of an area that would benefit from more systematic research examining how consultants did (or did not) package and sell their ideas to the public sector.

22.3.2 Networking and Lobbying Strategies

As the demand for consultancy in government became more important in countries like Britain, Canada, or Australia, most consulting firms, as well as the MCA, began in the 1980s to develop various institutions and practices designed at building networks of contacts with government officials. Their networking has been examined to a varying degree in the extant literature.

The British case is one of the better studied. Following the introduction of Margaret Thatcher's 'Efficiency Strategy' in 1980, it was noted that 'the Management Consultancies Association (MCA) moved swiftly to consolidate its position by developing its network of contacts within the civil service' (Smith and Young 1996: 142). In the early 1980s, the MCA actually created within its organization a 'Public Sector Working Party' (PSWP) to develop a more co-ordinated strategy for promoting management consulting to government. The PSWP consisted of various 'sub-groups', one of which was directly linked to the Cabinet Office; its role was to make sure, in the words of the MCA director, that there was 'a regular dialogue between the MCA and members of Cabinet and with senior officials' (MCA 1995: 3). Following the example of their business association, MCA member firms began, in the 1980s, to organize various lobbying activities targeted at Whitehall officials, and created 'Government Services Divisions' within their organizational structures. As Bakvis (1997: 109) observes, these divisions are often made up of 'former bureaucrats and others with public sector expertise [who] have been hired to develop a rapport with civil servants and to sell the firms' many and varied services'.

As the government became a more important client, management consultants increasingly sought to get inside knowledge and to obtain information on Whitehall's current and future plan for management reforms. Halloran and Hollingworth (1994: 198) highlight the fact that, in this search for information, MPs became important assets to help to secure valuable insights into government policies and practices vis-à-vis consultants. They provide the example of Tim Smith, a Tory MP and consultant to Price Waterhouse, who in 1988 asked no less than eighteen government departments parliamentary questions about their relationship with management consultants. The answers disclosed the nature of the contracts, the selected consulting firms, their specific assignments, and the government expenditures involved.

For Britain, some authors have highlighted the 'revolving door' between government and management consulting firms. They point to the fact that, for instance, Margaret Hodge, now Lady Hodge, was a senior consultant at Pricewaterhouse Coopers before becoming a Member of Parliament in 1994 and Minister for Children in 2003; and that Patricia Hewitt was research director at Andersen Consulting, now Accenture, prior to joining parliament in 1997, the government the following year, and the Cabinet in 2001 (Simms 2002: 34). Incidentally, the current foreign secretary and former Conservative leader, William Hague, is an ex-McKinsey consultant. Large consultancies also offer some of their staff for free on secondment to various government departments. An investigation by the *Observer* in 2000, which led to the 'staff for favours row' (Barnett 2000), found that firms like PricewaterhouseCoopers and Ernst & Young, which had donated staff free to departments, had subsequently won lucrative government contracts. One consultant to the Treasury is quoted in the *Observer* article as follows: 'I did work on policy issues and got amazing access [...] It is now much easier for me to ring up Treasury officials and get the information I need' (reported in Barnett 2000).

Much less is known about networking and lobbying activities in other countries. At the European level, the national associations of management consulting firms are regrouped in an organization called the European Federation of Management Consulting Associations (FEACO for its French name Fédération Européenne des Associations de Conseils en Organisation), which is based in Brussels. FEACO is organized into various committees, one of which is the European Community Institutions Committee (ECIC), which became very active following publication of the White Paper on Reforming the Commission in 2000—a reform exercise based on four guiding principles of efficiency, accountability, service, and transparency (Metcalfe 2000). The action plan of the ECIC following the White Paper sounds like an emulation of the strategy followed by the British MCA (see above)—which is not surprising since the MCA is one of, if not the, most important member association of FEACO:

> The main objective of the ECIC should be to monitor, influence and provide input into the modernization of the European Commission [...] The ECIC should maintain close contacts with key persons in the European Commission [...] and maintain close contacts with the European Parliament by inviting MEPs to lunches and organize meetings with them, to help them better understand the role of consultants and their contribution to the improvement of the efficient management of the EU. (FEACO 2000)

Perhaps most surprising is the absence of academic research about the networking and lobbying of public sector consultants in the United States, given the attention the literature has paid to those activities by other businesses. What is known so far comes from non-governmental organizations (NGOs). Financial contributions to parties and candidates for Congress seem a common practice among the large consulting firms. In the 2000 election cycle, for example, the so-called 'Big Five' accounting and consulting firms (see McDougald and Greenwood, Chapter 5, this volume) donated $8 million to the two major political parties: 61 per cent to the Republicans and 38 per cent to the Democrats (Center for Responsive Politics 2002). More recently, Accenture created its own 'political action committee' (PAC), which is the name given to a private group, regardless of size, organized to elect political candidates. Under the Federal Election Campaign Act, an organization becomes a PAC by receiving contributions or making donations to political campaigns. Accenture gave $313,380 to federal candidates in the 2005–6 legislative election: 63 per cent to Republicans, 37 per cent to Democrats. It gave close to $700,000 in the 2008 election. Accenture also spends millions of dollars on lobbying government officials (see OpenSecrets.org).

22.4 THE IMPACT OF PUBLIC SECTOR CONSULTING

Another question addressed by the extant literature concerns the impact the relationship between consultants and governments has had on them both. In terms of the impact on government, opinions seem to be quite contradictory. On the one hand, public officials and consultants argue that the use of consultants in the policy process is a way of strengthening the policy capacities of governments by mobilizing expertise that is often unavailable internally. Also, consultants are seen as providing flexibility: they are brought in at the discretion of the department or body concerned, and they can be selected according to specific needs (Villette 2003). But, on the other hand, critics are suggesting that consultants are weakening the capacities of government, because they are possibly usurping policy functions. Consultants, along with other external advisers, are seen as part of a 'shadow government' (Guttman and Willner 1976) that has effectively taken the policy-making function away from elected officials and bureaucrats (Craig 2006). This view is partly linked to the 'hollowing out' of the state thesis, which argues that because of globalization, the state is 'being eroded or eaten away' (Rhodes 1994: 138).

As it is often the case with such debates, the reality probably lies between these two positions. Policy capacity concerns the intellectual dimension of governance (Painter and Pierre 2004). It is a tricky concept, encompassing both staffing issues and organizational matters. It is difficult to measure precisely whether consultants are solidifying or undermining policy capacity. It is likely that no broad generalization can be made, and that consultants can either strengthen or weaken policy capacity, depending on the particular case one is studying. But one thing that seems more certain is that consultants are contributing to the expansion of the *political capacities* of decision-makers in government. Observers and critics often look at consultants as manipulators who are seeking to influence policy-makers to make more money. But what about the opposite scenario? Consultants allow policy-makers to diffuse blame and provide a layer of protection from attack on proposed policies by political adversaries (Martin 1998).

Concerning the impact on consultants, their growing use in the policy process in the past decades has made government a better—or at least, a more knowledgeable—buyer of consulting services (Kipping and Saint-Martin 2005). Various reports, either from government agencies or audit offices, have highlighted ways of getting more value for money in the engagement of external consultants. As a result, the consulting industry now faces more administrative procedures and rules when doing business with government for public sector contracts (Jarrett 1998).

And, finally, one paradoxical development in the relationship between consultants and government is what can be called the 'think tank-ization' of management consultancy: the idea that large consulting firms are becoming more and more like think tanks. The paradox is that if consultants have contributed to the 'privatization' of government, facilitating the introduction of business management practices in the public sector, their more or less intimate relationship with government has transformed them into somewhat less 'private' and more 'public' actors. In the past twenty years or so, a number of large consulting firms have developed not-for-profit research institutes that produce research on key public policy issues. This includes the PricewaterhouseCoopers (now IBM) Endowment for The Business of Government, the Accenture Institute of Public Service Value and the KPMG Centre for Government Foundation, the latter created in 1995 in Canada, and the publication of journals such as the *McKinsey Quarterly* or Accenture's *Outlook*. Whether this new, more visible, policy advocacy role is simply a public relations strategy designed to show that consulting firms are good 'corporate citizens' who care about the collectivity, is an open question. But the fact is that in developing closer interactions with government, management consultancy is no longer what it was thirty years ago.

22.5 CONCLUSION AND DIRECTIONS FOR FUTURE RESEARCH

This broad comparative overview has mainly focused on the relationships between consultants and governments and has reviewed the literature examining the reasons why this link has been closer in some countries than in others. It seems that countries can be categorized in terms of the more or less open character of their policy advisory system. More open systems (United States, Britain) make greater use of outside consultants, while at the other end of the continuum, countries like France, with a much stronger civil service tradition, tend to rely more on the advice of senior bureaucrats to manage their public sector. Countries like Australia and Canada seem to be located between these two poles. Nevertheless, more research on the demand side is necessary to confirm or, possibly, modify these first impressions. It seems actually surprising that more academic work has not focused on this area given the fact that governments have to disclose much more information on their interaction with external consultants than private sector organizations. This should enable systematic and even quantitative studies about the role of consultants in the public sector. But, as the above review of the extant literature has shown, so far much of the interest in uncovering their influence has come from (investigative) journalists.

Access to relevant information seems much more problematic, when it comes to the supply side, since consultants have been reluctant to disclose information for confidentiality reasons and/or to avoid the above mentioned 'bad press'. Nevertheless, more needs to be and can be done. There has been some discussion about the 'revolving door' between consulting and government in the UK, but to gain deeper insight into this issue here (and elsewhere), it seems necessary to obtain quantifiable information about former consultants working in the public sector and the extent to which they are involved in the procurement of consulting services. So far, the available evidence is very scarce and largely anecdotal, focusing on a few high-profile individuals. In terms of the ideas sold to governments, research should in future try to examine whether these are indeed similar to those applied in the private sector, as the very limited available examples suggest. And while the literature on new idea generation in consultancies has not made any distinction between those applied to the private and the public sector (Heusinkveld and Benders, Chapter 13, this volume), recent in-depth case study research, which included looking at a local authority in the UK, draws attention to the importance of 'sector knowledge' (Sturdy et al. 2009: ch. 5).

Last but not least there is the broader question as to what extent consultancies treat the public sector differently because of its special nature or if, as has been suggested in a 2006 study by the UK National Audit Office on the central government's use of consultants, consultants just 'tend to target public sector business when there is a downturn in their private sector income' (NAO 2006: 5). This leads to another big question concerning the interaction between supply and demand. Given the public sector purchasing and audit requirements, has that interaction been institutionalized in a way different from the 'normal' pattern involving reputation and relationships as a way to reduce risk (see Clark 1993; Nikolova and Devinney, Chapter 19, this volume)?

In sum, given the importance of the public sector for consultancies noted at the outset, much therefore remains to be done to fill the remaining gaps in the corresponding research.

References

Abiker, D. (1996). *Les consultants dans les collectivités locales.* Paris: Université Panthéon-Assas (Paris II), L. G. D. J.

Aucoin, P. (1986). 'Organizational Change in the Machinery of Canadian Government: From Rational Management to Brokerage Politics'. *Canadian Journal of Political Science*, 19/2, 3–27.

Aucoin, P. (1990). 'Administrative Reform in Public Management: Paradigms, Principles, Paradoxes and Pendulums'. *Governance*, 3/2, 115–137.

Audit Office (1994). 'Employment of Consultants by Government Departments'. In *Report of the Comptroller and Auditor General: Third Report for 1994.* Wellington: Government Publishing, 44–67.

Bakvis, H. (1997). 'Advising the Executive: Think Tanks, Consultants, Political Staff and Kitchen Cabinet'. In P. Weller, H. Bakvis, and R. A. W. Rhodes (eds), *The Hollow Crown: Countervailing Trends in Core Executives.* London: Macmillan, 84–125.

Barnett, A. (2000). 'Staff for Favours Row Hits Treasury'. *Observer*, 25 June. Available at http://www.guardian.co.uk/Archive/Article/0,4273,4033309,00.html accessed 1 October 2011.

Baumgarten, J. and Chui, M. (2009). 'E-Goverment 2.0'. *McKinsey Quarterly*, July. Available at http://www.mckinseyquarterly.com/E-government_20_2408 accessed 1 October 2011.

Beale, D. (1994). *Driven by Nissan? A Critical Guide of New Management Techniques.* London: Lawrence & Wishart.

BearingPoint (2002). Homeland Security Testimonials. Statement of S. Daniel Johnson, Executive Vice-President, Public Services, Committee on House Government Reform. Available at http://www.bearingpoint.com/about_us/features/home_sec_testimony.html accessed 1 October 2011.

Bissessar, A-M. (2002). 'Globalization, Domestic Politics and the Introduction of New Public Management in the Commonwealth Caribbean'. *International Review of Administrative Sciences*, 68/1, 113–125.

Blumberg, D. F. (1994). 'Marketing Consulting Services Using Public Relations Strategies'. *Journal of Management Consulting*, 8/1, 42–48.

Böhlen, M. H. Gamper, J., Polasek, W., and Wimmer, M. A. (2005). *E-Government: Towards Electronic Democracy.* Berlin: Springer.

Campbell, C. and Wilson, G. K. (1995). *The End of Whitehall: Death of a Paradigm?* Oxford: Blackwell.

Carr, D. K. and Littman, I. D. (1991). *Excellence in Government.* Washington, DC: Coopers & Lybrand.

Centre for Responsive Politics (2002). 'Enron and Andersen'. Available at http://www.opensecrets.org/news/enron/index.asp accessed 1 October 2011.

Clark, T. (1993). 'The Market Provision of Management Services, Information Asymmetries and Service Quality: Some Market Solutions: an Empirical Example'. *British Journal of Management*, 4, 235–251.

Craig, D. (2006). *Plundering the Public Sector: How New Labour are Letting Consultants Run Off with £70 Billion of Our Money*. London: Constable.

Deakins, E. and Dillon, S. (2006). 'Management Consultants' Performance in Local Government'. *International Journal of Public Sector Management*, 19/1, 40–56.

Djelic, M-L. (1998). *Exporting the American Model: The Postwar Transformation of European Business*. Oxford: Oxford University Press.

Dunleavy, P. and Margetts, H. (2000). 'The Advent of Digital Government: Public Bureaucracies and the State in the Internet Age'. Paper presented at the 2000 Annual Meeting of the American Political Science Association, Washington, DC, 4 September.

Dwyer, A. and Harding, F. (1996). 'Using Ideas to Increase the Marketability of Your Firm'. *Journal of Management Consulting*, 9/2, 56–61.

The Economist (1995). 'Manufacturing Best-Sellers: A Scam Over a "Best-Selling" Business Book Shows How Obsessed Management Consultancies Have Become with Producing the Next Big Idea'. 5 August, 57.

The Economist (2005). 'From Big Business to Big Government: How Public-Sector Work is Reshaping Management-Consultancy'. 8 September, 66.

Efficiency Unit (1994). *The Government's Use of External Consultants: An Efficiency Unit Scrutiny*. London: HMSO.

FEACO (Fédération Européenne des Associations de Conseils en Organisation) (2000). 'ECIC Action Plan 2000'. Available at http://www.feaco.org/ECICAction2000.pdf

FEACO (Fédération Européenne des Associations de Conseils en Organisation) (2007). *Survey of the European Management Consultancy Market 2007–2008*. Brussels: Federation of European Management Consultancies Associations.

Fischer, F. (1990). *Technocracy and the Politics of Expertise*. Newbury Park, CA: Sage.

Fountain, J. E. (2001). *Building the Virtual State: Information Technology and Institutional Change*. Washington, DC: Brookings Institution Press.

Fry, G. K. (1993). *Reforming the Civil Service: The Fulton Committee on Home Civil Service*. Edinburgh: Edinburgh University Press.

GAO (Government Accountability Office) (1992). *Government Contractors: Are Service Contractors Performing Inherently Governmental Functions?* Washington, DC: United States General Accounting Office.

Giddens, A. (1998). *The Third Way: The Renewal of Social Democracy*. Cambridge: Polity.

Gross, A. C. and Poor, J. (2008). 'The Global Management Consulting Market'. *Business Economics*, 69 (October), 59–68.

Guttman, D. and Willner, B. (1976). *The Shadow Government: The Government's Multi-Billion Dollar Giveaway of its Decision-Making Powers to Private Management Consultants, 'Experts', and Think Tanks*. New York: Pantheon Books.

Hall, P. A. (ed.) (1989). *The Political Power of Economic Ideas*. Princeton, NJ: Princeton University Press.

Halligan J. (1995). 'Policy Advice and the Public Service'. In B G. Peters and D. J. Savoie (eds), *Governance in a Changing Environment*. Montreal and Kingston: McGill-Queen's University Press, 138–172.

Halloran P. and Hollingworth, M. (1994). *A Bit on the Side: Politicians and Who Pays Them? An Insider's Guide*. London: Simon & Schuster.

Hawker, G., Smith, R. F. I., and Weller, P. M. (1979). *Politics and Policy in Australia*. Brisbane: University of Queensland Press.

Heclo, H. A. (1977). *A Government of Strangers: Executive Politics in Washington*. Washington, DC: Brookings Institution.

Heinz, J. P Lauman, E. O., Nelson, R. L., and Salisbury, R. H. (1993). *The Hollow Core: Private Interests in National Policy-Making*. Cambridge, MA: Harvard University Press.

HoC (House of Commons) Committee of Public Accounts (2007). 'Central Government's Use of Consultants'. Thirty-first report of Session 2006-7, HC 309.

Holman, K. (1997). 'Day of the Gurus'. *The Guardian*, 12 November, 9.

Howard, M. (1996). 'A Growth Industry? Use of Consultants Reported by Commonwealth Departments, 1974-1994'. *Canberra Bulletin of Public Administration*, 80 (September), 62-74.

Huntington, M. (2001). 'Careers: Public Sector—Working in the Public Eye'. *Management Consultancy*, 3 December. Available at http://www.accountancyage.com/aa/feature/1786872/careers-public-sector-working-public-eye accessed 1 October 2011.

IDC (International Data Corporation) (2002). 'Survey: IT Purchasing Patterns in Western European Public Sector'. IDC # PP08J. Available at http://www.idcresearch.com/getdoc.jhtml?containerId=PP08J accessed 1 October 2011.

Jarrett, M. C. (1998). 'Consultancy in the Public Sector'. In P. Sadler (ed.), *Management Consultancy: A Handbook of Best Practices*. London: Kogan, 369-383.

Jones, G. W. (1991). 'Presidentialization in a Parliamentary System?' In C. Campbell and M. J. Wyszomirski (eds), *Executive Leadership in Anglo-American Systems*. Pittsburgh: University of Pittsburgh Press, 111-138.

Kennedy Information (2007). 'Global Consulting Marketplace 2007-2010: Key Data, Trends and Forecasts'. Available at http://www.consultingcentral.com/researchreport/topconsultingservicelines?C=LYmcqabg4aEIsnb accessed 1 October 2011.

Kipping, M. and Bjarnar, O. (1998). *The Americanization of European Business: The Marshall Plan and the Transfer of US Management Models*. London: Routledge.

Kipping, M. and Engwall, L. (2002). *Management Consulting: Emergence and Dynamics of a Knowledge Industry*. Oxford: Oxford University Press.

Kipping, M. and Saint-Martin, D. (2005). 'Between Regulation, Promotion and Consumption: Government and Management Consultancy in Britain'. *Business History*, 47/3, 449-465.

Mackenzie, G. C. (1987). *The In and Outers: Presidential Appointees and Transient Government in Washington*. Baltimore: John Hopkins Press.

Martin, J. F. (1998). *Reorienting a Nation: Consultants and Australian Public Policy*. Aldershot: Ashgate.

MCA (Management Consultancies Association) (1995). *President's Statement and Annual Report*. London: Management Consultancies Association.

MCA (Management Consultancies Association) (1998). *President's Statement and Annual Report*. London: Management Consultancies Association.

Metcalfe, L. (2000). 'Reforming the Commission: Will Organizational Efficiency Produce Effective Governance?' *Journal of Common Market Studies*, 38/5, 817-841.

Nader, R. (1976). 'Introduction'. In D. Guttman and B. Willner (eds), *The Shadow Government: The Government's Multi-Billion Dollar Giveaway of its Decision-Making Powers to Private Management Consultants, 'Experts', and Think Tanks*. New York: Pantheon Books, 3-14.

NAO (National Audit Office) (2006). *Central Government's Use of Consultants*. London: The Stationary Office.

Newman, J. (2001). *Modernising Governance: New Labour, Policy and Society.* London: Sage.

Osborne, D. and Gaebler, T. (1992). *Reinventing Government: How the Entrepreneurial Spirit is Transforming the Public Sector.* New York: Plume.

Painter, M. and Pierre, J. (eds) (2004). *Challenges to State Policy Capacity: Global Trends and Comparative Perspectives.* London: Palgrave Macmillan.

Pal, L. A. (1992). *Public Policy Analysis: An Introduction.* 2nd edn. Scarborough, ON: Nelson Canada.

Parliament of the Commonwealth of Australia (1990). *Engagement of External Consultants by Commonwealth Departments.* Report 302, Joint Committee of Public Accounts. Canberra: Australian Government Publishing Service.

Pattenaude, R. L. (1979). 'Consultants in the Public Sector'. *Public Administration Review*, 39/3, 203–205.

Peters, B. G. (1996). 'The Policy Capacity of Government'. Canadian Centre for Management Development, Ottawa, Research paper no. 18.

Plowden, W. (ed.) (1987). *Advising the Rulers.* Oxford: Blackwell.

Plowden, W. (1991). 'Providing Countervailing Analysis and Advice in a Career-Dominated Bureaucratic System'. In C. Campbell and M. J. Wyszomirski (eds), *Executive Leadership in Anglo-American Systems.* Pittsburgh: University of Pittsburgh Press, 219–248.

Pollitt, C. (1996). 'Antistatist Reforms and New Administrative Directions: Public Administration in the United Kingdom'. *Public Administration Review*, 56/1, 81–87.

Power, M. J. (1997). *The Audit Explosion.* Oxford: Oxford University Press.

Prince, M. (1983). *Policy Advice and Organizational Survival: Policy Planning and Research Units in British Government.* Aldershot: Gower.

Reuters (2003). 'Governments Around the World will Spend an Estimated $550 Billion on Homeland Security in 2003'. Washington, DC, 7 July. Available at http://www.world-am.com/body_03-04-2.html accessed 1 October 2011.

Rhodes, R. A. W. (1994). 'The Hollowing Out of the State', *Political Quarterly* 65/2, 138–151.

Saint-Martin, D. (2001). 'How the Reinventing Government Movement in Public Administration Was Exported from the US to Other Countries?' *International Journal of Public Administration*, 24/6, 573–604.

Saint-Martin, D. (2004). *Building the New Managerialist State: Consultants and the Politics of Public Sector Reform in Comparative Perspective.* 2nd edn. Oxford: Oxford University Press.

Schlegelmilch, B., Diamantopoulos, A., and Moore, S. A. (1992). 'The Market for Management Consulting in Britain: An Analysis of Supply and Demand'. *Management Decision*, 30/2, 46–54.

Simms, A. (2002). *Five Brothers: The Rise and Nemesis of the Big Bean Counters.* London: New Economics Foundation.

Smith, T. and Young, A. (1996). *The Fixers: Crisis Management in British Politics.* Aldershot: Dartmouth.

Stone, D. (1996). *Capturing the Political Imagination: Think Tanks and the Policy Process.* London: Frank Cass.

Sturdy, A., Handley, K., Clark, T., and Fincham, R. (2009). *Management Consultancy: Boundaries and Knowledge in Action.* Oxford: Oxford University Press.

Tewksbury, H. (1999). 'Survey: Public Sector–Public Sector Go Slow'. *Management Consultancy*, 2 November. Available at http://www.accountancyage.com/aa/news/1783251/survey-public-sector-public-sector-slow accessed 1 October 2011

Villette, M. (2003). *Sociologie du conseil en management.* Paris: La Découverte.

Wilding, R. W. L. (1976). 'The Use of Management Consultants in Government Departments'. *Management Services in Government*, 31/2, 60–70.

Williams, N. (1999). 'Modernising Government: Policy-Making within Whitehall'. *Political Quarterly*, 70/4, 452–459.

Willman, J. (1994). 'Con Artists or Cost-Cutters? Do Whitehall's Outside Consultants Provide Value for Money?' *Financial Times Weekend*, 30 April, 7.

Zeitlin, J. and Herrigel, G. (eds) (2000). *Americanization and its Limits*. Oxford: Oxford University Press.

PART 6

NEW AVENUES
FOR RESEARCH

CHAPTER 23

....

THE FUTURE RESEARCH
AGENDA

....

ANDREW STURDY*

23.1 INTRODUCTION

....

OTHER chapters in this volume have pointed to further research opportunities in the specific areas they have addressed. The aim of this chapter is to look at the field of management consulting research more broadly and identify future research agendas. Given that the future is necessarily uncertain, this is, of course, highly problematic. Nevertheless, it is possible to speculate in an informed way by examining those drivers of research that have shaped the field to date and to identify areas of continuing neglect and emerging importance. So, what has led consulting research until now?

Until the 1990s, management consultancy received sporadic academic attention except, indirectly, for its association with often controversial organizational reforms (Jackall 1986) and, directly, through largely prescriptive accounts of organizational development and change (e.g. Schein 1969; Lippitt and Lippitt 1986; Armenakis and Burdg 1988). However, as consultancy expanded numerically as an occupation (in the USA, UK, and, increasingly, elsewhere), and its public and organizational profile increased, it became the focus of more analytical research—theories *about* consulting more than theories *of* consulting. This correspondence between consulting activity and consulting research reflects a key characteristic of the latter in that management consulting is not an academic discipline, but an occupation—a type of management—or an industry. Thus, research tends to be led by empirical phenomena and/or reflect theoretical and conceptual concerns of different academic disciplines or perspectives. Thus, for example, the growth of global consulting firms is of interest in the context of theoretical debates about transnational institutions (Morgan, Quack, and Sturdy 2006), or client–consultant interactions are explored in relation to, say, the anthropological concept of liminality (Czarniawska and Mazza 2003; see Czarniawska and Mazza, Chapter 21, this volume). Such an emphasis on theoretical contribution or novelty can be a source of frustration for consultants, clients, and policy-makers who, understandably, have more pragmatic interests. To a large extent, these concerns have not been addressed in the recent wave of academic consultancy research (O'Mahoney et al. 2007).

This is not to say that academic consulting research has nothing to offer a wider audience, including the public and media. Indeed, a key contribution of research has been to challenge the claims of consultants, clients, and the media, and other taken-for-granted assumptions of consultancy such as that of the objective, concrete, and/or innovative nature of consulting expertise (Clark 1995; Alvesson 2004; Sturdy et al. 2009). Furthermore, some academic consulting research is more empirically led, using preferred and sometimes implicit theoretical perspectives to make sense of developments in the industry, such as the changing nature of the client–consultant relationship (Werr and Styhre 2003). Indeed, some of this research is more applied, such as in the case of client purchasing practices (Werr and Pemer 2007).

What frustrates academics, however, relates to a second key characteristic of consulting research—the inaccessibility or secrecy of consultancy in terms of both client and consultant practices and reliable statistical data at firm and industry levels. Indeed, while research over the last twenty or so years has shed considerable light on consultancy as a phenomenon, in many respects, it has barely touched the surface. Most has relied upon post hoc interviews and documentary evidence and focused on the specific domains of the consulting project (Sturdy et al. 2009), the industry structure (Kipping and Engwall 2002), and, to a lesser extent, product development (Heusinkveld and Benders 2005; Anand, Gardner, and Morris 2007) and HR practices in consulting firms (Kinnie et al. 2006; Domsch and Hristozova 2006). The lack of empirical depth of much consulting research is illustrated in the contrasting richness in, albeit mostly sensationalist, accounts of former consultants (e.g. Pinault 2001; Craig 2005). Indeed, at the micro-level in particular, almost any consultant or client can shed more light on consulting practice than the leading consultancy researchers. The partial exception here is that of historical research studies (e.g. Kipping 2002a; Kipping and Armbrüster 2002; McKenna 2006), although these have other limitations such as a reliance on documentary sources and a common focus on individual firms.

The inaccessibility of consulting arises mostly from concerns of commercial, political, and existential sensitivities. However, there is also an element of competition between consultants and academics in that both sustain an identity based on claims to expertise (Kieser 2002). Thus, while consulting firms may be interested in what academics might contribute to their understanding of a particular client sector or organization within it, they are generally as sensitive about research on consulting as academics would be of consulting advice on academic practice. This does not mean that the best research is that performed by consultant-academics. While this can offer considerable empirical insight (which is often neglected by non-practitioners), it almost always serves to justify a particular consulting approach and consultancy in general. An 'outsider' view of consultancy is neither better nor worse, but different (cf. Merton 1972).

While relative inaccessibility to consulting practice will continue to hamper the future potential of much consulting research, the developing importance and profile of the sector, combined with its increasing geographical spread and a growing interest from different academic fields, mean that there is considerable scope for future work. Indeed, some consulting studies are already focused thus *by default*, in that the main focus is a related empirical domain or an area of policy such as management innovation (Birkinshaw, Hamel, and Mol 2008), small firms (Crucini and Kipping 2001; Christensen and Klyver 2006), or business and professional services (Løwendahl, Revang, and Fosstenløkken 2001). The following explores the possibilities for the future by examining some of the key drivers of research activity of particular relevance to the field of management consultancy.

The chapter is organized by addressing distinct, but closely related, themes. Firstly, empirical areas of neglect are identified, including new developments in the sector. This is followed by the related issue of under-used sources of data and research methods. Some theoretical concerns are then discussed along with the possible contribution of related fields of academic enquiry. Finally, practitioner concerns are discussed, both in terms of the consulting industry and client groups, before examining the areas of policy and explicitly political issues. The account is necessarily selective, reflective of some personal theoretical and political interests and, as already noted, partly speculative. It is, however, based on a longstanding and ongoing reading of consulting and related literatures in English (cf. Villette 2003); continuing involvement in empirical research and other writing projects; and a personal involvement in the consultancy policy issues of state, sector, and occupational organizations and forums in the UK, USA, and elsewhere. These activities have revealed a number of areas of empirical neglect in the academic literature to which we now turn and which could form the first basis for future research agendas.

23.2 EMPIRICAL AREAS: NEGLECT AND NEW PROSPECTS

The difficulty of gaining research access to consultancy in action, which was mentioned above, combined with institutional pressures within academia, which tend to discourage intensive and longitudinal research, means that some core consulting activities remain neglected. For example, despite years of calls to examine the client–consultant relationship in action, through observation for example, there remain very few studies which actually do this (see, for a discussion, Sturdy et al. 2009; Nikolova and Devinney, Chapter 19, this volume). In particular, given that consultants are typically seen as key agents in the promotion of management ideas, their formal and informal sales pitches to prospective clients and other interactive practices, in projects and presentations for example, are a surprising area of neglect. Indeed, except perhaps for an often overlooked study by de Jong and van Eekelen (1999) and consultant exposés, very little is known about what consultants, especially at senior levels, exactly do day to day.

This echoes the call by Mintzberg (1973) over forty years ago about research on managers. Similarly, consultant's recruitment, training, performance evaluation, and development have been largely overlooked (cf. Armbrüster 2006; Alvesson and Robertson 2006; Alvesson and Kärreman 2007). Client practices, except perhaps in relation to purchasing (Macdonald 2006), have been, at least until recently, even more neglected (see special issue of *Scandinavian Journal of Management* (2009) on the consulting client). Indeed, here, we even lack the resource of practitioner exposés to shed light on the life of clients. Similarly, consultancy as an occupation has been overlooked. Some research has been directed towards professionalization and, to a lesser extent, the subjective experience of consulting work (Kirkpatrick, Muzio, and Ackroyd, Chapter 9, this volume; also Meriläinen et al. 2004; O'Mahoney 2007), but broader structural concerns with the supply and demand of consultants and with consulting careers have been neglected (cf. Kitay and Wright 2007; Sturdy and Wright 2008).

Although often partially hidden under the label of professional service firm research, we do know a little about the organization of consultancy, in terms of organizational structures in large firms for example (cf. Greenwood, Suddaby, and McDougald 2006). However, some recent research on global firms suggests, perhaps unsurprisingly, that these structures do not work in the way that is typically claimed or assumed. In particular, whether based on partnership or corporate models, firms are far from transnational in relation to how they mobilize their human resources, but instead are strongly shaped by 'local' profit motives or fiefdoms (Boussebaa 2009). This, combined with similar critiques of knowledge-management systems and structures (Morris 2001; Fosstenløken, Løwendahl, and Revang 2003), highlights the need to get beyond formal accounts, based on interviews with senior staff and public documents, towards an understanding of firms *in practice*. This applies particularly to small consulting firms and sole practitioners where research is least evident, but where access might be less problematic (cf. Ram 1999). Indeed, empirical variation within the field of management consultancy is another area of research neglect in that studies tend to make claims about consultancy in general regardless of whether or not this is justified methodologically.

At the same time, although there has been some interesting research on the corporate promotion practices of firms, through their websites for example (Bäcklund and Werr 2004), the branding practices of large firms especially is another surprising area of neglect (cf. Kärreman and Rylander 2008), not least because of its likely importance in the sustainability of the industry in that much rests on reputation (Glückler and Armbrüster 2003). Indeed, although a number of empirical studies of the industry have pointed to some of the key ways in which consultancy has changed over time (e.g. Kipping 2002a), there remains space to develop accounts of sector dynamics further, especially when the sustained period of industry growth comes to an end, as it must do at some point. Indeed, market uncertainty exists for some firms even in the context of a buoyant sector, yet such experiences have been ignored. Finally and relatedly, in terms of core dimensions of consultancy where empirical neglect presents a prospect for further research, it is important to note the *non-use* or rejection of consulting at individual, organizational, sectoral, and regional levels (cf. Furusten and Werr 2005; Armbrüster 2006). For some time, for example, Japan and Germany were low users of management consultancy (as well as MBA graduates) although their economies were strong; however, this level of analysis is rarely explored (cf. Wood 2001; Kipping 2002b; Wright and Kwon 2006; Kipping and Wright, Chapter 8, this volume) even though global statistical data has become more available (see Gross and Poor (2008) for various sources). Non-use may occur for a number of reasons, including active resistance to the use of consultants or, simply, because alternatives are used. Here, there has been some recent attention to the use of internal consultants (Wright 2009) in favour of externals and, as we shall see, it has periodically been an area of policy concern in the public sector especially. In addition, the non-use of consultancy is evident in some historical and comparative studies, which point to the role of alternative channels such as firm networks or state bodies (see Kipping and Wright, Chapter 8, this volume), especially in 'peripheral' nations (Kipping, Engwall, and Üsdiken 2009; Frenkel and Shenhav, Chapter 26, this volume). However, there is rarely any mutual recognition between research on consultancy and that on other forms and sources of innovation (cf. Birkinshaw, Hamel, and Mol 2008), or on human resource planning or skills development and transfer for example. In short, what are the alternatives to the various consultancy processes and to what extent are they adopted or consciously considered?

23.3 DEVELOPMENTS IN CONSULTING PRACTICE

Having identified some of the core, *ongoing* features of consultancy, which have been neglected in research, we now turn our attention to new and emerging developments. These have often stimulated research in the past, and therefore current trends and emerging issues in the industry are likely to shape future research. Outlining these is necessarily highly speculative, not least because of the uncertainty created by changing economic conditions over time. Nevertheless, I shall suggest a few themes here and return to this topic when considering practitioner concerns later on. Firstly, while the scope of what constitutes consultancy has long been ambiguous or contested, it is clear that consulting has increasingly become concerned with the practical implementation of organizational reforms as well as simply advising clients or engaging in facilitation. Indeed, change implementation, combined with IT and related outsourcing income, means that consulting as advice represents only a fraction of the fee income of most large management consulting firms (see McDougald and Greenwood, Chapter 5; Galal, Richter, and Wendlandt, Chapter 6; both this volume). At the same time, the extension of what might constitute management consultancy has coincided with the recent emergence of offshoring and outsourcing of consultancy itself, as part of a broader development within professional services, especially in terms of analytical work.

Indeed, more generally, although consultancy has been compared with other professional and business services in terms of professionalization (McKenna 2008; Muzio, Ackroyd, and Chanlat 2008), product development, and client relations (Løwendahl, Revang, and Fosstenløkken 2001; Miozzo and Grimshaw 2006), another area of potential interest is the interactions and interrelations between these different occupational groups in practice. For example, multi-party projects might include accountants, bankers, lawyers, and IT staff (Coffee 2006). Studies of such relations could shed light on the nature of consultancy in much the same way that situations, where cultures meet reveal otherwise unnoticed dimensions of each one. However, even this situation may be changing, with some recently suggesting a blurring of boundaries between professional services (Gross and Poor 2008), although, following Enron, for example, and a longer history of maintaining occupational demarcations, regulatory developments may impede this development.

What certainly is evident in practice and has some potential as an empirical focus are interrelations between consulting firms. This occurs in various contexts such as net-working, tendering, firm partnerships/joint ventures, and the not uncommon phenom-enon of consulting projects, where consultants from more than one firm are employed. In the latter case, although this is apparently still quite rare, consultants—third party, counter, or meta-consultants—can be used to assess consultancy usage itself (Mohe 2007). Likewise, relations between internal and external consultants have only just begun to be explored as a particular variant of the client–consultant relationship (Sturdy and Wright, 2011). Here too, interesting developments may be in progress in terms of consultancy beginning to be seen as part of a more general management (i.e. potential client) skill, approach, or discourse. This has long been the view or aspiration of Schein (1988; see also Butler 2010) in his articulation of process consultancy as integral to organizational change. It has also been debated in the context of accountancy and other management occupations (Stevens 1981; McKenna 2006).

This is also evident in more recent developments. Firstly, the growth of project work-ing means that a key dimension of consultancy, project management, has become more widespread (Hodgson 2005). Secondly, the human resource management (HRM) func-tion has tentatively appropriated consultancy discourse alongside business partnering (Wright 2008), and similar developments are evident in internal auditing and the emerg-ing field of business improvement (Selim, Woodward, and Allegrini 2009). Thirdly, in the UK at least, the consultancy occupation's own professionalization strategy marries consulting and management skills in general—the Institute of Consulting (formerly the Institute of Management Consultants) is part of the Chartered Management Institute. Fourthly, there is some evidence that ambitious managers identify more with a consult-ant role (along with notions of enterprise, change, and leadership) than with that of 'manager' (Sturdy and Wright 2008; Brocklehurst, Grey, and Sturdy 2010)—perhaps 'we are all consultants now' or, at least, becoming so (Sturdy, 2011; cf. Grey 1999)?

23.4 RESEARCH METHODS
AND DATA SOURCES

The empirical topics discussed above as areas of research neglect or emerging developments in consulting can each be researched using a variety of methods and sources of data, even if some may suit certain topics more than others. However, under-utilized methods and data sources open up the possibility of new insights into consultancy and, therefore, new research agendas. Indeed, the problems of research access in consultancy have sometimes stimulated more innovative approaches to empirical research, such as the study of firms' websites (Bäcklund and Werr 2004) or of publicly available tenders for business, and, in the case of consulting methods, even the use of simulation (Werr 1999). Nevertheless, given the dominance of the interview method, there remains considerable scope for further innovation in methods and sources of data.

In particular, and perhaps surprisingly given its growth and variety in organization studies more generally, discourse analyses of consultancy remain relatively rare. Whatever theoretical approach is adopted, many consultant discourses and discourses about consultancy are widely available. The business media, including the internet (e.g. consultancy blogs), newspapers, and specialist magazines as well as consultant exposés, prizes, and prescriptive texts can be seen to shape both our understanding and the nature of consultancy. And yet, aside from some limited consideration of humour and critique in the media—the consultancy joke (Sturdy et al. 2007; Sturdy 2009)—very few popular discourses have been examined. Similarly, the representative bodies of consultants and of their firms, as well as consulting firms, networks, and individuals themselves, produce vast amounts of potential data that could shed light on empirical developments or trends and, for example, on how clients and consulting careers are conceived or constituted.

Other publicly available and, as yet, under-used sources include documents that might have been made accessible through freedom of information legislation, such as public bodies' documents surrounding consultancy projects and selection. In addition, aside from the high-profile example of the book *Dangerous Company* (O'Shea and Madigan 1997), which was based almost entirely on sources in the litigious context of the USA, legal documents may sometimes become available. Finally, a combination of publicly available sources might be used to study individual consultants and social networks, both of which have hardly been explored, except in the case of high-profile guru/celebrity consultants perhaps. Here, individual careers or consulting histories might be tracked, through biographies and name searches for example. These might be combined into, or inform, a more systematic social network analysis, which could yield important insights into what is typically only claimed anecdotally—the interplay of senior consulting and business/political careers (Jones 2003; Craig and Brooks 2006). Indeed, as others who seek to revisit debates on social elites have pointed out, senior consultants form an important part of the top strata of many Western societies (Henry 2002; Williams and Savage 2008).

The above may seem to be quite specialized or esoteric approaches while there remains huge scope for more mainstream research on day-to-day consultancy practice. For the latter, data is less easily accessible and there is no reason to suppose that research access will get any easier (and consultancy is by no means unique in this regard). However, my own experience is that significant access to consultancy can often be gained through client organizations or potential/former clients (Sturdy et al. 2009). Here, for example, access may be granted to consulting reports and bids and internal documents relating to projects such as project evaluations, again, not often examined in research except in some historical studies. In addition, as the purchasing function in many large client organizations becomes more important and systematic, it holds new sources of data such as prior assessments of firms and individual consultants (see Bäcklund 2003).

More challenging, but not uncommon in other organizational research, is access to less formal client communication such as email correspondence or conversations over coffee about, and with, consultants. These are sometimes reported in in-depth studies of management in organizations (e.g. Jackall 1986), but lack the consultancy focus. In addition, there is some scope (and certainly a need) for observational research such as sitting in on consultant bids and meetings (Whittle 2005; Sturdy et al. 2009), even following them around (Crucini and Kipping 2001), or, if not, then perhaps through shadowing a client. The latter method may be perceived as less of a threat or concern by consultants or, at least, as more commonplace. Alternatively, of course, a standard methodological approach in dealing with restricted access is the use of participant diaries and yet, to my knowledge, there are no studies of consultancy (clients and/or consultants) using this method. These issues obviously also apply to consulting activities that occur away from client interaction, in consulting and client organizations such as product development, preparing bids, and research and training.

At the other end of the methodological scale, there are still very few large-scale survey studies of consultancy, matching consultants and their clients or exploring perceived outcomes for example. There are various studies carried out by industry bodies (e.g. the Management Consultancies Association (MCA) in the UK), commercial research organizations (e.g. Kennedy Information in the USA), and the consulting media, but these are mostly focused on practitioner themes and are often poorly targeted or lack methodological rigour. Similarly, although we know something of management consultancy in different geographical locations, especially in different countries (Wood 2001; Kipping and Engwall 2002), there are very few cross-national comparisons of any aspect of consultancy or studies of the same firm in different locations (see also Mohe 2008; Kipping and Wright, Chapter 8, this volume).

In short, notwithstanding access difficulties, there remains much to be done in terms of exploiting research methods and data sources beyond that of the research interview. Furthermore, even the interview method could be used for new areas of research focus, both in terms of many of the empirical themes outlined in the previous section and others, such as more theoretically informed topics, to which we now turn.

23.5 CONSULTANCY RESEARCH BY DEFAULT

For some, particularly those who span the practitioner–academic boundary, it is both possible and desirable to develop a theory of management consulting, as intervention, meaning-making, or 'improvement' for example (e.g. Lundberg 1997). However, its highly ambiguous, contested, varied, and political nature means that such a task is futile or, at best, likely to lead to an overly generic approach founded on a particular perspective. Thus, and as noted earlier, aside from a few empirically based and practitioner accounts, consultancy research is typically informed or led by wider theoretical debates and perspectives in the social sciences and organizational studies especially. As a result, typical questions for consulting research do not focus on empirical dimensions and developments of consultancy or new data sources such as those outlined above, but broader conceptual concerns. This is evident in a study of academic consulting literature by O'Mahoney and colleagues (2007: 39), which summarizes common foci of research:

- How are consulting identities formed?
- How do structures such as the law, the economy and culture affect the actions of consultants?
- How might institutions (such as the professions) affect industries?
- How can rational choice economics explain consulting strategies?
- How do management ideas spread through the consulting industry?

Some theoretical perspectives have dominated the literature, such as institutional theory, transaction-cost economics, psychodynamics, and social constructionism (see Armbrüster (2006) for one of the few explicit discussions of theory in consulting research; also Faust, Chapter 7; Saam, Chapter 10; both this volume). These give rise to a focus on various core concepts such as isomorphism, identity, translation, knowing, and boundaries. Clearly, such a pattern is likely to continue, subject to the dynamics and vagaries of academic fashions and debate. There is not the scope here to outline possible theoretical and conceptual developments across the various disciplines, although some themes appear to be (re)emerging as foci for consulting research such as elites, space, discourse, innovation, and ethics. In addition, as management research becomes more established and driven by user agendas, it is possible that more positivist research will emerge on the outcomes of consultancy (cf. Sturdy 2011).

In addition to consulting-specific questions and issues, there are considerable opportunities to be gained from research in other empirical fields of organizational studies, both in general, but especially when they touch or focus on management consultancy— what was labelled earlier as consultancy research *by default*. Insights have already been achieved in this way across a wide spectrum of activities such as small firms (e.g. Christensen and Klyver 2006), inter-organizational relations (e.g. Nooteboom 2004), and purchasing (e.g. Werr and Pemer 2007), but are most evident in four related areas of study and debate. Firstly, consultancy is seen as a part of the broader field of professional and business services (e.g. O'Farrell and Moffat 1991; Furusten and Werr 2005; Muzio, Ackroyd, and Chanlat 2008) where emphasis varies between debates over the nature of professions and of service processes. Secondly, consultants are typically seen as central to, if not emblematic of, knowledge work and associated debates around the organization of knowledge-intensive firms (KIFs), knowledge workers, and associated knowledge-management processes (e.g. Alvesson 2004; Kinnie et al. 2006; Kipping and Kirkpatrick 2008). Thirdly, and as already noted, a number of studies of organizational change, particularly ethnographic accounts, have pointed to the often crucial and controversial role played by management consultants in various rationalization and strategy processes (e.g. Pettigrew 1985; Czarniawska and Sevón 1996; Born 2004) although, surprisingly perhaps, labour process research has rarely focused on this. Fourthly, research on the diffusion or translation of management ideas, practices, and innovations sees consultancy as a key element or mediator in the management knowledge industry or system, alongside business schools, management gurus, and the business media (e.g. Sahlin-Andersson and Abrahamson 1996; Suddaby and Greenwood 2001; Engwall 2002; Sturdy 2004; Birkinshaw, Hamel, and Mol 2008; Kipping, Engwall, and Üsdiken 2009).

These fields of enquiry—business services, knowledge work, organizational change, and management innovation—have informed and even come to constitute consultancy research and will continue to do so. However, further links could be made here, especially in the area of change management and change agency. Moreover, other areas of research, even within the silos of management disciplines could help develop consultancy research further, both empirically and theoretically. For example, and as noted earlier, project management has grown as a discipline and occupation (Hodgson 2005) and is, arguably, a core element of consultancy skills and practice, for both clients and consultants (Sturdy et al. 2009). Similarly, while there has been some overlap between consultancy and business services research, marketing issues and activities are of obvious relevance to consultancy, as noted earlier in relation to branding and corporate identity. Similar points could be made about accounting and the consultancy business model, and international business. Global integration and links with HRM have already been mentioned. Finally, although much consultancy research is more or less explicitly grounded in the social sciences, these links tend to be implicit and more theoretical than empirical. This means that there is scope for developing an understanding of themes in, say, sociology, through consulting research (e.g. Newton 1996). Indeed, until recently at least, broader social and political concerns in particular have been more evident outside of management disciplines, in sociology, public policy, and social theory for example, and yet are highly relevant to management consultancy. The following section will examine some of these concerns.

23.6 Practitioners, Policy, and Politics

This chapter has so far considered empirical, methodological, and conceptual/disciplinary influences on academic research on management consulting and noted how the concerns of the industry (client and consultants) and those of other non-academic groups such as public policy-makers have had relatively little apparent impact. Of course, both have had some impact, in part due to the fact that research often has some level of applied significance in order to secure grant funding. The focus on knowledge and innovation in consultancy is a case in point here. This is likely to continue, if not increase, in many contexts. In addition, many management academics are inclined to conduct research that they consider practically relevant.

Indeed, while there are strong arguments to support a liberal tradition of 'pure' academic research, there are also more instrumental, moral, and political arguments, which push for a more applied focus. To many, this means addressing the needs and interests of the industry, in this case, employers, consultants, their representative bodies, and, perhaps, managers or clients (e.g. Heller 2002). O'Mahoney and colleagues (2007), for example, chart a number of areas of interest raised by consulting industry spokespeople (strategic change, procurement, professionalization, operations, innovation, and people management) and decry the fact that very few academic articles examine these concerns in consulting (twenty-seven from over ten thousand between 2000–8). In short, it appears that the consulting literature is polar in character, with prescriptive non-academic accounts based on practical experience at one end and non-applied academic research at the other. Industry concerns differ in some significant respects, however, not least between those of the large firms and small firms/individual practitioners, especially over professionalization (cf. Gross and Poor 2008; McKenna 2008; Kirkpatrick, Muzio, and Ackroyd, Chapter 9, this volume). But some common themes are evident. For example, the following have been expressed to me in recent years: future sources of growth; the changing role of client purchasing; clients as competitors; outsourcing/offshoring of consultancy; and the holy grail for all management occupations, how to demonstrate their value and contribution to organizations and society (MCA 2010). Meanwhile, clients are also concerned with value, but extend their interest to the question of alternative forms of management innovation.

The question of identifying a contribution or, perhaps, specifying outcomes is one of the few areas of interest shared between practitioners and those with a more critical, political, or policy-oriented perspective (Sturdy 2011). In the latter group, broad-ranging critiques of the key role and lack of accountability of management consultancy in contemporary capitalism and government are expressed using such terms as 'commissars of capitalism' and 'consultocracy' (Froud et al. 2000; Saint-Martin 2004; Thrift 2005; Sennett 2006). But there is very little data on the specific consequences of consultancy. Such critiques might be worthy of research in themselves. They are sometimes expressed in the form of protest such as the demonstrations against McKinsey in Germany or the protest group called 'The Redundants' mentioned by Mohe (2008). Typically, they are articulated more tentatively, however, in the media or as humour. Nevertheless, these more popular criticisms cannot be wholly accounted for as a form of defensiveness or resentment. They suggest some implicit concerns and values. For example, the accusation that consultancy plays a neo-imperialist role in spreading managerial discourse points to notions of the 'integrity of the local'. Likewise, critiques over the lack of accountability of consultancy points to issues of the transparency and legitimacy of power. As I have argued elsewhere, such issues could inform a wider basis for critical perspectives on consulting, such as an exploration of whose voices are dominant and absent in consulting practice and outcomes (Sturdy 2009).

Such a critical approach would include, but significantly extend beyond, the common debate in and around consultancy: that is, that it works best when both parties are 'professional' or 'ethical' in their dealings with each other and recognize their respective interests. This rather conservative view dominates the concerns of the public sector especially, where, in the UK at least, periodic efforts are made to contain and make more effective the use of consultancies including the issue of skills transfer (NAO 2006). Again, however, such issues have been largely neglected in consulting research (cf. Kipping and Saint-Martin 2005; Saint-Martin, Chapter 22, this volume). Furthermore, and as noted earlier, little attention is given to exploring or specifying alternative ways of organizing than that which is currently achieved through, or claimed of, consultancy. In the field of consulting ethics, for example, this is clearly more than a question of individual conduct and responsibility and extends towards the role of institutions and regulation (O'Mahoney 2010; Freeman and Krehmeyer, Chapter 24, this volume).

The question of how to organize consultancy seems to have been left entirely to consultants. This is somewhat surprising in that, generally, organization studies and other disciplines are more vocal in this regard, especially in relation to issues of diversity and representation or exclusion. Some attention has been given to the exclusion of women, ethnic minorities, and the working classes in professional services (Hanlon 2004), including consultancy (Kumra and Vinnicombe 2008). But such work is rare and newly emerging. What, for example, constitutes a feminine form of consultancy (Marsh 2008; Kelan, Chapter 25, this volume)? Furthermore, although there have been a few critical studies of management consultancy in the context of international 'development' (Reilly 1987; Gow 1991), this is another largely unexplored area and one where postcolonial theory may have some purchase (Frenkel and Shenhav, Chapter 26, this volume). Finally, we might consider the absence or exclusion of various other groups from consultancy processes more generally, such as client employees, unions, citizens, and customers. If consultancy is as influential as is often claimed, then more participation and visibility is required as well as more research.

23.7 CONCLUSION

Nothing dates more quickly than predictions of the future. This is evident in looking back at previous predictive analyses of consultancy (e.g. Czerniawska 1999; Heller 2002). Although a number of these prior observations have proved insightful or remained accurate, looking forward is always as much about the present as the future. In this chapter, therefore, I have concentrated on identifying *possibilities* through an analysis of the main influences on, and characteristics of, consultancy research in the current context. In particular, consultancy research has been largely pushed by the high profile and status of the occupation/industry and its rapid growth, at least in contexts where organization studies are prevalent. As already intimated, continual expansion at previous rates seems impossible, except perhaps in new regions, as consulting remains highly concentrated (FEACO 2009). If one adds to this the currently emerging debates around the economic crisis, which question financialization in favour of greater managerial agency combined with new regulatory mechanisms, then consultancy research may no longer be based around a context or assumption of rapid growth. Research on occupations in stability or decline is likely to have a different tone at least. One wonders, for example, whether such occupations would warrant a handbook of research?

By focusing on that which influences consultancy research, this account has been as much a commentary on the existing field as an outline of its future possibilities. This is particularly evident in the identification of areas of, firstly, empirical and, then, methodological, neglect. Here, a wide range of options were identified, which did not rely upon an overly optimistic view of gaining research access. Rather, inaccessibility can prompt methodological innovation. What seems certain, however, is that there is plenty of room for non-interview-based studies. Empirical and methodological areas are obviously linked to some of the theoretical and conceptual issues and possibilities, which were then discussed, although here attention was also drawn to the role of other related research fields, both within management/business and more generally. If consultancy discourse and practice continue to extend beyond conventional occupational or disciplinary boundaries, this will surely open up the field, but also threaten its coherence.

While empirical, methodological, and disciplinary/conceptual issues can be seen to open up numerous possibilities for further research on consultancy, some additional and quite basic questions about consultancy remain in need of some attention or, where they have been examined, further scrutiny. The following list is by no means exhaustive, but illustrates the potential or undeveloped nature of the field:

- What is understood by 'management consultancy' and how does this vary according to context such as cross-nationally? Can it be understood in relation to other forms of advice giving or issue selling (Marsh 2008)?
- Why has management consultancy grown and changed in the ways that it has (cf. Wood 2001)? What are the limits to its future growth?
- What is the substantive nature of management consultant knowledge and how does this relate to efforts to standardize and/or professionalize consultancy (Fincham 2006)?
- How do early consulting methods and their development compare with those currently used (Kipping 2002a; Wright and Kipping, Chapter 2, this volume)?
- What is the relationship between organizational development and other forms of management consultancy (Clegg, Rhodes, and Kornberger 2007)?

Furthermore, as the previous section outlined, a wide range of areas of neglect in relation to the concerns of practitioners, policy-makers, and politics is evident. In particular, establishing more precisely the outcomes of, and alternatives to, consultancy, remains crucial, albeit from the point of view of different groups. Much is claimed of consultancy by its proponents and critics alike and yet little is known, perhaps necessarily so, with any degree of precision. Nevertheless, I would argue that more could be done. Moreover, the occupation attracts its fair share of critics in public discourse and yet equally critical academic research on consultancy is quite rare (Sturdy 2010). That is, there is relatively little research which draws on critical theory or engages with issues of an inequality or exploitation of power, however defined. There is some emerging work in these areas, however, including that discussed in the following chapters. More generally, research of all types is likely to be strongly influenced by the future of the sector, whether this be in continued growth, decline, and/or transformation. Will consultancy continue to appear as politically significant, successful, or distinctive to warrant the attention of scholars is a key question.

NOTE

* I would like to thank Joe O'Mahoney, Robin Fincham, Chris Wright, Andreas Werr, Michael Mohe, Mehdi Boussebaa, and the editors for their comments and suggestions on an earlier draft of this chapter. The chapter is partly based on research funded by the ESRC (RES-000-22-1980A), whose support is gratefully acknowledged.

REFERENCES

Abrahamson, E. (1996). 'Management Fashion'. *Academy of Management Review*, 21/1, 254–285.

Alvesson, M. (2004). *Knowledge Work and Knowledge-Intensive Firms*. Oxford: Oxford University Press.

Alvesson, M. and Kärreman, D. (2007). 'Unravelling HRM: Identity, Ceremony, and Control in a Management Consulting Firm'. *Organization Science*, 18/4, 711–723.

Alvesson, M. and Robertson, M. (2006). 'The Best and the Brightest: The Construction, Significance and Effects of Elite Identities in Consulting Firms'. *Organization*, 13/2, 195–224.

Anand, N., Gardner, H. K., and Morris, T. (2007). 'Knowledge-Based Innovation: Emergence and Embedding of New Practice Areas in Management Consulting Firms'. *Academy of Management Journal*, 50/2, 406–428.

Armbrüster, T. (2006). *The Economics and Sociology of Management Consulting*. Cambridge: Cambridge University Press.

Armenakis, A. A. and Burdg, H. B. (1988). Consultation Research: Contributions to Practice and Directions for Improvement. *Journal of Management*, 14, 339–365.

Bäcklund, J. (2003). 'Arguing for Relevance: Global and Local Knowledge Claims in Management Consulting'. Doctoral thesis, no. 100, Uppsala University.

Bäcklund, J. and Werr, A. (2004). 'The Social Construction of Global Management Consulting: A Study of Consultancy Web Presentations'. In A. F. Buono (ed.), *Creative Consulting: Innovative Perspectives on Management Consulting*. Charlotte, NC: Information Age Publishing, 27–50.

Birkinshaw, J., Hamel, G., and Mol, M. J. (2008). 'Management Innovation'. *Academy of Management Review*, 33/4, 825–845.

Born, G. (2004). *Uncertain Vision: Birt, Dyke and the Reinvention of the BBC*. London: Secker & Warburg.

Boussebaa, M. (2009).'Struggling to Organize Across National Borders: The Case of Global Resource Management in Professional Service Firms'. *Human Relations*, 62/6, 829–850.

Brocklehurst, M., Grey, C., and Sturdy, A. J. (2010). 'Management: The Work That Dares Not Speak Its Name'. *Management Learning*, 41/1, 7–19.

Butler, N. (2010). '"Lessons for Managers and Consultants": A Reading of Edgar H. Schein's *Process Consultation*'. In P. Armstrong and G. Lightfoot (eds), *'The Leading Journal in the Field': Destabilizing Authority in the Social Sciences of Management*. London: MayFlyBooks.

Christensen, P. R. and Klyver, K. (2006). 'Management Consultancy in Small Firms: How Does Interaction Work?' *Journal of Small Business and Enterprise Development*, 13/3, 299–313.

Clark, T. (1995). *Managing Consultants: Consultancy as the Management of Impressions*. Buckingham: Open University Press.

Clegg, S. R., Rhodes, C., and Kornberger, M. (2007). 'Desperately Seeking Legitimacy: Organizational Identity and Emerging Industries'. *Organization Studies*, 28/4, 495–513.

Coffee, J. C. (2006). *Gatekeepers: The Professions and Corporate Governance*. Oxford: Oxford University Press.

Craig, D. (2005). *Rip Off! The Scandalous Inside Story of the Management Consulting: Money Machine*. London: The Original Book Company.

Craig, D. and Brooks, C. (2006). *Plundering the Public Sector*. London: Constable.

Crucini, C. and Kipping, M. (2001). 'Management Consultancies as Global Change Agents? Evidence from Italy'. *Journal of Organizational Change Management*, 14/6, 570–589.

Czerniawska, F. (1999). *Management Consulting in the 21st Century*. Basingstoke: Macmillan.

Czarniawska, B. and Mazza, C. (2003). 'Consulting as Liminal Space'. *Human Relations*, 56/3, 267–290.

Czarniawska, B. and Sevón, G. (eds) (1996). *Translating Organizational Change*. Berlin: De Gruyter.

De Jong, J. A. and van Eekelen, I. M. (1999). 'Management Consultants: What Do They Do?' *The Leadership and Organization Development Journal*, 20/4, 181–188.

Domsch, M. E. and Hristozova, E. (eds) (2006). *HRM in Consulting Firms*. Berlin: Springer.

FEACO (Fédération Européenne des Associations de Conseils en Organisation) (2009). *Survey of the European Management Consultancy Market, 2007/2008*. Brussels: FEACO.

Fincham, R. (2006). 'Knowledge Work as Occupational Strategy: Comparing IT and Management Consulting'. *New Technology, Work and Employment*, 21/1, 16–28.

Fosstenløkken, S. M., Løwendahl, B. R., and Revang, O. (2003). 'Knowledge Development through Client Interaction: A Comparative Study'. *Organization Studies*, 24/6, 859–880.

Froud, J., Haslan, C., Johal, S., and Williams, K. (2000). 'Shareholder Value and Financialization: Consultancy Promises, Management Moves'. *Economy and Society*, 29, 80–110.

Furusten, S. and Werr, A. (eds) (2005). *Dealing with Confidence: The Construction of Need and Trust in Management Advisory Services*. Copenhagen: Copenhagen Business School Press.

Glückler, J. and Armbrüster, T. (2003). 'Bridging Uncertainty in Management Consulting: The Mechanisms of Trust and Networked Reputation'. *Organization Studies*, 24/2, 269–297.

Gow, D. (1991). 'Collaboration in Development Consulting: Stooges, Hired Guns or Musketeers?' *Human Organization*, 50/1, 1–15.

Greenwood, R., Suddaby, R., and McDougald, M. (2006). 'Introduction'. In R. Greenwood and R. Suddaby (eds), *Research in the Sociology of Organizations*. Volume 24: *Professional Service Firms*. Oxford: JAI Press, 403–431.

Grey, C. (1999). '"We Are All Managers Now?"; "We Always Were": On the Development and Demise of Management'. *Journal of Management Studies*, 36/5, 561–586.

Gross, A. C. and Poor, J. (2008). 'The Global Management Consulting Sector'. *Business Economics*, 43/4, 59–68.

Hanlon, G. (2004). 'Institutional Forms and Organizational Structures: Homology, Trust and Reputational Capital in Professional Service Firms'. *Organization*, 11/2, 187–210.

Heller, F. (2002). 'What Next? More Critique of Consultants, Gurus and Managers'. In T. Clark and R. Fincham (eds), *Critical Consulting: New Perspectives on the Management Advice Industry*. Oxford: Blackwell, 260–271.

Henry, O. (2002). 'The Acquisition of Symbolic Capital by Consultants: The French Case'. In M. Kipping and L. Engwall (eds), *Management Consulting: Emergence and Dynamics of a Knowledge Industry*. Oxford: Oxford University Press, 19–35.

Heusinkveld, S. and Benders, J. (2005). 'Contested Commodification: Consultancies and their Struggle with New Concept Development'. *Human Relations*, 58/2, 283–310.

Hodgson, D. (2005). 'Putting on a Professional Performance: Performativity, Subversion and Project Management'. *Organization*, 12/1, 51–68.

Jackall, R. (1986). *Moral Mazes: The World of Corporate Managers*. New York: Oxford University Press.

Jones, A. (2003). *Management Consultancy and Banking in an Era of Globalization*. Houndsmills: Palgrave Macmillan.

Kärreman, D. and Rylander, A. (2008). 'Managing Meaning through Branding: The Case of a Consulting Firm'. *Organization Studies*, 29/2, 103–125.

Kieser, A. (2002). 'On Communication Barriers between Management Science, Consultancies and Business Organizations'. In T. Clark and R. Fincham (eds), *Critical Consulting: New Perspectives on the Management Advice Industry*. Oxford: Blackwell, 206–227.

Kinnie, N. et al. (2006). *Managing People and Knowledge in Professional Service Firms*. Research report. London: CIPD.

Kipping, M. (2002a). 'Trapped in Their Wave: The Evolution of Management Consultancies'. In T. Clark and R. Fincham (eds), *Critical Consulting: New Perspectives on the Management Advice Industry*. Oxford: Blackwell, 28–49.

Kipping, M. (2002b). 'Why Management Consulting Developed So Late in Japan and Does It Matter?' (in Japanese). *Hitotsubashi Business Review*, 50/2, 6–21.

Kipping, M. and Armbrüster, T. (2002). 'The Burden of Otherness: Limits of Consultancy Interventions in Historical Case Studies'. In M. Kipping and L. Engwall (eds), *Management Consulting: Emergence and Dynamics of a Knowledge Industry*. Oxford: Oxford University Press, 203–221.

Kipping, M. and Engwall, L. (eds) (2002). *Management Consulting: Emergence and Dynamics of a Knowledge Industry*. Oxford: Oxford University Press.

Kipping, M. and Kirkpatrick, I. (2008). 'From Taylorism as Product to Taylorism as Process: Knowledge Intensive Firms in a Historical Perspective'. In D. Muzio, S. Ackroyd, and J-F. Chanlat (eds), *Redirections in the Study of Expert Labour*. Basingstoke: Palgrave Macmillan, 163–182.

Kipping, M. and Saint-Martin, D. (2005). 'Between Regulation, Promotion and Consumption: Government and Management Consultancy in Britain'. *Business History*, 47/3, 449–465.

Kipping, M., Engwall, L., and Üsdiken, B (2009). 'The Transfer of Management Knowledge to Peripheral Countries'. *International Studies of Management & Organization*, 38/4, 3–16.

Kitay, J. and Wright, C., (2007). 'From Prophets to Profits: The Occupational Rhetoric of Management Consultants'. *Human Relations*, 60, 1613–1640.

Kumra, S. and Vinnicombe, S. (2008). 'A Study of the Promotion to Partner Process in a Professional Services Firm: How Women are Disadvantaged'. *British Journal of Management*, 19/1, 65–74.

Lippitt, G. and Lippitt, R. (1986). *The Consulting Process in Action*. San Diego: University Associates Inc.

Løwendahl, B., Revang, Ø., and Fosstenløkken, S. (2001). Knowledge and Value Creation in Professional Service Firms: A Framework. *Human Relations*, 54, 911–931.

Lundberg, C. C. (1997). 'Towards a General Model of Consultancy Foundations'. *Journal of Organizational Change Management*, 10/3, 193–201.

Macdonald, S. (2006). 'Babes and Sucklings: Management Consultants and Novice Clients'. *European Management Journal*, 24/6, 411–421.

Marsh, S. (2008). *The Feminine in Management Consulting: Power, Emotion and Values in Consulting Interactions*. Basingstoke: Palgrave Macmillan.

MCA (Management Consultancies Association) (2010). *The Value of Consulting: An Analysis of the Tangible Benefits of Using Management Consultancy*. London: Management Consultancies Association.

McKenna, C. (2006). *The World's Newest Profession: Management Consulting in the Twentieth Century*. Cambridge: Cambridge University Press.

McKenna, C. (2008). 'Give Professionalization a Chance! Why Management Consulting May Yet Become a Full Profession'. In D. Muzio, S. Ackroyd, and J-F. Chanlat (eds), *Redirections in the Study of Expert Labour*. Basingstoke: Palgrave Macmillan, 204–216.

Meriläinen, S., Tienari, J., Thomas, R., and Davies, A. (2004). 'Management Consultant Talk: A Cross-Cultural Comparison of Normalizing Discourse and Resistance'. *Organization* 11/4, 539–564.

Merton, R. K. (1972). 'Insiders and Outsiders: A Chapter in the Sociology of Knowledge'. *The American Journal of Sociology*, 78/1, 9–47.

Mintzberg H. (1973). *The Nature of Managerial Work*. London: Harper & Row.

Miozzo, M. and Grimshaw, D. (eds) (2006). *Knowledge Intensive Business Services and Changing Organizational Forms*. Cheltenham: Edward Elgar.

Mohe, M. (2007). 'Meta-Consulting: Idea, Functions and Limitations of a New Business Model in the Consulting Market'. Paper presented at the Workshop on Innovative Capabilities and the Role of Consultants in the Information Economy, ZEW Mannheim, Germany, 19–20 November.

Mohe, M. (2008). 'Bridging the Cultural Gap in Management Consulting Research'. *International Journal of Cross Cultural Management*, 8/1, 41–57.

Morgan, G., Quack, S., and Sturdy, A. J. (2006). 'The Globalization of Management Consultancy Firms: Constraints and Limitations'. In M. Miozzo and D. Grimshaw (eds), *Knowledge Intensive Business Services and Changing Organizational Forms*. Cheltenham: Edward Elgar, 236–264.

Morris, T. (2001). 'Asserting Property Rights: Knowledge Codification in the Professional Service Firm'. *Human Relations*, 54/7, 819–838.

Muzio, D., Ackroyd, S., and Chanlat, J-F. (eds) (2008). *Redirections in the Study of Expert Labour: Established Professions and New Expert Occupations*. Basingstoke: Palgrave Macmillan.

NAO (National Audit Office) (2006). *Central Government's Use of Consultants*. London: The Stationary Office.

Newton, T. (1996). 'Agency and Discourse: Recruiting Consultants in a Life Insurance Company', *Sociology*, 30/4, 717–739.

Nooteboom, B. (2004). *Inter-Firm Collaboration, Learning and Networks*. London: Routledge.

O'Farrell, P. N. and Moffat, L. A. R. (1991). 'An Interaction Model of Business Service Production and Consumption'. *British Journal of Management*, 2, 205–221.

O'Mahoney, J. (2007). 'Disrupting Identity: Trust and Angst in Management Consulting'. In S. Bolton (ed.), *Searching for the Human in Human Resource Management*. London: Sage, 301–326.

O'Mahoney, J. (2010). *Management Consultancy*. Oxford: Oxford University Press.

O'Mahoney, J., Adams, R., Antonacopoulou, E., and Neely, A. (2007). 'A Scoping Study of Contemporary and Future Challenges in the UK Management Consulting Industry: ESRC Business Engagement Project'. Swindon: ESRC.

O'Shea, J. and Madigan, C. (1997). *Dangerous Company: The Consulting Powerhouses and the Businesses they Save and Ruin*. London: Nicholas Brealey.

Pettigrew, A. M. (1985). *The Awakening Giant*. Oxford: Blackwell.

Pinault, L. (2001). *Consulting Demons: Inside the Unscrupulous World of Global Corporate Consulting*. Chichester: John Wiley & Sons.

Ram, M. (1999). 'Managing Consultants in a Small Firm: A Case Study'. *Journal of Management Studies*, 36/6, 875–897.

Reilly W. (1987). 'Management Consultancies in the Developing World: The Case of a Training Needs Assessment'. *Management Learning*, 18, 289–298.

Sahlin-Andersson, K. and Engwall, L. (eds) (2002). *The Expansion of Management Knowledge: Carriers, Ideas and Circulation*. Stanford, CA: Stanford University Press.

Saint-Martin, D. (2004 [2000]). *Building the New Managerialist State: Consultants and the Politics of Public Sector Reform in Comparative Perspective*. Oxford: Oxford University Press.

Schein, E. (1988 [1969]). *Process Consultation: Its Role in Organization Development*. 2nd edn. Reading, MA: Addison-Wesley.

Selim, G., Woodward, S., and Allegrini, M. (2009). 'Internal Auditing and Consulting Practice: A Comparison between UK/Ireland and Italy'. *International Journal of Auditing*, 13/1, 9–25.

Sennett, R. (2006). *The Culture of the New Capitalism*. London: Yale University Press.

Stevens, M. (1981). *The Big Eight*. New York: Macmillan.

Sturdy, A. J. (2004). 'The Adoption of Management Ideas and Practices: Theoretical Perspectives and Possibilities'. *Management Learning*, 35/2, 155–179.

Sturdy, A. J. (2009). 'Popular Consultancy Critiques and a Politics of Management Learning?' *Management Learning*, 40/4, 457–463.

Sturdy, A. J. (2010). 'Studying Consulting Critically'. In J. O'Mahoney, *Management Consultancy*. Oxford: Oxford University Press, 293–295.

Sturdy, A. J. (2011). 'Consultancy's Consequences? A Critical Assessment of Management Consultancy's Impact on Management'. *British Journal of Management*, 22/3, 517–530.

Sturdy, A. J. and Wright, C. (2008). 'A Consulting Diaspora? Enterprising Selves as Agents of Enterprise'. *Organization*, 15/3, 427–444.

Sturdy, A. J. and Wright, C. (2011). 'The Active Client: The Boundary-Spanning Roles of Internal Consultants as Gatekeepers, Brokers and Partners of their External Counterparts'. *Management Learning*, 42/5, 485–503.

Sturdy, A. J., Clark, T., Fincham, R., and Handley, K. (2007). 'Management Consultancy and Emotion: Humour in Action and Contexts'. In S. Fineman (ed.), *The Emotional Organization*. Oxford: Blackwell, 134–152.

Sturdy, A. J., Clark, T., Fincham, R., and Handley, K. (2009). *Management Consultancy, Boundaries and Knowledge in Action*. Oxford: Oxford University Press.

Suddaby, R. and Greenwood, R. (2001). 'Colonizing Knowledge: Commodification as a Dynamic of Jurisdictional Expansion in Professional Service Firms'. *Human Relations*, 54/7, 933–953.

Thrift, N. (2005). *Knowing Capitalism*. London: Sage.

Villette, M. (2003). *Sociologie du conseil en management*. Paris: Editions la Decouverte.

Werr, A. (1999). 'The Language of Change: The Roles of Methods in the Work of Management Consultants'. Doctoral thesis, Stockholm School of Economics.

Werr, A. and Styhre, A. (2003). 'Management Consultants: Friend or Foe? Understanding the Ambiguous Client–Consultant Relationship'. *International Studies of Management & Organization*, 32/4, 43–66.

Werr, A. and Pemer, F. (2007). 'Purchasing Management Consulting Services: From Management Autonomy to Purchasing Involvement'. *Journal of Purchasing and Supply Management*, 13, 98–112.

Whittle, A. (2005). 'Preaching and Practising "Flexibility": Implications for Theories of Subjectivity at Work'. *Human Relations*, 58/10, 1301–1322.

Williams, K. and Savage, M. (eds) (2008). *Remembering Elites*. Oxford: Blackwell/*Sociological Review*.

Wood, G. (1998). 'Consultant Behaviour: Projects as Communities: Consultants, Knowledge and Power'. *Impact Assessment and Project Appraisal*, 16/1, 54–64.

Wood, P. (2001). *Consultancy and Innovation (in Europe)*. London: Routledge.

Wright, C. (2008). 'Reinventing Human Resource Management: Business Partners, Internal Consultants and the Limits to Professionalization'. *Human Relations*, 61/8, 1063–1086.

Wright, C. (2009). 'Inside Out? Organizational Membership, Ambiguity and the Ambivalent Identity of the Internal Consultant'. *British Journal of Management*, 20/3, 309–322.

Wright, C. and Kwon, S-H. (2006). 'Business Crisis and Management Fashion: Korean Companies, Restructuring and Consulting Advice'. *Asia Pacific Business Review*, 12/3, 355–373.

CHAPTER 24

....

CONSULTING AND ETHICS

....

DEAN KREHMEYER
R. EDWARD FREEMAN

24.1 INTRODUCTION

IN an ever more complex, global, and dynamic world, the influence of advisors on business organizations has grown dramatically. Organizations are increasingly looking to management consultants for their knowledge, independent perspective, innovation, or even just their affirmation in making decisions and taking actions (see Kipping and Clark, Chapter 1, this volume). As management consulting has dramatically expanded in both the industries it serves and the functional expertise it provides, this formerly supporting industry has grown in stature and prestige. The top students in business schools continue to strongly seek employment in management consultancies, and former consultants are highly sought after for senior executive positions in corporations and governments (ibid.).

As the influence of management consulting has increased, so has the public critique of the industry's responsibilities in many prominent corporate ethics crises. Following Enron Corporation's 2001 bankruptcy filing, several prominent business publications questioned the role of their consultant, McKinsey & Co., in the energy company's historic collapse. *Business Week* questioned whether the eighteen-year consulting relationship between Enron and McKinsey blinded the consultancy to any potential red flags of the pending Enron fraud and collapse, specifically citing factors such as Enron CEO Jeffrey Skilling previously being a McKinsey partner, McKinsey's involvement in developing Enron's 'asset-light' strategy, 'loose–tight' culture, debt securitization practices, a McKinsey partner in attendance at several Enron board meetings, and, in particular, Enron paying as much as $10 million in annual fees for McKinsey (Byrne 2002). While Enron's auditor, Arthur Andersen & Co., bore the brunt of being the gatekeeper who had failed the public, resulting in the accounting firm facing bankruptcy itself, many continued to question whether 'Enron'-like scandals and ethical lapses were in the consulting industry's future (Coffee 2002; Czerniawska 2003). *Business Week* listed additional McKinsey client failures, including Swiss-Air, Kmart, and Global Crossing, in inquiring whether such trusted advisors were suffering lapses of judgement in dispensing advice (Byrne 2002).

Gatekeepers typically refer to those firms that provide formal verification and certification services for companies; for example, accountants, debt rating agencies, or security analysts. However, consultancies, particularly those with longstanding, well-known, and strategic client relationships, may contribute to similar public expectations of the 'reputational intermediary' responsibilities of gatekeepers (Coffee 2002: 5). Furthermore, as the financial benefits of acquiescence to client demands increases, so too do the number of gatekeeper failures (Coffee 2002: 28; Leicht and Lyman 2006). In addition to gatekeeper failures, the frequent complaints against consultants of hawking management fads, being a rubber stamp for management decisions, and disenfranchising client employees, among other critiques, further highlights the tarnished image and lack of trust that impact many consulting engagements (Shapiro, Eccles, and Soske 1993; Ashford 1998; Craig 2005; Hagenmeyer 2007; Jung and Kieser, Chapter 16, this volume).

Such industry prominence and scrutiny has, in turn, led to new academic inquiry into questions relating to ethics issues within management consulting. Management consultancy has made attempts to address ethics issues through its professional organizations. For example, the UK-based Institute of Consulting, formerly the Institute of Management Consultants (IMC), requires that members adhere to the Institute's Professional Code of Conduct and Practice (Institute of Consulting 2011). The literature, however, remains inconclusive in evaluating whether consulting has achieved professional closure. Analyses revealing less than full membership in professional consulting associations (Kubr 2002), as well as questions around a lack of a common body of knowledge and standard education qualifications (Kyrö 1995) continue to be addressed by researchers. Additionally, in consulting as in other management practices, professional rules may serve as guidelines, but often fall short of addressing the most complex and pressing contemporary ethical issues. Such issues, as noted above in the case of client relationships with Enron, Swiss-Air, and other companies, include conflicts of interest, confidentiality, and consultant objectivity, to name a few.

The purpose of this chapter is to discuss some current approaches in analysing ethics issues in management consulting, including the potential shortcomings of such frameworks. Utilizing a representative, albeit not an exhaustive, list of ethics issues in management consulting, the chapter will first identify many leading ethical dilemmas that have emerged as management consulting itself continues to grow in both sheer influence and complexity. Academic inquiry on such issues specific to management consulting is limited, as the subsequent section will show in its review of existing research. The chapter will then discuss a stakeholder framework as an approach for more effectively addressing issues that occur at the intersection of management consulting and ethics. It will apply such a stakeholder framework specifically to management consulting and illustrate why the stakeholder view effectively highlights the ethics issues of the industry. Finally, the concluding section provides some future directions for research.

24.2 Ethical Issues in Management Consulting

As has been noted throughout this Handbook, management consultants operate in a very dynamic environment characterized by uncertainty, client relationships, organizational strategic challenges, development and application of new knowledge, and ever-present revenue and growth pressures (Clark 1995; Poulfelt 1997). Such complexities create a setting that is both full of ethical dilemmas and, at the same time, incongruent with simply applying one-size-fits-all ethical rules. However, many consulting firms do have such rules included in their marketing and communication statements, such as 'Put the client's interest ahead of our own' (McKinsey 2009), and 'We work in deep partnership with our clients' (BCG 2009). While such rules may provide directional support for ethical decision-making, the challenge for ethics is in the interpretation of such rules and the resulting behaviours (Poulfelt 1997; Hagenmeyer 2007). Poulfelt (1997) identifies seven frequently experienced ethical dilemmas, based upon research among consultants and clients, as follows:

- Maximum income (for the consulting firm) versus the best solution (for the client)
- The optimal approach versus the client's budget
- Professional ethics versus the client's interest
- Clients' needs versus organizational needs
- Confidentiality versus being impaired
- Proximity versus keeping a distance
- Full knowledge versus incomplete knowledge

Each of these is a 'dual-ethics' issue, tightly related to the set of ethics and values of both the client and the consultant (Poulfelt 1997: 69). Thus, consultants face conflict-of-interest issues in their own firm and industry, as well as encountering the additional conflicts of interests encountered by their clients. Stated more dramatically, the fundamental moral dilemma for consultants is that 'they, like their clients, compete directly with other players in their chosen market. As such, they are permanently in danger of providing advice that runs counter to their clients' best interests—of seeking to optimize their ... profits rather than (primarily) to solve the customer's problem' (Hagenmeyer 2007: 111).

At the core of many ethical dilemmas in consulting is the critical need for consultants to correctly identify their client upon each engagement. Schein (1987), for example, identifies the following types of clients: (1) contracting client, (2) intermediate client, (3) primary client, and (4) ultimate client; several of which may be present on a consulting assignment. The inability to answer this seemingly simple question, often due to the varied interests of different client stakeholders (Poulfelt 1997), is a key contributing factor to most, if not all, of the issues identified earlier. Consider the ambiguity and related ethical issues in the example of a consulting project that is approved by a CEO, led by an executive team-steering committee, implemented by a day-to-day working group of mid-level employees and consultants, and which will potentially result in the job displacement of many company factory workers. While certain research suggests that the ultimate payer is the client (Bell and Nadler 1979), other authors provide for a categorization of clients, such as the model of contracting, intermediate, primary, and ultimate clients suggested by Schein (1987; Fincham, Chapter 20, this volume).

24.3 CURRENT RESEARCH ON MANAGEMENT CONSULTING AND ETHICS

A review of the academic literature related to ethical issues in management consulting reveals limited research specific to industry issues, perhaps due to the 'extraordinarily eclectic' nature of consulting (Exton 1982: 211). However, the broader work in examining ethical issues and frameworks applied to similar professions, including accounting and marketing, and to management as a practice, provides more extensive literature that is useful for researchers of consulting activity (Exton 1982).

As management consulting has grown in practice and prominence, it has also taken on many of the ethics issue resolution mechanisms of other occupational groups, most notably in the adoption of codes of ethics for both the industry and individual firms. In addition to most, if not all, notable consulting firms having their own code of ethics, several trade associations, including the International Council of Management Consulting Institutes (ICMCI), a membership network of over forty national management consultancy associations and institutes worldwide who have a common purpose and shared values and goals (ICMCI 2010), have codes of conduct or ethics. Such codes include standards for confidentiality, independence, conflicts of interest, integrity, financial arrangements, client expectation-setting, and standards of product and service delivery (McKinsey 2009; ICMCI 2010).

Codes may legitimize the activity and interests of consultants, thus promoting the stature of consultants, or codes may fulfil clients' expectation of the consulting profession 'to set high standards of conduct for its members [...] and to enforce a higher discipline on themselves' (DeGeorge 1990: 384). However, the empirical support for the effectiveness of codes of ethics is inconclusive. In a review of nineteen different studies evaluating whether corporate codes of ethics (for a broad-based set of organizations, not specifically consulting firms) impacted behaviour, eight of the nineteen (42 per cent) found that codes were indeed effective in influencing behaviour; however, nine (47 per cent) indicated no significant relationship, and the remaining two showed only a weak relationship (Schwartz 2001: 249). A more recent review of twenty studies revealed that eleven of the twenty (55 per cent) reported a positive effect of codes of ethics on ethical decision-making, while the others indicated mixed results or no significant influence (O'Fallon and Butterfield 2005: 397).

Beyond the lack of widespread empirical support on the effectiveness of codes of ethics, research has specifically been conducted on the impact of the values and behaviours of consultants, which codes are intended to influence. Allen and Davis (1993) studied the causal relationships between individual values, professional ethics, and consulting behaviour. Their findings, in which an individual consultant's values correlate positively to one's professional ethics, but correlate negatively to the consultant's behaviour, raise further doubts on the impact of codes of ethics. They ascertained that 'while a consultant can maintain high personal and professional values which are positively related to professional ethics, they somehow disintegrate when actual ethical dilemmas are faced in the marketplace' (ibid.: 456). These results, which cast doubt on any significant relationship between consultants' professional ethics and their actual business consulting behaviour, also therefore raise questions about the effectiveness of codes of ethics for consultancies. The researchers surmise that 'unless ethical codes and policies are consistently reinforced with a significant reward and punishment structure and truly integrated into the business culture, these mechanisms would be of limited value in actually regulating unethical conduct' (ibid.).

The disintegration identified by Allen and Davis may be due to a number of factors. Among those are self-interest, employee dissatisfaction, a company environment of peer pressure, competing company financial interests, or just ignorance of violations (Schwartz 2001: 254). Another theory of 'moral seduction' suggests that a lack of awareness on the part of individuals of a gradual accumulation of pressures, from conflicts of interest and other ethical dilemmas, will slant one's conclusions and actions (Moore et al. 2006: 11). Acknowledging these potential disintegration factors, the question remains as to how a consultant chooses their behaviours and '"justifies" his/her actions when making critical decisions that have ethical implications?' (Allen and Davis 1993: 456). Thus, Allen and Davis' question highlights the need for an alternative framework to address individual actions taken to respond to the ethical issues faced by management consultants. One avenue for counsel is in the theories of business ethics.

24.4 ETHICAL THEORY AND FRAMEWORKS

Within the business ethics literature, moral philosophy provides the foundation for a number of frameworks individuals use for making ethical decisions. Indeed, managers frequently use philosophical theories in making ethical or unethical decisions, as do management consultants. How consultants collect competitor information, make assessments on the impacts on factory and plant closings, and determine the credibility of management assertions throughout a consulting project are all examples in which consultants wrestle with issues of right and wrong, benefits and harms, and a person's integrity—all of which are based on theories of moral philosophy.

Among the philosophies used to provide insight into ethical decisions and actions are three primary theoretical streams, each of which provides key insights into ethical decision-making, along with certain limitations in its practical application (Wicks, Harris, and Parmar 2003). The three different streams emphasize:

1. The *principles*, or standards of conduct, for guiding one's behaviour
2. The influence of an individual's or organization's *character*, and
3. The *consequences* of a particular decision or action.

Following a brief discussion of the three streams individually, a summary model of the interconnections of all three provides a more thorough framework for addressing ethical dilemmas faced by management consultants, which may also contribute to potential avenues of further academic inquiry for researchers.

When consultants are interviewing mid-level client staff, perhaps they must decide what 'rights' the interviewees have to know the nature and likely outcomes of the project. Specifically, does the consultant tell the interviewee that management has hired the consulting firm to help reduce costs by eliminating staff, or does the consultant lie and provide a different answer? Deontology is the stream of ethical theory, which focuses on this and similar ethical decisions that an individual makes, and attempts to determine their acceptability relative to the principles and standards of conduct held by an organization, community, or society (Wicks, Harris, and Parmar 2003). Thus, using a deontological approach, the issue for the consultant is simply whether lying is morally defensible, not whether one answer or the other will produce the more favourable project outcome.

While deontology's focus is on what is inherently good or bad, most often for managers and consultants facing ethical dilemmas, the conflicts arise between two or more compelling and morally justifiable principles; rather than between good versus bad standards. Most organizations have codes, standards, and principles—formal and informal—for sorting out competing, relevant moral claims and selecting a course of action. Thus, one initial challenge for consultants working in client environments is to understand the standards of conduct where managers and consultants operate together. In the same way that consultants often prepare for client engagements by understanding their financial performance, strategy, and the like, they must also understand and respect how ethical dilemmas are raised, addressed, and resolved.

Beyond principles and standards of conduct, this theory also suggests that ethical decisions and actions rest on issues of character—the virtues and qualities of an individual. Within moral philosophy, this perspective, sometimes called virtue ethics, focuses on how an individual is defined by their behaviour patterns, including strength of character, virtues, and integrity, and what makes one a 'good person' (Wicks, Harris, and Parmar 2003). The virtue ethics stream of theory seems particularly important to management consultants, whose codes of conduct often promote their attributes of integrity, courage, trustworthiness, and partnership with the client (McKinsey 2009; BCG 2009). Their behaviours and actions, under the lens of virtue ethics, allow them to demonstrate whether they indeed 'walk the talk'.

The third stream of ethical theory centres on the consequences and outcomes of actions that result from ethical dilemmas. As one example of the theory, utilitarianism, based on the concept of utility and comparisons of value, assesses ethical decisions not on the intent or motive of the decision-maker, but on the consequences of such decisions (Velasquez 1982). For example, it may be appropriate for a consultant to recommend closing a less productive factory to save costs, despite not considering the public relations fallout a client would face in the community. Utilitarianism and other consequentialism theories feature two core elements: (1) establishing morally defensible purposes; and (2) creating favourable consequences towards realizing the purpose (Wicks, Harris, and Parmar 2003). The purposes and consequences of actions are key business considerations for managers, and thus also for management consultants. As part of the consulting process, the consultant, with the client, determines the purposes for the engagement or project, and then the project itself consists of taking the necessary actions that are most likely to help achieve the desired consequences or purpose.

Moral philosophies, including deontology, virtue ethics, and utilitarianism, are featured throughout the business ethics literature as frameworks to guide individual decision-making (Beauchamp and Bowie 1979; Poulfelt 1997). However, the measurable impact of such stand-alone philosophies specifically on individual decision-making is unknown (Ferrell and Gresham 1985), perhaps due to the organizational differences and 'dual ethics' that are certainly prominent in management consulting. Against this backdrop, stakeholder theory, both as an organizing perspective of moral philosophies and a framework for ethical decision-making that addresses the complexities of such situations, may provide a more suitable approach to understanding the ethical issues in consulting and provide a basis for future research.

24.5 Management Consulting and the Stakeholder Framework

To provide a more thorough approach, we propose understanding management consulting, and the ethical issues faced by consultants, through a stakeholder framework, in which the consulting process operates as a set of relationships among groups with a stake in the activities that make up the consulting practice. Researchers can use this framework to describe the ethical issues faced by consultants. The consulting firm and the individual consultant operate within and among the stakeholder groups—clients, other consultants, and the industry, among others—to create value. Thus, understanding the stakeholder relationships and how value gets created for the stakeholder groups is necessary to understand the consulting process as well as the consulting profession.

An analysis of client views on management consulting bears out the usefulness of a stakeholder approach to consulting. Simon and Kumar (2001) surveyed Australian executives to determine the primary reasons for which consultants are hired. Their findings reveal that the two leading reasons were (1) insufficient in-house expertise; and (2) independent and objective advice. Additional motivations for consultancy activity beyond this *expert consulting* include experience-sharing, brokering, process consulting, and learning facilitation in which greater emphasis is placed on relationship-building rather than one-off project solutions (Schein 1987; Bessant and Rush 2000; Nikolova and Devinney, Chapter 19, this volume). The conclusions drawn have strong implications for management consultants facing ethical issues. Simon and Kumar (2001: 371) conclude that when clients engage management consultants,

> they are looking for something they have not the capacity to do or undertake in their own firm. They are truly in a position of dependence and vulnerability. Therefore, consultants have certain duties toward their clients:
> * they must put the client's interests first;
> * they must truly benefit the client; and
> * their own interest, while important, must not take precedence over those of the client.

Firstly, from this viewpoint, consultants must be attentive to many of their client's stakeholders, including the client's customers, employees, financiers, suppliers, and communities. This occurs directly through the consultant–client relationship. And while consultants have similar responsibilities to the client's stakeholders, they often do not share a similar level of authority with the stakeholders as their client counterparts.

It may be instructive to consider some of the earlier identified management consulting ethics dilemmas within the stakeholder framework. In doing so, it should be noted that an initial objective of the framework is to not view ethical dilemmas consistently as trade-offs, or 'versus' situations, as the list presented by Poulfelt (1997) describes. Instead, the framework views a manager's, and therefore a management consultant's, objective as balancing and aligning stakeholder interests over time to create value, demonstrating that profits and ethics are intrinsically linked (Primeaux and Stieber 1994; Freeman 2001). Just a quick snapshot reveals a number of stakeholders for consultancies, including the client firm, client executives, individual consultants, the consultancy industry, and, via the management advisory relationship, all of the stakeholders of the client firm—customers, suppliers, employees, communities, and financiers (shareholders). De Jong and van Eekelen (1999) find that consultants have office days, days at clients, and hybrid days. Additionally, they note that while most literature focuses on client relationships, consultants spend a 'great amount of interaction with colleagues [and] receive important backing from their colleagues' (ibid.: 186). The number of stakeholder interests creates an 'agency issue' for management consultants, namely, as agents of management do consultants privileging client management above all other groups? Further, does such privileging contribute to the 'conflict-of-interest' issues faced by consultants, and discussed earlier in the chapter? This is a question that is appropriate for further research and inquiry (see Fincham, Chapter 20, this volume).

Using the stakeholder as the unit of analysis makes it especially difficult to ignore issues of ethics that plague management consultants. Since the stakeholder framework focuses on specific human relationships, ethics is always in play. As McVea and Freeman

(2005) suggest, stakeholders have names and faces and are fully moral beings. Within the stakeholder framework, the primary responsibility of the consultancy and the consultant is to maximize the creation of stakeholder value such that no stakeholder interest is viable in isolation of the other stakeholders' interests (Freeman, Harrison, and Wicks 2007). The stakeholder management framework of consulting differs from many other perspectives, including aspects of the three moral philosophy streams discussed earlier, which separate 'business' decisions from 'ethical' decisions. As Allen and Davis (1993) demonstrated, a consultant's personal values are related to their professional ethics. The 'separation thesis' further suggests that one cannot usefully analyse the 'business' decisions and actions of consultants as if they are separate from the personal and professional 'ethics' that inform such decisions and actions (Freeman 1994). Consultants must face the consequences of their recommendations even if they are based on 'pure economics' or 'pure scientific' reasoning. The human consequences and responsibilities remain. Testing this separation thesis merely requires asking some basic questions about the decision (Freeman, Harrison, and Wicks 2007):

1. If this decision is made, for whom is value created and destroyed?
2. Who is harmed and/or benefited by this decision?
3. Whose rights are enabled and whose values are realized by this decision (and whose are not)?
4. What kind of person will I (we) become if we make this decision?

In short, stakeholder theory is a useful framework that has as its basis what might be called 'the integration thesis'—most business decisions, or analyses about business, have some ethical content, or an implicit ethical view, and most ethical decisions, or analyses about ethics, have some business content or implicit view about business (Freeman 2001). Adding even further complexity, consultants, as members of their own practice and profession, have their own set of stakeholders as well (Fincham, Chapter 20, this volume). This creates a dual-stakeholder network for consultants.

One may visualize an example of this dual-stakeholder network in practice for a typical, but unnamed, leading global consultancy. Its hundreds or thousands of individual consultants probably travel each week to work for a client, a similarly large and global organization. The consulting team works closely with key client executives, and surely the team periodically gets conflicted over whether their 'client' is the group of key executives or the organization itself. As the project progresses, the consulting team gathers data and interview information from internal consulting firm colleagues, client managers, and external resources. They develop a number of recommendations and potential solutions, all the while being very aware of how many billable hours they are charging against a fixed-fee contract, which directly affects the project's and the firm's profitability.

In the case of management consultants, the balancing of the unique dual-stakeholder network, while not making ethics dilemmas go away, does allow the consultant to see and act on such issues more clearly and effectively. The managing of the stakeholder's framework is grounded in people and relationships, or 'names and faces' (Freeman 2001), which serve as the basis for approaching decisions and actions. This foundation serves to align rather than face-off ethical dilemmas similar to those noted above.

24.6 DIRECTIONS FOR FUTURE RESEARCH

As management consulting continues to grow and gain influence, what are the critical issues for future research, particularly in support of a stakeholder management framework? The leading theoretical issue, for researchers and consultants, is addressing the 'separation thesis' (Freeman 1994). Researchers, particularly in business ethics, are hindered in their efforts to better understand the most pressing ethical dilemmas under a thesis that separates ethics from business. These deeply embedded topics must be addressed together, recognizing that the personal values of individuals and the guiding principles of firms must be taken into account in the business and consulting decisions that are made. Not integrating these values and principles in further research into ethics and consulting will continue to lead to analyses in which all decisions are viewed as trade-offs in which the creation of value is neutral at best.

A second direction for further research is in continuing to build a pragmatic approach to addressing ethical issues in management and consulting. One example for researchers is in delving more deeply into the 'agency issue' consultants continually encounter (see also Fincham, Chapter 20, this volume): Do consultants privilege management over the interests of the other client organization's stakeholders? The earlier example of McKinsey's role in Enron's strategy, growth, and ultimate demise seems to suggest that the answer to this question may not be as clear cut towards management as historically believed.

Finally, as we see more consultants utilizing a stakeholder management framework in addressing issues of consulting and ethics, academics may seek and receive greater access for research into the day-to-day field work of consultants (de Jong and van Eekelen 1999). Such inquiry may provide even more complete qualitative and quantitative insight into the decision-making actions of the actors in the field—consultancies, project teams, and individual consultants, heretofore 'a world that has otherwise remained largely invisible to all but the participants' (Sturdy et al. 2009). Such research will continue to inform further theory development for management consulting and the ethical dilemmas that consultants encounter.

REFERENCES

Allen, J. and Davis, D. (1993). 'Assessing Some Determinant Effects of Ethical Consulting Behavior: The Case of Personal and Professional Values'. *Journal of Business Ethics*, 12, 449–458.

Ashford, M. (1998). *Con Tricks: The Shadowy World of Management Consultancy and How to Make it Work for You*. London: Simon & Schuster.

BCG (Boston Consulting Group) (2009). 'Global Expertise, Deep Client Partnerships'. Available at http://www.bcg.com/about_bcg/vision/approach.aspx accessed 11 August 2009.

Beauchamp, T. and Bowie, N. (1979). *Ethical Theory and Business*. Englewood Cliffs, NJ: *FT* Prentice Hall.

Bell, C. R. and Nadler, L. (eds) (1979). *The Client–Consultant Handbook*. Houston: Gulf Publishing Co.

Bessant, J. and Rush, H. (2000). 'Innovation Agents and Technology Transfer'. In M. Boden and I. Miles (eds), *Services and the Knowledge-Based Economy*. New York: Continuum, 155–169.

Byrne, J. A. (2002). 'Inside McKinsey'. *Business Week*, 8 July, 54–62.

Clark, T. (1995). *Managing Consultants: Consultancy as the Management of Impressions*. Buckingham: Open University Press.

Coffee, J. C. (2002). 'Understanding Enron: It's About the Gatekeepers, Stupid'. Working paper. Available at http://ssrn.com/abstract_id=325240 accessed 11 August 2009.

Craig, D. (2005). *Rip Off: The Scandalous Story of the Management Consulting Money Machine*. London: Original Books Company.

Czerniawska, F. (2003). 'Is There an "Enron" in Consulting's Future?' *Consulting to Management*, 14/1, 1–4.

DeGeorge, R. T. (1990). *Business Ethics*. New York: Macmillan.

De Jong, J. A. and Van Eekelen, I. M. (1999). 'Management Consultants: What Do They Do?' *Leadership & Organization Development Journal*, 20/4, 181–188.

Exton Jr, W. (1982). 'Ethical and Moral Considerations and the Principle of Excellence in Management Consulting'. *Journal of Business Ethics*, 1/3, 211–218.

Ferrell, O. C. and Gresham, L. G. (1985). 'A Contingency Framework for Understanding Ethical Decisions Making in Marketing'. *Journal of Marketing*, 49, 87–96.

Freeman, R. E. (1994). 'The Politics of Stakeholder Theory'. *Business Ethics Quarterly*, 4/4, 409–421.

Freeman, R. E. (2001). 'A Stakeholder Theory of the Modern Corporation'. In M. Snoeyenbos, R. F. Almeder, and J. M. Humber (eds), *Business Ethics*. 3rd edn. New York: Prometheus Books, 101–114.

Freeman, R. E., Harrison, J., and Wicks, A. (2007). *Managing for Stakeholders: Survival, Reputation, and Success*. New Haven, CT: Yale University Press.

Hagenmeyer, U. (2007). 'Integrity in Management Consulting: A Contradiction in Terms?' *Business Ethics: A European Review*, 16/2, 107–113.

ICMCI (International Council of Management Consulting Institutes) (2010). 'About ICMCI'. Available at http://www.icmci.org/about_icmci accessed 29 April 2010.

Institute of Consulting (2011). *Code of Professional Conduct and Practice*. Available at http://www.iconsulting.org.uk/sites/default/files/upload_documents/Downloadable%20documents/IC%20code%20of%20conduct.pdf accessed 19 April 2011.

Kubr, M. (2002). *Management Consulting: A Guide to the Profession*. Geneva: International Labour Office.

Kyrö, P. (1995). *The Management Consulting Industry Described by Using the Concept of 'Profession'*. Research Bulletin 87. Helsinki: University of Helsinki

Leicht, K. T. and Lyman, E. C. M. (2006). 'Markets, Institutions, and the Crisis of Professional Practice'. *Research in the Sociology of Organizations*, 24, 19–47.

McKinsey & Co. (2009). 'About Us: Our Values'. Available at http://www.mckinsey.com/aboutus/whatwebelieve/ accessed 11 August 2009.

McVea, J. F. and Freeman, R. E. (2005). 'A Names-and-Faces Approach to Stakeholder Management: How Focusing on Stakeholders as Individuals Can Bring Ethics and Entrepreneurial Strategy Together'. *Journal of Management Inquiry*, 14/1, 57–69.

Moore, D., Tetlock, P., Tanlu, L., and Bazerman, M. (2006). 'Conflicts of Interest and the Case of Auditor Independence: Moral Seduction and Strategic Issue Cycling'. *Academy of Management Review*, 31, 10–29.

O'Fallon, M. and Butterfield, K. (2005). 'A Review of the Empirical Ethical Decision-Making Literature'. *Journal of Business Ethics*, 59, 375–413.

Poulfelt, F. (1997). 'Ethics for Management Consultants'. *Business Ethics, A European Review*, 6/2, 65–71.

Primeaux, P. and Stieber, J. (1994). 'Profit Maximization: The Ethical Mandate of Business'. *Journal of Business Ethics*, 13/4, 287–294.

Schein, E. H. (1987). *Process Consultation*. Volume II: *Lessons for Managers and Consultants*. Reading, PA: Addison-Wesley.

Schwartz, M. (2001). 'The Nature of the Relationship between Corporate Codes of Ethics and Behaviour'. *Journal of Business Ethics*, 32, 247–262.

Shapiro, E. C., Eccles, R., and Soske, T. (1993). 'Consulting: Has the Solution Become Part of the Problem?' *Sloan Management Review*, 34/4, 89–95.

Simon, A. and Kumar, V. (2001). 'Clients' Views on Strategic Capabilities Which Lead to Management Consulting Success'. *Management Decision*, 39/5, 362–372.

Sturdy, A., Handley, K., Clark, T., and Fincham, R. (2009). *Management Consultancy, Boundaries and Knowledge in Action*. Oxford: Oxford University Press.

Velasquez, M. (1982). *Business Ethics*. Englewood Cliffs, NJ: *FT* Prentice Hall.

Wicks, A., Harris, J., and Parmar, B. (2003). 'Moral Theory and Frameworks (UVA-E-0339)'. Darden Business Publishing technical note. Charlottesville, VA: Darden School Foundation.

CHAPTER 25

GENDER IN CONSULTING: A REVIEW AND RESEARCH AGENDA

ELISABETH KELAN

25.1 INTRODUCTION

THIS chapter provides an overview of the literature on gender, work, and organizations and on gender in consulting in particular, with a view to developing a research agenda for gender in consulting. The burgeoning literature on gender in organizations has highlighted many elements through which organizations are gendered. Whilst there is a lot of literature on gender at work and in organizations, there is limited research that explores gender in consulting and professional service firms. The chapter is structured as follows. Many of the gender issues in consulting are similar to issues found in the wider work context, which makes it important to review the literature on gender and work in general first. The literature on consulting and professional service work is then discussed. The final part of the chapter develops a research agenda to explore gender in consulting.

25.2 GENDER IN ORGANIZATIONS

The labour market is generally seen as being segregated vertically and horizontally in regard to gender (Anker 1998). Vertical segregation refers to the fact that men tend to be at the top of hierarchies and women at the bottom. This is often associated with the widely referenced glass ceiling (Meyerson and Fletcher 2000; Liff and Ward 2001; Dreher 2003). The glass ceiling is a metaphor for why women do not reach the top echelons of organizations: there is an invisible yet solid barrier that keeps women from advancing to the top jobs. Others argue that women do not face single barriers to advancement but rather a labyrinth consisting of twists and dead ends (Eagly and Carli 2007) in which women get lost. Most of these arguments refer to vertical gender segregation in organizations and occupations.

Horizontal segregation in contrast refers to the fact that women and men tend to work in different areas. For instance, women are less likely to work as managers in organizations and more likely to work as support staff, such as in administration. There is also often a prestige difference. Women tend to be found in areas that are seen as less prestigious. When women enter male-dominated occupations, this is generally associated with a loss of status for these occupations (Reskin and Roos 1990). The recent influx of women into medicine is, for instance, said by some commentators to have led to a loss in status for medicine as a profession (e.g. McGeoch 2008).

The burgeoning research on gender, work, and organizations has identified various ways through which organizations are gendered. Whilst this chapter does not aim to provide an exhaustive review of this literature, it is worthwhile looking at three areas, which are often seen as being particularly gendered. First, there are issues related to work–life balance and career progression. Given the perceived scarcity of women in leadership positions, it has been argued that the career model that is currently used in organizations was designed with men in mind (Wajcman 1998). Men's lifecycle has been described as linear while women's lifecycle shows interruptions and greater concern for work–life balance (O'Leary 1997). It has also been argued that the time when traditional careers are developed in organizations coincides with the time when women usually have caring responsibilities. It appears that when the need for work–life balance might be greatest, organizations do not allow this flexibility (Hewlett and Luce 2005). Many organizations have started to introduce work–life balance policies as a central component of their personnel management. However, these debates often have gendered undertones, which means that it is mainly women who take up flexible working (Smithson and Stokoe 2005). Those who want to work flexibly are often sidelined when it comes to career progression and their commitment to work is questioned (O'Leary 1997).

A second area that has attracted a lot of research attention relates to the gendering of skills. Early research on gender in organizations has demonstrated that the gender of the worker plays a central role when it comes to the way in which skills are valued (Phillips and Taylor 1980). These authors showed that work that was performed by women attracted lower pay in spite of the fact that it was similar to the type of work that men did. Research on gender and skills in the information and knowledge society in particular has pointed to the rising importance of social skills, which are commonly gendered feminine (Fletcher 1999; Woodfield 2000; Kelan 2008a). However, studies have shown that while social skills are seen as feminine, women rarely get credit for displaying these skills (Fletcher 1999; Kelan 2008a, 2008b). Supposedly feminine skills such as people skills are commonly seen as 'just normal' in women. When women display these skills, they just seem to do what is normal for women and rarely get credit for it.

Third, there is the concept of the 'ideal worker', which has been used fruitfully in debates on gender and organizations. Acker (1990) suggested that organizations are built around a disembodied 'ideal worker', who is available full time, is highly skilled, and is work-oriented. Building on Acker's research, scholars have started to argue that organizations have a gender subtext (Benschop and Doorewaard 1998a; Bendl 2008; Kelan 2008c). While organizations pretend to be gender neutral, the gender subtext shows that within the daily reality of work, those characteristics correspond with men rather than women. The gendered subtext has been explored in regards to who can be an ideal worker in the contemporary management literature (Kelan 2008b). This study, exploring how gender is portrayed in the management literature, has shown that while women are often said to be the new ideal worker, the subtext of the literature is such that it continues to construct men as the ideal worker. This means that the abstract form often used to speak for all workers, is in fact something that matches men more closely than women. There is also a growing area of work that unmasks masculinity in organizations. This research takes as its starting point the fact that masculinities in organizations are often invisible and hidden from view and by making them visible the ideal worker can be exposed (Hearn and Morgan 1990; Collinson and Hearn 2000; Knights and McCabe 2001). This means that rather than accepting those abstract notions of the ideal worker as gender neutral, the research shows that the ideal worker is more of a man than a woman.

To summarize so far, research on gender and organizations has regularly stressed the fact that organizations are not gender-free zones but instead are gendered. By showing how men's lifecycles are underlying current conceptions of career, how skills are gendered, and how an ideal worker functions as an exclusionary mechanism in organizations, it is possible to develop a view on organizations that allows us to see them as gendered. Such an approach is highly useful when it comes to studying gender and consulting as will be demonstrated in the following section.

25.3 GENDER IN CONSULTING

While the research on gender and organizations has flourished and produced many insightful studies, very few of these studies look specifically at consultancies. Consulting is a rather wide term and this chapter will refer mainly to business and management consulting, which is the business of providing advice to organizations on how to run more effectively (Kipping and Engwall 2002; Kubr 2002; Kipping and Clark, Chapter 1, this volume). This chapter will also include other professional service firms, particularly accountancy firms given their historically close association with management consultancies (see McDougald and Greenwood, Chapter 5, this volume).

As in other sectors, there seems to be a 'leaky pipeline' to the top of consulting firms as Table 25.1 suggests. The leaky pipeline refers to the phenomenon that women enter organizations in almost equal numbers to men, but drop out of organizations as they progress up the hierarchy (Rudolph 2004). While almost as many women as men enter consulting, women usually constitute less than 15 per cent at the partner

Table 25.1 Percentages of women in consultancies

Entry Level	40% Boston Consulting Group, UK
	40% KMPG, UK
	46% Capgemini, UK
	50% PriceWaterhouseCoopers, global
Consultants Overall	20% McKinsey, global
Partner Level	10% Accenture, global
	12% KPMG, UK
	15% PriceWaterhouseCoopers, global
	13% Ernst & Young, UK

Source: Accenture 2008; BCG 2008; CapGemini 2008; Ernst&Young 2008; KPMG 2008; McKinsey 2008; PricewaterhouseCoopers 2009.

level. As some research has shown, women are also working in areas other than strategy consulting or even within certain segments in consulting (Armbrüster 2006). For instance, many women work in human resources, diversity, or organizational development consultancies (Waclawski, Church, and Burke 1995; Rudolph 2004; Marsh 2008). One explanation for this is that women are leaving major consultancies to set up their own business or join other consultancies, which they feel are better fits. As highlighted by Marsh (2008), this leads to a situation where women tend to work in smaller and specialist consultancies rather than in the major strategy firms. Moreover, the specializations where women can be found are more likely to be stereotyped as feminine due to their strong focus on people.

Professional service firms seem to have recognized the lack of women in senior positions as a problem. For example, PriceWaterhouseCoopers researched this issue using a flow model that was developed internally and that set out to find blockages in a system, where women were no longer advancing (Opportunity Now 2009). This model found that the drop-out rates of men and women were not particularly different, but what was different was the fact that women were not promoted to certain levels, for instance from senior to top management. In this case the pipeline was not leaking but blocked. Subsequently, targeted initiatives such as bias- and stereotype-awareness training were developed in order to unblock the pipeline (ibid.).

The limited available research suggests that gender-specific issues in consulting firms arise from three different areas: the up-or-out culture, the client-facing nature of consulting, and the dominant idea that men rather than women are consultants. Related to the first, recruiting women into top consultancies does not seem to be an issue, but there is a 'leaking pipeline'. According to Kumra and Vinnicombe (2008), much of this has to do with the 'rat race' of making partner, which dominates many consulting firms. They point out that this leads to excessive working hours, with aspiring partners working eighty hours and more a week, leaving little room for activities outside work. In this culture, work takes priority over other aspects of life. Others have also pinpointed consultants as having 'extreme jobs', that is, working long hours in a fast-paced, unpredictable environment with tight deadlines and 24/7 client demands (Hewlett et al. 2007). This culture, they argue, suits workaholics well but it is hard to combine with having a personal life. Moreover, career structures are extremely inflexible and there are limited if any possibilities to go 'off- and on-ramp', that is, to take time out temporarily while remaining connected to the organization and not missing out on training (Hewlett 2007). The up-or-out promotion processes, typical for so many consulting firms, clearly leave little flexibility and off-ramping options—either for women or men. They seem particularly unsuited for the former, due the ebbs and flows commonly associated with women's career trajectories (ibid.).

Moreover, in these up-or-out systems, competition is fierce (Ibarra 1999) and the criteria used for promotion disadvantage women (Berry 1996). Thus, a study on the promotion to partner in one of the 'big four' professional services firms has shown that women are held back by two factors (Kumra and Vinnicombe 2008). First, career processes are largely self-managed and the individual has to be proactive to succeed. This, however, contradicts the feminine gender stereotype of modesty. Consequently, if women act in the required way and actively manage the impression they leave on others, they are not seen as feminine enough. If, by contrast, they are modest, they are not seen as fulfilling the success parameters (see also Jamieson 1995). Second, Kumra and Vinnicombe (2008) argue that women have to fit a success model that was designed for men, which makes it difficult for women to succeed.

Based on research in Germany, Rudolph (2004) also concluded that the need for impression management is damaging for women, since much of this career development takes place in informal networks outside of normal working hours, which is said to be problematic for women with caring responsibilities. Armbrüster (2006) goes even further, arguing that the potential sexualized undertones during these semi-private meetings generate problems for both men and women. This means that out-of-hours and out-of-office conversations between men and women can easily be misconstrued as sexual advances. Instead of exposing themselves to risk, such meetings might not take place when women are involved. Women thereby miss out on important networking events. Given that networking is highly relevant for a career in consulting (Kumra and Vinnicombe 2008), this can have detrimental effects on the careers of women.

Some argue that another important reason for the leaking pipeline in consulting firms is the potential preference by their clients for male consultants (Rudolph 2004; Armbrüster 2006). The client is the central figure for most consulting transactions (Fincham, Chapter 20; Nikolova and Devinney, Chapter 19; both this volume). Client contact increases with progression in the consulting hierarchy, which, as a number of studies have suggested, tends to disadvantage women. Thus, for instance, Gealy, Larwood, and Elliott (1979) show that male clients prefer male consultants, while female clients prefer female consultants—which means that it is in the economic self-interest of consultancies not to have women in client-facing roles, given the continued predominance of men in top management (see above). In their survey Larwood and Gattiker (1985) also found that clients believe that men provide a better service and, consequently, prefer to work with male consultants—which means that female consultants will have difficulties displaying the client management and retention skills essential for promotion to senior consulting roles. Similarly, based on interviews with senior personnel in a range of professional service firms, Quental (2010) identified client biases as a potential barrier for the career progression of female consultants. These studies might explain why women tend to be put in low-risk situations (Berry 1996) and, more generally, point to the consultant–client interaction having a gendered nature (see also Marsh 2008). However, more research is needed to better understand underlying gender dynamics in this key aspect of consultancy work.

Finally, there is a suggestion that the ideal template for a consultant is based on masculine characteristics, attributes, and attitudes, which means that women will have difficulties matching this ideal—similar to the 'think manager–think male' phenomenon (Schein 1976, 2001). In consulting women are perceived to be no problem as long as they 'fit in', but it is actually this fitting in that seems to be the main problem (Rudolph 2004). Thus, women in consulting have started to talk about the impact of stereotypes in their work environment, which leads to them not being taken seriously by colleagues and clients (Harris 1995; Kaplan 1995; Stringer 1995; Waclawski, Church, and Burke 1995). A recent study has confirmed these impressions by examining the discursive possibilities that are available to men and women in consultancies (Meriläinen et al. 2004). The researchers found a normalizing gender discourse about who can be a consultant, which included being addicted to work and being assertive. Thus, if the 'ideal consultant' is constructed as implicitly masculine, this has an exclusionary effect for those who are different. This is another area for future research, which could examine not only the symbolic discourses that associate consulting with practices of masculinity, but also look at specific masculine working practices in consultancies.

25.4 AN AGENDA FOR FUTURE RESEARCH ON GENDER IN CONSULTING

When compared to the flourishing research on gender, work, and organizations, summarized briefly above, the paucity of studies on gender and consulting becomes even more evident. Significant additional research is needed to elucidate how gender and consulting are co-constructed. While there are many open questions this section will focus on three key issues that deserve particular attention. Future research needs to explore: (1) the gender impact of the career model used in consultancies and its relationship to work–life balance; (2) how skills are constructed as gendered in consulting; and (3) how the ideal management consultant is constructed as masculine.

Related to work–life balance and career progression, it has been suggested that careers in consultancies are particularly difficult for women with family responsibilities

(Rudolph 2004). Further research needs to examine how having a family impacts on men and women in consultancies. It could be explored, for instance, how many mothers, fathers, or part-time workers are bypassed for promotion. There is also the question of to what extent female consultants without children experience similar issues. It has been argued that women are always at risk of being seen as 'potential mothers' (Gatrell and Swan 2008), regardless of whether they have, want to have, or can have children. Another possible question relates to arrangements in a consultant's private life. Anecdotal evidence suggests that senior female consultants outsource their family responsibilities to largely female nannies and helpers, which creates new gender relations that need to be studied. Research could, for instance, examine how financial means are used by some women, in this case senior female consultants, to buy them out of family responsibilities by employing other women. It could also be explored how far this changes the traditional division of labour in the household. For example, anecdotal evidence suggests that many senior women in consulting are the main breadwinner, meaning that their partners might take more responsibilities in the home. Those female consultants could then focus more on their careers, which might change their career patterns in consulting. This could prove an interesting area for further study.

As indicated earlier, the client relationship in consultancies in relation to gender is under-analysed and recent research is missing. Future research in this area should examine how much gender impacts on the client relationship. This is particularly pertinent as pressures from clients in terms of diversity might lead to a demand for more women and more minorities on their projects (United Nations Global Compact and UNIFEM 2008). It would also be interesting to contrast and compare consulting with other sectors, where women are hired specifically as they are seen as particularly good with customers. This has happened, for instance, in technology jobs, based on the rationale that stereotypically feminine characteristics—such as listening, and being empathetic and understanding—are useful when it comes to client interaction. At the same time, research has shown that these supposedly feminine emotional and social skills are often not valued in women and go unnoticed (Fletcher 1999; Woodfield 2000; Kelan 2008a). The question is to what extent the same is happening in consulting, given recent research that has aimed at highlighting feminine elements such as the importance of listening to clients (Marsh 2008).

Another under-researched area concerns the notion of the 'ideal worker', which has shown to be highly relevant in other sectors (e.g. Acker 1990; Benschop and Doorewaard 1998b; Kelan 2008a): Can the same (or a different) gender subtext be found in consulting? More generally, it might also be useful to conduct research that examines the masculine nature of consulting, which is often assumed but rarely shown. Such research could follow the research on men and masculinities in management, which sees unmasking the masculine subtext as a central area of concern (Collinson and Hearn 1994). Research on consultancies could explore how a certain brand of competitive masculinity is normalized and seen as a requirement to succeed, while those who are different are either not hired in the first place or let go because they do not fit it (i.e. the 'leaky pipe'). But one might also find that a successful consultant, rather than just drawing on masculine skills, needs masculine as well as feminine characteristics to succeed. Whatever the specific research focus and outcome, it is crucially important to avoid the reproduction of gender stereotypes.

In sum, the suggested studies could offer new insights into the co-construction of gender and consulting. Such research is critically required in order to better understand emerging issues surrounding gender in consulting and knowledge-intensive work more generally.

References

Accenture (2008). 'Accenture: Great Place to Work for Women'. Available at http://www. catalyst.org/publication/46/accenturegreat-place-to-work-for-women accessed 13 December 2008.

Acker, J. (1990). 'Hierarchies, Jobs, Bodies: A Theory of Gendered Organizations'. *Gender and Society*, 4/2, 139–158.

Anker, R. (1998). *Gender and Jobs: Sex Segregation of Occupations in the World*. Geneva: International Labour Office.

Armbrüster, T. (2006). *The Economics and Sociology of Management Consulting*. Cambridge: Cambridge University Press.

Bendl, R. (2008). 'Gender Subtexts: Reproduction of Exclusion in Organizational Discourse'. *British Journal of Management*, 19/S1, S50–S64.

Benschop, Y. and Doorewaard, H. (1998a). 'Six of One and Half a Dozen of the Other: The Gender Subtext of Taylorism and Team-based Work'. *Gender, Work & Organization*, 5/1, 5–18.

Benschop, Y. and Doorewaard, H. (1998b). 'Covered by Equality: The Gender Subtext of Organizations'. *Organization Studies*, 19/5, 787–805.

Berry, J. (1996). 'Women and Consulting: The Downside'. *Journal of Management Consulting*, 9/1, 34–38.

BCG (Boston Consulting Group) (2008). 'Is Consultancy for Me? An Event for Women'. Available at http://www.bcglondon.com/chapters/contact/events.html accessed 13 December 2008.

CapGemini (2008). 'Women in Management'. Available at http://www.capgemini.com/about/ our_people/diversity/women_in_management/ accessed 13 December 2008.

Collinson, D. and Hearn, J. (1994). 'Naming Men as Men: Implications for Work, Organization and Management'. *Gender, Work & Organization*, 1/1, 2–22.

Collinson, D. and Hearn, J. (2000). 'Critical Studies on Men, Masculinities and Management'. In M. J. Davidson and R. J. Burke (eds), *Women in Management Current Research Issues*, Volume 2. London: Sage, 263–278.

Dreher, G. F. (2003). 'Breaking the Glass Ceiling: The Effects of Sex Ratios and Work–Life Programs on Female Leadership at the Top'. *Human Relations*, 56/5, 541–562.

Eagly, A. H. and Carli, L. L. (2007). 'Women and the Labyrinth of Leadership'. *Harvard Business Review*, 85/9, 63–71.

Ernst & Young (2008). 'Support for Women's Leadership'. Available at http://www.ey.com/ global/Content.nsf/US/About_Ernst_Young_-_Offices_for_Flexibility_and_Gender_ Equity_Strategy accessed 13 December 2008.

Fletcher, J. K. (1999). *Disappearing Acts: Gender, Power, and Relational Practice*. Cambridge, MA: MIT Press.

Gatrell, C. and Swan, E. (2008). *Gender and Diversity in Management: A Concise Introduction*. London: Sage.

Gealy, J., Larwood, L., and Elliott, M. P. (1979). 'Where Sex Counts: Effects of Consultant and Client Gender in Management Consulting'. *Group & Organization Studies*, 4/2, 201–211.

Harris, M. E. (1995). 'What Has It Been Like to be a Woman Consultant Over the Last Two Decades?' *Journal of Organizational Change Management*, 8/1, 32–43.

Hearn, J. and Morgan, D. H. J. (1990). *Men, Masculinities and Social Theory*. London: Unwin Hyman.

Hewlett, S. A. (2007). *Off-Ramps and On-Ramps: Keeping Talented Women on the Road to Success*. Boston: Harvard Business School Press.

Hewlett, S. A. and Luce, C. B. (2005). 'Off-Ramps and On-Ramps'. *Harvard Business Review*, 83/3, 43–54.

Hewlett, S. A., Luce, C. B., Southwell, S., and Bernstein, L. (2007). *Seduction and Risk: The Emergence of Extreme Jobs*. New York: Centre for Work–Life Policy. Available at http://www.worklifepolicy.org/index.php/section/research_pubs accessed 23 February 2011.

Ibarra, H. (1999). 'Provisional Selves: Experimenting with Image and Identity in Professional Adaptation'. *Administrative Science Quarterly*, 44/4, 764–791.

Jamieson, K. H. (1995). *Beyond the Double Bind: Women and Leadership*. Oxford: Oxford University Press.

Kaplan, K. L. (1995). 'Women's Voices in Organizational Development: Questions, Stories, and Implications'. *Journal of Organizational Change Management*, 8/1, 52–81.

Kelan, E. K. (2008a). 'Emotions in a Rational Profession: The Gendering of Skills in ICT work'. *Gender, Work & Organization*, 15/1, 49–71.

Kelan, E. K. (2008b). 'The Discursive Construction of Gender in Contemporary Management Literature'. *Journal of Business Ethics*, 18/2, 427–445.

Kelan, E. K. (2008c). 'Gender, Risk and Employment Insecurity: The Masculine Breadwinner Subtext'. *Human Relations*, 61/9, 1171–1202.

Kipping, M. and Engwall, L. (eds) (2002). *Management Consulting: Emergence and Dynamics of a Knowledge Industry*. Oxford: Oxford University Press.

Knights, D. and McCabe, D. (2001). 'A Different World: Shifting Masculinities in the Transition to Call Centres'. *Organization*, 8/4, 619–645.

KPMG (2008). 'Financial Woman Magazine'. Available at http://www.auroravoice.com/pressarticle.asp?articleid=491 accessed 13 December 2008.

Kubr, M. (2002). *Management Consulting: A Guide to the Profession*. Geneva: International Labour Office.

Kumra, S. and Vinnicombe, S. (2008). 'A Study of the Promotion to Partner Process in a Professional Services Firm: How Women are Disadvantaged'. *British Journal of Management*, 19/S1, S65–S74.

Larwood, L. and Gattiker, U. E. (1985). 'Rational Bias and Interorganizational Power in the Employment of Management Consultants'. *Group & Organization Studies*, 10/1, 3–18.

Liff, S. and Ward, K. (2001). 'Distorted Views Through the Glass Ceiling: The Construction of Women's Understandings of Promotion and Senior Management Positions'. *Gender, Work & Organization*, 8/1, 19–36.

Marsh, S. (2008). *The Feminine in Management Consulting*. Basingstoke: Palgrave Macmillan.

McGeoch, G. (2008). 'Women Doctors and the Decline of Medical Professionalism'. *Oxford Medical School Gazette*, 56/1. Available at http://www.medsci.ox.ac.uk/gazette/previousissues/56vol51/Part54/ accessed 13 December 2008.

McKinsey(2008). 'Women FAQ'. Available at http://www.mckinsey.com/careers/women/faqs/faqs1/index.aspx/#5 accessed 13 December 2008.

Meriläinen, S., Tienari, J., Thomas, R., and Davies, A. (2004). 'Management Consultant Talk: A Cross-Cultural Comparison of Normalizing Discourse and Resistance'. *Organization*, 11/4, 539–564.

Meyerson, D. E. and Fletcher, J. K. (2000). 'A Modest Manifesto for Shattering the Glass Ceiling'. *Harvard Business Review*, 78/1, 126–136.

O'Leary, J. (1997). 'Developing a New Mindset: The "Career Ambitious" Individual'. *Women in Management Review*, 12/3, 91–99.

Opportunity Now (2009). PriceWaterhouseCoopers. Available at http://www.opportunitynow.org.uk/awards/awards_2009/2009_case_studies/advancing_women_in_business_award/pricewaterhousecoope.html accessed 20 January 2009.

Phillips, A. and Taylor, B. (1980). 'Sex and Skill: Towards a Feminist Economics'. *Feminist Review*, 6, 79–88.

PricewaterhouseCoopers (2009). 'Women at PricewaterhouseCoopers'. Available at http://www.pwc.com/extweb/home.nsf/docid/6E4B7AC62BA3EE0985257364006A43AD accessed 20 January 2009.

Quental, C. (2010). 'Gender, Knowledge Work and Partnership: The Gendered World of Professional Services Firms'. Paper presented at the 26th EGOS Colloquium, Lisbon, 1–3 July.

Reskin, B. F. and Roos, P. A. (1990). *Job Queues, Gender Queues: Explaining Women's Inroads into Male Occupations*. Philadelphia, PA: Temple University Press.

Rudolph, H. (2004). 'Beyond the Token Status: Women in Business Consultancies in Germany'. Available at http://www.wzb.eu/gwd/into/pdf/spiii_2004_202.pdf accessed 13 December 2008.

Schein, V. E. (1976). 'Think Manager: Think Male'. *Atlanta Economic Review*, 26/2 (March–April), 21–24.

Schein, V. E. (2001). 'A Global Look at Psychological Barriers to Women's Progress in Management'. *Journal of Social Issues*, 57/4, 675–688.

Smithson, J. and Stokoe, E. H. (2005). 'Discourses of Work–Life Balance: Negotiating "Genderblind" Terms in Organizations'. *Gender, Work & Organization*, 12/2, 147–168.

Stringer, D. M. (1995). 'The Role of Women in Workplace Diversity Consulting'. *Journal of Organizational Change Management*, 8/1, 44–52.

United Nations Global Compact and UNIFEM (2008). 'Calvert Women's Principles'. Available at http://www.unglobalcompact.org/docs/issues_doc/human_rights/Meetings_x_events/05Mar2009_Guiding_Principles_for_Business_to_Advance_Women.pdf accessed 13 December 2008.

Waclawski, J., Church, A. H., and Burke, W. W. (1995). 'Women in Organization Development'. *Journal of Organizational Change Management*, 8/1, 12–23.

Wajcman, J. (1998). *Managing Like a Man*. Oxford: Blackwell.

Woodfield, R. (2000). *Women, Work and Computing*. Cambridge: Cambridge University Press.

CHAPTER 26

MANAGEMENT CONSULTING IN DEVELOPING AND EMERGING ECONOMIES: TOWARDS A POSTCOLONIAL PERSPECTIVE

MICHAL FRENKEL
YEHOUDA SHENHAV

26.1 INTRODUCTION

WHILE the consulting market has until recently been a predominantly North Atlantic phenomenon, with the US and UK accounting for more than half of the world market, observers of the field of global management consultancy now argue that 'the fastest growing consulting economies are those described as "the rest of the world", including central and eastern Europe, Asia-Pacific, Latin America and Africa' (Curnow and Reuvid 2003: 10). Yet, despite the growing importance of consultancy encounters and experiences in the 'rest of the world' and the increased attention it has been receiving from consultancy firms and in texts aimed at practitioners (Golembiewski 2000; Kubr 2002; Curnow and Reuvid 2003), any systematic academic research of the subject is still in its infancy.

Studies of the global consultancy industry have mostly focused on its spread from the US, where professional consultancy knowledge and forms of conduct took shape, to other highly industrialized societies, such as the UK, Germany, and Japan (see Wright and Kipping, Chapter 2, this volume; Kipping 1999; Kipping and Engwall 2002). The few studies devoted to the diffusion of this industry in the 'rest of the world' (Wright and Kwon 2006; Donadone 2009; Wang 2009) have commonly drawn on the theoretical framework developed to account for diffusion in advanced societies, and have attributed the difficulties experienced by the big multinational consultancies in entering the 'developing world' to cultural and institutional distances, to the 'otherness' of the consultant, to technological backwardness at the non-Western client's end, and to resistance grounded in political interests and local industrial relations, largely *disregarding* the conflict-riven historical and geopolitical context that is echoed in the process of foreign consulting in the 'third world'.

The present chapter first draws upon empirical studies of management in emerging and developing economies in general in order to set out the baseline for a better understanding of the field. The next part of the chapter introduces ideas and theoretical insights from postcolonial theory—which has recently come to inspire general studies of management in peripheral and semi-peripheral societies—in order to offer new theoretical directions for the understanding of the encounter between foreign consultancies and local clients in third world contexts. More specifically, it is suggested that the first-world third-world encounter should be studied, as this is characteristic of much of the global consultancy experience in the 'rest of the world'. The encounter created a third space of 'in-between' (Bhabha 1994), in which knowledge, culture, and social identities developed in different social and economic contexts were intertwined with one another, thereby creating a new institutional environment that can no longer be traced back to its cultural origins.

26.2 CONSULTANCY IN EMERGING AND DEVELOPING SOCIETIES

26.2.1 Why Does it Matter?

Due to differences in definitions and difficulties in data collection, it is hard to estimate the share of emerging and developing (E&D) societies in the global consultancy market. According to consultancy expert Markham, the 'rest of the world' now accounts for up to 35 per cent of the worldwide consulting market (Curnow and Reuvid 2003), while Gross and Poor (2008) provide a more modest estimation of the markets outside North America and the EU, arguing that they are currently responsible for about 18 per cent of the global consulting market. However, despite these differences, most commentators in the field agree that, given the rapid economic growth of new economic giants such as China, India, and Brazil—previously considered parts of the 'rest of the world'—the market for global consultancy in these societies is likely to grow much faster than in any other part of the world. Under such circumstances, the construction of a theoretical and analytical framework that allows for a better understanding of consultancy in this unique context is thus more relevant now than ever before.

Furthermore, the growing market for consultancy in 'peripheral' societies constitutes an interesting and potentially innovative research domain, not only because of the quantitative transformation of the field of global consultancy, but also because of the ethical, political, and practical questions it raises. Thus, for example, in criticizing the excessive expenditure of third world countries on management consultancy, Ayittey (1999) has claimed that, by 1989, the total number of expatriate consultants and experts employed by the World Bank to try and solve Africa's economic problems had reached a staggering 80,000, costing cash-strapped African governments between US$1 billion and US$4 billion in fees and compensation per annum: 'Less than one-half of one percent of these management consultants were Native Africans', he stated (ibid.: 585–586), illustrating both the global importance of this market and the problem it has raised. While the cross-national transfer of management knowledge via management consultants within the core of the world system has met with criticism, mostly concerning its contribution to the clients efficiency and profitability and because of the micro-power relations between consultants and clients due to historical circumstances, in the context of the 'rest of the world', (foreign) consultant–client encounters are more likely to raise macro-political tensions.

Whether or not we regard the transfer of the World Bank's investment back to the 'West' as problematic, Ayittey's analysis highlights three very important aspects that have characterized consultancy in E&D societies: (1) clients are (more often than not) international organizations rather than local firms or local governments, therefore consultants are hired to advise a third party who is not necessarily interested in such a service and in the transformation it seeks to promote; (2) consultancy involves an extensive cross-cultural encounter, which is heavily embedded in hierarchical core-periphery relations; and (3) this complex cross-cultural encounter often generates resistance that is different in essence from that which consultants usually encounter in their own societies. Indeed, recent writings by practitioners on the experience of consultancy in developing countries suggest that while the global big brand consultancies make considerable investments in order to enter these expanding markets, are preferred by multinationals and international agencies, and enjoy high levels of legitimacy as carriers of advanced knowledge (see, for example, http://www.kennedyinfo.com/ accessed 1 October 2011), they tend to encounter more difficulties in markets in 'the rest of the world' than had been the case in new European markets (Gross and Poor 2008; Wang 2009). Likewise, in a survey of 574 organizational development (OD) projects, hundreds of which were carried out in third world countries, Golembiewski (2000: 536–537) found that while in the general population 40 per cent of the cases yielded 'high positive and intended effects', in third world countries only 18.7 per cent yielded such an effect, while a sizable majority of 58.1 per cent were described as having a balance of positive and negative effects.

26.2.2 What Do We Already Know?

As mentioned above, academic research that focuses on consultancy in E&D societies is very much in its infancy. Nevertheless, studies of the cross-national transfer of management models and ideologies often look at the role of management consultants (although not necessarily of consultancy firms) in spreading the new professional gospel in the global periphery (or third world). Thus, for example, in their historical analyses of the professionalization of management in Latin America, Gantman (2005, 2010), Wood and Caldas (2002), and others have mentioned the role of US consultants, invited by US aid agencies and private foundations (such as the Ford Foundation), in transforming management studies in these countries as part of the expanding US influence in its back-yard countries (see also Caldas 2006; and for a dissertation, published in Portuguese, on the role of consultants in Brazil; summarized by the author in Serva 1992).

While the role of these consultants in introducing new managerial models in Latin America is mentioned in these studies, and while the fact that, at least in Argentina, US-trained management professors find themselves spending more time consulting with locals than teaching or doing research—which is the core of Gantman's critique of management education in his home country—none of the English-language studies reviewed for this chapter either focuses on the consulting process itself, seeks to contribute directly to the expanding academic writing on consultancy, or attempts to study the consulting process in detail. Similarly, studies of the introduction of management models in Turkey (Erçek and İşeri 2008), India (Srinivas 2008), and Israel (Frenkel 2008b) all mention the role of management consultants as representatives of foreign aid agencies in the 1950s and global consultancies in the 1980s and onwards in spreading management models such as scientific management, human relations, workers' participation and others, but avoid an in-depth discussion of the consultancy process and its potential uniqueness in these contexts.

In another account, Mir, Banerjee, and Mir (2009) mention the role of foreign consultants in transferring and legitimizing US-originated techniques in an Indian subsidiary of a US-based multinational corporation. Taking into consideration the geopolitical power relations between India and the US, and the automatic professional authority that is often associated with managers and consultants who represent the 'first world', Mir, Banerjee, and Mir show how foreign consultants sometimes impose unnecessary, irrelevant, and more expensive forms of action, when the local institutional knowledge had actually been serving the organization better. While consultants can be seen as having played a major role in transferring knowledge from developed to developing regions, this study, as with others, does not delve into their everyday involvement, and only touches on their role in passing.

Another set of studies that may prove relevant to the understanding of management consultancy in the 'rest of the world' comes from recent research into global professional service firms (PSFs). Boussebaa (2009) has pointed out that while one might expect that consulting multinationals would send their top experts from the more advanced economies to share their knowledge with less advanced societies, the opposite is in fact the case. Since each national office must demonstrate that it is profitable, and since consultancy services in advanced and rich societies are likely to raise more income, managers of local offices try to maximize their profit by sending their star consultants to advanced societies, and prefer to hire consultants from less advanced countries, where salaries are smaller, to provide services in poorer societies. Thus, against conventional wisdom, which focuses on the role of consultants in diffusing management knowledge from the centre to the periphery, this study suggests that the logic of profit centres, as applied in global PSFs, may lead to the removal of internationally qualified consultants from the national reservoir in poorer countries.

Finally, a small number of studies have recently sought to contribute directly to the understanding of the consultancy process in E&D societies. Thus, for example, in their interesting account of their own work as consultants in emerging economies, Lendvai and Stubbs (2006: 2) focus on 'transnational consultancies as a site for critical scrutiny and empirical investigation'. They see such consultancies as representing an important signifying practice for new forms of governmentality, located in trans-local, interstitial spaces. These transnational consultancies do not simply transfer knowledge and models from one society to another. Rather, they are engaged in translation. They view transnational consultancies as part of a network of translators involved in a continuous process through which individuals transform the knowledge, truths, and effects of power each time they encounter them.

Another perspective on the role of foreign consultants as middlemen (or 'cultural brokers') moving between East and West, South and North, can be found in Styhre's (2002) study of the adoption of Japanese human resources (HR) practices in a Swedish firm. In his study, he argues that throughout the introduction of the Japanese practices, the managers and consultants were the group most inclined to talk about the Japanese and Japanese society, thereby contributing to the construction of an image of the Other that was shared across the organizational tiers. While Styhre's study deals with consultancy in a highly developed economy, it points to the role consultants may have in constructing cultural differences rather than bridging them.

Last, but not least, is Wang's (2009) dissertation on global management consultancy in China. This recent study is, to the best of our knowledge, the most systematic account of global consultancy in an emerging economy, and one that seeks to contribute directly to the growing literature on management consultancy. Analysing the encounter between foreign consultants and the Chinese institutional environment, Wang found that while foreign consultants' attempts at importing global knowledge assets mostly had positive effects at the market and firm level of practice, they caused a mix of benefits and challenges during the actual consultation process due to insufficient and inappropriate adaptation.

Taken together, the above studies mark three main challenges that any future systematic study of global consultancy in the 'rest of the world' should take into consideration: the conceptualization of relevant knowledge (subaltern/indigenous versus canonic-professional); the notion of culture and cultural encounters; and the question of power relations, that is, juxtaposing professional power relations with geopolitical ones. Not surprisingly, these are also the questions at the heart of recent studies of management in the rest of the world. In this more mature field of studies, the postcolonial perspective has often proved useful in offering a fresh vocabulary and theoretical frameworks that have helped in analysing the complex West–rest encounter that characterizes this unique environment.

26.3 Outline of a Postcolonial Perspective on Consultancy

In its widest sense, 'postcolonial theory involves a studied engagement with the experience of colonialism and its past and present effects, both at the level of ex-colonial societies as well as the level of more general global developments thought to be the aftereffects of empire' (Quayson 2000: 2). From this point of view, given that the binary opposition between 'Western' and 'Oriental' was constituted and institutionalized as part of the asymmetric power relations between colonizer and colonized throughout the colonial era (Said 1987), most West–rest relations, as experienced today, are still sustained, in one way or another, by the colonial heritage. Thus, despite much internal variation, different postcolonial theories share an interest in the ways that international and ethnic hierarchies of economic and political power are maintained and reproduced.

In recent years, a growing interest in ethnic and racial inequality in organizations in general, and in multinational organizations in particular, has led students of management and organizations to draw on postcolonial insights in their own studies. Existing postcolonial analyses in management studies have pointed (among other issues) to the exclusion and silencing of non-Western organizational knowledge (Calas and Smirich 1999; Westwood 2004; Frenkel and Shenhav 2006; Frenkel 2008a; Varman and Biswatosh 2009); the oversimplistic representation of 'the Other' in Western management discourses (e.g. Kwek 2003; Prasad 2003a; Westwood 2006); and the fallacies resulting from the application of 'Western' notions and definitions in non-Western contexts (e.g. Calas and Smirich 1999; Banerjee 2002, 2003). Critiquing international management discourse, especially in relation to developing countries, is one of the central foci of this approach (Calas and Smirich 1999; Westwood 2001, 2004; Banerjee 2002, 2003; Jack and Lorbiecki 2003; Kwek 2003; Jack and Westwood 2006; Peltonen 2006; Frenkel 2008a). Scholars in this tradition have also attempted to study subaltern managerial knowledge, defined in postcolonial studies as knowledge generated and produced by '[t]hose subjects which occupy a position so marginal and whose voice is so fragmented in relation to a dominant culture and language that they are potentially forever silenced and spoken for by the dominant culture' (Bernard-Donals 1998: 112).

It is important to note here that the use of the notions of the 'West', 'the rest', and the 'third world' in this chapter does not imply that these categories and distinctions are objective classifications representing an ontological cultural or developmental difference. They are not intended to homogenize either the West or the rest. These notions are used historically, to delineate and mark out the 'effects of hegemonic representations of the Western self rather than its subjugated traditions' (Hall 1992: 276, cited in Wong 2005: 127). It is also important to note that while several 'Western' societies, such as the US, Canada, New Zealand, and Australia, are themselves the outcome of European colonialism, their histories have made them part of the 'West', turning the West–rest divide into an internal characteristic of these societies and the racial and ethnic divisions upon which they are constructed. Similarly, the notion of the third world is not applied in postcolonial studies to represent the inferiority of those societies vis-à-vis the more developed first world, but rather as a *salute* to the act of self-identification through which the leaders of the third world set themselves apart from the two parties fighting the Cold War. The term 'postcolonial' should not be taken as implying that the era of colonialism has ended; rather, it seeks to develop a different discourse that speaks in a different language from that of colonialism, thereby exposing the basic colonialist assumptions that are embedded in modern structures of knowledge.

While rarely considered in these postcolonial analyses (for exceptions, see Wong 2005; Banerjee, Chio, and Mir 2009; Mir and Mir 2009), management consultancy should also be seen as a natural target for such a critique. The continuity between the 'civilizing mission' that characterized the colonial regimes and the modern consulting process in formerly colonized societies is particularly striking. In both cases, experts from European or North American states and organizations are urged to pass on their superior knowledge to the less developed, where that knowledge is seen as technically and objectively superior to indigenous know-how (see Kerr 2008). Moreover, in both cases, the bearers of this knowledge rarely make do with the implementation of technical models, aiming instead at the moral and cultural improvement of the 'under-developed' subject (see, for example, the 1998 memoirs of one of the most influential foreign consultants in south-east Asia, Rolf Lynton, *Social Science in Actual Practice: Themes on My Blue Guitar*). As depicted by scholars such as Wong (2005), Mir, Banerjee, and Mir (2009), Wang (2009), and others, the encounter between the global expert and the rest-of-the-world client is often loaded with a sense of supremacy and, in many cases, soft racism. In both instances, the unsuccessful implementation of imported know-how is often attributed to the clients' lack of development and their inferior capabilities, rather than to their active and conscious resistance to the people bringing that knowledge to them (e.g. Kerr (2008), on the transfer of public management knowledge from the UK to China). Finally, in both the colonial 'civilizing mission' and the modern consulting process small local elites at the client end are instrumental in promoting and legitimizing the transferred knowledge and techniques.

This parallel between the colonial 'civilizing mission'—which is stronger in some specific contexts than others—and modern consultancy in developing and evolving economies, makes the close interrelations stressed by postcolonial studies between *knowledge*, *culture*, and geopolitical *power* especially relevant for understanding cross-national consultancy. The subsequent parts of this section will discuss these issues in some more detail.

26.3.1 Rethinking Knowledge Construction and Transfer

At least three focal points, which have characterized postcolonial analyses of knowledge creation and implementation, are highly relevant to the understanding of consultancy knowledge and its role in the reproduction of the global 'West–rest' hierarchy: (1) the generation of Western knowledge about the colonized 'Other' as part of the very construction of the hierarchical 'West–rest' divide (Said 1978); (2) the marginalization of indigenous knowledge as a way of silencing the subaltern's voice and ability to control their own destiny (Spivak 1988; Prakash 1994; Chakrabarty 2002); and (3) the implementation of 'Western' knowledge in the third world as part of the colonial system of control and its transgressed implementation as a form of colonized resistance (Bhabha 1994).

Consultancy studies are mostly concerned with the nature of professional consultancy knowledge and its status vis-à-vis general management knowledge (see also Werr, Chapter 12; Jung and Kieser, Chapter 16; both this volume). Students of consultancy history have often pointed to the connection between management fads and fashions and the institutionalization and transformation of the consultancy industry (e.g. Kipping and Engwall 2002). While managerial bodies of knowledge from scientific management and management by objectives to Total Quality Management (TQM) and Business Process Re-engineering (BPR) have undoubtedly affected the popularity of management consultancy and its methods, students of consulting discourses have shown that consultants' professional authority vis-à-vis managers is also grounded in the former's ability to claim the possession of cutting-edge knowledge and specific problem-solving skills. Yet, while students of management knowledge have recently begun to study the construction of management knowledge about the 'Other', and the stressful encounter between Western (i.e. US-originated) and indigenous knowledge throughout managerial and consultancy processes (Prasad 1997, 2003b; Neu 2001; Lendvai and Stubbs 2009), students of consultancy knowledge still seem to assume that such knowledge has not emerged outside the developed world. A fertile avenue for a study of consultancy knowledge from a postcolonial perspective might therefore delve into local philosophies about how advice is taken and given in different cultures and regions, and how this may affect the consultancy process in those areas.

26.3.1.1 *Knowledge of the 'Other'*

One of the earliest insights of postcolonial studies can be found in Edward Said's book *Orientalism* (Said 1978). There, he examines the bodies of knowledge that developed in the West concerning cultures external to it and the manner in which these bodies of knowledge simultaneously create both the Orient and the ostensibly homogeneous identity of the West. According to Said (1978: 3),

> Orientalism can be discussed and analyzed as the corporate institution for dealing with the Orient—dealing with it by making statements about it, authorizing views of it, describing it, by teaching it, settling it, ruling it: in short, Orientalism as a Western style for dominating, restructuring, and having authority over the Orient.

He also tries to show that European culture gained in strength and identity by setting itself off against the Orient as a sort of surrogate and even underground self. Indeed, as often mentioned in consultancy studies, consultancy theory and mainstream academic writing about consultancy have by and large ignored the potential distinctiveness of the consultancy process in the third world, assuming instead that the process is universal, thus legitimizing the big brand consultancies' claim for superior professional skills, a claim that has given them a competitive edge in winning lucrative contracts with international organizations and multinational firms (Ayittey 1999; Styhre 2002; Kerr 2008; Wang 2009).

However, while consultancy theory produces hardly any academic knowledge about the non-Western Other, in their practice, management experts and consultants are found to be an important source of stereotypical knowledge about the Other. As mentioned above, Styhre (2002: 259) has shown how Swedish

> managers and consultants were the group most inclined to speak about the Japanese and Japanese society. Blue-collar workers basically shared the managers' and consultants' views but these groups were more eloquent in their accounts of the Japanese. The construction of the image of the other was still shared across the organizational tiers, although the blue-collar workers offered [...] more scattered, less conclusive views [of the Japanese] without a clear story-line compared with the consultants and managers.

According to Styhre, the construction of knowledge about the non-Western Other was not accidental, nor does it reflect individual racist perceptions. Rather, according to this study, the construction of the Other was part of the consultants' professional practice, aimed at mediating 'the differences between Japanese and Swedish culture' (ibid.: 257). As part of this 'mediation', 'the image of the other, the generalized view of the unfamiliar subject, is constructed in order to estrange and eliminate ambiguities in the culture of the other and to facilitate the adaptation of Japanese human resource management practices' (ibid.: 257).

26.3.1.2 *Silencing subaltern knowledge*

As mentioned above, giving voice to subaltern groups has been one of the central themes of postcolonial studies. One of the significant aspects of the silencing of subaltern groups is the marginalization of the knowledge they produce. One result of this process of marginalization is to treat subaltern techniques as inferior to those offered by the hegemonic groups and the imposition of foreign knowledge, even in cases in which local know-how has been proven to be efficient (Mitchell 1988).

Following our earlier work (Frenkel and Shenhav 2006), one way of understanding the Western self-identification of the purportedly universal body of consultancy knowledge is as based on a system of omissions and exclusions of knowledge produced outside the West and its academic and professional institutions (see also Calas and Smircich 1999). Such understanding may be applied to the analysis of existing practitioners writing about the Other's knowledge. Thus, a close reading of representative consultancy textbooks for practitioners can demonstrate this general tendency to uphold the knowledge they contain as modern and superior. For instance, a chapter on 'Ethics: guidelines for practice', which appeared in a practitioners' handbook entitled *Management Consulting: A Guide to the Profession* and published by the International Labour Office in Geneva (Kubr 2002), highlights the importance of developing a broad range of competencies, including applied behavioural science, leadership, management, administration, organizational behaviour, system behaviour, and organization/system development (Gellermann, Frankel, and Ladenson 2002). However, while the chapter also stresses the importance of acquiring knowledge about multiculturalism, gender, and cross-cultural issues, it never considers the need for consultants to equip themselves with locally produced knowledge and techniques (ibid.: 332–334).

An even more explicit distinction between the types of knowledge that may be acquired in the first and third worlds is found in Chisholm's (2000) chapter on action research, published in the *Handbook of Organizational Consultation*. 'Action research' combines management consultancy with the generation of new scientifically legitimized and generalizable knowledge. In such research, consultant–client symmetry in knowledge transfer is stressed. However, following Brown (1993), Chisholm distinguishes between two distinct perspectives on action research: (1) a northern hemisphere/'first world camp'; and (2) a southern hemisphere/'third world camp'. Action research in the two traditions is said to pursue fundamentally different purposes. While traditional (first world) action research attempts to improve organizational performance and generate social science theory—that is, to change organizations and social science—researchers who operate from a third world perspective attempt to raise levels of consciousness, explore new approaches to basic social problems, empower the underprivileged, and increase market equality through social change (Chisholm 2000: 193). Thus, while knowledge acquired in action research in the developed world is considered a potential contribution to the general professional body of knowledge, knowledge generated in a very similar research context in the developing world is seen as ungeneralizable and as relevant only to those parts of the world.

This lack of interest is especially endemic given the growing attention to the existence and relevancy of indigenous management knowledge in the Southern hemisphere and to its potential contribution to the success of organizations the world over. Thus, for example, in their recent book, Banerjee, Chio, and Mir (2009) point to the variety of environmental conservation techniques applied by different subaltern groups that could have been adopted by international organizations and multinationals in their sustainable development projects, not only around the third world, but in the 'developed world' as well. When international bodies got involved in these projects, the authors argue, the affordable and accessible techniques, which were less vulnerable to local weather changes, were substituted by foreign, more expensive, and less durable ones, grounded in Western and academically legitimated knowledge promoted by foreign consultancies (see also Mir and Mir 2009). Likewise, in studies of several international projects in South Africa, Jackson and his colleagues (Jackson, Amaeshi, and Yavuz 2008; Jackson 2009) have shown that attempts by foreign aid agencies to introduce advanced management models and foreign models of accountability have not led to the desired results, due to locals' tendency to apply indigenous philosophies of 'collective' management associated with the general local philosophy of 'Ubuntu', and because of a reluctance on the side of the foreign agencies to accept 'Ubuntu' as a valid and efficient model of management.

In general, from a postcolonial perspective this omission of the subaltern's knowledge, often depicted in consultants' reports as a process of upgrading or modernization, can be seen as part of the reproduction of Western superiority, and as a direct continuation of the colonial discourse of mimicry (Bhabha 1994), as the next subsection discusses in more detail.

26.3.1.3 *Mimicry and the imposition of foreign knowledge*

Postcolonial theorist Homi Bhabha argues that, as part of their historical and institutional justification for their rule over the colonies and their mission to civilize the non-Western Other, the colonial superpowers sought to canonize in the colonies' texts and practices that they identified with their own cultural superiority, and to force the colonial subject to emulate a Western role model (for an extended review of the idea of the third space in the context of international management, see Frenkel 2008a).

According to Bhabha, the colonizing nature of the transfer of knowledge may also explain the resistance to the proper implementation of this knowledge. From this point of view, the disrupted, disturbed, and inappropriate ways in which the imposed knowledge, discourses, and practices, including those offered by consultants, are articulated in colonized/third world societies are not only the expression of the colonizers' ambivalent needs, but also of active and sometimes conscious resistance by the colonized. Beyond merely accounting for the failure rates of consultancy in the developing world, which are far higher than in the developed world (Golembiewski 2000), critical studies of consultancy should focus on the relations between the nature of the transfer process, the transferred knowledge, and resistance. Such studies should look at managers' and workers' actual conceptualization of the foreign consultants and the solutions they offer to the problems that organizations face.

26.3.2 Culture

The general tendency of recent consultancy studies to overlook the uniqueness of consultancy in E&D societies also results in a lack of attention to questions of cultural differences that consultants must bridge. In practitioners' textbooks, however, the embeddedness of the consulting process within a broader and possibly conflict-ridden cultural encounter is explicitly articulated (e.g. Kubr 2002; Sadler 2001; Curnow and Reuvid 2003). In contrast to early conceptualizations of managerial and consultancy knowledge as culture-free (e.g. Harbison and Myers 1959), the prevalent contemporary professional attitude is one of cultural relativism and tolerance. Drawing specifically on the cross-cultural management literature and on Hofstede's definition of culture as 'the collective programming of the human mind that distinguishes the member of one human group from those of another group' (Hofstede 1980, cited in Kubr 2002: 11), practitioners' textbooks often take the centrality of culture in consultancy work for granted, along with the heightened risks of cultural miscommunication when clients and consultants do not share a cultural background, and especially when they represent different poles of the West/rest, North/South, developed/developing dichotomies (see, for example, chapter 5.3 on 'Facing culture in consulting assignments' Kubr (2002: 121); and Adams (2003), in Curnow and Reuvid (2003)).

Culture appears in these practitioners' textbooks, and indeed in most writings in the field of international management, as a stable part of any society that the foreign consultant must take into account. The schema of the Western consultant/non-Western client—which is by far the most prevalent case of the West–rest encounter in consultancy—is the only imagined possibility in these practitioners' textbooks. Thus, for example, in a book published by the International Labour Office, the imagined consultant, who is naturally seen as coming from the West, is advised to be 'culture-conscious', 'culture-sensitive', or 'culture tolerant':

> Your client may know that a first contact with an American consultant will be quite different from a contact with a Japanese consultant. However, there is no guarantee that your particular client is 'culturally literate' and culture-tolerant. It is therefore wise to find out beforehand how he or she expects a professional adviser to behave. (Kubr 2002: 121)

The critique of the notion of 'culture' in international management studies and cross-cultural management studies has occupied much of the postcolonial analysis of management discourse (Kwek 2003; Wong 2005; Frenkel 2008a), and should serve as a warning sign for future studies of consultancy in the 'rest of the world'. Two main perspectives have dominated these analyses: the Saidian perspective, underlining the role of 'cultural profiling' in constructing the colonized 'Other' and reifying (or naturalizing) the borderline between the West and the Orient, and a Bhabhaian perspective that challenges the very possibility of the existence of pure, authentic 'local' cultures in a globalizing world.

From a (partially) Saidian point of view, Wong (2005) has recently argued that, while scholars of cross-cultural management have indeed introduced greater cultural sensitivity to their studies of cultural difference and have suggested a greater awareness of institutional practices, their view of culture is frequently oversimplified (Wong 2005: 133). This oversimplification often 'gloss[es] over its internal cleavages (race, class, gender and regional) with no recognition of conflicting interests and with a silencing of dissenting voices'. This representation, it is argued, constitutes an attempt 'to reduce the menace of the difference of otherness by means of constituting the colonized (i.e., the Other) in terms of images that are already familiar to the colonizing consciousness' (see also Prasad 1997: 294; Kwek 2003; Westwood 2006).

The Bhabhaian point of view takes this critique even further, arguing that the West's attempt to shape the Other in its own (not quite precise) image, and the historically situated continuous encounter between the West and its Others throughout the colonial and neo-colonial era, constitute a third space, which is not entirely governed by the laws of either the ruler or the ruled. It is a space in which a hybrid culture is constructed that belongs neither to the ruler nor the ruled, but which is instead a fusion of the two. From this perspective, *culture* is seen as an *ongoing process of interpretation and reinterpretation* rather than as a fixed feature of any given society. Two main features of the practitioners' textbooks seem to lend themselves to a Bhabhaian cultural analysis. Against the essentialist cultural assumptions associated with Hofstede's analysis, Kubr (2002) notices that, in many cases, the local elite in a developing society has been socialized in Western systems and thus shares the system of meaning that the 'Western' consultant brings with him/her. This understanding suggests that the local subject may tolerate and be attentive to the consultant's culture at least as much as the consultant may understand the client's culture.

It seems that while consultancy practitioners are aware of the constant processes of hybridization, which construct and reconstruct cultural spaces that are subjected to different cultural repertoires at the same time, textbooks aimed at training consultants are still generally trapped in a colonial cosmology in which a stable Western and rational culture is seen as (at least technically) superior to 'Other' cultures, and as responsible for the better economic and managerial outcomes associated with the developed world. Due to the focus of academic studies of consultancy on consultancy in the first/developed world, the geopolitical power structure that allows for the reproduction of this underlying assumption in consultancy theory and practice is still largely overlooked in the field's literature.

26.3.3 Power and Otherness

As suggested by the previous discussions of alternative notions of knowledge and culture as presented in postcolonial studies, the most fundamental insight shared by all students in this field is the need to consider historically situated or constituted geopolitical and ethnic power relations as the general structure that shapes all international and interracial exchanges and relations (although this influence is by no means homogenous, unilinear, or constant). It is this understanding of West–rest power relations and their role in shaping cross-cultural consultancy encounters that is most conspicuously lacking from most studies of international consultancy—but see discussion of the 'dominance effect' by Kipping and Wright, Chapter 8, this volume. They point to the widely held view of consultants as representatives of a transnational community with a similar educational and professional background, or as global elite that shares 'a dominant "Western" sensibility' with other agents of neo-liberal capitalism. This draws attention to the fact that geopolitical relations should be understood as a crucial frame within which the process of consulting takes place. However, in most other academic consultancy studies, client–consultant power relations—to the extent that they are discussed at all— are usually seen as subject to oscillations of supply and demand and market conditions, as well as to questions about the size, legitimacy, and economic strength of both the knowledge supplier and the consumer (for an extended discussion of client–consultant power relations, see Nikolova and Devinney, Chapter 19, this volume).

This lack of recognition of the developing–developed power relations within which client–consultant power relations are embedded can be seen in the discussion of the notion of 'the burden of otherness', as it was recently formulated to account for client–consultant tensions (Kipping and Armbrüster 2002; Wang 2009). Developed to account for general cases of client–consultant relations, and not necessarily in the context of cross-cultural or cross-national encounters, the 'burden of otherness' is seen as resulting from the conceptualization of the consultant as a stranger to the organization and its interests, as serving management interests against those of the employees, and as someone who lacks an understanding of the organization's own local knowledge and habits. It is the consultant, regardless of his/her professional and cultural resources, who is considered the 'Other' and as requiring the assistance of an 'insider' to reduce resistance to him/her. While studies in 'peripheral' countries have repeatedly shown us that foreign managers and consultants are seen as foreigners who lack the knowledge and cultural understanding that are crucial in order to lead a successful reorganization (Mir, Banerjee, and Mir 2009; Mir and Mir 2009; Wang 2009), a postcolonial perspective would focus on the ways in which the embeddedness of the global consultancy industry, its clients, and especially the funding agencies, in the general structure of geopolitical and ethnic hierarchy leads to the presentation of the third world clients—rather than the foreign consultants employed to assist them—as the ultimate 'Others', whose knowledge is less relevant.

While the point of departure for any postcolonial analysis is the recognition of the historically grounded Western/Northern hegemony and the influence this hegemony has on any West–rest encounter, the different postcolonial perspectives are divided as to the omnipotence of 'Western' domination. Here again the Saidian and Bhabhaian perspectives appear to differ in their emphases. While the Saidian perspective focuses on the West's ability to construct the world in keeping with its own interests and outlooks, a Bhabhaian perspective opens the way for an analysis of collaboration, agency, and resistance among the colonized. A postcolonial analysis based on this perspective would not simply assume that the power resources available to foreign consultants advising in E&D economies mean that they will successfully impose their own views on their clients, even when these resources combine legitimate knowledge, the conceptualization of the consultants' cultural background as superior to that of their clients, and the structural support of the international, governmental, or non-governmental organization (NGO) sponsor of the consulting process. Rather, a research programme analysing this situation should take into consideration not only the geopolitical power structure, but the resources available to the different actors in the specific context and the available repertoires of resistance, ranging between rejection, transgression, hybridization, and the failure of the consultancy process.

Wang's (2009) recent depiction of the experience of foreign consultants in China, underlining the problems and difficulties that accompanied the consultancies' interventions, may be reinterpreted through this perspective. While Wang associates the difficulties experienced by major global consultancies and their expatriate consultants in China as resulting from the early stage of development of the consulting market in China and the lack of understanding of management consulting services, on the one hand, and from the general reluctance of the Chinese to trust foreigners who are not part of their family or their close social network, on the other (ibid.: 138), a postcolonial analysis of the kind offered here would highlight the complex ways in which the mutual conceptualizations of clients and consultants—both 'infected' by stereotypical views of the 'Other' that can be seen as the after-effect of the colonial encounter in China—might provide a potential explanation of these difficulties. More empirical research is needed to shed some light on the complexity of power relations as they are affected by the West–rest schema.

26.4 Concluding Remarks

The growing market for foreign consultancies in developing and emerging economies, together with the problems that so often accompany attempts by leading global consultancy brands to enter these developing markets, requires much more theoretical and empirical research. This chapter has offered an alternative theoretical direction that may lead to a shift not only in the terminology applied when referring to third world clients and their encounters with foreign consultants, but also in the methods used to conduct research in third world consulting sites.

Following Bhabha, it is suggested that foreign consultancy in the rest of the world should be understood as a concrete manifestation of the abstract idea of the third space of in-between. If the consultancy encounter is conceptualized as a hybrid space that is not entirely governed by the laws of either the foreign consultant or his local client, a better understanding of the consulting process may emerge. As part of such a conceptualization, academic students of consultancy should be sensitive not only to the way that foreign consultants and local clients in third world contexts stereotypically imagine each other's national culture, but also to national and cultural general collective memory and the way this memory may shape identities and positions within the consultancy process. This kind of understanding entails a recognition of the fact that while client–consultant power relations may be affected by specific market conditions, the broader and historically situated geopolitical context should always be taken into consideration.

Similarly, while most studies of consultancy in the third world tend to accept consultancy theory's propensity to focus on consultancy knowledge developed in the US and Europe, alternative definitions of knowledge should also be taken seriously so as to make room for subaltern knowledge, whose relevance should be evaluated not only in relation to local but also global enterprises. Only when these conditions are met will the academic study of consultancy in the rest of the world yield more fertile theoretical perspectives, which may even shed new light on the process of consultancy in the developed world.

References

Adams, C. (2003). 'Consulting in the Developing World'. In B. Curnow and J. Reuvid (eds), *International Guide to Management Consultancy*. 2nd edn. London: Kogan Page, 359–366.

Ayittey, G. B. N. (1999). 'How the Multilateral Institutions Compounded Africa's Economic Crisis. (Symposium: Sub-Saharan Africa in the Global Economy.)' *Law and Policy in International Business*, 30/4, 585–600.

Banerjee, S. B. (2002). 'Organisational Strategies for Sustainable Development: Developing a Research Agenda for the New Millennium'. *Australian Journal of Management*, 27 (special issue), 105–117.

Banerjee, S. B. (2003). 'Who Sustains Whose Development? Sustainable Development and the Reinvention of Nature'. *Organization Studies*, 24/1, 143–180.

Banerjee, S. B., Chio, V. C. M., and Mir, R. (2009). *Organizations, Markets and Imperial Formations: Towards an Anthropology of Globalization*. Cheltenham: Edward Elgar.

Bernard-Donals, M. F. (1998). *The Practice of Theory: Rhetoric, Knowledge, and Pedagogy in the Academy*. Cambridge: Cambridge University Press.

Bhabha, H. K. (1994). *The Location of Culture*. London: Routledge.

Boussebaa, M. (2009). 'Struggling to Organize across National Borders: The Case of Global Resource Management in Professional Service Firms'. *Human Relations*, 62/6, 829–850.

Brown, L. D. (1993). 'Social Change through Collective Reflection with Asian Nongovernmental Development Organizations'. *Human Relations*, 46/2, 249–273.

Calas, M. B. and Smirich, L. (1999). 'Past Postmodernism? Reflections and Tentative Directions'. *Academy of Management Review*, 24/4, 649–671.

Caldas, M. P. (2006). 'Conceptualizing Brazilian Multiple and Fluid Cultural Profiles'. *Management Research: The Journal of the Iberoamerican Academy of Management*, 4/3, 169–180.

Chakrabarty, D. (2002). *Habitations of Modernity: Essays in the Wake of Subaltern Studies*. Chicago: University of Chicago Press.

Chisholm, R. F. (2000). 'Applying Action Research to Public Sector Problems: International Perspectives'. In R. T. Golembiewski (ed.), *Handbook of Organizational Consultation*. New York: Marcel Dekker, 187–197.

Curnow, B. and Reuvid, J. (2003). *The International Guide to Management Consultancy: The Evolution, Practice and Structure of Management Consultancy Worldwide*. 2nd edn. London: Kogan Page.

Donadone, J. C. (2009). 'Brazilian Consulting Cartography and the New Recontextualization and Internationalization of Interchanges and Managerial Contents'. *Corporate Ownership and Control*, 6/4, 302–308.

Erçek, M. and İşeri, S. A. (2008). 'Discursive Ambiguity, Professional Networks, and Peripheral Contexts: The Translation of Total Quality Management in Turkey, 1991–2002'. *International Studies of Management & Organization*, 38/4, 78–99.

Frenkel, M. (2008a). 'The Multinational Corporation as a Third Space: Rethinking International Management Discourse on Knowledge Transfer through Homi Bhabha'. *Academy of Management Review*, 33/4, 924–942.

Frenkel, M. (2008b). 'The Americanization of the Antimanagerialist Alternative in Israel: How Foreign Experts Retheorized and Disarmed Workers' Participation in Management, 1950–1970'. *International Studies of Management & Organization*, 38/4, 17–37.

Frenkel, M. and Shenhav, Y. (2006). 'From Binarism Back to Hybridity: A Postcolonial Reading of Management and Organization Studies'. *Organization Studies*, 27/6, 855–876.

Gantman, E. R. (2005). *Capitalism, Social Privilege, and Managerial Ideologies*. Aldershot: Ashgate.

Gantman, E. R. (2010). 'Scholarly Management Knowledge in the Periphery: Argentina and Brazil in Comparative Perspective (1970–2005)'. *Brazilian Administration Review*, 7/2, 115–135.

Gellermann, W., Frankel, M. S., and Ladenson, R. F. (2002). 'A Statement of Values and Ethics by Professionals in Organization and Human System Development'. In M. Kubr (ed.),

Management Consulting: A Guide to the Profession. 4th edn. Geneva: International Labour Office, 329–337.

Golembiewski, R. T. (2000). *Handbook of Organizational Consultation.* New York: Marcel Dekker.

Gross, A. C. and Poor, J. (2008). 'The Global Management Consulting Sector'. *Business Economics,* 44/3, 169–176.

Hall, S. (1992). 'The West and the Rest: Discourse and Power'. In S. Hall and B. Gieben(eds), *Formations of Modernity.* Cambridge: Polity, 275–320.

Harbison, F. H. and Myers, C. A. (1959). *Management in the Industrial World: An International Analysis.* New York: McGraw-Hill.

Hofstede, G. (1980). *Culture's Consequences: International Differences in Work-Related Values.* Beverly Hills, CA: Sage.

Jack, G. and Lorbiecki, A. (2003). 'Asserting Possibilities of Resistance in the Cross-Cultural Teaching Machine: Re-Viewing Videos of Others'. In A. Prasad (ed.), *Postcolonial Theory and Organizational Analysis: A Critical Engagement.* New York: Palgrave Macmillan, 213–232.

Jack, G. and Westwood, R. (2006). 'Postcolonialism and the Politics of Qualitative Research in International Business'. *Management International Review,* 46/4, 481–501.

Jackson, T. (2009). 'A Critical Cross-Cultural Perspective for Developing Nonprofit International Management Capacity'. *Nonprofit Management and Leadership,* 19/4, 443–466.

Jackson, T., Amaeshi, K., and Yavuz, S. (2008). 'Untangling African Indigenous Management: Multiple Influences on the Success of SMEs in Kenya'. *Journal of World Business,* 43/4, 400–416.

Kerr, R. (2008). 'Transferring New Public Management to the Periphery'. *International Studies of Management & Organization,* 38/4, 58–77.

Kipping, M. (1999). 'American Management Consulting Companies in Western Europe, 1920 to 1990: Products, Reputation, and Relationships'. *Business History Review,* 73/2, 190–220.

Kipping, M. and Armbrüster, T. (2002). 'The Burden of Otherness: Limits of Consultancy Interventions in Historical Case Studies'. In M. Kipping and L. Engwall (eds), *Management Consulting: Emergence and Dynamics of a Knowledge Industry.* Oxford: Oxford University Press, 203–221.

Kipping, M. and Engwall, L. (2002). *Management Consulting: Emergence and Dynamics of a Knowledge Industry.* Oxford: Oxford University Press.

Kubr, M. (2002). *Management Consulting: A Guide to the Profession.* 4th edn. Geneva: International Labour Office.

Kwek, D. (2003). 'Decolonizing and Re-Presenting Culture's Consequences: A Postcolonial Critique of Cross-Cultural Studies in Management'. In A. Prasad (ed.), *Postcolonial Theory and Organizational Analysis: A Critical Engagement.* New York: Palgrave Macmillan, 121–146.

Lendvai, N. and Stubbs, P. (2006). 'Translation, Intermediaries and Welfare Reforms in South Eastern Europe Paper'. Presented at the ESPANET conference, Bremen.

Lendvai, N. and Stubbs, P. (2009). 'Assemblages, Translation and Intermediaries in South East Europe: Rethinking Transnationalism and Social Policy'. *European Societies,* 11/5, 233–256.

Mir, R. and Mir, A. (2009). 'From the Colony to the Corporation'. *Group & Organization Management,* 34/1, 90–113

Mir, R., Banerjee, S. B., and Mir, A. (2009). 'How Does Knowledge Flow? A Critical Analysis of Intra-Organizational Knowledge Transfer'. In S. B. Banerjee, V. C. M. Chio, and R. Mir (eds), *Organizations, Markets and Imperial Formations: Towards an Anthropology of Globalization*. Cheltenham: Edward Elgar, 98–131.

Mitchell, T. (1988). *Colonising Egypt*. Cambridge: Cambridge University Press.

Neu, D. (2001). 'Banal Accounts: Subaltern Voices'. *Accounting Forum*, 25/4, 319–333.

Peltonen, T. (2006). 'Critical Theoretical Perspectives on International Human Resource Management'. In I. Bjorkman and G. Stuehl (eds), *Handbook of International HRM Research*. Cheltenham: Edward Elgar, 523–535.

Prakash, G. (1994). 'Subaltern Studies as Postcolonial Criticism'. *American Historical Review*, 99/5, 1475–1490.

Prasad, A. (1997). 'The Colonising Consciousness and Representations of the Other: A Postcolonial Critique of the Discourse of Oil'. In P. Prasad, A. J. Mills, M. Elmes, and A. Prasad (eds), *Managing the Organisational Melting Pot: Dilemmas of Workplace Diversity*. London: Sage, 285–311.

Prasad, A. (2003a). 'The Gaze of the Other: Postcolonial Theory and Organizational Analysis'. In A. Prasad (ed.), *Postcolonial Theory and Organizational Analysis: A Critical Engagement*. New York: Palgrave Macmillan, 3–44.

Prasad, A. (2003b). *Postcolonial Theory and Organizational Analysis: A Critical Engagement*. New York: Palgrave Macmillan.

Quayson, A. (2000). *Postcolonialism: Theory, Practice, or Process?* Cambridge: Polity.

Sadler, P. (2001). *Management Consultancy: A Handbook for Best Practice*. 2nd edn. London: Kogan Page.

Said, E. W. (1978). *Orientalism*. London: Routledge and Kegan Paul.

Serva, M. (1992). 'A importação de metodologias administrativas no Brasil—uma análise semi-ológica'. *Revista de Administração Pública*, 26/4, 128–144.

Spivak, G. C. (1988). 'Can the Subalten Speak'. In C. Nelson and L. Grossberg (eds), *Marxism and the Interpretation of Culture*. Urbana: University of Illinois Press, 271–313.

Srinivas, N. (2008). 'Mimicry and Revival: The Transfer and Transformation of Management Knowledge to India, 1959–1990'. *International Studies of Management & Organization*, 38/4, 38–57.

Styhre, A. (2002). 'Constructing the Image of the Other: A Post-Colonial Critique of the Adaptation of Japanese Human Resource Management Practices'. *Management Decision*, 40/3, 257–265.

Varman, R. and Biswatosh, S. (2009). 'Disciplining the Discipline: Understanding Postcolonial Epistemic Ideology in Marketing'. *Journal of Marketing Management*, 25/78, 811–824.

Wang, Y. (2009). 'Global Management Consultancy in China'. Master thesis, School of Organization and Management, University of New South Wales.

Westwood, R. (2001). 'Appropriating the Other in the Discourse of Comparative Management'. In R. I. Westwood and S. Linstead (eds), *The Language of Organizations*. London: Sage, 241–282.

Westwood, R. (2004). 'Towards a Postcolonial Research Paradigm in International Business and Comparative Management'. In R. Marschan-Piekkari and C. Welch (eds), *Handbook of Qualitative Research Methods for International Business*. Cheltenham: Edward Elgar, 56–83.

Westwood, R. (2006). 'International Business and Management Studies as an Orientalist Discourse'. *Critical Perspectives on International Business*, 2/2, 91–113.

Wong, L. (2005). '"Globalizing" Management Theories: Knowledge, Ignorance, and the Possibility of a Postcolonial Critique'. *Copenhagen Journal of Asian Studies*, 21, 124–147.

Wood, T. and Caldas, M. P. (2002). 'Adopting Imported Managerial Expertise in Developing Countries: The Brazilian Experience'. *Academy of Management Executive*, 16/2, 18–32.

Wright, C. and Kwon, S-H. (2006). 'Business Crisis and Management Fashion: Korean Companies, Restructuring and Consulting Advice'. *Asia Pacific Business Review*, 12/3, 355–373.

INDEX

7